W9-DCI-892

SOCIOLOGY:

INQUIRING INTO SOCIETY

Ben Shahn

SOCIOLOGY:
INQUIRING INTO SOCIETY

Peter I. Rose Smith College

Myron Glazer Smith College

Penina Migdal Glazer Hampshire College

CANFIELD PRESS San Francisco
A DEPARTMENT OF HARPER & ROW, PUBLISHERS, INC.
New York Hagerstown London

Sponsoring Editors: Howard Boyer, Roger Williams
Designer: James Stockton
Photo Researcher: Kay Y. James
Composition: Typothetae
Printing and Binding: W. A. Krueger

Library of Congress Cataloging in Publication Data

Rose, Peter Isaac, 1933–
Sociology : inquiring into society.

Bibliography.
Includes index.
1. Sociology. I. Glazer, Myron, joint author.
II. Glazer, Penina Migdal, joint author. III. Title
HM51.R8246 301 75–36051
ISBN 0–06–387882–8

---

76 77 78 10 9 8 7 6 5 4 3 2 1

Dedication

This book is dedicated to
our dear friend
and esteemed colleague
Ely Chinoy

(1921–1975)

CONTENTS

PREFACE

The purpose of any social science is to render human experience intelligible and coherent. An introductory sociology text has the dual purpose of making the concepts and methods of sociology intelligible to the college reader and of providing insight into the workings of society. Because so many students in an introductory sociology class will never take another course in the discipline, it is essential that an introductory text convey the social utility of sociology. Thus we hope the student will discover that sociology has a human value, that knowledge in this field can explain his or her own social existence as something more than a random series of arbitrary or personal choices and habitual ways of doing things.

Why should a college reader care whether the concepts and methods of sociology are intelligible and exciting? One of the major thrusts of the text is to show how the discipline sheds light on some of the most complex and momentous issues faced by our society—among them racial prejudice, sexual inequality, and differences in the opportunity to obtain wealth, power, and prestige in this country. We are interested in confronting head-on some of the "conventional wisdoms" surrounding these questions, and the tools of the sociologist can be used for systematically analyzing, exploring, and evaluating suggested solutions to these problem areas. This disciplined way of thinking is revealed in the pages that follow, and we hope it will excite and engage the student.

As we wrote the text, we had in mind the nonmajor—the student who takes one or at most two courses in sociology. Composed of fifteen chapters of roughly equivalent length, the text should lend itself well to both one-quarter and one-semester introductory courses. To suit the needs and interests of a wide variety of readers, the text is supplemented by a tripartite structure: margin notes, captioned photographs, and activities.

The margin notes form a running glossary (a complete glossary appears at the end of the book). When a concept is introduced in the text, it is identified and defined in the margin. The reader can thus review all the major concepts in a chapter by checking the margins of that chapter. If further clarification or detail is desired, the student can quickly refer to the fuller context in which the idea is presented. When a concept is repeated in an important new setting, it is redefined in the margin, often with a cross-reference to the place where it was initially presented.

Photographs are no longer an unusual feature in sociology texts, but their use in this book is, we think, unique. They are not simply decorations; rather they supplement the text. There are individual and paired photos, mini-essays (three to five photos), and full photo essays. It is a commonplace that students have an increasingly visual orientation. When the unfamiliar is being discussed, or when the familiar is being discussed in unfamiliar terms, photographs are used to remind the reader of the concrete, vibrant—often vexatious—realities that sociology analyzes. The captions are intended to point up the ways in which the sociological perspective makes concrete experiences intelligible. We have also used the photographs to emphasize the cross-cultural applicability of sociological concepts, and we hope they will counteract some of the ethnocentrism that appears to infect our society, like all others.

Throughout each chapter the reader will find numerous "activities": challenges to the student to become involved in sociology by simulating the activities of a sociologist or by mentally grappling with a conceptual problem like those the sociologist constantly confronts. Many of these activities suggest individual research; others require the participation of the entire class as a unit; still others demand that the class be divided into several units. There are more activities in any chapter than can be done within the time normally allotted to a chapter. The instructor can thus use discretion in assigning or suggesting the projects to be done by various kinds of students. Specific suggestions for the use of the activities are given in both the *Instructor's Manual* and the *Student Study Guide,* prepared by Rosalie Gross. Instructors who want more detailed treatment of methodology than the description in Chapter 2 will welcome the extensive coverage in the Appendix, "The Research Process." The text also contains an annotated bibliography, a glossary, and an index.

Certain other features of our organization and emphasis warrant explanation. Many topics, concepts, and areas of concern recur in different contexts and several chapters. For example, some recent texts treat sex roles in a separate chapter. Although this gives the topic greater immediate visibility at a time when it is receiving much social attention, we favor treating sex roles and their emergent transformations as they occur in life—in many social contexts and in relation to many different concepts. Thus they receive attention in Chapters 1 (perspective), 4 (values and norms), 5 (roles and groups), 6 (social institutions), 9 (childhood and adolescent socialization), 10 (adult socialization), 14 (social change), 15 (social movements), and the Epilogue.

This same recurrence, or "spiraling," of analysis is applied to virtually all concepts and issues of moment. Our use of this technique led us to an unorthodox arrangement of topics: socialization is treated only after we have given a full macro view of the society, thus encouraging the student to place the operative concepts in a social context of class, ethnicity, and social institutions and groups. We could then devote two chapters to the chronological experience of socialization: the first discussing childhood and adolescence; the second extensively treating the adult years—the world of work, marriage and the family, retirement and old age.

Other areas of emphasis will, we think, interest teachers and students alike. Chapter 3, for example, explores the symbol systems by which culture is transmitted and gains its hold on members of a society. Only then are the normative and value components of culture examined.

We have also devoted most of Chapter 11 to a topic that generally gets only brief obligatory mention in introductory texts: resocialization in controlled environments or total institutions. Historians and social scientists generally credit this century with the origination and perfection of totalitarianism. Today's newspapers, magazines, and books frequently convey the worldwide concern with this topic, and certain controlled environments in our own society have received intense scrutiny. This text examines the individual's experience within the social structure of controlled environments and raises questions about their functions and goals. Are prisons necessary? Are they intended to rehabilitate or to punish? What is their actual effect? Likewise, does the characteristic structure of mental institutions fulfill or subvert their manifest functions?

We invite the reader's attention to the Epilogue, an imaginary symposium of three sociologists who look at our society from three different perspectives, coming to divergent conclusions about its values and its performance in relation to those values. Our intention and hope is that, as much as anything else in the book, this discussion will bring the practice and relevance of sociology alive to the student. Indeed, instructors might encourage their students to read the Epilogue first and return to it for reconsideration at the end of the course.

An undertaking of the scope of this text naturally involves many people. Jack Jennings, publisher, Russ Wilkens, George Levesque, and Howard Boyer, then sociology editor, persuaded us to come to Canfield, as did the reputations of Ken Burke, of Ken Burke Associates, and Jim Stockton, the designer. Once at Canfield, much energy, talent, and intelligence were devoted to refining the manuscript to its ultimate effectiveness. Kevin Gleason, developmental editor, Kay Y. James, photo researcher, and Zipporah W. Collins, copy editor and production editor, worked closely with us and with Roger Williams, social sciences editor-in-chief, and Laura Argento, manufacturing manager, to help make this book what it is.

Also valuable were the reviews by Michael Lewis, University of Massachusetts: Peter Chroman, College of San Mateo; Maurice Garnier, Indiana University; William Scalappino, College of Marin; Mark Chesler, University of Michigan; and sociologists Rosalie Gross and Butler Crittenden. Hedy Rose served as a sounding board and close adviser throughout the planning and writing of the book. Martha R. Fowlkes assisted in the development of the mental hospital section of Chapter 11. Agnes Shannon and Norma Lepine performed perhaps the most Sisyphean of tasks in publishing a book: typing draft after draft. To all these people our sincere thanks.

NOTE TO THE STUDENT

Throughout this book you will find material printed in a different color from the text. We think of these sections as activities, because they are meant to involve you actively in the process of sociological reasoning and investigation. Some activities involve doing research, either individually or as a class or as groups within a class; others give you practice in designing research; still others ask you to think in a systematic way about the issues, perspectives, or methods under discussion.

Each chapter contains more activities than any reader or class is likely to do. Thus you have a variety to choose from. Whatever their form, and whichever ones you choose to do, all have the same purpose: to persuade you that everything in this book is the product of systematic investigation and careful observations. Our aim is to encourage you to become familiar with those sociological methods and tools by using them to answer a wide array of questions.

For a discussion of the sociologist's research methods, see Chapter 2, "Methods, Models, and Theories." For a more detailed description of those methods, see the Appendix, "The Research Process."

You will also notice that most pages carry one or more brief notes in the margin. Many of these are concise, glossary-style definitions of concepts introduced nearby in the text; many others are repeated definitions of concepts introduced earlier and being used again nearby. Often these notes also remind you where the original discussion of the concept is located, or inform you where a concept or topic is treated further on in the book. These notes should enable you to keep in mind the central concepts around which a given description or analysis is organized—and to remind you indeed of the rigorous conceptual basis of all sociology.

Welcome to your first disciplined exposure to the study of society! We hope you will find this exploratory journey an exciting, memorable, and enjoyable experience.

A busy career in sociology has taken Peter Rose all over the world, most recently in an extensive study of the Fulbright Scholars Program for the State Department.

He began his academic career with graduate study at Cornell, where he completed his Ph.D. Currently he is Sophia Smith Professor of Sociology and Anthropology at Smith College and a member of the graduate faculty of the University of Massachusetts. He has been active in the American Sociological Association as a member of the Executive Council and has served as vice president of both the Society for Social Problems and the Eastern Sociological Society, and as president of the Massachusetts Sociological Association.

Peter has published two anthologies, The Study of Society *and* Seeing Ourselves, *widely used in introductory sociology courses. He has also studied race and ethnic relations extensively, writing* They and We, The Subject Is Race, The Ghetto and Beyond, Americans From Africa, Nation of Nations, *and* Strangers in Their Midst. *He has served as consulting editor to Random House and Time-Life Books.*

Peter, his wife, Hedy, who teaches at Hampshire College, and their two teenage children live in Northampton, Massachusetts. Their house is filled with art, books, and mementos from around the world. During the summer months the family shares a passion for sailing on Cape Cod Bay.

Like many sociologists, Myron Glazer has devoted much of his career to sociological research, but he has also examined the personal, ethical, and political aspects of social science research. He describes these in his book The Research Adventure.

While a graduate student at Princeton, he traveled throughout Latin America doing research on radical students for his book Student Politics in Chile. *He returned to Princeton for his Ph.D. in 1964 and subsequently coauthored* Latin American University Students: A Six Nation Study.

Mickey is presently chairman of the Department of Sociology and Anthropology at Smith College and a member of the graduate faculty at the University of Massachusetts. Now that their collaboration on this text is complete, he and his wife, Penina, hope to devote more time to their children, travel, cross-country skiing, and visiting with their large extended family.

Penina Migdal Glazer is dean of the faculty at Hampshire College, where she has been a faculty member since the college was founded six years ago. While she continues to teach, Penina is also involved in research in female friendships.

Penina completed her Ph.D. at Rutgers with a study of radical movements of the 1940s. She has continued to study radicals and reformers, writing articles on the new left, radical pacifists, women in the labor movement, and Chilean student activists. A sabbatical in Israel provided the basis for a study of Israeli war resisters.

As the mother of two children, Penina has managed to fill work and family roles. She finds the challenge of a dual career rewarding and has learned that each area of experience benefits the other. Penina has succeeded in developing her own interests outside the family setting and would encourage every woman to do so.

Art Acknowledgments

Cover "Spring" by Ben Shahn, 1946. Tempera. Albright-Knox Art Gallery, Buffalo, New York, Room of Contemporary Art Fund. © Estate of Ben Shahn.

Frontispiece "Paterson" by Ben Shahn, 1953. Lithograph in black. New Jersey State Museum. © Estate of Ben Shahn.

3 "Triple Dip" by Ben Shahn, 1952. Serigraph in black with hand coloring. New Jersey State Museum, gift of Mr. and Mrs. James E. Burke. © Estate of Ben Shahn.

53 "Memories of Many Nights of Love" (Rilke Portfolio) by Ben Shahn, 1968. Lithograph in black. New Jersey State Museum. © Ben Shahn Trust.

99 "Scientist" by Ben Shahn, 1957. Serigraph in black with hand coloring. New Jersey State Museum. © Estate of Ben Shahn.

271 "Headstand on Tricycle" by Ben Shahn, 1968. Lithograph in black. New Jersey State Museum, Gift of The Frelinghuysen Foundation. © Estate of Ben Shahn.

407 "Many Cities" (Rilke Portfolio) by Ben Shahn, 1968. Lithograph in black. New Jersey State Museum. © Ben Shahn Trust.

Photographic Acknowledgments

xx *top* Dan Rose
xx *middle* Gabriel Amadeus Cooney
xx *bottom* Gabriel Amadeus Cooney
4 Ken Heyman
5 Bill Owens, BBM Associates
7 James Motlow, Jeroboam
8 Ken Heyman
20 David Seymour, Magnum
24 Guy Le Querrec, Viva
25 *top left* Guy Le Querrec, Viva
25 *bottom left* Ken Heyman
25 *right* Gilles Peress, Magnum
29 Constantine Manos, Magnum
33 *left* Ken Heyman
33 *right* Leonard Freed, Magnum
42 Bruce Davidson, Magnum
46 State Historical Society of Wisconsin
47 Suzanne Szasz
55 Bill Owens, BBM Associates
56 Leo Hetzel
57 *top* Kent Reno, Jeroboam
57 *bottom left* Burk Uzzle, Magnum
57 *bottom right* Arthur Tress, Magnum
58 Burk Uzzle, Magnum
59 Leo Hetzel
60 Ken Heyman
61 Richard Kalvar, Viva
65 *top left* Imperial War Museum
65 *top right* Nacio Jan Brown, BBM Associates
65 *center* Wayne Miller, Magnum
65 *bottom* Charles Harbutt, Magnum
66 Charles Gatewood, Magnum
67 New York State Historical Association, Cooperstown, N.Y.
68 *left* Bruce Davidson, Magnum
68 *right* Paul Conklin
69 *top left* Burk Uzzle, Magnum
69 *top right* Eileen Christelow, Jeroboam
69 *center right* Jeffrey Blankfort, BBM Associates
69 *bottom left* Leonard Freed, Magnum
69 *bottom right* Henri Cartier-Bresson, Magnum
72 Library of Congress
73 Martin Eiter, Anthro-Photo
77 *top* Bill Owens, BBM Associates
77 *bottom* Bruce Davidson, Magnum
78 Hiroji Kubota, Magnum
79 *top left* Burt Glinn, Magnum
79 *top right* John Rees, Black Star
79 *bottom left* Dennis Stock, Magnum
79 *bottom right* Ken Heyman
82 Bill Owens, BBM Associates
83 *top left* Ken Heyman
83 *top right* Chris Maynard, Magnum
83 *bottom* Ken Heyman
85 *top* Roger Lubin, Jeroboam
85 *bottom* Stephen Shames, Black Star
90 Erich Hartmann, Magnum
91 *left* Ken Heyman
91 *right* Susan Ylvisaker, Jeroboam
92 *top* Ken Heyman
92 *bottom* John Dunlop
100 Leo Hetzel
102 Homer Sykes, Magnum
105 Helen Keller Collection, American Foundation for the Blind
108 *left* Inge Morath, Magnum
108 *right* Constantine Manos, Magnum
110 Ken Heyman
113 Leonard Freed, Magnum
116 Ken Heyman
117 *top* Ken Heyman
117 *bottom* Bill Owens, BBM Associates
125 Ken Heyman
126 Alex Webb, Magnum
131 Margaretta Mitchell
134 Cathy Singer
135 *top* Martine Franck, Viva
135 *bottom* Menard, Asia Photo
137 Doug Muir, BBM Associates
139 *top* State Historical Society of Wisconsin
139 *bottom* Alain Dagbert, Viva
142 *left* National Archives
142 *right* Dorothea Lange Collection, The Oakland Museum
148 Cornell Capa, Magnum
149 *top* The Kansas State Historical Society, Topeka
149 *bottom* Suzanne Szasz
153 Charles Gatewood, Magnum
154 Bhupendra Karia, Magnum
155 John Dunlop
158 Chicago Historical Society
159 National Archives
160 Leo Hetzel
162 Marilyn Silverstone, Magnum
163 *left* Elliott Erwitt, Magnum
163 *right* Information Service of India
169 Eve Arnold, Magnum
170 *left* Elliott Erwitt, Magnum
170 *right* Guy Le Querrec, Viva
172 Wycliffe Bible Translators, Magnum
173 *top* Martin Eiter, Anthro-Photo
173 *bottom* Earl Dotter, BBM Associates
176 Charles Moore, Black Star
180 Cornell Capa, Magnum
185 Marilyn Silverstone, Magnum
187 Danny Lyon, Magnum
191 *top* Paul Conklin
191 *bottom left* Leo Hetzel
191 *bottom right* Leo Hetzel
192 *top* Inge Morath, Magnum
192 *bottom* Cornell Capa, Magnum
196 Ken Heyman
197 Erich Salomon, Magnum
202 Bruce Davidson, Magnum
203 *top* Bruce Davidson, Magnum
203 *bottom left* Paul Conklin
203 *bottom right* Bruce Davidson, Magnum
205 Erich Salomon, Magnum
208 Bill Owens, BBM Associates
211 Paul Conklin
213 *left* Earl Dotter, BBM Associates
213 *right* Paul Conklin
214 *top* Burk Uzzle, Magnum
214 *bottom* Ernest Lowe, BBM Associates
217 *top* Constantine Manos, Magnum
217 *bottom left* Ken Heyman
217 *bottom right* Constantine Manos, Magnum
218 Ken Heyman
224 Sepp Seitz, Magnum
225 *top* Paul Conklin
225 *bottom left* Constantine Manos, Magnum
225 *bottom right* Earl Dotter, BBM Associates
229 Ilke Hartmann, Jeroboam
233 Ken Heyman
234 Danny Lyon, Magnum
235 *top* Dennis Brack, Black Star
235 *bottom* Ken Heyman
239 The Kansas State Historical Society, Topeka
242 Library of Congress
243 The Metropolitan Museum of Art, Gift of Mr. and Mrs. Wolfgang Pulverman, 1969
245 Bob Adelman, Magnum
247 Bruce Davidson, Magnum
249 Charles Moore, Black Star
250 Ken Heyman
251 Edward S. Curtis photograph, Philadelphia Museum of Art
252 National Archives
254 Ken Heyman
257 *top* State Historical Society of Wisconsin
257 *bottom* Bruce Davidson, Magnum
260 Bruce Davidson, Magnum
262 U.P.I.
263 *top* Roger Malloch, Magnum
263 *bottom* Hap Stewart, Jeroboam
267 Susan Ylvisaker, Jeroboam
273 Doris Allen
274 Eileen Christelow, Jeroboam
275 Eileen Christelow, Jeroboam
276 Ken Heyman
277 *top* Burt Glinn, Magnum
277 *bottom* Ken Heyman
279 Ken Heyman
280 Peeter Vilms, Jeroboam
281 Bill Grimes, Black Star
284 Ken Heyman
286 Abigail Heyman, Magnum
287 *top* Bill Owens, BBM Associates
287 *bottom* Eileen Christelow, Jeroboam
289 Leo Hetzel
291 Suzanne Szasz
293 *top left* Ken Heyman
293 *top right* Ken Heyman
293 *bottom* Leonard Freed, Magnum
296 Ken Heyman
297 *top* Ken Heyman
297 *bottom left* Burk Uzzle, Magnum
297 *bottom right* Paul Conklin
299 Mark Haven, Magnum
301 Earl Dotter, BBM Associates
303 Suzanne Szasz
307 Ken Heyman
310 *top left* Ken Heyman
310 *top right* Ken Heyman
310 *bottom* Charles Harbutt, Magnum
318 Ken Heyman
322 Paul Conklin
323 John Dunlop
327 Bill Owens, BBM Associates
328 Ken Heyman
330 Martine Franck, Viva
333 Ford Motor Company
337 Bruce Davidson, Magnum
341 Ken Graves, Jeroboam
343 *top* Charles Harbutt, Magnum

(continued following bibliography)

For as far back as the records go, human society has been a subject of study, but only some 150 years ago were the principles and methods of science applied to that study. Sociology was created as the systematic study of human groups and the patterns of interaction within them. To study human groups, sociologists have developed many concepts that make special use of words found in everyday speech, such as society, culture, institutions, groups. Sociologists define these terms precisely as aids to organizing their perceptions of the multitude of human activities that they study.

The major premise shared by all sociologists is that every human being becomes human only by learning—learning accomplished by interaction with others. Although we think of ourselves as unique individuals (and we are), we are also in good part products of our social environments—of the beliefs, values, and rules of conduct we have learned from those around us.

In Part 1 we see why sociology is called a systematic study of social interaction.

1

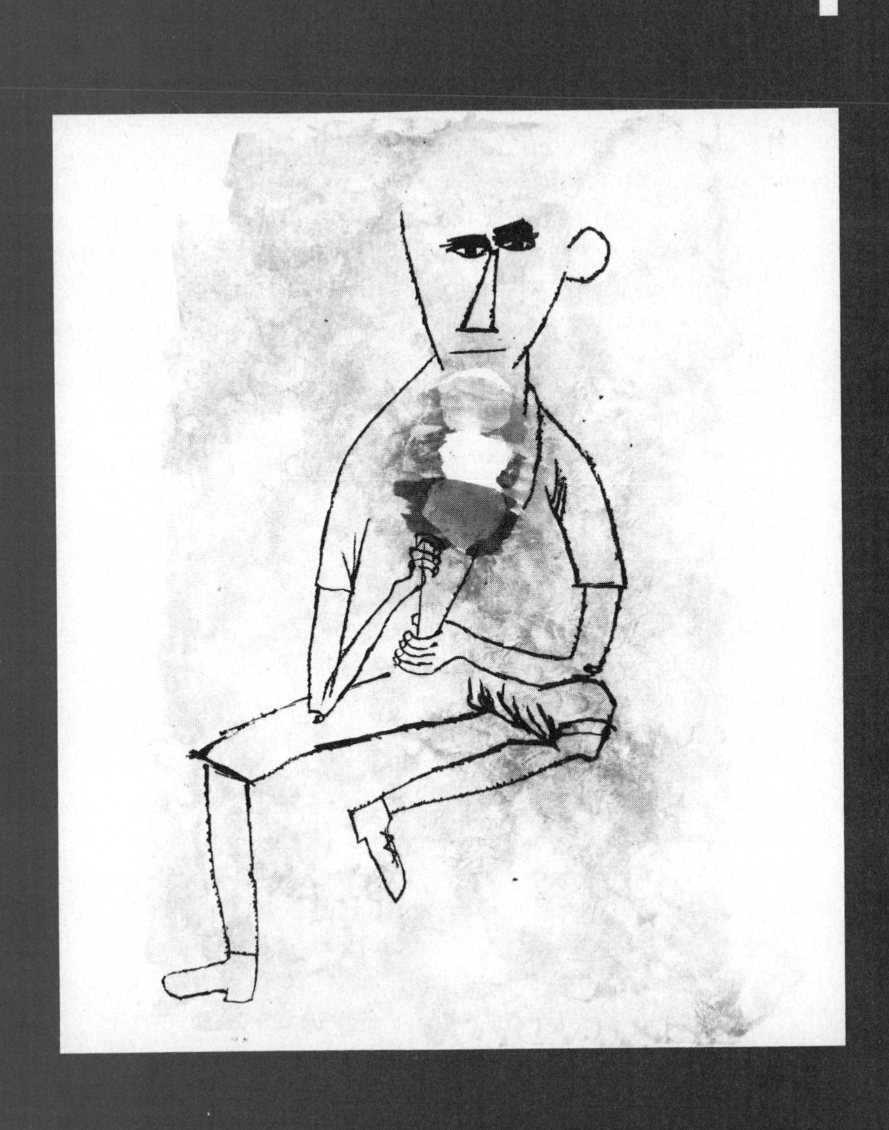

THE SOCIOLOGICAL PERSPECTIVE

Several years ago a college professor drove his wife to the local train station. As he began to pull away from the curb, two young women with suitcases noticed his faculty bumper sticker and called after him.

"Are you going back to the college?"

"Yes," he said, "hop in."

As they drove up the hill, one of the students asked the driver what he taught.

"Sociology," he replied.

"That's interesting. My boyfriend is taking sociology at State."

"What's it all about?" the second girl asked.

"Well," the first one responded with a smile, "he says it's just a lot of organized common sense."

"How's he doing?" asked the professor.

"Well, to tell you the truth, he's flunking the course."

Social roles: the behavior expected in each of the many positions a person holds in a society, such as parent, worker, or student.

The student was probably flunking because he assumed that what was being covered—the rules of society, the roles of individual members, the relationships of people—was so familiar to him from his own experience that he didn't have to pay attention. If he had paid attention, he might have found out a good deal that he didn't know. He might have learned to separate myths from social realities (and to explain the bases for the myths). He might have learned how the seemingly weird things some people do are not so crazy after all. He might even have come to enjoy the excitement of applying the scientific method to one of the most fascinating and elusive of all subjects—human behavior—by doing research on one of many interesting questions. Sociologists ask such things as why certain people seem to have a greater fondness for alcohol than others; why some students "drop out," others become active in movements to bring about social change, and still others are basically satisfied with things the way they are; or why ardent believers in God tend to be more patriotic than nonbelievers.

Each member of a society has many experiences that provide an essential basis for studying sociology. Each of us is, after all, a man or a woman, a member of a family, a participant in various social groups, a college student,

Sociology: the systematic study of society and patterns of human interaction.

perhaps a spouse, perhaps a parent. To get along with others we must know and follow many social rules. We know how to behave at home and in school and on the job. We have beliefs and opinions about all sorts of things: sex, politics, religion, education, the state of the economy, and the state of the world. Each of us is a socialized human being—or at least one who has undergone a significant amount of socialization. Socialization, moreover, is a lifelong process and is part of the definition of being human.

Socialization is the never-ending process by which we learn all the things we need to know to be adequately functioning members of society. It is discussed in detail in Chapters 9–11.

Thus, you already have a great deal of familiarity with your society. But philosophers and sociologists are aware that there is a difference between being familiar with something and truly understanding it.

THE SOCIOLOGICAL PERSPECTIVE

Understandably, in any society most assumptions about what is right and wrong, good and bad, pretty and ugly, pleasant and distasteful have come from "conventional wisdoms," that is, the ideas that people are repeatedly exposed to. In most of the ordinary activities of their daily lives, habit and considerations of convenience greatly influence their behavior. People tend to accept and act according to the rules that are passed on to them. Rarely do they

Two different cultures; two different notions of beauty, each of which has meaning only to members of the same or similar societies. Cultures vary as markedly in every other trait: beliefs, rules for behavior, ways of doing things, ideas of good and bad, right and wrong. Moreover, in a heterogeneous culture like ours, diversity abounds. Most feminists and their sympathizers find beauty contests offensive; many people have long considered them vulgar and meaningless.

challenge the conventional wisdoms.

In their daily lives, sociologists are pretty much like everybody else in this respect. But in their sociological work they do not take their own—or anyone else's—behavior for granted. They ask why most people conform to the norms of society. And they ask why some people deviate from the norms.

Sociologists must make the explicit assumption that anything that has to do with human beings has a *social dimension*—that is, that reality, as experienced by any human being, is *socially constructed.*[1] What does this mean? It means not only the obvious fact that such things as tools, instruments, and buildings are human creations, but also that all language, philosophy, science, religion, and social rules are equally the products of human invention.

Order: in science, the governing of phenomena by "natural laws" —accurate, general descriptions of how given phenomena occur and why.

Moreover, as we shall see throughout this book, the process of becoming, and remaining, members of a society influences the way we perceive the world. Since we derive such mental components as our beliefs, values, desires, and expectations from our membership in a society, it is clear that between individuals and the world stands an array of socially constructed filters or screens.

Sociologists do not deny the possibility of other forces in human existence as well—forces such as human evolution or "Mother Nature" or unseen divinities. Sociologists focus their attention, however, on the social sources of what they study. As scientists, they look for the order underlying human behavior.

Scientific method: a set of premises and methods of observation and experimentation used to arrive at accurate, verifiable descriptions of events.

Thus, the sociologist works from the belief that there is more order within the social reality than first meets the eye, and that it can be found and described with a useful tool: the scientific method.

Most of us, as participants in the social process, rely much of the time on common sense perceptions of our social world. The use of common sense to explain anything is a hazardous undertaking. Common sense stands, on the one hand, for our basic powers of observation and reasoning applied to everyday experiences. Common sense also stands for much knowledge that has never been carefully thought about. Thus, by its very nature it stands for the swamps and thickets of myth and prejudice: beliefs and judgments about the world that we have learned to make a part of our own frame of reference.

[1]For a comprehensive examination of the social construction of reality, see Alfred Schutz, *Collected Papers,* Vols. I and II (The Hague, Netherlands: Nijhoff, 1962–64). Schutz was a philosopher who explored the philosophical foundations of sociology. See also Peter L. Berger and Thomas Luckmann, *The Social Construction of Reality* (Garden City, N.Y.: Doubleday, 1966).

Pornography violates many values in a society like ours: the dignity of the person; the emotional components of sexual attraction; ideas about morality. But does it produce social harm? The evidence says no. On the contrary, legalized pornography has benefited certain societies, as measured by decreases in sex-related crimes. Sociology and other disciplines have the ability to demonstrate things that many people do not want to believe.

Let us make a short list of beliefs and assumptions that many people in our society consider reasonable—the kinds of ideas that people just "pick up"—and see how they fare under sociological analysis.

1. The widespread availability of pornography increases the number of sex crimes.

2. Most of the poor in the United States are nonwhite minority group members.

3. Blacks have a special set of grievances against Jews that makes them dislike Jews more than they dislike other whites.

4. Second marriages are more likely to be successful than first marriages.

Appearances can be deceiving. Several years ago it appeared that the United States had virtually no poor folk: they were visible only to each other, until around the early 1960s. Then the media often gave the impression that the poor were mostly nonwhite minority group members. Not true: most of the poor are white. However, higher percentages *of nonwhite minority groups are poor people.*

The first assumption is reasonable to a large number of people. Pornography offends their moral and religious beliefs by depicting lustful, forbidden acts. It degrades the act of love by making public what should be private and by isolating the physical aspects of sex from its emotional circumstances. Moreover, goes the argument, because it is intended to stimulate the viewer, an inevitable consequence of legalizing pornography must be an increase in sex crimes, particularly rape.

This last argument has been persuasive even with people who have no moral objections to pornography. But is the argument correct? No one could say yes or no until several years after Denmark legalized pornography in 1967. In 1970, it was reported that, from 1967 on, the incidence of sex crimes in that country had *dropped* sharply.[2] The President's Commission on Pornography and Obscenity stated in its 200-page report: "Extensive empirical investigation . . . provides no evidence that exposure to or use of explicit sexual materials plays a significant role in the causation of social or individual harms such as crime, delinquency, sexual or nonsexual deviancy or severe emotional disturbances."

The president and Congress both vehemently rejected the report. Said President Nixon: "The Commission tells us that the proliferation of filthy books has no lasting effect on a man's character . . . . Centuries of civilization and ten minutes of common sense tell us otherwise."[3] As a way of knowing, common sense still has its advocates.

The second assumption, that most poor people in the United States are members of nonwhite minority groups, is understandable. The media in particular have concentrated on the social problems of minorities. Their poverty is chief among their lasting problems. Moreover, since most of the urban poor are of minority status, and, since most of the United States population lives in urban areas, the nonwhite poor are more visible.

This is a readily tested assumption. All we need are Labor Department statistics showing the numbers of people above and below the poverty line by race. It turns out that most poor people in the United States are white.

Although far more poor people are white, another fact of American life is that poor whites are a much smaller *percentage* of whites than poor nonwhites are of nonwhites. For example, in 1972 some 19 million whites and 4 million blacks were defined as poor by the federal government. Since there are

[2]See *New York Times,* November 9, 1970, p. 4, for an account of the report by the President's Commission on Pornography and Obscenity.

[3]*New York Times,* October 25, 1970, p. 71.

some 180 million whites and 12 million blacks in the population, poor whites were only 9 percent of the white population, while poor blacks were 33 percent of the black population.

Consider the third commonsense belief: Blacks have a special set of grievances against Jews that makes them dislike Jews more than they dislike other whites. This assumption gained particular credence during the late 1960s, when some confrontations arose between Jews and blacks in New York. But it has been tested time and again using systematic surveys. Even during the height of those troubles, blacks remained favorably disposed toward Jews.

According to sociologist Gary Marx, there are three assumptions that most surveys of blacks set out to test: (1) that anti-Semitism is equally common among blacks and whites because it stems from the same cultural source; (2) that blacks have a special set of grievances against Jews that makes them dislike Jews more than they dislike other whites; or (3) that a special affinity between Jews and blacks makes blacks less anti-Semitic than whites and indeed makes blacks prefer Jews to other whites.

Marx's own study[4] involved an extensive survey of attitudes and opinions conducted face-to-face with both black and white respondents. Among many questions asked were those pertaining to Jews and other whites. Anti-Semitism was measured by the degree of agreement with a set of statements about Jews, such as "Jews have too much power in the United States," "Jews don't care what happens to anyone but their own kind," "Jews are more willing than others to use shady practices to get what they want." Answers to a number of such questions provided the researchers with an anti-Semitism score for each respondent.

Marx found that on measures based on stereotypes blacks and whites seemed to be similar in their views of Jews. "No case could be made for the prevalent notion that anti-Semitism is more widespread among Negroes than among whites, any more than it could be shown that they single out Jews for special enmity.[5] Marx went on to suggest:

> On measures not involving stereotypes, however, Negroes consistently emerge less anti-Semitic. Compared with whites, they more frequently opposed passage of a law to stop further Jewish immigration, more frequently said they would vote against a congressional candidate who declared himself against the Jews, and more frequently said they would not mind if their party nominated a Jew for President. In addition, Negroes expressed greater opposition to occupa-

[4]Gary T. Marx, *Protest and Prejudice: A Study of Belief in the Black Community* (New York: Harper and Row, 1967), especially Chap. 6.

[5]Ibid., p. 147.

tional and social club discrimination against Jews than did whites. It seems that their position as a persecuted minority leads black Americans to reject discrimination against Jews, if not always negative stereotypes.[6]

Let's go on to the fourth assumption we listed—the one about second marriages. Presumably, people who have erred once are more careful in their second choice. In addition, they have learned through difficult experience how to compromise in order to make a stable marriage. Finally, those engaged in second marriages are now older and more mature.

While we might thus predict a higher success rate for second marriages based on these and other factors, statistics reveal that the trend is in the other direction. While more than one third of first marriages end in divorce, statisticians predict that the rate for second marriages will reach 59 percent. As is often the case, an analysis of socioeconomic factors is enlightening. While the failure rate of second marriages among the affluent is very close to that of first marriages, couples at the lower end of the socioeconomic scale are far more likely to fail a second time. Financial concerns prove to be a relationship's undoing: for the less affluent the financial drain of child support and alimony from the first marriage is much more of a burden on the second marriage than it is for the more affluent.[7]

We see, then, that beliefs that seem entirely reasonable can be proved incorrect by use of the sociological method. Sociologists, of course, are not in the business of disproving generally held beliefs. But in their efforts to better understand the workings of a given society, their methods often yield a more accurate set of facts than commonsense deductions from the appearances of things.

Can we conclude from this that the world's societies lay in ignorance of themselves until the birth of sociology? To think so would do an immeasurable disservice to human intellectual history. Sociology is a very recent discipline in that history, and would not have been possible without all that went before it. For example, it rests on principles that emerged from the scientific revolution of the sixteenth and seventeenth centuries, which developed out of nearly 2,500 years of philosophical inquiry, beginning in Greece in the seventh century B.C. Indeed, we can divide the ways of forming ideas about the world, and about human societies, into three categories: the *nonscientific,* the *prescientific,* and the *scientific.* Sociology falls into the third category. The

[6]Ibid., pp. 147–48.

[7]See Leslie Aldridge Westoff, "Two-Time Winners," *New York Times Magazine,* August 17, 1975, p. 10.

distinctions among the ideas generated by these categories are not in the amounts of truth they contain but rather in how they come about and why they are believed.

THE HISTORICAL ROOTS OF SOCIOLOGY

Why are sociological ideas called scientific? We have already given some answers. They are based on observation, and they can be verified by testing, to name just two crucial features. How do these features differ from those of *non*scientific ideas and *pre*scientific ideas? Nonscientific ideas are derived and supported in ways that are inadmissible in science; prescientific ideas are derived in ways that resemble and anticipate scientific methods.

The Nonscientific: Myth, Religion, Tradition

Tradition as a social force is examined in Chapter 12 on community.

The story of the seven days of Creation, of Adam and Eve, and of their eviction from the Garden of Eden is familiar to virtually everyone in Western societies. This story is only one of many creation myths. In every culture a story can be found that describes how and why the world came into being. Myths need not be about creation or the origins of society. A *myth* is any story that has anonymous sources deep in the society's past; that involves elements of the supernatural, such as gods or magic; and that is kept alive by the strength of *tradition.* In other words, people have no reason to disbelieve what has been believed in the past. Indeed, the credibility of an idea may rest on nothing more than the fact that it was believed in the past.

Religion is discussed in more detail in Chapter 6 on social institutions.

A *religion* is more than a collection of myths. Many devout Christians and Jews, for example, no longer believe that the Bible's descriptions of the seven days of Creation and the Garden of Eden are true. They may accept evolutionary theory, or they may simply be indifferent to the conflict between that theory and the biblical story of creation. Yet they believe that the religion of their choice—or of their birth—expresses fundamental truths about human existence and its relation to a supernatural being. They also accept a set of rules for dealing with that being (prayer, ritual) and with their fellow humans (moral codes prescribed by the religion).

By labeling religious beliefs nonscientific, we are not labeling them either true and correct or false and incorrect. On the contrary, most of the religious beliefs held by members of our society are beyond either proof or disproof. Is there a God? Over the centuries the existence of the diety has been proved and disproved by various philosophers, but the issue is beyond the methods and concerns of science. Does every human have a soul? Is there an afterlife? Do heaven and hell exist? Whatever urgency such questions have for the individual (the scientist included), they cannot be answered one way or the other by science.

Religious conviction is fundamentally a matter of choice: one chooses to believe. Even religious thinkers who have sought to use reason to prove the existence of God or the truth of a religion have declared that reason alone is not sufficient for belief. Blaise Pascal, the seventeenth-century French Catholic mathematician and philosopher, stated:

> The metaphysical proofs of God's existence are so remote from man's reasoning and so complicated that they make no great impression. Even if some men are affected by them, the effect does not last beyond the moment in which they see the proof; an hour later they are afraid they have been taken in.[8]

Thus, nonscientific ideas are those that are not held primarily on the strength of evidence. Myths are credible chiefly because they have been believed in the past; they have the force of tradition. Religion, which supposedly has long been in conflict with science, gains fervent believers because it deals with many profound concerns that are beyond the realm of science.

The Prescientific: Intuition, Rational Speculation, Authority

In the early seventeenth century, when Blaise Pascal was planning his defense of Christian beliefs, our society reached the peak of what we call *pre*scientific thinking. The distinctive feature of prescientific ideas is their motivation by *doubt,* the very opposite of what motivates nonscientific thinking. The impulse to doubt was vividly felt by another French mathematician and philosopher, René Descartes, a contemporary of Pascal's, and generally considered the founder of modern philosophy. Descartes resolved to doubt everything; he accepted nothing on the basis of tradition or authority. In this way he intended to construct a philosophy based on certainty:

> My first rule was to accept nothing as true which I did not clearly recognize to be so; to accept nothing more than what was presented to my mind so clearly and distinctly that I could have no occasion to doubt it.[9]

Descartes accepted anything that was clear and distinct enough *to his mind* to overcome his doubt. He rejected "the fluctuating assurance of the senses" in favor of *intuition.* What did he mean by intuition? In his own words, it is "the conception, without doubt, of an unclouded and attentive mind, which springs from the light of reason alone." Thus the sensory

[8]Blaise Pascal, *The Pensées,* trans. J. M. Cohen (Harmondsworth, England: Penguin, 1961), p. 31.

[9]Quoted in J. Bronowski and Bruce Mazlich, *The Western Intellectual Tradition* (New York: Harper, 1960).

perceptions that modern science is ultimately based on (beneath all its sophisticated methods) were distrusted by prescientific thinkers.

Although Descartes stands at the beginning of modern philosophy, his methods and assumptions are in many ways like those of the earliest philosophers in the Western tradition. These thinkers, too, distrusted the appearance of things and looked beyond or beneath for a more accurate description of reality. In doing so, they distinguished themselves from people who accepted uncritically the myths and traditions that described and explained the world. Yet by modern standards the methods of these philosophers were crude and naive—they mixed impressive insights and ambitious speculations but used little or no observation. Nevertheless, some prescientific philosophers arrived at ideas that resemble modern scientific theories.

For example, Democritus, in the fifth century B.C., speculated that all matter, regardless of how solid it seemed, was in truth composed of atoms. His speculation predated experimental proof of the existence of the atom by more than twenty centuries.

It may be puzzling that an ancient philosopher would be studying the same subject that a modern atomic physicist studies today. Modern philosophers are more concerned with moral and ethical questions and problems of language and meaning. But philosophy was the foundation of most of the physical and social sciences. For many centuries scholars pursued knowledge in any and all areas of inquiry; and their methods of inquiry varied little from subject to subject. For example, Aristotle wrote extensively on physics, astronomy, zoology, ethics, political theory, poetics, linguistics, logic, and metaphysics.

Authority in its variety of forms is discussed in relation to the political institution in Chapter 6.

Aristotle was known for many centuries simply as "the Philosopher." His lasting fame—which in effect stalled further inquiry for centuries—illustrates another prescientific source of belief: authority. The body of Aristotle's work was accepted by the thinkers of the Catholic church in the early Middle Ages. The church, which then held virtually all social and political power throughout Europe, had a monopoly on education and literacy. The fundamental motive for all speculation—doubt—fell into disuse, because the prime objective of Catholic philosophers was to reconcile faith and reason: they took the Holy Scriptures and the teachings of the church fathers to be the absolute truth, and their task was to demonstrate that rational speculation would support rather than refute those truths.

Several different sources of authority can be seen at work here: first, the Scriptures have sacred authority because they are the word of God; secondly, the church has moral and political authority, because it has the power to declare ideas heretical and to punish heretics; thirdly, Aristotle has intellectual authority because his view of the world was most compatible with the philosophical needs of the medieval church. It was this array of authority that Descartes—himself a lifelong, devout Catholic—sought to replace by his method of systematic doubt.

The Scientific: Observation, Verifiability, Replication

With the scientific revolution, in the sixteenth and seventeenth centuries, tradition and authority were replaced by observation. Methods of observation became increasingly precise, partly because mathematics became the language of much description and partly because various instruments were perfected to expand the powers of the senses. The rules of logic were the basis for reasoning. Intuition remained useful, but only as a source of ideas to be tested by observation and experiment. Experimentation achieved the highest importance, because it is observation under extremely controlled circumstances.

Because methods of observation and the language of description became more precise, scholars could reproduce each other's results by repeating, or *replicating,* the steps of observation or experimentation. Because a scientist's claims were no longer acceptable on the basis of authority the methods *had* to be repeatable. This also enabled later experimenters to discover the shortcomings or oversights in the original method that affected the accuracy of the results.

With the rise of controlled, precise methods of observing the world, it was only natural that each field of inquiry would become specialized and increasingly differentiated from the others. The microscope is of no use to the astronomer, the telescope of no use to the biologist, the cyclotron of no use to the sociologist. But where does the sociologist fit into this scheme? What are the roots of sociology in nonscientific, prescientific, and scientific thinking?

The Science of Society: The Beginnings

Ideas about human behavior and human societies fall into the same three categories we have been discussing. Myths and traditions—nonscientific forms of belief—maintain the social order without necessarily asking or answering questions about why it should be as it is and not otherwise. Similarly, believers may differ in their interpretation of divine revelation ("the word of God"), but they have a basic belief that it is the source of truth about how people should behave and how societies should be run.

In some advanced ancient societies, the king or lawgiver set down formal social codes that govern behavior, as Hammurabi did in Babylonia around 2000 B.C. Usually such codes were outright statements of firmly held values and customs; they added the force of authority to the strength of tradition.

Prescientific thinking about human behavior and social structures has been characteristically devoted to describing what *should be* rather than to studying what *is*. Plato, for example, in *The Republic*, described in detail his view of the perfect society. It would be very strictly run on Plato's ethical rules and would be governed by a "philosopher-king." Up until the nineteenth century, most political and social theory was similarly concerned with redesigning society according to the philosopher's own favored system of conduct rather than carefully observing how a society actually operates.

Jean Jacques Rousseau, the influential eighteenth-century Swiss-born French philosopher, showed where such prescientific thinking could lead. He argued that human beings were "naturally good" and were made bad only by social institutions. He theorized that there was a creature called the "noble savage," who lived uncorrupted by society, in a state of innocence and goodness—in "a state of nature." Where was this state of nature to be found, so that its effects and benefits could be observed and studied? Nowhere: it is "a state which exists no longer, perhaps never existed, probably never will exist, and of which none the less it is necessary to have just ideas, in order to judge well our present state."[10]

Thus Rousseau felt able to propose as a "fact" that humans are "naturally good" but that the proper circumstances for demonstrating this truth do not exist and probably never did and never will. This is precisely the combination of statements that no sociologist could make or accept. Scientific thinking is, as we have already said, firmly based on observation of the real world. The French philosopher Auguste Comte coined the term sociology in the 1830s when he first proposed the discipline as a way of gathering accurate knowledge of society. Comte thought of sociology as the highest ("the queen") of the sciences because its subject of study—all of society and social behavior—is the most complex. He also believed human thought evolved through three stages: theological (religious), metaphysical (philosophical), and positive (scientific). (Comte's three categories correspond to our nonscientific, prescientific, and scientific stages. But whereas his terms imply that each stage makes previous ones obsolete, our terms do not.) Evolution applied not only to modes of thought but also to societies, which Comte thought evolved from simple to complex structures. The notion of social change was prominent in sociological thinking from its very beginnings.

Social change and its sources are examined in Chapter 14.

[10]Quoted in Bertrand Russell, *A History of Western Philosophy* (New York: Simon and Schuster, 1945), pp. 687–88.

Sociology came into being at a time when the societies of western Europe were racked with tumultuous political change and much economic and social misery. Comte looked to sociology to provide a scientifically accurate description of a society through theory and observations, and from this, he felt, rational, effective plans for social reform could be formulated. Sociology was to be the scientific means to an orderly, harmonious society.

Another prominent figure in early sociological thought, the Englishman Herbert Spencer, differed from Comte on the role of planning in social change. His theory of social change was based on "Social Darwinism," the notion that "survival of the fittest" applied to human societies as well as to the natural world. For the government, or anyone, to try to direct social change was to tamper with the natural evolution of the society into a higher form. The wealth and power of the "haves" was evidence of their natural superiority over the "have nots." To redistribute wealth and power, by providing such social services as public education, would misdirect social evolution by favoring the weak over the strong. Thus Spencer was the first *functionalist,* believing that any social arrangement that had evolved (in the absence of "artificial" planning) was acceptable.

The two rival perspectives, structural-functionalism and conflict theory, are studied in Chapter 2.

Karl Marx, the first *conflict theorist,* shared Spencer's belief in the inevitability of social evolution. But whereas Spencer saw the Darwinian process of "natural selection" as justifying social inequality, Marx saw this inequality as unjustified and the cause of conflict among social classes. He defined social classes in economic terms—according to whether or not they owned "the means of production" (factories, machines, and capital for investment). The capitalists, the owners of capital, were in conflict with the workers (the proletariat), who owned nothing but the labor they sold (at prices set by the capitalists). Marx predicted that the next stage of social evolution would occur by revolution. Members of the working class would understand the causes of their common plight, band together, and overthrow the capitalist class. From the dictatorship of the proletariat that was to follow, a classless society would finally emerge.

Among these three prominent figures of what is called sociology certain common traits are evident. All three favored the features that sociology inherited from prescientific thinking. First, each propounded a sweeping theory to explain the state of modern society, to describe its past, and to foresee its future. Secondly, each urged comprehensive social reforms, as the prescientific social thinkers had. (Although Spencer urged government and planners to keep their hands off social change, it was in the interest of promoting "natural" social change rather than of resisting change.)

Social classes are defined in detail in Chapter 7 on social stratification.

The Science of Society: The Mature Phase

Not until the last decades of the nineteenth century did some social theorists seek to discipline their theorizing and subdue their concerns for social reform with rigorous methods for systematically observing the society around them. The German sociologist Max Weber, for example, collected exhaustive data to demonstrate that the economic performance of a segment of a society is related to its dominant religious system. Weber compared the Protestant portions of Germany with the Catholic portions, and found the Protestants wealthier. To explain this fact he examined how each religion accepted the values and norms that underlie capitalism. He noted strong parallels between the capitalist ethic and the Protestant ethic (specifically the Calvinist form of Protestantism).[11] Calvinists believed that each soul was foreordained to salvation or damnation at birth. People did not know what their eternal fate was to be, but worldly success was taken as a sign that a person was among the "elect," the saved. Thus, ambition, hard work, thrift, and self-discipline were valuable traits among Calvinists. These very traits (plus the desire for worldly success) were equally valuable to the growth of capitalism. In contrast, Catholicism stressed ritual and repentence for sin; it did not place high value on ambition, wealth, and success on earth.

Bureaucracy and formal organizations are considered in Chapter 5.

Weber also studied the organizational structure that characterizes the modern industrial society: bureaucracy.[12] His descriptive analysis of the structure and purpose of bureaucracies remains the starting point for contemporary analysis of these large formal organizations.

Durkheim's study of suicide is described in Chapter 2.

The nineteenth-century French sociologist Emile Durkheim performed one of the earliest empirical studies in sociology. His work *Suicide* remains a classic in its close application of the scientific method to test his hypothesis that the varying suicide rates of different groups are related to the degree of social cohesion experienced by group members.

Durkheim also sought to study social evolution empirically by comparing societies in their degree of specialization of function, differentiation of labor, and reliance on formal contracts. He approached the territory of the early sociological thinkers, who formulated grand theories of social evolution, but he did so with more of the tools of systematic observation at hand.

During the latter decades of the nineteenth century when Weber and Durkheim were undertaking their studies, sociology was developing particular

[11]Max Weber, *The Protestant Ethic and the Spirit of Capitalism,* trans. Talcott Parsons (New York: Scribner's, 1958).

[12]Max Weber, *The Theory of Social and Economic Organization,* trans. A. M. Henderson and Talcott Parsons (New York: Oxford University Press, 1947).

features and emphases in the United States. Because this nation was then undergoing rapid, unsettling changes—industrialization, urbanization, internal migration, and immigration—the earliest American sociologists were more concerned with social problems than with perfecting scientific methods. (To this day, many Americans mistakenly consider sociology to be the same as social work.)

American sociology displays the variety of perspectives found in its European counterpart. Lester Ward was a forceful advocate of "applied" sociology of the sort advocated by Comte. William Graham Sumner shared Herbert Spencer's Social Darwinism in his thinking on social evolution. The prominent twentieth-century Americans Talcott Parsons and Robert K. Merton work within the functionalist perspective formulated by Spencer. C. Wright Mills, the most notable advocate of the "power elite" theory, worked within Marx's conflict perspective.

Whatever the differences in perspectives, contemporary American sociologists have long devoted their energies to compiling systematic analyses of social structures rather than to advocating policies of social reform. Sociologists now draw on an array of sophisticated data-gathering techniques. And all share a few premises on which sociological thought is based.

INDIVIDUALS IN A SOCIAL CONTEXT: SOCIAL VARIABLES

Culture includes thoughts and feelings, the things people create, possess, and use, and the rules of conduct by which they organize their lives.

If there is a single key to sociological understanding, it is the idea that the personal traits, beliefs, and values that govern behavior are products of an interaction between individuals and their social environment. All human beings receive a double inheritance at birth: a biological one and a social one. This social legacy is part of what we call *culture.*[13] Culture involves all that surrounds a person: beliefs, rules for behavior, ideas of right and wrong, material objects. Many of the things people know and want and do are taught to them by their parents. Others are instilled by teachers, preachers, and friends. Still others are learned through the give-and-take of daily living. As we see in the next few chapters and in Part 4, the habits and abilities people absorb as members of a society have a much greater influence on who and what they are—and think they are—than their genetic inheritance.

There is a long-standing debate among social scientists about how much—if any—of the mental process that underlies people's behavior is determined by genetic inheritance—that is, how much of a person's mental abilities (for instance, "intelligence," "creativity," and "the need to achieve") is genetically

[13]For a detailed discussion of culture defined as "social heredity," see Ralph Linton, *The Study of Man* (New York: Appleton-Century-Crofts, 1936), pp. 69–90.

People experience themselves as unique individuals; they value this and, in our society, often strive to express or enhance their individuality. Sociologists are aware of how the lives of individuals are affected by social variables: social class; ethnic background; rural, urban, or suburban residence; religious affiliation; and generation. These variables and others influence what sociologists call the social basis of individual behavior.

determined and how much is dependent on the individual's particular social environment? The proportion of genetic inheritance versus social learning is unknown. Social scientists debate the degree of emphasis to be placed on genetic factors in explaining social behavior. Despite the absence of clear-cut conclusive evidence on this issue, the debate remains alive. Why is the question of special concern to sociology? Because, if the bulk of human behavior is learned, virtually all sources of individual or group behavior are, at least potentially, observable. The sociologist does not, then, have to assume that complex behavior is the product of invisible forces.

Few individuals spend much time speculating on how much of their behavior is genetically determined. They are more concerned with themselves as unique individuals. Sociologists would agree that each person is unique. But such uniqueness is not the major focus of their research. Their main concern is how people, individually or collectively, act, react, and interact. As scientists, sociologists assume *causality:* that human attitudes and behavior (including thoughts, desires, and feelings) are products of what has happened before and of the individual's social environment. For example, suppose that a woman was born into a devout Catholic family. She has grown up to be a sincere, reverent believer in God. She prays and often attends worship services. She feels that God watches over her, is pleased by her good acts, and is displeased by her sins. She feels her religious beliefs in an intensely personal way, and she believes that her acceptance of the values of her religion is her own individual, free choice. Yet, from the sociological perspective, there is an important relationship or *correlation* between those personal beliefs and a set of circumstances that sociologists call *social variables:* being born into a Catholic family; belonging to a particular social class; living in a particular area; going to a particular type of school.

Social variables: the elements of a society that affect human behavior.

Émile Durkheim was one of the first to recognize the significance of these variables for understanding social life. He called them *social facts* and first used the concept in his book *The Rules of Sociological Method* (1895).[14]

Social class: a person's position as measured by social rewards of wealth, power, prestige, and life-style. See Chapter 7.

Social variables are any observable and measurable social phenomena that help explain group-based patterns of behavior. Among the many social variables are race, religious affiliation, social class, sex, age, level of education, and occupation. As we saw earlier, divorce rates can be linked to the social variable of membership in a given social class. Likewise, social class can be a social variable that influences a person's occupational goal: a middle-class or upper-class person has greater expectations of entering one of the prestigious

[14]Émile Durkheim, *The Rules of Sociological Method* (New York: Free Press, 1962).

and financially rewarding professions than does a working-class or lower-class person. Being white and being male further increase that likelihood in our society. Thus, race and sex are also social variables affecting occupation.

Society: The Invisible Teacher

To further understand the relationship between individual behavior and social variables, let us examine an issue that deals with half the population: women. We now recognize that in many societies women and men have not been regarded as equals. Women often have been considered less intelligent, less able to control their emotions, less capable of taking care of themselves, and, with a few exceptions, unable to succeed in such pursuits as business, politics, and the arts. They have frequently been considered "good" only for doing housework, rearing children, gossiping, and giving emotional support and comfort to "their men."

For centuries this view of women has been persuasive to overwhelming numbers of people—both men and women. After all, most women seemed to act in ways that fit this description, which served as a proof to many people. From a sociological perspective, however, this conclusion from observation is too simple. In order to formulate fuller explanations of the behavior of persons or groups, sociologists look at certain social variables. In this case, they would look for social variables within the *socialization* process—for example, the attitudes of the parents about appropriate behavior for males and females and the respective sex role of each parent. From this analysis they would conclude that women are taught to behave as they do. Their observed behavior neither proves nor disproves that they are inferior to men by birth. It proves only that women have been socialized into the roles that their society has defined as appropriate for them.

Sex roles are discussed in detail in Chapters 9 and 10.

Sociologists studying why women behave as they do would also be likely to examine practices outside the family and education systems, where other agents of socialization exist. Patterns of discrimination can be found in the marketplace, the news and entertainment media, and the political arena. Those who carry out practices that keep women down—and out—reinforce the social definition of a "woman's place."

Proof that men and women learn their social roles would not, by itself, answer the question of whether men and women are innately (by birth) different in their abilities and temperaments, however. What about the biological inheritance of each sex? Isn't it likely that, despite variations in detail from society to society, men and women are fulfilling built-in, instinctive roles? Isn't there a maternal instinct? Aren't men naturally aggressive and competitive?

Although there are still no definitive answers to these questions, significant progress was made when anthropologist Margaret Mead published *Sex and Temperament in Three Primitive Societies* in 1935.[15] In her comparative studies of three New Guinea tribes, the Arapesh, the Mundugumor, and the Tchambuli, Mead found evidence to overthrow the traditional assumptions about the influence of biological inheritance on male and female behavior.

She found that, among the Arapesh, both men and women exhibited a gentleness toward each other and toward children that in our society is considered a feminine characteristic. Among the Mundugumor, on the other hand, she found that both men and women showed traits characterizing our own notions of masculine behavior: aggressiveness, competitiveness, and indifference to children. Among the Tchambuli, men and women differed in their behavior, but with a shocking twist for an observer from our society: Tchambuli men fit the traditional stereotype of women in our society, while Tchambuli women fit our stereotype of men. The men were emotional, flighty, concerned with attractive appearance, and dependent on the attentions of women. The women were aggressive, practical, responsible for the well-being of the tribe, and tolerant but patronizing toward the men.

Model: in sociology, a description that incorporates the essential features of a complex phenomenon and excludes the unimportant or incidental variants. Models are discussed further in Chapter 2.

Thus, Mead's application of the scientific method permitted observation of social variables that cleared up a long-standing ambiguity. The Mead study was the first of many to seriously challenge the view that biological inheritance is the determining factor in the behavior of men and women in a society.

Mead's study of these New Guinea tribes can illustrate yet another trait of any social science: it is systematic. Her detailed descriptions and her conclusions would be of little value if they were based on hasty impressions or even on recurrent impressions that she did not test for accuracy. In Chapter 2 we look briefly at sociological methods of research, and these are described in still greater detail in the Appendix, "The Research Process."

A MODEL FOR SURVEYING HUMAN BEHAVIOR

In addition to methods of observation, sociologists need a clear notion of behavior itself, and of the level (or levels) at which they will explain what they observe.

To organize the study of human behavior the sociologist J. Milton Yinger has proposed a *model:* a structure of interrelated generalizations.[16]

[15]Margaret Mead, *Sex and Temperament in Three Primitive Societies* (New York: Morrow, 1963).

[16]J. Milton Yinger, *Toward a Field Theory of Behavior* (New York: McGraw-Hill, 1965), especially Chap. 2.

The biological fact of gender is subject to many social influences. Each society socializes people into the sex roles of its culture. In some traditional societies, such as those of Algeria and India (shown here), male and female roles are changing slowly and generally remain well-defined. The American women here involved in civic work, the young Frenchwoman in motorcycle garb, and women in other industrial societies have wider options, which sometimes present them with a confusing array of inconsistent demands and opportunities.

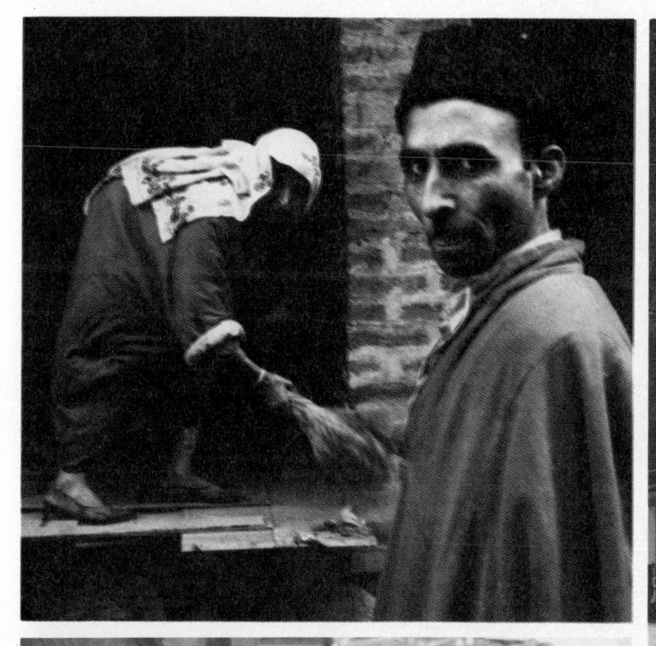

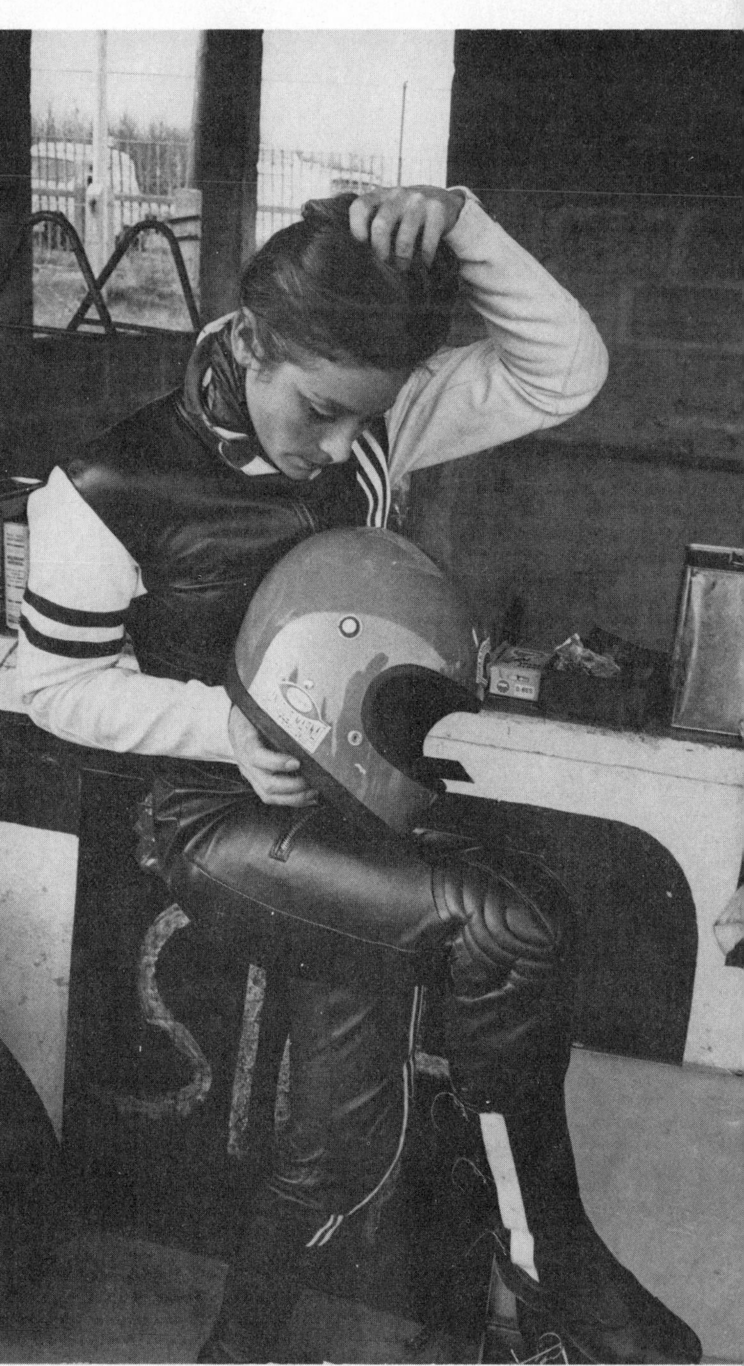

Yinger's model breaks the study of human behavior into four areas:

1. culture (norms and values)
2. society (structure)
3. personality (individual)
4. biology

In this model, behavior can be explained or described at any of four different levels or some combination of the four. Each area clearly differs from the others in how abstract or concrete it is. Human biology, for example, is concrete, based on direct observation of biological processes and on experimentation. Culture is a comparatively abstract concept: a sum of beliefs, rules, values, and objects.

To describe human behavior in relation to culture a sociologist must not only generalize from an enormous number of observed instances of behavior, but also observe how those instances spring from cultural components.

The study of social organizations and societies, focusing on the structure of group and individual interactions, is less abstract than that of culture, because what is studied is closer to direct observation. The social variables mentioned earlier are the structural elements—social class, religion, ethnic background, and rural or urban or suburban residence, for example.

At the individual (or personality) level, the sociologist considers the psychological principles that operate when a person interacts with his or her social structure and culture. Culture and social structure affect the individual. In turn, as we know from personal experience, individuals affect their social structure and culture. Thus, between the individual and society there is a *dialectic*, a never-ending tension between opposite forces.

Dialectic: an ongoing interplay of opposing forces that produces constant change in each. For example, individuals are influenced by their society, which in turn is the product of their patterns of interaction.

The fourth level of Yinger's model, the biological, focuses on the genetic and physiological characteristics of humans, such as their neurological processes (brain waves, brain chemistry, and the human nervous system). As we have mentioned, sociologists consider genetic inheritance to be a relatively minor factor in human social behavior. This in no way diminishes the soundness of scientific research on this factor; but as sociologists see things inheritance plays a limited role in explaining *variations* in behavior—whether from individual to individual or from group to group.

In any event, sociologists concentrate their attention on the first two levels, the cultural and structural, with occasional reliance on the third level, the individual or personality. We will refer to Yinger's model again later to help orient our approach to sociology.

SUMMARY

Sociologists are far from being the first students of humanity and human societies. They are, however, the first who adopted an empirical perspective (what we call the sociological perspective) and the scientific method in such studies. By use of the sociological perspective sociologists seek to get behind social appearances to the social facts or variables. They thus systematically avoid the pitfalls inherent in common sense and conventional wisdom: the beliefs based on uncritical conclusions drawn from the appearances of things.

All sociologists share a premise basic to this perspective: that however unique individuals feel they are, they nevertheless are products of interaction with others. What they believe, what they value, what rules of conduct they follow (or break) are learned through their membership in groups and their socialization into a culture.

For this reason sociologists favor the cultural and structural levels on Yinger's model of the study of human behavior. They occasionally choose the psychological level and rarely the biological level. Sociologists, in short, study the group basis of human behavior.

METHODS, MODELS, AND THEORIES

In Chapter 1 the sociological perspective was described. It should be clear that such a perspective is meaningless without a method or set of methods. Sociologists need well-defined tools of observation and data collection. But they also need intellectual tools, such as theories, models, and hypotheses. All these are the subject of this chapter. We will distinguish models from theories, referring to Yinger's model for the study of human behavior, discussed in Chapter 1, and examining Durkheim's theory of suicide. The chapter concludes with an examination of the two major theoretical models in sociology: structural-functional theory and conflict theory.

THE SOCIOLOGICAL METHOD

Sociological perspective: the viewpoint that individual behavior is explainable as a product of group interaction and can be studied by systematic observation and experimentation.

How do sociologists actually go about their tasks, and why do they claim that their approach is scientific? In the Appendix, "The Research Process," the scientific approach to sociology is given much more detailed treatment. Here we give only a brief sketch.

The sociologist's use of the scientific method involves:

1. defining issues and areas of investigation, usually within the perspective of a larger theory;
2. specifying and operationalizing concepts;
3. formulating questions and hypotheses;
4. collecting and analyzing data.

Defining Issues and Areas of Investigation

Sociologists range in their research from the micro (small) view of society to the macro (large) view. They may study the interaction of two-person groups (such as friends or spouses) or the role of education in an advanced industrial society. No society is wholly intelligible to an observer if only the overall view is studied and the details of life within it are ignored. At the same time, a vast collection of details tells us little unless they are placed in a larger framework. The sociologist begins his or her research by trying to define what is to be

In the village of Olympos, in Karpathos, Greece, all of the villagers participate joyously in a wedding dance. From this and myriad other customs and patterns of interaction that characterize life in tiny human settlements, sociologists have derived a model of the community (studied at length in Chapter 12). Models, if properly constructed, enable researchers to simplify complex phenomena to their basic observable and defining features.

studied and how it might fit within the larger context of society as a whole.

The two major frameworks used by sociologists are model and theory. Models are *descriptions;* theories are *explanations.* A model is an artificial, convenient reduction of something to its structure of essential parts and their interrelationships. (Another term for models is *ideal types.*) For example, in physics one of the first models to be studied is that of the atom: the model shows each part of the atom in relation to the other parts. In sociology the nuclear family and the extended family are models.

The classic sociological theory, Durkheim's theory about suicide, is discussed later in this chapter.

A theory, on the other hand, attempts to explain the elements and relations found within a model. For example, Karl Marx proposed a model to describe the class structure of his society (and societies like it) in the mid-nineteenth century. The model provoked him to ask questions about how this class structure came about and what it was likely to become. His explanation of why the class structure took the form he had observed was his *theory* of social class. Marx also made *predictions,* based on his theory, about future forms of class structure. Thus Marx performed the same intellectual tasks required of all sociologists. They try to describe society accurately as a basis for explaining the relations between individuals and groups and between groups and groups, and they often make predictions based on these explanations.

Prediction can mean two different things. A prediction can be made simply to test a hypothesis or theory, or it can be proposed as a practical solution to a social problem. For example, a sociologist might predict that if welfare rules didn't deny payments to families with resident male heads of household then the family structure would be strengthened among welfare recipients. Then if the welfare rules were changed and the affected families did indeed seem strengthened, two things would have occurred: first, a hypothesis relating a certain family problem to a certain welfare rule would have been validated; and, secondly, a solution to a social problem would have been found.

Defining and Operationalizing Concepts

Operationalize: to define a concept by observable specifics (for example, to define "rich" to mean "having an income of $35,000 or more per year") so that the concept can be used in empirical research.

Scientists in every discipline must specify their concepts and *operationalize* them (define them in such a way that they can be the basis for observation or research). For sociologists this task is especially important, because so many terms have no single, clear, agreed meaning in popular usage. For example, to study some aspect or consequence of poverty, a sociologist would first have to formulate a clear, precise definition of poverty. Everyone knows that the poor are those with too little money. But what precisely is "too little money"? Many members of our consumer-oriented society feel discontented with their ability to buy goods. Is everyone who feels the need for more money to be considered poor? To add to the confusion, we often hear—chiefly from media commentators—that the so-called poor in our society are much better off than the poor in most other societies. Their point seems to be that the poor in our society are not really poor; they only *think* they are.

The United States government provides the sociologist with one of many possible operational definitions of poverty. In 1972, for example, any nonfarm family of four with a total income of less than $4,275 was operationally defined as living in poverty. Why $4,275? Because in 1972, according to the government, that income could not provide adequate nutrition, health care, clothing, and entertainment for a family that size. Thus, the government operationally defines poverty according to the current United States standard of living (such as having indoor plumbing) and the purchasing power of income. Although the figures in the government's definition and the assumptions behind them are disputed by many people, the definition itself is operationally precise.

Ideal types. To aid in research and conceptualization, the sociologist Max Weber formulated what he called *ideal types,* lists of all possible traits or characteristics of a phenomenon, such as all the characteristics of a bureaucracy. To probe beneath the apparent differences on the surfaces of two things to their hidden similarities, an ideal type was invented. Then the researcher could compare significant features of each against the model (the ideal type). For example, the Roman Catholic church (or any formal religious denomination) and the United States Army are very different in many ways, but when studied against the ideal type of bureaucracy they are revealed to share the traits of a strong bureaucratic structure.

To see how well you understand what we have been discussing, try the following activity (you'll find many others throughout the text).

Compose an ideal type of, say, a democratic political system. Try to be precise in developing your concept. Some library research might be valuable.

Using further library research, compare the United States political system with your model. Also compare some other system that is supposed to be democratic. How well does each fit your model?

Formulating Questions and Hypotheses

Hypothesis: a statement of expected relationship between two or more variables or sets of variables to be tested by observation or experiment.

A hypothesis is a statement of expected relationship between two or more variables (measurable characteristics, such as sex and wealth) or sets of variables that a researcher proposes for testing. For example, Durkheim formulated a hypothesis that suicide rates vary with the degree of social cohesion within a given social group: the more cohesion, the lower the suicide rate. (We will examine his research of this hypothesis later in this chapter.) Another example of a hypothesis is: There is a relationship between certain child-rearing practices that socialize us to the sex roles in our culture and the fact that certain jobs are sex-specific. (*Sex-specific* is a label that must be operationalized. We might say, "By sex-specific, we mean behavior that is related to either males alone or females alone and is not shared by both.")

Sociologists usually start their research with a hypothesis in mind. They suspect that two social variables are related, and are related in a particular way. Their research is intended to test the hypothesis—to prove it or disprove it.

Not all research starts from hypotheses, however. Sociologists sometimes investigate an issue or area of research without any particular expectations to be confirmed or disproved. This is called *exploratory research.* But because sociologists, like all people, have commonsense ideas about almost any subject they might study, these ideas often become early working hypotheses.

Collecting and Analyzing Data: Research Techniques

Once the sociologist has decided on the topic and the area of investigation, has drawn a plan for examining a problem, has set forth ideas to test, and has specified the concepts involved, he or she is ready to begin gathering data to be analyzed. First the data-base (the source of information) must be selected. Then the researcher must decide which of many data-gathering techniques would be most appropriate to the needs of the study.

Suppose you have formulated the hypothesis we described about sex-specific jobs. Its terms are defined and operationalized, and you are ready to test it. First, you must have a source of data to investigate. You want to get information about how people see themselves and others. You might use people in your college, in your town or city, or somewhere else in the country (or, if you are comparing broader groups, overseas).

Like other scientists, you must decide which techniques will best help you to test your hypothesis. Sociologists use a wide variety of techniques. One is participant observation: the researcher participates fully in the lives of those being studied (for example, by taking a job that few or no people of the sociologist's gender choose and observing the reactions of coworkers and customers). Another technique is experimentation (for example, a researcher interested in sex-specific jobs could have men and women subjects call a female telephone operator and call a male operator, and observe the differences or similarities in the subjects' reactions). The researcher can interview selected individuals with a battery of questions (for example, probing their beliefs and attitudes about sex-specific occupations). Or the researcher can select a thousand people randomly and survey them by mail to find out how they would react to hearing a male telephone operator, or whatever questions are relevant to the research topic.

The many research techniques are discussed further in the Appendix, "The Research Process."

If you want to know the opinions of a true cross section of American society, and know them in a month, the survey of a random sample of the population is the best way to go about it. However, if you want to get a sense of how children are taught sex roles, observation in private homes and day-care centers over lengthy time periods would make much more sense than asking people to answer a battery of yes or no questions or to reminisce about what they did with their children—or what their parents did to them.

These two photographs represent the contrast between the two chief modes of observation. In each photograph the position of the camera represents that of the sociological observer. In participant observation the sociologist becomes a part of the phenomena to be observed, playing roles like those of the persons being observed. Thus to study, say, patterns of interaction among office workers, the participant observer would become an office worker for the time being. In nonparticipant observation the researcher stands outside and seeks an overview of the phenomena. Each method has its advantages and disadvantages, which is why a combination of the two is often used.

Types of data. Sociologists often refer to their data as *soft* or *hard.* Soft data are qualitative; they are based on material that is difficult—though not always impossible—to measure. Observations, impressions, comments, and oral histories come under the general category of soft data.

Hard data are quantifiable; that is, either they are numbers to begin with (such as rates of suicide, divorce, or crime) or they are readily converted into numbers (such as scores given to responses to a public opinion poll). Most

PUBLIC OPINION POLL OF ADULT ATTITUDES TOWARD MARIJUANA LAW

	Percentage Expressing Approval of			
Category Polled	*Civil Penalties, as Is Now*	*Possession of Small Amounts Legal*	*Sale and Possession of Small Amounts Legal*	*Stiffer Penalties*
Total adults	31	18	9	40
By age:				
18–29	27	30	17	26
30–44	35	21	8	34
45–59	42	9	5	41
60 and over	23	6	5	63
By usage:				
Have used	23	44	24	9
Currently use	9	54	35	2
Never used	34	11	5	48

Source: "Survey of Marijuana Use and Attitudes: State of Oregon," December 1, 1975.

survey findings—that is, the answers to questions on questionnaires—are ultimately changed to statistics and analyzed in terms of percentages and probabilities. The percentages then show the views or behavior of particular groups (like Democrats) or categories (like husbands) of people compared to other groups (Republicans) or categories (wives). The probability statistics specify the likelihood that the comparisons are mere accidents or mean something significant. Soft data may be written up as case studies—descriptions of processes that are more thorough than surveys can be.

Whether soft or hard, the data are used for one purpose: to help answer the questions posed in the original study plan—to test the hypothesis.

Consider the following hypothesis: "Students who return to college after a prolonged absence (say because of military duty or the need to work) are more likely to take the required course work seriously than students who have come to college directly from high school."

1. Do you agree with the statement? If not, what alternative hypothesis would you suggest?

2. Imagine that interview questions and written questionnaires have been suggested as alternative methods of collecting data to test the hypothesis (or your substitution). What do you think are the advantages and disadvantages of each method for this study?

Although you are not a trained sociologist, you should already have some feeling for the challenge of doing a piece of research and some idea about how to do it. You will have ample opportunity throughout this book to become more familiar with sociological methods. Many of the activities in each chapter require one or more of the techniques sociologists use to obtain data and to make the information usable for their analyses.

In testing the hypothesis about respective attitudes toward college work, some of you may have chosen to talk to a number of your friends informally; others may have planned a survey asking specific questions of a larger number of people.

Not all research is done through observation or experiment or sample surveys. Much important work actually goes on in the library. There, both primary (original) and secondary source materials often provide valuable information. Library research is most suitable for such areas as statistical and historical research. A researcher might study changes in the composition of the labor force, or population changes due to migration, or changes in the birth and death rates. Census figures and other statistical data regularly compiled by government agencies are the sources for such research.

Historical research likewise involves library research: diaries, autobiographies, official records, and other material from archives are the chief sources—often the only sources—for research into the past. The library is also the best place to begin any empirical field research, to find out what previous researchers have discovered or concluded on the topic.

Correlations: relationships asserted between two or more variables.

All sociological research requires planning, testing, and data collection, as the research of any scientist does. And the goal of sociologists is like the goal of those in other fields: to analyze carefully collected data in order to answer or test carefully defined (operationalized) questions or hypotheses.

Correlation versus causality. The questions sociologists seek to answer often concern *correlations:* relationships between one social variable and another without any assumption that one *causes* the other, at least not in any direct way. We have referred to correlations earlier; a person's religion can be correlated to his or her social class, ethnic background, geographic region, and other social variables; Durkheim found that suicide can be similarly correlated to social variables.

Variable: anything that is measurable and subject to change in such ways as to affect research findings.

Do individuals raised in permissive homes have fewer sex biases than those raised in rigid ones? Do those educated in the days before the popularity of Dr. Spock's book on child-rearing have different attitudes toward sex-specific jobs from those educated in later times? Do men and women have views on what is appropriate and inappropriate for men and women to do?

Independent variable: the variable believed to produce a change in particular circumstances; the causal variable.

An analysis or testing of hypotheses on these questions requires a series of comparisons between certain *variables* (measurable characteristics) that differ (such as sex—male and female) or change (such as opinions about a particular issue). In the hypothesis about college students there were two principal variables: (1) presence or absence of prolonged interruption of education; and (2) attitudes toward course work. Sociologists would call the first variable independent and the second dependent. That is, it is assumed that whether an individual goes to college immediately or delays beginning a college education is the variable that affects the student's attitude toward course work. The latter is dependent upon (an effect of) the former. In the graph below, there are three variables: education and age are the independent variables and income is the dependent variable.

Mean Income of Males by Education and Age, 1966

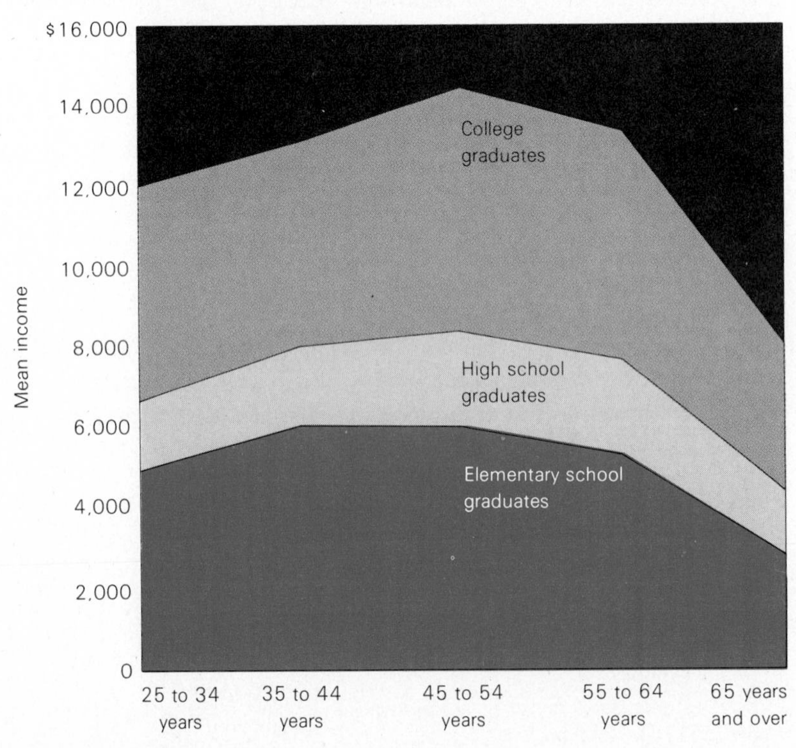

Source: Everett K. Wilson, *Sociology*, rev. ed. (Homewood, Ill.: Dorsey, 1971), p. 271.

Dependent variable: the variable believed to be affected by another variable in given circumstances; the effect variable.

A CLASSIC OF SOCIOLOGICAL METHOD: DURKHEIM ON SUICIDE

We can sum up our discussion of perspective and method, and of model and theory, by looking at Émile Durkheim's study *Suicide,* published in 1897.

From his examination of records in France and elsewhere in Europe, Durkheim noticed that people in certain social categories had higher rates of suicide than others. He found, for example, that as percentages, fewer Catholics committed suicide than Protestants; fewer married persons than single; and fewer civilians than military persons. He noted also that in times of economic depression suicide rates were higher.

So far Durkheim was compiling statistics, getting a purely descriptive picture of suicide. Next was the crucial step from descriptive to theoretical sociology. In effect Durkheim asked: Why would lower percentages of Catholics, married persons, and civilians commit suicide than of Protestants, single, widowed, and divorced persons, and soldiers? And why would the suicide rate in an economic depression in France be ten times worse than it is in Spain, a chronically poor nation?

A popular explanation for suicide in Durkheim's day was couched in biological terms. It was widely believed that the urge to commit suicide was passed genetically from parent to child. Durkheim considered this possibility, for there were so many cases of a grandfather, father, and son who each committed suicide at the same age and by the same means. But from his perspective as a sociologist Durkheim could not believe that members of the same family would be genetically disposed to use the same weapon. Rather it was more likely that each family member was imitating the earlier example.

To explain suicide, then, Durkheim decided to consider the structure of society, the different groups and situations in which the suicides had been participants. He sought to understand why there seemed to be something different about the behavior of those in certain social categories: religious, marital, and the like.

Durkheim next framed a hypothesis, a tentative statement of relationships between social variables that he expected his further research to confirm: Differences in suicide rates are directly related to the different levels of social integration, or feelings of closeness with others, experienced by persons in each opposite set of circumstances—Protestants versus Catholics, or married versus single persons, for example. Durkheim expected to find that suicide rates varied with the degree of integration of a social group. The American sociologist Robert K. Merton summarizes Durkheim's reasoning as follows:

1. Social cohesion provides psychic support to group members subjected to acute stresses and anxieties.

2. Suicide rates are functions of *unrelieved* anxieties and stresses to which persons are subjected.

3. Catholics (and other specified additional groups) have greater social cohesion than Protestants.

4. Therefore, lower suicide rates should be anticipated among Catholics than among Protestants.

Before Durkheim's theory could be tested he had to define his terms, such as social cohesion, psychic support, stresses and anxieties, and group membership. He had to make explicit his assumptions, such as that all humans have a basic need to relieve anxieties, and that failing to do so they might feel suicidal. He had to operationalize such concepts as the level of cohesion among Catholics and Protestants. And he had to restate his general hypothesis in terms of working hypotheses. The general hypothesis, that suicide varies with the degree of integration of a social group, was made more specific for testing: suicide varies by religious affiliation (or Protestants are more likely to commit suicide than Catholics). Did the statistics support this specific hypothesis? Durkheim found they did. This was also true for specific hypotheses about divorced persons and soldiers.

In terms of Yinger's four levels of study of society, Durkheim's theory explains suicide at the social or structural level, but his primary assumption is at the level of personality: Humans have a deep need to release anxiety. Durkheim rejected the biological level, as we said. He also rejected the cultural level as a source of differential suicide rates, because the norms and values of Protestantism and Catholicism, of married and unmarried persons, were equally condemning of suicide.

He concluded that Protestant values supported individualism (thus less group interaction in personal lives) and upward social mobility (thus more uncertainty and risk) and provided a less warm and more competitive congregational setting, because worldly success was measured by material wealth. Catholicism, on the other hand, focused more on family, community, and parish life and less on competition and individualism. Catholics were more inclined to accept their class position, were thus subjected to less uncertainty and risk, and were encouraged to stress cooperation over competition. Not only did parish life provide more social contact but the confessional provided penitents with a sense of absolution, forgiveness for their sins, which was certainly intended to release anxiety.

Durkheim relied heavily on logical reasoning and scholarly analysis of library sources to arrive at these conclusions. Although he may have talked informally to members of the groups under study, he made no formal survey or test of the social cohesion of each group. You may have noticed that Durkheim's research seems to complete a big circle, using the very data he began with—suicide rates in various groups—to prove his point. This circularity is more apparent than real, because there were many intermediate steps of logical analysis in which he considered possible reasons why his theory was wrong and further elaborated the differences between pairs of groups to support his theory. Many field surveys since have lent empirical support to Durkheim's classic study.

MAJOR MODELS AND VIEWPOINTS

While all sociologists are "theorists" of sorts, not all see society in the same theoretical framework. As we mentioned in Chapter 1, those called *structural-functionalists* see society as fundamentally a smoothly working set of interrelated institutions, groups, and classes.[1] *Conflict* theorists, on the other hand, see society as an arena of groups and social classes in conflict, each seeking dominance and achievement of its own goals.[2] Most sociologists make partial use of both perspectives.

Sociologists also differ among themselves in the scope and breadth of their studies. Some seek to understand society on a large scale (macro); others study the smallest possible (micro) components of a society—the roles of individuals and the interaction in small groups; and many choose studies between these extremes.

[1]Debate among structural-functionalists was begun by Kingsley Davis and Wilbert Moore, "Some Principles of Stratification," *American Sociological Review* 10 (1945): 242–49. For modifications of the structural-functionalist approach to stratification, see Melvin Tumin, *Social Stratification* (Englewood Cliffs, N.J.: Prentice-Hall, 1967), and Talcott Parsons, "A Revised Analytical Approach to the Theory of Social Stratification," in *Class, Status and Power,* ed. Reinhold Bendix and Seymour Martin Lipset (New York: Free Press, 1953).

[2]For extensive discussion of the conflict theorists' position, see Lewis Coser, *The Functions of Social Conflict* (Chicago: Free Press, 1956); Ralf Dahrendorf, *Class and Conflict in Industrial Society* (Stanford, Calif.: Stanford University Press, 1959); id., "Toward a Theory of Social Conflict," in *Social Change,* ed. Amitai Etzioni and Eva Etzioni (New York: Basic Books, 1964); and G. William Domhoff, *Who Rules America?* (Englewood Cliffs, N.J.: Prentice-Hall, 1967).

Perhaps we can see these differences best by drawing two bisecting axes (crossed lines), one running between the conflict and the functional theories to represent a sociologist's theoretical perspective, and the other running between macrosociology and microsociology to represent his or her scope of study.

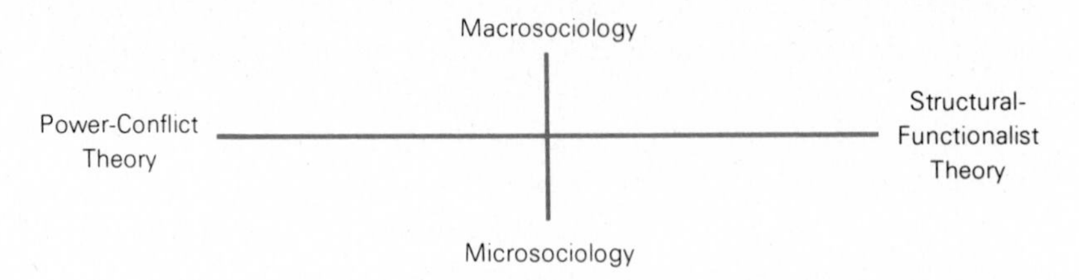

The labels *macrosociology* and *microsociology* indicate the poles of the vertical axis. Macrosociologists are concerned with whole societies and large organizations—the big issues. They study the structures that hold societies together and the tensions that lead to instability. Microsociologists are more interested in the smaller units within the social order, interpersonal rather than intergroup relations, or how individuals learn the roles they are to play and how they play them in particular social settings.

Suppose two sociologists wanted to study race in contemporary society. One of them could do microsociology by studying the patterns of interaction in a classroom that has been integrated by busing. The other sociologist could do macrosociology by studying the change of roles and participation rates that a minority group has experienced—in the economy as consumers and workers and in politics as voters and officeholders, for example.

The horizontal axis of the diagram represents the range between opposite theoretical perspectives of society. The structural functionalists and the conflict theorists can look at the same society or social component and usually see two different things. They do so because their perceptions are influenced by opposite assumptions or concerns.

The structural-functionalists work from the assumption that every feature of society serves a purpose within it. From this perspective, functionalists examine society mainly to see how it works, how each part contributes to holding the society together as a smoothly running, balanced organism. In so doing, sociologists distinguish between two different kinds of social functions: *manifest* and *latent* functions. Manifest functions are the obvious, intended functions of a social arrangement, latent functions are the unintended, often unnoticed functions. For example, the manifest function of compulsory education in an industrial society is to guarantee a pool of skilled labor to meet its productive needs. One of its latent functions is to act as a "baby-sitter," allowing many more adults to remain in the labor force who otherwise would have to remain at home meeting full-time parental obligations.

1. Can you find any other latent functions in the educational institution?

2. List the manifest and latent functions of:

education	**pets**
the Vietnam war	**automobiles**

Suppose, for example, that the functionalists are looking at social stratification—the division of a society into classes according to the life-style, wealth, power, and prestige of people. Because stratification can be found in almost every known society, functionalists argue that a system of unequal social rewards serves a manifest purpose in each society. The argument rests on the notion that some tasks are more important to a society than others, requiring more training, skill, and commitment.

Functionalists take for granted that such a system is necessary for the equilibrium (balance) of the society. Equilibrium is a key consideration to functionalists. They assume that it is a condition that every society strives to maintain. As we mentioned earlier, they see society as a smoothly running, balanced organism. This comparison of a society to an organism, a biological entity whose survival depends on the proper relationships among parts, goes back to the early years of sociology.

Not all sociologists believe that things mesh as well as the functionalists contend or that everything is functional for all members of a society. Indeed, some writers—Karl Marx was one—maintain that certain institutions (such as the economy) and certain social classes (such as capitalists, the land- and wealth-holding class) tend to dominate a society. This dominance creates inequalities that may be functional for those in power (for example, the slaveowners in our own history) but very unfortunate and unfair for those lacking the power to determine their own destinies (such as the slaves). Marx analyzed the evolution of societies from the conflict theory perspective. He maintained that, in every stage, except the ultimate stage, communism, one group was dominant. Historical change occurred, he believed, when one group was defeated by another group, which in turn became powerful for a time.[3]

[3]For the basic concepts in Marx's theory of class, see Karl Marx, *Early Writings* (New York: McGraw-Hill, 1964).

Not all conflict theorists necessarily agree with Marx's philosophy or the contention that the workers will one day launch a successful revolution that will ultimately produce a classless society. Nevertheless they share Marx's view that society is characterized by conflict and change rather than harmony and stability.

A look at a contemporary issue from one perspective and then the other should make each view clear. As an example, let's take the system of welfare.

Consensus theorists and conflict theorists observe social phenomena from two fundamentally opposite perspectives. The consensus theorist sees inequities as essential to social order, believing that, without stratification (unequal distribution of social rewards), the more demanding positions in society would not be adequately filled. The conflict theorist sees the poverty and squalor endured by many ethnic minorities and lower- and working-class people as symptoms of an exploitive social structure.

The welfare system takes income gathered from taxation of the working members of society and redistributes it to those who are not working.

The functionalists would see welfare as contributing to overall social equilibrium by sustaining the economic well-being of those who are unable to work. The society thus carries out some of its professed goals by preventing starvation and homelessness among the poor. At the same time it forestalls social disruption. If poor people without jobs receive the minimum amount they need to live, they are less likely to riot or commit other violent acts out of prolonged desperation. The society demonstrates its kindly concern for the well-being of its members; deprivation because of unemployment or the loss of the family wage earner is unbearable to only a minority of the poor. These few react in various ways: mental illness, rebellion, and crime. The rest learn to adjust to the deprivation of a welfare existence.

The conflict theorist looking at the same system would have a very different interpretation. The welfare system would be viewed as a tragic example of the injustices of social stratification. From the conflict perspective, many persons at the top of the social ladder have no need to work because they are so wealthy, and many persons at the bottom are unequipped to work by lack of education or opportunity (for example, mothers without husbands and with children needing constant parental care). The system maintains this condition of dependence by providing a minimal amount of money, just enough to sustain life but too little to allow most people on welfare to find alternatives, whether by going back to school or by paying for child care so that the parent can find work. Moreover, in many places a family cannot receive welfare payments if the unemployed father lives at home. This rule favors broken homes and keeps the welfare rolls full. And the system creates a permanent state of hopelessness and apathy in children as well as adults, again achieving the unintended effect of keeping the system supplied with clients.

While we were comparing the functionalist and conflict theory viewpoints, you may have noticed the macro and micro viewpoints as well. Both theorists can see the welfare system from the viewpoint both of the society and of the individual. The macro functionalist view is that welfare decreases the grounds for social strife; the macro conflict theorist sees welfare as an extreme symptom of an uneven distribution of social rewards characteristic of our social stratification. From the micro view, the functionalist sees the individual gaining economic well-being despite nonparticipation in the economic institutions; the micro conflict theorist sees the individual losing self-esteem and motivation as well as family stability.

To check your understanding of the different perspectives and approaches discussed above, take several of the social issues listed below and try to figure out how a functionalist and a conflict theorist would approach them. Then see if you can guess the sources of data you might use to study these issues from both macro and micro sociological perspectives.

1. The seniority system in a labor union or congressional body

2. The problem of environmental pollution

3. A land use problem (for example, strip-mining an area instead of using it for farming)

4. Keeping traditional sex roles (man the breadwinner, woman the homemaker and mother)

5. The military-industrial complex (that is, the close ties among the defense industry, the military, and Congress)

In the chapters to follow we occasionally offer theoretical perspectives other than those of the functionalists and the conflict theorists. We look not only at the extremes of the micro-macro continuum but also at issues that fall in the middle ground between those extremes. One such area of study that we examine is the realm of institutions, where in every society certain universal human needs must be fulfilled: in the family, through religion, through economic and political arrangements, and through education.

Consider one last continuum that underlies much of the work in this book. This continuum puts the concept of social institutions approximately in the middle of the macro-micro axis. Thus we can study the interactions between each extreme and the middle:

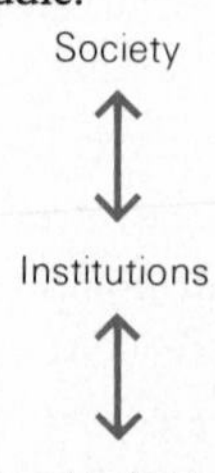

The arrows indicate relationships. We look at institutions from both "above" and "below"—that is, we study both how they perform essential functions for the society and how each institution governs the roles of people who participate in it.

THE IMPACT OF SOCIOLOGY

Sociologists are concerned with all aspects of social life—the ordinary and the unusual, the normal and the abnormal, the simple and the complex. Any aspect of a society or culture can be studied. Nothing is too sacred or too remote.

Today sociologists are at work in many countries studying everything from the political systems of developing nations to the dating patterns of Australian young people. Recent studies have focused on the attitudes of northwest Canadians toward the ecology movement; police behavior in various industrial societies; communes in the United States and Israel; child-rearing practices in Southeast Asia; protest and power in black Africa; and marriages east and west. Sociologists at work in the United States are doing thousands of studies on various aspects of American life. Books in almost any sociologist's office have titles that illustrate the range of topics covered: *The Conduct of the Corporation; The Politics of Unreason; Automobile Workers and the American Dream; The Adolescent Society; The Social Order of the Slum; The Tenacity of Prejudice; The Protestant Establishment; And the Poor Get Children; The Rise of the Unmeltable Ethnics; The Feminine Mystique.*

Sociologists share their basic working principles and methods with other scientists—and some of their problems as well. They are well aware of the risks they run in reporting unusual or unpopular findings to an often suspicious public. They know the troubles encountered by Galileo, Darwin, Einstein, and many other scientists who unsettled not only the scientific community but the wider world as well.

In the present age, when most people have not yet become disillusioned with our massive technology, it may be hard to remember that many past scientific discoveries and theories disturbed the cultures in which they were made. Galileo came into conflict with the Roman Catholic church for confirming that the earth circled the sun and not vice versa. Darwin scandalized his contemporaries by suggesting, and seeking to demonstrate, that humans originated in a way quite different from the biblical account.

Today, a discovery in the physical sciences is unlikely to cause a stir of indignation. But, in the social sciences, opportunities for controversy still lurk around every corner. Perhaps sociologists are especially sensitive, since their principal activity is poking into people's personal, professional, and public lives. When sociologists come up with something that many think is commonplace knowledge, they are accused of elaborating the obvious. But woe unto those whose findings and theories run counter to conventional wisdoms. Their studies are often attacked as having been done improperly. And when

The family is one of many social phenomena that can be studied from a macrosociological or microsociological perspective. The microsociologist might study patterns of interaction among family members and how the size and functions of the family influence those patterns. The macrosociologist would more likely be concerned with the role of the family in relation to other social institutions in fulfilling the functional prerequisites of society (discussed in Chapter 6). The two perspectives combined yield a thorough description of a given social phenomenon (here, the family) and its changing condition through time.

people accept the results of the studies, they often express regret that the research was undertaken.

Some studies have revealed a gradual increase in what was once forbidden behavior. Many people believe that publicizing these findings encourages more people to engage in the practices discussed. Thus, the revelation that most people have had sexual intercourse before marrying, or the claim of most psychologists that, on the basis of evidence, it is better for the children of an unhappy marriage if the parents get divorced, upsets people who want premarital virginity to remain a social value or divorces to be prevented at all cost. Suppose, for example, it is found that crime is increasing everywhere, including in middle-class schools. We disapprove of this trend, of course. What if we believe that publicizing it will only encourage more people to consider crime acceptable and thus increase the trend? Should sociologists publish the finding anyway? Or should they publish it only if they have also worked out a series of suggestions for dealing with the problem?

Sociologists are often involved in research on such controversial subjects. Recent studies have explored problems in school desegregation, civil disorders, crime and violence, and pornography. Some of these were conducted by presidential commissions and other governmental bodies. Most sociologists who worked on these studies hoped their analyses and recommendations would be reviewed and acted on by the authorities. Others who investigate similar matters have been unwilling to do so under the sponsorship of government agencies (or private firms) because they *fear* the uses to which their findings may be put. Some will do such "contract" research only when they feel they have the full support of their *host communities,* that is, the people they are investigating. And some sociologists are reluctant to engage in any sort of "applied" research altogether, believing that their primary responsibility is inquiry, not application—application is something to be left to others.

1. Despite the disagreement among sociologists about what should be published and how, the fact remains that sociological findings can have an impact on society. In your view, should sociologists be problem-solvers, mixing their "pure science" with "social policy"? Or should they pursue knowledge for its own sake, hoping it has beneficial consequences but taking no responsibility if it doesn't?

2. If you think that sociologists should "get involved," would you think the same if you were, say, a conservative Republican and you

found that most sociologists were liberal Democrats or political radicals? If you think that sociologists should act as pure scientists, is it because you have some kind of faith that knowledge can never harm us ultimately?

These issues are important, because there is evidence to indicate that sociologists' findings influence social behavior. Just think of how pollsters' findings feed into the political bandwagon effect, helping certain candidates for office and sometimes thwarting the campaigns of others. Or consider the trend of trial marriages: the English philosopher Bertrand Russell advocated trial marriages years ago, but only a few were persuaded by his ideas. Then sociologists and others reported that increasing numbers of couples were living together unmarried. The behavior and experiences of couples who tried such experiments, once reported and picked up by the media, influenced the behavior of many more persons.

Clearly, to observe a society and report the findings is to influence that society. To the problems we have just discussed we can add still another—one that has plagued sociologists with controversy. Although sociologists aspire to the methods and detachment of other scientists, how closely can they approach this ideal—and if they cannot come close, what should they do about it?

Consider, for example, what happened in 1969 when the educational psychologist Arthur Jensen reported his findings that, despite variations among individuals, members of the black race, *on the average,* displayed lower intelligence (as measured by standardized group tests) than members of the white race.[4]

The controversy that followed was due in good part to the fact that Jensen's findings ran contrary to those of accepted research. There were many methodological criticisms of Jensen's research as well as questions about the assumptions of generalizing from the available data. But much of the controversy—and certainly much of the heat that infused it—was due to the fact that a basic value was being challenged, one held by most sociologists and other social scientists. Until Jensen's report was published, most recent research had been strengthening the scientific foundation of the value enunciated in the preamble to the Declaration of Independence, "that all men are created equal."

[4]Arthur R. Jensen, "How Much Can We Boost IQ and Scholastic Achievement?" *Harvard Educational Review* 39 (winter 1969): 1–123. There have been a number of responses to Jensen's article. An early group of them is collected in "Environment, Heredity, and Intelligence," *Harvard Educational Review,* Reprint Series no. 2 (1969). For a recent critique, see Philip Green, "The Pseudoscience of Arthur Jensen," *Dissent* 23 (summer 1976): 284–97.

Value judgments: evaluation of facts or events according to a belief system.

Controversy continues to swirl around Jensen's report, contesting the interpretation of data it gave. Our point here is that sociologists, like other social scientists, face a dual role: as systematic social observers and as citizens, members of a given society with their own opinions, attitudes, and values. Can these ever be entirely eliminated from their performance as scientists? Or do sociologists inescapably impose their own value judgments on the structure of their research and the interpretation of their findings?

Consider again our discussion of the disagreement between the structural-functionalist and the conflict theorist looking at the social welfare system. From the same data each draws very different conclusions, because each has a very different theoretical perspective. Their theoretical perspectives are built into their analyzing and interpreting processes. Without them, no data or phenomenon could become intelligible. But with them, the two groups will never come to any fundamental agreement about or interpretation of a given society.

Value-free sociology: the belief of many sociologists that they can and should examine a society without allowing their values to influence their analysis in any way.

Thus, the question seems to have only one persuasive answer: sociologists can no more completely erase their values from their work than the rest of us can when we participate in society. Because of this inescapable feature of human study of human societies, many sociologists propose that there is only one remedy.[5] Sociologists, they say, must avow their biases at the same time that they strive to minimize the influence of those biases on research and interpretation of data. Once it is admitted that personal values play a role in research, it is only reasonable to expect sociologists to focus their attention on controversial social issues.[6] Whether they become problem-solvers themselves or not, it is argued, they should concentrate on providing data and conclusions that can be useful to problem-solvers.

[5]See, for example, Howard S. Becker, "Whose Side Are We On?" *Social Problems* 14 (winter 1967): 239–47, and Irving Louis Horowitz, *Professing Sociology: Studies in the Life Cycle of a Social Science* (Chicago: Aldine, 1968).

[6]See Philip M. Hauser, "On Actionism in the Craft of Sociology," *Sociological Inquiry* 39 (spring 1969): 139–47.

SUMMARY

Sociologists seek to apply the scientific method to their study of human interaction. All science is ultimately based on empirical observation (no matter how diverse is the range of instruments thus used from one science to another). The scientific method is a series of interrelated steps. Data collection is only a part of this method. Model building and theorizing are other integral parts. A model attempts to give the clearest, most accurate possible description of some set of phenomena. For the actual gathering of data sociologists have several methods (and various combinations of them) at their disposal: participant and nonparticipant observation; random sample surveys, by interview or questionnaire; and others.

With their shared perspective and methods, it might seem that sociologists would produce a unified view of any society, but this is hardly the case. Sociologists adhere wholly or in part to one of the two major rival models of society: the structural-functional model or the conflict model.

The structural functionalists examine a society chiefly to see how its many elements combine to enable the whole to function in a state of balance. Conflict theorists, on the other hand, expect to discover in that society the conflicts among groups and classes that those in power seek to suppress.

Sociologists can also differ in the scope of their investigations. Macrosociologists study the larger constituents of the society—its institutions—and how they interrelate. Microsociologists study how individuals interrelate with one another in small groups or how they, in turn, function within the social institutions.

Should sociologists, like their peers in the physical and mathematical sciences, pursue knowledge for its own sake? Or should they concentrate instead on seeking solutions to the problems that beset a society? This issue is another area of disagreement among sociologists. Some of them say scientists should be value-free in their work: they should not take sides on an issue. But to try to solve problems is to take sides. Moreover, many others doubt that, even when trying to be purely scientific, a sociologist can put aside his or her values in choosing the issue for study, making assumptions, and drawing conclusions.

The sociological perspective and its accompanying methods of data collection yield, ideally, the most accurate description of a society. Implicit in the sociological perspective is a major division of social phenomena into the cultural and structural components. Culture represents the symbols that are used to communicate and the content of that communication: beliefs; ideas about what is good and bad, beautiful and ugly, valuable and worthless; and standards of proper and improper behavior. In Part 2 we examine in detail what sociologists mean by culture, how it is transmitted, and how it differs from social structure.

2

3

SYMBOLS AND SUBSTANCE

We have seen that sociologists make use of a particular perspective, the sociological perspective, and the scientific method, adapted to the study of human behavior and its group basis. We have said also that they concentrate chiefly on the structural dimension of human behavior: the patterned ways of interacting that predominate in a given society or groups within it. But these patterned ways of interacting are related to cultural components, that is, to the beliefs, rules, and values that affect behavior. Before we study these (in Chapter 4) we must examine the cultural components that transmit them: language, gesture, and symbol.

CULTURE DEFINED

Culture: the sum of a society's learned beliefs, values, norms, and ways of doing things.

Most people in our society, if asked what they think the word *culture* means, would be likely to reply, "Shakespeare, Beethoven, ballet, opera," and the like. In common usage, that is, culture suggests the most ambitious achievements of intellectual and emotional investigation and expression. It does not suggest "I Love Lucy," deodorants and toothpaste, rock and roll, ten-speed bicycles, large powerful-engine cars, the belief in an almighty God, or the belief in "progress" (the notion that most change is for the better). Sociologists, however, do include such traits as part of a people's culture.

Sociologists, like other social scientists, define a culture as a complex whole that, in the words of the anthropologist Edward B. Tylor, "includes knowledge, belief, art, morals, law, custom, and many other capabilities and habits acquired by man as a member of society."[1] Consider, for example, this jingle from a 1975 radio and TV commercial:

> Baseball, hot dogs,
> Apple pie, and Chevrolet . . . .

Here is a glimpse at some other dimensions of culture that most Americans can relate to. A scant few visual and verbal clues call forth a whole pattern of

[1]Edward B. Tyler, *Primitive Culture: Researches into the Development of Mythology, Philosophy, Religion, Language, Art and Custom* (London: John Murray, 1913), 1:1.

The notion of culture is popularly associated with achievements in the arts and appreciation of those achievements. To sociologists, however, culture encompasses all the prevailing beliefs, values, rules for living, and material objects of a society—in short, anything we can pass along to our children.

responses—at least this is the intention of the advertiser. Using a familiar tune and listing items the audience is presumed to like (baseball, hot dogs, and apple pie), the advertiser hopes to get us to associate well-known aspects of our culture with the company's product. People in other societies might find the combination of baseball, hot dogs, apple pie, and Chevrolet absurd (even if they understood what the words themselves meant).

Why can we relate so easily to this ad, while other people cannot? We are not born loving baseball, hot dogs, or apple pie, much less Chevrolets. We *learn* about them, just as we learn about thousands of aspects of our culture. Whatever our own feelings about these cultural traits—that is, whether we like or dislike baseball, hot dogs, and apple pie—we learn to associate them with our way of life. Any culture, then, is not only its highest, most revered achievements but also the entire array of what its members believe; what they consider good and bad, beautiful and ugly, pleasant and unpleasant; what they think they must do and must not do; and their tools, clothes, and playthings.

DIFFERENCES AMONG CULTURES AND WITHIN CULTURES

We are all aware of the infinite variety of cultures throughout the world. We find small tribal hunting societies in which members believe in many gods, they put their trust in a priest–medicine man, many relatives live together as a family, and all or most property is shared by everyone. In contrast are societies like our own: large, industrial ones, in which property is privately owned, most knowledge is sought by reason and evidence, and many different systems of religious beliefs coexist.

Cultures differ not only between two very different societies such as these but also among societies that are similar in many ways. In each society

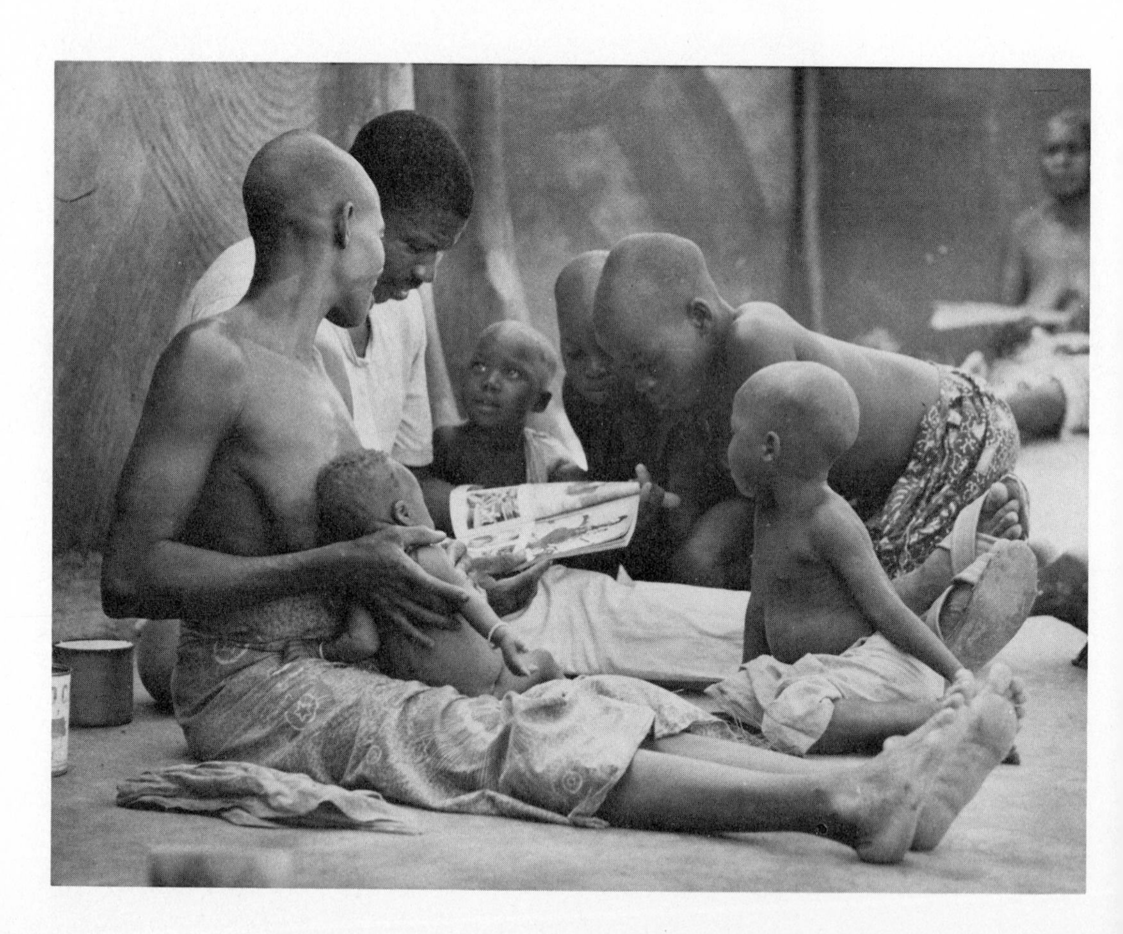

the beliefs, the ways of doing things, and the traits, objects, and experiences that people value will differ from those of a generally similar society.

Having lived in the United States, we know that there are cultural differences *within* societies as well as *between* them. American society, for example, contains a wide assortment of people who originally came from many parts of the world. They brought their own "cultural baggage" with them. Although, in time, much of it was lost or replaced, much was kept. In addition to differences based on our countries of origin, or nationalities, we can see differences in the religious beliefs and practices of various American groups. City dwellers often have some different values and norms from rural dwellers. People from different cities or different parts of the country (New York and New Orleans, Maine and Montana) have regional traits, such as different accents, that set them somewhat apart from one another.

No two cultures are entirely alike. Each one transmits unique combinations of ideas, values, and norms.

In heterogeneous societies like that of the United States, many subcultures (cultures within cultures) can be found. Subcultures may incorporate important elements of the larger culture, but they maintain distinctive traces of their roots elsewhere as these Italian-American bocce players and these celebrants of Chinese New Year show.

Whereas subcultures combine elements of the society's mainstream culture with elements of a past or foreign culture, countercultures incorporate elements in opposition to the mainstream culture. A counterculture may, for example, reject private property, accepted marital or sexual norms, materialistic values, and reliance on machine production.

Subculture: a system of norms and values that distinguishes one group in a society from others in it.

Because all these special qualities—based on national origin, religion, economic class, residence, or region—are variations on the basic American cultural "model," we say they are *subcultural.* Members of the subculture share many of the cultural elements of the mainstream society, but they replace others with their own, whether these come from the foreign country of their birth or ancestry, or have evolved through generations of particular kinds of experiences. Working-class and upper-class people, for example, show subcultural variations from the large middle class in our society. In one social class or ethnic or religious group, worldly success may be much less important than it is in others. In some, family unity may be far more important instead.

Counterculture: a set of norms and values that contradicts and rejects many or all norms and values of the mainstream culture.

Whatever the cultural differences that mark a subculture as a variant from the mainstream, the subculture is not opposed to the basic elements of that mainstream. In many societies, however, people come together on the basis of a shared opposition to mainstream culture. They create or adapt a *counterculture* (often also called a *contraculture*) that expresses their rejection of the basic values, norms, and patterns of interaction found in the mainstream culture. The most visible American countercultures of recent times have been the so-called longhairs or freaks who reject our culture's ideas of worldly success and private property, and often reject sexual fidelity, the nuclear family, modern technology, and urban life.[2]

[2]For a detailed discussion of the differences between subculture and contraculture, see J. Milton Yinger, "Contraculture and Subculture," *American Sociological Review* 25 (1960): 625–35.

1. Considering only the town or city where you live, write down as many examples of subcultural variations as you can.

2. To what extent are the traits you listed *subcultural* rather than cultural? That is, how much does each vary from the main cultural pattern?

3. How would a foreigner classify these same traits? Would he or she see them as variations on the American model or, perhaps, be surprised to learn that most Americans did not behave in this way?

4. Try to find an example of a counterculture movement in your area. What are its distinguishing traits? What cultural elements of the mainstream do its members reject? How successful do they seem to have been in establishing their own culture?

A culture is transmitted and sustained by communication. Spoken and written language is the most prevalent form of communication, but other ways exist as well. Physical gestures are often an important way of expressing ideas, desires, and attitudes, as these Spanish women show. Cultures differ in the reliance they place on gestures and their "vocabulary" of gestures.

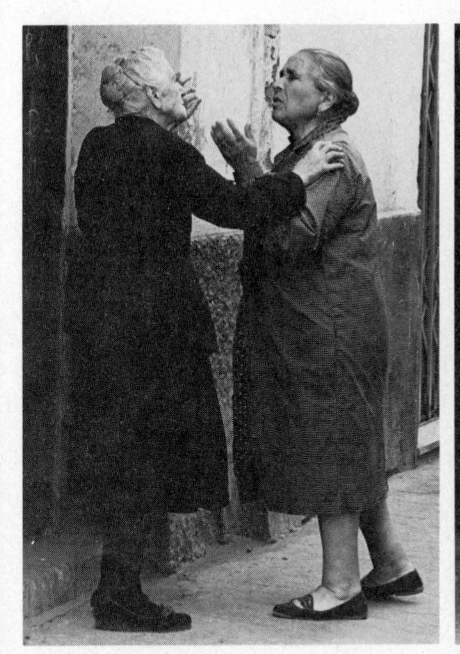

Language: any system of communication that uses signs or symbols whose meanings can be understood by others. As you read these words, you understand their meanings, and communication through language is occurring.

TRANSMITTING CULTURE

Symbols: things that stand for other things—usually ideas or values. The Statue of Liberty is a large statue, an image of a woman, and a symbol of our nation's professed value of political liberty.

Entire ways of living depend largely on what we learn. Those who teach us transmit what they consider to be "correct" attitudes and "proper" thoughts and behavior. Successful socialization—as we see in Part 4, which deals exclusively with this process—depends on how easy or difficult it is to convey to others what they should know. It also depends on whether they have the proper tools with which to learn.

The most basic aspect of the learning process is communication itself. Language, gestures, signs and other symbol systems are ways of transmitting ideas. Because of the ability of human beings to develop, to use, and to teach others to use complex symbol systems, they can both inherit the ideas of others and perpetuate them. Culture—that combination of ideas, inventions, and objects—is understood and passed on by symbolic communication.

Without a system of symbols for communication, no culture—or human society—would be possible. No society could survive more than a single generation without some means of transmitting its knowledge, beliefs, values, and behavioral rules to others. This transmission takes many forms—from simply living and doing things in the presence of children, to encouraging youngsters to imitate their elders, to explaining complicated ideas in lengthy discussions. Regardless of what is being taught or shared, some form of

In two different cultures people experiencing the same emotion may resort to different accepted ways of expressing it.

communication must be used to transmit ideas from one person to another.

While all animals communicate, most do so only at a very elementary level. The human brain has a greater capacity to absorb, store, and use information to engage in highly sophisticated communication than that of any other animal. Humans learn to speak the same way that they learn almost everything else—through their contact with their social environment and with those responsible for their socialization. By four or five years of age, children have learned to express themselves in culturally appropriate ways. For example, they know how to give fairly elaborate answers to questions about "what they want to be when they grow up." Soon after birth they begin to learn how to express displeasure or joy. Within a short time they learn the particular forms of such expression that are used in their own society or group within it. This is because so much of communication is based on cultural expectations. Few men in our society use anything more expressive than a handshake to display pleasure at seeing one another. Yet, in other societies, and in some ethnic groups in our own society, men feel comfortable expressing this pleasure by embracing and kissing each other.

Something is culturally specific when it has special meaning in a certain culture, or exists only in that culture. It can be an idea, a thing, or a value.

People frequently invent and use culture-specific symbols—symbols that only those raised in their particular culture can fully understand. This is true of language, gestures, signs, and even, as we shall see, certain material objects.

Language

ΟΥΚ ΕΣΠ ΤΛΩΣΣΑ ΑΜΗ Η·Η ΕΜΗΜΚΗ

Do you know what is written above? If you are thinking, "It's Greek to me," you are correct. It is Greek, and translated it means, "There is no language other than Greek."

If you had been raised and schooled in Greece you would have had no difficulty understanding the symbols that make up the words or the words that make up the sentence. A Greek who hadn't been taught English would be unable to read this book: he or she would find the letters, words, and sentences incomprehensible.

However important language is for communicating ideas, for expressing ourselves, for receiving and passing on information, it is only one of several arbitrary message systems.

Language reflects culture. For example, by examining our language—the words we use, how we say them, and how we interpret them—we can learn a great deal about our culture.

1. List the words that men have used for the term *woman,* and discuss their cultural implications. Can you tell how men feel about women by means of the words they use and how they say them? What generalizations might be drawn about male cultural attitudes toward women from the ways they label and describe them?

2. Make a list of words that women use to refer to men. Is it shorter than the list in question 1? If so, why? Discuss.

Since our language is English, we communicate with its symbols. We know our ABCs. We know how to put them in particular orders to make words. *Ngorinca* means nothing to us; neither does *gug* or *nov shmos kapop.* But *road* has an understandable meaning; so does *drive* and *stop light.*

While all human beings possess the ability to communicate by language, languages differ from one another, and any language is unintelligible to those who have not learned it. (That is why most Americans could not read the Greek phrase we quoted.) In addition, a language can take various written shapes. Although we assume that the only way to write English is with letters, it isn't. Thus,

·—·|——|·—|—·· —··|·—·|··|···—|·
···|—|——|·——· ·—··|··|——·|····|—

are the same three familiar terms: *road, drive,* and *stop light.* But they are written in Morse code. They might have been written in braille or some other system of designating letters, such as the semaphore code, or words like those conveyed in the hand signals of the deaf.

When words are "spelled out" they conjure meaning in our minds. Think of what flashes into your head when you read the word *automobile.* Now think of that same word with a modifier, such as *antique automobile.* Did you visualize a Model T or a Model A Ford, or does your antique car look like something from the 1940s? Now think of a *sports car.* Do you see it? Is it a boxy old MG TD or a new Porsche 911? Is it red or blue—or didn't you "color" it until we mentioned the words for certain colors?

If you stop to think about it, it is really amazing what knowledge of a common language can do. But we must not make it sound too easy: simply knowing the words is not enough, since some words and phrases have different meanings in different societies whose members speak the very same language.

If a young man asked a waitress for the bathroom in an English pub, she would probably be quite surprised. If she figured out what he wanted, she might retort: "A bathroom is where you bathe, luv. What you want is the 'Gents.'"

Consider some other examples of English that the British use. Write down what you think the following English words mean (they are all related to automobiles and driving):

1. hooter
2. boot
3. bonnet
4. mudguard
5. roundabout

If you called the first a horn, the second what we call a trunk, the third a hood, the fourth a fender, and the fifth a traffic circle, you would score 100 percent. How did you make out?

Of course, a similar test could be done giving American English examples to British students. What would they think of words like *turtleneck* or *undershirt?* Would they understand that they mean exactly the same as their own words *roll collar* and *vest?* What would they make of *mags, sissy bar,* and *do a wheelie?*

Gestures

A gesture is any culturally expressive physical act. Examples include waving a hand, opening a door for another person, and saluting the flag.

Even words may be inadequate to express a meaning fully. Sometimes they are of little help without the use of gestures. Try, for example, to explain what is meant by the words *spiral staircase* without using your hands. Difficult, isn't it? Gestures are very important in communicating ideas and are therefore an important part of any culture. For example, a Japanese person acknowledges an introduction or a departure with a bow; most people in Western societies shake hands.

Sometimes the importance of gestures becomes painfully apparent—for instance, when you extend your hand and get no response from the other person. How embarrassing it is to stand there with that limp thing at the end of your arm. How you wish it would fall off or disappear!

A kiss is like a handshake—at least certain kinds of kisses in certain kinds of company. Did you ever go to a wedding where you were introduced to some distant aunt and neither you nor she knew whether to shake (too formal) or kiss (too intimate)? Did you end up trying to suppress both your blush and your anger at the awkwardness of your position?

Many other gestures have specialized meanings. When we see a woman holding the palms of her hands together, fingertips pointing up, with her head bowed, we know immediately what she is doing, even though we can't hear the words of her prayer. Yet we might not recognize the gestures for praying used by orthodox Jews or Japanese or Africans. These people would never clasp their hands in the gesture that many of us think is the universal pose of prayer.

Religious gestures are not the only ones that are culturally specific—that have a particular meaning in a particular culture. Until the beginning of World War II, Americans pledged allegiance to the flag with their right arms stretched before them.

Why do you think Americans were asked to stop pledging that way? What did an extended arm come to represent? This gesture was the salute widely used by the Fascists in Italy and the Nazis in Germany before and during World War II. Americans wanted to show that they were very different from the totalitarian, warlike societies of Germany and Italy at that time.

Throughout history, salutes have been used to show respect and allegiance. The Roman legionnaire made a fist and tapped his heart before and after addressing an officer. So did the senators who spoke to Caesar. The medieval knight saluted by lifting the visor of his helmet, and since then many

Even within a culture a single physical gesture can assume many, often opposite meanings. The V-sign, made famous in World War II by Winston Churchill, first meant victory. Some twenty years later it was used to mean peace (in opposition to the Vietnam war). The clenched fist, adopted by the Black Panthers, stood for resistance to racism and oppression. Other counter-culture groups next gave it a broader meaning: revolutionary struggle.

persons have used a modification of this gesture, touching the forehead with the back or front or side of the hand.

In many cultures an open hand is a sign of peace and friendship. Indeed, the handshake is said to have originated from the notion of showing to all that one's hand held no weapon.

Another familiar gesture in which the symbolic meaning changed was the two-fingered salute. During World War II, the British Prime Minister Winston Churchill made the two-fingered salute a V for victory. Twenty years later it meant peace and opposition to war.

1. List other symbolic gestures that would appear natural to people in our culture but might not be understood by someone from a different culture.

2. Do you know any symbolic gestures of another culture that seem strange to Americans? Write them down or describe them.

Here, Abbie Hoffman, an outspoken radical, makes a novel combination of the salute and the clenched fist, as if to say revolution is patriotic.

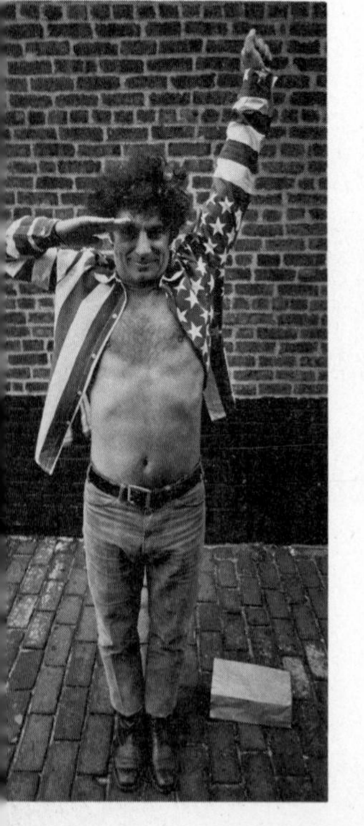

Symbols

In virtually every culture symbols can be found. A symbol is any thing or gesture that stands for something else. Some things become symbols by association. Certain cars, for example, have always been status symbols because they cost so much that only people who have gained material success can afford them. Such a car is desirable not only because it is supposed to be more reliable but also—perhaps mostly—because of its symbolic function.

Other objects or gestures do not *acquire* symbolic status but are instead deliberately *created* to fill the need for a symbol. The national flag is a perfect example. We all pledge allegiance to the flag, and we have special rules about how to handle it, fly it, fold it, and dispose of it when it is worn out. During the Vietnam war, some people saw the flag as a symbol of military power. Most people, however, still see it as a symbol of the American people. They have emotional feelings about it, even though they may be reluctant to discuss them openly.

Once, many years ago, a professor tried an experiment with a class of college students who seemed reluctant to admit to themselves that so impersonal an object as a piece of cloth with stars and stripes on it could have near-sacred qualities. They were almost as matter of fact about such matters as today's young people.

One of the major rules about the flag in our country is that Old Glory must never touch the floor; certainly we must never drag it on the ground. To make his point, the professor took a flag from a nearby classroom and walked into his own room dragging it behind him. The students did not laugh. Nor did they applaud this apparent gesture of defiance. As many of them as could be observed, seemed to gasp a bit or swallow or gape in disbelief.

In a discussion of the episode a few minutes later, several voiced the opinion that even to make a point the professor had gone too far. Said one, "I guess it bothered me to see somebody purposely pull the flag across the floor." Said another, "It hit me—that's *our* flag!" Said a third, "You know what—it's hard to explain, but I felt a bit sick."

And so did the professor. Like the students, he found it very difficult to break a rule that had been drilled into him early in life, especially since this rule concerned an important symbol in his society. The flag was a revered symbol in his culture. Dragging it across the floor indicated disrespect for the flag and, by implication, for the entire country it symbolized.

Symbols—words, gestures, and other methods of expression—exist in many different forms. They provide clues that not only guide or limit our attitudes and behavior but also help the social scientist to understand our culture and that of others.

The American flag is the symbol of the United States. For many people the flag also symbolizes their feelings about this country. It evokes their loyalty and patriotism, and wearing it or displaying it expresses those feelings. But what exactly is "our country"? What is symbolized by the flag, and what is not? Does the flag stand for the principles and structures encompassed in the Declaration of Independence and the Constitution; for democracy; for "the American way of life"; for the present political administration? All of these? Some of these? Who decides? As strong a symbol as it is, it stands for something that has never been operationally defined. This fact was made clear in the late 1960s and early 1970s during conflict over the war in Vietnam. In each of these pictures, try to analyze what the flag stands for to the people involved. If some seem ambiguous—if could be interpreted in more ways than one—what interpretations are more plausible to you, and why?

THE SIGNIFICANCE OF SYMBOLS AND SYMBOLIC ACTS

The symbols we have been discussing and the means by which people learn and use them are of critical significance to sociologists trying to understand human behavior in different social settings. Consider the following description of religious ritual among members of the Temple of Islam, otherwise known as Black Muslims. These black Americans decided to leave the Christian churches in which they were raised and instead to accept the teachings of Elijah Muhammad, the leader of the Black Muslims. The reasons for their conversion were many. One was certainly that the Muslim faith offered a very different view of black people, indeed of all people, from that of Christianity, which preached brotherhood but actually looked down on nonwhites and helped to perpetuate their servitude. Black Muslims firmly believe in self-help and self-realization. Black is beautiful, and Allah is God. The entire religious service is made up of symbols of purification and devotion.

Muslims are instructed to prepare themselves for prayer:

> Washing the hands to the wrist;
> Rinsing the mouth three times;
> Cleansing the inside of the nose with water three times;
> Washing the face three times;
> Washing the arms to the elbows three times (the right arm should be washed first);
> Wiping over the head with wet hands;
> Wiping the ears with wet fingers;
> Wiping around the neck with wet hands; and
> Washing the feet (the right one first) to the ankles.*

The officer marches briskly down the aisle, comes to a stop, salutes the other guards, and shows the visitor to a seat. Male visitors normally sit on the front rows in the aisle to the right of the speakers' platform, separated from the followers and believers. Female visitors sit immediately behind the male visitors, separated from them by a few rows of empty seats unless there are too many visitors to maintain this separation of the sexes. The registered Muslim women sit in the center aisle behind the Temple officers, who occupy the front row of this aisle. All male registered Muslims and believers sit in the left aisle. Other men may also sit in the balcony on a crowded day. Women are separated from the men partly because this is the tradition of Islam and partly because undivided attention is required. The Temple is not a place for socializing; mixing the women and men together might cause distractions. . . .

. . . An American flag appears in the upper left corner of the blackboard and directly below it, painted against a white background, a tree with a black man hanging from a branch. This symbolizes justice under the United States govern-

*Elijah Muhammad, *Muslim Daily Prayers* (Chicago: University of Islam, 1957), pp. 9–11.

ment. Opposite the tree is the cross, another symbol of oppression, shame, suffering, and death. Below the cross appears the word "Christianity." In the upper right corner the flag of the Nation of Islam is painted—the moon and stars in white against a red background which represents the sun. The letters, I., F., J., and E. are inscribed on the flag, one on each corner. These stand for Islam (Peace), Freedom, Justice, and Equality. Below the flag and directly opposite the word "Christianity," is inscribed "Islam." Between the two flags and the names of the two religions is a large question mark with the question: Which One Will Survive The War of Armageddon?

The two guards are posted on each side of the speaker's stand. They face the audience and are relieved every thirty minutes. A guard relieving another marches forward, stands at attention, and exchanges a salute. They lean toward each other and whisper some words. The guard to be relieved then marches swiftly up the aisle and the other does a smart about-face and takes his place. This goes on throughout the meeting. . . .

Seriousness of purpose and sincerity in prayer are emphasized.

There is no singing. "Shouting and wailing" is considered characteristic of Negro Christian preachers who want to arouse the emotions of their congregations in order to get money "which is tied up in churches and Cadillacs.". . .

After the prayer, the minister salutes the congregation again, saying, "As-Salaam-Alaikum," to which the followers respond, "Wa-el-Alaikum-Salaam." Frequently the minister asks the congregation, "How do you feel, my dear brothers and sisters?" and makes impromptu remarks to establish rapport. His duty is to bear witness to the teachings of Muhammad and to affirm that "Allah is our God and the Most Honorable Elijah Muhammad is His Last and Divine Messenger."[3]

This description by sociologist E. U. Essien-Udom includes many of the cultural traits analyzed earlier in the chapter. Note the significance of washing as an actual and symbolic preparation for entrance into the temple; sex-segregation as an enactment of the value that no distraction is to be tolerated; respect among the guards as shown by the salute; the flag's portrayal of positive and negative forces; and the language that introduces the prayer, emphasizing that the devotees have entered into a special ceremony.

CULTURE IS A COMPLEX WHOLE

Like archaeologists, sociologists and anthropologists spend a good deal of their time studying the cultural characteristics of people in different parts of the world. With pad and pencil, sometimes with tape recorder and camera, they try to capture the essence of life in a given culture. In social worlds rather different from their own, they have to rely on other people's answers to their

[3]E. U. Essien-Udom, *Black Nationalism* (Chicago: University of Chicago Press, 1962), pp. 212–19.

Try some cultural analysis on these two pictures. What is going on in the first picture? People are gathered around a dinner table; their plates hold turkey, yams, and mashed potatoes; there is a pitcher of what looks like apple cider. On the sideboard are many kinds of pies. It could be just an ordinary, old-fashioned Sunday meal, but it looks like Thanksgiving dinner, because all the cultural items just mentioned combine to symbolize that holiday to us. (Add a decorated pine tree to these to evoke Christmas.)

What of this other picture? What is happening? We see people of different ages standing and holding candles in a dimly lit place, but unless we know what culture they belong to, and unless we know

questions, their own observations of behavior, and a listing of cultural items.

Although a single symbol may tell much about a culture, it does not make a culture. Cultures, as we said, are *complex wholes* that include "knowledge, beliefs, art, morals, law, custom, and any other capabilities and habits acquired by man as a member of society."[4] Cultures consist of a combination of factors that, taken together, tend to form coherent patterns. The sociologist and the anthropologist who go into "the field" must put together the various pieces. Often they must begin by trying to "decode" the symbolic characteristics, to figure out their meaning in the particular setting.

Try your hand at some cultural analysis: Read the following description,

[4]Tylor, *Primitive Culture,* 1:1.

that culture well, our description can go no further. Is it a religious ceremony? If so, one of joy or one of mourning? Is it a tribal or village ceremony to reaffirm the solidarity of community life? In fact, it is a religious ceremony, in the village of Gomba, in East Nepal. These people have gathered to fulfill a vow made to a deceased family member. One year after his death they offer these butter lamps to help him achieve a favorable reincarnation.

These villagers, if shown the photo of the family at Thanksgiving dinner, would have been just as incapable of describing more than the bare physical facts. Thus, even the simplest, most unexamined things in a culture can have meanings unique to that culture.

written by anthropologist Horace Miner, of several aspects of the daily life of the group called the Nacirema.[5]

They are a North American group living in the territory between the Canadian Cree, the Yaqui and Tarahumare of Mexico, and the Carib and Arawak of the Antilles. Little is known of their origin, although tradition states that they came from the east. According to Nacirema mythology, their nation was originated by a culture hero, Notgnihsaw, who is otherwise known for two great feats of strength—the throwing of a piece of wampum across the river Pa-To-Mac and the chopping down of a cherry tree in which the Spirit of Truth resided.

[5]Horace Miner, "Body Ritual among the Nacirema." Reproduced by permission of the American Anthropological Association from *The American Anthropologist* 58 (3), 1956: 503–7.

Nacirema culture is characterized by a highly developed market economy which has evolved in a rich natural habitat. While much of the people's time is devoted to economic pursuits, a large part of the fruits of these labors and a considerable portion of the day are spent in ritual activity. The focus of this activity is the human body, the appearance and health of which loom as a dominant concern in the ethos of the people. While such a concern is certainly not unusual, its ceremonial aspects and associated philosophy are unique.

The fundamental belief underlying the whole system appears to be that the human body is ugly and that its natural tendency is to debility and disease. Incarcerated in such a body, man's only hope is to avert these characteristics through the use of the powerful influences of ritual and ceremony. . . .

While each family has at least one such shrine, the rituals associated with it are not family ceremonies but are private and secret. The rites are normally only discussed with children, and then only during the period when they are being initiated into these mysteries. . . .

The focal point of the shrine is a box or chest which is built into the wall. In this chest are kept the many charms and magical potions without which no native believes he could live. . . .

Beneath the charm-box is a small font. Each day every member of the family, in succession, enters the shrine room, bows his head before the charm-box, mingles different sorts of holy water in the font, and proceeds with a brief rite of ablution. . . .

The Nacirema have an almost pathological horror of and fascination with the mouth, the condition of which is believed to have a supernatural influence on all social relationships. Were it not for the rituals of the mouth, they believe that their teeth would fall out, their gums bleed, their jaws shrink, their friends desert them, and their lovers reject them. They also believe that a strong relationship exists between oral and moral characteristics. . . .

In addition to the private mouth-rite, the people seek out a holy-mouth-man once or twice a year. These practitioners have an impressive set of paraphernalia, consisting of a variety of augers, awls, probes, and prods. The use of these objects in the exorcism of the evils of the mouth involves almost unbelievable ritual torture of the client. The holy-mouth-man opens the client's mouth and, using the above mentioned tools, enlarges any holes which decay may have created in the teeth. Magical materials are put into these holes. If there are no naturally occurring holes in the teeth, large sections of one or more teeth are gouged out so that the supernatural substance can be applied. In the client's view, the purpose of these ministrations is to arrest decay and to draw friends. The extremely sacred and traditional character of the rite is evident in the fact that the natives return to the holy-mouth-man year after year, despite the fact that their teeth continue to decay. . . .

A distinctive part of the daily body ritual is performed only by men. This part of the rite involves scraping and lacerating the surface of the face with a sharp instrument. Special women's rites are performed only four times during each lunar month, but what they lack in frequency is made up in barbarity. As part of this ceremony, women bake their heads in small ovens for about an hour.

1. What clues help you discover, and prove, who the Nacirema actually are?

2. What do you think the author's purpose was in writing "The Nacirema"? Do you think he meant to show, satirically, how risky it can be for an observer to look into a society and culture from outside, to try to interpret and explain a society very different from his or her own? Was Miner also poking some fun at our cultural obsession with cleanliness?

3. Watch a few hours of network television and pay particular attention to the commericals. (When there is programming on one channel, flip the dial to find other commercials.) Note what people's concerns are in these commercials (bad breath, dandruff, easy-to-use furniture wax, and so on). From your impressions of these commercials, try writing a satirical description of the values, norms, and roles of "TV commercial" culture.

SUMMARY

Sociologists define culture as the beliefs, values, rules of conduct, and material objects shared by most members of a society. The world's peoples show a wide diversity in all of these cultural elements, and—especially in large, complex societies—marked diversity among the groups within a single society.

However different one culture may be from another, they all share one fundamental feature: they are transmitted from the grown to the young by systems of communication. Humans communicate by manipulating systems of symbols: things that stand for other things. The symbols may be sounds, marks on a page, physical gestures, or objects created to embody a symbolic meaning. A language itself is a system of symbols. Thus, before we can begin to learn the content of our culture, we must begin to learn the systems of communication within it.

4 VALUES AND NORMS

In Chapter 3 we surveyed the ways in which people transmit and maintain a culture: by manipulating systems of symbols. In this chapter we examine the components of a culture—values and norms—and how they are interrelated to make a complex whole.

A survey of the world's cultures reveals an immense variety of values and norms. Sociologists study any cultural trait in relation to the overall culture. They judge the trait by its function and suitability in that society, not according to its acceptability or nonacceptability in any other society. This position is called *cultural relativism.* Cultural relativism can put sociologists in a dilemma, however, as we see in this chapter. How should the sociological perspective deal with such phenomena as, say, the atrocities of Nazi Germany? Is it proper or improper to discuss such an event purely in terms of its function for the particular society at the particular time?

COMPONENTS OF CULTURE

Imagine that you are an information officer in the United States Foreign Service. The head office in Washington has asked you to go on special assignment to a remote atoll in the Pacific, where a tiny settlement of people has recently been discovered. Researchers learned that these people were mostly the descendants of British sailors lost at sea in 1757 and never heard from again. To their discoverers' amazement, the islanders appeared to be living in the eighteenth century. Their homes, their dress, and their language, though modified in various ways, were all clearly reminiscent of that earlier period.

A number of the community members were suffering from a rare disease, and it was decided that they should be offered the opportunity to come to the United States for treatment. They were not quite sure what this meant, especially since they had never heard of the United States, though they knew of the American colonies. After much deliberation, the mayor of Bristol Town, as they called the place, agreed to have his people taken by boat to America. But he begged that they be given some preparation for what he was beginning to realize was a whole new world.

The voyage to the west coast of the United States would take approxi-

These few images convey only fragmentary pictures of the breadth and diversity of the American culture. In these pictures many material objects of our culture can be seen. If you pay some attention, many values and norms should also become visible to you. Look for them, and look for continuities within the diversity. Are there any discontinuities and contradictions as well? Are any of the cultural elements depicted here idealizations of dying or obsolete ways of thinking or behaving? Are any elements subcultural or regional traits? Are any elements universal—found throughout our society?

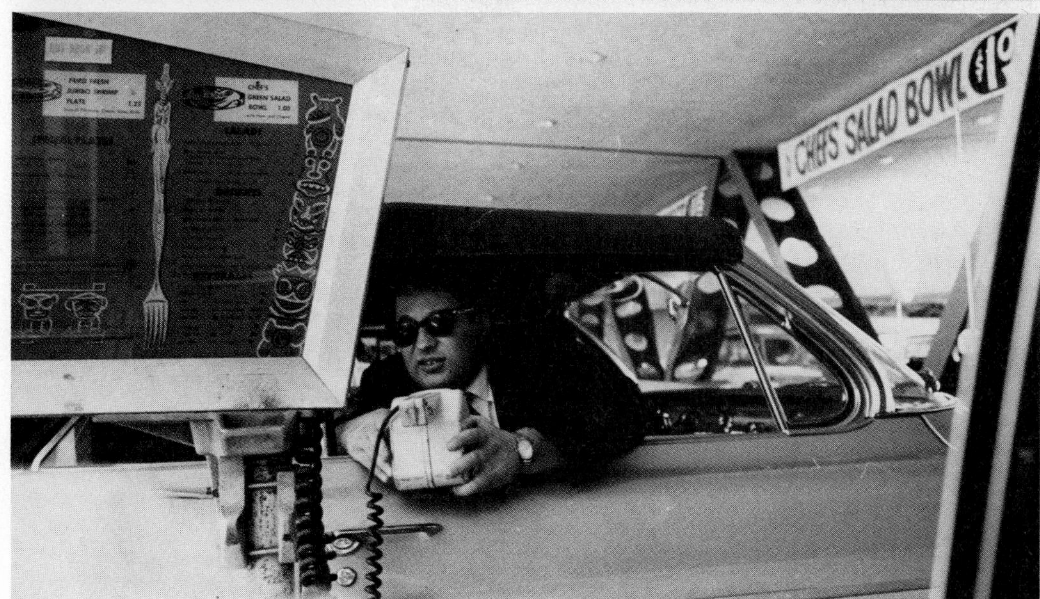

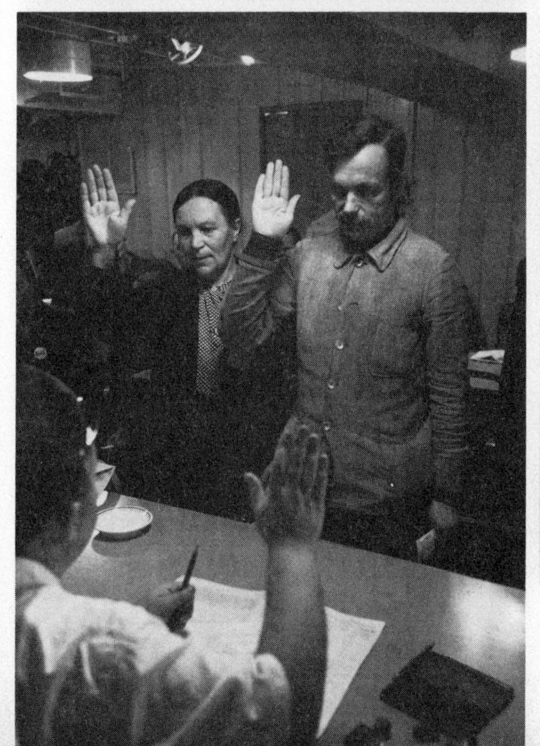

STANB
for HEADA
please"
Come In!
PALL MALL
COLD —
DRINKS
55¢
BUGLER

mately two weeks. Your assignment was to be on board the boat to prepare the people as much as possible.

How would you go about it? Remember that the people are English and have retained the language (though to your ear it is quite strange). Beyond this they are completely bewildered. In the two weeks' orientation, you have to give them a real introduction to American society and culture.

Where would you begin? What would you tell them? What beliefs and values, what rules of conduct should they be made aware of?

Values: the preferred or desirable goals, conditions, and modes of behavior of a culture.

In your description, what elements of our culture did you emphasize? Did you mention cherishing certain values such as equality of opportunity, the importance of work, and pride in our country? Did you say that Americans have a political system called democracy, rather than a monarchy? Did you describe our capitalist economic system? Did you mention the mass production of goods, assembly lines, and automation? Were you specific, saying that Americans liked ice cream, hot dogs, apple pie, baseball and football, jazz and rock music? Did you mention the flag, the Constitution, or the Fourth of July? Did you name certain objects typical of our "material" culture, such as automobiles, ranch and split-level houses, drive-in fast-food places, and colonial furniture, or smaller objects, such as transistor radios, cassette tape players, and cameras?

The cultural components you listed tell a great deal about how people view their own societies. They can highlight the generally held beliefs, values, and norms of a culture. Cultural *beliefs* are, as might be expected, those things that most people in a society believe to be true, such as that the world is round; that democracy is the best form of government; that most progress is for the good. Cultural *values* are the things generally considered desirable or important. For example, in teaching about the United States you might have mentioned the value of racial equality, no matter what your judgment is about how well it is practiced. Or you might have noted the value of material success, of striving to get ahead and being able to afford the good things in life. Your list might also describe cultural *norms*—the rules that people are expected to follow. For example, American children attend school from about age six until age sixteen or older.

Norms: the rules of behavior that govern members of a society.

Many norms apply in all sections of society, but some are limited to particular spheres of life. For example, parents are expected to provide support, love, and guidance to their children. But in the role of employer, a parent is not expected to behave this way toward employees.

DEFINITIONS AND EXAMPLES OF CULTURAL TRAITS

		Examples		
Term	*Definition*	*Education*	*Politics*	*Religion*
Value	An abstract idea of the relative desirability of (1) various goals or aims, and (2) means for achieving them.	Education should not be entirely utilitarian.	Democracy is better than totalitarianism.	It is better to obey the laws of God than the laws of man.
Norm	A rule prescribing appropriate or prohibiting inappropriate behavior.	Stand in front of the class.	It is illegitimate to buy votes directly.	Confessions should not be violated.
Position	That part of culture that defines the attributes and/or behavior to be displayed by an individual member of a social system in his relationships with other position occupants in that system.	Professor	Party boss	Priest
Attitude	A positive or negative orientation toward an object, person, or idea.	I like to read.	Republicans are no good.	Satan is evil.
Belief	An idea about an objective state of the world that is acted upon as if it were true, whether or not it actually is.	Man is a rational animal.	Communists are out to conquer the world.	There is a God.
Symbol	An object or act that stands for something else.	Cap and gown	Democratic donkey	Communion
Tool	A physical object that is necessary in order to perform the behavior associated with the position.	Book	Campaign poster	Prayer book

Source: Adapted from *Understanding American Society* by Robert C. Atchley. ©1971 by Wadsworth Publishing Company, Inc., Belmont, California 94002. Reprinted by permission of the publisher.

Our culture influences the way we define what a male is and what a female is. Some people think that even within the same culture men and women perceive appropriate male and female traits differently.

1. Have each person in the class take a sheet of paper. On the left side write five traits that you consider a successful male in American society today would have. On the right side write five traits of a successful female.

2. On the back of the sheet note your own sex.

3. Hand all the papers to one person to separate into "male" and "female" piles. Analyze with your classmates what characteristics are specified about men by men and by women. Do the same for characteristics about women.

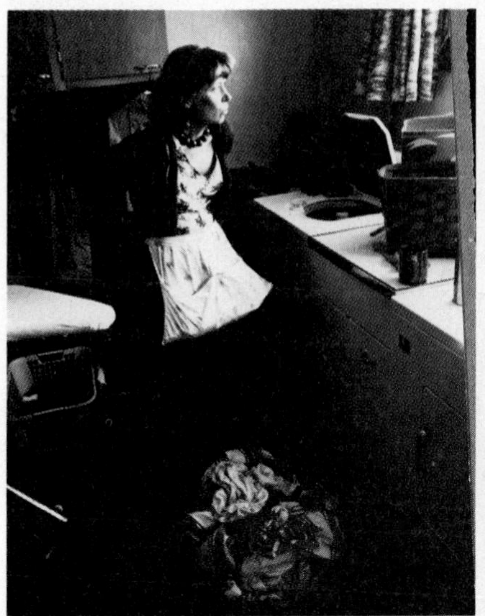

Traditional sex roles made clear distinctions between male behavior and female behavior. What traits or activities in each of these photographs fit the traditional stereotypes for males and females?

CULTURAL VALUES AND NORMS

Sex roles: the expected behavior of society's members according to whether they are male or female.

Whatever you found in your study, why do you think there were some differences in perception? Why were certain things much more important to males than to females (and vice versa)? The norms of this society say that males are supposed to conduct themselves in one set of ways and females in another. In recent years male and female perceptions of appropriate social roles have been changing. Did these changes show up in differences between male and female perceptions of their own roles and those of the opposite sex in your class?

People get their ideas about themselves and others and learn the norms (the appropriate rules of conduct) of their society from the people who are responsible for their socialization. Some of the rules reflect the most basic values of the society (core values). Others may be less important but are widely used as guides for behavior. Consider, for example, the difference between the norm of respecting your parents (or "Honor thy father and thy mother") and driving on the right side of the street.

Classifications of Norms

Sociologists often classify social norms by three significant characteristics: *range of acceptance,* that is, how widely the norm is followed; *enforceability,* that is, how great the pressure is for people to comply and how great the punishment is for not doing so; and *salience,* that is, the importance of the particular norm to society. The last characteristic obviously links norms and values, for the norms that are considered most salient are clearly related to our most important values.

Many norms rate high on all three of these scales. For example, "Thou shall not kill" is a norm with an immensely wide range of acceptance, with severe punishment for violation, and with high salience. None of our other values having to do with social order and harmony and with the worth of the individual would have meaning if human life itself were not considered of the highest value and its protection were not one of our most widespread, enforceable, and salient norms.

Some norms are accepted by most people and are most important to the functioning of society. If people violate these norms, they are severely punished. "Thou shalt not kill" is such a norm; it has a wide range of acceptance, high salience, and high enforceability.

1. **In what cases can individuals legitimately challenge even this norm?**
2. **Name two or three other norms that have high levels of all three**

characteristics. In what circumstances can individuals legitimately challenge them?

3. What statement can you make regarding the rigidity or flexibility of norms or values?

Ideas, modes of behaving, and styles of dress that come and go are termed fashions. Usually the word suggests frivolity or superficiality, but such fashions in behavior as jogging, bicycling, and tennis are beneficial to their practitioners. Fads, *however, are in fact short-lived and frivolous. Remember hula hoops? Streaking? Wearing overalls and mechanics' coveralls as everyday clothing?*

The Range of Salience: Mores and Folkways

Some of our cultural norms reflect essential or basic values. They have what sociologists call high salience. They reach deep into the histories of the cultures that our culture is drawn from—back to Hebrew laws (such as the Ten Commandments), Greek thought, Roman law, and Christian teachings. Such norms are either *prescriptions,* rules about the things people must do ("Honor thy father and thy mother") or *proscriptions,* rules about the things people must not do ("Thou shalt not steal").

Other norms are considered less essential to the continued existence of society, though they are still very important. Examples are norms dealing with the behavior of men and women toward one another, the behavior people must follow to get good grades or to prove their importance to the company, the use of harmful drugs, and the acceptable clothing for various situations.

Still other cultural norms shade into the trivial and temporary, such as fads and fashions in dress, behavior, and even ideas. For instance, wearing "bells," or "baggies" was important to a person's image in many places only a few years ago; acting cool—nonchalant and detached—was just as important; and claiming that LSD or other hallucinogenic drugs were doorways to the truth about everything was once considered important to the images of many young people.

Up to this point, we have been concerned with cultural norms and rules for behavior. We have not mentioned situations in which there are no rules for behavior (so that people don't know how they are supposed to act in a culture) or where there are too many different sets of rules for behavior (so that people don't know which is the best set of rules to follow). *Anomie* describes both of these situations.

Some people today think that there are no guidelines (or rules) to tell people how to behave in dating relationships. They feel there are too many different possible ways for people to behave on a date. List all the rules you can (even if they are competing sets of rules) that our culture gives us for dating relationships. Do you believe a state of *anomie* exists in this area of social life?

If we try to rank the norms of our culture in order of their importance, and if we separate the prescriptions from the proscriptions, we wind up with something like a U-shaped curve. The most important "dos" and "don'ts" are at the top of either side of the U. As we get down into the dos and don'ts that are less important to society and to each of us, they begin to mingle with our personal preferences.

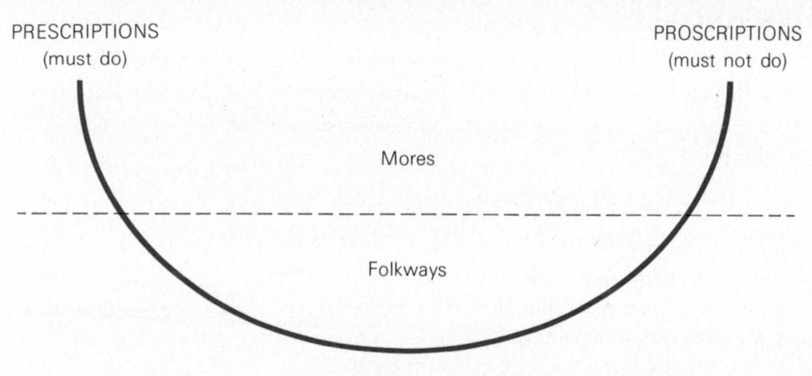

Mores: the major essential norms of a culture.

The norms closest to the extremes of the U have the strongest moral sanctions (punishments) attached to their violation. These strict prescriptions and proscriptions are called *mores* (pronounced "more-ays"—a word derived from the same Latin root as the word *morals*). Below mores in the diagram is the word *folkways.* These are customs—traditional, expressed ways of doing things, rather than absolute, strictly enforced rules.[1] A person who robs a liquor store violates one of our mores; someone who gets loud and obnoxious at a party violates one of our folkways.

Folkways: less essential norms derived from tradition and custom.

The broken line in the diagram above symbolizes the fact that it is often hard to pinpoint where mores end and folkways begin. Using the second diagram as your guide, see if you can set down a range of norms on various points along the U.

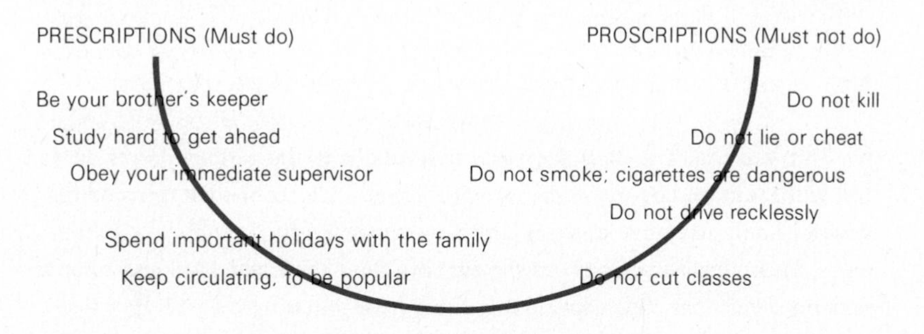

[1]These concepts—mores and folkways—were originally introduced by William Graham Sumner in *Folkways* (Boston: Ginn, 1906).

Think of the last time you violated a norm. Was it one of our folkways or mores? Write down the incident. What did you do? How did you know you had broken a rule? What reaction, if any, did you get from other people? Were any sanctions imposed on you?

Read the following familiar story. Then see if you can plot the various mores and folkways described along a U-shaped curve.

The alarm clock rings at 7:15 on Friday morning, and Dan leans over to shut it off. "Ten more minutes," he mutters to himself, "ten—" but he is interrupted. His mother is calling, telling him he'd better get moving. "You've already missed your eight o'clock engineering class three times this month," she says, "and you admitted that those absences haven't helped your progress."

Dan dawdles for a few minutes, rolls out of bed, hurriedly gets dressed, goes downstairs, and starts out the door. His mother calls again. "Come on, Dan, you should have some breakfast. You'll still be on time. You need to eat."

"Look, either I eat and my instructor gives me the evil eye again, or I don't and you tell me I'll waste away. I gotta split."

He runs out, revs up the engine of his old car, and takes off for campus. Preoccupied with thoughts about a calculus test he forgot to study for, he almost runs through a red light. Screeching to a halt, he hears someone yell, "You want to kill somebody? Damn kids, shouldn't have cars!"

At 7:57 he rolls into the campus parking lot. Since he is late, he heads for the nearest section, which is reserved for faculty members. A campus guard tries to stop him, but Dan waves, saying, "Listen, I'm late; I gotta get to class. Please don't give me a citation. I'll move it in an hour, right after class." The guard starts to argue, "Listen, kid, can't you read? That sign there says—" but Dan is gone.

He bounds up the stairs to room 211 and flops into a chair near the door, a minute before the instructor enters the room. "I trust you've all got your slide rules this time," the teacher says dryly as she opens her notes.

If you read this short narrative with an eye to the various norms on and below the surface you can come up with a pretty impressive list, considering it describes only forty-five minutes from one person's life.

Most obvious perhaps are the formal rules—the traffic laws and campus parking regulations. But doing things from habit often makes us forget that we're following rules. For example, most students follow the norms of attending classes and of showing up for them on time pretty well. The rule of punctuality relates to not disrupting the class and not missing class material. The rule of attendance may be formal (enforced by roll-taking and cut limits) or informal (enforced by our knowing that frequent absences indicate our indifference and lack of disipline). In either case it relates to the larger social norm that society is supposed to be run by educated persons. Few of us are going to college for the sheer love of learning alone. If we're in college to learn how to get ahead, it's only reasonable that we'd better attend classes.

In the hurried conversation between Dan and his mother we find one obvious norm and a couple that are less obvious. We're expected to eat the right amounts of the right kinds of food. Parents are expected to watch over their offspring. Thus Dan's mother shows concern for both his diet and his punctuality. In turn, children are supposed to respect their parents. Thus Dan responds to his mother's concern (though perhaps he has an edge of frustration in his voice) rather than ignoring her by running out the door in silence.

Identify six norms that affected Dan's day. Plot them along a U-shaped curve.

Laws: Norms Put into Writing

Laws: norms that are formally codified and enforced by police and courts.

We have seen that norms can be divided into prescriptions (must do) and proscriptions (must not do). We have also seen that both kinds can be further divided into mores and folkways. Where do laws fit in? Are they separate from mores and folkways? If not, does each more and folkway have a law to back it? The answer to both questions is no. Laws *codify* our mores and some of our folkways—that is, they set down the prescribed and proscribed behavior in precise terms and often include specific guidelines for the kind and length of punishment to be given to violators.

It would be hard to find a norm that is clearly one of our mores but is not codified into law. For example, "thou shalt not kill" states one of the mores that have high acceptance and salience. It is intimately related to our values surrounding human life. Any behavior that is threatening to the lives of others becomes a matter of social concern. Every state has laws prohibiting murder and establishing severe punishments.

On the other hand, only a few folkways are given the force of law. If you look at any crowded downtown sidewalk or campus walk or corridor, you can see that people pass one another either on the left or on the right, without paying attention to which side it is. (Even the folkway that a man should walk on the outside—curb side—of the sidewalk when with a woman companion is dying out.) But put those same people in cars on the road and such indifference would be life-threatening. So a folkway of road travel became codified into law. In some societies, such as England, Australia, and Japan, motorists drive on the left side of the road; in the United States, France, Italy, and most other countries, they drive on the right. The side that is chosen is unimportant, but it is very important that the arbitrary choice be followed by everyone.

1. Consider the following laws, and indicate whether you believe they are mores or folkways:

Everyone is entitled to freedom of religion.

Everyone earning an income above a certain amount must pay income tax.

No one may discriminate against a person because of race, religion, or national origin.

All dogs must be on leashes within city limits except in designated areas.

Alcoholic beverages may not be purchased by minors.

Cars must be inspected twice a year.

Pedestrians have the right-of-way at a crosswalk.

Children over seven years old must be enrolled in school.

2. List three laws that reflect our mores.

3. List three laws related to folkways that make good sense but do not evoke strong feelings, such as driving on one side of the road or the other.

4. Can you make any generalizations about the differences?

5. Can you think of any former mores that have become folkways in the course of time?

In the situations shown, the participants have clear ideas about the appropriate behavior. Sociologists define social institutions as clusters of norms that apply to major areas of human interaction. Through socialization, members of a society learn the rules of behavior that apply in each of these areas: in the family; at work; at places of worship and spiritual union; in education; at parties or celebrations; and in government.

NORMS IN INSTITUTIONAL CONTEXTS

By now we've seen that we are continuously surrounded by rules. These rules—whether they are mores or folkways, laws or customs—show immense variety in their range of acceptance, enforceability, and salience (the sociologist's three measures).

Many norms apply to all of us just about all the time. For example, "Thou shalt not kill" is a norm that is suspended only for soldiers in wartime, police defending themselves in hazardous duty, and citizens defending themselves against extreme violence. But other norms apply more in some situations than in others; they go with particular *social contexts.* They deal with what goes on (and what a person is supposed to do) in certain spheres of social activity. How is a person supposed to behave in these spheres:

1. a house of worship
2. a school
3. a party
4. a political rally
5. on the job

Most people would answer the first question with words like "quiet" and "reverent"; the second with "cooperative," "interested"; the third with "relaxed," "cool," "wild"; the fourth with "earnest," "eager," "involved"; and the last with "interested," "aggressive," "reliable."

People know they are supposed to act differently according to the particular social context in which they find themselves. They do act differently, for they are taught that there are appropriate norms for different social contexts. Not only do we *behave* differently in church, at school, or at a party but, as we shall see, we even think differently.

A STRUCTURAL MODEL OF MORAL REASONING

How are norms and values related? We could say logically that norms are enactments of values: the rules of behavior that support a given value system. For example, if human life is highly valued in a culture, then such norms as "thou shalt not kill" would have broad currency and high salience. Is this close relationship between values and norms true in practice? Do people's rules of behavior reflect the values they hold? Lawrence Kohlberg found that they did in every one of the cultures or groups he studied.[2]

[2]Lawrence Kohlberg, "The Child as a Moral Philosopher," *Psychology Today,* September 1968, pp. 25–30.

Kohlberg was actually studying stages of moral development in children, but his findings, which also apply to our discussion of socialization, yield a model of how the two cultural elements, norms and values, are related. Kohlberg's study, which lasted twelve years, followed seventy-five boys from the time they were ten to sixteen years old until they were twenty-two to twenty-eight. His method of testing was to interview his subjects every three years and ask them the same set of moral questions. He applied a structural approach: that is, he was seeking a description of "general structures and forms of moral thought which can be defined independently of the specific content of particular moral decisions or actions."

From his interviews, Kohlberg was able to discern three moral levels:

1. *Preconventional:* The child behaves according to his or her expectations about the physical consequences of the behavior: reward or punishment. The rules followed hold no importance of themselves; the child is responding to superior physical force.

2. *Conventional:* The child comes to value conformity to the rules for its own sake. The rules of behavior held by the group are seen as valuable in their own right, and the child feels it is extremely important to maintain them and support the social order.

3. *Postconventional:* The individual sees norms as having a validity in themselves independent of the authority of the groups that support them. The individual sees moral principles as self-evident because they relate to values held.

Within each level Kohlberg discerned two stages, making six stages in all. To illustrate, let's trace the progress of moral reasoning through each stage on the issue of "motive given for rule obedience or moral action":

1. Obey rules to avoid punishment.

2. Conform to obtain rewards, have favors returned, and so on.

3. Conform to avoid disapproval, dislike by others.

4. Conform to avoid censure by legitimate authorities and resultant guilt.

5. Conform to maintain the respect of the impartial spectator judging in terms of community welfare.

6. Conform to avoid self-condemnation.

Kohlberg concluded that this sequence illustrates a structural model, because he found the same sequence everywhere he looked, not only in our society but also in Great Britain, Canada, Taiwan, Mexico, Turkey, and among Malaysian aboriginals. Despite the wide range of cultural content (in norms and values) this same sequence was followed in the moral reasoning of all individuals. The only difference Kohlberg found within cultures (say between middle-class and working-class people or between rural and urban dwellers) or between cultures (say between a modern industrial democracy and a small tribal village) was in the *rate* of passage through the stages.

Kohlberg then asked why there should be "such a universal invariant sequence of development." He answered, "Each step of development . . . is a better cognitive organization than the one before it, one which takes account of everything present in the previous stage, but making new distinctions and organizing them into a more comprehensive . . . structure." The more inseparable norms are from the values that support them, the higher a person goes on Kohlberg's scale, and this appears to be true in every society and culture. Thus Kohlberg concludes that the progression is a structural characteristic of the human mind.

CULTURAL RELATIVITY: THE SOCIOLOGIST'S DILEMMA

Cultural relativity: the acknowledged absence of absolute standards of behavior and the consequent need to judge behavior within its cultural setting.

Today few people in our society are unaware of the cultural diversity to be found in the world. For example, television alone has brought us documentaries about different cultures all over the globe. Virtually every human practice, including murder and incest, enjoys cultural approval at some time, in some place. For centuries the people who most often came into contact with exotic cultures were explorers, traders, and missionaries. Their modern counterparts in this respect are anthropologists and ethnographers.

What is the chief difference between the attitude of, say, a missionary and that of an anthropologist toward some alien culture? Missionaries seek to introduce a religious and moral order that they consider superior to that of the natives; they want to convert the population to their beliefs. Sociologists or anthropologists (or other social scientists) study the system of beliefs, values, and practices that constitute the society's culture and structure; they are not seeking to make changes. The social scientist is a cultural relativist.

Cultural relativism is the position that there are no universal standards of right and wrong. The American sociologist William Graham Sumner made the classic statement of the cultural relativist position: "Everything in the mores of a time and place must be regarded as justified with regard to that time and place."[3] Thus, instead of judging and seeking to promote change, the social scientist seeks to explain patterns of human behavior.

The ethical neutrality imposed by cultural relativism may be acceptable to most of us when it is applied to distant preliterate societies in remote jungle highlands or frozen, barren tundras, but we may be troubled by its application to our own and related societies. Should a sociologist remain ethically neutral on racism in our society, on extremes of wealth and poverty, on the totalitarianism and the atrocities of the Nazis, or on other controversial issues of the present or recent past?[4]

If Sumner's injunction is followed, the sociologist is forced to maintain the detachment of the "innocent" bystander in his or her own society as well as in alien ones. But in practice most sociologists are scientists only part of the time. They are also members of a given society and share many of its cultural values.

Of course, the fact that sociologists have more thorough knowledge of various social issues often gives them a clearer picture of the social consequences of various courses of action. For example, if a sociologist is aware of the social consequences of racism and its related patterns of discrimination, he or she is likely to be more opposed to racism than many well-meaning but less-informed citizens.

Thus, Sumner's statement of the relativist perspective can be adhered to only so far: the sociologist seeks to understand the structural basis of any pattern of behavior, whether racism, anti-Semitism, drug addiction, conspicuous consumption, or whatever. But explaining does not logically lead to approval (or invalidate *dis*approval).

[3]William Graham Sumner, *Folkways* (Boston: Ginn, 1906), p. 65.

[4]For further discussion of this issue, see John Horton, "The Dehumanization of Alienation and Anomy," *British Journal of Sociology* 15 (December 1964): 283–300.

SUMMARY

Taken together, then, the values people hold and the norms they follow tend to form clear patterns—patterns of culture. We can describe American culture, for example, by identifying the norms most Americans consider important and the rules that guide their behavior.

We also recognize that cultural norms vary in their importance to us: those most important are called mores; those less so, folkways. Sometimes these norms are specified in law. Sociologists classify norms according to their range of acceptance, their enforceability, and their salience. Not all norms are followed by everyone all the time. Some are relevant only to certain segments of the society. Many are specific to particular spheres of social life or institutions.

A model of the stages in a person's moral development has been devised by Lawrence Kohlberg. It consists of six stages at three levels and was found in every society that Kohlberg studied. While all humanity seems to share in this process of developing moral reasoning, there is diversity in the *content* of cultures. Sociologists accept the perspective of cultural relativism: the position that there is no single universal set of moral standards.

Norms are also specific to certain groups within a society. In Chapter 5, we discuss these groups and examine the social relationships within them. The groups range from family, religious, and ethnic groups to work and political groups. In all of them, members are assigned a particular set of behaviors—their social roles.

All human beings have certain basic, permanent needs: to be fed, clothed, and sheltered; to learn the rules and skills essential to survival in their environment; to deal with the pervasive mysteries of life (and death); and to achieve and maintain some kind of harmonious order with other individuals and groups. Each society evolves what sociologists call social institutions: systems of rules and patterns of interaction directed toward satisfying one or more of these needs. Sociologists distinguish five major institutions: the family; education; religion; the economy; and government. Although all societies have these institutions, the forms they take can vary greatly from one society to another.

All societies share another feature: structured inequality. That is, the social rewards—wealth, prestige, and power—available within a society are distributed unequally among its members. Differences in distribution can vary from slight to immense. In simple, tribal societies, everyone may be nearly identical in each of these measures of social reward. In others, a few people may dominate in all three measures, while many are poor, despised, and powerless. In such a society there is little chance for a person to rise from a lowly status to a higher one. This is a closed society. In other societies, like our own, the rich and the poor are both far fewer in number than the vast majority in between. In such a society it is possible to move up (or down) the social ladder by acquiring more wealth or prestige or power. Sociologists call this kind of society an open society.

Most societies today contain groups that are distinguished from one another by physical characteristics (color, facial features, hair texture) or by national origin, religion, or cultural background. In no society do all such groups live together in complete harmony and equal sharing of social rewards. Instead, most suffer to some extent from racial and ethnic prejudice, the belief that members of one group are basically inferior to members of another. Discrimination is the social pattern by which one group minimizes another group's access to the social rewards of wealth, power and prestige.

3

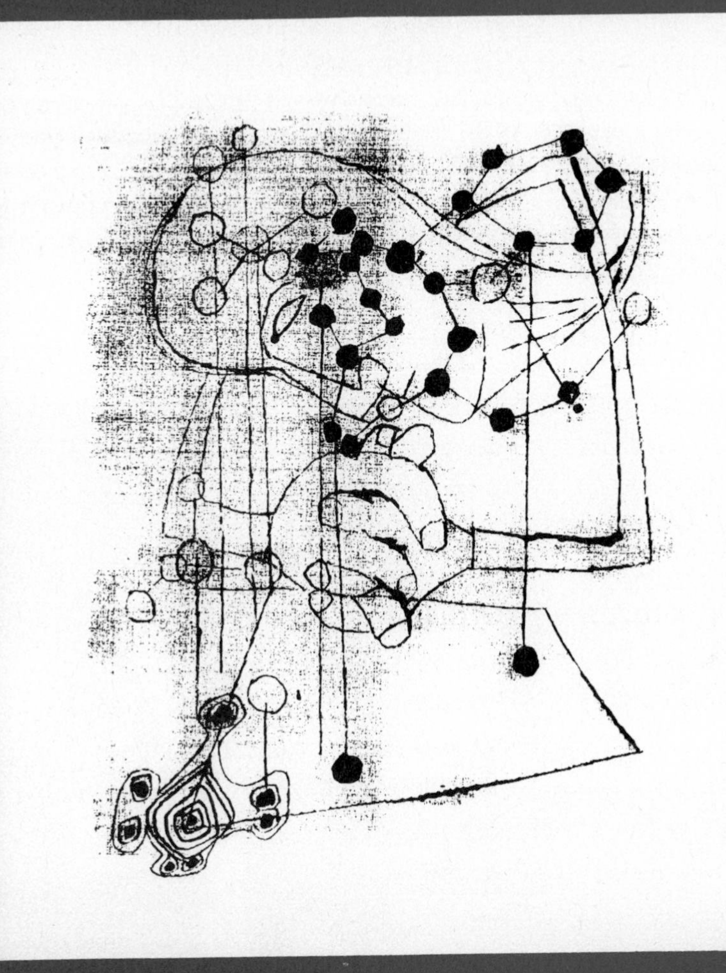

5 ROLES AND RELATIONSHIPS

Our discussion of the sociological perspective, and its cognitive and research tools, and our discussion of the components of culture and its transmission have shown that all human social behavior has a group basis and group context. Our beliefs, values, and norms are derived from our membership in groups, and our patterns of behavior are exhibited in the context of groups of one size or another.

Because of this fact sociologists define much of our behavior as *roles:* behavior that others expect of a person in a given context. We occupy various

Parents, siblings, and others who watch a child grow from the helplessness of infancy often believe they witness the unfolding abilities of the child. But it is not that simple. Even the earliest, most ordinary acts of physical coordination result from interaction between the child and people around it. Almost all human behavior is learned, mainly in group contexts. This generalization is explored further in Chapters 9, 10, and 11.

roles–son or daughter, student, spouse or single person, mother or father, worker (or, more specifically, plumber, teacher, artist, and so on), to name a few. In this chapter we discuss the sociological components of roles, the model of the group, and the group context of roles.

LEARNING THROUGH SOCIAL INTERACTION

The seventeenth-century poet John Donne wrote, "No man is an island." To be truly what we think of as a human being, each of us needs others. This fact was known centuries before the beginnings of sociology. But sociologists have made a special study of socialization: the process of interaction with others by which we acquire our culture–and our humanity.

Few people choose to live apart from society. Certainly without others no one can *learn* to live. We are born totally helpless–physically feeble and with a narrow range of instincts. We simply couldn't survive more than a few hours without the help of others.

Children raised in isolation bear little resemblance to socialized human beings. They do not know or understand the symbols of their society–the spoken language, the written word, or the physical gestures. They know nothing about the existence of values or social norms of behavior. They are human *creatures,* by a biological definition, but they aren't people–if by that term we mean humans who have begun the process of learning a culture (beliefs, skills, values, and norms). Why should this be so?

From our helpless state at birth to the present day we have undergone a process that every mentally and physically normal person undergoes in every society. At first we were taken care of because we were totally dependent; as we grew and our mental and physical abilities developed, we were taught activities that made us increasingly self-sufficient and decreasingly dependent on the time and skills of others. Our parents expressed excitement and pleasure when we were able to feed ourselves, use the toilet, and dress ourselves. Since those early years, our learning and the demand that we learn have continued steadily.

Learning to take care of ourselves as little children evolves into preparing to take care of ourselves (and our families) as adults, in such a way that we also contribute to the well-being of society. Throughout this process we interact with our culture, as it is represented to us by fellow members of society. To see how important this interaction is, we can look at two case studies of children who were raised in isolation until their discovery a few decades ago by authorities (who relocated them in different environments). Their cases were reported by Kingsley Davis.

A Child in Isolation: Anna

Anna was the child of unmarried parents. Her maternal grandfather was so ashamed of his daughter's "misbehavior" that he ordered the baby be kept isolated in an upstairs room. Sociologist Davis reported on this "case of extreme isolation."[1]

> As a result [of her isolation] the infant received only enough care to keep her barely alive. She was seldom moved from one position to another. Her clothing and bedding were filthy. She apparently had no instruction, no friendly attention.
>
> When finally found and removed from the room at the age of nearly six years, Anna could not talk, walk, or do anything that showed intelligence. She was in an extremely . . . undernourished condition, with skeleton-like legs and a bloated abdomen. She was completely apathetic, lying in a limp . . . position and remaining . . . indifferent to everything. She was believed to be deaf and possibly blind. She of course could not feed herself or make any move in her own behalf.

After being discovered and removed from her virtual imprisonment, Anna was given a good deal of love and attention. As Davis reports:

> By the time Anna died . . . , approximately four and a half years later, she had made considerable progress as compared with her condition when found. She could follow directions, string beads, identify a few colors, build with blocks and [tell the difference] between attractive and unattractive pictures. She had a good sense of rhythm and loved a doll. She talked mainly in phrases but would repeat words and try to carry on a conversation. She was clean about clothing. She habitually washed her hands and brushed her teeth. She would try to help other children. She walked well and could run fairly well, though clumsily. Although easily excited, she had a pleasant disposition. Her improvement showed that socialization, even when started at the late age of six, could still do a great deal toward making her a person.

During Anna's first six years she was virtually alone. She had no contact with those who represented the culture of her society. She was given almost no experiences that would teach her how to relate to others. Yet, as Davis reports, she needed others desperately: her condition at the time of her discovery showed how biological resources alone help little to make a "complete person." In his analysis of Anna's case, Davis emphasized the importance of *communication* with people. Contact alone was not enough: Anna had limited physical contact with those who fed her, but almost no social contact—no communication.

[1]Kingsley Davis, *Human Society* (New York: Macmillan, 1948), pp. 204–5.

Because of Anna's early death (from hemorrhagic jaundice at age ten and a half) it is impossible to know how much the learning process would have gained speed once she learned to talk well. It is clear, however, that interaction with and stimulation from others are essential steps toward a human being's participation in social life.

Learning after Isolation: Isabelle

A second case history of a child raised in isolation is also reported by Kingsley Davis.[2]

> The other case of extreme isolation, that of Isabelle, helps in the interpretation of Anna. This girl was found at about the same time as Anna under strikingly similar circumstances when approximately six and a half years old. Like Anna, she was an illegitimate child and had been kept in seclusion for that reason. Her mother was a deaf-mute and it appears that she and Isabelle spent most of their time together in a dark room. As a result Isabelle had no chance to develop speech; when she communicated with her mother it was by means of gestures. . . . Her behavior toward strangers, especially men, was almost that of a wild animal [showing] much fear and hostility. In [place] of speech she made only a strange croaking sound. In many ways she acted like an infant.

Like Anna, Isabelle was rescued from her life of isolation. She was brought to an institution to be cared for and taught. At first those who worked with her were certain she was feebleminded. Yet, as Davis reports,

> the individuals in charge of her launched a systematic and skillful program of training. The task seemed hopeless at first but gradually she began to respond. After the first few hurdles had at last been overcome, a curious thing happened. She went through the usual stages of learning characteristic of the years from one to six not only in proper succession but far more rapidly than normal. In a little over two months after her first vocalization she was putting sentences together. Nine months after that she could identify words and sentences on the printed page, could write well, could add to ten, and could retell a story after hearing it. Seven months beyond this point she had a vocabulary of 1,500–2,000 words and was asking complicated questions. Starting from an educational level of between one and three years . . . she had reached a normal level by the time she was eight and a half years old . . . She eventually entered school where she participated in all school activities as normally as other children.

Both cases show how important it is for people to interact with others and to be stimulated by them. Much human behavior that appears "natural" —that is, unlearned—is in fact taught and encouraged by those with whom an individual comes into contact.

[2]Ibid., p. 206.

Imagine being blind and deaf from infancy, deprived of the two most important senses for interacting and learning (not to mention the pleasures these senses allow). Helen Keller was so, and yet throughout a long life (88 years) she distinguished herself. She learned sign language played on the palm of her hand, and by this means of communication and braille writing managed to graduate cum laude from Radcliffe College in 1904. She spent most of her life writing and working on behalf of blind and disabled people. Her life vividly illustrates the importance of interaction with others in becoming human. Here she manually reads the lips of her teacher Anne Sullivan while communicating, also manually, with Alexander Graham Bell.

1. Imagine yourself training a child like Anna. What activities would you begin with? What skills would you have to teach?

2. Can you think of any behavior or rules of conduct that people do not learn from other human beings?

POSITIONS AND LABELS

Social position: a position within a social structure that is accompanied by a set of expected behaviors.

Anna and Isabelle were both deprived of social relationships during their years of isolation. Isabelle's only social relationship, according to Davis, was with a deaf-mute mother. When she was finally released from her isolation, he reports, "Her behavior toward strangers . . . was almost that of a wild animal." In contrast to such isolated children, the ordinary child by age six has related to many other people who occupy a variety of positions in their social worlds: father, mother, brothers, sisters, grandparents, aunts, uncles, friends, teachers, and others.

Positions and Roles

Positions are often called *statuses* by sociologists. This term, however, also suggests "prestige" in general usage; so in this chapter we give preference to the term *position.*

Even as young children we come to see ourselves as occupying positions. Our interactions with parents teach us the social position of being a child. We learn that, as children, we are expected to obey our parents' statements about what we can and cannot do, while they are not expected to obey us. We learn that, although they teach us to do things for ourselves more and more, they still take care of our needs.

Our social positions are always defined in relation to others according to a pattern of interaction: parent-child; teacher-student; boss-worker; friend-friend; and so on. We can easily label a position—"mother" or "father," for example—but we actually learn the defintion of such a position by the behavior of the person who occupies it: fathers and mothers care for their children, prepare their meals, clean their clothes, tell them what they can and can't do, and provide affection and protection. These positions cannot be separated from the *roles* that go with them.

Enacting the roles of almost any position brings a person into interaction with many others. In the role of mother or father a person interacts not only with his or her children but also with teachers, doctors, clothing store clerks, and others. Likewise the child interacts with other children, teachers, baby-sitters, and doctors. Thus, in a single position we can have many quite different roles.

Social role: the sum of behaviors expected of a person in a given social position.

As children grow, they become more and more aware of the people around them, and they come to recognize that these individuals often occupy more than one position. Father is also a worker, a baseball fan, a PTA member, and a Republican precinct committeeman. Brother is also a son, a high school student, a tennis fanatic, a collector of rare butterflies, and a friend to many others.

Ascribed and Achieved Positions

Ascribed positions: those assigned to a person by the society or by nature.

In every society, some positions are biologically determined. For example, we are born either male or female; we become old only through the passage of time. We cannot reverse the aging process no matter how we may try to do so. These positions are *ascribed*—that is, assigned. (Yet even these ascribed positions allow for exceptions or modifications, as in sex-change operations and cosmetic surgery to make a person look younger.) On the other hand, a person may become a doctor or writer or scholar by special training or by cultivating a skill. These positions are *achieved.*[3]

Achieved positions: those acquired by a person through individual effort.

Even sex, race, and age, the major ascribed positions, are affected by the society and its culture. These positions are not simply a matter of biology. Being a woman in Israel is different from being a woman in Japan. Being a black in the Republic of South Africa is quite different from being a black in Ghana. The concept of age and treatment of the elderly differ drastically in our society from that of the mountain people in the Soviet Republic of Georgia.

Labels

Everyone occupies a number of social positions. If you were asked to describe yourself, you might start with your name and your physical characteristics. If you were pressed to continue ("Yes, but who *are* you?"), you would eventually have to recite some or all of the *labels* defining your positions. For example, you might say, "I am a white, female, Catholic student; I am a music major, a Young Democrat, and a part-time school librarian."

When we want to know about somebody, we generally expect to get a description of the person by such designations. "Bill Smith? Oh, he's one of the Smiths from Highland Village. He's about twenty years old, goes to State, plays football, drives a red Corvette. Sure you know him. He's the guy who was the lifeguard at the pool last summer."

This list of labels is a useful source of information about another person. It tells us what he or she is like. It helps to place the other person in a recognized social slot. Labeling also tells us what kind of behavior to expect.

Often, signs are used to designate a person's position. No one wears a badge saying "grandfather," but professors often have their titles on the door. In department and discount stores, salespeople often wear smocks or buttons or

[3]The concepts of ascribed and achieved positions were first distinguished by Ralph Linton, in *The Study of Man* (New York: Appleton-Century, 1936).

Sociologists distinguish between two kinds of positions, or statuses: ascribed, *or given, positions, such as sex, race, age, and nationality; and* achieved, *or earned positions, such as occupation. The distinction can be misleading, however, because an ascribed position—for example, female sex—can mean very different things in different cultures. Traditionally Iranian women had to cover their faces in the presence of men (the photographer is a woman). Even today they have very few personal and legal rights. Although American women are not yet free from discrimination, nevertheless some, like this woman executive, have achieved exceptional success in fields traditionally dominated by men.*

badges to show that they are not customers; otherwise it would be hard to tell the two apart. Military personnel are required to salute officers of higher rank (whether the person in the higher position is kind or gruff, respected or hated). In order to tell the rank at a glance, they wear uniforms and insignia that indicate their positions. People in other lines of work often wear clothing that indicates their positions also.

Leonard Bickman performed several experiments on unknowing subjects to measure the effect of dress on patterns of interactions.[4] In one experiment, a dime was left in full view in a public phone booth. After someone picked it up, a male or female student dressed in either high-status or low-status clothing would try to reclaim the dime. The sex of the claimant had no effect

[4]Leonard Bickman, "Clothes Make the Person," *Psychology Today,* April 1974, pp. 49–51.

on response, but the mode of dress did: 77 percent of those approached by a well-dressed student returned the dime, whereas only 38 percent of those approached by the poorly dressed did.

Bickman also performed several experiments to test the influence of uniforms. He found that experimenters dressed as security guards got much higher compliance (83 percent) to aggressive commands (such as "pick up this litter" or "give that man a dime for the parking meter") than did persons dressed as milkmen or as ordinary citizens (46 percent).

While relatively few people wear obvious emblems of position, we often look for *some* clue to tell us how to relate to them. We constantly observe and judge others according to the symbols they display that indicate their positions in the social order.

A man might introduce himself by saying, "Hello, I'm Steve Stern." Frequently, however, people give us clues about their positions that tell us how to respond to them. Notice the difference if a man says, "Hello, I'm Dr. Stern," or "Hello, I'm Steve Stern, Assistant to the President," or "Hello, I'm from Thanatos Life Insurance Comapny; Stern's the name."

Labels apply to many spheres of life. Here are a few from several categories:

Category	*Examples of Social Positions*
Sex	Male, female
Race	Oriental, white, black
Nationality and ethnic background	American, French, French-Canadian, Mexican-American (Chicano), Polish-American, Greek, German, Cuban
Age	Infant, child, adolescent, young adult, senior citizen
Kinship	Mother, father, son, daughter, husband, wife, brother, sister, grandparent, cousin, aunt, uncle, mother-in-law, firstborn, middle child
Occupation	Stenographer, farmer, clerk, manager, minister, doctor, lawyer, merchant, police chief, plumber
Education	High school student, graduate assistant, associate professor, dean of students, college president, alumnus
Economics	Employee, unemployed, retired, welfare recipient, millionaire, dependent
Religion	Protestant, Catholic, Jew, Muslim, rabbi, priest, elder, deacon, layperson, parishioner, bishop, abbot
Club or association	President, vice-president, secretary, treasurer, committee chairperson, member
Government	Citizen, prime minister, king, senator, judge, bureaucrat, commissioner, mayor, governor

Consider six positions you occupy. List three that you occupy because you have done something to earn them (achieved) and three that were given to you because of your sex, race, age (ascribed).

POSITIONS AND SOCIAL FUNCTIONS

How is it decided what social positions we will occupy? What are their sources? Our positions are determined by the requirements of social living in a particular cultural context.

The kinds and number of positions differ from one society to the next. In highly religious societies, like those of India and Bali, many people occupy positions of religious significance. In totalitarian societies, like that of Nazi Germany, police and military organizations require many functionaries with varying responsibilities. In Switzerland, where tourism is a primary industry, a wide range of people is needed to provide services to travelers. Among the

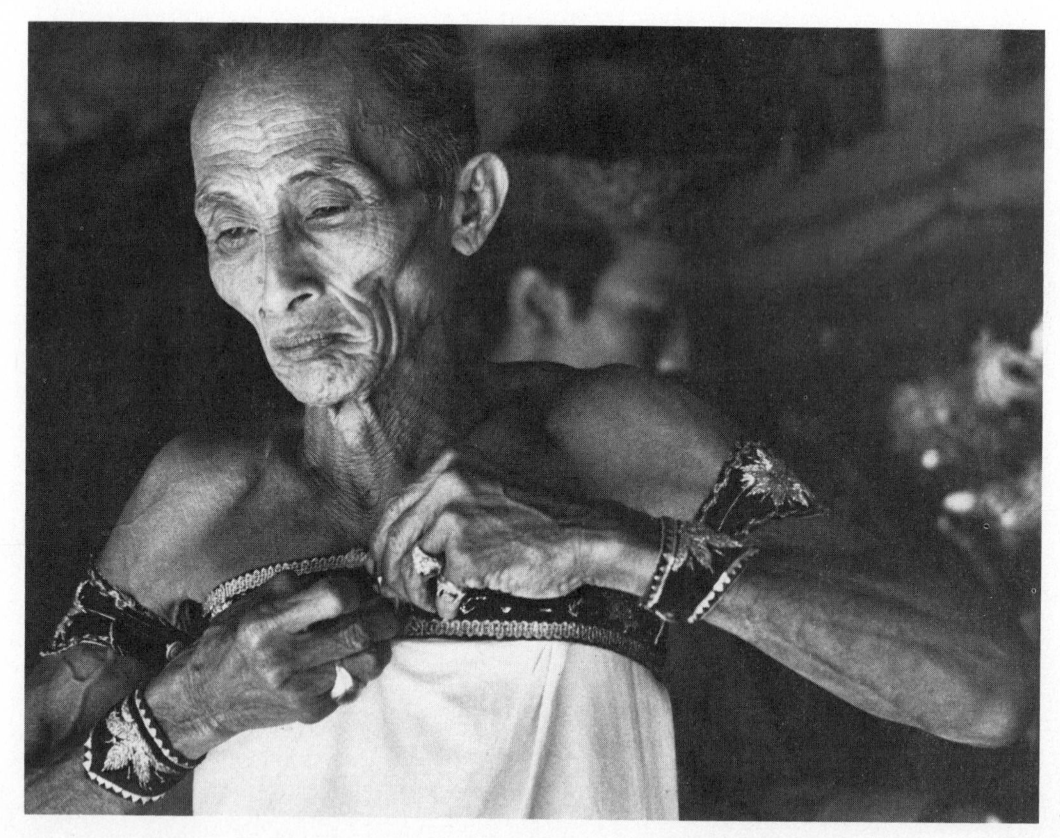

Prestige is a quality accessible to some people in virtually every society. But sources of prestige differ from one society to another. The traditional culture of Bali places high value on religion. Thus, eminence in religion bestows prestige.

nomadic tribes who live in North Africa, no business executives or congressional representatives will be found. No taxi drivers are needed on the upper Amazon or camel drivers in London. Shepherds wander the arid, barren hills of biblical Palestine; hunters, not shepherds, stalk the savanna grasses of the Kalahari Desert.

In complex societies like our own, individuals occupy many positions. Take your sociology instructor, for example: he or she may be a parent and is also the grown child of parents; a college instructor is required to play roles in both the educational and economic institutions, since teaching is an educational activity and a source of income. Your instructor is also likely to be a voter, a supporter of a political party, a believer in a particular religion, and a member of several clubs and associations.

Some social positions—for example, son and daughter—are found in every society. Yet a survey of several societies reveals that there is great variety in the expected behavior related to these positions in different cultures. Child-rearing practices, attitudes toward the behavior of children of a given age, beliefs about whether and how parents should express their love to the child—in these and many other matters no two cultures are exactly alike.

Societies also vary in how one position relates to others and in the roles characteristic of a given position. In our society, some mothers work outside the home, and others do not; in some societies, all women are sheltered in the home and allowed hardly more authority than children have (in fact, they sometimes have less authority than their own sons). In our society the position of uncle has a flexible array of social roles and is not generally considered important to the institution of the family; in some other societies an uncle is extremely important and is expected to be partly father and partly schoolteacher to his nephews.

Have students take the following roles and enact impromptu situations. Note the different types of social relationships that develop. In acting out these three types of role relationships, notice how the definition of each person (the position, or what we are) changes as the social relationship changes. Notice how the role (what we do) changes when the position changes.

1. **saleswoman and customer.**

2. **doctor and patient (who was a saleswoman from nine to five).**

3. **child and mother (who works as a saleswoman and went to the doctor).**

Reciprocity among Roles

People interacting according to a set of roles have clear expectations about how they each will behave. They know (or should know) the limits. We can see this in the doctor-patient relationship, for example. Patients expect that a doctor will be well-trained and expert in applying medical knowledge to the diagnosis and treatment of their problems. Patients also expect a doctor to prescribe medicine that is helpful. The doctor is not supposed to be concerned with how much profit a druggist can make on one kind of medicine as opposed to another; physicians are supposed to be concerned only with their patients' health.

Doctors also have a set of expectations about the behavior of patients, and they act accordingly. They expect patients to be honest and thorough in discussing the symptoms and history of their medical problems. A doctor will often tell a patient, "Unless you tell me everything truthfully, it is impossible for me to help you."

Reciprocity between role performers does not always go smoothly, however. Often, for example, a patient wants a more thorough explanation of the condition and its treatment than the doctor is willing to give. Eliot Freidson contends that doctors in hospitals tend to see their patients as children who should have faith in the doctor's judgment and should not inquire about things beyond their understanding.[5] The patients, on the other hand, often feel more fearful and helpless because of this approach.

Adopting New Roles

Doctor-patient, doctor-nurse, and doctor-doctor relationships are largely controlled by expectations known to all parties in the interaction. We don't even need to be actual doctors or patients or nurses to know how to act the part in relation to another person. All we need to know is the setting of interaction and the positions of the actors.

1. In small groups, role-play a situation requiring several different actors. For example, assume that a person accused of rape is before a judge. Also present are the alleged victim, the prosecutor, the defense attorney, and a police officer. Spend twenty to thirty minutes acting out the sequence of events, without rehearsing beforehand.

[5]Eliot Freidson, "Dominant Professions, Bureaucracy, and Client Services," in *Organizations and Clients*, ed. W. R. Rosengren and Mark Lefton (Columbus, Ohio: Charles E. Merrill, 1970), pp. 71–92, especially pp. 79–82.

Each social position involves roles: patterns of expected or obligatory behavior. But most positions allow some degree of role tolerance: behavior that does not fit the position but also does not violate the norms that apply to the position, like this snowball fight between two priests in Rome.

2. How did you know how to act the role that you were assigned to play? How much of your performance was based on external sources of information—say, television screenplays on the subject or books or magazine articles? How much came from imagining yourself in that position and playing it by ear? How much came from the cues that you received from the other role-players?

You can see how quickly you learn to play socially defined roles, even those you've never played before. You might also have noticed how much your actions depend on the position of the other person—defendant, police officer, lawyer, witness, judge—with whom you are interacting.

In the following situations, someone is called on to play a new role with special expectations. From the following examples, describe as carefully as you can the expectations of the role-players, the relationships, and the interaction that will result.

1. A college senior is being interviewed by campus recruiters from various large corporations, such as Prudential Life, IBM, and General Foods.

2. Marcie's parents are politically conservative. She is going home during spring recess and bringing her boyfriend, who is very radical compared to her parents. Marcie doesn't entirely agree with her boyfriend's political ideas. However, she wants her parents to realize that she has a mind of her own and that her feelings must be respected.

ROLE STRAIN AND CONFLICTS

Role conflict: conflict between opposing demands within a role or between two roles occupied by the same person.

Most of the roles we play are related to specific social situations and relations within them. We are generally expected to behave differently as a member of a family group, as a friend, as a church-goer, as a student, as a buyer or seller, as a voter. In other words, we are expected to play roles that are appropriate to the positions we occupy in different areas of society. Sometimes the requirements of one role conflict with those of others. Then we are confronted with the dilemma of *role conflict.*

Competing Norms

When a role conflict occurs, a person is often forced to violate the norms of one role to fulfill the norms of another. An extreme example is the conflict experienced by a Catholic priest when a man confesses that he has committed heinous crimes, indicating he has a pathological personality and is likely to harm others. By the laws of the Catholic church, the privacy of a confession is sacred. If the criminal refuses to surrender to authorities, the priest cannot identify him or locate him for the police without violating his vows as a priest. Yet not to report the criminal surely endangers other lives.

In the following situation, identify the roles of the person in conflict and describe the norms that conflict.

A young black police officer is assigned to a beat in an urban ghetto. He is sworn to uphold the law, and he believes in the social necessity of order and justice. But he is also aware of conditions in the ghetto, and he understands the despair and cynicism about "the system" felt by many ghetto dwellers. Hearing a burglar alarm go off in a nearby appliance store, the officer runs toward it. He sees a figure dart out of the store and into the adjacent alley. He pursues the fleeing figure and traps a black youth of about sixteen who is carrying a portable television set.

Ideally, what should the police officer do? In reality, what options are open to him? Which option do you think he will choose?

Often we find ourselves in roles that do not produce outright conflict but nevertheless produce strain. For example, a college professor has the competing roles of teaching and publishing (the "publish or perish" syndrome). Each demands much time and energy. As a teacher he or she must constantly improve and update teaching materials and techniques, devote time to student conferences outside the classroom, and attend departmental and faculty meetings. Publishing requires time and energy for original research, intensive study of the work of others, and organizing and writing the materials in publishable form. Most of this activity is likely to be too narrow or specialized to be of use in the professor's courses.

Role Priorities

Role priorities: the ranking of role demands in order of importance to minimize role conflict and strain.

Attempts to resolve role conflict and strain usually require setting *priorities.* When two norms conflict in a given role, a person must choose which one is to be given preference over the other. The priest must decide whether his vows of silence about what is said in the confessional should outweigh his duties as a citizen. (Doctors, lawyers, psychologists, psychiatrists, and reporters, while they don't take religious vows, may face the same ethical conflict, because the same guarantee of privacy is virtually "sacred" in their relations with clients and news sources.) The professor must decide whether to spend more time on teaching or on research and writing.

For most priests, the role conflict we described probably never occurs. But for the people who occupy many other positions role conflicts and the need to set priorities are constantly present. Most people try to achieve consistency in the priorities they give to conflicting values, norms, and roles. One professor may be a good teacher but offer little time to students outside the classroom, while another is very popular and active with students but is regularly in peril of losing the job for lack of scholarly output. One office supervisor may favor the judgments and decisions of upper management instead of those of the supervised workers and therefore lose their trust, while another supervisor may risk being considered "soft" by management for the amount of consideration he or she gives the workers. In these and many other instances of role strain, we decide which of two conflicting norms matters most to us as individuals, and then we give priority to that one in balancing our behavior.

Compartmentalization and Tolerance Limits

Compartmentalization: isolation of competing or conflicting norms by considering two or more social roles as separate.

Setting priorities occurs even more commonly in conflicts between positions than in conflicts within them. We might say that setting priorities among roles of different positions is compartmentalizing our behavior. That is, in dealing with conflicting norms, we stress one set of norms when we occupy one position (often related to a particular social institution) and stress a different, conflicting set of norms when we occupy another position. Each set of norms has its own compartment in our social lives. We are able to compartmentalize this way, because there is a margin of tolerance for differences in behavior in the roles of most of our positions.

Role tolerance: the margin of acceptable variances in performance of a role. Behavior exceeding the tolerance limits is deviance, which is discussed in Chapter 11.

While we are learning the social roles for the positions we occupy, we are also learning the margins allowed between the ideal performance of each role and outright violation of it. The width of these margins of tolerance are not agreed on by everyone. Taxpayers probably take a more tolerant attitude toward "creative" tax returns than IRS agents do. As heads of families, taxpayers would prefer to spend their money on immediate needs—food, clothing, car payments, house repairs, and so on—than have it withheld from their paychecks or demanded on April 15. Businesspeople and advertising agency employees, whose goals are to increase product sales, have different priorities from those of consumer groups, who want to increase the value of each dollar by eliminating shoddy merchandise and false or misleading advertising.

Each of these three collections of persons displays the sociological traits of a group, whether a couple of Samburu (Kenya) tribesmen who are friends, an American family, or members of the Elks Club, a voluntary association. Each particular group has more or less resemblance to its defining ideal type, of course. In some families, for example, there may be far less spontaneity and intimacy than in others; nevertheless, a family most closely resembles a group at the primary end of the spectrum of groups.

Changing Role Priorities

Sometimes social pressures make us change our priorities. Consider the following situation in which a person is under pressure to follow opposed sets of norms and, therefore, to play roles differently.

Archie Raggers is a twenty-two-year-old law student who lives with his parents, mainly for financial reasons. His parents are pleased with Archie's goals and performance as a student, and they accept his living at home. He has worked his way through school and has contributed money toward the household expenses. He gets good grades and has earned the praise of both college and law school teachers. But his parents have never been able to accustom themselves to Archie's hair, which he wears shoulder length, as do many of his friends. ''What's happening these days?'' the parents ask. ''The boys all have *long* hair, and the girls have *short* hair!''

Over the years, discussions about Archie's hair and clothing (jeans, denim jackets, workshirts, and hiking boots) have become less frequent, chiefly because they tended to repeat each other word for word. ''Archie, you're a man now, but you sure don't look it,'' his father would say. ''You look like some long-haired freak, some doped-up rock musician. We know you're okay, but your mother and I have an awfully hard time explaining you to our friends—especially since we ourselves don't understand why you want to look that way. You and your friends look like fugitives from Woodstock. You're just a bit too old for that now.''

To which Archie would reply, ''C'mon, Dad. You and your friends should get it together. Why do you worry so much what other people think? What do they know? I'm not going to live my life to please them, any more than you should. My friends and I *like* long hair. We don't see anything wrong with it, or any reason to apologize for it. Why should we walk around with our ears sticking out, like we had to do when we were kids?'' On and on it would go, a merry-go-round of dispute going nowhere.

Imagine the surprise and delight of Archie's parents one day when he came home with a haircut. His ear lobes were visible for the first time in years, as was part of his neck. His parents beamed with pleasure. ''You look terrific, Archie. How come you did it?''

''Well, I was offered this really great job for the summer as research clerk with the local American Civil Liberties Union chapter. But they said that, things being what they are, appearances are somewhat important there, since the ACLU is unpopular with a lot of people to start with.'' Archie shrugged his shoulders. ''So I got a haircut.''

''Well, I hope you won't get mad,'' his mother said, ''but your father and I will find it a lot easier to have you around now that we won't always have to defend you to our friends and neighbors.''

''Uh—well, Mom, I'm not going to be here much longer. I'm moving into a flat downtown that's closer to campus and the ACLU office.''

''But how will you manage that, Archie? I mean, financially?''

''Oh, I'm moving in with four people already there. You know them,'' Archie said, with a twinkle in his eye, ''Chuck, Dominic, Sandy, and Donna.''

"But Sandy and Donna are—"

"Right. Girls."

"But, Archie . . . ."

"C'mon, Mom. We're all too busy studying law to do what you're thinking. It's strictly financial. That was the understanding when the four of them first got the flat together, and it's stayed that way all along. Even Lisa doesn't mind. And if my own girlfriend isn't upset, you sure have nothing to worry about. The family is safe."

"Well, if you don't mind, Archie," his father replied dryly, "I don't think we'll mention to our friends that Sandy and Donna are among your roommates."

1. Have you ever been in a position similar to Archie's? Describe it. What were the conflicting views on the behavior considered appropriate? (Note how the topics we have discussed so far—norms and values, institutional requirements, cultural symbols, and role expectations—all intertwine.)

2. When you were in that norm conflict position, what determined your priorities? On what basis did you decide how to act? Who had the greatest influence on your decisions?

3. Why do you think Archie would do something for the ACLU that he wouldn't do for his parents? If you had been Archie, would you have acted in the same manner?

THE GROUP CONTEXT OF ROLES

If we change our perspective slightly to look at Archie Raggers's problems in relation to different and competing roles, we can see another element in the sociological description of human interaction. That is, as a member of his family, as a person with friends, and as a potential worker for the American Civil Liberties Union, Archie is dealing with groups.

Like Archie, we all live much of our lives in close proximity with others. We wait in lines to go to a movie, ride a bus, and buy groceries. We rub elbows with others on subways and trains. We gather in classrooms, libraries, and stadiums. We congregate in offices and factories. We meet with friends. We make love. For most of us, daily life involves constant contact and considerable interaction with other people.

The notion of groups is another concept that sociologists take from the everyday world and make useful by operationalizing it for their specific purposes. In common speech we often use the word *group* to mean nothing more than a gathering of people. Think, for example, of the newspaper statement, "A larger group showed up for the opening night performance than was expected." The people who make up such a gathering are there because they have an interest in a certain event. They are gathered only briefly and their interaction is minimal. Like those who take an elevator or ride a bus together, people going to the theater have only a few rules to observe in their interactions. They know they are supposed to join the line at the end, move forward as those in front do, resist the temptation to push and shove, and move aside for officials. Other than these minimal norms, they are not required to interact at all with the others who are gathered.

The Sociological Concept of Groups

Group: two or more people who interact in patterned ways, share beliefs, values, and goals, and have a sense of membership.

Archie's associations in the story were more complex than associations among people attending a play together. They came closer to the sociological definition of a group, which is more than a mere gathering of persons for a specific purpose. For a gathering to be a group in the sociological definition, it must meet three requirements:

1. it must have recurrent patterns of interaction;
2. its members must hold shared or similar beliefs, values, or goals; and
3. the members must be conscious of their membership in it.

Archie's family and friends and the ACLU share these three requirements, although in different degrees. In any family, patterned, recurrent interaction means that people behave toward one another (at least ideally) according to the norms that govern the family as an institution in their society or sector of it: the parents take care of the children, the children respect and obey the parents (within limits), and they show affection and support for each other. Although Archie and his parents clearly do not share all the same values and beliefs (about appearance, for example, and about living with friends of the opposite sex), they probably agree on the goals of the family.

We usually do not even think about these goals consciously. A college-age sister who is asked to stay home with a younger brother may refuse because there is something more pressing she has to do but not because she feels no responsibility to help in the child's care and protection. Goals such as these underlie the patterned interaction within a family.

1. How does a local ACLU chapter meet the three requirements of a sociological group?

2. Think of a group that you belong to. Is it a sociological group? Why or why not?

Group Structures

A friendship clique, or group, like that of Archie and his close friends, also depends on clear patterns of interaction, common outlooks and a special sense of belonging or membership. But, unlike a family, it is a voluntary association. There is an old saying that "you can choose your friends but not your relatives." It's true we don't choose our parents, cousins, or children; in many societies, we would even have little to say about who we were going to marry.

Another difference between relatives and friends is that the roles of relatives (how they are expected to interact with us) are generally well defined. "Parent" usually includes the notion of authority over children; "child" includes showing respect for parents. In most societies fathers and mothers have specific responsibilities that they are expected to carry out.

In many ways friends are different. We choose them according to personal preferences. Affection for each other is the basis of the relationship. Among friends, we interact more as equals (peers) than as superiors and inferiors. Friendship cliques are considerably more equal in power distribution than families, even nuclear families (parents and children alone). This doesn't mean that friends have no obligations to each other or that they don't set up leader–follower situations among themselves. Of course they do. But, by and large the norms are more flexible; not so many are imposed by the requirements of society. Therefore the "structures" of friendship groups tend to be *idiosyncratic*—that is, particular to each group, not the same for all.

Groups have a set of norms governing behavior and impose penalties on members who don't comply with the norms. In 1952, psychologist Solomon Asch tested the pressure members feel to conform by enlisting one real subject and various numbers of people posing as subjects. All were asked about the comparative lengths of sticks being held up to view. The pseudosubjects expressed incorrect judgments. This put the real subject in a dilemma: should he or she express his or her own judgment and risk being different from the group, or should he or she conform to the group's judgment? Asch found that there was substantial conformity on the part of the real subjects and that the amount of conformity depended on the size of the opposition. If one person was opposed to the subject's judgments, the subject rarely

yielded. When the majority of a group expressed contrary judgments, the subjects' conformity became pronounced. Some subjects conformed to group judgment even though they still believed that their own view was correct and the group was incorrect.[6]

Try to test this theory with groups of different sizes, each time having only one real subject. Arrange with the other "subjects" that they will all take off their sweaters, put their books on the floor, or stand up with no command. Test the reactions of the real subject as the number in the group increases; correlate reactions and responses with the size of the test group. Compare your findings with Asch's.

THE GROUP CONTINUUM: PRIMARY TO SECONDARY

In our daily lives we participate in all sorts of groups—from family and friendship groups to schools and businesses. But not all our relationships take place in groups. Not every person with whom we interact is a member of one of our groups. The doctor and the outpatient in a large hospital may discuss very personal matters, but they do not constitute a group any more than a prostitute and her client or a clerk at the Motor Vehicle Bureau and an applicant for a license do. On the other hand, highly impersonal organizations, such as giant corporations, labor unions, and government agencies, may well possess the characteristics of groups despite the impersonality and brevity of the interactions within them.

Primary group: two or more persons who interact in intimate, spontaneous ways that provide emotional involvement.

Clearly, groups can possess all the criteria for existence—patterned interaction, shared values and goals, and a sense of membership—and still differ enormously in size, complexity, and purpose. Recognition of this fact has led sociologists to distinguish groups according to the kind and quality of relationships in them. The opposite poles in this distinction are primary groups and secondary groups.[7]

Relations within a primary group are characterized as spontaneous, intimate, emotionally involving, and rewarding. They are not directed to specific tasks but exist for their intrinsic value (their worth just for themselves).

[6]Solomon Asch, "Effects of Group Pressure upon the Modification and Distortion of Judgments," in *Readings in Social Psychology,* ed. Eleanor E. Maccoby, Theodore M. Newcomb, and Eugene L. Hartley (New York: Holt, Rinehart and Winston, 1958), pp. 174–83.

[7]See Charles Horton Cooley, *Social Organization* (New York: Schocken Books, 1962). Cooley is credited with coining the term *primary group.* Its opposite, *secondary group,* gradually came into use.

The family unit is often portrayed as the ideal example of a primary group. But not all families achieve this ideal or even aspire to it. Perhaps the Russian novelist Leo Tolstoy had this fact in mind when he wrote in *Anna Karenina*, "Happy families are all alike; each unhappy family is unhappy in its own way."

It is true that most people view the family, the nuclear family (parents and children) at least, as the place of deepest love, support, and intimacy among all members. The trouble is that many families lack the one other quality mentioned above, spontaneity—the ability of members to be completely themselves with others in the group. Problems between children and parents often seem to prevent a free and fair exchange of ideas and outlooks, fears and desires.

For this reason, the smallest possible group, the couple (what sociologists call a *dyad*—a group composed of two), whether husband and wife, lovers, or best friends (of whatever sex), often comes closer to being a truly primary group than the nuclear family.

Do you agree or disagree with this last statement? With whom do you feel the closest bonds and the most inclusive relationships? Is there any group in which you experience all three characteristics of the primary group?

Secondary group: a group in which interaction is task-oriented, formal rather than spontaneous, and lacking in intimacy.

At the other end of the continuum are secondary groups. They too have the core characteristics of groups, but the relationships of members are more formal, more emotionally restrained, and goal- or task-oriented. While secondary relationships, like primary ones, can be rewarding to members, the rewards are usually more tangible than those derived from a primary group. Rather than giving or withholding love and affection, those in positions of influence in secondary organizations offer varying degrees of prestige and, sometimes, wealth and power to other members.

The American Civil Liberties Union is a secondary group. It is task-oriented; its entire reason for being is the task of preserving civil liberties through the legal system. Its members have clearly defined roles related to this central purpose, and their relationships are limited to playing these roles. If friendships or love relations arise among members, these are independent of the members' official roles and are supposed to have no effect on the performance of their jobs.

Imagine a primary-secondary continuum as a ruler.

Primary 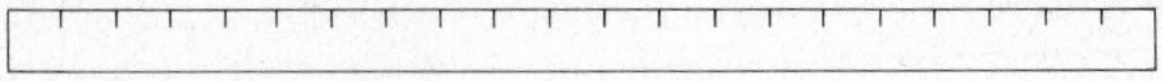 Secondary

1. List the characteristics of primary and secondary groups.

2. Think of five social groups to which you belong. Plot them along the continuum. It is easier to plot the groups that fall close to the extremes, because they possess most of the characteristics you listed above.

3. Consider the groups that fall somewhere between the primary and secondary extremes. What kinds of intimate behavior take place in each of these groups? What impersonal characteristics are present?

Perhaps the most striking difference between primary and secondary groups is that members of primary groups have such complete commitment to the group and need so little formality to maintain it. Secondary groups, on the other hand, require highly structured interactions. Rules for behavior and task assignment seem to be taken for granted when we are parents or close friends. But at work or in school elaborate regulations define what we are supposed to do, where we are supposed to be at given times, and where we stand in relation to others. Sociologists call these secondary groups *formal organizations.*

Formal Organizations

Formal organization: a secondary group in which rules of interaction are explicit and there is a hierarchy of authority.

Let's return to Archie Raggers once again. The group Archie is going to work for is fairly easy to describe and to map. It is a formal organization, which means that it has a clearly stated set of values and goals, an internal structure, and a defined membership. The American Civil Liberties Union exists as a chartered organization with a stated goal of enforcing the norms explicitly stated in the Bill of Rights of the United States Constitution, primarily through court action. It is hierarchically organized, like most formal organizations, with a fixed *table of organization.* The ACLU's table is an arrangement of status designations and functions in rank order according to authority over subordinates. The names attached to the positions can be readily replaced by others without altering the structure. Thus, the ACLU exists apart from the personalities of its members and, ideally, will outlast any of them.

Like other groups, the ACLU has patterns of interaction among members engaged in the activities aimed at fulfilling its goals and between its representatives and clients or potential clients in civil liberties cases. Members also

In a formal organization, positions, lines of authority, and division of labor are clearly defined. People interact according to their positions and in order to fulfill their designated tasks. Spontaneity and intimacy have limited relevance to the functioning of a formal organization.

interact with others in preparing briefs, planning court strategy, and keeping in touch with contributors who help support the organization. Within the internal structure, responsibilities are divided among various staff members: there are administrators, supervisors, clerks, secretaries, fund raisers, lawyers, and researchers, at national, regional, and local levels. Group membership is equally explicit: there are staff members and dues-paying supporters.

Bureaucracies

We have already noted that although the Motor Vehicle Bureau clerk and the license applicant are involved in an interaction, they do not constitute a group. However, a woman who is a license clerk is a member of a group—a formal

The common image of the modern bureaucracy: long lines, "red tape," impersonality, and anonymity. Nevertheless, bureaucracies exist to carry out a complex array of tasks most efficiently. Whatever the real or imagined faults in such formal organizations, bureaucracies appear to be necessary to the functioning of a modern, industrial society.

Bureaucracy: a formal organization that incorporates clearly defined, separate tasks assigned to positions within an explicit hierarchy of authority.

organization. She has certain clearly defined connections to it, follows its rules, and sees herself as a part of the bureau. She is a member of a complex organization, a giant secondary group. She is literally a bureaucrat.

Max Weber,[8] one of the founders of sociology, studied the modern bureaucracies that emerged with the growth of nationalism and the industrial revolution. He defined bureaucracy as a type of formal social organization, one that attempts to achieve maximum efficiency in carrying out complex administrative tasks by making interactions impersonal, rational, predictable, and reciprocal. Bureaucracies exist in government, in large private corporations, in public services such as sanitation departments, police forces, and fire departments, in many church organizations, in the army and navy, in schools, colleges, and universities.

All these bureaucracies share certain common characteristics, which Weber analyzed. In listing them, Weber was treating bureaucracy as an ideal type. He was describing how these organizations were meant to operate to serve their intended purposes, rather than how any specific bureaucracy actually operates.

Ideal type: a model of a complex entity incorporating the essential elements that underlie variants among particular examples of the entity.

Characteristics of the ideal type. The ideal type of bureaucracy has five characteristics, according to Weber. In the first place, bureaucracies are organized into carefully defined positions or offices. Each position has certain tasks, responsibilities, and authority. These don't change when one person leaves the office and another is hired. People interact on the job as occupants of the positions, not on the basis of likes or dislikes. The only criterion the person must meet is competence to handle the tasks of the position efficiently.

The ideal type of bureaucratic organization is divided into a hierarchial order. Lines of authority and responsibility are clearly defined from the top, where the ultimate authority rests, to the bottom, where positions have no authority. Every position in between must answer to the position above and be answered to by the position below.

A third characteristic of bureaucracy, Weber noted, is that personnel are selected on the basis of their skills. In a bureaucratic organization positions are reciprocal—that is, completion of tasks requires interaction between two or more positions. Because of this, each position must be occupied by someone with the specialized skill and training for it. Standardized tests are often given applicants to be sure the most qualified person gets the job.

[8]See Hans H. Gerth and C. Wright Mills, eds., *From Max Weber* (New York: Oxford University Press, 1958); and Max Weber, *Essays in Sociology*, ed. and trans. Hans H. Gerth and C. Wright Mills (New York: Oxford University Press, 1958).

In a bureaucracy, rules and regulations state how the business of the agency is to be carried out. When we apply for a driver's license or a passport, the bureaucrat who receives our application does not use his or her judgment of our looks or wealth or family background to decide whether we deserve to have our request fulfilled. Rather, specific rules tell both the bureaucrat and the applicant what must be done to gain the document wanted. Even within the organization, personnel interact, on business, according to rules and regulations. If an employee has a question about procedures or some other matter, his or her immediate superior is the only source of information. This allows for control and predictability. It also means that secondary relationships prevail among people in bureaucracies.

Finally, to encourage employees to work as efficiently as possible, each member in the organization is eligible for a raise or promotion only on the basis of merit, further examinations, or seniority. Personal preferences, friendships, and dislikes are not bases for granting or denying advancement to a worker. Those who work in public or government bureaucracies are often given tenure (permanent job security) after a probationary period. This privilege, which is central to our civil service, was purposely introduced so that people wouldn't be subject to political pressure in carrying out their jobs.

Informal relationships in formal organizations. Although we can find ample evidence of each of these features in bureaucratic organizations, nevertheless not everyone in bureaucracies limits relationships to those of the secondary kind, not everyone performs exactly the tasks assigned, and not everyone follows the precise channels of authority to get things done.

Think of how often people try to "bend the rules" in order to "cut through the red tape" to get something done at school or on the job. Breaking or getting around the rules is what has been called "bureaucracy's other face." Within the limits established by the table of organization of a bureaucracy, its members find areas of flexibility in which personal preferences can be expressed. For example, friendships may begin on coffee breaks or during business hours while employees are doing the routine tasks that require them to interact. Informal pressures lead people to modify the explicit norms of the organization, to open new channels of communication, and to create new groups based on shared experiences and close relationships.

In recent decades, organizational planners have abandoned their earlier fear of primary relations within secondary groups. Many no longer see them as potentially disruptive to efficiency and order. In fact, they are recognized as contributing to morale and group solidarity within an organization.

SUMMARY

Culture refers to the way people live; social organization refers to the way they live together. While culture defines the patterns of social behavior, actual human interaction occurs in clearly defined social settings. Without others no cultural ideas would be transmitted, no values would be instilled, no rules would be learned.

With others—and through others—we learn the many parts or roles we are to play on the stages of life. We learn how each of these roles is related to a particular position in the social structure. These positions or statuses sometimes exist before we come on the scene, and we are "assigned" to them. Other positions we achieve through our personal efforts.

Sometimes the requirements of one position conflict with those of others. We are placed into situations of role conflict, because opposing behaviors are expected in different social contexts. Often these social contexts are what sociologists call groups. They range from small, intimate primary groups to large, impersonal bureaucracies. These are formal organizations in which individuals' roles are clearly and narrowly defined. Ideally, relations within bureaucracies are of the secondary variety; the organizational structure is fixed and stated; role performance is directly related to the hierarchy of clearly defined positions; and the bureaucracy is formed with the efficient performance of specified tasks in mind, according to rules of procedure.

Even in bureaucracies, however, members often suffer from (or delight in) informal pressures to humanize their behavior. Informal groups frequently develop in the most highly organized settings, establishing their own rules and relationships according to how individual members see the organization and its goals.

This same idea applies on a much wider scale. In the next three chapters we look more broadly at the structures of whole societies, concentrating on institutional compartmentalization, social stratification, and other patterns of inequality and how individuals and groups react to such facts of social life.

6 SOCIAL INSTITUTIONS

Human behavior is seen through the sociological perspective as group-based. Our culture—our beliefs, values, and norms, and our patterned ways of interacting—all of this is learned by transmission from others. Much human behavior is seen by sociologists as roles—the behavior expected of people in various social positions. Much of this behavior occurs within the groups we are members of—families, friends, coworkers, formal organizations, religious bodies, and so on.

Sociologists also categorize human behavior another way: according to *social institutions,* unified systems of rules and patterns of interaction that are directed toward satisfying one or more of our basic, permanent needs. Thus, while a particular family is a group, the family as an overall pattern of interaction is a social institution.

The term *institution* is an elusive one. It is used in a variety of ways. For instance, you may have heard people say:

Yankee Stadium is an institution, it would be a shame to tear it down.

The family gathering at Thanskgiving is an American institution.

Her brother? I didn't know he was in a mental institution.

The family is an institution under severe challenge.

In the first statement, the word is used to identify an important landmark, something that has existed for a long time and that would be missed if it were allowed to disappear. The second use of the word identifies a time-honored tradition that is cherished by many people in our culture. The third is a specific place or building with a special purpose. The fourth use is considerably broader than the other three. It refers generally to an aspect of social life that, without being spelled out in detail, conjures up complex relationships among people and rules governing those relationships.

Social institution: a system of norms and values that pattern behavior toward fulfilling some basic, enduring human need.

While sociologists also use the word *institution* in the first three ways, for analytical purposes they tend to keep to the last: a social institution is a system of norms and patterns of social interaction that are related to particular and important spheres of social life. Thus, we speak of family, educational, political, economic, religious institutions—and sometimes others.

FUNCTIONAL PREREQUISITES

Functional prerequisites: the basic needs that must be met by a society if it is to survive.

Every society, in order to function, has to have ways of meeting such needs as its own continuation, the care and training of the young, the distribution of cultural, economic, and political resources, and the explanation of events that seem incomprehensible. These *functional prerequisites*, as they are sometimes called, are universal; they are shared by all human societies.[1] But the ways in which people meet these needs vary markedly from one society to another. For example, when we think of the norms surrounding family life in American society, we tend to think of ideas such as free choice, romantic love, obligations to dependent children, and controversies about abortion, divorce, and the relative positions of men and women. Similarly, when we think about the American economic system, concepts such as capitalism and free enterprise come first to mind.

Our attitudes about the family and the economy are largely set by our culture. The way we perceive the family and the economy and the way we behave in these realms of life are largely determined by what we have learned to be "our" institutional arrangements.

All societies work out their own approaches, their own *functional alternatives*. If we asked a Navajo Indian to describe the family in Navajo society, his or her response would be very different from the response of most other Americans. Instead of ideas about romantic love and choice or controversies about abortion, divorce, and the relative positions of men and women, the Navajo might well discuss how marriage is arranged, the sacredness of the bond, and the importance of clan ties. A member of the Red Guard in the People's Republic of China, if asked about the economic system, would hardly begin with discussions of free enterprise. Instead, he or she would explain the nature of socialism and its importance in satisfying the economic needs of China's vast land.

There is inevitably a certain amount of integration (meshing) among the institutions of each society. As Karl Marx and others have shown, institutional requirements in one sphere affect those in others. To boost production in a labor-intensive farming society (that is, one requiring large amounts of human labor for a given output of goods), it is logical to favor large families, which provide many hands. In a highly automated, capital-intensive industrial society (that is, one requiring large investments in plants and machinery), it is just as logical to attempt to lower the birth rate. The amount and content of educa-

[1]See D. F. Aberle et al., "The Functional Prerequisites of a Society," *Ethics* 60 (January 1950): 100–111 (reprinted in Bobbs-Merrill Reprint Series in the Social Sciences).

tion is often influenced by economic considerations. And so is the political order.

INSTITUTIONS AND PEOPLE

We can categorize societies according to the character of their institutions. But we must realize that the networks of norms that make up the institutions are meaningless without people. Societies are social units made up of people—people who relate to one another in particular ways, who act, react, and interact in groups and associations. Thus, every society has not only familial institutions (norms surrounding family life) but also actual families; each has not only economic norms but also actual units of people who engage in the production, consumption, and distribution of goods; each has not only ideas and rules relating to religious practice but also actual churches that people attend and religious organizations in which they participate. The rules and norms of the institutions govern the constant interplay among the actual people who carry out institutional functions.

Unlike many tribal and preindustrial societies, industral societies generally require a high degree of specialization of their members. The family group is located in the home; the educational functions are carried out in schools;

FUNCTIONS AND STRUCTURAL ELEMENTS ASSOCIATED WITH MAJOR SOCIAL INSTITUTIONS

Function	*Institution*	*Major Roles*	*Physical Traits*	*Symbolic Traits*
Bearing and rearing children	Family	Father Mother Child	House Furnishings	Ring Wedding Will
Providing food, clothing, and shelter	Economic	Employer Employee Consumer Producer	Factory Office Store	Merit award Emblem Trademark
Enforcing laws, rules, and standards	Political	Ruler Subject	Public building Public works	Flag Codes Charter
Promoting cooperative attitudes, faith, hope, charity	Religious	Pastor Member	Cathedral Temple	Cross Altar Bible
Socializing persons into basic values and practices of society	Education	Teacher Student	School College Books	Diploma Degrees

Source: George Lundberg, C. Schrag, O. Larsen, and W. Catton, Jr., *Sociology*, 4th ed. (New York: Harper and Row, 1968), p. 709.

religious functions in places of worship; economic functions in factories, offices, shops, and markets; and government functions in city halls, police stations, courthouses, legislatures, federal and state agency offices, and the like. Each social institution has become the basis for one or more different social groupings.

In this chapter we examine the background and characteristics of the major social institutions in our society.

THE FAMILY

The biological needs of infants have remained the same throughout the course of human existence. So has their need to be socialized into their cultures in order to become contributing members as they grow older. While families fulfill these basic biological and socializing needs as they always have, the structure of the family has undergone profound changes in many parts of the world, especially in the last 150 years, when technological change has occurred more and more rapidly.

This change has reduced the traditional functions of the family so greatly that in some societies the old-fashioned family unit seems on the verge of disappearing. Other societies have tried to alter the pattern of family life to make it serve changing goals. Some alterations have been rather dramatic: for example, Soviet leaders after the Bolshevik Revolution in 1917 tried to rid their new society of the family tradition of inheritance and the dependence of each generation on previous ones. Some Zionists in Israel have substituted communal arrangements on the kibbutz for those of the traditional Jewish family; this frees mothers, in particular, from their time-worn role.[2] The

[2]For a detailed examination of family life in the Soviet Union and Israel, see David Mace and Vera Mace, *The Soviet Family* (New York: Doubleday Dolphin, 1964), and Bruno Bettelheim, *The Children of the Dream* (Toronto: Macmillan, 1969).

In the Soviet Union, in the People's Republic of China, and on some kibbutzim in Israel, much of the traditional socializing function of the family has been taken over by the state or community. Parents have more limited roles—although they remain very important as sources of affection.

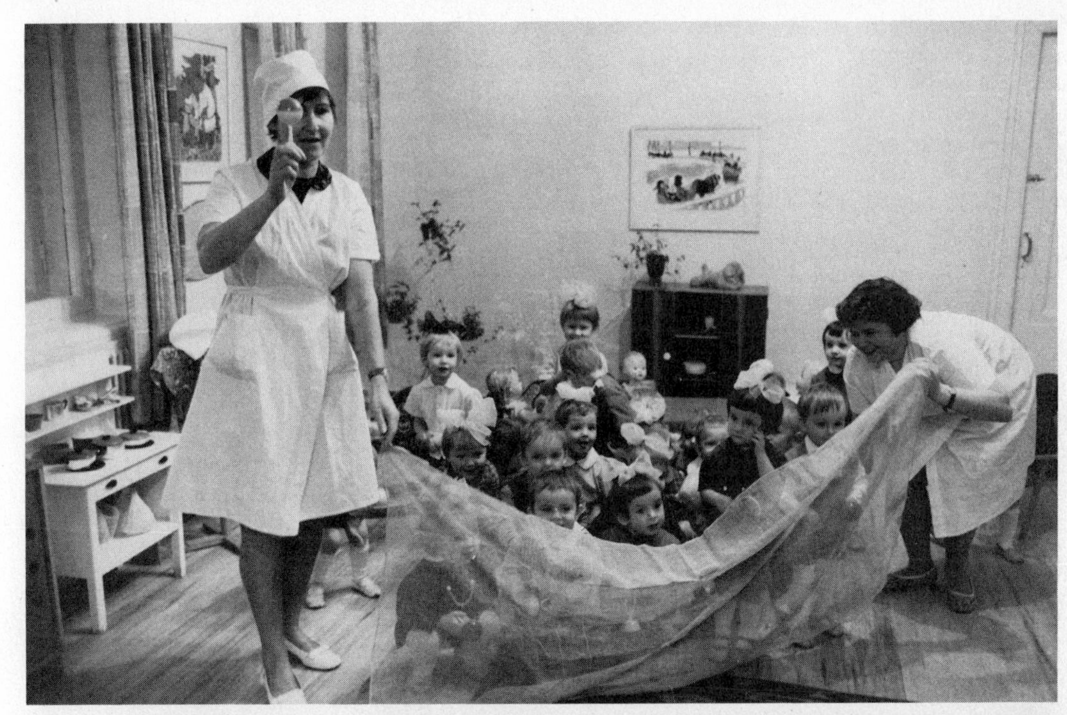

Extended family: a family structure that includes more than one nuclear family or includes three or more generations of people linked by birth.

People's Republic of China is trying to change its families' traditional intense reverence for parents and grandparents (called *filial piety*) to a reverence for the state and dependence on the community, to serve the nation's social and political needs.

The goals of the Soviets, Israelis, and Chinese were never fully achieved. Certain functions continued to be met in traditional ways despite ideological pressures from the authorities. Nevertheless, parents are seen chiefly as sources of affection and personal warmth, while villages or schools serve to transmit the values and norms of the wider society to the children.

Family Size in the United States Since 1920

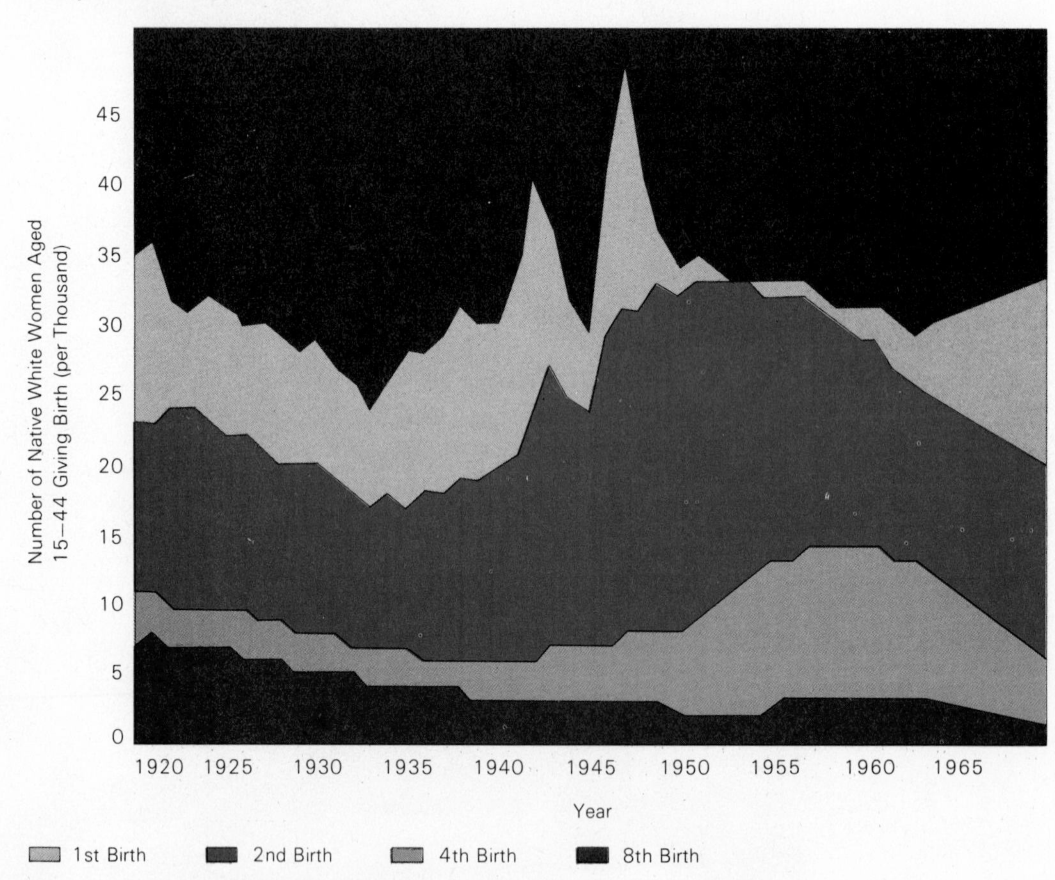

Sources: United States Department of Health, Education, and Welfare, *Vital Statistics of the United States*, vol. 1, *Natality* (Washington, D.C.: U.S. Government Printing Office, 1964), pp. 1–11; *Statistical Abstract of the United States* (Washington, D.C.: U.S. Government Printing Office, 1970), p. 50.

Although in American society there has been no deliberate effort to reduce the role of the nuclear family as a socializing agent in the early life of the child, the changing role of women in the work force has created the demand for more child-care centers.

The American Family

In our own society, and in many others in advanced stages of industrialization, change has been less deliberate, although almost as dramatic. The family that serves as an economic unit of production—once common—is now rare. Ties to the large extended family have become more limited. The nuclear family has gradually become smaller as the average number of children has declined. Unusual today are families of four or five children. Unlike nineteenth-century parents, couples now can control the number of children they will have and can be fairly confident their children will survive until adulthood.

Nuclear family: two parents and their children.

BIRTH, DEATH, MARRIAGE, AND DIVORCE RATES

	Rate per Thousand Population			
Year	*Birth*	*Death*	*Marriage*	*Divorce*
1910	30.1	14.7	10.3	0.9
1915	29.5	13.2	10.0	1.0
1920	27.7	13.0	12.0	1.6
1925	25.1	11.7	10.3	1.5
1930	21.3	11.3	9.2	1.6
1935	18.7	10.9	10.4	1.7
1940	19.4	10.8	12.1	2.0
1945	20.4	10.6	12.2	3.5
1950	24.1	9.6	11.1	2.6
1955	25.0	9.3	9.3	2.3
1960	23.7	9.5	8.5	2.2
1965	19.4	9.4	9.3	2.5
1970	18.4	9.5	10.6	3.5
1973	15.0	9.4	10.9	4.4

Source: United States National Center for Health Statistics, *Vital Statistics of the United States* (Washington, D.C.: U.S. Government Printing Office, annual).

Social mobility: movement up or down in the system of social stratification.

Other changes in the family include the shifting role of women, the growing rate of divorce, and the increase in one-parent families (sometimes called *subnuclear families,* since the single parent assumes the traditional roles and responsibilities of both father and mother).

Social rewards are discussed more fully in Chapter 7 on social stratification.

Evolution of the nuclear family. Among the sociological theories that explain these family changes in industrial societies, that of William Goode is most representative.[3] Goode and others point out that an industrial society needs people who can move from place to place easily—people with geographic mobility. They must be able to change locations to get their particular kind of work. A metallurgical engineer may study this subject in southern California, but he or she might work wherever such training is needed—in Seattle, Houston, or Boston. The engineer's mobility makes it very difficult for him or her to have close ties with an extended family.

Extended family ties are weakened not only by geographic mobility but also by social mobility. Our metallurgical engineer may achieve much higher social rewards—in wealth, prestige, and power—than others in his or her family. The engineer's way of life, values, and friendship groups are likely to change as a result. Brothers, sisters, and cousins may occupy different social strata as adults although they were alike as children.

We include the development of suburbs as part of the urbanization phenomenon (see Chapter 13), although it occurred only in recent decades.

Urbanization has also affected the family structure. As large numbers of people moved to cities in the early stages of industrialization, they began to rely more and more on institutions other than the family. Goode explains that the number of children per family decreased when the crowding of city populations put a strain on dwelling space. As compulsory education and child labor laws were enacted, they kept children out of the job market for far more years than before. Children became consumers of family income rather than contrib-

OPINIONS ON IDEAL NUMBER OF CHILDREN PER FAMILY, 1973

Respondent's Answer	*Percentage of Respondents*
One, Two	46
Three	23
Four	14
Five, Six, or more	3
None	1
No Opinion	9

Source: George Gallup, "Few Favor Large Families," reported in the *Salt Lake Tribune,* February 5, 1973. Reprinted by permission of Gallup Poll (American Institute of Public Opinion).

[3]William J. Goode, *World Revolution and Family Patterns* (New York: Free Press, 1963).

Changes in one social institution produce changes in other institutions. Once the extended family (several generations of relatives living together or close to one another) was common in American society. The family was important as an economic unit. More children meant more workers, whether on the farm or in the city's factories and sweatshops. As the family's productive role diminished, so did its size.

utors to it, especially as improvements in medicine allowed more children to survive. Large families found it harder to live within their income than small ones. Gradually people changed their ideas about the number of children a family should normally have. By 1973, 46 percent of the Americans surveyed in a Gallup poll thought the ideal number was one or two children.

Our description of the changes in the family does not apply uniformly and without exceptions. It consists of generalizations—statements that describe the overall pattern. For example, family size has changed at different rates among different groups, and the average family size continues to vary by group.

1. Survey your own family's past, going back several generations, if you can. Record the number of children. Note the number of children who died at birth or in their early years. List the father's and mother's occupations and social class (upper, middle, working, or lower), based on income and community prestige and power. Were they rural, city, or town dwellers? Did the children serve an economic function?

2. Do you see a trend toward smaller families in successive generations of your family? Ask your parents and grandparents their reasons for having the number of children they had and their ideas about the reasons of their ancestors.

Sex roles and the rapidly increasing changes in these roles in contemporary society are examined at length in Chapters 9 and 10.

Women in the labor force. Industrialization and urbanization have affected not only family structure and size but also family values and norms. In the past several generations these have also changed significantly. The middle-class conception of American nuclear family life has also shifted recently. Whereas many working-class and lower-class women have always had to work for financial reasons, a wage-earning father and a homemaking mother were once the middle-class norm. Now more and more middle-class women, both single and married, have careers outside their homes.

This growing proportion of working married women was accelerated by World War II. Motivation for women to work came from both outside the family and inside it. The country needed labor for heavy war production, while immense numbers of men were taken from the labor force to serve in the military forces. Women, who used to be excluded from most roles in the job market, were suddenly invited to fill this vacuum.

Why did women respond so readily to the nation's need for their labor?

Marital Status of Gainfully Employed Women

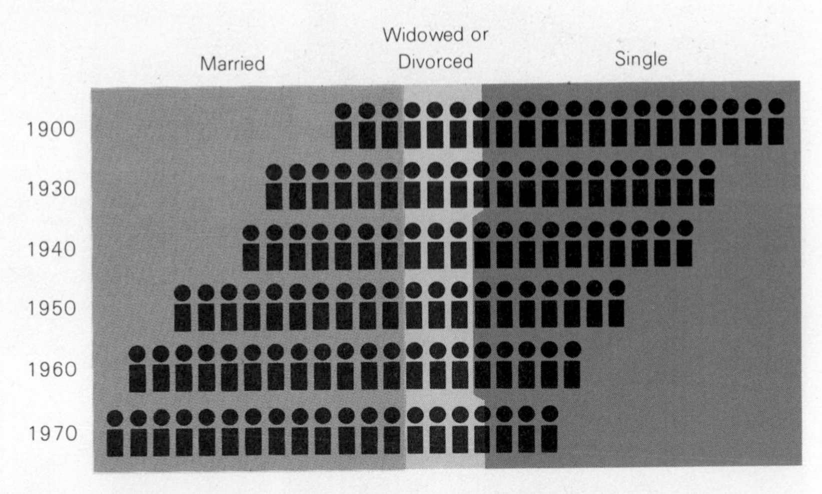

Source: United States Department of Commerce, Bureau of the Census.

Was it simple patriotism? Was it a real but unexpressed feminist desire for "liberation"? Perhaps these were motives for some women, but most saw the chance to serve their country by helping their families. Industrial production for the war effort was bringing the country out of ten years of the Great Depression. After suffering from rampaging unemployment and struggling to survive, virtually everyone was eager to earn money. Women wanted to work outside their families partly to satisfy the material needs of those families.

After the war there was a general return to prewar norms, at least for a time. With men reentering the labor force and resettling into traditional routines, women were pushed out of the work place. This change was reinforced by a glorification of traditional sex roles, especially in advertising and the media.

The work force is sexually integrated today, but discrimination persists, both in pay scales and in opportunities for women to hold certain positions, as we see in Chapter 10.

Many husbands went to college under the GI Bill, a government program subsidizing education for veterans. Better education meant better jobs. In the postwar boom years, there were plenty of opportunities for workers eager to improve their lot. More consumer goods of a wider variety were available than ever before. With new labor-saving devices, housekeeping became somewhat less time-consuming, and the advantages of a higher standard of living lured people who were entering the middle class to spend more money for goods and services. Many wives again found reasons to work outside their homes.

Under pressures created by World War II, women were encouraged to change their work roles—but not their self-images, as the idealized portrait and caption of the poster show.

Dorothea Lange Collection, The Oakland Museum

HIGH SCHOOL AND COLLEGE GRADUATES

	High School			College		
		Number (Thousands)			Number (Thousands)	
Year of Graduation	Percentage of 17-year-olds	Male	Female	Percentage of high school graduates	Male	Female
1900	6.4	38	57	28.4	22	5
1920	16.8	124	188	15.8	32	17
1940	50.8	579	643	15.3	110	77
1950	59.0	571	629	36.0	329	103
1960	65.1	898	966	21.0	254	138
1965	74.0	1,314	1,351	19.9	316	214
1970	75.7	1,433	1,463	28.6	484	343
1975 (projected)	75.4	1,569	1,593	31.8	564	440
1980 (projected)	75.9	1,536	1,560	34.2	582	477

Sources: United States Office of Education, *Earned Degrees Conferred* (Washington, D.C.: U.S. Government Printing Office, annual); id., *Digest of Educational Statistics* (Washington, D.C.: U.S. Government Printing Office, annual); id., *Projections of Educational Statistics to 1982–83* (Washington, D.C.: U.S. Government Printing Office, n.d.); and unpublished data.

With higher living standards and more family income, college education became a possibility not only for men but also for increasing numbers of middle-class women. As young women learned sophisticated skills for use in the world of work, paid employment developed a new importance in their images of themselves. More and more women saw careers as desirable and permanent parts of their lives—not just as ways to pass the time while waiting for the right man to come along, marry them, and take them "away from all this."

Increasing divorce rates. The social changes we have discussed—the decline of family size and the increase in the number of middle-class women holding jobs—are related to another change, the current high divorce rate in the United States. According to recent census figures there is roughly one divorce for every three marriages.

Increase in Divorce Rates

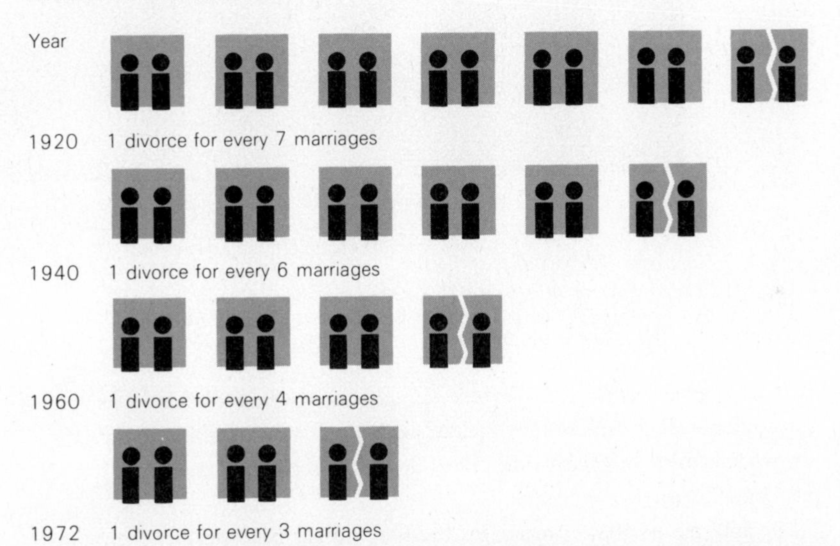

Source: United States Department of Commerce, Bureau of the Census.

What do these figures actually mean? The data presented do not say that one out of every three marriages fails but rather that at a given time, say 1972, the United States Bureau of the Census recorded one couple getting a divorce for every three couples getting married. If we look more deeply into the situation, we discover that recently married couples have a very high chance of divorcing, while those married for some time have a very low likelihood of getting divorced. In conjunction with this, we find that as the number of chil-

Number of Divorces by Duration of Marriage

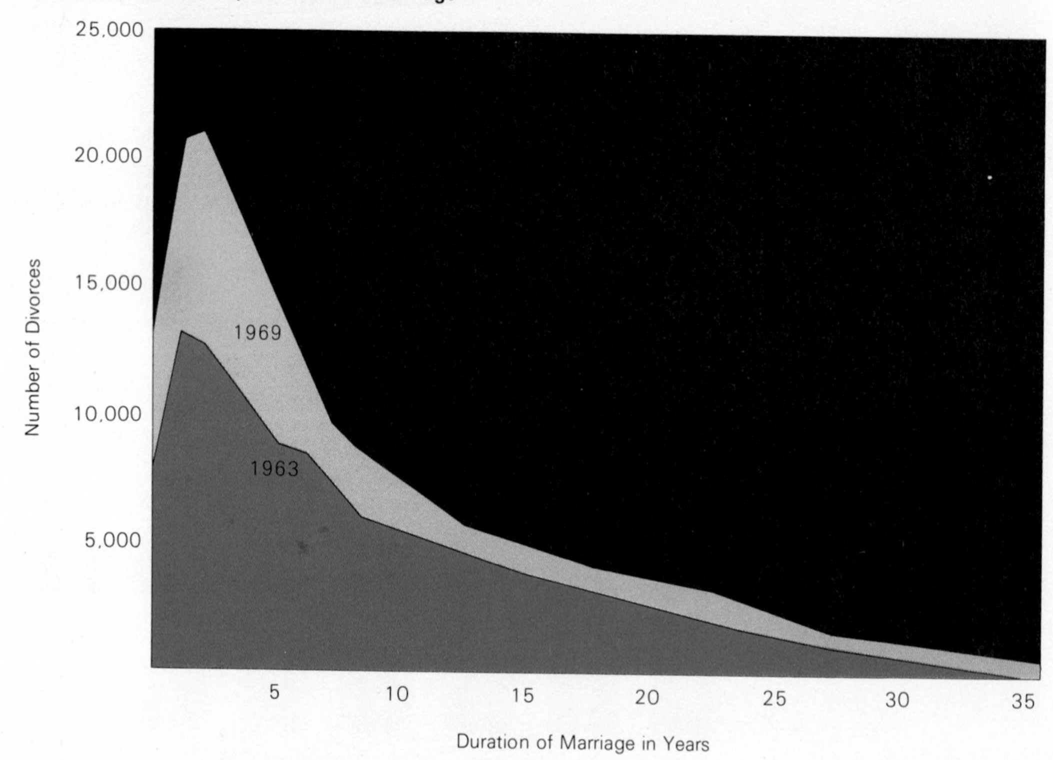

Source: United States Department of Health, Education, and Welfare, *Divorces: Analysis of Changes, United States, 1969,* Vital and Health Statistics Series 21, no. 22 (Washington, D.C.: U.S. Government Printing Office, 1969), p. 22.

dren in a family goes up, the divorce rate goes down. Raw divorce rates are further misleading because they include individuals who obtain a divorce for the second, third, or fourth time. They do not indicate how many first marriages actually stay together.

Still, the number of marriages breaking up has been steadily increasing. Sociologists have offered several explanations for this. Marriages based on romantic love have always been acknowledged gambles. In earlier times, unhappy couples were kept together by religious rules, state laws, and social sanctions (penalties) that were applied to divorced people. These sanctions are far weaker today. Major barriers to ending marriages have been removed. States have accepted broader and more lenient grounds for divorce, and most churches (the Roman Catholic church is a notable exception) do not condemn divorce.

Number of Divorces by Number of Children, 1963 and 1969

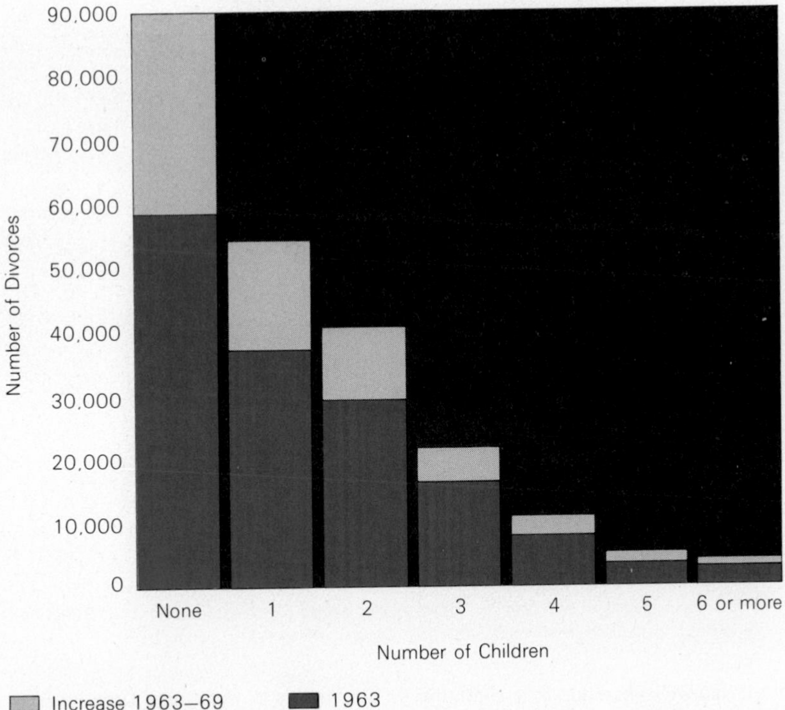

Source: United States Department of Health, Education, and Welfare, *Divorces: Analysis of Changes, United States, 1969,* Vital and Health Statistics Series 21, no. 22 (Washington, D.C.: U.S. Government Printing Office, 1969).

In addition, many working women are financially independent. They don't feel bound to their husbands for their livelihood, so they are freer to seek divorces. Women who are not financially independent also get divorced, of course. Many welfare recipients, for example, are divorcees. Husbands and wives today are less likely to see value in preserving unhappy marriages "for the sake of the children."

For all these reasons, divorce has become more common. Indeed, it has become a socially acceptable solution to difficult marital problems.

Survival of the family. What are we to make of all these changes? The extended family has become less important than the nuclear family, and the nuclear family has shrunk in its urban environment; significant numbers of women have entered the work force; the divorce rate has steadily increased.

MARRIAGES AND DIVORCES

Marriage and Divorce	*1940*	*1950*	*1955*	*1960*	*1965*	*1970*	*1973*
Marriages							
Number (thousands)	1,596	1,667	1,531	1,523	1,800	2,163	2,277
Rate per thousand population	12.1	11.1	9.3	8.5	9.3	10.6	
Percentage married, 18 and over							
Male	66.1	71.8	56.7	76.4	76.2	75.0	74.5
Female	65.4	70.9	71.9	71.6	70.5	68.5	68.1
Median age (years) at first marriage							
Bride	21.5	20.3	20.2	20.3	20.6	20.8	21.0
Groom	24.3	22.8	22.6	22.8	22.8	23.2	23.2
Divorces							
Number (thousands)	264	385	377	393	479	708	913
Rate per thousand population	2.0	2.6	2.3	2.2	2.5	3.5	
Percentage divorced, 18 and over							
Male	1.4	1.8	1.9	2.0	2.5	2.5	3.0
Female	1.8	2.3	2.4	2.9	3.3	3.9	4.5
Median duration of marriage (years)		5.3	6.2	7.1	7.2	6.9	
Divorced persons per thousand married	25	29	31	35	41	47	56

Sources: United States National Center for Health Statistics, *Vital Statistics of the United States* (Washington, D.C.: U.S. Government Printing Office, annual); United States Department of Commerce, Bureau of the Census, *Current Population Reports,* series P—20, periodic.

Is the family dying? Or is it changing to new forms to meet new functions?

Sociologists differ on these questions. Some, like Pitirim Sorokin, see the rising divorce rate and declining birth rate as signals of attitudes that will one day spell the death of the family.[4] Others, like Talcott Parsons, see the institution of the family evolving gradually to serve more limited functions. The two main functions Parsons has in mind are providing early socialization for the young, and meeting the emotional needs of both children and adults.[5]

EDUCATION

The norms, values, and structure of education, like those of the family, have undergone many changes in recent years.[6] Compulsory education is only a few generations old in our society. And college education has been available to large segments of the population for less than a generation.

[4]See Pitirim Sorokin, *Social and Cultural Dynamics* (New York: American Books, 1941).

[5]See Talcott Parsons and Robert Bales, *Family Socialization and Interaction Process* (Glencoe, Ill.: Free Press, 1955).

[6]See, for example, Lawrence Cremin, *Transformation of the School* (New York: Knopf, 1961).

Annual Divorce Total, 1954–71

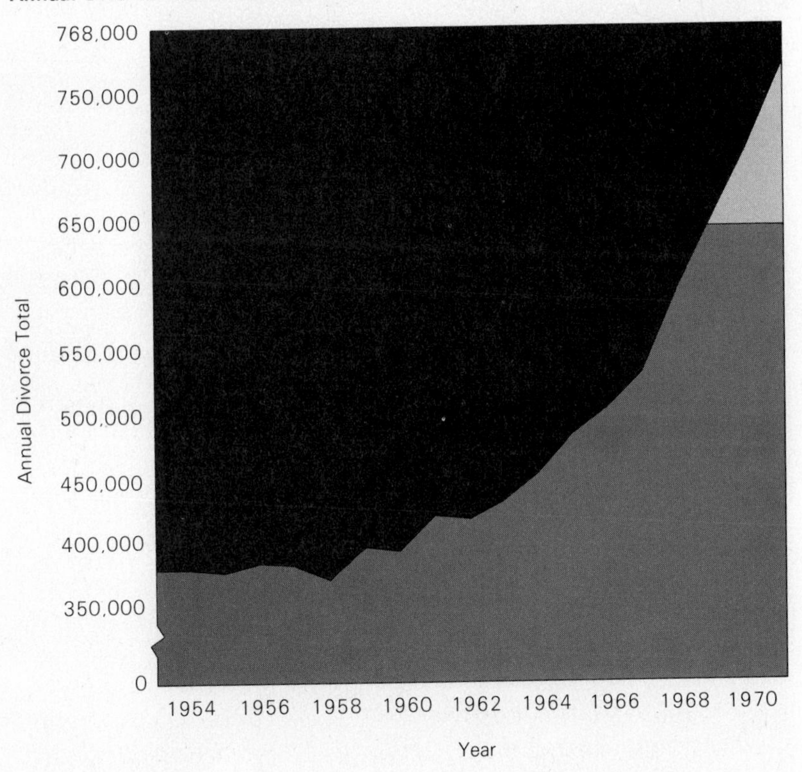

Provisional data

Source: United States Department of Health, Education, and Welfare, *Divorces: Analysis of Changes,* Vital and Health Statistics Series 21, no. 22 (Washington, D.C.: U.S. Government Printing Office, 1969), p. 1.

Humans have always needed to learn virtually everything. But what, and how, and how much they learn has varied a great deal. So have the teachers and the places of learning. In a small, preliterate (nonreading) society, parents (or other relatives) are usually the teachers of children. There is no need for classrooms and grades: the bush where game lurk, the field to be planted and harvested, the flock and its pastures, and the home are "schools."

In a few pre-Christian societies, such as those of ancient Greece and Rome, circumstances conspired to create the need for a certain number of formally educated persons. In its classical period, Greece was a collection of city-states in constant need of administrators and statesmen, who generally were drawn from among the young of wealthy families. To serve their func-

In every society the educational institution fulfills the need to transmit the culture to the young. In tribal, preliterate societies, the family may fulfill this need, transmitting not only beliefs, values, and norms but also basic productive skills. In other societies the educational institution takes the form of schools. Even within a given society differences may occur. Today some traditional schools look very much like the late nineteenth-century classroom shown here, but other schools are much more informal and are directed as much toward socializing "the whole person" as they are toward teaching skills.

sing
the garden

tions they needed to acquire formal knowledge. (You may be amused to learn that our word *school* comes from the Greek *scholē,* which means, among other things, leisure.) Likewise, the later Romans provided schools to educate people to meet the bureaucratic needs of their immense empire.

Most formal education in its early stages was training of the sons of the elite to assume positions of leadership. This training was not "vocational" in the modern sense; it was truly "classical," aimed at improving the mind. Philosophy and mathematics were more important than applied skills.

Social control: the various methods of ensuring and reinforcing conformity to a society's norms.

After the fall of the Roman Empire in the fifth century, the only people in Europe to receive schooling were those going into the service of the Christian church. The church was the one extensive agent of social control in all Europe. Secular (nonreligious) education did not begin in Europe until the fourteenth century. Then schools and universities were established for the education of aristocrats. Over the centuries, more and more members of the rising middle class gained entry to the schools.

Still, until well into this century, education was extremely limited by every measure: the average number of years; the range of the curriculum; the percentage of children who were able to go at all; and the amount of funds allocated to schooling. Schooling remained the province of the elite. This was true at all levels, but it was particularly acute at the university level.

American Education

At first, American society was chiefly agricultural and rural. Children learned the values and norms of society at home. Skills of farming and crafts—shoemaking, tinkering, blacksmithing, and the like—were learned by the apprentice method (young workers taught on the job by experienced farmers or craftsmen). There was little need for formal schooling, although communities did provide elementary schools so that children could learn to read the Bible. Higher education was almost solely for training clergymen, doctors, lawyers, and other professionals.

Growing industrialization required more and more new skills to be taught—from mathematics and spelling to engineering and personnel management. Without tracing the growth of the American curriculum in chronological detail, it should be clear that education was usually linked to social needs. At first these were essentially religious needs; then they were basically economic needs. Later, when vast numbers of people flocked to the United States from Europe and Asia, education shifted to the task of preserving the dominant culture by instilling its values. Schools became basic agencies for socializing the young immigrants to the beliefs, values, and norms of American society.

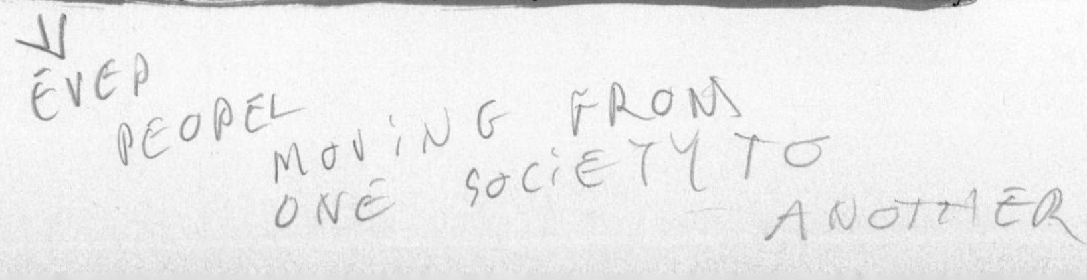

Traditionalists and progressives. As education began to assume a larger part in socializing this heterogeneous (diverse) population to live in an increasingly complex society, debates raged about the proper direction and focus of schooling. Some theoreticians, like John Dewey, argued that there was too much emphasis on "dogma and obsolete knowledge." A philosopher and an advocate of "progressive education," Dewey proclaimed that learning must be an active process, attuned to the needs of students and their changing society.

For decades the controversy has continued between the traditional, skills-oriented approach and the progressive notion of "educating the whole person." Traditionalists argue that training in basic skills, especially, in the three Rs—reading, 'riting, and 'rithmetic—is the primary function of education. Schools should not be expected to become substitutes for parents but only to provide what most parents cannot give themselves. The progressives reply that schools are necessarily socializing agents, no matter how narrow and technical their training seems to be. The traditional school's treatment of students and the behavior it demands of them—docile obedience, pretended interest, unquestioning observance of arbitrary rules or curriculum choices—prepare students for a social existence that is rigid and unchanging. Education needs to produce students attuned to the spirit of open inquiry and democratic ideals, say the progressives. Two virtues are claimed for progressive education: it socializes the students in democratic norms; and it makes them more independent thinkers in a constantly changing world. Traditionalists, on the other hand, maintain that progressive education fails to teach the basic skills adequately. Although progressive schools can perhaps produce imaginative people, traditionalists argue that too many of these students lack self-discipline and competence in fundamental, practical skills.

In Chapter 9 we see how schools have acted as a significant force in socializing the young into traditional sex roles.

Channeling for roles. As students are being socialized and taught useful skills, they are also being selected and channeled for various roles in life. Guidance counselors, different courses of study (adademic, general, and vocational tracks, for example), and grading systems are all used to differentiate students in ways that affect the positions they will eventually occupy.

Try to list all the decisions that you or someone else (a parent, teacher, or counselor, for example) made about your future role or direction in school. List all tests you were given for these purposes (IQ tests, college boards, and so on).

1. How did you feel about the decisions made? Did you agree with some and disagree with others?

2. How much control do you feel you had?

3. How meaningful do you think each test was as a guide to the course your schooling should take?

4. How important were your family income, ethnic background, and social class in these educational choices?

There is no overestimating the importance of the schools in making these selections for both individuals and society. In general, a person's lifetime income can be directly correlated with the total number of school years completed and the degrees received. There are further correlations with subject majors. In this crucial tie with the economic institution of our industrial society, education has the effect of reinforcing our class structure. Schools often reflect middle-class values, and teachers frequently seem to favor those who come closest to these values.

Thus, once again we see how different social institutions can overlap to interact with and support one another. Our performance in the economic system is largely based on how we use the educational system. Our performance in school is in turn influenced by our family background and economic position.

INCOME OF MALES BY YEARS OF SCHOOL COMPLETED

Income (Thousands of 1972 Dollars)

	Years Completed					
	Elementary School		*High School*		*College*	
Year	*Less than 8*	*8*	*1–3*	*4*	*1–3*	*4 or more*
Lifetime income, from age 18 to death						
1956	$202	$275	$311	$376	$428	$573
1961	212	287	330	383	469	636
1967	244	326	369	444	510	706
1970	256	331	374	450	532	715
1972	280	344	389	479	543	758
Annual mean income, 18 and over						
1956	3.9	5.5	6.2	7.3	7.8	11.7
1961	4.1	5.8	6.6	7.5	8.5	13.1
1967	4.5	6.4	7.2	8.8	8.9	14.6
1970	4.7	6.4	7.2	8.8	9.0	14.6
1972	5.2	6.6	7.5	9.2	9.2	15.2

Source: United States Department of Commerce, Bureau of the Census, *Current Population Reports,* series P–60, no. 92 (Washington, D.C.: U.S. Government Printing Office, n.d.).

In the 1970s, busing children to schools in other neighborhoods proved a controversial way of achieving racial integration. This issue demonstrates a clash among several institutions: the family, government, and education. Other educational issues raising interinstitutional conflicts have been sex education in the schools; the Darwinian theory of evolution versus the biblical account; and—perennially—the teaching of basic skills versus broader socializing activities.

THE INDUSTRIAL ECONOMY

In late 1974, "stagflation" (recession plus inflation) was at its height in the United States economy and provoked a furious search for solutions to its problems.[7] Secretary of the Treasury William Simon appeared before a Senate committee in response to congressional proposals that American taxpayers receive rebates (partial refunds of their withheld taxes) so that consumers would have more spending money. Economists hoped that the consumers would use the extra money to stimulate the sinking economy. Simon created a stir by proposing that Congress return most of the proposed $60 billion in rebates to upper-middle-class taxpayers instead of to lower-middle-, working-, and lower-class people. Why keep the money from those who presumably need it most in inflationary times? Because those people would only spend it on more of the goods they're already buying—nondurables (food, clothing, rent). The upper-middle-class consumers, on the other hand, would probably spend

[7]Before the experience of the 1970s, inflation (a steady, broad rise in prices) and recession (a decline in purchases, output, and employment) had never occurred at the same time: in times of recession prices fell; in times of inflation output and employment rose.

this extra money on durable goods (cars, major appliances, houses) in the sectors of the economy most in need of stimulation.

From the sociological perspective, what can we conclude about this idea of withholding consumer income from those who need it most in favor of those who need it least? It can teach us several things about an advanced industrial economy and its norms of interaction. For one thing, the statement was made by one member of government, the secretary of the treasury, to a branch of government, the Senate. We thus get an indication of how interrelated our economic and governmental institutions are. For another, it illustrates a warning voiced by economist John Kenneth Galbraith that "our wants will be managed according to the needs of the industrial system . . . . The state will add its moral, and perhaps some of its legal, power to their enforcement."[8]

[8]From "Where Do Mergers of Corporations Lead?" *Christian Science Monitor,* March 5, 1969, p. 10.

Historical Development

Throughout this text we have pointed to various functions of the economic institution—to promote the physical well-being of the members of society, to manage its resources, and to distribute its goods and services. We have touched on the variety of forms the institution can take, from hunting and gathering activities to the affairs of gigantic corporations.

The history of modern economics shows links between the earliest forms of economic activity and current patterns. When human beings first domesticated plants and animals (developed agriculture), they made the first truly permanent human settlements. Later, as they accumulated food surpluses in the fertile valleys of the Near East and Asia, some of their population could live without farming or herding, and the first cities were born. People began to specialize in their economic activities and to trade on a much larger scale—exchanging goods they produced for other goods. Artisans, craftsmen, and merchants became essential role-players in city economies.

From these urban roots bloomed the first great empires of China, Persia,

Two very different activities in two very different societies, yet both illustrate the economic institution. The peasants in western India winnowing wheat are more clearly involved in providing physical sustenance than are the milling hordes on the floor of a stock market, but in an industrial, consumer-oriented, private enterprise economy, investor activity is essential.

Social strata: levels within a society that are distinguished from one another by their share of social rewards (wealth, power, prestige). See Chapter 7.

and, later, Rome, and the complex, sophisticated cultures of ancient Egypt and Greece. Later, in Christian Europe, economic progress was irregular. For many years the feudal economic and social system prevailed. People were divided into distinct social strata (castes), and each member of society was expected to be content with his or her position.

Gradually nation-states with increasingly powerful rulers developed. The system of expansive mercantilism emerged in the fifteenth and sixteenth centuries. The Protestant Reformation brought forth values that favored the economic norms of capitalism. In the cities, two new classes developed: the bourgeoisie and free laborers. The bourgeoisie owned the tools and places of production from which goods could be made and sold. The free laborers owned no tools but sold their services in the marketplace to the highest bourgeois bidder. These groups gradually replaced the aristocracy and the serfs or slaves of feudal times.

The sixteenth and seventeenth centuries were times of exploration and colonization. Each European nation competed with the others to find new sources of raw materials and wealth, particularly gold and silver. By the seventeenth century, the commercial systems of England, France, Holland, and later other European states were expanding into more and more markets and sources of raw supplies.

The industrial revolution erupted in the late eighteenth and early nineteenth centuries. Invention after invention (from the cotton gin to the steam engine) was put to commercial use, producing and transporting goods. Cities swelled to gigantic size, as the majority of laborers switched from agricultural to industrial work, first in England, then in the United States, France, and later Germany.

The American Economy

Today, the vast majority of Americans live in cities. Labor is divided and specialized to an unprecedented degree. The complexity and variety of occupations are astounding. Innumerable new organizations have developed to deal with human wants and human needs. Science and technology have given us a greater chance of controlling our environment and increasing our production. Labor unions, pension plans, and insurance programs have been created to protect workers. Americans have more social mobility—more ability to change from one social class to another—than members of any preindustrial society have had.

Mixed economy. The norms that govern the American economic system today are those of a mixed economy. That is, our economy is based on the free enterprise system (private ownership of the means of production and free workers), but in practice it is "mixed" because the government controls many aspects of the economy.

Theoretically, in a free enterprise system, prices are determined by market pressures—by the interplay of supply and demand. A product that is in great supply and for which there is little demand will sell at a low price. If demand is high and the supply is low, the price will be high. In this system, competition among sellers is supposed to safeguard the consumer. If two producers offer the same product, the consumer will choose the cheaper one. This pressures the producers to try to keep their prices low. If they both sell at the same price, the buyer will choose the better quality product. This pressures producers to keep their quality high.

This, briefly sketched, is the ideal mechanism of the free enterprise system. Why, then, do we have a mixed economy instead of a free enterprise model? In the history of our economy, the system didn't follow the ideal pattern. Around the turn of the twentieth century, the nation experienced an industrial, transportation, and commercial boom. An age of corporate giants emerged, in which producers voluntarily limited competition among themselves and fixed very high prices on all sorts of goods and services. Large companies merged to become even larger, so that they dominated or controlled their fields. Consumers of everything from oil, steel, and rail transportation to finished goods were charged enormous prices by these combines, trusts, monopolies, and cartels; competition was dead in many industries. The free enterprise norms described earlier were abandoned. Government then stepped in by means of legislation to regulate the size and particularly the behavior of businesses. It also played a role in the disputes between industrialists and early labor unions, acting generally on the side of the industrialists, often with force, until the 1930s.

The Great Depression of the 1930s substantially increased government involvement in all facets of the economy. To restore employment, support the unemployed, and stimulate production, trade and investment, the government enacted a wide variety of programs.

Since then the government has kept its hand in the economy. The sudden collapse of a corporation or an industry can have widespread effects on the country, and the government sometimes takes steps to avoid this. When a firm such as Lockheed or Boeing folds, whole cities can be affected. Thousands of workers are laid off. They stop paying income taxes and start drawing unemployment or welfare checks. This happened in Seattle in the late 1960s. Partly to prevent these consequences, the government has underwritten failing com-

From its beginnings, the United States government has been involved in the economy, through such activities as releasing public lands for private farming, and subsidizing the building of transportation systems—first canals and then railroads. Government at all levels lent its force to industrialists and businessmen in resisting union organizing and breaking strikes, such as the 1904 Chicago stockyard strike shown here. To pull the country out of the Great Depression of the 1930s, the government virtually directed the economy, seeking to restimulate it by providing jobs for many thousands of manual laborers, office workers, and even artists.

panies such as Penn Central Railroad. To prevent similar occurrences, with the possibility of more widespread repercussions, the federal government came to the aid of New York City in 1975 and 1976.

Capitalism as a model. Despite the exercise of government controls, our economic system is basically capitalist, and the vast majority of citizens seem wedded to it. We are committed to and believe in free enterprise and the profit motive. We learn these norms from our families and schools. We persistently elect people to government who share these views. No wonder, then, that we don't see much deviation from the capitalist norm in our economy. When changes occur, they are generally intended to preserve the system.

Of course, other societies have entirely different concepts of economic planning and performance. Some reject the idea of private ownership altogether. Some see individual competition as an obstacle to meeting broader social goals. In a socialist system, for example, in its ideal state, each member of society is guaranteed an equitable share in the goods and services produced by government-controlled industries. Under the communist system, in its ideal form, people produce according to their abilities and receive shares of the goods and services produced according to their needs, both under complete government control.

THE POLITICAL INSTITUTION

Our sketch of the economic institution indicated the importance of the government's role in defining and enforcing the norms of that institution. Anyone who pays more than casual attention to the news media is aware that the government is a major participant in the American economy in another respect: as an employer. The federal government employs over a million persons; state and local governments employ many thousands more. Government is so highly visible in our lives that it may require a leap of imagination to see anything corresponding to this institution in many primitive societies.

We must remember, however, that in our society each institution, while closely interacting with the others, is visibly distinct from the others. This is not necessarily true of other societies. An institution, we said, is a collection of norms clustered around a permanent social function. The permanent function of government is to permit decision-making while maintaining social control by enforcing the norms of society. Sociologists agree that a government or political system is found in every society. It may be a tribal council or a town meeting or a royal court. Whatever its form, the political system includes a set of rules and some apparatus for keeping social order, distributing power, and allowing decisions to be made.

This king of Abomey, in Dahomey, Africa, represents a political system. He has several roles that in the United States system, for example, are divided among distinct branches of government employing thousands of persons. He may be magistrate, police chief, and commander of the army.

Power: the ability to manipulate the behavior of others with or without their consent.

Authority: the formally recognized right to exercise power.

Power and Authority

NO

Power and political institutions are intimately related. The German sociologist Max Weber distinguished power from authority. He defined power as the ability to control others, even to the point of being able to make them do something against their own desires or interests. Such power is coercive; that is, it threatens punishment for disobedience. Weber suggested that coercion by itself was the least effective form of social control. What people in power need is *legitimacy*. In other words, the rulers must be recognized as having the right to control other people. That right is *authority*. Weber described three kinds of authority: traditional, charismatic, and rational-legal.[9]

Traditional authority. Traditional authority is based on the traditional beliefs of a society. For example, the authority of a council of elders might come from a firmly held, unchallenged belief that the elders possess a store of wisdom accessible only to the aged. Traditional authority is the basis of legitimacy for tribal or clan chiefs, kings and queens, and others who inherit their offices. These people do not draw their authority from their personal characteristics or the office they hold but rather from being persons whom the society traditionally considers rightful leaders.

Charismatic authority. The second basis of legitimacy that Weber distinguished is charismatic authority. Individuals who have all or many of the personal qualities that are valued or desired in a culture have charisma. The full meaning of the word can be seen by returning to its roots. *Charisma* in Greek means favor or gift. It comes from another Greek word, *charis*, meaning grace in the sacred sense of the word. Charisma, then, is the persuasive force that a particular personality exercises over the members of society.

In our own society, John F. Kennedy and, to a lesser extent, his brother Robert displayed charisma. In earlier periods, Thomas Jefferson, Abraham Lincoln, Sojourner Truth, Theodore Roosevelt, Jane Addams, Dwight D. Eisenhower, Eleanor Roosevelt, and many others have shown this quality. History books are studded with charismatic figures: Jesus Christ, Joan of Arc, Winston Churchill, Adolph Hitler, Charles de Gaulle.

Charismatic authority is, by its very nature, fleeting—it disappears with the individual who possesses it. Any movement or government founded solely on such a leader is therefore doomed to falter and fail when the leader is gone. For example, the nonviolent movement to emancipate India and all Indians faced a doubtful future when its charismatic leader, Mahatma Gandhi, died.

[9]Max Weber, *Essays in Sociology*, ed. and trans. Hans H. Gerth and C. Wright Mills (New York: Oxford University Press, 1958), pp. 181–95.

Authority can come from one of three sources. The Shah of Iran exercises authority based on tradition. People believe, as their ancestors believed, that the Shah has the right to rule them, to wield power over them. Mahatma Gandhi was a major force in the movement to gain independence for India from Great Britain. Gandhi's authority came from his charisma: his personal qualities of benevolence, integrity, and shrewdness inspired multitudes to join his campaigns of nonviolent resistance against the British, who were the legal-rational authority. The American political system is based on legal-rational authority, from the president to the police officer on patrol.

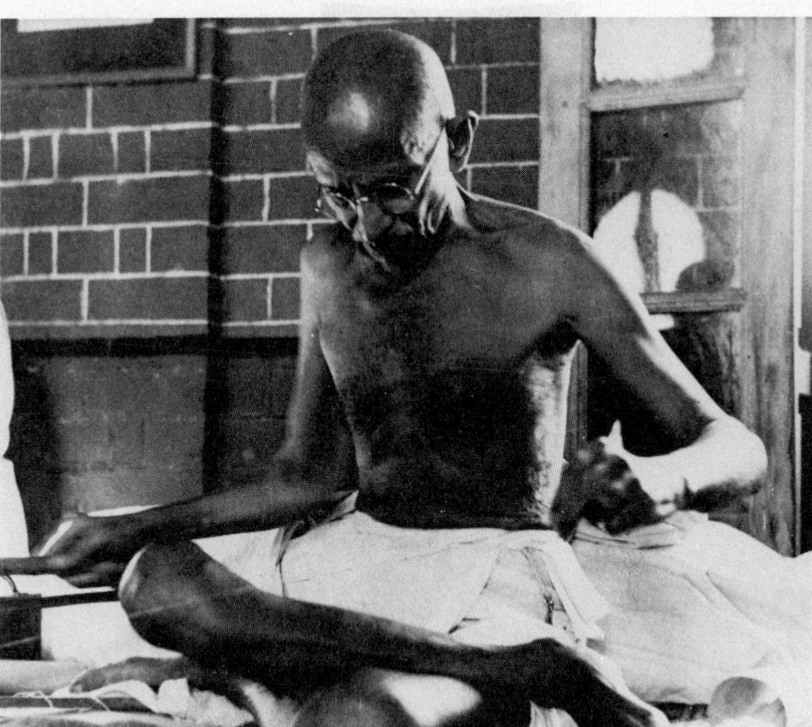

Rational-legal authority. The third basis of legitimacy distinguished by Weber is rational-legal authority. This authority is granted by the position; it is not in the person. As we already know, individuals occupy a wide array of positions in their daily lives. Some of these are particularly political—they have to do with the exercise of power and with forms of social control. Being a policeman, a magistrate, a member of Congress, or a secretary of defense each represents a rational-legal position in the political structure. The rights, privileges, and obligations come with the office. When an individual leaves that office, the next person to occupy it is granted those same rights and obligations.

While in an office of authority, a person is expected to behave in accordance with certain rules. Richard Nixon, who occupied the highest and most privileged office in the United States, was forced to resign under threat of impeachment for wrongdoing. He had violated the rules of behavior that were required of a person in his position and lost all powers and privileges. Within hours of his resignation, Gerald Ford assumed the presidency and received the authority of the office.

In most sectors of our society, the office, not the person, is most important. Traditional authority plays a very small part in our political arena. There are, however, a few instances of powerful American families handing their power down from one generation to the next, the Rockefellers and the Kennedys, for example. Charismatic authority may help candidates to win their elected positions or give them added ability to accomplish their goals once elected. Television campaigning brings out a need for candidates to display charisma. But the primary authority in our political system is rational-legal.

In addition, the social control functions of government in our society also have a rational-legal character. Rules are written down in ordinances, codes, and laws. This codification is one of the primary foundations for the legitimacy of our political institutions; the law is there to be followed by all. Anyone who violates it risks punishment. In a democracy, one of the claims to legitimacy is the equality of all citizens before the law.

1. List five people who have authority over you (for example, your parents, your mayor, your dean). Which of Weber's three types is the principal source of that authority in relation to you? Does each of these people exercise other kinds of authority in his or her life?

2. Try to list the values that underlie our political norms. Then, on a separate sheet, list the norms. Ask five to ten people you know to write down (anonymously) ratings of their support of each norm. (You should make up a rating scale: for example, very important; of some

importance; of little importance.) Then have them rate the values underlying the norms by the same scale. Compare the two sets of ratings by each person. Does the rating for each norm match that for its underlying value?

The American Political System: A Conflict between Models

Throughout the middle years of our education, civics courses inform us that our political system is a democracy in which equality and justice prevail. Yet ordinary citizens often feel that, at best, they are helpless pawns in a gigantic political power game or, at worst, they are habitually defrauded and robbed by "those crooks," the politicians. Which view, if either, is correct—the idealized picture of democracy in action or the cynical view of the political system?

No political scientist or political sociologist seriously proposes that either view hits the mark. The school book description of our political system often omits a candid account of its limitations and complexities in operation. Students are socialized to believe in an idealized description of the system. Little wonder if they are later confused or embittered by experiences in the real political world. On the other hand, sociologists do not adopt the cynical view either. Few of them spend time examining the criminality or virtue of politicians as individuals or as a class. This issue may be of interest to journalists and concerned citizens, but sociologists concern themselves more with the structured patterns of social interaction in the political system.

Both sociologists and political scientists have formulated several major, rival models of the system. Each model accepts as fundamental the legal-rational government branches (legislative, executive, judicial) at the local, state, and federal levels, and a franchised electorate. What these models describe (and their area of disagreement) is how the decision-making powers of government are allocated by the social structure. The debate is three-way: between pluralists and mass society theorists on one hand, and between pluralists and power elite theorists on the other hand.

Pluralist model versus mass society model.

Proponents of the pluralist model acknowledge that the individual in a democratic system is virtually powerless. The system works nevertheless, they claim. Let's examine the premises and arguments of a leading pluralist, sociologist William Kornhauser.[10]

Kornhauser distinguishes four types of industrial societies, based on the relationship found between the people and their leaders. These relationships in turn derive from the prevailing social structure. He calls the people—all of

[10]William Kornhauser, *The Politics of Mass Society* (New York: Free Press, 1959).

those who are not leaders—the *nonelites.* The leaders are called *elites.* Kornhauser found four combinations of relationships between the two groups, as shown in the diagram below. The nonelites may be *available*—that is, easily whipped into action or support of a movement—or they may be difficult to mobilize. The elites may be *accessible*—in direct contact with nonelites and thus vulnerable (that is, easily voted down or thrown out)—or they may be able to maintain their power no matter what the people think or want. The diagram shows Kornhauser's names for the possible combinations of variables.

Kornhauser's Model of Societal Types

		Accessibility of Elites	
		Low	High
Availability of Nonelites	Low	communal society	pluralist society
	High	totalitarian society	mass society

Clearly for our system today the two most important variants to examine are the pluralist society and the mass society. In the pluralist society the nonelites have low availability (are not easily mobilized), because they are organized in interest groups with overlapping loyalties and because they know that, within a reasonable length of time, they can either influence or replace leaders who do not satisfy them.

The elites of a pluralist society, in turn, are highly accessible, but they are protected from becoming mindless extensions of the nonelites because competition among interest groups keeps any one group from total dominance and because elites are expected to have ideas of their own and to lead. The pluralist model thus resembles a working democracy with its checks and balances.

In the mass society model, the nonelites are easily mobilized to action and the elites are highly accessible and vulnerable to losing power unless they respond to nonelite demands. What causes this difference from the pluralist society? For one thing, the mass media reach the nonelites directly, bypassing intermediate interest groups. Also, the government is so large and remote that people feel powerless at the local level. They become discouraged and impatient with any technique but direct action to get results.

Pluralism: in political sociology, the sharing of power by rival voluntary associations favoring different interests.

The elites in such a society are accessible because they are put in power to deal with specific issues. They thus have unstable constituencies: their

Mass society: in political sociology, a volatile society composed of an organized elite that is readily accessible to a disorganized, unintegrated, nonelite mass.

backers are capable of losing interest and fading away or of rejecting leaders who fail to show immediate results. In short, a democracy without much stability is in operation. Social programs tend to adopt extreme goals and methods, and compromise is scorned. Political activists (those who can make or break the elites) are concerned only with their own causes, not with those of others, and not with maintaining a smooth, stable system. Kornhauser maintains that mass societies tend to move toward totalitarianism.

What is the underlying distinction between these two different models? To pluralists it lies in the social structure. Kornhauser states:

> We can conceive of all but the simplest societies as comprising three levels of social relations. The first level consists of highly personal or primary relations, notably the family. The third level contains relations inclusive of the whole population, notably the state. The second level comprises all intermediate relations, notably the local community, voluntary association, and occupational group. These intermediate relations function as links between the first and third levels.

A society that has many strong interest groups (which is what Kornhauser chiefly means by "voluntary associations") will be pluralist, and a society with strong primary groups and a strong state but with few or no strong interest groups will be a mass society. Sociologists disagree on whether United States society resembles the pluralist society model or the mass society model more, chiefly because the data are so complex and loaded with ambiguity (fitting two mutually exclusive definitions). To further complicate matters, some sociologists propose yet a third model.

Power elite: in theory, an interlocking of elites sharing and protecting common interests by monopolizing political power.

Power elite model. The power elite theorists are closely related to the mass society theorists but base their model on relations within the elites, rather than on relations between elites and nonelites. Thus, while the pluralists maintain that contending elites shape policy through sharing power and making compromises (since no single elite is powerful enough to get its way), the power elite theorists say this is naive. C. Wright Mills, the sociologist who coined the term *power elite,* proposed the opposite of what Kornhauser was later to say. Mills stated:

> The top of American society is increasingly unified, and often seems willfully coordinated: at the top there has emerged an elite of power. The middle levels are a drifting set of stalemated, balancing forces; the middle does not link the bottom with the top. The bottom of this society is politically fragmented, . . . increasingly powerless.[11]

[11]C. Wright Mills, *The Power Elite* (New York: Oxford University Press, 1956), p. 324.

As partial evidence, Mills and the elite theorists argue that it is people from similar backgrounds and of similar political and economic interests who are in control of the major oganizations of American society. Not only do the corporation executives, generals, and high government officials frequently come from the same class background, attend the same parties, and belong to the same clubs, but they also tend to move from a position in one elite to a comparable position in another. High-ranking military men retire to become executives in defense-related corporations. Corporation presidents in turn become cabinet officers as heads of regulatory agencies. They may change jobs, but they continue to serve the interests and maintain the perspectives of the groups from which they came. To illustrate, Mills quoted Charles Wilson, the president of General Motors who became secretary of defense in the Eisenhower administration: "What's good for General Motors is good for the country." This, claimed Mills, shows how the people who make the critical decisions in this country actually believe that the interests of the government are identical with those of major corporations.[12]

Ironically, Eisenhower, who had appointed Wilson his secretary of defense, added to the belief in a power elite by warning against a "military-industrial complex," the enormous combination of power that the Pentagon, large defense-related corporations, labor, and universities had built up throughout the cold war.

But the major point at issue among sociologists is not whether elites share a community of interests. (We should not be very surprised if they do.) Clearly what divides pluralists from mass theorists and elite theorists is their views on what is happening in Kornhauser's "second level" or Mills's "middle levels." Are they stalemated and drifting, as Mills maintained, or balancing and compromising among themselves in the political arena, as Kornhauser suggests?

Pluralists point to several kinds of power exercised by the "second level" groups: lobbying power (the ability to push through programs the group wants), countervailing power (the ability to neutralize the power of opposing groups), and veto power (the ability to stop programs the group doesn't want). Many power elite theorists acknowledge these types of power but contend that there is also a higher level of power beyond the measurement of the pluralists. This "higher power" is almost impossible to document, however, so the debate continues.

[12]Ibid., p. 168.

Religion is the institution that deals with the mysteries of human existence, from sweeping questions, such as how the world was made and why, to questions of personal urgency, such as the nature and meaning of death. Religion can provide believers with solace when they are afflicted with disease, grief, or loneliness. Ritual is a body of practices by which people maintain a proper relationship with the supernatural powers. But religion often has the additional effect, the latent function, of giving support to the society's values and norms—or, in times of change and cultural diversity, usually giving support to its traditional cultural traits.

RELIGION

Religion, in a rich collection of forms, is found in every known society of the globe. The French sociologist Émile Durkheim, in *The Elementary Forms of Religious Life,* published in 1912, defined religion as "a unified system of beliefs and practices relating to sacred things, uniting into a single moral community all those who adhere to those beliefs and practices."[13]

The sacred: that which transcends the natural world and is awe-inspiring.

A "unified system of beliefs and practices" is a coherent philosophy about the relation of human beings to things beyond their immediate grasp. It does this by introducing the concept of the *sacred* by which it offers explanations for life and death and rules for moral behavior. It details the behavior that will give active expression to beliefs. When this philosophy is specifically "sacred" (that is, dealing with "mysterious and awesome power,

[13]Émile Durkheim, *The Elementary Forms of Religious Life* (New York: Free Press, 1954), p. 47.

other than man and yet related to him")[14] it is religion. Usually religions specify rituals that believers are to follow. For example, to show proper reverence to their god-figure, people pray in various ways, as we noted in Chapter 3. They may bow their heads, bend their knees, or prostrate themselves—before a priest, before an altar, or in a particular direction (toward Mecca, for example).

Moreover, religious practices often involve making an ordinary act extraordinary. A person who believes that the wafer or the bread and wine offered in a Christian communion service is the body and blood of Jesus Christ offered for his or her redemption receives it with reverence. People who believe that certain objects or creatures are taboo—that they possess a supernatural power to cause suffering or misfortune—carefully avoid them or treat them with the required respect.

According to Durkheim's definition, these beliefs and practices relate to "sacred things"—the Torah of the Jews, the crucifix of the Christians, or the

[14]Peter L. Berger, *The Sacred Canopy* (New York: Anchor, 1969), p. 25.

several gods of the Hindu religion. For pantheists, the sacred can be in all things that exist, a divine spirit that unifies the many in one. In such Eastern religions as Buddhism, the sacred can be certain beliefs or guides to behavior rather than any personal supernatural spirit. What makes all these things sacred is that they are believed to have some existence or powers beyond the ordinary reality of the senses.

Religion gives the individual believer an explanation of life and a guide for ethical behavior. All people experience items in the catalog of timeless human sorrows: disease, poverty, the death of loved ones, and the certainty of death for each are a few examples. Religion attempts to make sense of these human burdens. It offers explanations that cannot be understood by reason alone.

Many religions also offer rules for believers to follow. These are supposed to protect the believer from various unhappy events. They may claim to prevent troubles from occurring or to enable the believer to replace sorrow with serene indifference. Some religions promise an afterlife infinitely more pleasant than this life for observers of the faith.

Durkheim's statement that a religion unites believers "into a single moral community" means two things: first, they all follow, or try to follow, the norms that derive from their beliefs about the sacred (such as, "Love thy neighbor as thyself"); secondly, they feel a sense of community, they share a common bond to the sacred things. Each is bound both to the object of worship and to the fellow worshipers. A religion provides a community of persons within which the believer interacts and from which he or she derives emotional support. Its rituals give reaffirmation in the face of misfortune and grief. Death, for example, is met by prescribed rituals of mourning. Whether it is the austere Jewish ritual of "sitting shibah" or the more high-spirited Irish Catholic wake, it unites members of a sect by shared beliefs and norms. Peter Berger, in fact, maintains that death is the ultimate concern of religion, because it is the ultimate mystery for all people.

The sense of community is discussed in its secular form in Chapter 12.

American Religion

In the United States, our freedom to worship in our own way is a fundamental guarantee of the Bill of Rights. We have a wide range of religious organizations. They vary in structure from the vast bureaucracy of the Roman Catholic church to small, transitory, and loosely organized Protestant sects in storefront churches. Some religious bodies in this country are fundamentalist, accepting the Bible as literal truth. Others are more liberal, interpreting sacred writings and theology as symbols of broader meanings.

Death awaits each of us, and virtually every society has some ritual to signify the ending of a life. Like other cultural traits, the ritual serving this function can be performed in many different ways, as these funerals in New Guinea, East Nepal, and the United States show.

FIELD

UNITED STATES RELIGIOUS GROUPS

Religious Body	*Year*	*Number of Churches*	*Membership (Thousands)*
Total		329,299	131,425
African Methodist Episcopal Church	1951	5,878	1,166
African Methodist Episcopal Zion Church	1970	4,500	940
Albanian Orthodox Archdiocese in America	1971	13	62
American Baptist Association	1973	3,336	956
American Baptist Churches in the U.S.A.	1972	6,029	1,484
American Carpatho-Russian Orthodox Greek Catholic Church	1972	70	108
American Lutheran Church, The	1972	4,825	2,492
The Antiochian Orthodox Christian Archdiocese of New York and All North America	1970	92	100
Apostolic Overcoming Holy Church of God	1956	300	75
Armenian Apostolic Church of America	1972	29	125
Armenian Church of America, Diocese of The (incl. Diocese of California)	1972	58	372
Assemblies of God	1973	8,871	1,110
Baptist General Conference	1972	686	111
Baptist Missionary Association of America	1972	1,437	200
Buddhist Churches of America	1970	60	100
Bulgarian Eastern Orthodox Church	1971	13	86
Christian and Missionary Alliance, The	1972	1,154	136
Christian Church (Disciples of Christ)	1972	4,569	1,352
Christian Churches and Churches of Christ	1973	5,479	1,036
The Christian Congregation, Inc.	1972	297	53
Christian Methodist Episcopal Church	1965	2,598	467
Christian Reformed Church	1972	750	287
The Church of God	1973	2,035	76
Church of God (Anderson, Ind.)	1972	2,261	156
Church of God (Cleveland, Tenn.)	1972	4,152	297
The Church of God in Christ	1965	4,500	425
The Church of God in Christ (International)	1971	1,041	501
The Church of God of Prophecy	1973	1,711	60
Church of Jesus Christ of Latter-day Saints, The	1972	5,112	2,186
Church of the Brethren	1972	1,037	180
Church of the Nazarene	1972	4,861	405
Churches of Christ	1968	18,000	2,400
Congregational Christian Churches, National Association of	1972	344	85
Conservative Baptist Association of America, The	1970	1,127	300
Cumberland Presbyterian Church	1972	879	89
Episcopal Church, The	1972	6,891	3,063

UNITED STATES RELIGIOUS GROUPS

Religious Body	*Year*	*Number of Churches*	*Membership (Thousands)*
Evangelical Covenant Church of America, The	1972	523	69
Evangelical Free Church of America	1972	562	70
Free Methodist Church of North America	1972	1,091	65
Free Will Baptists (National Association of)	1973	2,275	203
Friends United Meeting	1972	515	69
General Association of Regular Baptist Churches	1973	1,473	214
General Baptists (General Association of)	1973	834	70
Greek Orthodox Archdiocese of North and South America	1972	502	1,950
Independent Fundamental Churches of America	1972	598	78
International Church of the Foursquare Gospel	1963	741	89
International General Assembly of Spiritualists	1956	209	164
Jehovah's Witnesses	1972	5,794	431
Jewish Congregations	1972	5,000	6,115
Lutheran Church in America	1972	5,788	3,034
Lutheran Church, Missouri Synod	1972	5,741	2,781
Mennonite Church	1972	1,036	90
Moravian Church in America (Unitas Fratrum)	1972	148	58
National Baptist Convention of America	1956	11,398	2,669
National Baptist Convention, U.S.A., Inc.	1958	26,000	5,550
National Baptist Evangelical Life and Soul Saving Assembly of the U.S.A.	1951	264	58
National Primitive Baptist Convention, Inc.	1971	2,198	1,645
North American Old Roman Catholic Church	1973	121	60
The Old Roman Catholic Church (English Rite)	1972	186	65
The Orthodox Church in America	1972	370	1,000
Pentecostal Church of God of America, Inc.	1967	975	115
Pentecostal Holiness Church, Inc.	1972	1,340	74
Polish National Catholic Church of America	1960	162	282
Presbyterian Church in the U.S.	1972	4,284	947
Primitive Baptists	1950	1,000	72
Progressive National Baptist Convention, The	1967	655	522
Reformed Church in America	1972	911	373
Reorganized Church of Jesus Christ of Latter-Day Saints	1972	1,031	180
Roman Catholic Church	1972	23,880	38,460
Romanian Orthodox Episcopate of America, The	1972	45	50
Russian Orthodox Church in the U.S.A., Patriarchal Parishes of the	1972	41	50
The Russian Orthodox Church Outside Russia	1955	81	55

UNITED STATES RELIGIOUS GROUPS

Religious Body	*Year*	*Number of Churches*	*Membership (Thousands)*
Salvation Army	1972	1,101	359
Serbian Eastern Orthodox Diocese for the U.S.A. and Canada	1967	52	65
Seventh-day Adventists	1972	3,278	449
Southern Baptist Convention	1972	34,512	12,065
Syrian Orthodox Church of Antioch, Archdiocese of the U.S.A. and Canada	1972	10	50
Triumph the Church and Kingdom of God in Christ (International)	1972	495	54
Ukrainian Orthodox Church in the U.S.A.	1966	197	88
Unitarian Universalist Association	1969	1,076	265
United Church of Christ	1972	6,635	1,895
United Free Will Baptist Church	1952	836	100
The United Methodist Church	1972	39,626	10,335
United Pentecostal Church (International)	1972	2,650	250
The United Presbyterian Church in the U.S.A.	1972	8,732	2,909
The Wesleyan Church	1970	1,898	84
Wisconsin Evangelical Lutheran Synod	1972	991	385

Source: United States Department of Commerce, Bureau of the Census, *Statistical Abstract of the United States: 1974*, 95th ed. (Washington, D.C.: U.S. Government Printing Office, 1974), pp. 46–47.

Religiosity. Roughly 96 percent of Americans say they have a religion. Roughly two-thirds are Protestant; about forty million people are Roman Catholics; and approximately six million are Jews. However, measuring *religiosity* (the strength of religious beliefs) in our society has been a complex problem for sociologists. They have not operationalized the concept of religiosity in a way acceptable to most. Should stated church affiliation be the test? Should attendance at services be an additional test? Would, say, a farmer who travels twenty miles four Sundays a year to go to church be considered more or less religious than a city dweller who goes once a month to a church up the street? Should detailed knowledge of religious beliefs and practices be included? For example, would a Catholic be required to know the teachings of St. Aquinas, St. Augustine, and St. Ignatius in detail before being considered religious? Would a Southern Baptist have to be able to recite Bible passages word for word?

Keep in mind that correlation is not causality. Our choice of religion does not necessarily cause our choice of a political party or occupation. How these choices correlate with social class is discussed in Chapter 7 on social stratification.

Sociologists have, however, discovered substantial correlations between a person's religion and his or her participation in other social institutions. Family size, extent of education, choice of career, lifetime income, and political party affiliation can all be correlated with religious denomination.

INTERCONNECTIONS

We can use Christmas to illustrate, once again, how social institutions and the groups associated with them are intertwined in a culture—even in a complex society like ours.

First of all, Christmas is a religious festival of great significance. To Christians it is a celebration commemorating the birth of the key figure in their beliefs. For many it is a time of reverence and reflection. For others it is simply a festive occasion when people feel the warmth of human fellowship.

We sing carols not only in church but also in school, although our Constitution requires us to keep religious doctrines and dogmas out of schools (which are run by the state). Most Americans accept this intrusion. Of course, the majority are Christians themselves, and the Christmas story is part and parcel of their cultural heritage. The Nativity scene in the school yard is offensive to some Americans of other faiths. Still, even non-Christians often accept it as part of an "American" holiday.

Christmas is an official national holiday. The government personnel who determine when Americans shall work and when they shall "rest" long ago declared Christmas Day a legal holiday. They did so, of course, in response to social pressure. Imagine what would happen here if the authorities decided that Christmas was a working day, as those in the Soviet Union did.

Christmas is also a business. The amount of money retail merchants make in a year is directly related to the Christmas season. "Without Christmas," one storekeeper stated, "I would be out of business in a minute." Large stores and small depend on the "spirit" of gift-giving to sustain them. In fact, whole industries have developed specifically for this holiday: growing Christmas trees, producing tree ornaments, and printing Christmas cards, for example.

Finally, Christmas is a family time. It is the season when we reaffirm ties to kin, visit old friends and relatives, send cards and presents to distant family members.

Religion, education, politics, economics, and the family all have their connections with the phenomenon called Christmas. There is a place for the norms of each. Generally they mesh to form a coherent pattern of behavior. It may seem strange to an outsider, but for most of us it seems to work.

The example of Christmas illustrates how our activities in separate institutions of American life are interdependent. That, as we noted much earlier, is what institutions are basically all about. They are separable in theory and even in practice—each answering certain social needs and fulfilling certain social functions. Yet the institutions of a society tend to form coherent patterns, based on basic cultural assumptions. Though teaching and preaching, merchandising and legislating relate to different sectors of life in the United States, they often seem to be variations on a common theme—"the American way of life."

SUMMARY

In this chapter we took a close look at a concept introduced in the first part of the text—the concept of social institutions—and showed its significance to an understanding of social life.

In every society certain basic functions must be carried out. These so-called functional prerequisites require us to find ways of perpetuating the group, training the young, producing, distributing, and consuming goods, allocating and exercising power, and the broader matter of finding meaning in life. No two societies meet these needs in exactly the same way. Cultural values often dictate the character of institutional norms. Consider the different economic institutions in capitalist and communist states or the different religious institutions in India, Spain, Japan, and Scandinavia.

American institutions have their own characteristics. Many of the rules we are expected to observe in various spheres of life stem from the Western tradition and the font of Judeo-Christian ideas. Some have been developed during the evolution of the United States itself and show marks of being "made in America."

In many ways, institutions are like the organs of the body. Each has its particular set of functions but all are related to the whole. We can learn much about the social corpus (the social body) of the United States, for example, by studying its family, educational, economic, political, and religious systems. As we see in the following chapter, we can also learn much by studying the society's patterns of ranking among people, its system of social stratification.

7 SOCIAL STRATIFICATION

The sociological perspective gives us a way of looking at a society and organizing our perceptions by means of certain concepts. We see how the components of a culture relate to the structure of society—the recurrent patterns of interaction among its members. We also see how widely diverse societies accomplish similar functions by the use of different patterns—how certain social institutions are part of every kind of society and differ among societies.

Another structural feature that sociologists find in virtually every society is *social stratification:* the unequal distribution of the social rewards of wealth, power, and prestige. Sociologists were certainly not the first or only ones to notice stratification, but the sociological perspective and method enable them to refine their understanding of stratification, its different systems (open and closed), social mobility, and its consequences—what sociologists call *life chances.*

SOCIAL CLASS: PATTERNS OF INSTITUTIONAL INEQUALITY

Social rewards: the wealth, power, and prestige distributed among the members of a society.

What does *social class* mean? There are distinct differences between the ghetto dweller and the suburbanite, between the unskilled worker and the plant manager, between the corner druggist and the president of Johnson and Johnson Products. If we try to organize our sense of what the differences are and where they come from, we come up with the concepts sociologists use in analyzing social stratification.

People differ from one another not only in their occupations and styles of living but also in the *social rewards* they receive. There is a vast spread of income and wealth among the people just mentioned, ranging from the poor to the wealthy. There is also a wide variation in prestige, or social honor and respect. Some have little or none, while others are accorded high esteem. After even closer study, we will see that there is a spread in the distribution of power. Some of these people have great ability to control the behavior and destinies of others according to their own purposes or desires, while others have little or no such ability.

Social class: a number of people within a society who are grouped together because they have similar amounts of wealth, power, and prestige and similar life-styles.

Sociologist Max Weber identified these three measures of social rewards—wealth, prestige, and power—as the major components of social class.[1] Earlier Karl Marx had argued that a person's social class was determined by his or her relationship to the means of production: people were either property owners (bourgeoisie) or workers (proletariat) whose labor provided surplus value (profits) for owners. Most American sociologists interested in social class have tended to use Weber's approach. They study the distribution of wealth, prestige, and power and the interrelationship of these three dimensions.

Both Max Weber and Karl Marx argued that a social class is more than a measure of social reward. Class interests and class consciousness are other important facets in understanding the sociological significance of social class.

[1]See Hans H. Gerth and C. Wright Mills, eds., *From Max Weber* (New York: Oxford University Press, 1958). For further literature on social stratification, see Reinhard Bendix and Seymour M. Lipset, eds., *Class Status and Power,* rev. ed. (Chicago: Free Press, 1966), and Kurt B. Mayer, *Class and Society* (Garden City, N.Y.: Doubleday, 1955).

Class interests are policies and actions that benefit members of a particular social class. For example, it is in the interest of the working class to have strong unions and to have legislation restricting the importation of foreign-made goods that sell for lower prices than union-made products. Similarly, it is in the interest of the upper class to be allowed tax deductions for capital gains, business-related entertaining, and travel.

Class interests may not always be recognized by members of that class. Some workers aspire to be members of the middle class and reject efforts at unionization. When a significant number of people in a class recognize that they form a special group—when they feel bound to each other by similar interests, similar needs, and the potential to use their power—then sociologists say in Marx's terms that class consciousness exists.

Some American sociologists argue that class is not a useful mode of analysis for the United States. They recognize that inequality is a feature of the society, but they believe that so many interests divide members of the same social class and unite others across class lines that class identification no longer is meaningful. Race, ethnicity, region of the country all undercut class, they argue. For example, an Italian Catholic businessman may identify with Italian Catholic workers on certain issues and with businessmen of other religions and ancestries on others.

Social scientists who follow this line of argument generally talk about social strata or socioeconomic status (SES) to denote differences in wealth and prestige and to examine how these differences influence life-styles, values, and behavior.[2]

Socioeconomic status: a measurement of a person's position in a system of social stratification that does not have clearly defined classes.

Despite the difficulty of drawing very precise class lines in a complex society, many believe it is a useful way of understanding inequality in most social systems. The sociologist A. B. Hollingshead and his coworker Frederick Redlich formulated a two-factor index as a convenient, reasonably objective means of measuring socioeconomic class.[3] The two factors are: level of education reached and occupation. (Hollingshead and Redlich also devised a third factor that made the index more accurate, but it was more difficult to determine, since it required direct observation of an individual's life-style: area of residence, quality of furnishings, and other indicators.) Following is a much-abbreviated version of Hollingshead's two-factor index to indicate how

[2]See Milton M. Gordon, *Assimilation in American Life: The Role of Race, Religion and National Origins* (New York: Oxford University Press, 1964).

[3]August B. Hollingshead and Frederick C. Redlich, *Social Class and Mental Illness: A Community Study* (New York: Wiley, 1958), pp. 387–97.

HOLLINGSHEAD'S TWO-FACTOR INDEX OF SOCIAL CLASS STANDING (ABBREVIATED)

Educational Index

1. Professional (M.A., M.S., M.E., M.D., Ph.D., LL.B., etc.)
2. Four-year college graduate (A.B., B.S., B.M.)
3. 1–3 years college (also business schools)
4. High school graduate
5. 10–11 years of school
6. 9 or fewer years of school

Occupational Index

1. Higher executives of large concerns, proprietors, and major professionals
   A. Higher executives (value of corporation $500,000 and above as rated by Dun and Bradstreet)
      Bank: presidents, vice-presidents, assistant vice-presidents
      Business: directors, presidents, vice-presidents, assistant vice-presidents, executive secretaries, research directors, treasurers
   B. Proprietors (value over $100,000 by Dun and Bradstreet)
   C. Major professionals
2. Business managers, proprietors of medium-sized businesses, and lesser professionals
   A. Business managers in large concerns (value $500,000)
   B. Proprietors of medium businesses (value $35,000–$100,000)
   C. Lesser professionals
3. Administrative personnel, owners of small businesses, and minor professionals
   A. Administrative personnel
   B. Small business owners ($6,000–$35,000)
   C. Semiprofessionals
   D. Farmers ($20,000–$35,000)
4. Clerical and sales workers, technicians, and owners of little businesses (value under $6,000)
   A. Clerical and sales workers
   B. Technicians
   C. Owners of little businesses ($3,000–$6,000)
   D. Farmers (value $10,000–$20,000)
5. Skilled manual employees and small farmers (value under $10,000)
6. Machine operators, semiskilled employees, and smaller tenant farmers who own little equipment
7. Unskilled employees and sharecroppers

Class Scale

High	I	11–17
	II	18–31
	III	32–47
	IV	48–63
Low	V	64–73

HOLLINGSHEAD'S TWO-FACTOR INDEX OF SOCIAL CLASS STANDING (ABBREVIATED)

Example

	Scale Score	×	Factor Weight	=	Partial Score
Occupation	e.g. 3	×	7	=	21
Education	e.g. 3	×	4	=	12
					33

Source: Adapted from Charles M. Bonjean et al., *Sociological Measurement: An Inventory of Scales and Indices* (New York: Chandler, 1967), pp. 442–48.

Closed stratification system: a system in which there is virtually no social mobility, where people remain in the social position of their parents.

it is used. A numerical value is assigned to each factor (education and occupation), and each is multiplied by a factor weight. The two products are then added, and their sum places the person on the rank of classes from I (highest) to V (lowest).

In your opinion, how useful is it to think in terms of social class? List five people you know well. Can you easily identify their social classes? Do you think they consider themselves lower, working, middle, or upper class? Do they tend to associate with others of the same class? Can you think of values they hold or interests they have that are directly correlated to their social class? Do they have any values and interests that you would argue are contrary to their class but derive from other sources?

SYSTEMS OF SOCIAL STRATIFICATION

The type of stratification system can vary enormously from one society to another. Sociologists usually distinguish at least two types of societies: closed and open. In a closed system, each member has an ascribed social position or caste. In other words, a person remains for life in the caste that he or she was born into. Rarely is there social mobility. In the open system, strata or classes do exist but people have the possibility of changing to a higher (or lower) one. Social position is achieved rather than ascribed. People who have a combination of ambition, skill, talent, education, and the like are supposed to be able to achieve a higher social position than they were born into. The open system is sometimes called a *meritocracy,* because a person's social position is supposed to depend on merit, or achievement.

Open stratification system (or meritocracy): a system of stratification in which social mobility is possible and is based on personal achievement.

In this chapter we examine several types of stratification. Then we look at social stratification in our own society, to see whether we have as open a system (offering unlimited mobility) as we often claim.

Despite legal emancipation of the Untouchables of India over twenty-five years ago, they remain in low socioeconomic positions and menial, unprestigious occupations. Brahmans, on the other hand, retain their privileged status.

Caste system: a closed stratification system usually sanctified by religion (as in India) in which a person's parentage determines his or her social position for life. "Castelike" systems also exist, often based on racial group membership instead of religion.

CASTE SYSTEMS

The most striking example of a caste system existed for centuries in India, where religious doctrine divided people into groups or castes from which they could almost never move.[4] To believers in the system it was functional, for each person had a place in the order of things. In the words of Manua, the great Hindu lawgiver:

> For the sake of the prosperity of the worlds, he [the Lord, the divine Self-existent] caused the Brahmana, the Kshatriya, the Vaisya, the Sudra to proceed in turn from his mouth, his arms, his thighs, and his feet. . . . But in order to protect this universe, He, the most resplendent one, assigned separate [duties and] occupations to those who sprang from his mouth, arms, thighs, and feet.
>
> To Brahmana he assigned teaching and studying [the Veda], sacrificing for their own benefit and for others, giving and accepting [alms]. The Kshatriya he commanded to protect the people . . . . The Vaisya to tend cattle . . . . One occupation only the Lord prescribed to the Sudra, to serve meekly even these [other] three castes.[5]

In such a rigid system, with its foundations in religious dogma, there is little or no hope for an individual to advance. A person's place is fixed by birth, and each marries someone within his or her caste (that is, marriage is *endogamous*). Someone who is born a Brahman, the highest Indian caste, is assured of wealth, honor, and power for life. Someone born a Sudra, the lowest caste, is assured of a lowly, but recognized, place. Someone born an Untouchable, however, is "outcaste," below everyone, and can expect a life of poverty and powerlessness. As the quotation indicates, each caste is also differentiated by the kinds of work it must and must not do. The Untouchables were considered so unclean that the other castes wanted no physical contact with them. The castes feared both actual and ritual pollution from touching an outcast.

While these castes were functional for the religious order, they were most unfair for those born into perpetual misery and ostracism. Yet few people ever challenged the Indian caste system. One who did was the late Mahatma Gandhi, a champion of the Untouchables and a chief opponent of castes. Gandhi led a movement both to win India's independence from England and

[4]For a Weberian explanation of the Indian caste system, see Gerth and Mills, *From Max Weber,* pp. 396–415.

[5]Quoted in Gerhard Lenski, *Power and Privilege* (New York: McGraw-Hill, 1966), p. 4, from *The Laws of Manua,* trans. G. Buller, in *Sacred Books of the East,* ed. Max Müller (Oxford: Clarendon Press, 1886), 25:13–14 and 24.

This decayed storefront in a southern city symbolizes the castelike structure of race relations in our recent past. Like the Untouchables of India, American blacks no longer face such forms of legal discrimination, yet many are denied full participation in society because racist attitudes have not been eliminated.

to democratize the nation. Although the laws supporting castes were changed in 1949, religious and traditional sanctions keep people in caste divisions, and the outcast Untouchables remain in their lowly state.

Japan has a variation of the Indian caste model.[6] There, members of an

[6]See John B. Cornell, "Individual Mobility and Group Membership: The Case of the Burakumin," and George A. De Vos, "The Outcast Tradition in Modern Japan: A Problem in Social Self-Identity," in *Aspects of Social Change in Modern Japan* (Princeton, N.J.: Princeton University Press, 1967), pp. 337–410.

"occupational caste," the *Buraku-min*, are traditionally referred to as *Eta* (a word akin to "nigger" in our society), meaning "dirty ones." Although the *Buraku-min* are neither racially nor culturally distinct from other Japanese, they are treated as if they were both.

The Buraku-min have always been the low caste. They were traditionally assigned the dirty work of society—as slaughterers, tanners, sweepers, and grave diggers. Since their supposed emancipation in the 1880s, they have remained poverty-stricken, powerless outcasts in many sectors of Japanese society.

Japan has a highly efficient census system: all Japanese must register births, marriages, deaths, and job changes at the local district registry. A person's status as a member of the Buraku community is always recorded. This easily enables the Japanese to maintain their pattern of discrimination, even though it is officially illegal.

A Castelike System

The Untouchables of India and the Buraku-min of Japan are familiar to few Americans (and Indians and Japanese do not like to discuss them). But in their circumstances they resemble a group that is familiar to Americans: blacks in the United States.

Blacks and other minorities are discussed in Chapter 8.

Black Americans were emancipated from slavery some twenty years before the Buraku-min. But, until recently, they seemed to be locked into a caste system rather than members of an open system of social stratification.[7]

In his classic study of a southern community, published in 1937, John Dollard found that blacks were essentially members of a caste that could never rise to share the power or privileges of white members of the community. While there was also stratification within each caste, white and black, the caste line could never be crossed. Formal rules and informal customs kept the black population "in its place." Although many blacks worked as domestics in the homes of whites and took care of the children of white families, such intimate behavior was never considered a step toward real fraternization. Neither blacks nor whites could marry members of the other racial group (like castes in India). Each race had to send its children to separate schools and had to use separate parks and facilities.

[7]Gerald D. Berreman, in "Caste in India and the United States," *American Journal of Sociology* 64 (1960): 120–27, uses the concept of caste to suggest cross-cultural structural similarities between India and the southern part of the United States, though the two systems differ in origin and content.

Dollard gives a glimpse of the detailed restrictions imposed on both races in their interactions:

> Caste etiquette . . . is compulsory for Negroes. A white friend gave me some instruction on this score immediately after I arrived in Southerntown. Never, he said, address a Negro man or woman as "Mr." or "Mrs." and do not refer to them thus in talking to a white person; don't shake hands with a Negro (except in the case of an old Negro friend who has been gone for a long time, and this would be rare); don't tip your hat to a Negro, man or woman, but call him or her by the first name whenever you know it. If you walk on the street with a Negro keep a serious demeanor as though talking business. You may go to a Negro's house on business and even sit down, but Negroes are careful in this case to offer you the best chair, not sit near you, and, if they are your tenants, not to sit while you are sitting. After this familiarity or the handshake cited above, the Negro must be careful not to presume on the exception the next time you meet, but must show that he recognizes caste etiquette.[8]

According to Dollard, whites received several advantages from maintaining their castelike system. First of all, they made money from the exploitation of black workers. They paid blacks low wages and reaped large profits from their labor. They also gained a certain amount of self-satisfaction, even prestige, from the system. Even the poorest whites prided themselves that they were superior to the outcast group. Their egos were inflated by the lowliness of others. And there was a third advantage. Southern mores placed the white woman on a pedestal and viewed the black woman as an easy prey for white men. White men could boast of the purity of their women while enjoying illicit affairs with blacks whose families could do little to protect them.

In recent years, challenges to the racial caste system in the United States have dramatically altered these exploitive relationships. Blacks grew increasingly outraged, and eventually rose up to challenge the system that kept them in a state of exclusion and humiliation. Whites could no longer ignore the gap between their claims that ours is a nation in which all are equal and the reality of racial oppression.

See the discussion of the civil rights and black power movements in Chapter 8.

Dollard maintained that a castelike system of social stratification existed in the South. Do you think that, despite recent gains by blacks, both blacks and whites preserve a castelike mentality to a certain extent? What are some indicators that this mentality still exists or no longer exists?

[8]John Dollard, *Caste and Class in a Southern Town* (New Haven: Yale University Press, 1937), p. 343.

FEUDAL SYSTEMS

Feudal system: a closed system of stratification in which social position is ascribed, strata are distinctly defined, mobility is difficult, and wealth is based heavily on land ownership.

Other systems of stratification can be found in the present and the past that closely resemble the caste system. Feudal, or estate, systems of stratification present the same marked distinctions in wealth, life-style, occupation, and education that characterize the strata in a caste system. The main difference between caste and estate systems is that, although the stratification of estates is justified by strong traditional beliefs, the racial distinctions found in a caste system are absent. Instead the structured inequality is considered a part of the natural or divine order, as expressed in this medieval English verse:

> The rich man at his castle,
> The poor man at his gate.
> God made them high or lowly
> And ordered their estate.

Events in the Bible were also used to justify the estate system. For example, in Genesis 9:20–27 Noah hurls an angry curse against Canaan, making him "a servant of servants . . . unto his brethren."

Estate systems are called this because ownership of land is the source of wealth and power in them. In a preindustrial society, little else produces wealth. A typical feudal system existed in medieval Europe before the age of capitalism. There were three estates: the nobility; the Catholic church; and the third estate, composed of peasants, merchants, craftsmen, and soldiers. Members of the nobility were the chief landholders. The church was the secondary landholder. Members of the third estate owned no land and thus were dependent for their livelihood on the other two estates.

Variations of this system have survived into the modern era. In Asia, Africa, and Latin America, colonial powers have seized political and economic control of native populations and natural resources, imposing a system that amasses wealth for themselves (the top stratum) and keeps others in distinct lower strata. There is almost no social mobility from one stratum to another.

Bolivia, in South America, has a feudal system surviving into the modern era. Only twenty years ago Bolivian newspapers carried advertisements for ranches listing for sale not only the buildings and animals but also the peons (peasants). Although in such a feudal system the peasants are not legally slaves, the landowner has many of the rights over them that a southern slaveholder had before the emancipation. The landowner has the right to punish a peasant for any failure to fulfill his or her obligations. As punishment, the landowner can confiscate the peasant's personal property, such as blankets or farm animals, or have the foreman beat the peasant physically.

Three images of the feudal system. The lot of most members of a feudal society consists of grinding poverty and hard work. Property is the chief source of wealth, but few people who work the land own it.

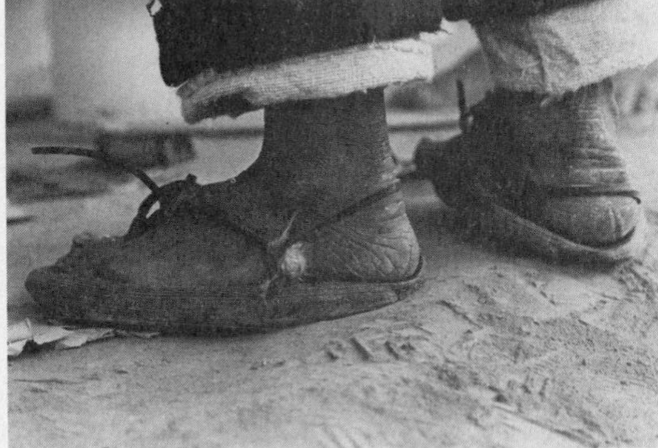

Despite the official ideology of the Soviet Union, structured inequality demonstrably exists. Although it is not truly a classless society, the largest percentage of the population is within the middle of the social strata. In these views of a Moscow museum and a government department store, what elements of an open stratification system are visible or suggested?

The landowner and peasant are bound together by the land, despite their inequality in wealth and rights over one another. The peasants must spend a certain number of days a year tending the owner's land and animals and must give the landowner a percentage of the year's crop harvest. In return, the landowner must provide the peasants with housing, land for their own farming and pasture, seed for sowing, and a chapel for religious ceremonies.

What cultural elements maintain these patterns of social interaction? In a feudal society, tradition is the major cultural force. Social arrangements of great inequality are accepted because they have always been what they now are. Added to this, often, is the influence of a religion emphasizing that people should accept their earthly lot and hope for their rewards in an afterlife.

OPEN STRATIFICATION SYSTEMS

In the industrialized society—as an ideal type—the main characteristic of the stratification system is that it is open. Sociologist Melvin Tumin has described the ideal type of such a system.[9] In it, the most important factor determining a person's social class is his or her achievement. Although there is marked difference between rich and poor, the differences between any two adjacent classes are not sharp and distinct.

Inequality is always present, but the ideals of equality and equal opportunity exist. Mobility among the classes is approved. A person can move up the social scale through good business ability, education, marriage, special talents, determination, political ability, or luck. Although most people tend to interact with others in their class, friendships can form across class lines.

People generally believe mobility is possible, and they do not see themselves eternally tied to their present class by fate. The primary impediment to upward mobility for lower-class members is lack of resources such as money and cultural background (the education, manner of speech, and personal bearing associated with the middle and upper classes).

1. Consider stratification in the United States. How close do you think it comes to the description of an open class system?

2. In your view, what factors play an important part in a person's access to various occupations? Think specifically of the institutions that are most directly involved. (You might find a brief review of Chapter 6 useful.)

[9]Melvin M. Tumin, *Patterns of Society: Identities, Roles, Resources* (Boston: Little Brown, 1973); id., "Some Principles of Stratification: A Critical Analysis," *American Sociological Review* 18 (1953): 387–94.

STRATIFICATION IN AMERICAN SOCIETY

No one claims that all Americans are or even should be perfectly equal in the rewards they control. But there is debate over whether the system is becoming increasingly equalitarian. Some argue that in recent years progressive taxation, welfare legislation, the civil rights movement, and legislation requiring equal employment opportunities have helped to remove class barriers and to make this a land of more equal opportunities. Others maintain that the cards are still definitely stacked against the lower classes. Those who are rich can buy all the right connections; others are simply out in the cold. Few have made it from rags to riches.

Using some of the sociological concepts we have learned, let's look at the American class structure more systematically, examining each of the three major components of class—wealth, prestige, and power—to see what the contemporary stratification system looks like.

Income Distribution

Sociologists and other social scientists (such as economists) have various ways of measuring wealth and tracing how it is distributed. Two ways that we will discuss here are: median income and wealth of each fifth of the population. Each of these measures gives us a particular kind of information.

A look at the table at the top of page 195 shows that in 1959 the median income of American families was less than $6,000 (that is, half the families were earning more than $6,000, and the other half were earning less.) By 1970 the median income had risen to almost $10,000 and by 1972 to over $11,000.[10] Even allowing for inflation, the overall standard of living was rising. Until the recession of the 1970s, the "pie" itself was getting a good deal bigger.

But the table tells only part of the story of income distribution. Suppose we look at how much of the total personal income in the United States goes to the top fifth (20 percent) of families and how much goes to the lowest fifth. The next table shows this income distribution from 1947 to 1972.

Over the past few decades the average income of American families has gone up—at the bottom level, at the top, and in between. In fact the 1974 *Economic Report of the President* notes that "between 1947 and 1972 median family income, adjusted for the rise in prices, doubled."[11] But the proportion

[10] United States Department of Commerce, Bureau of the Census, *Statistical Abstract of the United States, 1974,* 95th ed. (Washington, D.C.: U.S. Government Printing Office, 1974), p. 382.

[11] *Economic Report of the President* (Washington, D.C.: U.S. Government Printing Office, 1974), p. 139.

DISTRIBUTION OF INCOME OF FAMILIES

Family Income	Percentage of Families	
	1959	*1972*
Under $1000	5.1	1.3
$1000 to 1999	8.3	2.2
$2000 to 2999	9.3	3.7
$3000 to 3999	10.1	4.5
$4000 to 4999	11.7	4.9
$5000 to 5999	13.2	5.0
$6000 to 6999	11.0	5.2
$7000 to 7999	8.4	16.8
$8000 to 9999	10.6	16.8
$10,000 to 14,999	9.1	26.1
$15,000 to 24,999	2.4	23.0
$25,000 and over	0.7	7.3

Source: United States Department of Commerce, Bureau of the Census.

going to each fifth of the population has not changed a great deal.

Let's take our analysis one step further. Even within the upper fifth of income distribution, each family does not get an equal share of the big slice of income pie. In 1972 the top 20 percent of families received about 41.4 percent of the country's total income. But even many of these people are not really wealthy. The table of income levels above on this page indicates that most of the families in the top 20 percent in 1972 were earning family incomes higher than $15,000, but still below $25,000. A large segment of wealth is controlled by a small number of rich families.

Most of the families in the top 5 percent of income distribution were receiving over $25,000 a year before taxes. Obviously within this category there are great differences. It includes the family in which two members earn in-

SHARE OF INCOME BY EACH FIFTH OF FAMILIES

Income Rank	Percentage of Total Income				
	1947	*1950*	*1960*	*1966*	*1972*
Lowest fifth	5.1	4.5	4.8	5.6	5.4
Second fifth	11.8	11.9	12.2	12.4	11.9
Third fifth	16.7	17.4	17.8	17.8	17.5
Fourth fifth	23.2	23.6	24.0	23.8	23.9
Highest fifth	43.3	42.7	41.3	40.5	41.4
Highest 5 percent	17.5	17.3	15.9	15.6	15.9

Source: *Economic Report of the President* (Washington, D.C.: U.S. Government Printing Office, 1974), p. 140.

Every society has certain sources of prestige. The high umbrella symbolizes high social status or membership in royalty in traditional Japan.

Wealth alone often fails to bestow prestige (long-time wealthy families often see the nouveau riche as objects of amusement or scorn). Wealth combined with government service brought prestige to the Kennedy family, beginning with Joseph P. Kennedy.

come—perhaps each in the $10,000–$15,000 range. Their combined earnings put them into the top 5 percent. It also includes the 4,000 or so families that earn more than $500,000 and the 400 or so whose incomes are above $1,000,000 (according to Internal Revenue Service figures). Their wealth derives from corporate stocks, property rents and sales, tax-exempt local or state bonds, and similar sources.

In general we can see that the United States stratification system is far from equal in the distribution of income. Some people control a much larger share of the wealth than others. Furthermore, there has been very little change in the last two decades. The differences are not as marked as those in developing countries, but they are similar to those in other advanced industrial nations, such as Sweden, England, Canada, and Switzerland. As the United States has moved into advanced stages of industrialization, its total wealth has increased. Mass-produced items make a reasonable standard of living available to many, but by no means all, strata. Large sectors of the working and middle classes defend the system because it provides them with decent jobs, homes, food, clothes, automobiles, and services. They also believe improvements are possible. In a later section we look at the strata of society who do not share this abundance.

Prestige

Prestige: the degree of honor and respect accorded a person.

According to our definition of social class, people are stratified by other factors in addition to wealth. One of these is prestige. Sociologists refer to prestige as the honor or respect that an individual is given by others in the community. Prestige is a subjective quality. It is not based on census figures or other precise measures. Instead, it is based on how most people in a society *feel* about a particular activity. The criteria for high prestige vary in different cultures. In some societies it may come from birth. For example, in feudal societies the highest prestige goes to members of the nobility. In other social systems, religious activities may be the primary source of high prestige. Holy men in India and rabbis in orthodox Jewish communities have great prestige because of this.

In many societies, wealth and power are sources of prestige. This is true in the United States. Wealthy families—such as the Rockefellers, Vanderbilts, and Mellons—automatically have high prestige. However, it is possible for a wealthy person to lose prestige while retaining wealth. This happened to John D. Rockefeller at the time of the Ludlow Massacre in 1914. Miners at Rockefeller's Colorado Fuel and Iron Company in Ludlow went on strike, and the company used strong-arm tactics to break the union, attacking and burning the workers' tent colony. Men, women, and children were killed in a confrontation between state troops and miners on April 20, and public sympathy for the strikers was aroused. Outrage focused on Rockefeller, who was heaped with contempt and hatred. The Rockefeller family found its scorned position intolerable and set about building a prestigious public image through philanthropy and favorable publicity.[12]

[12]See Edward Jay Epstein, "The Great Rockefeller Power Machine," *New York*, November 24, 1975, especially pp. 46–50.

For most people in our society, and other industrial societies, prestige derives from the person's occupation.[13] Doctors, judges, and scientists have high prestige occupations. Street cleaners, janitors, and ditchdiggers have low prestige occupations.

1. Rank the following ten occupations according to the amount of prestige you think each one has in American society (rank as first the one with the greatest prestige, tenth the least).

automobile mechanic	**janitor**
musician in a symphony orchestra	**police officer**
owner of a factory that employs about 100 people	**manager of a small store in a city**
lawyer	**truck driver**
bookkeeper	**Supreme Court justice**

2. What criteria did you use in ranking these occupations? Why?

3. Consider our society's dependence on proper garbage disposal. Think for a moment of a garbage strike in New York City, where tons of trash pile up on the streets if a pickup does not come. There is danger of spread of disease, a proliferation of rats, the unpleasant odor of rotting food. Clearly garbage collectors are central to the maintenance of our health. If this is true, why don't they have the same social position as doctors–who are also involved in the maintenance of society's health? Explain.

Measuring occupational prestige. In a 1963 nationwide random sample survey, respondents were given a list of ninety occupations, covering a wide range. They were asked to rate each occupation as excellent, good, average, below average, or poor. The results were tallied, and each occupation was given a score depending on how many times it was mentioned in each category. From this, the occupations were listed in order of their prestige in our society. Here are the rankings of sixty of the ninety occupations.

[13]See Alex Inkeles and Peter H. Rossi, "National Comparisons of Occupational Prestige," *American Journal of Sociology* 61 (1956): 329–39.

OCCUPATIONAL PRESTIGE RANKS IN THE UNITED STATES

Rank	*Occupation*
1.0	United States Supreme Court justice
2.0	Physician
3.5	Nuclear physicist
5.5	State governor
8.0	United States representative in Congress
8.0	College professor
11.0	Chemist
11.0	Lawyer
14.0	Dentist
14.0	Architect
17.5	Psychologist
17.5	Minister
17.5	Member of the board of directors of a large corporation
17.5	Mayor of a large city
21.5	Priest
21.5	Airplane pilot
24.5	Banker
29.5	Accountant for a large business
29.5	Public school teacher
31.5	Owner of a factory that employs about 100 people
31.5	Building contractor
34.5	Musician in a symphony orchestra
34.5	Author of novels
39.0	Electrician
44.0	Farm owner and operator
44.0	Undertaker
44.0	Welfare worker for a city government
46.0	Newspaper columnist
47.0	Policeman
48.0	Reporter on a daily newspaper
49.5	Radio announcer
49.5	Bookkeeper
51.5	Insurance agent
53.0	Carpenter
54.5	Manager of a small store in a city
57.0	Mail carrier
57.0	Railroad conductor
57.0	Traveling salesman for a wholesale concern
59.0	Plumber
60.0	Automobile repairman
62.5	Barber
62.5	Machine operator in a factory
62.5	Owner-operator of a lunchstand
65.5	Garage mechanic
67.0	Truck driver
70.0	Clerk in a store
70.0	Streetcar motorman
72.5	Restaurant cook
74.0	Singer in nightclub
75.0	Filling station attendant
77.5	Night watchman
77.5	Coal miner
80.5	Restaurant waiter
80.5	Taxi driver
83.0	Janitor
83.0	Bartender
86.0	Soda fountain clerk
87.0	Sharecropper—one who owns no livestock or equipment and does not manage a farm
88.0	Garbage collector
89.0	Street sweeper
90.0	Shoeshiner

Source: Based on Robert W. Hodge, Paul M. Siegel, and Peter H. Rossi, ''Occupational Prestige [in] the United States,'' 1925–63, *American Journal of Sociology* 70, no. 3 (November, 1964) 286–302, table 1. Reprinted from Theodore Caplow, *Elementary Sociology* © 1971, pp. 388–89, by permission of Prentice-Hall, Inc., Englewood Cliffs, N.J.

1. How did your ranking of the ten occupations we listed compare with their ranking in the table above? If there are major differences between them, how do you account for the differences?
2. Look at the first five and the last five occupations in the prestige rating table. Rate each of these as high, medium, or low in the following characteristics:

The degree of education required to hold this job.

The amount of money earned by a person with this job.

The power held by a person in this position.

The degree to which the work is "clean" (rather than "dirty").

3. Can you draw any generalizations about the characteristics that generally surround a high prestige position?

Income and job prestige. In our society, high income and high occupational prestige usually go together, as do low income and low prestige. But not always. In an advanced industrial system like ours, a skill that is in demand and that therefore produces a high income may still command only low prestige. An owner of a trash-collection business, for example, might earn more than a teacher, but the teacher generally has more prestige because of the "clean," intellectual nature of teaching work. Plumbers, electricians, and carpenters frequently earn as much as or more than store managers, social workers, and librarians, but society generally accords less prestige to skilled manual workers than to white-collar workers.

Because of these exceptions to the link between wealth and prestige, Americans cannot be rigidly divided into upper, middle, working, and lower classes. Our class is decided not only by how much we earn, but also by how we earn it. This is less true for very wealthy and very poor people. They almost always fit the criteria for upper and lower classes respectively. For large portions of the population, however, wealth alone is not a clear indication of social class. Sociologists also use occupational prestige, life-style, and educational background to help determine whether a person is working class or middle class. The sociologist's use of multiple factors to determine social class is borne out by the behavior of many people in our society who acquire wealth but have been denied prestige. Dismissed as *nouveau riche* (new rich) by those with wealth *and* prestige, they try to obtain for their children the social status to accompany their wealth.[14]

[14]See, for example, Daniel Bell, "Crime as an American Way of Life," in *The End of Ideology* (Glencoe, Ill.: Free Press, 1960).

This business executive draws prestige from his job, among other social rewards, whereas the sanitation worker derives little or no prestige from his. Teachers often receive more occupational prestige than income from their work. Some teachers have now adopted the strategies of other workers and have organized unions to bargain for better pay. Because of their unions, construction and other skilled workers generally make handsome incomes, at least while they are actually on the job, although they do not receive high prestige.

Power

In Chapter 6 we defined the third component of social class, power. It is the ability to control others, the authority or force that can make others do things, even against their own wishes or interests. In Weber's words, power is "the chance of a man or of a number of men to realize their own will in a communal action even against the resistance of others who are participating in the action.[15]

Power is often related to control of wealth. In capitalist societies, control over basic industries (steel, oil, and others), large landholdings, and ownership of transportation systems (railroads, airlines) have been primary sources of power. Power enables a group to defend its interests. It gives people the ability to maintain and increase their wealth and prestige. This may be done by influencing government activities (lobbying for protective legislation, winning major government contracts) or by affecting private business.

For example, many professional groups have gathered the power to protect their members. The American Medical Association wields enormous power to determine who will receive a license to practice medicine. It also has power to limit the number of people who become doctors, even when others feel that more physicians are needed. Over the years it has exercised its power to restrict national health legislation, which has been sought by presidents since Harry Truman first proposed it in the 1940s.[16]

Power has become dispersed into pockets among the working, middle, and upper classes. Does this mean that power, unlike wealth and prestige, is equally distributed throughout society? Hardly.

Upper income groups have always had a disproportionate share. For instance, a study of the Eighty-ninth Congress, made in the 1960s by William Domhoff, revealed that 15 percent of our senators were members of the upper class (the top 5 percent of the population). Of eight secretaries of state appointed between 1932 and 1966, five were listed in the Social Register–a privately published listing of the nation's elite families. Similarly, of thirteen secretaries of defense, eight have been listed in the Social Register, and four out of seven Treasury Department heads were members of the upper class.[17] Domhoff gives comparable figures for other important public and private positions.

[15]Gerth and Mills, *From Max Weber,* p. 180.

[16]See Eliot Freidson, *The Profession of Medicine* (New York: Dodd, Mead, 1970).

[17]G. William Domhoff, *Who Rules America?* (Englewood Cliffs, N.J.: Prentice-Hall, 1967), pp. 98–99, 111.

William Randolph Hearst, a man of immense wealth and power, is credited with creating the Spanish-American War (in 1898), by the use of his newspapers—certainly an accomplishment that amply fulfills Weber's definition of power.

The Watergate scandal revealed how many directors of major industries had contributed illegally to political campaigns to gain influence over the White House. These same people are very powerful in the private sphere—as directors of foundations, civic organizations, churches, and colleges, to name a few examples. Their power is not unlimited, however. Law and competing groups are important factors restricting it.

SOCIAL MOBILITY

Our overview of American society indicates that on all three dimensions—wealth, prestige, and power—the United States is highly stratified. Despite vast differences among the strata, however social mobility is not automatically denied. That is the last measure we should look at in discussing stratification here: mobility—movement from one stratum to another.

Intergenerational mobility: change in a person's social class from that of his or her parents.

Just how much social mobility is there in American society, and how do sociologists measure this? Although there are no exact measures, sociologists have designed several indicators, or rough measurements (usually of from five to seven bold categories), to help them judge the amount of mobility. The most frequently used method is to make an occupational rating scale and to compare the occupations of fathers and sons. Since occupations are highly correlated to wealth and prestige, the amount of movement from one occupational category to another between generations should indicate the amount of social mobility.

This movement is called *intergenerational* mobility, because it compares the social or occupational prestige of one generation with that of the previous one. Another kind of mobility is *intragenerational*–movement up (or down) within a person's own working life.

Intragenerational mobility: change of a person's social class within his or her own working life.

The following table shows the percentage of sons in each occupation whose fathers had that occupation. Draw conclusions from the table cautiously. It gives us a picture of upward and downward mobility, but its occupational categories are very general. Nevertheless, we can make some judgments about the opportunities for children at the upper end of the social scale and those at the lower end. We can also pinpoint where mobility is most likely to occur.

MOBILITY FROM FATHER'S TO SON'S OCCUPATION, 1962 AND 1973

Year and Father's Occupation	Son's Current Occupation: Upper White Collar	Lower White Collar	Upper Manual	Lower Manual	Farm	Total	Column Percentage
1962							
Upper white collar	53.8%	17.6%	12.5%	14.8%	1.3%	100.0%	16.5%
Lower white collar	45.6	20.0	14.4	18.3	1.7	100.0	7.6
Upper manual	28.1	13.4	27.8	29.5	1.2	100.0	19.0
Lower manual	20.3	12.3	21.6	43.8	2.0	100.0	27.5
Farm	15.6	7.0	19.2	36.1	22.2	100.0	29.4
Total	27.8	12.4	20.0	32.1	7.7	100.0	100.0
1973							
Upper white collar	52.0	16.0	13.8	17.1	1.1	100.0	18.2
Lower white collar	42.3	19.7	15.3	21.9	0.8	100.0	9.0
Upper manual	29.4	13.0	27.4	29.0	1.1	100.0	20.5
Lower manual	22.5	12.0	23.7	40.8	1.0	100.0	29.7
Farm	17.5	7.8	22.7	37.2	14.8	100.0	22.6
Total	29.9	12.7	21.7	31.5	4.1	100.0	100.0

Note: Data are from March 1962 and March 1973 Current Population Surveys and Occupational Changes in a Generation Surveys. Occupation groups are:

upper white collar: professional and kindred workers and managers, officials and proprietors, except farm

lower white collar: sales, clerical and kindred workers

upper manual: craftsmen, foremen and kindred workers

lower manual: operatives and kindred workers, service workers, and laborers, except farm

farm: farmers and farm managers, farm laborers and foremen.

Source: Robert M. Hauser and David L. Featherman, "Occupations and Social Mobility in the United States," Institute for Research on Social Poverty, Paper 336–76, March 1976. This table and a related discussion will also be published in David L. Featherman and Robert M. Hauser, *Opportunity and Change* (New York and London: Academic, forthcoming).

1. On the basis of the table, what percentage of upper white-collar fathers have sons who are also upper white-collar? What percentage of unskilled workers have sons who entered upper white-collar occupations? What does this tell us about opportunities for mobility?

2. Which groups have the greatest number of sons remaining in the same category? Which have the greatest mobility?

3. Do all groups have a certain amount of upward mobility from fathers to sons? Is there downward mobility in all occupational categories?

4. What differences, if any, do you observe between the 1962 and the 1973 data?

The father owns the gas station; the son works there. If the son goes on to other jobs that bestow higher social rewards, intergenerational mobility will have been achieved. Intragenerational mobility could be measured by listing the sequence of occupations of either of the men throughout their lives and noting changes in their social rewards.

Social structure: the recurrent pattern of relations within a group or a society that constitutes its organization.

Structural Sources of Mobility

Sociologists have drawn several conclusions from these large-scale surveys of occupational mobility. First, there is considerable intergenerational mobility—movement of sons into an occupational category different from that of their fathers. In no category do most sons have exactly the same jobs their fathers had. Yet rarely are there great spurts up or down the occupational ladder. Sons tend to move into categories close to those of their fathers.

MOBILITY BETWEEN MANUAL AND NONMANUAL WORK. BY COUNTRY

	Nonfarm Populations		
Country	*Percentage Showing Upward Mobility (Nonmanual Sons of Manual Fathers)*	*Percentage Showing Downward Mobility (Manual Sons of Nonmanual Fathers)*	*Total Mobility Between Working and Middle Class*
United States	33	26	30
Germany	29	32	31
Sweden	31	24	29
Japan	36	22	27
France	39	20	27
Switzerland	45	13	23

Source: Seymour Martin Lipset and Reinhard Bendix, *Social Mobility in Industrial Society* (Berkeley, Calif.: University of California Press, 1959), p. 25. Copyright © 1959 by The Regents of the University of California; reprinted by permission of the University of California Press.

Contrary to popular belief, mobility rates in the United States are roughly comparable to those in Sweden, Great Britain, Denmark, France, Japan, Germany, and other industrialized countries. The factors that promote social mobility tend to exist in all the economically advanced societies. Long-term technological changes affect the economy, reducing the need for unskilled labor and farm workers and increasing the need for white-collar workers, technicians, and professionals. Thus, technology has been the major factor in promoting mobility. Also, birth rates differ among the social classes. Because upper- and middle-class groups frequently have small families, they do not produce enough people to fill all the new positions created. There is room for others to move upward. In addition, immigrants from foreign countries and migrants from rural areas to cities often provide unskilled labor, filling the jobs left vacant by the mobility of others.

Nevertheless, as we said earlier, rags to riches stories are rare in real life. Studies have shown, for example, that about 70 percent of the people who

Social variables: those variations in social background (race, sex, age, ethnic and religious membership, social class) that influence individual and group behavior.

make up the business elite in this country come from upper-class homes, about 20 percent come from middle-class homes, and about 10 percent from working-class homes. Some sons of manual workers have moved into professional jobs, through higher education, but the positions of the upper classes remain closed to most people not born into them.[18]

You probably noticed that mobility was measured only for fathers and sons. Women have not been mentioned at all. Why? Until recently it was commonly believed that women in American society derived their socioeconomic status from the positions of their fathers and their husbands. This was reinforced by the idea that the main work of women was homemaking and that their occupations were secondary. Although this view is now being challenged by women, comparable data are not yet available to discuss mobility trends of women.

LIFE CHANCES IN A STRATIFIED SOCIETY

Many of what we called social variables in Chapter 1 are affected by the positions we hold in the stratification system: they are *structural variables.* For instance, lower-class members arrested for a crime are much more likely to go to jail than are those of higher social classes.

Sociologists link this and other such consequences of social class membership by the concept of *life chances.*[19] This concept is simply that what an individual will become is strongly influenced by social circumstances—his or her location in the social class structure. This location has an economic, a political, and a cultural dimension.

Life chances: the statistical probability of certain events or patterns of behavior occurring because of an individual's or group's set of social variables.

For example, let us briefly examine the cultural dimension. Looking at education in relation to this dimension, we can see that values, norms, and attitudes of parents, teachers, and the individual student alike influence the student's ultimate performance and progress in the education system. But the economic dimension is also operating in determining the quality of schools available for the student. This in turn depends on the political dimension—the decision-making process by which school resources are allocated. Thus a person's life chances depend on how he or she stands in relation to all three of these dimensions—cultural, economic, and political.

[18]Paul Blumberg, ed., *The Impact of Social Class* (New York: Thomas Y. Crowell, 1972), p. 496.

[19]Max Weber defined life chances as the chances that an individual's life will follow certain patterns, determined most significantly by the individual's class position. See Max Weber, *The Theory of Social and Economic Organization* (New York: Free Press, 1957).

SOCIAL IMMOBILITY: THE VICTIMS OF AFFLUENCE

This society constantly socializes people to believe that anyone can get ahead by hard work. How, then, do workers respond when there is little actual opportunity to move up the social scale? One study of automobile workers, done by sociologist Ely Chinoy, helps us answer that question. Chinoy found that in the automobile industry there were very few chances for intragenerational mobility. Executives were not chosen from among the workers. Because unions bargained collectively, no individual could better his or her position by extra initiative.

Workers responded to the lack of mobility in several ways. First, they continued to hope their children would achieve more than they had. Some blamed themselves for not getting more of an education or for being attracted by wages that seemed high at first. Most began to define security and the acquisition of material goods as forms of getting ahead. Chinoy quotes from several of the workers: "If you can put away a couple of hundred dollars, so you can take care of an emergency, then you're getting ahead." Some began to work for small gains in the factory. "Getting ahead is working up to a job where you don't get kicked around."[20] Thus, buying a refrigerator, a color television set, or new furniture or gaining some slightly better factory job is substituted for gaining more money, better skills, and greater responsibility.

Groups in Poverty

Who are the poor in our society? There are several distinct groups, but their sources of poverty overlap. Nonwhite minorities probably come to mind first. Poor whites, however, outnumber poor nonwhites. There are rural poor as well as urban poor. And there are the unemployed poor as well as the working poor.

WHO ARE THE POOR?

Category	*Percentage Who Are Poor**
All Americans	12
Whites	9
Blacks	33
People 65 and over	19
Families in central cities	11
Farm families	13
Black farm families	43

*Based on official 1972 "poverty level"—$4,275 annual income for a nonfarm family of four, $3,643 for a farm family of four.

Source: United States Department of Commerce, Bureau of the Census, *Current Population Reports*, series P–60, no. 88 (Washington, D.C.: U.S. Government Printing Office, 1973).

Two sources of economic hardship are related to technology and the economy. For one, improvements in agricultural methods reduced the number of people needed to produce a given food output, so many workers were forced off the land into the cities. Movement occurred chiefly from the rural South to the cities of the North. Meanwhile the percentage of unskilled workers needed in our society decreased markedly in this century. People without money to obtain further education and training in marketable skills have had a hard time finding work. This is one cause of the high unemployment rate among nonwhites, particularly blacks.

[20]Ely Chinoy, *Automobile Workers and the American Dream* (Garden City, N.Y.: Doubleday, 1955), p. 125.

Hard work in hazardous conditions, low occupational prestige, and uncertain job security in a changing technology: the lot of miners in Appalachia, a region that has long known chronic poverty, unemployment, and work-related illnesses.

Coal miners. Others have also fallen victim to technology and economics. Industries can go from boom to bust, as the coal mining industry has in this century.

During World War II coal was in great demand. Jobs in the industry became plentiful. The boom lasted until the early 1950s. Then, many buyers began looking for other fuels, particularly oil and natural gas, to meet industrial and home heating needs. The reasons for the switch were complex. Strikes by the miners for higher pay and safer working conditions made it difficult for mine owners to maintain stable production and profit levels. Orders were frequently delayed by work interruptions, and prices rose. But the main reasons were that oil and gas were relatively cheap and were cleaner.

In the face of this competition, mine owners had to produce coal more efficiently. Bargaining with the United Mine Workers under John L. Lewis led to an agreement for increased mechanization of the mines in return for higher pay and benefits for the miners. By 1958 fewer than 200,000 men were needed to produce the nation's coal, whereas in 1910 coal production had provided jobs for 700,000 miners. As time went on, the situation of the unemployed miner became even worse. Appalachia, the region where so many coal mines once flourished, entered our vocabulary as a word evoking an economic backwater and hopeless poverty. Recently, the energy crisis and the high price of oil have led owners to reopen coal mines and create some new jobs.

Only in recent years have migrant workers obtained the right to organize in a few states. Low pay and poor living conditions are the rule. What are the life chances of the children of most farm workers?

Farm workers. The same technology that drove people from the countryside favored the large, corporate farms that have developed there. Successful competitive farming depends on mechanization, chemical fertilizers, and sophisticated techniques. But this combination requires heavy capital investment that small farms can neither justify nor afford. The self-employed small family farmers, the sharecroppers, and the migrant workers following the harvests share a burden of insecurity. Sharecroppers and migrant workers, however, are particularly vulnerable to bad fortune, because they do not even own the land they work or, usually, the tools they use.

Migrant workers move from place to place following the harvest seasons throughout the country. They often live in camps provided by growers, far from community stores, schools, and health services. Their low pay usually leads them into continual debt, generally to their own crew bosses, and prevents them from getting proper nourishment. Families often work from sunrise to sunset. They are rarely able to send their children to school regularly or to save money for hard times or to improve their situation. For the most part they remain tied to their work, unstable as it is.

Recently, a few states have passed legislation to protect migrants. In most states, however, they are not covered by minimum wage laws, proper health and safety provisions, or guarantees of the right to collective bargaining through unions. The nature of their work keeps migrants from casting off their economic insecurity and political powerlessness: moving from place to place makes it hard for them to form unions and hard even to vote in most elections.

In some states, legislatures have ended the worst abuses. There workers are covered by minimum wage laws and health codes. But, in spite of considerable improvement, a 1974 survey of the conditions of farm workers in the Northeast found poverty and improper living conditions to be serious problems.[21] Moreover, when minimum wage laws and health codes force up growers' costs, many of them replace human labor in the fields with machines wherever possible. Between 1965 and 1975 the number of migrant workers dropped about 50 percent.

Sharecroppers. A sharecropper farms land belonging to someone else in exchange for rent and a share of the crops. Sharecropper families generally live in grinding poverty. In many ways the sharecropper's life resembles that of the peasant in a medieval feudal society. The economic arrangement overwhelm-

[21]William H. Friedland and Dorothy Nelkin, *Migrant Agricultural Workers in America's Northeast* (New York: Holt, Rinehart and Winston, 1974).

ingly favors the landowner and disfavors the sharecropper, as we can see from this brief description:

> The Berryhill [family's] cash income is less than $800 a year—equal to what the average American family earns in six weeks—and the labor they perform in exchange for that paltry amount is back-breaking indeed. Sam clears $250 a year from his half-share of the cotton crop. The plantation owner—"The Man"—sells what Sam grows, then deducts from Sam's half what is supposedly owed for seed, fertilizer and other items advanced during the year. The remainder of the Berryhills' income derives from the $1.30 hourly wage Sam is paid for driving a tractor on the boss' other fields, and the $5 each Maude and the children get for an occasional day's work chopping cotton.[22]

Some families, after a lifetime of sharecropping, suddenly are evicted from the land. Many landowners have found that replacing sharecropping families with tractors and harvesters means less worry and responsibility and more productivity and profit for them. Or the federal government's "soil bank" policy makes it more profitable for an owner to leave the land idle than to plant crops. When landowners receive such farm support, the sharecroppers are generally sent off to fend for themselves.

Many of these displaced people have gone north to New York, Chicago, and Philadelphia, or to southern cities such as Atlanta. Some try to find new jobs there, others face unemployment and welfare. Their only skills are agricultural, and they find little work in the cities. They join masses of other unskilled workers whose jobs have been taken over by machines and who lack other work alternatives.

It is ironic that the technology and industrialization that promote an open class system with its greater promise of social mobility also produces poverty. However, the actual sources of poverty are our cultural values and norms. These dictate that economic efficiency is given priority over providing jobs for all. They also dictate how our wealth is distributed and how we measure wealth, power, and prestige. In another culture the wealth derived from technology might be shared by much more of the population.

Old age and poverty. In the late 1950s and early 1960s, Michael Harrington, sociologist and political activist, traveled throughout the United States to study those he called "forgotten Americans": the poor. In *The Other America*, published in 1962, Harrington reminded us that the prosperity that followed World War II did not come to all Americans. Millions of people in various

[22]Jack E. White, Jr., "The Unchanged South," *Ebony*, August 1971, pp. 126–32.

Constant hardship and indebtedness are built into the sharecropper economy. The circumstances and consequent life chances of sharecroppers are little different from those of peasants in a feudal system. The white family shown here is not part of the sharecropper economy: it owns its farm. But cutthroat competition from large corporate farms using advanced technology is driving the small farmer out of the market.

In our society, many elderly people are dispossessed. Fixed incomes (pensions, Social Security payments, savings) often prove inadequate for maintaining a decent standard of living. Can you think of any remedies?

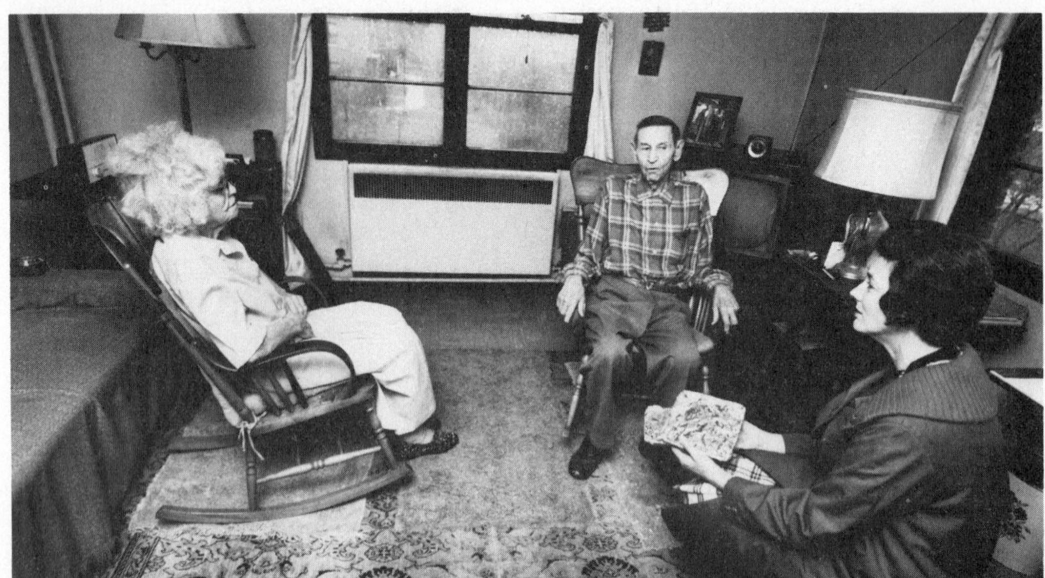

sections of the country, in different occupations, of many racial backgrounds, and of different ages continued to live in poverty.

The elderly poor were among the least visible, wrote Harrington. They were rapidly increasing, as medical advances kept people alive longer, yet we had not prepared to meet their special needs. Many employers impose compulsory retirement at age sixty-five, leaving healthy, potentially active people with sharply reduced income and little activity to fill their time. As we saw in Chapter 6, the nuclear family has replaced the extended family. In American society today the elderly no longer feel comfortable living with their grown children and grandchildren. Many families move far from their childhood homes for jobs and schooling, so that older people cannot even visit their relatives easily.

INCREASE IN THE ELDERLY POPULATION

Year	*Percentage of National Population 65 or Older*
1900	4.1
1960	9.2
1970	9.9

Source: Calculated from United States Department of Commerce, Bureau of the Census, *Historical Statistics of the United States, Colonial Times to 1957* (Washington, D.C.: U.S. Government Printing Office, 1960), and id., *Statistical Abstract of the United States, 1974,* 95th ed. (Washington, D.C.: U.S. Government Printing Office, 1974), p. 31.

Full Social Security pensions are generally not enough to live on. What is worse, many retired people receive only partial benefits, because they have not worked consistently and have not contributed sufficiently to the program. Social Security also favors the well to do in certain provisions. For instance, if a retired person earns more than $1,200 a year in wages, he or she loses a portion of Social Security benefits. This is supposed to keep retired people out of the labor market, to make room for younger workers. But money from stocks, bonds, or real estate is not counted, so the wealthier retired people who receive this income can still receive full pensions.

Relatively few elderly people have private pensions or personal savings. Many are forced to live in inferior housing, get inadequate health care, and suffer from poor nutrition as the cost of living rises. Some have no choice but to turn to welfare funds and public nursing homes.

Race, Sex, and Poverty

What are a person's chances of living in poverty? In large measure they are determined by two ascribed factors—race and sex. Today, 62 percent of the adults living in poverty are women. Of the families headed by women, 38.3 percent live in poverty, while only 8.3 percent of the families headed by men are poor. Some of these women are unemployed, but many work in very low-paying jobs: 1.6 million are domestics, maids, and servants, and more than a half million are farm workers.

White and Nonwhite Family Income Levels

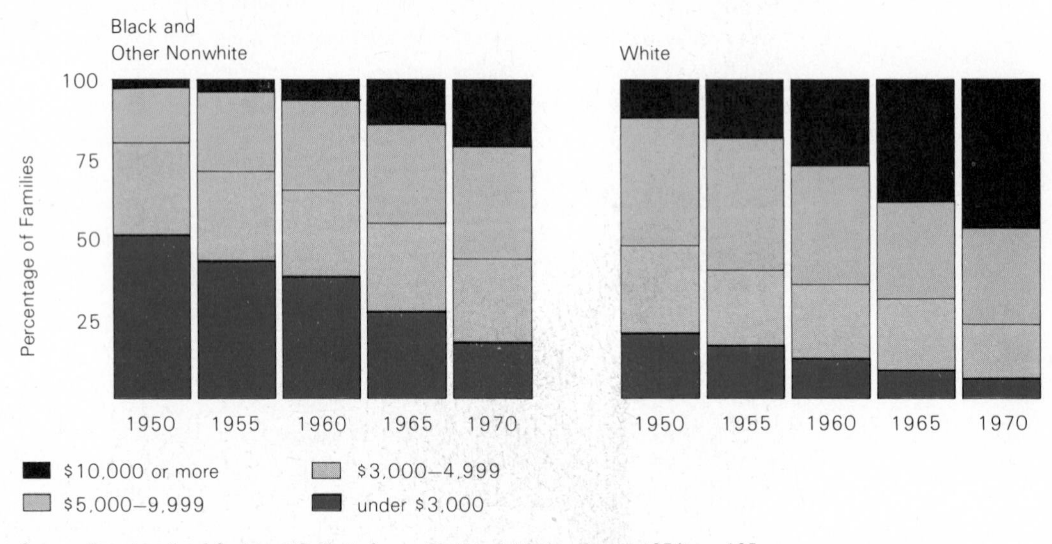

Source: *Encyclopedia of Sociology* (Guilford, Conn.: Dushkin Publishing Group, 1974), p. 135.

The statistics comparing poverty in the white and nonwhite populations are equally striking. True, millions of white Americans live in poverty. They receive the largest share of the welfare benefits distributed in the United States and have the largest number of unemployed. Yet blacks, Native Americans, and Puerto Ricans (all groups that are defined as nonwhite by the United States government for census purposes) have disproportionate percentages of people who live in poverty or near-poverty.

A child who is born to a nonwhite American family has a greater chance of dying in infancy, or receiving poor health care, of going to an ill-equipped school, and of living in crowded conditions than does a child born to white Americans. The nonwhite child is more likely to live in a high-crime neighborhood in an urban ghetto, to drop out before graduating from high school, and to have a difficult time finding a job. The nonwhite minority member in the United States has long been the victim of racial discrimination.

Families Below Poverty Line by Race and Residence, 1959 and 1969

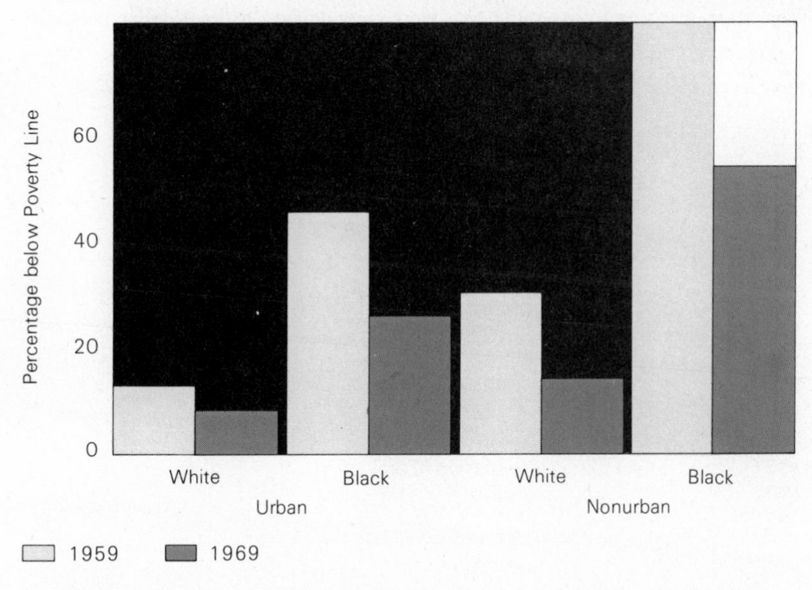

Source: *Encyclopedia of Sociology* (Guilford, Conn.: Dushkin Publishing Group, 1974), p. 220.

When the two variables, race and sex, are combined, we see that white men have the greatest chance for affluence and that black women are most likely to be poor. Nevertheless, some observers have noted significant progress among black people in the 1960s. Those who emphasize the gains point to higher levels of education and income and greater numbers of union members, craft workers, and white-collar workers in the black population.

Two statisticians, Ben Wattenberg and Richard Scammon, have concluded that most black people now are members of the working and middle

AVERAGE SALARIES EARNED BY WORKING MEN AND WOMEN, 1970

Type of Worker	*Average Salary*
Full-time, year-round	
White men	$9,375
Nonwhite men	6,598
White women	5,490
Nonwhite women	4,674
Full-time and part-time	
Men	$7,939
Women	3,785

Source: United States Department of Commerce, Bureau of the Census, *Current Population Report*, series P—60, no. 80 (Washington, D.C.: U.S. Government Printing Office, 1970), p. 129.

classes—that they have put poverty behind them and work in a vast array of jobs, from teaching to assembly line work, bus driving to bank teller positions. Wattenberg and Scammon argue that it is important to stress the gains that have been made as well as the gap that continues to prevail.[23]

THE INCOME GAP

	Median Income		
Year	*Blacks*	*Whites*	*Percentage of Black to White Income*
1964	$3,724	$ 6,858	50
1965	3,886	7,251	50
1966	4,507	7,792	58
1967	4,875	8,234	59
1968	5,360	8,937	60
1969	5,999	9,794	61
1970	6,279	10,235	61
1971	6,440	10,672	60
1972	6,864	11,549	59

Source: United States Department of Commerce, Bureau of the Census.

STRATIFICATION: FUNCTIONAL OR DYSFUNCTIONAL?

Poverty remains a constant feature of our system of stratification. Because of poverty and differences in life chances that are linked to stratification, sociologists feel some urgency about answering a question they have inherited from philosophers and social theorists: Must every society—at least every society of some size and complexity—be stratified? Sociologists disagree on the answer. For structural functionalists, stratification is functional; for conflict theorists, it is dysfunctional.

Even assuming that a persuasive argument can be made for stratification, must the differences between those at the top and those at the bottom be so great? Is it functional for a society to have some members who are enormously wealthy and to have many more members who live in constant poverty and misery, whose children are doomed, by their set of life chances, to repeat the pattern?

Structural functionalists see a system of inequality as integrative (holding the society together). They acknowledge that it causes strains and conflicts among members, but these are minor compared to the disorder that would

[23]Ben J. Wattenberg and Richard M. Scammon, "Black Progress and Liberal Rhetoric," *Commentary,* April 1973, pp. 35–44.

follow from a "leveling" of society. If our society became truly classless, if wealth, power, and prestige were distributed uniformly to all, how would enough people be induced to go through premed studies, medical school, and internship, for example? Why would anyone want the headaches and ulcers of running a giant corporation if the salary and prestige were the same as those for an assembly line worker? Indeed, the structural functionalists ask, how could jobs such as streetcleaner or gas station attendant—worthy and necessary as they may be—ever actually gain the prestige of jobs that require immense responsibility, constant skill, sharp intelligence, and clear imagination?

If power is uniformly distributed, can it be said to exist at all? Power, remember, is the ability to get others to do what you want, whether they want it or not. As we saw in Chapter 6, Weber distinguised coercive power from authority or legitimacy. Can a society operate without a delegation of power to the few who are entrusted (whether by vote or by coronation) to exercise it legitimately?

Karl Marx, the formulator of the conflict perspective, answered these questions directly. He claimed that modern capitalist societies were essentially exploitive. Indeed, Marx categorized previous stages of societies on the basis of who the exploiters and the exploited were: who owned the property and who owned none. Marx predicted that a classless, stable society would emerge after a revolution by the working class. The propertyless workers would seize the property and productive wealth of society. The state, representing the workers, would then control property, production, and exchange: it would hold the power. Since it represents all workers equally, stratification would cease to exist. Ultimately the central value of society would be that the free development of each is necessary for the free development of all.[24]

Marx's followers further rebut the functionalist argument for stratification. Not all conflict theorists are Marxists, however. Instead of attacking the structural functionalist assumptions head-on, non-Marxist conflict theorists stress the dysfunctional results of inequality, not only for those who suffer (like the poor) but also for the system as a whole.

The conflict theorists point out that the limited life chances of the lower-class members deprive society of an unknown quantity of talent. A poor family finds it cannot afford to educate a child for a professional career. The parents' expectations of success for the child are also far lower than those of parents in a higher social class, and their motivation to try is correspondingly lower.

[24]Karl Marx and Friedrich Engels, *The Communist Manifesto,* ed. Samuel H. Beer (New York: Appleton-Century-Crofts, 1955).

Today a Rolls Royce costs in the neighborhood of $60,000. What beliefs and values in our culture justify immense inequality in the distribution of social rewards? Does this inequality violate any cultural elements?

CHANEL

Thus, while society as a whole may have broad cultural definitions of success, the lower a person's social class, the lower his or her realistic expectations and definitions of success.

Who knows how many brilliant performers in all the socially valuable fields are lost to the society because they were born into its lower strata? It is naive, the conflict theorists claim, to think that talent and determination consistently rise to the top. In our society it is easier to climb to the top of the ladder if daddy owns the ladder. This may sound cynical, but its truth is borne out by statistical evidence, as we have seen.

Seeing a stratified society as exploitive (the upper strata exploiting the lower) and dysfunctional, conflict theories address themselves to the second question: Must a stratification system have the wide gap between its wealthiest and its poorest members that we see in our society and many others? Consider our welfare programs: we hear some people complain that these programs encourage unemployment (or "laziness") by paying people as much money for not working as they could make on some jobs. The critics claim that the welfare system should be abolished or drastically cut because of this.

A conflict theorist would say this is an effective argument against our class system rather than against the welfare program. After all, the vast majority of welfare recipients have no choice; there are no jobs available within their capabilities that will pay them a living wage. And what must certain job occupants think—of themselves *and* of the system—knowing that their tedious, unprestigious, dirty jobs pay them no more than is received by someone who doesn't work? The solution is not to abolish the welfare system, but rather to redistribute income even more; to reduce the immense differences between the top of the heap and the bottom, so that life chances become more equal; to finally break the chain of social variables that perpetuate poverty by making the children of the poor grow up to be poor themselves.

In your opinion, can the gap between upper and lower classes in the United States be closed? Should it be? If so, how? If not, why not?

SUMMARY

Structured inequality is a feature of virtually every society. That is, the major social rewards—wealth, prestige, and power—are unequally distributed among the members of a society. Sociologists study the number and distinguishing characteristics of the social strata in a society, the distance between top and bottom (measured by social rewards), the possibility of movement up or down among the strata, and the relative size of each stratum.

The two distinctive types of social stratification are the closed, or caste, system and the open system, or meritocracy. In the first, social mobility from one stratum to another is virtually impossible, and the spread of wealth is great, with a few rich and many poor. In an open system, social mobility is possible for everyone according to his or her efforts and abilities, and there are few rich and few poor, with the overwhelming majority living comfortably in between.

These two social systems are ideal types—models against which actual societies can be compared. Modern, industrial societies like our own approach the ideal type of the open system, because an industrial economy, to survive, must reward socially useful talent and skills rather than maintain privileges.

Although American society resembles the open system model, with a large middle class and comparatively few poor and fewer rich, it nevertheless does not offer as much chance for mobility as is generally believed. The lower a person's social class, the fewer the years of schooling, the lower the annual and lifetime income, the earlier marriage takes place, and the larger the number of children born. All these social variables make upward social mobility less likely.

8 RACE AND ETHNICITY

Societies are structured in several ways, as we have seen. They are divided into functional units (such as groups and organizations) and social institutions to meet permanent human needs. They are also divided according to the distribution of economic opportunities, social honor, and access to power. In most modern societies another dimension is important: membership in a particular racial or ethnic group.

Race and ethnicity are based on awareness of differences among people. Ethnic groups are those within a larger society that retain distinctive cultural and social traits. Races are groups of people characterized by shared inherited physical traits that distinguish them from other groups. Racism is an especially intractable modern problem because it is based on a confusion of physical traits and cultural traits.

DOMINANT AND MINORITY GROUPS

A striking feature of many modern nations—from Singapore to the Soviet Union, from Belgium to Brazil, from the Republic of South Africa to the United States of America—is their mixture of peoples. If we were to go down the list of all the countries of the world, we would be hard put to find any whose people were all—or even nearly all—sharers of the same beliefs, norms, and values. Not all are native born, members of the same race, adherents to the same religion, or speakers of the same language. There are few *homogeneous* societies, where everyone is the same in all these features.

Many people believe that *heterogeneity*—a mixture of differences—is preferable to homogeneity. An ideal society is often thought to be made up of people of different races, national origins, and religions living in harmony. Such societies can provide the enriching experience of cultural diversity, whether in the delights of many kinds of dining experiences or in profounder exchanges of insights and ideas among cultures—what sociologists call *cultural diffusion.*

Cultural diffusion: the adoption of a trait or traits from one culture by members of another (discussed in Chapter 14).

This ideal of harmony among different groups is difficult to achieve, however. In many societies throughout the world, races, religions, and ethnic groups often live in constant or intermittent conflict: Protestants and Catholics

in Northern Ireland; Chinese and Malays in Malaysia; Moslems and Hindus in India; blacks and whites in South Africa, the United States, Brazil. In Italy, North African laborers are looked down on; in Switzerland and West Germany, Italian and Turkish "guest workers" are also considered second class.

From our abbreviated list we can see that a feature common to many societies, including our own, is *intergroup conflict:* tensions among groups composed of members who share certain physical or cultural characteristics—such as race, religion, language, or national origin. In intergroup conflict, one group is dominant, having influence or even control over the social opportunities of the other groups. The dominant group almost always enjoys greater privileges. Its members have better schools, jobs, and neighborhoods; they monopolize the wealth, prestige, and power within the society.

Dominant groups usually justify their special position by claiming some kind of superiority. The white- or black- or yellow-skinned group claims that it is on top because it has superior physical, intellectual, or moral qualities. A religious group may claim that it has the only true system of beliefs. A tribe or other cultural group may claim that its value system and lifeways are better than those of others.

Conflict occurs when the subordinate groups reject the dominant group's assessment. Subordinates may say that, ideally, *they* should be on top: "Our people were here first. We have a right to be in control." Others simply seek some sort of equality—political, economic, or religious.

1. List five subordinate groups in our society. Indicate the criteria you use to define them as subordinate.

2. Do you think any of these groups contributes to its own subordination?

3. In what ways do the groups' members resist subordination?

Minority: a group sharing ethnic, racial, or social class status and subordinate to another group. (A "minority" group can actually have larger membership than the dominant group.)

Sociologists use a special term for subordinate groups: *minorities.* A minority may be much larger in sheer numbers than the dominant group. For example, the blacks in Rhodesia and South Africa are minorities in this sense although they vastly outnumber the whites. They are a numerical majority but a sociological minority: they get unequal treatment. Blacks outnumber whites in some parts of the southern United States and in some northern cities. So do Native Americans and Chicanos in some parts of the Southwest. And women are slightly more than half of our society. But if these groups remain subordinate they, too, are sociological minorities.

A minority group in one society may be the majority (dominant) group in another. Jews are dominant in Israel, but in the Soviet Union they are a minority. In Singapore, the Chinese are the most powerful group, while Malays, East Indians, and others are subordinate. But in Los Angeles, San Francisco, New York, and Boston, the Chinese and Chinese-Americans are a distinct minority group.

All minority groups, by definition, share the status of underdog in a society, whether they are a numerical minority or half the population or a numerical majority.

What is the dominant group in the United States? What characteristics (ascribed or achieved positions) do its members have that define them as "the best" or "ideal Americans"? How do these affect the members' attitudes toward different minorities in this country?

RACE: A SOCIALLY CONSTRUCTED REALITY

Socially constructed reality: our perceptions of the physical and social world as governed by our learned beliefs, values, and expectations about it.

From ancient times to the present, the Western world has tended to divide the human species into separate "races." The term *race* has yet to live down a history of careless, fuzzy use. Until only a few generations ago, it was common to hear people talk of the Irish race, the Italian race, and so on. Even today, references to the Jewish race can occasionally be heard, and many persons of Latin American descent refer to themselves as *la raza,* the race. Of course, the most frequently mentioned "races" are the black, white, and yellow.

What is the source of consciousness of "race"? Physical differences are immediately evident to the senses. But this fact hardly tells the whole story. Let's apply a perspective we introduced in Chapter 1, the notion that all reality is "socially constructed": that is, that our perceptions of the world are influenced by the components of our culture. This concept has particular relevance to our understanding of "race" (and of ethnicity, which we will soon discuss).

To begin with, our powers of observation enable us to notice innumerable characteristics of ourselves and others. Many of these characteristics are physical: eye color, height, body mass and muscularity, grace or clumsiness in movement, vitality or lethargy, and numerous others.

One feature that seems constant in human behavior is our mental tendency to organize our observations, to categorize things. Early in history (and probably before history), for a variety of reasons people began using a notion—race—to distinguish one set of physical traits from another, in much the same way that the term *sex,* or gender, distinguishes one set of physical traits from another.

Thus the concept of race was socially constructed: people arbitrarily chose certain physical traits as distinguishing, rather than others, such as height, eye color, or ear size. We have long since forgotten why these traits were chosen rather than others, and we now use the term *race* as if it had an objective validity. It is a socially constructed concept.

If the notion of race were an objective biological term, there would not be so little agreement on how many races there are. The number ranges anywhere from three or four, six or seven or nine, to the thirty-four that Theodosius Dobzhansky claimed to discern.

How useful can a concept like race be if even those who believe in its objective validity cannot agree on a unified description of human physical types? The social construction of the concept is especially evident in our society, where a person to whom minute percentages of "Negro blood" can be traced is considered "black." For example, until 1960 the United States Bureau

Race: biologically, an aggregate of persons who share a composite of genetically transmissible physical traits; socially, a group of people who share physical traits, are considered different from others because of this, and are treated differently.

of the Census gave instructions to its workers to use the following criteria in deciding who was to be listed as Negro: "In addition to persons of Negro and mixed Negro and white descent, this category includes persons of mixed American-Indian and Negro descent, unless the Indian ancestry very definitely predominates or unless the individual is regarded as an Indian in the community." A person who was part black and part Indian once commented bitterly, "Better to be red than black, even an off-shade of red."[1]

What can we conclude from the assertion that race is the product of a socially constructed reality? Clearly the evidence of our senses cannot be denied. People have physical differences, and large numbers of people resemble one another in ways that distinguish them from large numbers of other people. But what we need to keep in mind is the limited significance of that fact.

Many sociologists strive to minimize the importance placed on the notion of race, defining it as an aggregate of persons who share a composite of genetically transmissible physical traits. This rules out mental, moral, or social traits commonly attributed to members of a given race, because they are not genetically transmissible.

Where could such associations of physical traits with behavioral traits have come from? One hypothesis is that human societies have shown a long history of *ethnocentrism* (which we will soon discuss): suspicion of and contempt for other people whose ways are different—whether in language, dress, ideas, social institutions, or other areas. The early Greeks, for example, lumped all non-Greeks together as "barbarians." Now, if these observed cultural and social differences are exhibited by people having observed physical differences, it is likely that prescientific thinkers came to associate the two. This hypothesis is reasonable but not testable, because it involves events in the irretrievable past. If it is correct, then race and racism are as closely linked in their origins as they have been in the history of our society. Then, as now, the link derived from a confusion of physical and cultural traits.

To see how misleading it can be when we confuse physical and cultural traits, consider this: whites and blacks in the American South share more cultural traits with one another than white southerners share with their English ancestors or black southerners share with their African ancestors. They share religion, accent, intensity of patriotism, diet ("soul food" is poor southern cooking—not black or white but both). Yet many white southerners (and northerners) claim to see immense differences between black and white norms and values.

[1]See Brewton Berry, *Almost White* (New York: Macmillan, 1963), p. 161.

Racism: the assumption that those considered members of a given race are inferior to others in mental or moral capabilities.

Every person is physically unique; each looks exactly like no other. Yet gross similarities of skin color, hair texture and other traits often lead us to categorize people according to certain shared physical characteristics. They are labeled "races" by some scientists because they are "aggregates of persons who share a composite of genetically transmissible physical traits." Too often, however, such categories classify wholly unrelated cultural *differences as if they were* physical *differences.*

RACISM

Because of the common confusion of physical and cultural traits, sociologists and other scientists are very careful in defining the notion of race. It is a socially loaded concept, because consciousnesses of race and racism are only a step apart. Racism is the belief that persons in one racial category are, on the average, innately superior or inferior to persons in some other racial group. The most virulent form of this social phenomenon is *institutional racism.*

Consciousness of race and racism are only a step apart. These Ku Klux Klan members are in a sociologically untenable position because they act on the assumption that there are indeed "pure races." In fact, the existence of a pure race is very hard to demonstrate.

Institutional Racism

When the assumption that a minority is inferior is built into the society's ways of dealing with the minority, the resultant patterns of discrimination comprise what is called *institutional racism.* Thus, if our society treats blacks as inferior by herding them into ghettos, keeping them in neighborhood ghetto schools, giving those schools insufficient funding, facilities, and teachers, giving the

Institutional racism is the pattern of discrimination that keeps a racial group in unfavorable social circumstances—poor housing, malnutrition, inadequate education, and inferior job opportunities. "Sociological" racism is the failure to see that such social variables, and not the individual faults of minority group members, have created and maintained their disfavored circumstances.

Institutional racism: enduring patterns of social interaction that express racist assumptions and enforce racial subordination.

ghetto students inadequate training and skills to compete in the job market, and keeping black job applicants out of many higher level jobs because their intelligence or moral qualities are considered questionable (even if they have the required skills), then we have successfully built racism into the system. It has been institutionalized.

Institutionalized racism can be maintained without the force of law, as we have seen in recent decades in our society. Court decisions and federal and state legislation have virtually eliminated the legal bases of this racism. Yet prejudices, discrimination, and even active resistance to black equality have survived throughout our society.

Things were a lot worse for American blacks, however, when institutionalized racism carried the force of law as well. Only a generation ago segregation was established in the statute books. The process of erasing it there was completed only a decade ago. Before that, southern laws had maintained segregated public schools and public facilities. Both privately owned public facilities (such as restaurants, theaters, and department store lunch counters) and municipal facilities (such as swimming pools, playgrounds, transit terminals, and buses) would not serve blacks with whites. Blacks were effectively kept from voting by discriminatory voter registration laws and were forbidden to marry whites by some state statutes.

Institutional racism, by definition, influences dealings with the minority throughout the entire social order. Various segments of society—for example, schools, industries, churches—may systematically deny the minority equal opportunity or even access. Then *everyone* takes part in discriminatory acts simply by attending schools or churches, buying in stores, or working in industries where discrimination is practiced.

List the major social institutions. In which of these do you think certain people are discriminated against? Give three examples of discrimination that appears to be based on the personal behavior of certain individuals. Give three other examples of discrimination that appears to be the practice (stated or unstated) of that particular sphere of social activity.

If the discrimination is built into the basic functioning of that institution, then we can say that institutional racism exists.

An American social scientist, Pierre van den Berghe, doing research in South Africa, described how he felt involved despite himself in the discriminatory policies enforced by the white-dominated government:

I quickly became aware that, try as I may, there was no escape from the color bar, and that I must, however reluctantly, comply with segregation much of the time. Inviting arrest for violation of apartheid regulations would have defeated the purpose of my stay, and besides, jails are also segregated, so that even in prison I should have enjoyed against my will countless special privileges.

Probably to save my self-respect and allay my feelings of guilt, I decided that I would engage in some symbolic protest actions, that I would refuse "customary" white privileges, and that I would break some laws which I considered iniquitous or which exposed my non-white friends to embarrassment. For example, I refused to be served before non-white customers in shops or in government offices; similarly, I filled in the item labeled "race" on official questionnaires with the term "human" or "American," often to see it changed . . . to "white" by a state official who must have wondered at the stupidity of foreigners who do not even know that they belong to the master race. When I invited Africans to my house, I offered them alcoholic beverages, a criminal offense until 1962, and when in the company of non-whites, I always tried to avoid using segregated facilities, or, when I did, I used the non-white ones.

In addition, I broke other laws and regulations not so much on grounds of principle, but because compliance with them would have jeopardized my research more than their evasion. For example, whites are required to carry special permits to enter most African "locations" and "reserves." I entered such places countless times without ever asking for a permit. . . .[Whenever I was caught in a violation] my skin color . . . protected me. . . . , and I always got away with a warning. Most of the time I pretended to have lost my way, and the police gave me elaborate road directions, while commenting on the danger of traveling unarmed in "Native areas." Had I had a black skin, of course, I would have been repeatedly arrested and convicted for "pass" offenses. Even in my defiance of the law, I was given preferential and often deferential treatment, simply because of my lack of pigmentation.[2]

Sociological Racism

Sociological racism: the belief that individual members of a racial minority are responsible for their socially disadvantaged status.

Institutional racism is a self-fulfilling prophecy. When a society as a whole treats a minority as inferior and contemptible, the minority has little chance of behaving differently. Failure to recognize this fact has been called *sociological racism.* This recent social phenomenon, named by Howard Schuman, might better be called social racism, because it has nothing to do with sociology or sociologists.[3] It is the failure of people to attribute minority problems to the social variables that comprise institutional racism. The term describes the thinking of people who do not consider blacks innately inferior to whites but

[2]Pierre van den Berghe, "Research in South Africa," in *Ethics, Politics, and Social Research,* ed. Gideon Sjoberg (New York: Shenkman, 1967), pp. 185–86.

[3]Howard Schuman, "Sociological Racism," *Trans-Action,* December 1969, pp. 44–48.

nevertheless believe that blacks themselves are responsible for their disadvantaged position in society.

Schuman took as his starting point two surveys, one in 1942 and the other in 1956. Whites were asked whether they considered blacks to be as intelligent as whites. In 1942, some 42 percent thought they were; in 1956, it was 78 percent, with most of the increase in the South. Schuman then approached people with this survey question: "On the average, Negroes in this city have worse jobs, education, and housing than whites. Do you think this is mainly due to Negroes having been discriminated against, or mainly due to something about Negroes themselves?" The answers were:

54 percent: the problem was Negroes themselves

19 percent: it was that plus discrimination

19 percent: the problem was discrimination

4 percent: the premise was not accurate; blacks were indeed better off

4 percent: didn't know

To the question, "Why don't they do better?" the answers were:

8 percent: innate differences

25 percent: lack of education; poverty cycle

57 percent: lack of motivation

10 percent: didn't know

Social variables: the variables of societal membership, such as class, ethnicity, sex, religion, race, education, and level of technology, that influence the individual's behavior in a society.

Thus those who blamed lack of motivation outnumbered those who believed innate differences were the factor by seven to one. But those who saw social variables—institutional racism—at work numbered less than half those who laid the failing on blacks themselves.

ETHNICITY AND ETHNOCENTRISM

Often physical characteristics play little or no role in distinguishing one group from another in a heterogeneous society. Differences in national origin, whether or not accompanied by distinctive physical traits, have been the reason for ethnic groupings. Ethnic groups can be identified by any combination of distinctive patterns of family life, language, recreation, religion, and other customs. Many ethnic groups live—by force, by choice, or by lack of oppor-

Swedish immigrants to the United States often were confronted with the unpleasant stereotype of the "dumb Swede." Yet the people shown here are among those who founded the city of Lindsborg, Kansas, complete with a college, soon after their arrival.

Ethnicity: the condition of being distinct from other groups in the society in race, national origin, or religion.

tunity—in their own sectors or neighborhoods. Members of ethnic groups feel a closeness with those who share their traditions and their status in society.

Ethnicity refers to the importance of ethnic identity to individuals, groups, or societies. A person's ethnicity reflects how much he or she feels (or is made to feel) part of an ethnic group. Here is how one Polish-American worker describes himself:

> My family has been here for four generations; that's a lot. My great-grandfather came over here, from near Cracow. I've never been to Poland. I'll never go there. Why should I? It's in your blood. It's in your background. But I live *here*. My wife is the same, Polish. We're just like other people in this country, but we have memories, Polish memories, that's what my grandfather used to say: "John, don't let your kids forget that once upon a time the family was in Poland!" How *could* I forget? My wife won't let me. She says you have to stay with your own people. We don't have only Polish people living near us, but there are a lot. Mostly we see my family and my wife's family on the weekends, so there's no time to spend doing anything else. . . .
>
> I don't know who's *really* an American. There are guys I work with, they're Italian and Irish. They're different from me, even though we're all Catholics. You see what I mean? We're buddies on the job. We do the same work. We drink our coffee together and sit there eating lunch. But you leave and you go home and you're back with your own people. I don't just mean my family, no. It's more than your wife and kids; it's everything in your life.[4]

[4]Robert Coles, *The Middle Americans* (Boston: Little, Brown, 1971), pp. 43–44.

Immigration by Region of Origin, 1860–1920

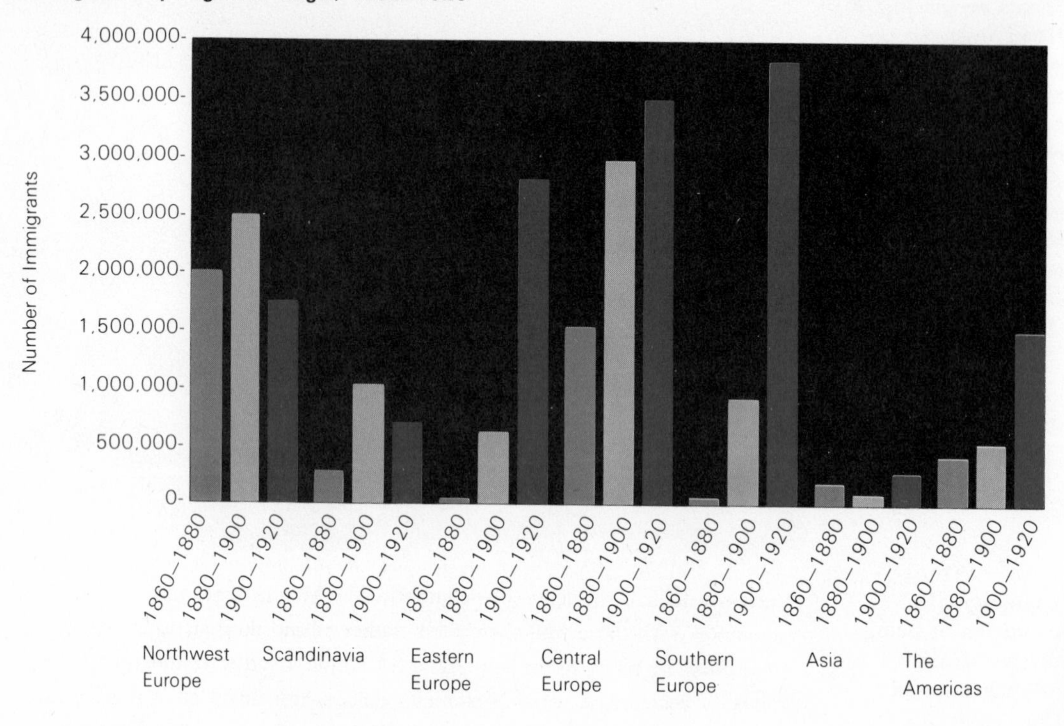

Northwest Europe = Great Britain, Ireland, Netherlands, Belgium, Luxembourg, Switzerland, France
Scandinavia = Norway, Sweden, Denmark, Iceland
Eastern Europe = Soviet Union, Latvia, Estonia, Lithuania, Finland, Rumania, Bulgaria, (European) Turkey
Central Europe = Germany, Poland, Hungary, Austria
Southern Europe = Italy, Spain, Portugal, Greece
Asia = China, Japan
The Americas = Canada, Newfoundland, Mexico, South America

Source: Allen Weinstein and R. Jackson Wilson, *Freedom and Crisis* (New York: Random House, 1974), p. 499. © 1974, reprinted by permission.

Ethnic pride is not limited to minority groups. Members of dominant groups may also express pride in their ancestry and the achievements of their people. Another American worker might describe himself and his "people" by saying:

> I'm an American. White. Protestant. American. My ancestors settled this country, and I'm proud of them. They brought civilization to this continent. They built it. I get excited when I go to Deerfield and see the old tavern or to Williamsburg. I love the fife and drum corps on the Fourth of July. After all, those are my people. No nonsense. Proud. Good American stock.

Ethnocentrism: the belief that our own group has superior moral standards, beliefs, or ways of behaving to those of others.

Ethnicity is yet another feature of the social construction of reality. Cultural differences are seen as crucial barriers, dividing lines between "us" and "them." Thus ethnicity can give rise to the same connection as in racism between difference and an assumption of inferiority. In 1906, the American sociologist William Graham Sumner introduced the concept of *ethnocentrism.* He defined it as a tendency by members of a group "to exaggerate and intensify everything in their own folkways . . . which differentiates them from others."[5] He emphasized that this sharpens distinctions between the members of the group and others, between "we" and "they." In such distinctions, there is obviously the implication of prejudice that follows from ethnicity. In our cities especially, wave after wave of immigrants arrived from foreign shores to find themselves unwelcome or only grudgingly accepted. The last ethnic group to arrive was generally the underdog and had to fight its way out of both poverty and disgrace for being Italian or Irish or Polish or Hungarian or Armenian or Jewish.

Ethnocentrism reached its most extreme form early in this century. A group of supposed scientists (later discredited), called *eugenicists,* claimed to have made tests of various immigrant groups awaiting entry into this country. They said they found high percentages of "feeblemindedness" among those from southern and eastern Europe. On the basis of these "findings" (and the popularity of the "science" of eugenics) the 1924 immigration laws set up quotas restricting entry of these groups. Later, in an age more sophisticated about testing, researchers discovered that the eugenicists' so-called intelligence tests were actually tests of a foreigner's familiarity with American culture![6]

[5]William Graham Sumner, *Folkways* (Boston: Ginn, 1906), p. 15.

[6]For an overview of American immigration patterns, policies, and problems, see Benjamin M. Ziegler, ed., *Immigration, an American Dilemma* (Boston: D.C. Heath, 1967).

(This same cultural bias raises problems in administering IQ tests to our own minorities today.)

A few familiar examples illustrate the results of narrow, ethnocentric thinking.

Jonathan's isolation. Jonathan Levy, now an adult, clearly remembers his first day in a rural school after his family moved to a border town in upstate New York. At recess, he and his classmates went out to the playground. One tall boy jumped on a step and shouted, "All you Hebes and Frogs over there; the rest of us good guys over here." He was kidding, but neither Jonathan nor the four French-Canadian boys in the class were very amused.

Nobody else came to school. The time was 1968. All schools in the state were being desegregated. Willie Jones's old school for the "colored children," Booker T. Washington Junior High, was being closed. Willie was pleased to be going to a new school, with good equipment, a decent library, and a science lab. He wanted to be a chemist.

With three other black youngsters, Willie set out for the junior high—and

In our society, ethnocentrism reached perhaps its strongest pitch in the early twentieth century, when eugenicists were offering "scientific proof" that immigrants from southern and eastern Europe were mentally and morally inferior to the older settlers from northwestern Europe. Time showed that many of the most valuable contributors to our intellectual and cultural life were the descendents of these "inferior" immigrants.

a new life—one bright day. He had heard there might be trouble, but he felt the rumor was being circulated merely to prepare him for getting the cold shoulder from his new white classmates. What he got was more than a cold shoulder. No one else showed up! The integration order at Robert E. Lee Regional had prompted a boycott by white parents and their children.

Czelusniak, Mary. Applications were being sorted for the job of receptionist at the Modern Talent Company. The supervisor, Sally Adams, was thumbing through the list of those who had come in that morning.

''Aldrich, Jane,'' she said under her breath.

''Andrews, Elizabeth,''

''Baker, Carol,''

''Brian, Margaret,''

''Czelusniak, Mary,''

''Danvers, Elizabeth,''

Ms. Adams paused for a moment. She flipped back to the previous card,

''Czelusniak, Czelusniak,'' she thought to herself. ''I really wonder if she'd fit in.''

ETHNIC STRATIFICATION

In the 1973 film comedy *Blazing Saddles,* a black sheriff agrees to take extraordinary measures to save a town from marauding bandits—on one condition: that the townspeople yield some agricultural land to several black railroad crew workers. The townsfolk resist the suggestion, but eventually their plight persuades them to agree. "All right," says their spokesman, "the niggers can live with us. But," he adds emphatically, "*no Irish!*"

This crude joke is true to history. We're used to thinking of nonwhites (blacks chiefly, but also Mexican-Americans, Puerto Ricans, Chinese-Americans, and others) as the lowest placed of our ethnic groups. However, in the mid-nineteenth century, the blacks in our northern cities commonly referred to the Irish as "white niggers."

Here we see a vivid illustration of what sociologists call *ethnic stratification;* a pecking order among ethnic groups. As we said earlier, the last ethnic group to arrive in this country has generally been the lowest on the social ladder. (Native Americans and blacks are notable exceptions.) Ethnic groups are not necessarily united with one another by their shared minority status or even outright oppression.

For example, the blacks are far and away our most numerous nonwhite minority: there are six times as many black Americans as Mexican-Americans, the next largest group (if this group is considered nonwhite). In the last two decades, blacks have been the most persistent, forceful, and successful of the nonwhite minorities in overcoming institutional racism. They led the way, finding techniques for confronting the system and for confronting the psychological results of racism within themselves. "Black power," "black pride," and "black is beautiful" entered the consciousness of Americans—black, white, Mexican-American, Native American, Chinese-American, Puerto Rican.

Ethnic stratification is found in many societies. In South Africa the descendents of the Dutch and English settlers have the favored positions. Then come the Jews (mostly from Eastern Europe), the Asians (mainly from India), and the Cape Coloured (people of mixed racial ancestry). At the bottom are the native blacks. Each group enjoys less power and social prestige than the one above.

In some new African nations, the rank order of various groups has changed. White colonials used to be on the top, followed by Asians, and then Africans. Now Africans are on top, then come whites, and Asians are at the bottom.

1. Does ethnic stratification exist in the United States? If so, how do you think various ethnic groups rank in social status?

2. How does ethnic stratification affect the distribution of social rewards—wealth, prestige, and power?

3. How would laws that forbade various kinds of discrimination (civil rights legislation) affect ethnic stratification in a society? Explain.

4. Has civil rights legislation been effective in breaking down ethnic stratification in the United States?

PREJUDICE AND DISCRIMINATION: ATTITUDES AND BEHAVIOR

Prejudice: negative attitudes toward all members of a given group.

We have discussed racism and ethnocentrism; both are particular forms of what is commonly called *prejudice.* As used by most sociologists, prejudice refers to negative attitudes toward a group of people. Like all attitudes, prejudice involves beliefs, feelings, and action orientations. Beliefs are things we think we know although we can't prove them (such as "America is the greatest nation

Whites, in Selma, Alabama, 1963, taunt two black girls in reaction to the civil rights movement, which was then approaching its peak. They are acting discriminatorily on the basis of their prejudiced beliefs about blacks.

Discrimination: social patterns or behavior that disfavors members of a group or groups.

on earth"). Feelings are emotional responses (such as getting anxious when we anticipate a meeting with a member of a particular group). Action orientations are the things we decide to do (such as avoiding contact, or putting on a good front, or punching somebody). Harmful action against a minority group is called *discrimination.*

Although they are frequently opposite sides of the same coin, prejudice and discrimination are separate concepts. They should not be confused. The difference between prejudice as an attitude and discrimination as behavior was summed up several years ago by an English judge. He was talking to nine young people convicted of race rioting in the Notting Hill section of London:

> Everyone irrespective of the color of his skin is entitled to walk through our streets with head held erect and free from fear. . . . These courts will uphold [these rights]. . . . Think what you like. . . . But once you translate your dark thoughts into savage acts, the law will punish you, and protect your victim.[7]

Discrimination includes any *outward* expression that affects others. The children's chant, "Sticks and stones may break my bones, but names will never hurt me," is simply not true. Name-calling, the use of words like "nigger," "kike," "spic," or "mex," hurt plenty. They are clear examples of discriminatory behavior. So are other verbal insults, such as the use of disparaging language ("jew him down"), colloquial expressions containing racial slurs ("nigger in the woodpile"), or ethnic jokes ("Did you hear the one about the two Poles . . . ").

Robert K. Merton[8] has offered a typology of four sets of belief and behavior patterns as they relate to prejudice and discrimination:

1. **the unprejudiced nondiscriminator**
2. **the unprejudiced discriminator**
3. **the prejudiced nondiscriminator**
4. **the prejudiced discriminator**

Think of examples to illustrate each of these four types, in light of your understanding of the meanings of *prejudice* and *discrimination.*

[7] *Time,* September 29, 1958, p. 58.

[8] See Robert K. Merton, "Discrimination and the American Creed," in *Discrimination and National Welfare,* ed. R. M. MacIver (New York: Harper and Row, 1949).

Avoidance

Avoidance: patterns of interaction that minimize contact between one group and another or others.

Not all discrimination is verbal. Direct action is often involved. It ranges from simple avoidance (members of the dominant group stay away from others) to violence—even mass violence. Exclusive clubs, fraternities, and other private organizations, whose membership is limited to those with the "proper" racial or ethnic credentials, are practicing avoidance (although they may employ members of the excluded minorities in subservient jobs: the black chef, the Puerto Rican busboy).

The avoidance pattern of behavior accounts for much of the move to the suburbs that has occurred since World War II. At first, people were primarily seeking more appealing and relaxed living conditions. Then, as whites who had the money to move left the city, *urban succession* occurred: nonwhites and ethnic minorities flocked to the central cities in search of jobs; as their numbers grew, more middle-class whites left the cities. For many of these, the desire for more pleasant surroundings was mingled with the desire to avoid contact with the minorities.[9]

[9]Robert Park and Ernest Burgess wrote extensively on the characteristic population distribution of urban areas. They found that, as ethnic groups came to the cities, they flocked together to form cultural islands (ethnic enclaves). See Robert E. Park, Ernest W. Burgess, and Robert D. McKenzie, *The City* (Chicago: University of Chicago Press, 1925.)

Segregation, legal isolation of one race from another, is a form of denial. Ironically blacks were employed in menial jobs in places where they would not be admitted or served as patrons.

Denial

Denial: avoidance achieved by excluding a minority group from participation in given social patterns.

Avoidance is directly linked to denial. To be exclusive means to deny others access—to certain organizations, places, forms of wealth, goals, and activities. When customs or laws forbid contact between certain groups, we call this practice *segregation.* In a segregated society, not only is access limited to a select few, but also barriers are set up to keep all members of a minority group "in their place." Residential segregation, school segregation, and occupational segregation are three obvious examples.

Patterns of residential segregation vary. The urban succession of nonwhites in the central cities of the North created ghettos—slum neighborhoods in which minorities, by informal pressure, are forced to live, because owners refuse to rent or sell housing to them in other areas of a city. This is known as *de facto* segregation: segregation by nonlegal means, as opposed to *de jure* segregation, which is segregation actually written into the laws of a city, county, state, or nation.

Segregation: maintaining separation of two or more groups by laws or strongly enforced customs.

Until 1954, separate schooling of blacks and whites was the accepted practice in the United States. Although the Supreme Court decision in *Brown* v. *Board of Education* that year forbade de jure segregation, de facto segregation has stubbornly resisted opposition for over two decades. Segregated residential patterns have made de facto segregation possible: if the neighborhoods are segregated, neighborhood schools will be, too. People fighting against busing children to schools out of their neighborhoods seek to maintain de facto segregation.

Children usually go to school in their neighborhoods, since these are the schools that are easiest to reach. Neighborhoods are usually composed of residents with similar economic situations. As people achieve more economic success, they usually attempt to move to "better" neighborhoods.

Advocates of busing often argue that children from poorer families would benefit from the type of schooling that more well-to-do children receive, as well as from contact with these better students in the classroom.

Foes of busing argue, in response, that they have worked hard to achieve economic success so that they can move out of the inner city and, as a result, want their children to remain in the neighborhood schools, close to home.

Have four students debate the following topic, in teams of two:

Resolved: Children should not be forced by law to leave their neighborhoods to go to school.

Physical aggression is one mode of maintaining a pattern of discrimination. Here black participants in the civil rights movement of the 1960s are blasted with the spray from fire hoses in Birmingham, Alabama. The high-pressure jets of water could inflict internal injuries. Elsewhere in the South electric cattle prods and police attack dogs were used against blacks in the movement.

Segregation at work follows from and is followed by other forms of discrimination. Minorities in segregated neighborhoods go to segregated schools, which often receive inadequate funding and provide inferior education. The children are less prepared for higher education or higher status work. Their lower paying jobs keep them in poverty so that they cannot move out of the ghetto even when segregation cracks a bit. Thus, as we saw in Chapter 7 on stratification, social status is perpetuated from one generation to another. Each form of discrimination contributes to the effectiveness of others. The concept of life chances, also examined in Chapter 7, demonstrates how segregation is maintained.

Physical Aggression

The most extreme form of discrimination is physical aggression directed at individuals of minority groups. Sometimes violence is spontaneous; often it is planned. Harassment, fighting, bombing, and lynching are but a few of the activities people have experienced under the heading of physical aggression.

The legal structure can assist in a pattern of aggression. Blacks in the South and in northern cities have been found guilty by all-white juries and been given harsh sentences by white judges for minor crimes, while whites, including law officers, who commit major crimes against blacks receive little or no punishment. In recent times, blacks have seen some improvements take place. For example, Joan Little, a young black woman, stabbed her white jailer to death with an ice pick after he allegedly forced her to perform an oral sex act. In the summer of 1975, she was acquitted of murder by a southern jury of six blacks and six whites.

THE SOCIAL ROOTS OF PREJUDICE

We've discussed the major social forms of prejudice—racism and ethnocentrism—and their frequent social consequence, discrimination. What accounts for prejudice, though? Why do real or imagined differences in physical or cultural characteristics lead us to have prejudices, to believe that people who are different are inferior?

Sociologists suggest three dimensions—the psychological, the cultural, and the structural—that may be at work singly or in combination creating patterns of prejudice. Let's look briefly at each.

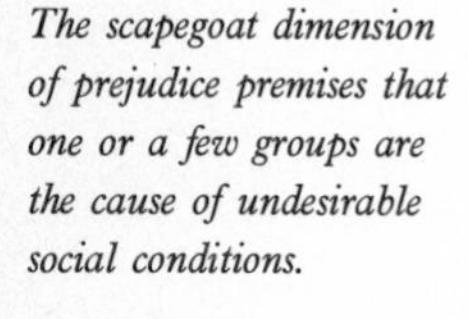

The scapegoat dimension of prejudice premises that one or a few groups are the cause of undesirable social conditions.

This nation's history contains innumerable instances of violation of Native American treaty rights. Settlers of European origin often deceived and brutalized the Indian. The Nez Percé was only one of many tribes that suffered greatly from governmental and civilian abuses. Its leader, Chief Joseph, was a man of great integrity and courage. At his death, the attending physician (a white man) said he had died of a broken heart at the wrongs his people had suffered. Yet settlers accused these "redskins" of being treacherous and warlike. This blight on United States history is an instance of projection: accusing others of traits we cannot admit to having ourselves.

Anti-Semitism goes back to ancient European history. At various periods Jews suffered ghettoization, institutional discrimination, and expulsion from continental nations. The Nazi ascent to power in Germany in the 1930s brought the greatest atrocities. Nazism stressed the notion of a superior race of Aryans and condemned Jews as a lowly "race." Millions were massacred by the Nazis in extermination camps.

The Psychological Dimension

Scapegoat: in relation to prejudice, a group wrongly blamed as the source of problems or frustrations.

Within the psychological dimension of prejudice there are three separate theories: the scapegoat; projection; and the authoritarian personality. In the scapegoat theory, when people are kept from achieving their goals but cannot directly attack the obstacle stopping them (whether it is an employer, say, or the state of the economy), they turn their frustration on another person or group. A man frustrated in his office work might abuse his wife or children instead of confronting his boss.

In the 1920s Germany suffered severe economic collapse when the victorious nations in World War I imposed punishing peace terms on the Germans. Anti-Semitism reached a fever pitch in the defeated country, especially among the marginal members of the middle class: those lowest in that class who suffered economic dislocations first and most severely. The Jews were blamed for the nation's economic and social disorders.

Projection: in relation to prejudice, ascribing to members of another group traits we cannot admit to having ourselves.

In the projection theory, when people cannot admit that they have undesirable characteristics or behavior, they assign these faults to others. Thus, in the South, white men were inhibited in their sex drives by puritanical codes that acclaimed the virtue of white women; they then developed the myth that black men were highly oversexed and obsessed with desire for white women.

In many Western cultures, Jews have been portrayed as greedy and untrustworthy in business. The "international Jewish banker conspiracy" once flourished alongside its opposite projection, "the international Jewish Communist conspiracy": Jews were supposedly obsessed with both amassing as much personal wealth as possible and trying to overthrow the government to establish

Authoritarian personality: a personality type that is very conventional, is intolerant of variants in behavior and custom, and believes in a strong central authority.

a system in which personal wealth could not be amassed at all.

The authoritarian personality theory was developed by the research of Theodor Adorno and others during World War II.[10] They hypothesized that a particular personality type—the authoritarian personality—was prone to prejudice. An individual with this personality type strongly believes that people need control by a powerful and severe central authority. Authoritarian people are extremely conservative and conventional, and they are intolerant of variety in behavior, values, or beliefs. Thus, if an ethnic group strays, in its culture, from the narrow, rigid norms approved of by an authoritarian, that group is a likely target of his or her hatred. The reaction is especially pronounced if the group's cultural differences are accompanied by physical differences.

Gordon Allport and Leo Postman conducted a study on the phenomenon of spreading rumors, using the technique called *serial reproduction.* They showed a subject a picture of a subway scene in which a white man and a black man were standing next to each other. The white was dressed in work clothes and had an open razor stuck in his belt. (This is a stereotype of *blacks* that many whites have.) The subject was asked to describe the picture to a second subject; the second subject described it to a third; the third to a fourth; and so on. After a series of descriptions had been made, the last one was compared with the original picture to see what differences had been introduced.

Conduct a similar study of your own. Select an appropriate picture, and test the results of serial reproduction of a description of it by various types of subject groups (such as blacks, whites, children, women, professors, randomly selected subjects). How do the final descriptions compare with the original picture? How does the composition of the subject group affect the comparison? How do you explain the differences in results from different groups?

(Allport and Postman found that, among white subjects, the final description in half of the experiments indicated that the black man had the open razor. Among black subjects and young child subjects this transfer did not occur.)[11]

[10]See Theodore W. Adorno et al., *The Authoritarian Personality* (New York: Harper and Row, 1950).

[11]Gordon W. Allport and Leo J. Postman, "Analysis of Rumor," *Public Opinion Quarterly* 10 (1946): 501–17.

The cultural dimension of prejudice is akin to sociological racism. Onlookers see the results of institutional racism and discrimination but place the blame on the victims rather than on social variables. Native Americans, stripped of their culture and placed on reservations, or forced to live in ghettos elsewhere, are seen as people who fail to adapt rather than as victims of discrimination.

The Cultural Dimension

Cultural prejudice: prejudiced attitudes and stereotypes absorbed during socialization.

During the process of socialization, when we are learning the beliefs, norms, and values of our culture, we are also likely to learn whatever prejudices are predominant in the society or region or in our social class. Our methods of learning are diverse. We may pick up the derogatory words that are applied to ethnic groups. The tone of their use clearly conveys the attitudes behind them. We may be told outright that certain people are beneath us, just too inferior for us to associate with.

We also learn prejudices from ethnic stereotypes: Italians are linked with the Mafia; the Irish are heavy drinkers; Indians are bloodthirsty savages; blacks are typified by Stepin Fetchit or Amos and Andy. The resentment of each group at this "type-casting" shows that such stereotypes can have a deep social impact.

Sociological racism, presented earlier in the chapter, clearly applies here as well.

Not only do stereotypes reinforce our attitude of prejudice, but they also affect our perceptions of minorities. When large numbers of blacks are unemployed, we may "see" that they are lazy, shiftless, and irresponsible rather than unable to find work. When Native Americans have a high rate of alcoholism, we may see this as a racially inherited moral weakness rather than as a response to the impotence, poverty, and despair of life on a reservation or in a ghetto.

Daniel Katz and K. W. Braly studied racial and ethnic stereotypes in the 1930s by asking subjects to choose the traits they associated with Americans, Blacks, Chinese, English, Germans, Irish, Italians, Japanese, Jews, and Turks.[12] They discovered a fair degree of unanimity about the traits listed below, which were associated with the groups identified by initials in parentheses.

scientific (G)
industrious (G, Je, A, Ja)
artistic (It)
sportsmanlike (E)
shrewd (Je)
cruel (T)
lazy (B)
superstitious (B, C)
stolid (G)
conscious of duty (G)
impulsive (It)
passionate (It)
warm-blooded (It)
musical (It)
religious (T)
treacherous (T)
happy-go-lucky (B)
ignorant (B)
pugnacious (Ir)
quick-tempered (Ir)
intelligent (E, A, Ja)
conventional (E)
traditional (E)
mercenary (Je)
materialistic (A)
ambitious (A)
democratic (A)
shy (C)
poor (C)
conservative (C)
progressive (Ja)

This study was done in 1933. If it were repeated in the 1970s, would the results be the same? Would the stereotypes hold up today? What changes would you expect to have taken place? Why?

Cultural prejudice can place a minority group in a double bind: the society discriminates against the minority to keep it in the low strata and then justifies its prejudice against the minority because it is so lowly in social position. This double bind brings us to the last dimension of prejudice.

[12]Daniel Katz and K. W. Braly, "Racial Stereotypes of 100 College Students," *Journal of Abnormal Psychology* 28 (1933): 280–90.

The Structural Dimension

Again, the structural dimension has to do with patterns of interaction that comprise the social organization.

In the mid-nineteenth century a southern apologist for slavery, George Fitzhugh, claimed that economically and socially the black slaves in the South were far better off than free, white workers of the North—who were "wage slaves." Fitzhugh wrote:

> We would remind those who deprecate and sympathize with negro slavery, that his slavery here . . . Christianizes, protects, supports and civilizes him; that it governs him far better than free laborers at the North are governed. . . . Our negroes are not only better off as to physical comfort than free laborers but their moral condition is better. . . . the masters in free society, or slave society, if they perform properly their duties, have more cares and less liberty than the slaves themselves. . . . our negro mechanics do not work so hard, have many more privileges and holidays, and are better fed and clothed than field hands, and are yet more valuable to their masters. The slaves of the South are cheated of their rights by the purchase of Northern manufactures which they could produce. Besides, if we would employ our slaves in the coarser processes of the mechanic arts and manufacturers . . . we would find a vent in new employments for their increase, more humane and more profitable than the vent afforded by new states and territories.[13]

Few northern workers were avid abolitionists. They were not indifferent to slavery or in agreement with southern slaveowners, but many believed that emancipation of the slaves would increase competition for work in the industrial cities of the North. Thus, the abolition of slavery threatened their job security.

The structural dimension of prejudice: economic, social, and political benefits that accrue to others through the exploitation of particular minorities.

This was one example of an economic motive for favoring discrimination in its most extreme form, slavery. Slaves provided cheap labor for the southern plantation owner and kept this part of the population out of the urban industrial job market. Now, long after slavery has ended, we can still theorize about the economic motives behind racism: to keep a class of people permanently at the bottom to do the dirty work of society.

The double bind we mentioned in discussing the cultural dimension of prejudice is related to this structural dimension. The cultural content of racism or ethnocentrism—our myths about a minority and our attitudes toward it—justify our patterns of exploitive stratification. These myths *rationalize* (give us reasons for) keeping a group or groups at the bottom of the social ladder.

[13]George Fitzhugh, *Sociology for the South, or Failure of Free Society* (Richmond, Va.: A. Morris, 1854), pp. 84–87.

The double bind of prejudice and discrimination: the stereotype assigned to a group justifies patterns of discrimination against it, and the consequences of discrimination in turn are used to "prove" the validity of the stereotype. Until only a few decades ago blacks were said to be lazy, childlike, happy-go-lucky creatures who "knew their place" (at the bottom of society). This patronizing stereotype was customarily embodied by whites in "black face" who performed as minstrels and sang such "darky tunes" as "Old Black Joe" (nearly all of which were written by whites). Today blacks are no longer assigned that image but their struggle for improved social status continues.

Gregory Razran performed a study in 1950 to test ethnic dislikes and stereotypes.[14] He took photos of thirty girls. Then he asked test subjects to judge each photo on a five-point scale indicating how they liked each girl generally and how they rated her beauty, her intelligence, her character, her ambition, and her ability to be entertaining.

He later showed the subjects the same photos labeled with ethnic surnames (Jewish, Italian, Irish, old American). He found that the labels affected the subjects' perceptions of the girls. The same photos were given different ratings on various traits associated with stereotypes of ethnic groups.

With the assistance of your instructor, select a dozen photos of people and draw up a questionnaire similar to Razran's. Identify a study population (your instructor will determine the number of subjects). Test your subjects' responses before and after the photos are labeled with ethnic names. Compare your findings with Razran's, referring to his article, if possible.

REACTIONS TO DISCRIMINATION

In the various societies that have patterns of ethnic stratification, minority groups make a variety of responses to their plight. The black poet Langston Hughes explored some of the reactions of an ethnic group that society keeps from fulfilling its dreams.

> What happens to a dream deferred?
> Does it dry up
> like a raisin in the sun?
> Or fester like a sore—
> And then run?
> Does it stink like rotten meat?
> Or crust and sugar over—
> like a syrupy sweet?
> Maybe it just sags
> like a heavy load.
> *Or does it explode?*[15]

For many black Americans, the dream deferred is "the American dream" of freedom, equality, and unrestricted opportunities for achievement.

[14]Gregory Razran, "Ethnic Dislikes and Stereotypes: A Laboratory Study," *Journal of Abnormal Psychology* 45 (1950): 7–27.

[15]© 1951 by Langston Hughes, reprinted from *The Panther and the Lash: Poems of Our Times,* by Langston Hughes, by permission of Alfred A. Knopf, Inc.

Submission

Submission: acceptance by a minority of the dominant group's stereotype of it.

Translating Hughes's poetic phrases into concrete examples, we note that some people "dry up," or submit to their treatment. A militant black leader of the early 1960s, Malcolm X, said that one of white people's worst crimes was to teach blacks to hate themselves.[16] Many minority group members internalize the stereotypes the majority has of them. In earlier decades, psychological tests of black children revealed they had low esteem for blackness. More recent tests, however, show much higher self-esteem among black children.[17]

With the rise of a broad-based, active, civil rights movement came an attack on minority members who submitted to the stereotypes and played the debasing roles. Such blacks were scornfully called Uncle Toms. Later, Mexican-Americans who behaved like their stereotypes were called Tio Tacos, and Native Americans who did so were called Uncle Tomahawks.

Other members of minorities, faced with prejudice and discrimination, seek to escape the stereotypes by separating themselves from the group. They may change their names (from Feldman to Mansfield, for example). Some have their eyes or noses "fixed" by plastic surgery to make them more like those of the dominant group. Some straighten their hair or attempt to lighten their skin color.

Sometimes minority members make these changes in an attempt to "pass" into the majority society. Then, they think, they will finally be accepted by those who say their group is inferior. More often than not, however, they find themselves trapped between the ethnic or racial world from which they want to escape and the majority's world in which they never feel quite comfortable. Their attempts at disguising or minimizing their membership in a minority group are often directed more at themselves than at others. They adopt the notions of beauty accepted (or imposed) by the majority. They become ashamed of their dark skin or kinky hair or Jewish nose and wish to improve their self-image by changing these features.

Some minority group members go farther still—quite literally. They leave the country, seeking refuge in places that are less hostile to their ethnic

[16]See Malcolm X, *Malcolm X Speaks: Selected Speeches and Statements,* ed. George Breitman (New York: Merit Publishers, 1965).

[17]See Kenneth B. Clark and Mamie P. Clark, "Emotional Factors in Racial Identification and Preferences in Negro Children," *Journal of Negro Education* 19, no. 3 (1950): 341–50; *Psychiatric Aspects of Desegregation,* report no. 37 (New York: Group for the Advancement of Psychiatry, 1957); James A. Banks and Jean D. Grambs, *Black Self-Concept: Implications for Education and Social Sciences* (New York: McGraw-Hill, 1972); Donald Cleveland, Jr., "Black Students," in *Through Different Eyes,* ed. Peter I. Rose et al. (New York: Oxford University Press, 1973), pp. 377–92.

Until black pride grew out of the civil rights movement, many blacks held an ideal of physical attractiveness that was based on white middle-class standards. This Harlem billboard advertised a black beauty contest in 1963.

group. American blacks settled in Europe, especially Paris, in the early part of this century and again, though in smaller numbers, after World War II. Thousands of Jews left their European homes to come to the United States, Canada, and Latin America in flight from Nazism in the 1930s. And in the early decades of this century there was a flourishing back-to-Africa movement among American blacks, inspired by Marcus Garvey.[18]

Imitation of the Dominant Society

Imitation: the creation by a minority group of patterns of behavior that parallel those of the dominant group.

Instead of submitting to the views of others or fleeing from the group or the country, many members of ethnic groups assert themselves in ways that parallel the dominant group. They set up separate schools, businesses, social clubs, and the like. A number of years ago, most campus fraternities and sororities excluded non-Christians from joining. Jewish students therefore created their own. The pages of black magazines, such as *Ebony, Jet,* and *Tan,* used to be filled with stories of fancy balls and parties that were mirrors of those held by and for wealthy white people. Perhaps these are the "syrupy sweets" Langston Hughes was talking about.

[18]See John H. Clarke, ed., *Marcus Garvey and the Vision of Africa* (New York: Random House, 1974); Amy Jacques Garvey, *Garvey and Garveyism* (New York: Collier, 1970).

Effect of 1965 Voting Rights Act on Registration of Southern Blacks

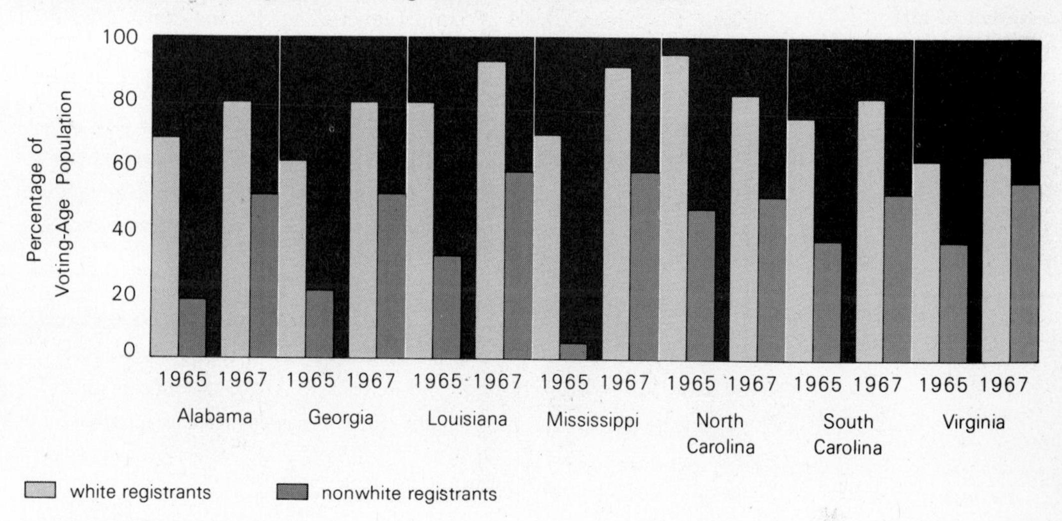

Source: From *American Political Behavior* by Howard D. Mehlinger and John J. Patrick, © Copyright, 1972, by Indiana University. Used by permission of the publisher, Ginn and Company (Xerox Corporation).

Challenging Discrimination

Many members of minority groups have grown tired of trying to reconcile themselves to continuing subordination. They want to lift the "heavy load" of discrimination from their backs, and they have reacted in a variety of ways. As Langston Hughes predicted, there have been explosions of pent-up frustration. The outbursts have taken many different forms and occurred in many different locations. Some of the explosions have been in the courts, some in the streets, some in the minds of both oppressors and oppressed.

Many of the changes that we have witnessed in recent years are the result of two types of challenges to discrimination: the civil rights movement challenged the system to practice the values expressed in the United States Constitution; the ethnic pride movements challenge minorities to stop accepting other people's definitions of their alleged inferiority, to discover and exult in their own accomplishments.

The civil rights and ethnic pride movements are two examples of social movements, which are discussed in Chapter 15.

The civil rights movement. Blacks were the earliest minority to launch both movements on a large scale. In fact, among blacks these movements began around the turn of the century. The civil rights movement included many different activities and organizations. Among the better known associations were the NAACP (the National Association for the Advancement of Colored People), which began in the first decade of the century, the Urban League,

Desegregation: removal of all legal and customary barriers to integration.

CORE (the Congress of Racial Equality), SCLC (the Southern Christian Leadership Conference), led by Martin Luther King, Jr., and SNCC (the Student Nonviolent Coordinating Committee). Over the years these groups sought their goals by various activities—from court challenges to boycotts to voter registration drives to sit-ins to mass marches. All used forms of nonviolent direct action. Whites and blacks marched together. Their shared goal was desegregation: the removal of all legal and informal barriers to full integration and equality. The civil rights movement reached its peak in the early and middle 1960s.

The black pride movement. Major efforts to instill pride in blackness also began early in the century.[19] Followers of Booker T. Washington, Marcus Garvey (who led a "Black Nation" and a "back-to-Africa movement" in the 1920s), and the Black Muslims of more recent times engaged in activities of a

[19] See, for example, Philip T. Drotning, *Black Heroes in Our Nation's History* (New York: Cowles, 1969).

The related movements of black pride and black nationalism have waxed and waned in popularity throughout this century. In the 1920s Marcus Garvey achieved great prominence with a black separatist program. From the 1950s on Elijah Muhammad has built the Black Muslim religion into a cultural force for blacks. In the middle 1960s the Black Panther Party, a political group with roots in the rural South, achieved national attention with its ideology of black liberation and political revolution.

different nature. Their basic creeds were also different. Rather than attacking the system directly, they urged black people to take pride in and improve themselves—in their words, to be "revitalized." Some leaders of the nationalist movement wanted to show whites that blacks were as good as they were. Some, especially in the past two decades, emphasized what they proclaimed as the moral superiority of blacks and the inferiority of whites.

The black power movement. Both the civil rights movement and the movement for black nationalism were only moderately successful. Each had attacked one part of the problem. Each had made some gains. There is little question that the civil rights movement was responsible for cutting through a number of segregation barriers, especially in the South, and for successfully obtaining new federal legislation to guarantee the voting and public accommodation rights of black citizens. And there is no doubt that the small black nationalist movement did succeed in raising the ethnic consciousness of many blacks, including the majority who were unaffiliated with any specific nationalist group.

But somehow protest and pride were never quite joined. Those in positions of leadership began to feel that the victories had been won at too great a cost. They called for a new orientation. It took shape in the mid-1960s, when events seemed to bring the issues and forces together in a strong black power movement. Among the issues were the slowness of the authorities to deliver on promises made, especially in the early days of Lyndon Johnson's administration, the lack of attention to the problems of ghetto dwellers in northern cities, the disaffection of some white supporters (who turned to other matters, such as Vietnam war protests and campus rebellion), and a new black awareness of the power that a tightly confined and segregated population could wield both in city halls and in the streets.[20]

In the late 1960s, disillusion with white resistance to desegregation turned many blacks away from the civil rights movement. Hope gave way to anger. In 1954, the Supreme Court had prohibited segregated schooling on the ground that "separate" facilities could not be "equal." More than ten years later, blacks found that most whites were determined to keep the races separate. Many blacks themselves now rejected integration as a goal.

Separatism again became a forceful movement among blacks. However, few now thought migration to Africa was a realistic goal. They were American, they knew; what they shared with black Africans was mainly physical

[20]See, for example, Robert H. Brisbane, *Black Activism* (Valley Forge, Pa.: Judson Press, 1974); Edward Peeks, *The Long Struggle for Black Power* (New York: Scribner, 1971).

traits. Cultural ties with Africa were buried deep in the past. Some black Americans decided to demand large land areas within this country. There they could set up their own nation within the nation. They also demanded large sums of money as repayment for a history of wrongs against the black population. Many non-Muslims began to express the Black Muslim belief that "whites are devils."

Ironically, racism was now a charge made by whites against blacks. Some whites were getting an idea of how it felt to be prejudged—to be victims of group prejudice. Many of the specific charges made by blacks were true, though. Integration and full equality were often acceptable goals for northern whites only when pursued in the South. When their own communities were affected, many lost their enthusiasm for civil rights.

The growth in ethnic pride and identity among blacks has not been matched by improvement in economic circumstances. In the late 1960s and early 1970s, the goals of black power advocates encompassed a broad range. Some sought separate political and economic power bases for blacks. Others embraced revolutionary philosophies that equate racial exploitation with capitalism and that offer Marxist or Maoist remedies. Today the political and psychological gains among nonwhite minorities appear to be considerably greater than their social and economic gains.

Critics of "affirmative action programs" argue that preferential treatment is given to minorities and that unqualified or less qualified applicants may be hired over more qualified whites. This, they contend, amounts to reverse discrimination. If you were an affirmative action officer, how would you answer these charges of reverse discrimination?

Assimilation or Separation?

Assimilation: a minority's replacement of its distinctive ethnic or subculture traits with those of the dominant group.

Many American minorities want to go beyond desegregation. They press for full equality, for the removal of all racial, religious, and other barriers that seem to divide people or keep them out. They argue for full integration, for a truly "color-blind" society in which racial, religious, and subcultural differences are no longer bases for discrimination. Some hold onto a "melting pot" theory of assimilation in America. As Daniel Patrick Moynihan and Nathan Glazer pointed out,

> the idea of the melting pot is as old as the Republic. "I could point out to you a family," wrote the naturalized New Yorker, M-G. Jean de Crevecoeur, in 1783, "whose grandfather was an Englishman, whose wife was Dutch, whose son married a French woman and whose present four sons have now four wives of

different nations. *He* is an American who, leaving behind him all his ancient prejudices and manners, receives new ones from the new mode and life he has embraced. . . . Here individuals of all nations are melted into a new race of men."[21]

Others, however, fear that through integration minorities will be absorbed or assimilated into the mainstream and will lose their unique characteristics. While still pressing for civil rights, they want to remain different. In the extreme, they emphasize their uniqueness and try to shut out the rest of the world as best they can. They represent modern continuations of old black nationalist and similar movements. They include not only black power advocates, but also brown power and red power supporters.

How do leaders of these movements justify their emphasis on separateness? Some explain that they really want to become like "white" ethnic groups, such as Italian-Americans, Polish-Americans, and Irish-Americans. These groups have been recognized as sharing two cultures and not being considered inferior or disloyal for maintaining their ethnic identities along with their American cultural traits. What they are talking about is *cultural pluralism:* the idea that a single society can afford to have a variety of people with somewhat differing norms, values, and interests living together in harmony. Horace Kallen, the social philosopher who used the term *cultural pluralism* to describe American society, saw it as a "multiplicity in a unity, an orchestration of mankind." Kallen compared each cultural group and nationality to an instrument in an orchestra, each instrument adding its unique sound to the whole (the United States).[22] A society might, indeed, benefit from this variety.

Cultural pluralism: the ideal of distinct ethnic groups living in harmony and equality in a society.

Affirmative Action Demands

Whether they seek integration or pluralism, minority group leaders see that improvement of their conditions must come from participation in the nation's economic and political institutions. In the early 1970s this goal was sought by obtaining "group rights" rather than "individual rights." That is, minorities argued that, to overcome the problems created by discrimination, those who have suffered most should now be given favored treatment. Advocates of favored treatment often look to the government to ensure opportunities for minorities. *Affirmative action plans* are one method of bringing groups into

[21]Nathan Glazer and Daniel Patrick Moynihan, *Beyond the Melting Pot* (Cambridge, Mass.: MIT Press, 1967), p. 288.

[22]Horace M. Kallen, *Culture and Democracy in the United States* (New York: Boni and Liveright, 1924), p. 124.

In many American cities on St. Patrick's Day "everyone is Irish." Yet the Irish have been virtually assimilated into the American culture. Other ethnic groups, however, no longer strive for assimilation. Like the Mexican-Americans shown here, they want full social equality without sacrificing their distinctive cultural heritage.

areas where they have been excluded. For example, any organization (corporation, college, state agency) that receives federal funds or does business for the government must have an affirmative plan—giving preference in hiring and promotion to minorities. It must prove it is making a special effort to hire members of groups that have been excluded in the past by custom or deliberate policy.

The new attempt to enforce affirmative action has had many effects. One of these is what some have called "the resurgence of ethnicity": a revival of emphasis on race, religion, and national origin by people who in the past played down their backgrounds and tried to see themselves simply as Americans. The black power movement and minority movements like it gave a new kind of legitimacy to ethnic separatism in the United States. We now have books on our "unmeltable ethnics."[23] Their authors describe American society as a collection of unassimilated racial and ethnic groups that have loyalty to the larger society but maintain their distinctive characteristics.

Integration is a much less common topic these days than it was in the past. And yet in a few years it might again become a major goal. It may then be defined in slightly different ways, however. As various nonwhite groups discover or rediscover their own heritages, they undergo a period of intense separatism. But they also find that they have more power than they thought they had. That power may force politicians, businesspeople, and union leaders to listen more carefully to grievances about discrimination. Minorities may also press the government to honor traditional values and norms of equality of opportunity. Should they succeed, the pluralist variety of integration may be achieved. This integration would be based on mutual understanding and respect among ethnic groups, not on the assimilationist idea that "if you throw off your strange ways and become like me, then we'll be as one."[24]

1. Would the United States be better off if there were no ethnic divisions among its people? What might be some advantages? Some disadvantages?

2. Assuming you think it would be better not to have ethnic divisions, how would you change the society we do have, which is made up of a variety of peoples?

3. If you agree that there is "strength in diversity," how do you think it could be made to work better for all people, especially in light of what you have learned about prejudice, discrimination, and ethnic stratification in this chapter?

[23]See Michael Novak, *The Rise of the Unmeltable Ethnics* (New York: Macmillan, 1971), and Andrew M. Greeley, *Ethnicity in the United States* (New York: Wiley, 1974).

[24]For a brief, yet thorough, presentation of assimilation in the United States (as seen through the theories of Anglo-conformity, the melting pot, and cultural pluralism), see Milton M. Gordon, "Assimilation in America: Theory and Reality," *Daedalus* 90 (1961): 263–85.

SUMMARY

Heterogeneous societies often include people of varying racial and cultural backgrounds. These differences may be used as the basis for a specific form of stratification, sometimes called ethnic stratification. Certain groups are seen and treated as superior and others as inferior. Those in control are called dominant groups. The subordinate groups are referred to as minorities. Ethnicity and race and their frequent consequences, ethnocentrism and racism, are manifestations of the social construction of reality that characterizes all social, and therefore all human, existence.

Minorities frequently suffer from the beliefs and actions of the dominant group. Sociologists refer to negative attitudes about groups of people as prejudices. Discrimination is differential treatment. Discrimination takes many forms, and so do the techniques used by minority group members and their sympathizers to overcome it. Among the most important techniques we have witnessed in recent years are the civil rights movement, the movement for ethnic pride, and the black power movement.

The study of reactions to prejudice and discrimination offers important insights into the nature of intergroup conflict, the ethnocentrism of those in power, and the ethnicity of those who seek to share it.

How do we learn the norms, beliefs, and values of our society? Why do most of us play our various roles more or less as we are expected to most of the time?

The agents who teach us about our society and culture include our parents, our peers, the school system, television, and other communication media. We learn from them how to act, what to think, what to like and dislike, even who we are as boys and men or girls and women. The process of socialization continues throughout our lives, as new situations and roles impose new demands on us and affect our sense of self.

Most of us conform to cultural norms, because we see ourselves as we think others see us and evaluate us. We are first influenced by the people close to us who are significant to us emotionally. Later we internalize the values and norms that these significant others have conveyed to us.

Some people do not conform to important norms; they deviate beyond the society's limits of tolerance. Sociologists have developed several theories to explain deviance, and societies have various ways of dealing with deviants. In our society, one method used with some deviants is to try to resocialize them in controlled environments, such as prisons or mental hospitals. Resocialization is the process of changing a person's behavior or self-concept drastically and rapidly. It is used in a variety of situations, some helpful and some harmful to the subjects.

4

EARLY SOCIALIZATION

So far we have gained a better understanding of life in societies by using the sociological perspective to analyze the various components. To do this we divided the components into those that are cultural–ideas, values, norms, and objects–and those that are structural–our patterned ways of playing roles, our interactions in social institutions, the structured inequality in social rewards, and the division of people by race or ethnic background.

The sociological perspective and its methods allow us to gain similar knowledge about how we are transformed from newborn infants into members of society. The fundamental components of socialization are universal: there are agents (those who socialize the young); there are methods; and each individual undergoes development of a self. But in every society, and in many diverse groups within a heterogeneous society, the cultural content of socialization is unique. Likewise the structural components of a society vastly influence the individual's socialization.

DEFINING SOCIALIZATION

Spare the rod, and spoil the child.

Children should be seen, not heard.

Boys will be boys.

Big boys don't cry.

What are little girls made of? Sugar and spice and everything nice.

These are only a few of the catchphrases that once had general currency in our society. They can still be heard today in some social classes and parts of the country. In many segments of our society, however, they have given way to guidelines from Benjamin Spock, Sigmund Freud (and his popularizers), A. S. Neill, and others granted authority on the basis of expertise. For instance, Spock advises: "Spoiling doesn't come from being good to a baby in a sensible way . . . . Spoiling comes on gradually when a mother is too afraid to use her common sense or when she really wants to be a slave and encourages her baby to become a slave driver."[1]

[1]Benjamin Spock, *Baby and Child Care* (New York: Simon and Schuster Pocket Books, 1958), p. 4.

Socialization: the process of learning the beliefs, values, norms, and social roles of a culture and society.

These quotes, whether from old folk wisdom or from experts in psychology and child-rearing, all have several points in common. They have to do with socialization of the young. Socialization, as we have seen frequently throughout this text, is easy enough to define: the process of learning the beliefs, values, norms, and roles of our culture and society. The definition is deceptively simple; the process is quite complex.

Socialization is something we experience in our everyday lives. Yet we rarely think about the factors that influence what we do, how we think, how we see ourselves. A sociological perspective helps us to understand the nature of the socialization process better.

Whether they are rules ("Spare the rod . . . ") or expressions of attitudes ("Boys will be boys"), the admonishing phrases we quoted not only teach the socializing agents what to do or what to expect, but also teach the

young about themselves and their society. For example, "Spare the rod, and spoil the child" implies that children are savages, so to speak, who must be disciplined into obedience by punishment or the threat of it. The child and society are adversaries, and society must overcome the child. The remark, "Boys will be boys," usually made after some piece of mischief has been traced to a male youngster, signals to him that he can expect a certain amount of tolerance for breaking some norms. It also signals to children of both sexes that adult tolerance and expectations differ according to a child's gender.

However, the variety of attitudes and norms displayed in these quotes indicates that changes are taking place in how people socialize their young into our society. In recent generations, many people have come to see that the choice of socializing methods influences the results—what kind of person the child will become. Most current views on socialization acknowledge that the

These two children reflect their socialization. No instinct directs the girl to draw a flower and the boy to draw the torso of a muscle man. The children have learned these sex-specific images and certain patterns of interaction between the sexes, just as they learned their physical and mental skills.

personality is far more complex than certain traditional child-rearing methods had assumed. Many parents in older generations believed there was something fixed already present in us at birth—something called human nature. They believed that human beings behaved in certain biologically determined ways: for example, that men were naturally aggressive, competitive, intellectual, and inventive; that women were passive, nurturing, emotional, and dependent on men for their survival; that people were inherently greedy and had to be taught to share; that it was only natural for people to want to improve their lot in life. Today such beliefs about human nature have been seriously challenged, although they may well remain the dominant view.

THE AGENTS OF SOCIALIZATION

On the basis of research in a wide variety of cultures, social scientists contend that the social environment is the critical factor in determining how people behave and what they believe.[2] Attitudes, values, and rules for behavior are learned, not inherited. The instructors and role-models—or *agents of socialization*—are parents, peers, teachers, and other figures with whom individuals come into direct contact. They may also be people who are more distant. The age of television gives us ample evidence of effective teaching at long range.

Parents

At first, parents do little more than care for the immediate physical and emotional needs of the infant—food, warmth, rocking, holding, and changing

[2]See, for example, John A. Clausen et al., *Socialization and Society* (Boston: Little, Brown, 1968).

Socialization begins at birth. It progresses from simple care of the infant, through teaching the child elementary tasks and skills (as this Eskimo grandfather oversees his grandchild's efforts at cat's cradle), to teaching the child the beliefs, values, and norms of the culture.

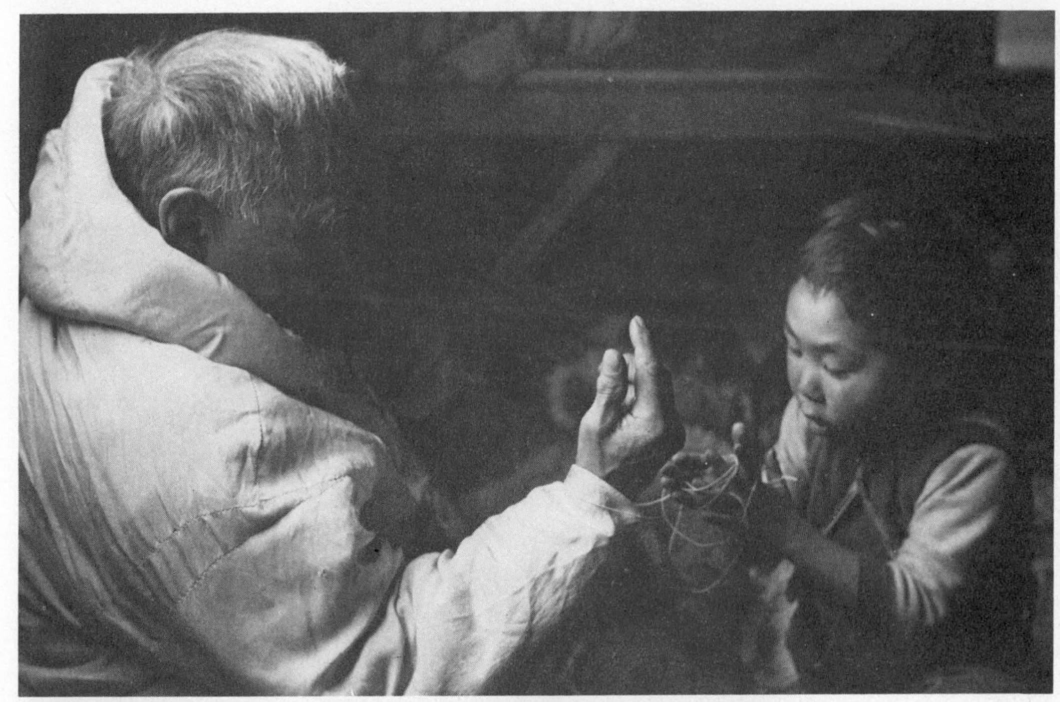

diapers—anything that will keep the baby from crying or fretting. Then, as the baby's capacities for physical coordination develop—sitting up, grasping objects, crawling, later walking—the child also begins to learn norms. At first they take a rather unimposing form: "Don't spit food out," "Don't drop your cup on the floor," "Don't touch that," "Everybody, see Lisa standing!" "Chuckie, can you walk to Daddy?"

As mastery of language grows, children begin to learn still more—other norms, values, and beliefs. Many of these are deliberately taught, but many others are picked up by observing what parents say and do. Children may be told that Santa Claus rewards good children and not bad. They may be taught that someone named God is always watching them and wants them to be good. They may observe their parents repeatedly expressing displeasure about soiled clothes or a dirty floor or expressing pleasure about the cleanliness of this or the shininess of that. They hear parents discussing their friends or business associates or the world in general: "Carl's a good worker; he carries his own load." "Prendergast never shows any appreciation no matter how hard you try." "At this rate we'll never get ahead. It's getting harder and harder just to keep up." They may see mother defer to father whenever decisions are made about finances or whenever the parents engage in discussions with friends and relatives.

For the younger child, tone of voice carries more meaning than the words. As a child grows older, tone and meaning become clearer and reinforce each other to convey ideas and attitudes. The child's ability to pick up information from surroundings is accelerated by lessons in school, where a deliberate effort is made to describe society in terms suitable to the student's limited powers of abstract understanding. But preparation for such learning starts long before school, as we have just seen.

Peers

For most people, peers (those who are more or less the same age) become socializing agents before schoolteachers do. Sometime in the first two or three years (earlier for those with brothers or sisters), children come into regular contact with playmates. How can little children be socializing agents? If socialization is learning, what can they teach each other? They know little, if anything, more than those they are socializing. Precisely. They introduce a new dimension into the socialization process. Until children interact with peers, they live in a condition of pronounced inequality: their parents have skills, size, power, and authority; children have little or none of these. Even the child's powers of coercion by charm or tears are only as effective as parents allow them to be.

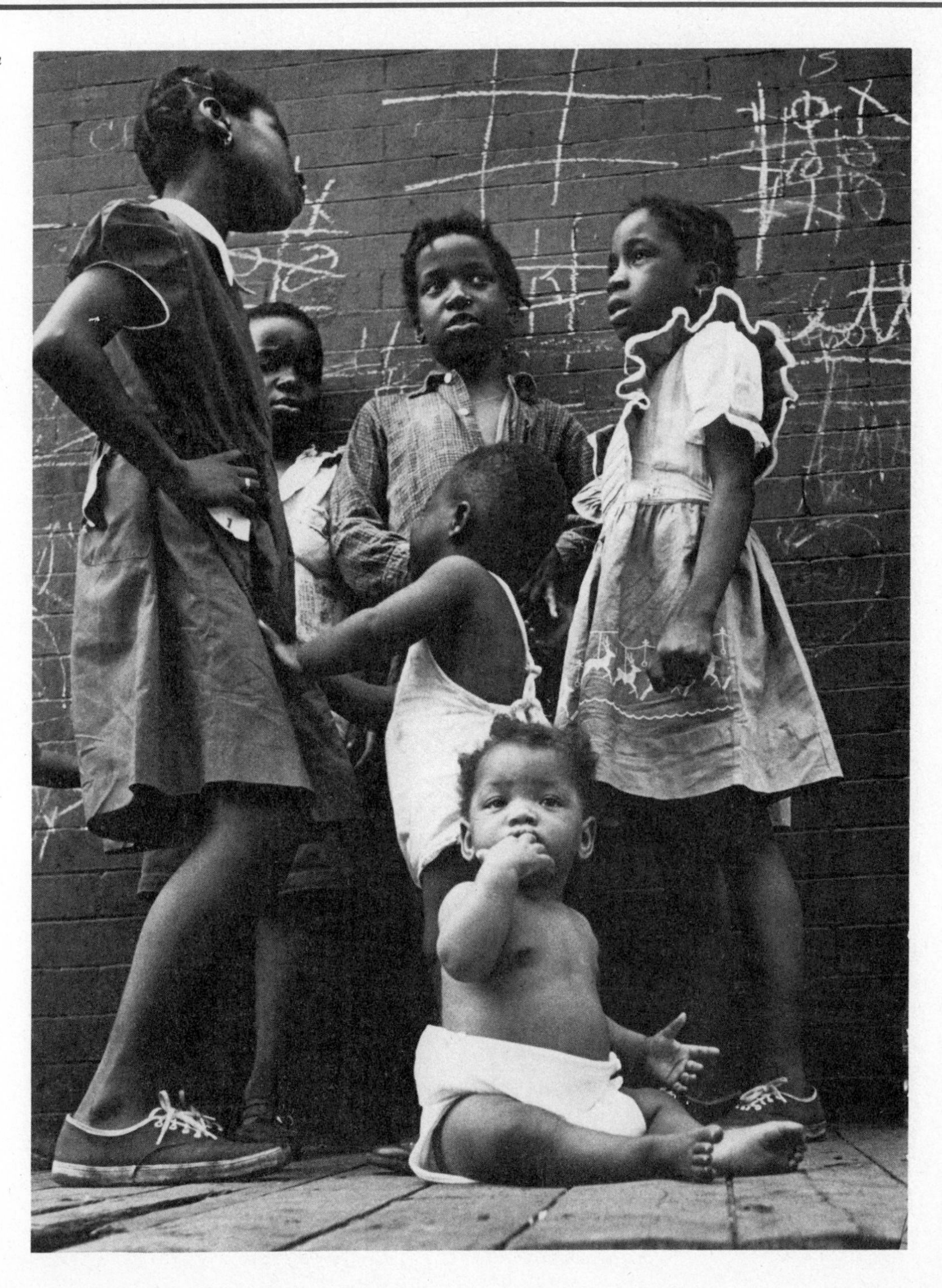

The process of socialization is extended through interaction with peers, which presents a child with new experiences in applying norms and in learning skills.

With peers, individuals first experience being equals among equals. They are taught new norms by their parents for dealing with this new condition. Children learn to share toys; not to take something away by force from someone else who is using or playing with it; not to hit or fight. They also begin to experience the reasoning behind the norms in our society: when a child takes a toy away from a friend, the deprived child angrily and tearfully experiences violation of a norm from the victim's point of view. (This experience of suffering from violation of a norm does not immediately translate into obedience to the norm, as anyone who observes young children playing together knows.)

Children also learn some of the more subtle norms that surround the role of friend, such as how to be a leader in some situations and a follower in others. Boys might have to learn if and when they can play with dolls, and girls have traditionally learned that they get more approval from peers and adults alike for acting "like a little lady" than for roughhousing with their brothers or neighborhood boys.

Schools

So far socialization has taken place within the context of primary groups.

School is a major prolonged agent of socialization in a modern society. Not only do the children learn the subject matter being taught but they also learn a succession of patterns of interaction.

Secondary group: a group in which participation and interaction tend to be impersonal, unspontaneous, and task-oriented (discussed in Chapter 5).

Parents, brothers and sisters, and playmates all fit the definition of primary role-players. But, in industrial societies like ours, sometime in the first six years children are introduced to their first major secondary group—the school. Whether it is a nursery school, kindergarten, or first grade, public school or private, traditional, progressive, or experimental, it places major demands on the children to learn new rules and roles.

In school, as in the family, children are taught to play special roles related to achieving immediate goals and to their preparation for the future. Slowly, through nursery school, kindergarten, and grade school, children are taught how to play the role of student. At first it means sharing the attentions of the teacher with a large group of classmates. It requires being at a particular place at a particular time and leaving when the school session is over. There are programmed activities and rules to learn. New norms are introduced as students receive ratings for their achievement (by grades and other means) and punishments if they do not follow the rules by which classes are conducted.

At home and among friends they learn to accommodate to the differences of others and to expect others to make the same kinds of allowances for their traits. In school a different set of priorities holds. Children must perform within the rules, and the rules are explicit and far less flexible. Their stated purpose is to allow the school to accomplish its socialization of the student with maximum efficiency. The school is thus an early model of the secondary groups that dominate adult institutions in an industrial society.[3]

One leading sociologist, Talcott Parsons, believes that achievement is the key variable by which the school works as a selection agency for future status. In the beginning, he believes, children in a single classroom are not differentiated by the teacher. All are exposed to the same program, and some achieve more than others. As time goes on, teachers begin to reward the achievers and guide them toward more education in the future.[4]

Later in this chapter we discuss tests of female attitudes toward female achievement in traditionally male-dominated roles.

Other researchers question Parsons's interpretation. They argue that the school is not neutral in its attitude toward its students, simply selecting the highest achievers for advancement. Rather, it is biased toward middle-class values and often discriminates against those who deviate from the norms reflecting those values. Similarly, schools encourage academic achievement in men more than in women, despite the superior performance of girls over boys up to high school and sometimes throughout the high school years. As evidence, critics note that 75 percent of the intellectually qualified people who do

FUTURE PLANS OF MEN AND WOMEN WITH B+ OR A AVERAGE, 1971

Future Plans	*Women (Percentage)*	*Men (Percentage)*
Highest degree expected		
Bachelor's	14	6
Master's	61	33
Academic doctorate	17	31
Professional doctorate	6	28
Other and no answer	3	2
Immediate postcollege plans		
Full-time work (including military)	64	41
Graduate study	27	29
Law or medicine	5	24
Other professional study	9	14

Source: Adapted from Leonard L. Baird, Mary Jo Clark, and Rodney T. Harnett, *The Graduates*,

[3]See, for example, Harry L. Gracey, "Learning the Student Role: Kindergarten as Academic Boot Camp," in *The American Elementary School, A Case Study in Bureaucracy and Ideology* (Washington, D.C.: National Institute of Mental Health, n.d.).

[4]Talcott Parsons, "The School Class as a Social System," *Harvard Educational Review* 29 (1959): 297–318.

not go to college are women.[5] Our textbooks consistently show more pictures of boys than girls. In science texts, for example, only 6 percent of the pictures included adult women.[6] Guidance counselors and teachers encourage many girls to take home economics rather than physics. A major proportion of the sports budget in most schools is geared to boys' teams. This tells women that physical development is not important for them. Even among women who go to college and receive good grades (B-plus or A averages), fewer expect to get doctorates or enter professions than men with those grades do.

Ask to see the readers and story books used in kindergarten and the lower grades of a nearby grade school. Examine them for sex-role stereotypes, such as women in passive situations and men in active ones, or men in dominant positions and women in subordinate positions. How might such stereotyping influence children's attitudes toward achievement?

Television

In the last decade or so, more children in the United States have entered school with better preparation for the new patterns of interaction it requires. Television has made an important difference. Studies have shown that television has a significant socializing effect on children who watch it for several hours a week. It provides child viewers with random factual information about our society and others. It also gives them more information on norms they have already learned and others new to them. It has also demonstrably accelerated the growth of their vocabulary.

Whether children watch chiefly "educational" programs designed to teach them (such as "Sesame Street"), or programs intended to entertain rather than educate them, or programs aimed at adults rather than children, television offers the most comprehensive view of the world that a child can obtain. A child watching a quiz program sees winning contestants burst with excitement as a car, a major appliance, or pictures of a trip to Hawaii for two are displayed. The child can hardly fail to sense that both material things and winning are desirable. A child watching a series program about a team of inner-city detectives is fairly certain to see a lot of action—chases on foot

[5]Lenore J. Weitzman, "Sex-Role Socialization," in *Women: A Feminist Perspective,* ed. Jo Freeman (Palo Alto, Calif.: Mayfield, 1975), pp. 106–44.

[6]Pamela Roby, "Structural and Internalized Barriers to Women in Higher Education," in *Women: A Feminist Perspective,* p. 121.

Television has become a major socializing agent in the last few decades. It brings children information about the world, expands their vocabularies, and begins to socialize them to the role of consumer.

across rooftops, car chases through city streets, shoot-outs, and fistfights. Several values are also being displayed, however: courage in the face of danger, dedication to the job, loyalty to the team, and the virtue of upholding the law. Thus, a child who regularly watches television is likely to be learning an array of stated and unstated values and norms far beyond his or her parent's expectations or, perhaps, desires.

The revolutionary effect of television comes chiefly from the fact that it supplies information without requiring effort or skills from the viewer. The painstaking and repetitive exercises required in learning to read are bypassed. Before television was commonplace, children who could not read had to rely on their parents much more for information. This required adult time and attention. Television is a substitute for both parental attention and reading skills. Even after they learned to read, children in past generations had access to only limited information. Books and magazines for young children are generally written with their limited cognitive skills and special subject interests in mind. Television, however, provides an immense variety of subjects and treatments.

Television contributes significantly to socialization not simply because it presents so much information, but also because of what so many children do with that information. As we see in the next section, on methods of socialization, the process of learning our culture involves more than gathering information. It includes becoming part of that information through mental and physical activities, such as imitation and role-playing. Television offers young viewers raw material for exercising these capabilities. Parents who are happy that their kids sit quietly before the screen and keep out of mischief have only a partial idea of what is happening in that room. Television is clearly more than a baby-sitter.

Watch several hours of television on weekday and Saturday mornings, when children's programs predominate. Also watch several early evening programs that children would be likely to watch or to join adults in watching.

1. Do some content analysis. Try to pick out and record the beliefs, values, and norms that are conveyed, however subtly.

2. Note any distinctions between the role models for boys and men and those for girls and women. Which occupations do men have? Which occupations do women have? How distinct are they? Do they project the traditional sex-role stereotypes (boys adventurous, aggressive; girls passive, timid, eager to please), or do they show an effort to erase them? Do you find inconsistencies from program to program? What about parental roles? What responsibilities do fathers have in the home? What responsibilities do mothers have in the home?

3. It has been said that television commercial jingles are the nursery rhymes of today's young children. Perform the same content analysis on these commercials, looking for the same cultural elements as in activities 1 and 2 above. Note how child performers are used in children's commercials? How do they behave? What values do they express? What role do you think they are socializing child viewers to imitate?

METHODS OF SOCIALIZATION

Role-playing: imitation by children of behavior they observe in the role occupants around them.

We have already become familiar with several of the important ways of becoming socialized. Whether at home or in the classroom or among friends children are deliberately taught many things. They learn facts (the earth is round; white light is composed of the spectrum of colors). And they learn skills (from tying their shoelaces to dissecting a frog). Much teaching and learning occurs without conscious effort—either to teach or to learn. As we mentioned briefly, children pick up attitudes and beliefs in their daily contact with parents and peers. Attitudes toward courage and timidity, attitudes and beliefs about racial and ethnic minorities or members of social classes, attitudes toward life itself can be taught the young unwittingly. Thus, they learn much of their culture without deliberately trying—often simply by imitating what others, such as parents, peers, or television characters, do and say and think.

Probably the most visible form of imitation in children between three and five years old is *role-playing.* A trip through a toy store would show that a

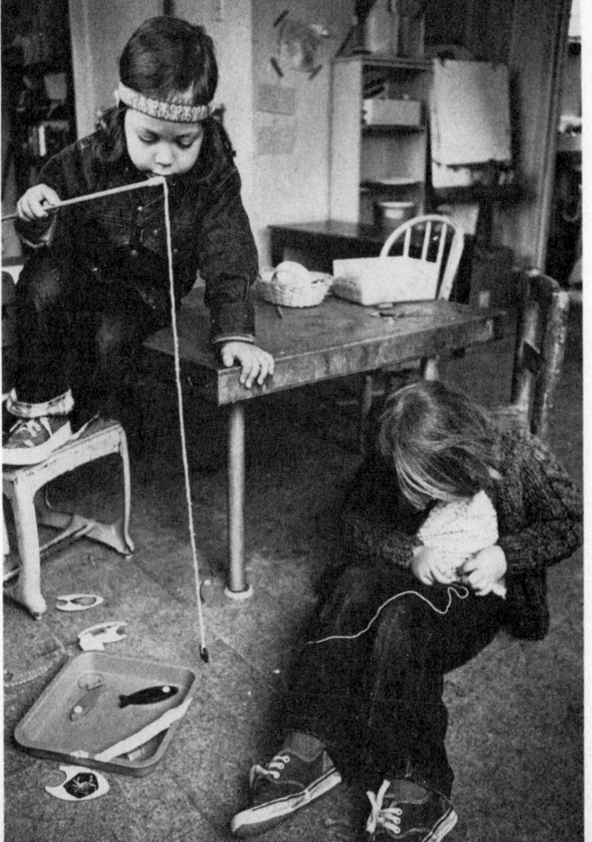

Role-playing is an essential component of socialization: by use of memory and imagination children "get inside" the roles they see around them in their immediate lives or in books, television, and films.

good part of the stock is scaled-down objects from the adult world—dolls and dollhouses, trucks and cars, tanks and guns, doctor's kits and housecleaning tools. By role-playing, children become more familiar with the "inside" of the roles that surround them in everyday life: mothers, fathers, older brothers and sisters, firemen, policemen, and so on. Children translate their surroundings into terms they can understand by copying the repeated ways of interaction they have observed. They imitate the tones of voice they associate with the role occupants most familiar to them.

Anticipatory socialization: behavior that prepares the individual for occupying future roles.

On their own initiative, children who are engaged in this make-believe are doing the same imitative exercises as the child learning to tie shoelaces. There is, however, one significant difference between the two kinds of imitation: the latter develops a skill of immediate use; the former is what sociologists call *anticipatory socialization.* Children imitating the roles they see around them are beginning a long preparation for assuming those or similar roles; they are learning future roles.

DEVELOPMENT OF THE SELF

The human ability to learn does not by itself explain why the process of socialization works so effectively for so many members of every society. Society depends on another complex process within each person being socialized: the development of the *self.*

We have noted that among the basic human needs is positive emotional interaction. While human beings are at first totally dependent on the care of others for their very survival, they gradually become more able to take care of their own needs. But, just as these needs continue to require people to interact with others within social institutions, their emotional needs work in a way that keeps them involved with society.

The Need for Acceptance

It may be helpful to review Lawrence Kohlberg's model of moral development of children, discussed in Chapter 4.

Starting very early, a child's behavior is increasingly dominated by cultural values, beliefs, and norms. Children accept these partly because of the possibility that others will punish them and partly from the constant desire for approval by others. Punishment is only sometimes physical: pain from a spanking, or hunger when the child is sent to bed without supper, or other means of physical deprivation. In addition, parents' anger is fearful in itself, because it raises the child's doubt about his or her acceptance by those who matter most. Children are often unable to distinguish anger from the absence of love. In fact, they often fail to make the distinction in their own feelings: they may express their anger by saying, "I don't like you" or "I hate you."

Children come to *internalize* the values and norms they are taught.

This girl of the Nupe tribe, in Nigeria, exemplifies the "looking-glass self" that Charles Horton Cooley theorized about: we think of ourselves as we think others see us and judge us. Perhaps this is part of the reason why cosmetics or adornments are an almost universal phenomenon in human societies.

Significant others: those whose attitudes and judgments about us are important in the process of our socialization.

Parents are important in this process not just because they are constantly present in the child's early life but also because they are what sociologists call *significant others.* At first parents are the sole significant others, but through successive stages of a child's development other status occupants assume that importance as well. These people appear in the make-believe imitations of young children discussed earlier.

The Looking-Glass Self

Looking-glass self: the self as a product of how we think others judge us and how we feel as a result of that judgment.

The American sociologists Charles Horton Cooley and George Herbert Mead were the first to develop enduring sociological theories about the self in the process of socialization.[7] Early in this century, Cooley formulated what he called the *looking-glass self,* and Mead later refined it by describing its components and the process of acquiring it. Combined, the two theories indicate how much of the personality is a social creation.

[7]See Charles Horton Cooley, *Human Nature and the Social Order* (New York: Schocken, 1964), and Anselm Strauss, ed., *George Herbert Mead on Social Psychology: Selected Papers* (Chicago: University of Chicago Press, 1964).

Internalization: the process of adopting a society's norms as part of the individual's personality and notion of self.

Cooley proposed that the looking-glass self is a product of what happens in our interaction with others. Although the self becomes well formed in the early years of our lives, it is constantly undergoing reevaluation. We internalize beliefs: our notions about what others think of us. That is, we gain feelings about ourselves, and thus a definition of our *self,* by three steps, according to Cooley: we form beliefs about how we appear to others; we then form beliefs about their judgments of how we appear to them; and finally, in response to the imagined judgment, we develop pride, shame, improved self-esteem, slightly damaged self-esteem, and other attributes of the self. Thus Cooley says we see ourselves as *we think* others see us.

The Development Process

Mead's development—or operationalization—of this theory distinguished the stages by which the self is developed. We have already seen some of his concepts: the significant others and the importance of make-believe in socialization. As soon as the infant in the first month or so of life becomes conscious of its own physical boundaries—of the distinction between itself and the world —the foundations for self have been laid. From then on, the infant is aware of its total dependence on others for everything: food, the comfort of dry diapers, cuddling.

The human powers of learning begin, and the infant starts to correlate its behavior with the reactions of others. Parents soon learn the "language" of crying—the difference between a cry that signals hunger or discomfort, the cry that signals anger when a response doesn't come, and the cry that signals fatigue. The infant is developing expectations while learning the expectations of others. It has entered into a pattern of interaction with the first of the significant others in its life.

The next stage in development of the self, according to Mead, is the make-believe play we have described. The child tests out the roles that fill its immediate surroundings—the roles of significant others—and internalizes them ("Mommy and Daddy don't want me to throw my food on the floor"). Soon after, at the age of four or five, the child begins to develop what becomes the "I/me" dialogue. The "I" is the spontaneous part of the self, generating immediate desires and wishes that must be dealt with by the "me" part, which represents the internalized norms of society—what Mead called the *generalized other* ("Nobody should throw food on the floor"). The generalized other represents the cumulative effect of the various early agents of socialization. In familiar situations the child knows what norms apply, and a dialogue between the "I" and "me" parts of the self settles what the child's behavior will be.

Generalized other: the individual's notion of what behavior is expected of him or her by society in general.

Make-believe is followed by the game-playing stage, in which participants must learn to coordinate their behavior with others according to the positions occupied and the rules of the game.

At this stage, at about seven to nine years of age, children change their patterns of play from make-believe imitations of roles to complex organized games, ranging from tic-tac-toe and hopscotch to baseball and soccer. This is another stage of anticipatory socialization. A child playing baseball is not imitating a role but rather is mastering a position involving interaction with others in sequences determined by rules. A player aware of the rules does not run to first base until after hitting the ball. A child playing tic-tac-toe tries not only to get three marks in a row but also to prevent the opponent from doing so. The child has mastered yet another stage of socialization: playing reciprocal roles—anticipating the behavior of others and playing the role according to the particular rules of the game or situation.

Observe and record the kinds of play and undirected activity done by children in a nursery school, a kindergarten, and a schoolyard or playground. For each age category, note the kind and amount of role-playing and imitation, and the role models that are imitated, if any. Observe the kind and amount of reciprocal interaction (that is, whether two or more children who seem to be playing together are actually participating in the same game or make-believe, or whether each is focusing on his or her own fantasy). Note the extent to which your observations of the children at different age levels coincide with the stages of development described by George Herbert Mead.

THE CULTURAL COMPONENTS OF GROWTH

The physical and mental differences between a grown man or woman and an infant are pronounced. The differences between an adult and an adolescent in our society are far less pronounced. Thus the biological basis for the condition we call adolescence may therefore seem somewhat doubtful. Not only is adolescence a cultural construct, or creation, but childhood is as well.

Childhood

The biological differences among infancy, puberty, and adulthood and between male and female cannot be denied. But the meaning, or lack of meaning, attached to each of these distinct biological states has a cultural dimension. In some societies, as soon as children acquire enough coordination and skills to take care of most of their daily needs, they cease to be given the special status of child; they are simply smaller adults, in need of further training in other socially useful skills.

Philippe Aries, in his book *Centuries of Childhood,* has shown that, in French society before the modern period (approximately the eighteenth to twentieth centuries) children older than seven were dressed like adults, were allowed at gambling tables, and witnessed adult nakedness, masturbation, and other practices that would be hidden from their sight today.[8] Only over the course of centuries did special ideas about childhood develop. Similarly, Ruth Benedict, in a classic anthropological article on socialization, has shown how a number of premodern cultures have much greater continuity between childhood and adult roles than Western societies do.[9] Among the Cheyenne, for example, little boys are given tiny bows and taught to hunt as they will in adulthood. Among the Papago, young children of both sexes are given respon-

[8]Philippe Aries, *Centuries of Childhood* (New York: Knopf, 1962).

[9]Ruth Benedict, "Continuities and Discontinuities in Cultural Conditioning," *Psychiatry* 1 (1938): 161–67.

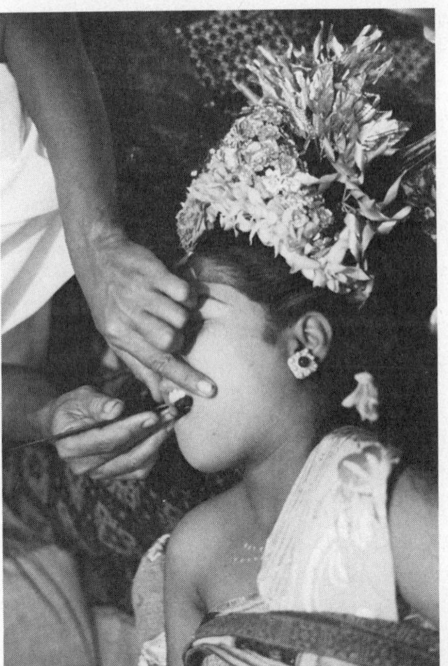

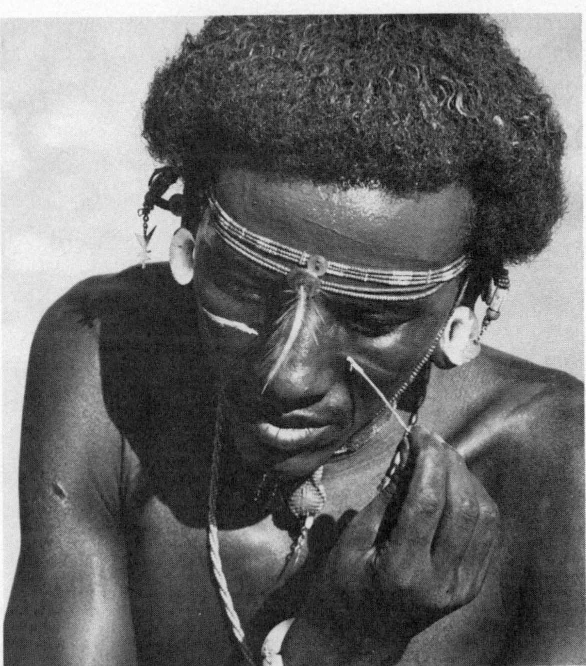

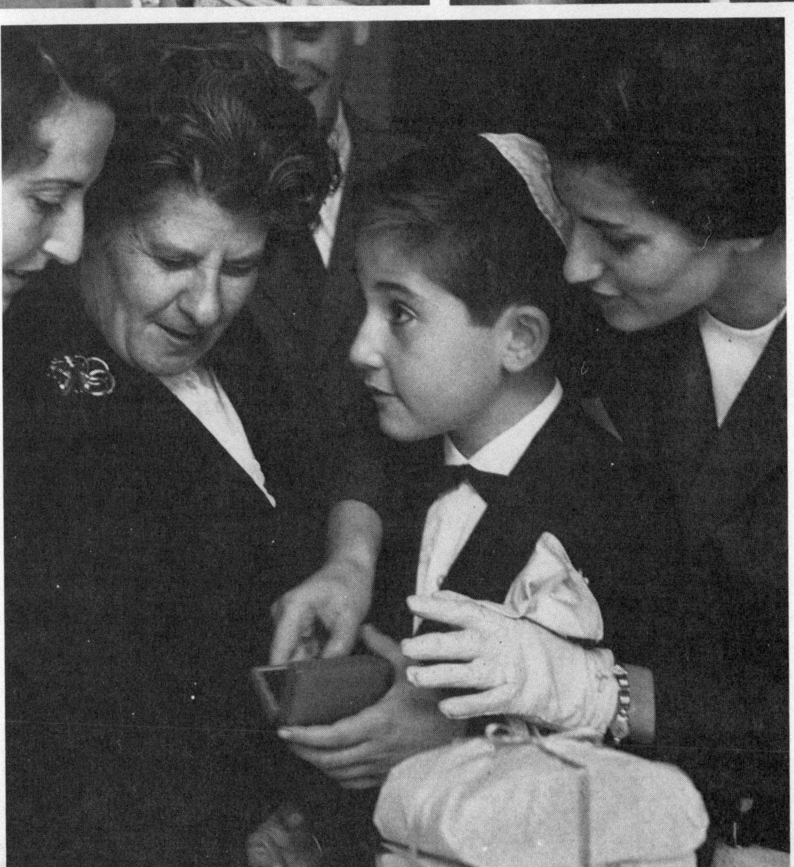

Many societies have rites of passage to mark transition from one stage of life to another. Girls in Bali undergo filing of their molars to mark passage from childhood to adulthood. A young Samburu (Kenya) designs his own pattern of facial decoration to mark his warrior status, once he reaches puberty. In secular, industrialized societies like ours, rites of passage are particularly notable in religious contexts. The Jewish bar mitzvah is a ceremony that marks the thirteen-year-old boy's passage into manhood.

Rite of passage: any ceremony that marks an individual's transition to a further stage of growth or social acceptance.

sibilities that are miniature versions of adult tasks. In such cases, when the time to enter adulthood occurs, *rites of passage* (ceremonies marking the transition to adult authority and privileges) are held. Although in our society adulthood is considerably delayed, remnants of such rites of passage survive: Jewish boys at age thirteen undergo the bar mitzvah, by which they symbolically become men and full-fledged members of the religious community; in many Christian denominations boys and girls of that age are confirmed as members of the church.

Even among premodern societies, however, a smooth and early transition was not always made. In colonial New England, young men were inhibited from marriage and full adult privileges and responsibilities until their mid-twenties. Because fathers needed the labor of their sons, they withheld the allotment of land and therefore full independence until very late.[10]

Adolescence: a culturally defined period between childhood and adulthood.

In a similar fashion, the transition from childhood to adulthood in modern societies occurs only gradually, in the stage of growth called adolescence. There are few clear-cut secular (nonreligious) ceremonies to signal the passage to adulthood. Certain events mark the transition: for example, entering high school, then graduating; the first date; obtaining a driver's license. Some of these take on the character of a rite of passage, even though that is not their main purpose.

Anthropologist Ruth Benedict studied societies that she called "age-graded"; that is, societies that group together persons of a similar age and demand different behaviors of the different age groups. In such a society, "an individual who at any time takes on a new set of duties and virtues is supported" by people his or her own age who are going through the same changes in life.[11] Moving from one stage of life to another with people of the same age helps an individual bridge the gap between the old behavior and the new behavior.

List three societal rites of passage from childhood to adulthood in the United States. Could these rites of passage be made more effective or meaningful for the participants and for society if ours was an age-graded society? Explain.

[10]See Philip J. Greven, Jr., *Four Generations: Population, Land, and Family in Colonial Andover, Massachusetts* (Ithaca, N.Y.: Cornell University Press, 1970).

[11]Benedict, "Continuities and Discontinuities," p. 165.

Adolescence

G. Stanley Hall was the first psychologist to study adolescence scientifically. In 1882 he wrote that adolescence was a biological period of "storm and stress." It was a time of "lack of emotional steadiness, violent impulses, unreasonable conduct . . . the previous selfhood is broken up . . . and a new individual is in process of being born."[12]

Later social scientists have contested some of Hall's theories. Anthropologist Margaret Mead has shown the strong cultural component in this notion of "storm and stress." Others have begun to see adolescence as related to historical development—an outgrowth of urbanization and industrialization.

As the need for unskilled labor decreased early in the twentieth century, there was an organized effort by unionized workers and progressive political groups to stop the use of child labor, a common source of cheap workers in the early factories and mills. Children, and even teenagers, it was argued, needed more education, protection from labor abuse, and special treatment from the authorities when they broke the law (juvenile courts, reformatories). As a result, adolescents were treated as a special legal category—one whose rights were very much restricted by specific rules and laws. Only in recent years have some adolescents come to demand the constitutional protections that other citizens assume as their natural rights.[13]

No matter how closely the legal rights of adolescents come to resemble those of adults, teenagers remain neither children nor adults. Not only do marked biological changes occur in adolescence, but also particular socializing experiences occur.

Characteristics of adolescence. Many people have tried to define the major characteristics of adolescence. Although there is not complete agreement about this definition, a number of social scientists have agreed that the following characteristics are very important.

Adolescence is a period of *biological maturation.* This is a period of sexual development, in which many physiological and hormonal changes occur in a relatively short period of time. The onset of puberty and its many secondary signs (rapid growth, sprouting hair, changing shape) are often accompanied by self-consciousness, pleasure, and fear. In order to cope with these changes

[12]G. Stanley Hall, "The Moral and Religious Training of Children," *Princeton Review,* January 1882, pp. 26–48.

[13]David Schimmel and Louis Fischer, *The Civil Rights of Students* (New York: Harper and Row, 1975).

Peer group: collectively, the individual's peers in their role as a significant other.

and emotions, adolescents must learn to play new roles or must change their old roles so that they are more appropriate: they must play the roles of date, friend, and gang or club member. The sex role, as we see later in this chapter, is central to the building of an identity.

Adolescents are *peer-group oriented.* As young people mature, they begin to rely less on their families and other adults. For some, adolescence is a time of fierce conflict with people of an older generation. Increasingly, adolescents learn norms, values, and styles from their friends. The special status of adolescents often encourages them to form cliques, gangs, and other kinds of friendship groups with whom they can share new experiences, face the future, and demonstrate loyalty, hostility, and love.

Adolescents have their *own styles and artifacts* (material objects). During the teen years in our culture certain styles and possessions are very important. Among American adolescents today, long hair, jeans, and boots are popular. There is a large youth market for popular music, posters, stereos, cars, motorcycles, and cosmetics. Mass communications and mass production have spread youthful styles and artifacts across this nation and to millions of young people in other lands.

Unlike other societies and other times, our society today places youths in a holding pattern called adolescence until they are about twenty-one years old. During this time they are neither children nor adults.

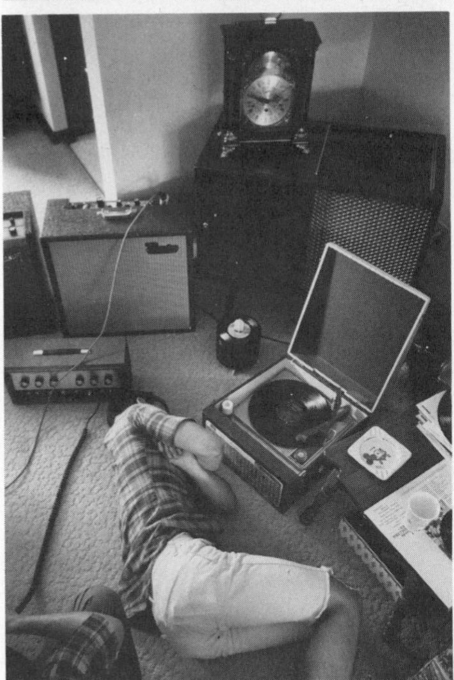

1. From your own past experiences or observations, can you list any other characteristics of adolescence?

2. What are some of the major problems of contemporary teenagers that derive from their social status as adolescents?

3. Do any of your past personal experiences highlight the contradictory values that adolescents are compelled to deal with? Which ones?

Adolescence is a period when individuals learn new role behaviors in anticipation of adulthood, but they are not fully liberated from childhood role expectations. Parents are often anxious for their children to plan careers for the future and to be succcssful with their peers so that they can look forward to forming new families at the appropriate time. This is a training period for independence and separation from the family.

At the same time adolescents are still financially dependent on their parents, usually living in their parents' households and subject to the authority of their elders as they were in childhood. In this way they remain dependent while they are training to be independent.

Tension between dependence and independence often continues outside the family. Young people are often openly critical of much around them, especially their schools. At the same time, many are aware that their performance in high school and college will have a crucial effect on their future work possibilities. As a result they are under pressure not to voice their displeasure but to go along with situations they find objectionable.

Adolescents are continually reminded they must grow up. Yet legally they are told they are too young to drink, vote, drive, have sexual intercourse, or participate in controlling the social institutions (such as schools) that affect their lives. Advertising and mass media glorify the youth culture and the world of the young. Those who promote styles of hair, clothing, and cosmetics, phonograph records, motorcycles, sports cars, magazines, movies, and books make special appeals to the youth market. Adults then begin to imitate the symbols of youth–to adopt the long hair, clothes, music, and dance associated with young people. No one wants to get old in our society. Thus, teenagers find themselves both scorned and idealized.

SOCIALIZATION TO SEX ROLES: THE CULTURAL AND INSTITUTIONAL COMPONENTS

Up to this point we have been talking about the socialization of children and adolescents in general terms. Sociologists have noted, however, that certain

Sex roles—the behavior assigned to members of each sex in a society—are discussed further in Chapter 10.

variables (factors) critically affect the way in which the individual is socialized. Although sex and social class are not the only important variables, they are crucial, and we will discuss them in some detail. In addition, we will briefly describe how international rivalries can influence the way in which young people choose their future work roles.

We have referred previously to the variability of sex roles from society to society. In nearly every society the essential tasks are divided into those for males and those for females. But the characteristic distribution in one society can be matched by the opposite distribution in another. As we saw in Chapter 1, anthropologist Margaret Mead discovered several New Guinea tribes who displayed sex role distributions quite unlike ours, and in fact one that was the direct opposite of ours.

The importance of her discovery for our time was not simply that different tasks and activities were assigned to men and women, but that the mental and emotional traits displayed by men and women varied. Among the Mundugumor people, both men and women exhibited exaggerations of what our society considers male characteristics: aggressiveness and competitiveness.

Among the Arapesh, both men and women displayed gentleness and submissiveness to the needs of others that are considered female traits in our society. And among the Tchambuli, the women were the aggressive, authoritative figures, and the men were the dependent, "flighty" creatures—the exact opposites of our own sex role stereotypes.

The components of socialization can combine to have such a profound and lasting effect on us that we cannot shake our beliefs and values about ourselves and others even when confronted by strong contrary evidence. In reading about Mead's accounts of the New Guinea tribes, many of you may have been struck less by the variety of possible patterns of human interaction than by an uneasy feeling that something was profoundly wrong with these strange patterns, particularly that of the Tchambuli. Even if you are sympathetic to feminist principles and claims, you may be affronted by a society in which men are treated as vain, flighty, helpless creatures.

Unpleasant as the notion may be to us, because we have internalized our own culture's beliefs and values into our self-images, the truth is that social and cultural influences are crucial in establishing how males and females act, think, and feel. Only their respective ways of participating in the act of reproduction—impregnation, gestation, birth, and nursing—are not interchangeable. But socialization into culturally determined sex roles begins so early in life that as young adults—or even as children—we lose the memory of the early process. For as far back as we *can* remember, we are pretty much like the finished product—a boy or a girl.

Parentally Instilled Stereotypes

By the age of two, children generally are being taught the norms related to their sex in their particular culture. The methods of socialization we discussed earlier in this chapter are addressed to sex-related norms as well as to values and norms of wider application: by instruction and imitation, by the different ways that significant others interact with them, later by role-modeling, and through all the stages of development of the self, individuals come to be cultural products that they think of as natural and unchangeable.

Some studies have shown that even from birth, the treatment of girls and boys is different.[14] Researchers have observed that mothers of six-month-old infant girls touch their babies much more than mothers of boys the same age. One researcher has demonstrated that this later causes little girls to seek more maternal contact, whereas little boys have internalized the expectation they will be independent.

[14]Weitzman, "Sex-Role Socialization."

The subtlest ways of interacting with an infant can influence later patterns of behavior.

Many of the norms about differences between boys and girls are reinforced in picture books. Studies have shown that most children's books and television programs portray very stereotyped images of women and men. Different expectations of different sexes are articulated in folk expressions, as we showed earlier ("Boys will be boys," "She's a perfect little lady," "Boys are better in math," "She's mother's little helper").

Not everyone in our culture develops the attitudes and beliefs that women should be dependent, however. One study found that children whose mothers work had less stereotyped ideas about sex roles. Similarly, girls whose fathers encourage high achievement and performance more often seek roles that are not typically female.[15]

Parents transfer their sex role expectations to their children in many ways, some deliberate, others unconscious. In traditional families that have not been influenced by the feminist movement, a crying seven-year-old girl is far more likely to get comfort and sympathy from her mother or father than a seven-year-old boy. A little boy may find his crying tolerated only if he is in pain. If he cries from frustration, fatigue, or disappointment, he often is

[15]Ibid., p. 136.

reproved, "Big boys don't cry, Paul. Do you want your father to think you're a sissy?" A little girl crying for similar reasons is likely to get a show of sympathy and parental efforts to direct her attention to some diversion. She probably will not be told that it is somehow wrong for her to cry.

As children get older, parental expectations about behavior of the sexes increase in scope and frequency. The toys children are given for their birthdays and other gift-giving holidays may also reflect traditional cultural norms: trucks, trains, bats, and balls for boys; dolls, dollhouses, tea sets, and little ovens for girls. The early stages of anticipatory socialization (of learning future roles by make-believe) are thus linked to future sex roles. So are other habits or patterns of play: boys are expected to be rambunctious, inquisitive about everything, hard to control; girls are expected to "play nicely," to be more subdued and obedient. The later stages of childhood socialization follow logically from these beginnings.

Reinforcement of Stereotypes

The role models and later the generalized other of a boy or a girl simply reflect the sex differences instilled a few years before. This process is reinforced by the images of the larger world in children's books, their music, and most of their television viewing. Thus, not only is their present behavior encouraged to reflect cultural sex role types, but also their childhood exposure to the grownup world gives them the same stereotypes.

Once children enter school, they are exposed to another source of sex role socialization. According to several research projects, the books used in the early grades to teach reading present the same sex role models that are found in preschool books.[16] The history books used throughout grammar school and high school present the past as one created by men. This neglect of women is only partly because they have been excluded from active participation in politics, war, business, and the arts. They have not been as uniformly absent as their neglect in the history books suggests.

Once children are in high school, guidance counselors and the tracking system come into play to reinforce the socialization accomplished so far. Boys and girls of equal demonstrated intelligence and similar aptitudes and interests may be channeled into different programs preparing them for different future

[16]Lenore J. Weitzman and Diane Rizzo, "Images of Males and Females in Elementary School Textbooks" (New York: National Organization for Women, Legal Defense and Education Fund, 1974); Terry Savo, Carol Nagy Jacklin, and Carol Kehr Tittle, "Sex Role Stereotyping in the Public Schools," *Harvard Educational Review* 43 (1973): 386–416.

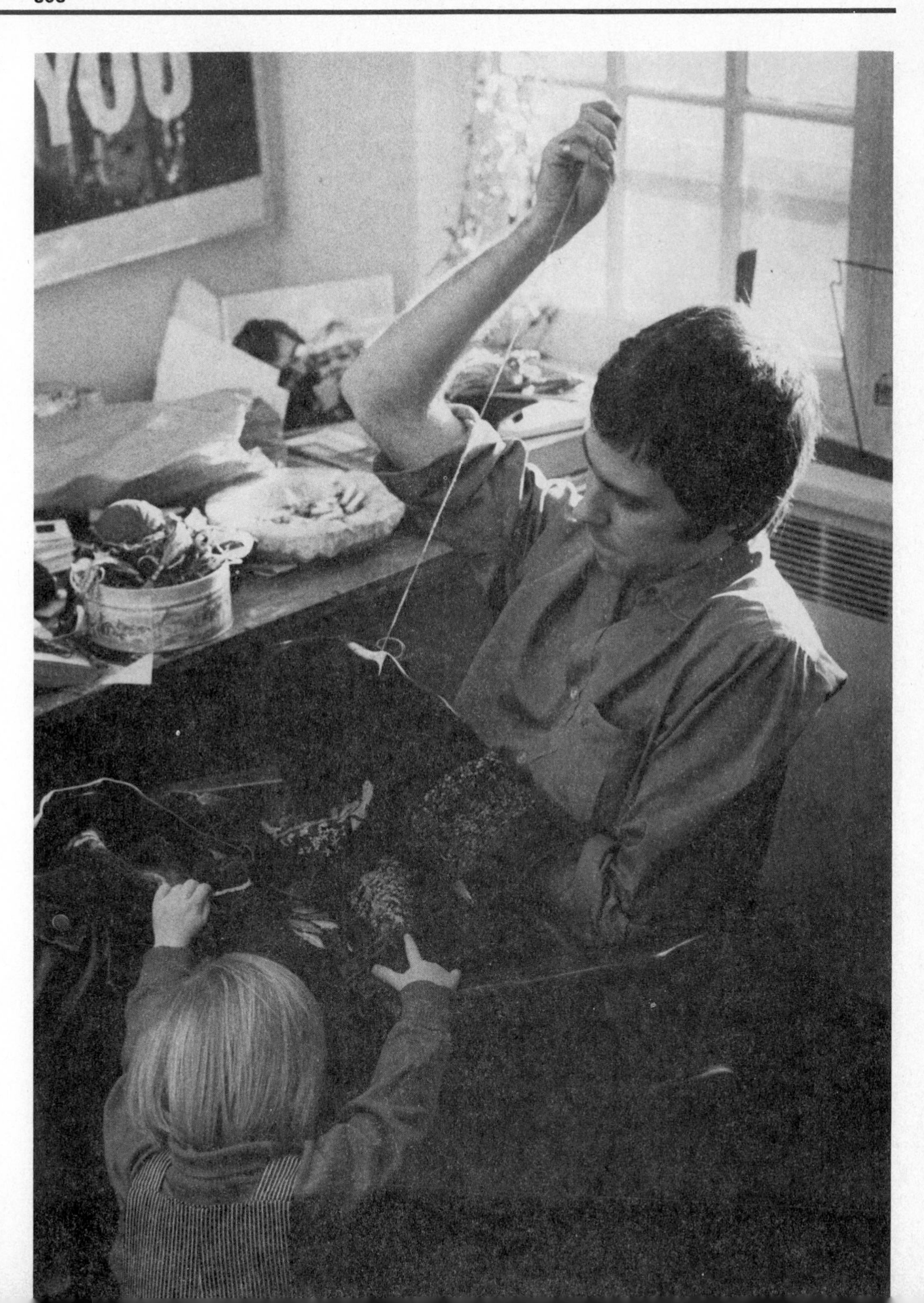

Sex roles are passed to the young by example as well as by precept.

occupations. Suppose a girl wants to become an engineer, a physicist, a mathematician, a doctor, or some other professional in an occupation that is almost exclusively male. Unless she attends a truly "liberated" high school and has parents similarly minded, she will face a great deal of resistance. (And her chances of being in such a high school depend heavily on her parents' social class.) Until the feminist movement became a visible cultural force, many young women succumbed to this resistance. Today fewer do.

Feminism in the last ten or fifteen years has also had an effect on sociology. Recently, significant attention has at last been given to the importance of socialization in transmitting sex-related norms (although Margaret Mead's study of the New Guinea tribes was published in the mid-thirties). The feminist movement has also influenced the beliefs and socializing goals of many parents, so that they now guard against limiting their children to traditional roles.

1. Assume you have a son and a daughter whom you want to raise to be free of traditional sex role stereotyping. Consider only their pre-school years. Make two lists for each child: one of traits you want to encourage; one of traits you want to discourage.

2. Try to describe the socializing methods you would use to convey your expectations to your children.

3. Compare your lists with the lists of the other students of your sex in the class. Is there a consensus in goals and methods for son and daughter? What significant differences appear, if any? Compile the consensus goals and methods.

4. Compare these consensus lists with those drawn up by the students of the opposite sex. How much agreement is there? What are the significant differences? How do you account for them?

Female Fear of Success

Matina Horner, a psychologist and the president of Radcliffe College, hypothesized that young women who were capable of success in careers were more fearful of it than comparably talented men.[17] Horner administered the following test to students at a leading university. Each male was asked to tell

[17]Matina Horner, "Fail: Bright Women," *Psychology Today*, November 1969, p. 36. For a later statement, see id., "Toward an Understanding of Achievement-related Conflicts in Women," *Journal of Social Issues* 28 (1972): 157–75.

a story based on the sentence, "After first-term finals John finds himself at the top of his medical school class." Over 90 percent of the male students wrote with delight about John's success. They predicted a great future for this wonderful guy.

Women students were asked to write a story given the same sentence, except that the name was changed from John to Anne. About two-thirds of the young women wrote stories that indicated they were worried about professional success. For example:

Anne is an acne-faced bookworm. She runs to the bulletin board and finds she's at the top. As usual she smarts off. A chorus of groans is the rest of the class's reply. . . . She studies 12 hours a day and lives at home to save money. "Well it certainly paid off. All the Friday and Saturday nights without dates—fun. I'll be the best woman doctor alive!" And yet a twinge of sadness comes through—she wonders what she really has.

Anne feels guilty. . . She will finally have a nervous breakdown and quit medical school and marry a successful young doctor.

Anne is talking to her counselor. Counselor says she will make a fine *nurse.*

Other young women pictured Anne as crippled or simply unable to do so well. One bright honors student wrote:

Anne starts proclaiming her surprise and joy. Her fellow classmates are so disgusted with her behavior that they jump on her in a body and beat her. She is maimed for life.

This study reveals how young adults are affected by their constant exposure to sex stereotypes. It used many other questions and activities, and all led to the finding that young women are affected by the notion that achievement is a masculine trait. They felt that even very bright women should be careful to play down their mastery of skills and knowledge to fit society's definition of what is feminine. Horner found, for example, that many female students scored higher on tests than males when men and women were tested in separate rooms. When women were given a similar test together with males in a more competitive situation, the women's scores went down significantly. For the men the opposite was true: over two-thirds were able to raise their scores when they were in a competitive situation. The study demonstrates additional psychological barriers that career-minded women face as a result of their socialization.

Horner saw some hope for the future in the women students who did not have a fear of success. Said one:

> Anne is quite a lady—not only is she tops academically, but she is liked and admired by her fellow students—quite a trick in a man-dominated field. She is brilliant, but also a woman. She will continue to be at or near the top, and . . . always a lady.[18]

Horner followed up her study of college students in a major American university by administering the same tests and questions to students in high schools and other settings. The responses quite clearly demonstrated that young men and women had very different learning patterns about what is appropriate for their sex and that many capable young women were taught to fear success.

Some of Matina Horner's material is preliminary. More studies are needed to understand the complexity of fear of success and fear of failure and their relationships to sex role socialization. Some social scientists have begun to offer critiques of her work—primarily based on her sample size and method. Yet her study is widely cited because it raises very disturbing hypotheses about the effects of sex role socialization. It also points to the kinds of questions social scientists must pursue.

OTHER SOCIAL-STRUCTURAL INFLUENCES ON SOCIALIZATION

Social-structural influences: the influence of social variables on the socialization of any individual in a society.

Our description of socialization has given the broadest outlines of the process. In a complex industrial society, however, considerable differences arise in how children are socialized. Methods and goals differ according to social class, ethnic background, religious affiliation, and even overall economic conditions and political moods.

International Competition

In 1957, the Soviet Union launched its first orbiting space satellite, Sputnik. In that cold war period, the fact that the Soviets had been first into space was considered a major embarrassment by the United States government and by much of our population. The government appropriated large sums of money for space-related research grants and studies on college campuses, and science and math programs assumed great prestige in high school. Bright high school students were strongly encouraged to major in the sciences (particularly those related to aerospace). Liberal arts departments in colleges had greater difficulty obtaining adequate funds, as new, expensive science buildings and laboratories mushroomed. Government space and military research funding continued to grow to the point where in the middle and late 1960s many campus protesters described their colleges as arms of the military.

[18]Horner, "Fail: Bright Women," p. 62.

Our society's dependence on technological skills has placed great emphasis on advanced education in recent generations. This concern has been fostered by the cold war of recent decades and the defense and aerospace rivalries of the major world powers.

What has all this to do with socialization? Simply that many youths who might have become doctors, writers, musicians, or teachers, were virtually pushed into high school science programs and then on to science majors in college. Moreover, the relative decline in the liberal arts has continued, so that monetary rewards and prestige still favor the sciences in college and beyond.

Technological Advances

From this example we can see how technology also influences socialization. If two national powers became enemies in earlier times, large numbers of men were recruited for combat, not for research. But the heavy reliance of countries on technological advantage over each other as a source of power has made national priorities more complex since World War II.

Technology has had other, more far-reaching influences on socialization. We saw in Chapter 5 that the technological evolution of our society in this century has drastically shrunk the need for unskilled labor. Thus, long formal schooling and adequate academic performance have become essential to economic success. This fact can produce different reactions from individuals, ranging from vigorous use of educational opportunities to apathy and a sense of hopelessness.

Social Class

Social class influences the cultural content and the methods of socialization. Not only do members of each class view society differently but so do their beliefs about the nature of children and the appropriate parent-child relationship differ. Class is also a critical variable in determining how adolescents see their possibilities for the future. Compare the values of two male adolescents who live two blocks apart in a major city, but who are separated widely in their class backgrounds and aspirations. The first says:

> I think about what I should do when I get out of school, and I just don't know. The people in my neighborhood, . . . they're all doing it wrong. And if one tries to get out, the rest laughs. Like they say, they tried and couldn't do it, so you're not going to do it either. And this guy feels, ''Well, maybe I can't do it,'' and he comes back into the slum. You figure, you know, they failed, man, I might as well give up. . . .
>
> But I don't know any boys from these big houses. As long as I'm living here, all the boys over there have been going to private schools and they're very snotty. They think they're way superior. They can't show it by a fight because they lose. . . . [A boy from those houses] has a lot of protection from his parents, and then, when he is away from them, he doesn't know how to handle himself. I usually go all the time away from my parents and I do pretty well.
>
> The way I see it, right now, I think I have it better than the other one. But when I was small, then he had it, and when I get *older,* he will have it still better. He will have a better education. He will have a better atmosphere.
>
> Like I wouldn't be able to go to a rich night club, or hire a night-club singer, or have a good career. He might turn out to be a lawyer or a doctor or something, whereas I could only be maybe a mechanic or a machinist. I might make money, but I won't make the same kind of money he makes.[19]

The second boy says:

> The one thing I'd like is to be finished with college and have all that worry behind me—all the difficulty of whether I'm going to get in, how my marks are going to be and all that over with. I'd like to be settled down in a good job with enough money to buy all the necessities and some luxuries. The thing I'd like is a lot of clothes, an awful lot of clothes. . . . Then I'd buy a car if I were old enough and a house of my own and, of course, a dog. I see myself in a life with a lot of friends around me and a good family. . . .
>
> I see myself with two or three children whom I can take care of financially, physically, and in every way. And the kind of girl I'd want to marry would be well-mannered, respectable, and good-looking, with a good personality.[20]

[19]Juan Gonzales and Peter Quinn, *Two Blocks Apart* (New York: Avon Books, 1965), pp. 104, 108–10.

[20]Ibid., pp. 117–18.

GROWING UP IN DIFFERENT COMMUNITIES

Why do the attitudes and plans of the two young men who live two blocks apart differ so greatly? The ideas they hold about themselves are a direct outgrowth of the socialization process they have undergone. More precisely a good deal of the variation between them results from their membership in different social classes.

Parents who believe that their children can be successful may socialize them to obey the rules, get good grades, and do all the things required to "get ahead." Other parents may not feel that getting ahead is the most important goal. They may teach their children to value family, friends, and neighborhood more than higher education, wealth, job prestige, and suburban living. Parents who are struggling to provide the basic necessities may believe either that their children are their only hope for improvement or that failure and bad luck are their lot in life. All these parents pass along their attitudes to their children. In short, most people teach their children to play roles according to what they think is valuable or necessary for life as they know it.

In this section we compare child-rearing practices in three distinct North American communities. The communities differ in social class and ethnic composition. One is a wealthy suburb, one is a working-class urban neighborhood, and the third is a lower-class public housing project.

As you read the descriptions, pay particular attention to the agents of socialization. Can you identify the socialization methods the young people are undergoing? What agents teach them about sex roles and future possibilities as they move through various age levels to adulthood?

Crestwood Heights: Growing Up Middle Class

Crestwood Heights, a wealthy suburb of Toronto, Canada, has many of the characteristics of the "American dream"—the houses, yards, schools, and shopping centers that typify American upper-middle-class suburbs. Here the criteria for prestige are a good education, an impressive home, and expensive possessions, such as elegant furniture, art objects, and books. Many families originally came from less well-to-do circumstances and have worked very hard to get where they are. Parents try diligently to prepare their children for a comparable life.

In the mid-1950s a group of researchers spent five years studying this community and its child-rearing practices.[21] They found that the number and spacing of births was usually planned and that children grew up in an environ-

[21]John R. Seeley, R. Alexander Sim, and Elizabeth W. Loosly, *Crestwood Heights, Toronto* (Toronto: University of Toronto Press, 1956).

Social class, ethnic and religious background, educational attainments of parents, and parental views of society are among the important social variables that influence the socialization of the young and their futures in the society.

ment that was watched over and carefully controlled by adults. These successful families placed great value on their material possessions. There were many things in the home that children were not permitted to touch and rooms in which they were not to play. Although freedom in the house was limited, children received expensive toys, often educational in design. Very early, then, children learned that property was valuable.

Parents took pains to pursue various activities with their young children, and the children quickly learned that life was well-ordered and took place on a scheduled basis. Organized activities began to dominate a child's life at a very early age. At three, children were sent to nursery school, where they were separated from their families for several hours a day. Since there were many children in a class, each had to learn to share the teacher's attention and act with some independence. Children at the nursery school were expected to get along with others, to share toys, and to explore their environment freely. The nursery school experience was designed to help the children overcome "aggressive impulses" and develop proper social attitudes and skills.

The parents deliberately turned over part of socialization to trained experts who were not nearly as emotionally involved in dealing with their children. This reduction of family involvement in child rearing accelerated the child's preparation for entering the larger world. There was a close relationship between parents' goals for the child and the attitudes and skills that the teachers tried to impart.

Nursery school was, of course, followed by grade school and a series of after-school activities, ranging from ballet lessons to clubs. Between school terms, the children went to summer camps. Children were expected to do well in their activities and to assume more and more responsibility as they matured.

From ages five to twelve, the values of responsibility and punctuality were stressed in many ways. Children learned that they were expected to be on time for a host of organized activities. Scouts, music lessons, religious education were all planned for after-school hours. Each of these activities helped the child develop a sense of responsibility. That is, while learning the norms of scouting or dancing or playing the piano, the child was also learning, again, the norm of doing what others expect to be done. As children grew older, their obligations were increasingly stressed. The parents were intent on teaching their children to be responsible for such things as doing their homework, helping around the house with assigned chores, and learning how to spend money (given in an allowance).

In discussions about the purposes of an allowance, junior high school students in Crestwood Heights showed how they had internalized the values of their parents, as these excerpts from the field notes show:

> A girl expressed the idea that an allowance should be considered from the viewpoint of training for later life; the student will learn the value of money through management of an allowance; if not all the allowance is spent, that part should be saved.
>
> . . . One boy felt an allowance helped develop a sense of responsiblity; boys could save if they had a purpose in mind, such as a gift for Mother's Day.[22]

1. Which significant others are involved in the socialization process in Crestwood Heights? What experiences outside the family have an impact on the children?

2. The researchers observed that parents in Crestwood Heights were particularly concerned that their children internalize the values of responsibility and independence. Parents used money as one means for socializing their children to these values. How do you think an allowance could help parents achieve their goal? What other means did the parents use? What means can you think of that they might have used?

3. According to your own observations of middle-class socialization, does the Crestwood Heights pattern accurately reflect American middle-class socialization in the 1970s? Explain.

West End: Growing Up Working Class

The West End is discussed in Chapter 12 as an example of an "urban village," a community within a city.

Among the Italian-American working-class residents of Boston's West End in the 1950s, sociologist Herbert Gans found the same unity between social class and socialization that was found in Crestwood Heights.[23] By participant observation as a temporary resident, Gans discovered that, although the redevelopment agencies called the area a slum, the occupants enjoyed the crowding. Many of the apartments were inexpensive and in reasonably good condition. In general, the income of these families was low, and less than a third of the workers had finished high school or studied in college. The men were factory workers or low-income service workers such as barbers.

Among the West Enders the nuclear family (father, mother, and unmarried children) tended to be large. Even so, a family did few things alone. Problems and pleasures were readily shared with neighbors and relatives, who formed an essential peer group. However, interaction was most common among members of the same sex.

[22]Ibid., p. 110.

[23]Herbert Gans, *The Urban Villagers* (Glencoe, Ill.: Free Press, 1962).

Although parents wanted their children to succeed and to live a good life, they did not make children the center of their existence. Parents were very concerned that their children not become "bums," that they be acceptable to the neighborhood peer group. They did not put great emphasis on education or having their children strive for a much higher social position than they themselves had. It was much more important that children not disgrace their families—that boys and girls learn behavior considered appropriate to their sex. For example, boys were taunted and called sissies if they did anything that was considered unmasculine, such as playing the piano or studying too much.

West End parents rarely intervened or involved themselves in the children's schools. Many children were sent to parochial schools, because parents valued the discipline and religious training these schools offered. Parents would become involved in the school, whether parochial or public, only if the child was in trouble. Children needed to learn enough to be able to get jobs. And jobs were defined according to the parental experience—unskilled, low-paying occupations requiring little schooling.

Parents spoke to their children as if they were adults and expected them to behave accordingly. Girls at age seven or eight were expected to help their mothers with housework and taking care of younger children. Boys were given considerable freedom to roam the neighborhood streets. The rules of good behavior that parents taught their children were often contradicted by the street rules learned from peer groups.

By the time they were in their teens, boys—and to a lesser extent, girls—spent little time in their homes. At home or in school, they were often withdrawn and quiet; on the street, they behaved much more boisterously. If, after age ten or so, boys got into trouble with the police or the priest, parents rarely felt responsible or guilty. They would blame their son for being a "bad kid" or having "bad friends." Similarly, parents didn't worry much about whether they were being too strict or too permissive. They were generally unconcerned about any later psychological impact of their methods of child-rearing or discipline. They told the child what they expected in as direct a way as they would have told an adult.

What, then, did the children learn from these kinds of socialization experiences? They quickly realized that, although certain behavior was expected of them in the home, much that was important in their lives would occur in their peer groups. These groups of friends of the same age and sex often determined acceptable individual behavior. For example, scholastic excellence was usually scorned as sissy behavior for boys. As a result, the studious young man had to find new friends or, more likely, play down (repress) his academic interests to stay in the group.

Teenage peer groups were segregated by sex. Because of this, Gans was able to learn much more about the male groups than the female ones. Also, the male groups were more visible on street corners and in public. Teenage boys loved to talk about girls and various sexual exploits, but they looked down on anyone who had a serious relationship with a girl that took him away from the group. In their late teens, however, boys began to date or "go with" girls. When they married, they temporarily left the group. Soon after, new groups of married men and women formed. Yet, for most of their social interactions the women were in one room and the men in another.

Like their parents, the children learned to value the community for the company and support the peer group gave them. Unlike children in Crestwood Heights, they were not taught to place much value on privacy, education, or achievements that would take them far from the community.

1. How do the West Enders' expectations of their children differ from those of the Crestwood Heights parents?

2. How does the type of education (and educational philosophy) offered to and sought by West End parents and children differ from the education in Crestwood Heights? What values are stressed and developed in both school settings?

3. What is the function of peer groups in the West End? How does this differ from the Crestwood Heights child's experience?

Blackmoor: Growing Up Poor

As Eskimo children must learn to deal with life in the cold arctic climate, and those in fishing villages must learn the dangers and benefits of rivers and oceans, so all communities must instruct their young in the realities of their life situations. Among some communities the dangers and difficulties are so great that children must be socialized quickly to protect themselves from the hazards of their environment. Such was the case in a poor urban housing project studied by sociologist William Moore.[24]

Moore studied life in Blackmoor, a large project in an urban ghetto of a midwest city. He wanted to analyze the effects of life in a high-rise slum on the children who grew up there. Furthermore, he hoped his research would increase public understanding about the difficulties of life in a ghetto project and would encourage the creation of new laws to benefit the urban poor. He

[24]William Moore, Jr., *The Vertical Ghetto* (New York: Random House, 1969).

sought answers to several questions: What is the meaning of growing up in a "vertical ghetto"? What values do children learn? How are they taught to adapt to this environment?

What Moore found was that Blackmoor parents were much less able to control the socialization process their children underwent than parents in Crestwood Heights or the West End. Many desperately wanted to protect their youngsters from exposure to violence or gambling but were unable to do so. Significant others outside the home became important agents in teaching children to survive in this very difficult environment.

Moore reported that the project was overcrowded and dirty, many of its facilities needed repair, and its halls and stairwells were scenes of gambling and crime. Families lived in very cramped conditions in most apartments. Sleeping space was at a premium, and bathrooms were in constant use. Rarely was there a quiet place for a child to study or be alone. The noise level throughout the building was very high. Children played in the halls, and music blared from radios and records. Outside, the streets roared with the sound of large trucks on their way to nearby depots and other local traffic.

Many of the fathers had no jobs. In fact, they frequently did not live with their families. They were driven from their homes by despair at their inability to support their families and by welfare regulations that gave financial aid to families only if there was no father in the home.

This disruption of the family relationships had a serious impact on the children. The boys particularly were deprived of the opportunity to learn from and identify with a father and use him as a role model. Although the girls were more fortunate in being able to identify with their mothers, they also faced some serious problems. Many of the mothers worked outside their homes for long hours each day. Girls at a young age were given responsibility for taking care of smaller children.

Youngsters had to grow up very quickly. With little opportunity for parental supervision, even preschool children soon became skilled, for example, at crossing busy streets to buy family groceries. Unlike other children, who are supervised by a baby-sitter when their parents are away, these children had to learn to take care of themselves for hours.

Play in the playground and on the streets was often rough, and fights were frequent. Children learned at an early age that they had to know how to defend themselves. In contrast, children from wealthier communities are constantly told that fighting is bad. They are encouraged to "get along" with other children. This type of socialization, suitable for the environment in Crestwood Heights, would have left youngsters poorly prepared for coping with the rough-and-tumble relations of ghetto life.

Blackmoor parents had hopes for their children's futures. Most parents, however, were unable to provide the environment or pass on the skills or motivations that would make such success possible. On the contrary, Moore believed that the harsh realities of growing up in a "vertical ghetto" like Blackmoor socialized children to attitudes and skills that were essential to survival there but were not often useful for succeeding in the larger society.

Moore cited, for example, the many instances in which Blackmoor's children saw their parents treated without respect by housing authorities, social workers, or police officers. The children knew their parents felt insulted and saw that they could not force others to deal with them as citizens worthy of consideration. The children experienced similar treatment themselves in neighborhood stores. Clerks looked on all the children as potential thieves. They were closely watched as they moved about the aisles or searched as they left the store. Moore writes that children who were treated like thieves often took up the challenge and actually outwitted the guards.

Blackmoor children did not generally know any parents who had solved their marital and economic problems. Rather, the children continually experienced family breakdown, community deterioration, and the distrust and lack of respect of those outside the project. Thus, according to Moore, most children did not learn to respect themselves or put much stock in their chances for the future. They saw few who had made it out of the vertical ghetto by means of education and a career. The Blackmoor children were given a legacy of failure by their parents, their immediate community, and the larger society. Their upbringing denied most of them the competence or vision to change the situation for themselves, their siblings, or their peers.

1. What important roles do "significant others" play in the lives of Blackmoor's ghetto children? How does this differ from the experience of the children in Crestwood Heights and in the West End?

2. How does Blackmoor socialize its children to attitudes and skills that are essential to survival but not necessarily useful in getting ahead in the larger society?

3. Compare your own upbringing with that of a friend or acquaintance whose family seems to follow a different style of life (different class, racial, ethnic, or educational background). How do you think these different socialization experiences affected the development of your values, beliefs, and behavior?

SUMMARY

Socialization is the process by which individuals learn the values, norms, and role expectations of their social environment. It begins as children interact first with parents and later with peers, teachers, and other adults. It also occurs as children are exposed to messages from television and other mass media. From these interaction and exposures the child's definition of self grows. Such concepts as significant other, generalized other, role-playing, and internalization all assist the sociologist in understanding the process.

Socialization is a lifelong process. In childhood the foundations of belief and behavior are laid. During adolescence the emphasis is on anticipatory socialization for future work and family roles. Young people are prepared for independence while they remain under the authority of families, schools, and other restrictive bodies. In societies like ours this seeming contradiction often leads to major discontinuities in the socialization process of teenagers.

In addition, certain social variables, such as sex, influence the outcome of the socialization process. Evidence indicates that parents and teachers relate differently to girls and to boys. Textbooks portray girls less frequently and usually show them to be passive and dependent. Teaching systems direct females into different careers from their male peers. Indeed, one important and provocative study reveals that success itself is viewed by many women with anxiety and fear.

Social-class background also looms large in its impact on young people. An individual's life experiences, aspirations, and opportunities differ according to the wealth, prestige, and influence of his or her family. In American society it makes a great deal of difference whether children grow up in a wealthy suburan area, a working-class urban community, or a lower-class housing project.

10 THE ADULT YEARS: FAMILY, WORK, AND RETIREMENT

Small children look forward to the day when they will no longer be considered children, when they will be on their own, when they will truly be adults. The anticipation is related to their conception of adulthood as a time of independence, of living life on their own terms, of choosing the kinds of jobs they want and making all sorts of decisions that affect their own lives. Once they are well established in that state of adulthood, they sometimes wish that, like Peter Pan, they could have remained children forever.

Between the idealized state of adulthood and the reality of life as a spouse, a parent, and a breadwinner, there is sometimes quite a difference. Adults quickly learn that the freedoms of majority are only relative. They have to make trade-offs between the independence they longed for and the responsibilities now required—even if these are only the obligations to provide for themselves and their families. Most important of all they learn that there is still much to learn!

Throughout their adult lives people must learn or master new,

unfamiliar roles and the norms that apply to them. Many of their values change. For example, note the different peaks of concern about health, marital appreciation, and wealth by adults of different ages in the graphs below. At the same time that people's values are changing, the values and norms of the society are also changing. This is a particular characteristic of a modern industrial society.

Clearly, then, by marrying and starting families (or adapting to life as an unmarried adult), by entering the job market, and by living in a society that is constantly changing, adults continue the process of socialization that was so much a central fact of childhood and adolescence.

Concern About Selected Issues by Age

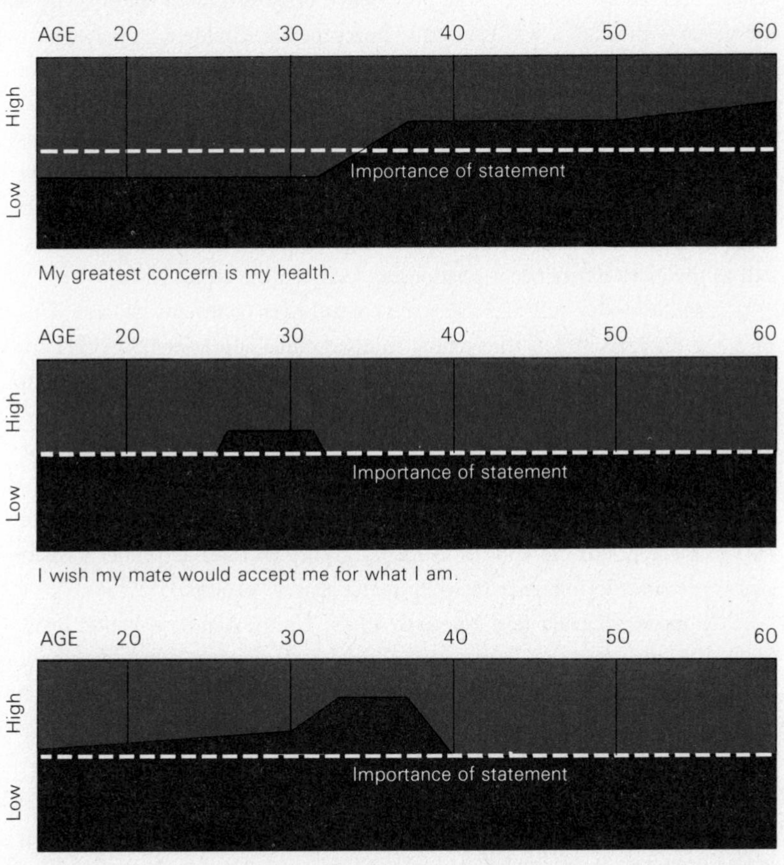

Source: Wilbur Bradbury and the editors of Time-Life, *The Adult Years* (New York: Time-Life Books, 1975), p. 69.

MARRIAGE

Almost every discussion of marriage in popular journals and books talks about the rising instability of marriage, the inadequacy of romantic interest as the guide for choosing marriage partners, the changing definitions of appropriate roles within a marriage, and new forms of marriage, such as open marriages and contract marriages. Let's try to retrace the sources of some of our modern ideas and beliefs about marriage.

From Arranged to Free-Choice Marriage

For hundreds of years in Europe most marriages were arranged by parents. Over the course of several centuries this arrangement underwent many changes. Even in colonial times in America, young people began to have some veto power. The parents chose, but the prospective bride or groom could speak out and object if the choice was personally unacceptable. Children exercised increasing independence as families moved to cities where young people met each other in schools, jobs, and churches.

Parental choice with possible child veto was then replaced by a proposal: a man first proposed marriage to the woman of his choice and then asked her father's permission to have the daughter's "hand." This ritual symbolized the continuing parental concern for a child's right choice of marriage partner as well as the more independent relationship between the sexes.

Families today still exercise some control over children's choices. They often use financial means, threatening to discontinue educational or other support, if their son or daughter marries an unacceptable partner. If parents have no property to hand down, their authority over the children's choices is decreased.[1] Observers have noted that in the Soviet Union, for example, the abolition of private property made decision-making within families more democratic and increased the power of the children.[2] Parents throughout the world, however, still use appeals to family loyalty and ties and other psychological pressures to influence their children's marital choices.

In modern Europe and especially in the United States, romantic love fused with other traditions surrounding matrimony. Factors other than "falling in love at first sight" continued to be important. Families of means sent their offspring to colleges and universities where they would be most likely to meet

[1]Friedrich Engels, in his classic work *The Origins of the Family, Private Property and the State* (Chicago: C. H. Kerr, 1902), noted that private control of wealth usually inhibits democracy in the family.

[2]Kent Geiger, "The Family and Social Change," in *The Transformation of Russian Society,* ed. Cyril E. Black (Cambridge: Harvard University Press, 1960), p. 450.

others of their station. Religious and ethnic groups brought together young people of marriageable age in social clubs and camps just as matchmakers or other arrangers used to do.

The move from arranged to free-choice marriage was not specifically an American phenomenon. Rather, it seems to have accompanied industrialization. In China, for example, marriages were traditionally arranged by parents, often when the children were very young. In 1950, one year after it came to power, the Communist government passed a comprehensive marriage law that attempted to modernize family relations. The law expressly forbade arranged marriages and insisted on free choice by wedding partners. When they went to register, each had to declare that the decision was his or her own. Parents initially resisted, and official policy was modified. Parents could still play a role in introducing young people. They were expected to exert some influence, such as disapproval and discouragement of a political outcast, but they nevertheless had to allow the bridal couple to make the final choice.[3]

1. Family control or involvement in an individual's marriage choice reflects a different set of values and beliefs from romantic love. According to the romantic tradition—often reinforced by popular magazines, books, and television—love conquers all. The conflict is classically drawn in *Romeo and Juliet,* where the two young lovers are denied the chance of marrying because their families are feuding enemies. A modern version of the theme was *West Side Story,* which substituted ethnic group conflict for family feuding as the force tearing lovers apart. Can you think of other books or plays where this theme is central?

2. What norms in choosing a marriage partner prevailed when your parents were married? Ask them or a member of their generation. What norms have changed since then? Describe today's norms.

What changes do you think might occur by the time your children are ready to marry? In answering, consider the increasing mobility of the young, the increasing economic independence of both men and women, the influence of the mass media, and changes in the interaction of different ethnic and racial groups.

[3]Martin King Whyte, "The Family," in *China's Developmental Experience,* ed. Michel Oksenberg, *Proceedings of the American Academy of Political Science* 31, no. 1 (1973): 175–92.

Contemporary Marital Norms

The opportunities for *exogamous* marriage (marriage outside the group) have grown in our society over the years. Marriages between individuals of different ethnic and religious backgrounds rarely create scandals anymore. Marriage is a means of social mobility, and people of different socioeconomic backgrounds often do meet, fall in love, and marry.

Yet the old factors are not dead. Many parents still do not want their children to marry "beneath them" socially. Religious concerns, educational background, and other factors influence an individual's choice. Interracial marriages are still relatively rare, accepted in a few communities but condemned in many others.

Courtship normally takes place during late adolescence and early adulthood. Young people then have to balance a variety of pressures in choosing a partner. The choice of a marriage partner is potentially quite stressful to young adults. Divorce rates may be rising, but individuals getting married still feel as if they are making lifetime choices, often at an age when they are continuing to grow and change intellectually and emotionally.

In contemporary society the traditional division of tasks between the sexes is gradually giving way, as this businessman doing household chores and this businesswoman at an industry luncheon attest.

The wedding is a rite of passage: the white gown and tuxedo, flowers, rice, a gathering of friends and family, a feast of good food all mark the acquisition of a new status ceremonially. Gifts of household items—pots and pans, silverware and dishes, linens, and toasters—are common recognition that the new couple are establishing their own home.

The new status means new roles. In the past, role expectations were quite specific. Women stayed home or worked a short time until they began having children. Their first obligation was to homemaking, whereas men's first duty was to bring home the bread. Now the expectations of wives and husbands are less well defined. Many families need two incomes to maintain their life-style, and many women have begun to resist the traditional definitions of their role as wives. The cultural changes have challenged the former division of labor between spouses.

Effects of Women's New Roles on Marriage

Just as marriages moved historically from an arranged to a free-choice system, so the nature of the marital relationship has moved from a highly unequal one, in which husbands had almost all the power and prerogatives, to a more evenly

balanced relationship. These characterizations, however, are two ends of a continuum. Certain women always held some power in their marital relationships—by virtue of the wealth or family connections they brought to the marriage or by virtue of their personal qualities. But by and large, until recent decades, power resided with husbands. Legally, wives could often not own property, have custody rights to their children in case of divorce, or exercise other minimal civil liberties. Mores reinforced this legal inequality. A double standard, for example, allowed much greater sexual freedom for men than for women.

The slow movement toward more equal relationships has been in process for over a century. Nineteenth-century feminists protested property, divorce, and custody prohibitions. Lucy Stone and Henry Blackwell in the 1850s drew up their own marriage contract because she refused to swear to the passive obedience required in the traditional oath. Instead, the couple published the following "Protest" on the occasion of their marriage:

> While we acknowledge our mutual affection by publicly assuming the relationship of husband and wife, yet, in justice to ourselves and a great principle, we deem it a duty to declare that this act on our part implies no sanction of, nor promise of voluntary obedience to, such of the present laws of marriage as refuse to recognize the wife as an independent, rational being, while they confer upon the husband an injurious and unnatural superiority, investing him with legal powers which no honorable man would exercise, and which no man should possess. . . .[4]

As feminists gained greater legal and political rights, changes in the character of the relationship between spouses were coming about. This changing relationship paralleled other changes for women, such as the increase in the number of women getting higher education and their growing participation in the labor force. Women with college education tend to have stronger feminist attitudes than those who do not go to college.

Still, today few marriages are totally equal.[5] The traditional division of labor keeps most women responsible for the private sphere of household management and most men responsible for the public sphere of economics and politics. This division is under extensive review by many couples, but it continues to influence most marital relationships. Couples usually will move

[4]From Alice Stone Blackwell, *Lucy Stone, Pioneer Woman Suffragist* (Boston: Little, Brown, 1930), pp. 161–68.

[5]For a review of the continuing sources of husband power, see Dan L. Gillespie, "Who Has the Power? The Marital Struggle," in *Women: A Feminist Perspective,* ed. Jo Freeman (Palo Alto, Calif.: Mayfield, 1975), pp. 64–87.

WOMEN'S BELIEFS ABOUT SEX ROLES, BY LEVEL OF EDUCATION

Belief	*College Women*	*Noncollege Women*
It's very important that a man be a good provider	56%	79%
It's very important that a man put his family before anything else	46%	70%
It's very important that a man show women courtesy and respect	45%	66%
It's very important for men to keep their feelings under control at all times	24%	43%
It's very important that a man make the decisions in the family	19%	36%
Having children without formal marriage is morally wrong	41%	62%
Having children is a very important value	35%	50%
Casual premarital sex relations are morally wrong	29%	41%
Women are discriminated against	63%	42%
Women should be free to take the initiative in sex	83%	67%
"Women's place is in the home" is nonsense	64%	47%

Source: Adapted from Daniel Yankelovich, *Changing Youth Values in the 70's*, Copyright © 1974 by the JDR 3rd Fund, Inc., pp. 34–35.

when the husband's job requires it, but not when the wife's job does so. Many more women than men take primary responsibility for cooking, cleaning, laundry, and shopping. Many people still feel men must earn more than their wives to maintain their self-respect. It is acceptable for a wife's educational background to equal her husband's but not for hers to exceed his. It is allowable for a man to marry a woman ten or even twenty years younger than he is, but a woman who marries a man that much younger is considered scandalous, or at least emotionally unstable.

The discrepancy between the ideal—an equal partnership—and the actuality—social contradictions that inhibit equality—creates many tensions in marriage. As part of the socialization process, each couple must come to terms with these tensions. They may simply accept a more traditional, unequal relationship and find ideological and psychological supports for it ("a woman's place is in the home"; "the main thing is that we respect each other"). Or they may struggle against such a relationship and consciously try to divide both work and decision-making power in the home evenly. A small minority of couples are attempting to change family structure more radically—experimenting with group marriage, communal living, role-switching, and other nonconformist marital styles.

PARENTHOOD

Becoming a parent for the first time represents a major change in a person's life cycle. Alice Rossi, a family sociologist, has analyzed the role of parent and compared it to that of spouse or worker.[6] Socialization for parenthood, she argues, is much more tension-ridden. In fact, she says, the "honeymoon" period of a marriage often ends when the wife becomes pregnant.

Why is socialization to parenthood so difficult? First, it is at this time that women in contemporary families experience a radical role change. Rarely do they stop working after marriage but rarely do they continue working for a time after childbirth. In addition, young adults undergo little anticipatory socialization that involves direct contact with infants; they receive meager preparation for the new role. Parents, especially mothers, are expected to love their infants and be totally involved in caring for them. Yet, childbirth is not preceded by the equivalent of a courtship—a period of growing intimacy in preparation for living together. Rather, the birth of an infant is abrupt, suddenly exerting enormous demands on the parents.

Finally, parenthood is one of the few adult roles from which there is no exit. Divorce or job changes are legitimate methods of ending a marital or occupational role that has become intolerable. For most people, accepting the role of parent means assumption of full-time responsibility on a scale they have not experienced before and recognition that they cannot cast it aside when they are tired of it.

Choice of Parenthood

In most parts of the world, birth of a child is an event that is expected to follow marriage quickly and automatically. Failure to have children may be a source of shame, may elicit community sympathy, and often is one of the very few legitimate reasons for divorce.

In highly industrialized countries, birth control has changed some of these patterns. Many couples carefully plan the number and spacing of their children. This tendency has accelerated in the last generation, as birth control pills became available, abortion controls were relaxed, and vasectomy and tubal ligation techniques were improved. Increasing concern in this country about overpopulation, the growth of organizations like Zero Population Growth, and feminist support for women who do not want to be mothers have combined to raise the issue, among some young couples, of whether to have children at all. Thus far, only very small numbers of middle-class couples seem to be

[6]Alice S. Rossi, "Transition to Parenthood," in *Family in Transition,* ed. Arlene S. Skolnick and Jerome H. Skolnick (Boston: Little, Brown, 1971), pp. 331–42.

choosing deliberately to forgo parenthood. Whether or not the trend will broaden is a subject worthy of future study.

The vast majority of young adults are socialized to the idea that marriage and parenthood are important stages in adult life. No matter what difficulties these new statuses present, most believe that to create a family is part of self-realization and fulfillment.

Changes in the Socialization Process

Who teaches adults to be parents? Much of the socialization is internalized while they are children. They tend to repeat a good deal of what their parents did. Some of their learning comes through folklore and advice from other parents. Pregnant women and new parents are often flooded with advice from friends and relatives. These admonitions are a good-natured attempt to help socialize the parents to their new roles. "You should nurse the baby for at least six months." "Don't tie yourself down." "You don't have to sterilize everything." "Heat the baby food." "Don't use baby food." Dozens of well-intentioned guides may be offered almost daily.

In earlier times, before families became so mobile geographically, the guides for new parents were their own parents. Although this remains true for many couples today, many more must rely on experts for guidance. This might seem unfortunate, since it makes learning to become a parent a less personal experience. But at the same time it allows more opportunity for parents to learn new and better ways of doing things than their parents followed. Here parents-to-be practice for the Lamaze method of natural childbirth.

Increasingly, in a complex, mobile society, socialization to parenthood becomes formalized. Prenatal classes are offered to teach prospective parents childbirth techniques and fundamentals of infant care. Books offering parents advice are recommended by obstetricians. Dr. Benjamin Spock's *Baby and Child Care* has sold millions of copies and been translated into many languages. It tells parents when to call the doctor, how to relax in the presence of an infant, what to do when the baby is teething—almost everything an inexperienced mother or father might want to know. Organizations like La Leche League give classes and offer advice to nursing mothers.

This outpouring of books, classes, and groups results partly from the decline of the extended family. In the past, new parents often had relatives nearby to help train them in their new roles. Today's formal training also serves to introduce new norms into the adult socialization process. Advocates

Day-care centers, like this one in the Soviet Union, intensify the child's early interaction with peers and magnify the socializing role of the society (as represented by the government) overshadowing the role of parents.

Extended family: a family that includes more than one nuclear family or includes three or more generations of people linked by birth, living together regularly.

of natural childbirth and permissive methods of child-rearing can present their views more widely and hope to overrule traditional advice from parents and grandparents.

Still, many questions raised by parents remain unanswered, and in some areas their expectations are unclear. Changing norms about working mothers and increased participation in child care by fathers are not always matched by flexibility in the social structure. Good child-care facilities are often unavailable. Few occupations match their working hours to school schedules or allow workers the flexibility of staying home to care for sick children. It is rare to see day-care centers at workplaces, so that parents can spend time with their children during coffee and lunch breaks. A bare beginning has been made in the struggles for paternity as well as maternity leave and for shared jobs or part-time work without loss of fringe benefits, raises, promotions, holidays, vacations, or sick leave.

Some societies have shown greater concern for building structures to meet new parental norms. Many communist and socialist governments provide day-care services as a part of their ideological commitment to having all adults work. The centers often serve also to teach children socialist group values rather than allow parents to pass on traditional beliefs. Thus, child-care facilities are much more numerous in the Soviet Union, China, Sweden, Denmark, and Israel than in the United States, where the tradition that mothers should care for their children full-time still greatly influences parental definitions of their roles.

WORKING

Learning how to play the role of wife or husband, mother or father is, of course, not the only challenge of adult socialization. Crucial learning of new roles also occurs on the job. The variety of occupations to be found in an industrial society is almost infinite. They can be classified, however, into a handful of categories by certain criteria: the difficulty of the work—that is, the kind of talent or training needed to acquire the skills used in the job; where the skills are acquired and how long it takes to acquire them; where the work is performed—in a factory, an office, a store, or elsewhere; and the prestige and money rewards that go with the position.

By these standards we can divide kinds of work into unskilled, semi-skilled, and skilled wage labor (the so-called blue-collar jobs); salaried office work and managerial positions (white-collar jobs); and professional occupations (whether within organizations or as forms of self-employment). How people become socialized to each kind of job, and how their norms and sense of self are affected, should emerge as we discuss each of these categories.

Jobs requiring little skill, like that of the French short order cook shown here, can sometimes offer a worker satisfaction, but few such jobs do. They also offer low prestige, low pay, and little opportunity for advancement.

The Unskilled Laborer

Several million American men and women perform relatively unskilled work that requires little formal education and only a few, basic abilities. Dish-washing, operating an elevator, carrying bricks, and cleaning a building are taught on the job in a very brief time, ranging from a few minutes to a few hours. The pay for these jobs is low, and so is the social prestige attached to them.

Costs and values. To study unskilled workers, sociologist Elliot Liebow became a participant-observer among black workmen in Washington, D.C.[7] He lived among them and their families for about eighteen months in the early 1960s, becoming intimate enough to learn of their joys and troubles, their dreams and frustrations. Most of the men did hard physical work for low pay. The jobs held out no hope of future advancement, and the men constantly shifted from one job to another. They were never able to make enough money for enough time to provide for their families adequately, to get satisfaction

[7]Elliot Liebow, *Tally's Corner* (Boston: Little, Brown, 1967).

In Chapter 5 we discussed the requirement that many roles be reciprocal and the problems that arise when they are not.

from their work, or to develop much self-respect.

From the employer's viewpoint, ideally these men were to be socialized to be cooperative, reliable, and respectful to the boss at work. They were supposed to be pleasant, to learn quickly, and to assert no independence in doing their work. This socialization was rarely achieved in reality. The study revealed that other attitudes about the work had more influence on the roles the workers played.

Liebow found that the men had little interest in specific details of a particular job beyond the size of the paycheck. A worker doing the menial tasks of society saw little difference between "pushing a mop and pulling trash in an apartment house, a restaurant, or an office building . . . or if he is a laborer . . . pushing a wheelbarrow, mixing mortar, or digging a hole." The men often did not work hard to succeed at these jobs and changed work frequently. Given the available alternatives in the unskilled labor market, they felt "a job is a job."

Images of failure. Liebow analyzed why the workers adopted the attitude of lack of job commitment. They had learned, he explained, that these jobs were considered worthless by the larger society. Not only were they low-paid tasks, but they also offered no prestige or opportunity for advancement. Most of society held dishwashing and janitorial work in contempt, and so did the men who worked at these jobs. Menial work seriously affected the men's view of themselves. After going from one job to another and making no headway in money or esteem, they began to regard themselves as failures. One described his situation this way:

> "I've been scuffling for five years from morning till night. And my kids still don't have anything, my wife don't have anything, and I don't have anything." "There," he said, gesturing down the hall to a bed, a sofa, a couple of chairs and a television set, all shabby, some broken, "There's everything I have and I'm having trouble holding onto that."[8]

Unemployed and underemployed unskilled workers like those described in *Tally's Corner* reflect one of the sharpest problems of our industrialized society—not everyone shares in the abundance that new technology offers. Indeed there is a high correlation between workers' skill levels and their likelihood of unemployment at some time. Among unskilled workers, it is the very young, the very old, and those with little schooling who are the first to be laid off and the last to be hired. Recessions and depressions hit them first and hardest.

[8]Ibid., p. 67.

In his conclusion Liebow challenges American society to deal with the problems of these workers. Some, he admits, have been crippled by their inability to find jobs that pay a living wage. These men need to be paid reparations (given public financial support), for they may be beyond help. But many thousands of others are young and eager enough to accept and benefit from training for more skilled work. Until this country takes steps to improve their condition there will remain a large group of poor, like the inhabitants of *The Vertical Ghetto* we discussed in Chapter 9, who have little hope and competence to pass on to their children.

Prestige in unskilled jobs. The men studied by Liebow make a sharp contrast to a morgue attendant studied by David Sudnow in a large county hospital.[9] The actual tasks in the morgue were quite simple, but learning how to behave on the job was a more subtle and important part of the work. This was accomplished by a complex socialization process.

The attendant's major tasks were to transport dead bodies from the wards to the morgue and to assist the pathologist in performing autopsies. The work itself was not difficult, and the attendant could learn it quickly. However, most people—staff members, patients, and visitors—were uneasy or upset in the presence of dead bodies. The attendant therefore had to learn a variety of ways of interacting with others so that they would feel more at ease. When entering a service elevator, for example, he would call out to the doctors and nurses telling them he was about to wheel in a body. They could decide to ride with him or wait for another elevator. As he walked through the halls, he learned to lower his head and avoid eye contact with others. This made it unnecessary for friends to greet him or engage him in conversation, which might be uncomfortable to them.

Sudnow reports that while the attendant was performing his official duties he was uneasy about meeting a nurse's aide he was dating. He explained that light conversation or joking in the presence of a dead body was inappropriate in public. Just as he had learned how to interact with others, he tried to make it clear to his friend that she had to act toward him a particular way when he was on the job.

Despite its many cautions, the work had many rewards. The morgue attendant's pay was better than that of other attendants. The pathologists in the morgue treated him with consideration. One pathologist jokingly, but respectfully, told others that this worker knew more pathology than he did. The attendant, in fact, did learn many technical details of human anatomy.

[9]David Sudnow, *Passing On* (Englewood Cliffs, N.J.: Prentice-Hall, 1967),Chap. 3.

Although he had not graduated from high school, this job made it possible for him to study surgical texts and even attend surgical operations.

What factors made the morgue attendant's job more satisfying to him than the jobs described in *Tally's Corner?* Could any of these factors be introduced into those unsatisfying jobs? What other unskilled jobs can you think of that offer satisfaction to the worker? What are their rewards?

The Semiskilled Worker

An essential feature of an industrial society is the assembly line, where dozens or hundreds of semiskilled workers are engaged in turning out complicated products, such as automobiles, airplanes, and washing machines. Usually each worker performs a specific operation on the product as it is passed by mechanical conveyor from one worker to the next. By organizing the tasks systematically and breaking them into simpler steps, which each worker does repetitively, this procedure turns out large numbers of the product per day.

The assembly line was perfected with two goals in mind: to improve the efficiency and speed with which products could be assembled; and to minimize the skills needed to assemble them. Once a worker has learned the few necessary skills, monotony can set in. Some manufacturers are seeking ways of alleviating this condition.

Some basic work tasks in the factories require more on-the-job training than unskilled tasks do. Operating a machine often demands more knowledge and attention than pushing a mop or washing dishes. The worker needs some understanding of the machine and how to operate it safely. While these may be learned within only a few days, they are crucial to producing an acceptable product; without them the worker cannot function on the job. Thus the jobs differ from unskilled labor.

Costs and rewards on the assembly line. Probably the best-known user of the assembly line is the automobile industry. Each year thousands of young men and some women enter auto plants. Learning their tasks is not difficult, but performing them day after day and week after week is hard. Automobile workers must cope with the tension, boredom, and pressure of working on a line. Although their pay is generally considered good, and their union secures fringe benefits for them, assembly-line workers nonetheless usually show the strain of laboring for eight or more hours a day at a difficult and repetitious task.

Sociologist Ely Chinoy, who studied automobile workers in Detroit, quoted one as saying, "The only reason a man works is to make a living. The things I like best about my job are quitting time, pay days, days off, and vacations."[10] The wife of another worker commented:

> I don't know much about what he does in the plant, but it does something to him. Of course I shouldn't complain. He gets good pay. We've been able to buy . . . a lot of things we couldn't have had otherwise. But sometimes I wonder whether these are more important to us than having Joe get all nervous and tensed up.[11]

These comments reveal the costs and rewards that accompany assembly-line work. What, then, are the socialization experiences of semiskilled assembly-line workers?

Learning the norms. In Chinoy's study, the workers said that the most difficult thing to learn was keeping up with the continually moving assembly line. Newcomers were socialized to do their joking and talking when the line broke down and to concentrate on the work when it was moving. "The line got into its swing. The fellows stopped joking and talking. There was no

[10]Ely Chinoy, "Manning the Machines—The Assembly-Line Workers," in *The Human Shape of Work*, ed. Peter L. Berger (New York: Macmillan, 1964), p. 75.

[11]Ibid., p. 66.

whistling or singing or horseplay—no time for nothing but work."[12]

A worker was not allowed to leave the line, even to go to the bathroom, unless a scheduled relief man took over. Foremen socialized workers to the norm of staying with the line under all circumstances, telling them to regulate their bodies' needs to the line and not to expect unscheduled chances to go to the bathroom.[13]

The work had little meaning. It was rarely possible for workers to relate their individual monotonous tasks to the finished product. "I'm just a cog in the machine," one worker said, to describe his relationship to the work. Workers quickly realized that they had to limit their expectations. The jobs were dead-ended. Those who had been around for a while did not look forward to promotions, more interesting work, or a more rewarding career, and they soon made this limitation known to newcomers.

1. Talk to friends who are semiskilled workers or try to talk to such workers at a gathering place in an industrial area—a cafe or diner, bowling alley or bar. (Discuss with your instructor the best ways of doing this tactfully and productively.) Ask the workers how they feel about their jobs. What do they like about their jobs? Are any discontented? If so, what kind of work would they prefer to do? What compensations are there to the work? What are their hopes and expectations for their children? Try to get an informal profile of the effect of this working role on the employee's self-image, norms, and values.

2. Some factories, such as the Saab auto plant in Sweden, have tried to relieve the monotony of semiskilled work by giving each worker a variety of tasks. For example, an entire Saab car is built by a team of five or six workers gathered in one area and allocating tasks among themselves. Do you think such an arrangement would change workers' feelings about their work? Why?

3. One assumption regarding work is that it ought to be a source of creative effort. Do you agree or disagree with this assumption? Explain your answer.

[12]Wessel Smitter, *F.O.B. Detroit* (New York: Harper and Row, 1938), quoted in Chinoy, "Manning the Machines," p. 62.

[13]Chinoy, "Manning the Machines," pp. 63–64.

Alienation (Marx): a condition of estranged detachment of industrial workers from their occupation or the goods they produce, and a resulting diminished sense of identity.

Alienation among blue-collar workers. The emphasis on worker alienation under capitalism was one of Karl Marx's lasting contributions to sociological thought. What does this concept include? Obviously alienation means many different things to different people. According to Marx's definition, labor becomes alienated under certain circumstances: modern factory work is repetitive and unsatisfying, the work is not an end in itself but merely a means to earning a livelihood, little democracy exists in the workplace, workers are under the authority of someone else, they do not own their tools, no part of the factory truly belongs to them, and they have no say about what happens to the product, to whom it is sold, or under what conditions.[14]

According to Marx, labor will not be alienated if its work is not for private profit and is socially useful. Workers need to have a relationship to the final product and to participate in decisions about what happens to it.

Worker discontent, such as that in the automobile assembly plant studied by Ely Chinoy, was an issue for American labor until the early 1970s, when economic recession caused massive layoffs. Workers then became more concerned about holding onto their jobs than reforming their conditions of work. During periods of economic upturn, the issue of job satisfaction tends to reassert itself.

Other cultures may use different methods of socializing workers to appropriate norms and values. Japanese workers in an electrical plant sing this song each morning:

For the building of a New Japan,
Let's put our strength and mind together,
Doing our best to promote production,
Sending our goods to the people of the world,
Endlessly and continuously,
Like water gushing from a fountain.
Grow, industry, grow, grow, grow!
Harmony and sincerity!
Matsushita Electric.

What norms are being stressed? What do you think workers are expected to learn from singing the verse? How do you think American workers would react if required to sing a similar song each morning in factories? Why?

[14]Paul Blumberg, *The Impact of Social Class* (New York: Crowell, 1972), pp. 428–29.

Skilled jobs, like those of the carpenter, plumber, and electrician, usually require years of training on the job as an apprentice to attain mastery. They often require the worker to exercise diagnostic and decision-making skills that the semiskilled worker never needs.

The Skilled Worker

Skilled labor is manual work that requires considerable training. The worker has to master the craftsmanship of the trade. Plumbers, electricians, carpenters, and ironworkers are skilled workers. They go through an apprenticeship or training period to learn their jobs. For certain trades a worker has to be licensed as a master before undertaking jobs alone or as a boss of others. This is true of master plumbers and master electricians. Many skilled workers are self-employed; others belong to unions that carefully regulate the types of work they can and cannot do and that protect them in a variety of other ways.

In contrast to work on an assembly line, in some of these jobs people have to work closely with each other. They have very strict norms governing their activities. Ironworkers involved in the construction of tall buildings, for example, work at great heights where safety is always a problem. It is essential that members of the work group develop a sense of mutual trust.

Socialization processes. John Haas studied, as a participant observer, how ironworkers socialized apprentices to become trustworthy members of their work group. Not everyone who applied was accepted as an apprentice. Usually preference was given to applicants sponsored by an ironworker relative or friend. Once chosen, the apprentice had to "punk" for experienced workers. This included going up on the steel beams and doing such chores as transferring tools or getting coffee. Newcomers learned that, to be accepted, they had to walk across the beams competently and without showing fear of working high above the ground.

As an essential part of the socialization process, called "binging," workers tease their apprentices to see if they can "keep their cool" when the going gets rough. If not, they cannot be accepted into the group for work on dangerous jobs. As apprentices slowly gain acceptance into the group, they are allowed to "bing" back, to begin acting as group members. One worker explained the purpose of binging this way:

> "I don't want to call it an initiation, but it's something like that. If you're going to work with a guy, you want to know whether he can take it or not, and just what kind of a guy he is."
>
> Dick, the newer apprentice, says, "Yeh, you're always a punk and they rib you pretty hard, but you've got to show them you can take it. Now sometimes they give me that and I'll just tell them, 'Hey, you know, back off, I'm not your slave.' Then they begin to appreciate you a little more and understand that you're a human being. I mean you can't get angry at them, because then they get on you worse. You've got to show that you can take it, but then you've also got to show that you can dish it out."[15]

Ironworkers develop values about their ability to do the job, coolness in dangerous situations, and loyalty to fellow workers both on and off the job. These values are made clear in the role expectations that ironworkers set for their apprentices. Those who want to be accepted must meet the expectations. Loyalty to the group, for instance, includes the expectation that an ironworker will gladly lend money to a fellow worker who needs help, that workers will spend time drinking together in bars, and that workers will pass along information on how to deal with particular contractors. They need each other on the job and enjoy each other's company after work.

Workers also begin to develop common attitudes about issues beyond the specific job they are doing. They often reach common conclusions about government officials, welfare programs, and minority groups. Ironworkers,

[15]John W. Haas, "From Punk to Scale: A Study of High Steel Ironworkers" (Ph.D. diss., Syracuse University, 1971), p. 102.

Haas found, stressed the values of masculinity and courage. These shared values and attitudes help to foster their group solidarity.

A crucial component of an industrial system is a well-trained, motivated, and satisfied blue-collar work force. We have presented some areas of satisfaction for members of this force and some sources of underlying discontent. Work on an assembly line or as an ironworker on high steel beams provides income for a good standard of living. Workers can afford many consumer goods. Skilled or semiskilled workers sometimes compare themselves to unskilled workers, who are poorly paid, and they feel they are doing well. But their margin for comfort is not great. Unemployment, a strike, or a serious illness can quickly wipe out a lifetime savings. Union protection built by many years of struggle can be weakened during economic recessions. Younger workers, members of minority groups, and women are often last hired and first fired. They are most likely to suffer layoffs when inventories pile up and production is cut back. Most blue-collar workers in contemporary American society continue to be vulnerable to the fluctuations of our industrial economy whatever the nature of their satisfaction or dissatisfaction on the job.

Assume you are to collect data for use by high school guidance counselors. You must describe the economic characteristics of certain representative skilled, semiskilled, or unskilled jobs. In the reference section in the library, consult the most recent volume of the *Occupational Outlook Handbook,* published by the Bureau of Labor Statistics of the United States Department of Labor. Make a chart comparing average wages, prospects for employment, and other pertinent data for several occupations at each skill level. Summarize your findings in a few paragraphs that might be useful to a vocational guidance counselor.

The White-Collar Worker

As our industrial technology has grown in the last century, so has the size of our business organizations. A business may have a small office with a handful of employees and one boss, or it may have several far-flung branches around the world employing thousands of office workers. In all such offices most of the employees are called white-collar workers. Their jobs and responsibilities revolve around "paperwork"—producing, recording, classifying, and storing information. (Today the term *paperwork* is only partly descriptive. Computers, using magnetic or electrical impulses rather than paper to convey information, have become essential to all large and many small organizations.)

PERCENTAGE OF WHITE-COLLAR WORKERS

Year	Percentage of Work Force
1950	37.5
1955	39.0
1960	43.4
1965	44.8
1970	48.3
1972	47.8
1973	47.8
1974	48.8

Sources: United States Department of Commerce, Bureau of the Census, *Current Population Reports*, series P–50 (Washington, D.C.: U.S. Government Printing Office, 1950–74); United States Department of Labor, Bureau of Labor Statistics, *Employment and Earnings* (Washington, D.C.: U.S. Government Printing Office, monthly since 1960).

White-collar workers are now the largest percentage of the work force in our society. White collar positions range from low-paid file clerk to executive secretary, computer programmer, and office manager. The tasks range from routine and tedious work, such as filing invoices, to responsible and varied problems, such as maintaining confidential records or responding to clients and visitors.

We have seen that semiskilled workers on the automobile assembly line have little control over their work. Office workers too are usually closely regulated within a definite hierarchy of authority, although not quite as much controlled as assembly-line workers. Secretaries, file clerks, and bookkeepers often have to produce a certain output continually. These white-collar workers usually do not have strong trade unions looking out for their interests in such matters as working conditions, salaries, health and pension plans, and other fringe benefits. An employee who protests may well be fired, because, like semiskilled factory workers, most white-collar workers can be quickly replaced.

Secretaries and other office workers learn that certain attitudes are an important part of their work roles. They must accept norms about dress, manner, and attitude toward work, as well as learning skills of stenography, typing, bookkeeping, or office management. Although there is a great variation in norms from office to office, white-collar workers are socialized to expect more pleasant and clean surroundings, more varied tasks, and more prestige than factory workers. At the same time, they learn that they are not the major decision-makers in the office and are usually supervised carefully in their work.

Costs and rewards. Depending on the temperament, values, and norms of the worker and the conditions on the job, white-collar work can be rewarding

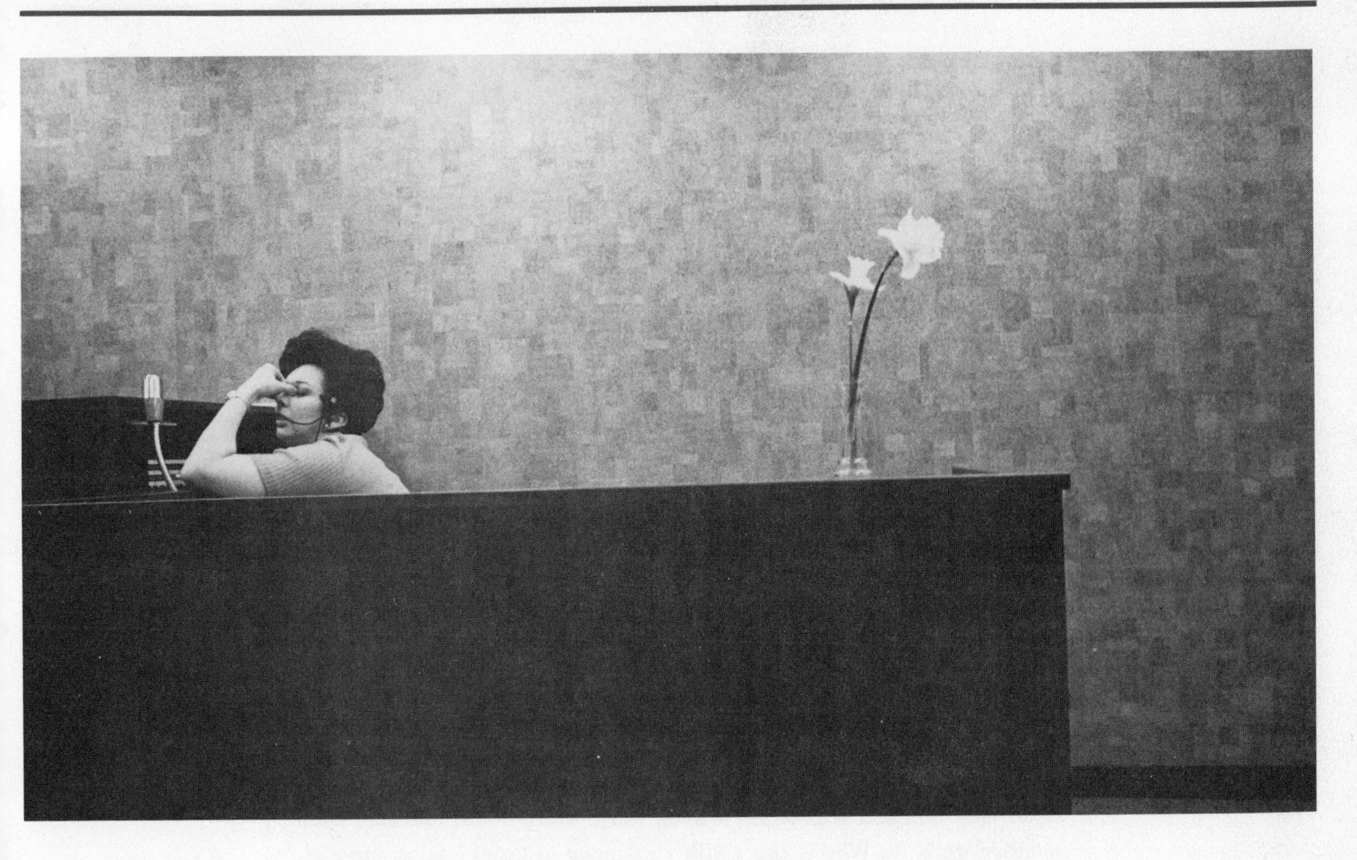

Low-level white-collar work is a mixed blessing to most employees. Neither the pay nor the prestige is outstanding. Great or rapid advancement is rare. The work is generally tedious and constant, and many workers feel insufficiently appreciated. On the other hand, office jobs generally have higher prestige than factory jobs.

or frustrating or a combination of the two. For example, a secretary to two physicians in England described her hectic schedule and overcrowded conditions at work. Although she was unhappy about the tiring pace and the variety of tasks she had to do, she was very satisfied with her job. "The reason, quite briefly, is that I feel I am doing a necessary job. But even that wouldn't be sufficient if I weren't lucky enough to be working for two such good doctors."[16]

In order to succeed at this job, the secretary had to learn to keep track of appointments, answer phone calls, make children in the waiting room comfortable, attend to correspondence, handle contacts with the hospital, and file records. In mastering both the secretarial skills and the ability to get along with a variety of people in the clinic, she gained respect and therefore self-esteem from her job.

[16]Catherine Dracup, "The Secretary," in *Work*, ed. Ronald Fraser (Harmondsworth, England: Penguin Books, 1969), 2:288.

One of the chief attractions of the job for me is the feeling of being in charge, feeling that I matter. Patients often comment that without me the surgery [clinic] would be in chaos . . . . I'd find it difficult to be just a small part of some large organization. In the four years I have worked at the surgery I have never been late, although in previous jobs I was never on time.[17]

Clearly, this woman found recognition and satisfaction in her job. Where these do not exist in white-collar jobs, tensions and frustrations can rise. Consider the following description by one dissatisfied secretary in a pamphlet by a Massachusetts feminist group:

The secretaries seem to control what is going on and do not seem easily intimidated . . . . But [this] does not change the nature of our work: boring, painful, degrading . . . the role of the secretary is the role of a servant. . . . [For example, you find yourself] being bugged on the intercom by an administrator who gives you a phone number which you are to dial while he waits at his desk. . . .

If a secretary should find herself mentally composing a letter without having first placed her fingers firmly on the typewriter keys and adopted an expression of intense readiness to type, she will also find that she is being watched disapprovingly by some superior who has been observing his servant-children for signs of idleness. A secretary is not evaluated by the amount or quality of the work she does so much as by her ability to look respectful, bland, and moderately busy at all times.

Union organization is growing among some white-collar workers such as office workers. Why is there still resistance to unionization among secretaries, bank tellers, and other white-collar workers? How would you counter their arguments?

The Manager

We examined the structure of formal organizations in Chapter 5.

All complex organizations give certain employees formal authority to make decisions and to supervise and manage the work of others. Managers hire and fire those who work for them, and grant them raises and promotions. High-level managers participate in major policy decisions of the organization. They are often held responsible for the success or failure of the branch of work they manage.

Socialization through management training. The conditions of work vary in different organizations, but most managerial positions are characterized by a high degree of responsibility, a good salary, and extensive training either in school or on the job. Studies show that most top managers in large companies

[17]Ibid., p. 233.

Near the top of the white-collar work force hierarchy are managers. Although they are below the top executives, who make the major, guiding decisions, middle managers do have decision-making responsibilities in running complex formal organizations. For this reason, they are required to have education and often special training. Usually they must also have years of experience on the job and a demonstrable ability to obtain the cooperation of others.

Executive positions at the top of the corporate ladder are neither easy to reach nor easy to keep. In addition to demonstrating decision-making skills and administrative talents on the way up the ladder, the would-be executive must usually make great personal sacrifices in time and energy. And the kind of role performance that wins such a position must generally be maintained to keep the position.

are college graduates with degrees in accounting, business, or engineering. To enter the managerial world, then, the young adult must have the opportunity to attend college, and probably must have taken courses that apply to a business career.

After college, new managers often have to enter a management training program within the company that hires them. The trainee learns technical skills for managing the events and people of the firm through such classes as personnel management, human relations, and public relations. In the course of the program, instructors and others will make critical decisions about the future of the trainees. Will this one be given routine work while that one is tapped for a future as an executive? What kind of learning makes a trainee become a successful manager?

William H. Whyte noted several norms and values in describing the elaborate training program of one of the largest corporations in the United States:

> The most noteworthy feature of the General Electric approach is the emphasis on the "professional" manager. As in all training programs, the bulk of the instruction is on specifics. Unlike most, however, there is considerable study in

subjects that cut across every kind of job. Trainees study personnel philosophy, labor relations, law, and most important, the managerial viewpoint. Only a minority of the trainees will ever become managers . . . . most of the thousands of young men trained during this time will never get further than middle management. Nevertheless, it is the future executive slots that the company is thinking of, and it makes its concern plain to the trainee. . . .

To get ahead, of course, one must compete—but not too much, and certainly not too obviously. . . . The trainee is, first of all, a member of a group, and the group is entrusted to a surprising degree with the resolution of his future. How well, the company wants to know, does he fit in? His fellow trainees provide the answer. . . . Trainees speak frequently of the way close fraternity life atmosphere is valuable in ironing out some trainees' aberrant tendencies. . . . In a few years the trainee will be released from this close association and *the social character that he has perfected will be a fundamental necessity;* he will be moving from one company branch to another, and he must be able to fit into the same kind of integrated social system. [Italics added.][18]

The incentives to do well are clear. The pay is good, prestige in the community is high, and the tasks of an executive are interesting. Thus the work has many attractive benefits. However, there are also strains associated with the job. The executive must think in terms of the company, considering the interests of stockholders, employees, customers, and the public. At times managers may have to engage in activities that conflict with their personal ethical standards. They may promote products of questionable value; arrange with other companies to fix prices illegally; or bribe foreign officials to obtain suitable market or labor conditions.[19]

Competition for managerial positions is intense. Only a few make it to the top. Looking up the corporate ladder, young managers quickly learn that success comes only to those who show a total commitment to the work. Family and relaxation must often take second place to career needs. In interviews with a variety of managers, one study found that top executives liked managers who worked a sixty- to sixty-five-hour week and then took more material home for study.[20]

[18]William H. Whyte, *The Organization Man* (New York: Doubleday, 1956), pp. 134, 136.

[19]John G. Fuller, in *The Gentleman Conspirators* (New York: Grove Press, 1962), describes the socialization process that facilitated illegal executive activity in the electrical industry. See also Robert Heilbroner et al., *In the Name of Profit* (Garden City, N.Y.: Doubleday, 1972). During 1975 and 1976 numerous instances of Unites States corporate bribing of foreign officials came to light.

[20]William H. Whyte, "How Hard Do Executives Work?" in *Organizations and Human Behavior,* ed. Gerald D. Bell (Englewood Cliffs, N.J.: Prentice-Hall, 1967), pp. 276–77.

1. People training for management positions that offer occupants great authority are the most intensely and thoroughly socialized of all the workers we have discussed. Why do you think this is so?

2. The General Electric management training program most closely resembles the childhood socialization practiced in Crestwood Heights (described in Chapter 9). Can you find areas of continuity between the two—how Crestwood Heights prepares for GE and how GE picks up the threads of Crestwood Heights? Think in terms of norms, values, and images of self.

The Professional

Learning a profession such as law, medicine, or engineering is not easy. Professionals, who are highly trained specialists, acquire their knowledge through years of schooling, normally in professional schools with difficult entrance requirements. Only a small percentage of the students who apply for admission are chosen, and future professionals are informed that those who survive the training are a select and privileged group.

Training teaches the students not only technical knowledge but also attitudes about proper behavior for future professionals. They learn, for example, what are considered acceptable conditions of professional work, norms of interaction with other workers in the field, and accepted behavior toward clients for their services.

Professionals achieve the greatest prestige in the world of work. Doctors and lawyers fit the standard image of the professional. Others share some but not all traits of the full professional. What of these stock analysts, for example? And what about artists, composers, writers, professors?

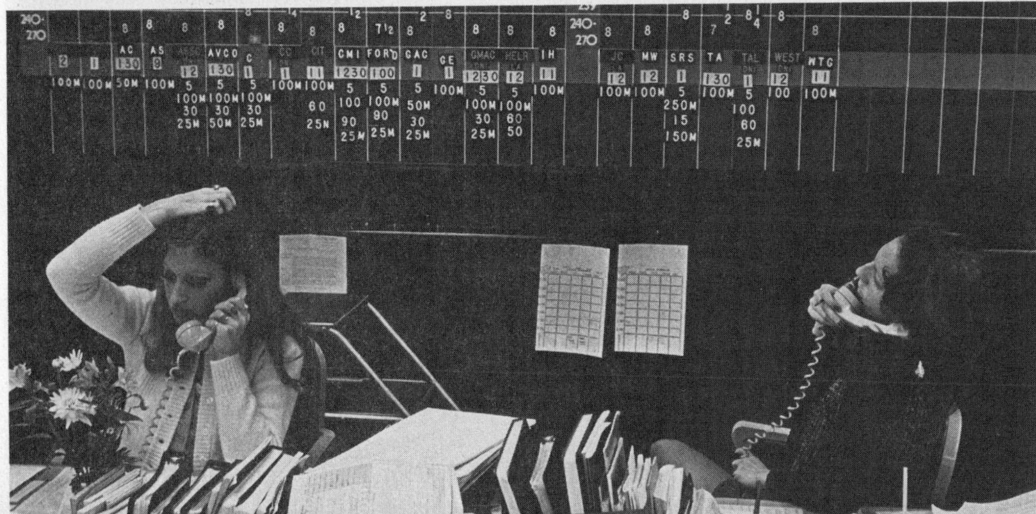

Control over work conditions. Professionals insist that the responsibility for decision-making on the job must be theirs. They believe that laymen, who have not gone through the years of specialized education, cannot determine the direction of professional work. Student doctors, for example, are taught that nonphysicians—whether government officials, hospital administrators, or patients—cannot be allowed to dictate proper medical procedures. This, they argue, would hamper them from providing good medical care. It would also reduce the respect the profession is given by the larger community.

Professionals often form organizations to protect their authority and interests. These groups may make sure that careful licensing procedures are established by the government and that the procedures are determined and regulated by members of the profession. Thus, the profession tries to keep nonprofessionals from being able to practice or to influence legally licensed practitioners. The limits are imposed, the professionals say, to protect the public from inadequate or shoddy services, but they also serve to protect professionals themselves. The number of practitioners of a profession can be controlled by school admissions and licensing procedures and standards.

Some professionals (teachers, librarians, and social workers, for example) are usually employed by organizations that regulate aspects of their work. Although they are not as independent as self-employed doctors or lawyers, these professionals also maintain associations to try to control their work conditions. Many lawyers and doctors, too, are not self-employed. Every large city has law firms employing many lawyers, sometimes more than 100, who are not partners. Many doctors, psychologists, and psychiatrists work for clinics or health groups rather than in private practices of their own. In recent years substantial numbers of professionals employed by the government or private industry—teachers, engineers, scientists, social workers, and others—have organized unions. Many professionals have come to believe that their interests cannot be sufficiently protected by their professional status, and they have begun to look to collective bargaining.

Ethical standards. Professionals hold a special place in modern industrial society because they are expected to be experts who offer services to those in need. Most people feel that professionals are entitled to a good income, but ideally they are not supposed to be highly influenced by the profit motive. Scientists, for example, are expected to want to contribute to knowledge. Doctors are supposed to be committed to preventing and treating disease. Whether engaged in private, clinic, or group practice, physicians are expected to be primarily concerned with the well-being of their patients. According to their code of ethics, for example, doctors must not exploit patients by prescribing treatments or drugs that enrich the physician but do the patient no good.

Professionals often fall short of these ethical goals. In recent years doctors have been criticized for charging excessive fees, particularly under Medicare programs. Malpractice suits against doctors have become so numerous and juries have awarded mistreated patients such large settlements that a crisis has been created. Insurance companies have doubled and tripled their charges for malpractice coverage, and doctors have threatened to quit practice rather than pay the new rates. Patients accuse the medical profession of failing to ensure the competence of its members. The doctors countercharge that lawyers are pushing clients to file malpractice suits that line the pockets of attorneys.[21]

The involvement of many lawyers in the Watergate scandal raised other questions about the ethics of the legal profession. Social scientists, too, have been criticized for not maintaining confidentiality about people they study, exposing their subjects to embarrassment or even punitive actions.

A few professional organizations have responded to criticisms by increasing their regulation of members. By policing themselves better, professionals hope to minimize scandals and avoid government or other interference in their working lives.

Women in the Work Force

Clearly, unskilled workers and white-collar workers have different experiences and get different social and personal rewards from their jobs. White-collar workers, in turn, differ from managers and professionals. Thus, social class is a major variable in understanding the different work lives of adults.

One other social variable determines access to the good jobs and influences a person's work experience: sex. The job market has never treated men and women equally—even when they were of the same social class.

Women workers tend to concentrate in certain areas of the labor force and historically have been virtually excluded from others. Women were most often household servants and agricultural workers before the twentieth century. Later they began to work in factories, offices, and a few professions such as teaching, nursing, and social work.

In every generation, social norms have determined what kinds of work were appropriate for women to do. Of course, rich women would not do the

[21]See the excellent series of articles in the *New York Times* during the week of January 26, 1976.

same work as poor women did. The norms about particular jobs often changed as the need for women in particular fields increased or decreased. Thus, in the nineteenth century many men thought women should never do office work. In the twentieth century, as the demand for office workers far outstripped the supply of men, women assumed most clerical and secretarial work, and the prestige of these occupations declined. They no longer were a natural route to upward mobility.

Sex discrimination in work. At present, women are heavily concentrated in clerical and service occupations. The vast majority of these jobs offer low prestige and poor wages. In the past few years there has been a concerted attempt to open new opportunities for women to enter certain fields. The Civil Rights Act passed by Congress in 1964 outlaws discrimination in employment based on sex or race. Large companies have been required to draw up affirmative action plans that reform their discriminatory personnel policies. Women have been accepted in larger numbers in medical, law, and other professional schools.

Nevertheless, the patterns of employment continue to differ substantially for men and women—particularly among craft workers, managers, and clerical and service workers.

OCCUPATIONAL DISTRIBUTION OF THE LABOR FORCE BY SEX, 1971

	Distribution (Percentage)	
Occupation Group	*Males*	*Females*
Total employed	100.0	100.0
White-collar workers	40.9	60.6
Professional and technical	13.7	14.5
Managers, officials and proprietors	14.6	5.0
Clerical workers	6.7	33.9
Sales workers	5.9	7.2
Blue-collar workers	45.9	15.4
Craftsmen and foremen	19.9	1.3
Operatives	18.3	13.3
Nonfarm laborers	7.7	0.8
Service workers	8.2	22.3
Private household workers	0.1	4.9
Other service workers	8.1	17.4
Farmworkers	5.1	1.7
Farmers and farm managers	3.2	0.3
Farm laborers and foremen	1.9	1.4

Source: United States Department of Labor, Manpower Administration, *Manpower Report of the President* (Washington, D.C.: U.S. Government Printing Office, March 1972), p. 173.

Women learn even before they begin their jobs that they do not have the same access to work that their brothers and husbands have. To enter certain fields a woman may have to exert extra effort, face a slimmer chance of success, and even be willing to go to court.

Women also confront discrimination in salaries. Although it is now illegal to pay women less than their male counterparts in the same jobs, statistics show that in 1970 women working full-time had a median income that was only 60 percent of the median among working men. In part, this reflects the small number of women in highly paid careers. Even in the same fields, however, discrepancies in pay levels exist, as the table on salesmen and saleswomen demonstrates.

WHITE AND NONWHITE MEN AND WOMEN WITH INCOMES OVER $10,000, 1972

	Men		*Women*	
Income	*White*	*Nonwhite*	*White*	*Nonwhite*
From wages				
$10,000–14,999	24.4	13.3	4.4	4.2
$15,000–24,999	11.3	2.8	0.6	0.5
$25,000 and over	2.8	0.4	0.1	0.2
From sources other than wages				
$10,000–14,999	1.4	0.1	0.8	0.1
$15,000–24,999	0.5	0.1	0.3	—
$25,000 and over	0.3	—	0.2	—

Source: United States Department of Commerce, Bureau of the Census, *Current Population Reports,* series P–60, no. 90 (Washington, D.C.: U.S. Government Printing Office, 1973), pp. 151, 152.

The reasons for this kind of discrimination are many. Women have been regarded as inferior to men in many spheres of society. Employers justify their unequal treatment of women in the labor force by the argument that women are not permanent workers. They claim women are either working temporarily until they marry and have children, or are picking up a little extra "pin money" to supplement their husbands' salaries. Thus, it would be foolish to train them for advancement to positions of responsibility and high reward.

Despite evidence to contradict these arguments, discrimination continues.[22] The percentage of women in the labor force has grown continually and is no longer restricted to women working until they have children.

[22]See Francine D. Blau, "Women in the Labor Force: An Overview," in *Women: A Feminist Perspective,* ed. Jo Freeman (Palo Alto, Calif.: Mayfield, 1975), pp. 211–25.

PROPORTION OF RETAIL SALESWOMEN AND SALESMEN BY SALARY LEVEL, 1970

Average Weekly Salary of Sales Occupations	*Saleswomen*		*Salesmen*	
	Number (Thousands)	*Per-centage*	*Number (Thousands)*	*Per-centage*
Over $120 (*e.g.*, motor vehicle dealers)	104.0	1.9	762.6	9.7
$110–119.99 (*e.g.*, building materials and farm equipment)	122.3	2.2	652.0	8.3
$100–109.99 (*e.g.*, furniture and home furnishings)	928.5	17.0	2,756.4	35.2
$90–99.99 (*e.g.*, mail order houses)	81.3	1.5	51.2	.7
$80–89.99 (*e.g.*, grocery, meat and vegetable stores)	593.8	10.9	1,168.0	14.9
$70–79.99 (*e.g.*, department stores)	1,667.5	30.6	1,235.5	15.8
$60–69.99 (*e.g.*, women's ready-to-wear stores)	313.7	5.8	65.0	.8
$50–59.99 (*e.g.*, eating and drinking places)	1,644.5	30.1	1,151.1	14.7

Note: Trades included in this table met the following criteria: (1) they provided information on the total number of men employed, the total number of women employed, and the 1970 average weekly salary; and (2) they did not include another more specific category that could be used.

Source: United States Department of Labor, Bureau of Labor Statistics, *Employment and Earnings Statistics for the U.S., 1909–1971*, Bulletin no. 1312–8 (Washington, D.C.: U.S. Government Printing Office, 1971).

The rationale that women are only earning "extra income" is equally open to challenge. Women constitute 62 percent of the adults who live in poverty. There are more than twelve million working women who are not supported by a man. The rising divorce rate has vastly increased the number of single-parent families, in which the women usually are responsible for child care.[23] In addition, many families depend on the income of both husband and wife to keep them above the poverty line. They cannot define the wife's salary as a source of extras or luxuries.

[23]Kathleen Shortridge, "Working Poor Women," in *Women: A Feminist Perspective*, pp. 238–53; see especially pp. 246–48.

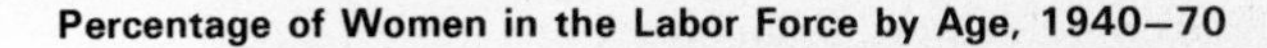

Percentage of Women in the Labor Force by Age, 1940–70

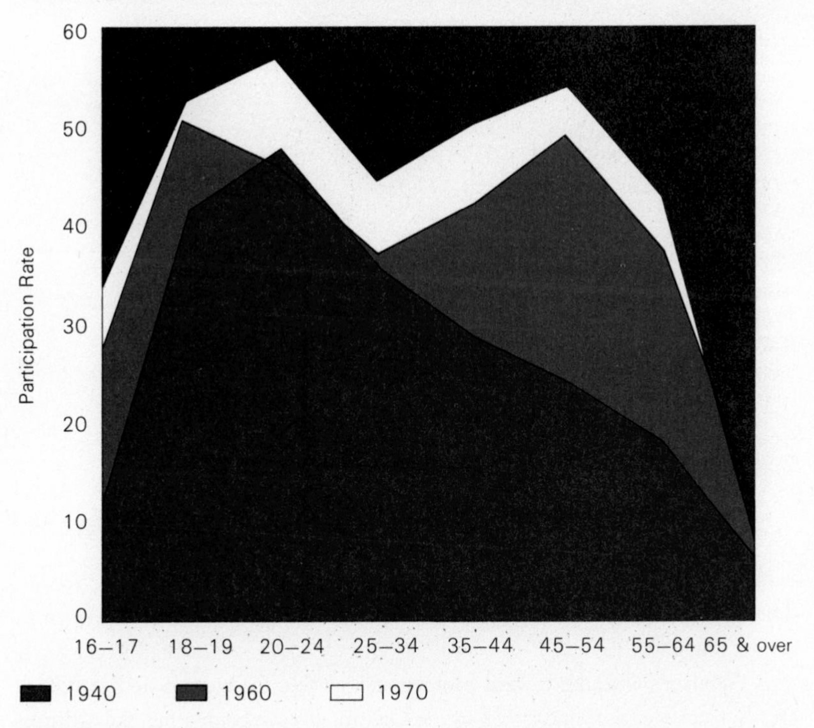

Sources: United States Department of Labor, Women's Bureau, *1969 Handbook on Women Workers* (Washington, D.C.: U.S. Government Printing Office, 1969), p. 18; United States Department of Labor, Manpower Administration, *Manpower Report of the President* (Washington, D.C.: U.S. Government Printing Office, March 1972), pp. 160–62.

Women in the professions. Recent studies have also addressed themselves to the situation of more privileged women. What happens to those who reach the upper levels? Almost all studies report that female scientists and other women with doctoral degrees advance more slowly in their careers than their male colleagues, despite equal productivity (for example, in published research).[24]

Several observers have noted that women lack access to "sponsorship"—special encouragement by a senior person in the field who informally teaches a young professional the trade secrets and helps to determine whether the newcomer is invited to conferences, is given a good hearing, and receives constructive suggestions on papers. Informal access to colleagues may be had

[24]Pamela Roby, "Structural and Internalized Barriers to Women in Higher Education," in *Toward Sociology of Women,* ed. Constantina Safilios-Rothschild (Lexington, Mass.: Xerox Publishing, 1972).

WOMEN IN THE CIVILIAN LABOR FORCE, 1890–1970

Year	*Number (Thousands)*	*Percentage of All Workers*	*Percentage of Female Population*
1890	3,704	17.0	18.2
1900	4,999	18.1	20.0
1920	8,229	20.4	22.7
1930	10,396	21.9	23.6
1940	13,783	25.4	28.6
1945	19,290	36.1	38.1
1947	16,664	27.9	30.8
1950	18,389	29.6	33.9
1955	20,548	31.6	35.7
1960	23,240	33.4	37.7
1965	26,200	35.2	39.2
1970	31,520	38.1	43.3

Sources: United States Department of Labor, Women's Bureau, *1969 Handbook on Women Workers* (Washington, D.C.: U.S. Government Printing Office, 1969), p. 10; United States Department of Labor, Manpower Administration, *Manpower Report of the President* (Washington, D.C.: U.S. Government Printing Office, April 1971), pp. 203, 205.

at lunches or over cocktails, when women are less likely to be present. Many women have reported that subtle forms of discrimination tend to keep them "out of the club."[25]

Women's attitudes toward professional success for women do not differ greatly from men's, as measured in the Gallup surveys below, but the attitudes of both sexes are substantially different from what they were forty years ago.

1. Would you be willing to enter a field that interested you if there were very few members of your sex in that career? If so, how do you think significant others (family, friends) in your life would respond to this decision? How would you deal with norms that make it more difficult for members of your sex to enter the field?

If you would not, defend your position.

2. Compare the answers of men and women in the class to the first question. Are there significant differences? If so, why do you think there are?

3. Do you feel that any division of labor according to sex is unfair? Defend your answer.

[25]Martha S. White, "Women in the Professions: Psychological and Social Barriers to Women in Science," *Science* 170 (1970): 413–16.

SURVEYS OF ATTITUDES ON WOMEN IN LEADERSHIP

Survey Question	Year of Survey	Male Respondents		Female Respondents	
		Yes	No	Yes	No
Would you vote for a woman for president if she were qualified in every other respect?	1937	27%	73%	41%	59%
If your party nominated a woman for president, would you vote for her if she were qualified for the job?	1971	65%	35%	67%	33%
If your party nominated a woman to run for Congress from your district, would you vote for her if she were qualified for the job?	1970	83%	13%	84%	13%

Sources: Compiled from George Gallup, *The Gallup Poll: Public Opinion 1935–1971* (New York: Random House, 1972), pp. 67, 131, 2139, 2261; National Opinion Research Center, University of Chicago, 1972, p. 27.

Media attention to feminist groups and concerns might give the impression that our society is making rapid progress toward full sexual equality. The fact is that most women who enter the world of work today are socialized to different roles and experiences from men.

RETIREMENT AND OLD AGE

As we move through the life cycle, we proceed from one status to another—from child to adolescent to adult, from single person to spouse to parent, from student to worker. In each of these statuses we are called on to play new roles and to interact within new primary and secondary groups. As we have seen, socialization is the ongoing process through which we are taught the norms, values, and expectations associated with the roles we are learning to play.

What happens when roles we have held for a long time suddenly end and are not fully replaced by new ones? How do people cope with *role loss?* This is a major issue for elderly people in modern industrial societies (and for many of the unemployed). As children grow up and form their own families, the role of parent is substantially reduced. At retirement, whether voluntary or mandatory, the role of worker is diminished or ends. Work and family roles are central to an adult's sense of self. The loss of these roles marks a momentous change in the life cycle.

Role loss: curtailment or reduction of a role that contributed to the individual's definition of self.

The elderly suffer not only role loss but also a decline in the prestige and social rewards associated with their former roles. Since people in our society are generally judged by their occupations, retirement often creates a feeling of uselessness. Pensions, Social Security payments, and personal savings substitute for salary or wages, and for a large portion of the population these do not offer the same standard of living as before retirement.

In some other societies, the elderly are honored because of their experience and their knowledge of tradition. But in a society that values change and progress, the elderly tend to be held in less esteem. Even in China the elderly are losing prestige as modernization occurs. In the traditional Chinese family, many generations lived together in a household.[26] Married sons and grandsons ideally continued to live under the authority of the eldest male. Today, although extended families frequently do live in the same house, especially in rural areas of China, the relationship is different. Parents may live with a married son and his children, but the authority now lies with the second generation. Age is respected, but it is no longer a source of veneration and power.

Socialization for Role Loss

Socialization to old age differs from socialization to other statuses. It involves coping with role loss and devaluation—by others and frequently by elderly people themselves. How do older adults learn to deal with this situation and to play new roles? What norms are established? Who are the socializing agents, the role models, and the significant others?

One recent book, *Socialization to Old Age* by Irving Rosow,[27] contends that the process is largely incomplete. Norms are not clearly defined, leaving individuals to face new roles without guidance about how they should behave. There are no established expectations, for example, about how husbands should redefine their participation in housework after retirement. Yet couples who are able to redistribute this work make better adjustments to retirement. Similarly, there are few expectations for the social role of widow or widower. It is often a norm, however, that married friends exclude widowed peers from their social activities.

Rosow outlines several other problems in the socialization process. For most roles in our lives, we have *anticipatory socialization* or role rehearsal well before we actually assume a status. However, no one likes to rehearse for getting old, becoming sick, being widowed, or becoming unemployed. There are few role models for aging gracefully. Consequently older people often try

[26] Martin King Whyte, "The Family," pp. 182–83.

[27] Irving Rosow, *Socialization to Old Age* (Berkeley: University of California Press, 1974).

Old age is a universal biological fact, but the cultural dimension makes it a different experience in one society from what it is in another. The kind and severity of role loss may be much greater in advanced industrial societies than in more traditional ones, just as the aged are more isolated from younger generations in modern societies. Continued participation in the society, which supports a person's sense of self, generally seems to keep the aged more vigorous.

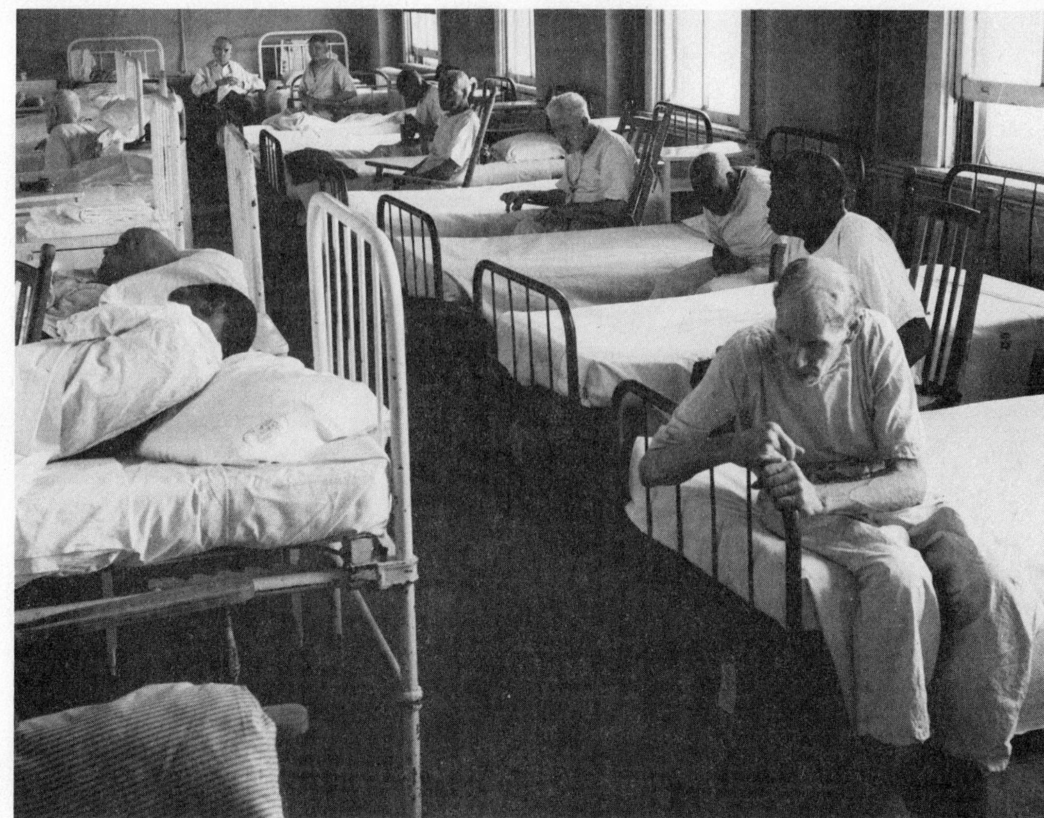

DANCE
AUCTION
SAT., SEPT. 10
AUCTION
SAT., SEPT. 10
HENRY T. SCHMITZ
THE BLUE BOYS
SATURDAY, SEPT. 3
DOERNER
COUNTY ATTORNEY
SEPT. 3
AUCTION
Saturday, Sept. 3
ALGON BALLROOM
DON'S BEVERAGE CO.
AUCTION
WED., SEPT. 7
COUNTY ATTORNEY
AUCTION
TUESDAY, SEPT. 6
Machinery and Equipment
LAUER
SHERIFF
SHERIFF
LAHR
SHERIFF
BENO
STEARNS COUNTY

MLW 128

Self: the composite of ideas and attitudes we have about ourselves that give us a sense of identity and worth.

Reference group: the people by whose standards we judge ourselves.

to use youthful role models and to define themselves as middle aged.

Perhaps the failure of the larger society to sustain the self of older members is a primary reason for the immense growth of "leisure villages" in the last generation. The elderly flock together for mutual peer support. Sharing the same problems, they serve as a reference group for each other. These communities are available only to those who can afford them, of course—those whose savings or pensions are large enough to pay the bills of such surroundings. Others sometime join golden age clubs or their equivalent in search of peer support. Many do not easily find satisfying relationships and must endure the prevailing loneliness of life in a small apartment, relieved occasionally, perhaps, by a visit to or from children and grandchildren. In addition women frequently suffer the loneliness of widowhood, since wives generally outlive their husbands.

Widowhood by Age Group, 1970

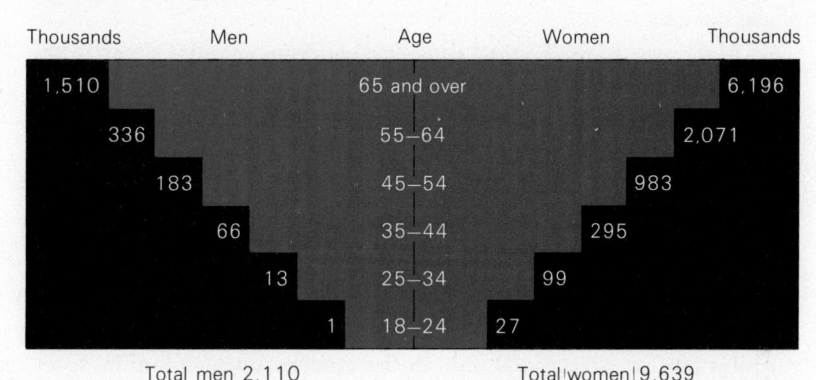

Source: United States Department of Commerce, Bureau of the Census.

For many of the elderly, once their families deem them unable to care for themselves, the final earthly destination is a nursing home for the aged. In recent years there has been a nationwide scandal over the abominable conditions found in many of these homes. Even the best have some of the significant traits that characterize total institutions—organizations in which individuals must yield control over themselves to a centralized authority. As we see in Chapter 11, the result is often an assault on the individual's self.

Most of us know one or more elderly people full of vitality and love of life, people who have remained involved with the young and continue to draw their respect. And despite the society's devaluation of the elderly and its intergenerational conflict, it is not uncommon for children to maintain love for and loyalty to their elderly parents and a genuine concern for their well-being. Nevertheless, the bleak description of the problems of aging in our society is real. Those with financial independence, strong family ties, and good health are less burdened than the poor, the sick, and the isolated. Even in the best of cases this society does not fully meet the needs of our growing population of elderly citizens. Those who live long enough must eventually come to terms with the fact that they are increasingly dependent on others and increasingly isolated from many social roles and institutions.

SUMMARY

Although socialization is generally experienced most intensely during childhood and adolescence, the process continues throughout life. As people enter adulthood they face new roles and must apply their store of values and norms to new social situations: marriage, parenthood, work, old age.

Marriages have changed considerably from colonial times to the present. Arranged marriages have given way to free choice, generally based on romantic attachment. Increasingly, couples are redefining marital roles in a search for greater equality. Although divorce rates have risen in recent years, sometimes creating the impression that traditional marriages are rare, many traditional norms still prevail.

Becoming a parent introduces another set of demands on each spouse. Artificial birth control methods enable married couples to plan the timing and number of their children. But there is little anticipatory socialization for parenthood and, in the modern nuclear family, few older, experienced persons nearby to offer guidance. New parents often rely on expert advice from books, classes, and other formal sources to teach them how to care for and socialize their children.

Much of an adult's self-concept may be determined by the social rewards of money, prestige, and power that derive from his or her occupation. Work has been traditionally divided between blue collar (manual labor) and white collar (office work), with a hierarchy of subdivisions within each category. Unskilled, semiskilled, and skilled blue-collar workers differ in the amount of training their jobs require, the prestige they enjoy, and usually their financial rewards. White-collar workers range from clerks and secretaries, to managers and executives, to professionals. Again, the three social rewards differ for different jobs in the hierarchy.

Women make up a large component of the modern work force, but they are generally overrepresented in the lower paid and less rewarding positons. In almost all positions women tend to be paid less than men doing the same work.

Our life span has lengthened, the nuclear family has replaced the extended family, and retirement from the work force in the mid-sixties has become the norm. Because of all three developments, aging has become an increasingly lonely experience for many people. Virtually no anticipatory socialization prepares us for the adjustments we need to make. Old age is a time of role loss and devaluation. For a great many it is a period of declining standards of living, as inflation reduces the purchasing power of their fixed incomes, declining health, and increasing dependence.

CONFORMITY, DEVIANCE, AND RESOCIALIZATION

A rich girl like Patty Hearst, somebody who has everything anybody could want, and she throws it all over for a bunch of crazy radicals?

A homosexual in the Air Force? Are you serious. He could be a real threat to national security.

But he always seemed to act normal. He had a good job, a nice family, belonged to the club. Then one day it turned out he had been embezzling company funds.

Sure she's poor and lonely. But becoming a call girl? Such a beautiful girl.

Can you believe they made him into a marine? He used to get tired walking to his car, hated regimentation, and was always wanting to have the last word. Somebody did a job on Charlie.

So far our concerns have been mainly on learning and playing roles that are considered appropriate according to the cultural dictates of the wider society or some sector of it that is particularly important to us—our social class, occupational category, or ethnic group, for example. We noted in Chapters 4 and 5 that most American children are instilled with certain feelings about their parents, their friends, their teachers, and their country. We saw in Chapter 6 that people are expected to behave in different ways at home, in church, in school, and at work and that, in general, they act in accordance with rules specific to each institution. We learned in Chapter 9 that, while there are class differences in socialization practices, young people at each level learn to do things that are appropriate for "people like us" and learn that other things are not appropriate. Members of ethnic and religious groups are also taught particular norms—often ones that enhance group solidarity and acceptance.

Of course, exceptions are made to what is required or expected in various spheres of life. Poor children may reject "the culture of poverty" and seek something better. Some people prefer homosexual relations to heterosexual

ones. Many executives would like to get away from the business rat race. A substantial number of American women want to be something besides housewives and mothers. Many minority group members try to shake loose the bonds that tie them so tightly to their ethnic or racial group and limit their interactions with others.

In all societies people dream of being what they are not. Sometimes they decide to challenge the system, to push out beyond the limits of tolerance established in law or tradition. The political radical, the gay liberationist, the corporate dropout, the feminist, and many others are willing to stand up and be counted as rejecting at least some of society's norms. They are willing to risk being labeled as troublemakers, queers, witches, or, simply, deviants. The embezzler, the professional thief, the bank robber also violate norms usually for different and often more private motivations. They usually don't want to change the world—just get a bigger share of the pie for themselves. They, too, are labeled deviants.

As these examples show, the label *deviant* is a broad term. While it is

Deviance: the violation of a society's essential norms.

often applied with some malice, it is also sociologically appropriate. Sociologists define deviance as behavior that violates an essential social norm or set of norms. Deviants, then, are those who go beyond the limits of socially acceptable behavior.

Resocialization: in this chapter, a rapid and extreme change in an individual's permitted behavior and a consequent change in his or her sense of self.

In this chapter we look briefly at the concept of deviance and the major sociological theories of deviance. We then consider what happens to many of those who are seen or see themselves as deviants—hospitalized mental patients, prison inmates, and others. Society's reaction to deviant behavior is often what sociologists call *resocialization:* the individuals are placed in controlled situations where extreme methods are used to teach them new roles according to the dictates of the new social environment. Although all controlled environments impose resocialization on their inmates, not all are intended to correct or punish deviance. Basic training camps, convents and monasteries, and concentration camps are places of resocialization with different goals, as we shall see.

THE PROBLEM OF DEVIANCE

If all children are socialized to observe the norms of their society, or their segments of it, why does deviance occur? There is no single satisfactory answer to this question. Although the operational definition of deviance is simple, deviant acts in real life are generally surrounded by ambiguitites—circumstances that can be interpreted in more than one way. No single act is forbidden at all times in every human society, not even taking another person's life.

SURVEY OF WHAT GROUPS ARE CONSIDERED DEVIANT

Response Given	*Percentage of Respondents*
Homosexuals	49
Drug addicts	47
Alcoholics	46
Prostitutes	27
Murderers	22
Criminals	18
Lesbians	13
Juvenile delinquents	13
Beatniks	12
Mentally ill persons	12
Perverts	12
Communists	10
Atheists	10
Political extremists	10

Source: J. L. Simmons, "Public Stereotypes of Deviants," *Social Problems,* 13:2 (Fall, 1965). table 1, 224. Reprinted by permission of The Society for the Study of Social Problems.

Deviance, then, is a highly relative concept. What is deviant in one place or at one particular time may be acceptable behavior elsewhere or at another time. For an act to be deviant it must be considered so by a large part of a society or group or by socially powerful persons who can influence a sufficient number of others to agree with them.

A behavior pattern may be seen as normal, even desirable, by some participants, while others consider it deviant. If a student spends a good deal of time doing library research, he or she may win a teacher's respect and appreciation but be scorned as a "bookworm" by other students. What is normal or desirable to the teacher can be deviant to fellow students. Some of those students—those who refuse to study—are deviant by the teacher's (and presumably the school board's and the parents') norms. The urban guerrilla may be scorned by most citizens and yet hailed as a revolutionary hero by his or her supporters.

List in detail several instances of behavior that is normal in one segment of conventional society but is considered deviant in other segments. Give the norms that support each pattern of behavior and those that are violated. For example: Men are supposed to remove hats as a sign of respect when entering a public building. Orthodox Jews, however, are required to keep their heads covered in order to show their reverence for God. You might also think about norms governing dress, sexual relations, and sex role behavior that differ in various subgroups.

Salience of norms was discussed in Chapter 4.

In certain circumstances, even violators of norms that have high salience in our society, and that generally carry high penalties, have escaped severe punishment—or any punishment. Not too many decades ago in the South a white who murdered a black or raped a black woman ran virtually no risk of being accused or tried for the crime. On the other hand, a southern black accused on the flimsiest evidence of murdering or raping a white faced a high risk of being lynched without even a trial.

More recently high-level corporate executives have been convicted of conspiring to fix prices in the electrical industry. Customers lost millions of dollars as a result of the actions of these directors. Few of the culprits actually went to prison, however, and all quickly returned to high-paying positions with their original or other industrial firms. While they had violated the law by conspiring to limit competition, they escaped with only mild punishment compared to offenders from lower social class backgrounds.[1] The price paid for transgression often depends heavily on who the offender is.

Thus, even among the high-salience norms within a society at a particular time, considerable variety can be found in what is acceptable or unacceptable behavior and what the punishment is for violation of the norm. Such variability is more characteristic of large, advanced, heterogeneous societies like ours than of small societies bound by a set of strong, shared traditions. Sociologist Émile Durkheim, in fact, related deviance itself to modernization. He believed that the variety and complexity of norms in an industrialized urbanized society and the predominance of impersonal, contractual relationships combined to weaken the individual's commitment to norms in general. It then became statistically more likely that an individual in that society would behave deviantly.

MAJOR THEORIES OF DEVIANCE

Anomie: (Durkheim): a condition of normlessness.

Durkheim's theory suggests that larger social conditions predispose some members of a society to higher rates of deviance than others. But Durkheim wasn't specific about how or why some individuals become deviant and others do not. Sociologists are still not able to answer such a question, but they have tried to draw a clearer, more detailed picture of the social mechanisms that lead to deviance. There are several major theories.

Anomie

To explain the occurrence of deviance, Robert K. Merton adopted Durkheim's concept of anomie.[2] Merton suggests that, in our society, in which success is measured largely by material possessions and in which competitiveness is a norm, many people are socialized to the goal of success but lack the means of achieving it. If their social class or ethnic group membership or lack of competitive ability deprives them of acceptable, legitimate access to the goal, they may, according to Merton, choose one of four behavior patterns: ritualism; retreatism; innovation; or rebellion.

Ritualism (Merton): going through the motions of a role with no hope of or interest in achieving its supposed goals.

By ritualism, Merton means the mechanical performance of acceptable behavior but without hope of success. Proper behavior becomes a ritual

[1]Gilbert Geis, "The Heavy Electrical Equipment Anti-Trust Cases of 1961," in *White Collar Crime*, ed. Gilbert Geis (New York: Atherton Press, 1968); see also James Boyd, *Above the Law: The Rise and Fall of Senator Thomas J. Dodd* (New York: New American Library, 1968).

[2]Robert K. Merton, *Social Theory and Social Structure* (New York: Free Press, 1968), Chap. 4. For further discussion of anomie as a cause of deviance, see Marshall D. Clinard, ed., *Anomie and Deviant Behavior: A Discussion and Critique* (New York: Free Press, 1964).

Durkheim theorized that in modern, industrialized societies the variety *of norms is sufficient to weaken general adherence to any one set of them. Deviance would naturally increase in such circumstances.*

In a deviant subculture, behavior that is considered deviant by most people in the society is both acceptable and required of subculture members. In the nineteenth century, Mormons were driven from place to place by legal harassment. They finally settled in the territory of Utah, not yet a state or under full United States law. Their deviance? Their religious belief and norm that a man should have more than one wife.

Like the Hells Angels and other motorcycle gangs, this gang from Oakland, California, shown on the next page, maintains norms that life in the ghetto often promotes: toughness, daring, and contempt for rational-legal authority.

Retreatism (Merton): abandoning socially prescribed behavior along with the socially held goals.

Innovation (Merton): acceptance of the broadly held social goals but use of illegitimate means to achieve them.

because it is divorced from the goals to which other members of society link it. An example is the bureaucrat who has given up hope of promotion but remains a stickler for the rules. By retreatism, Merton means the behavior pattern of the dropout: the alcoholic, the bum, the user of hard drugs such as heroin—each of these persons has retreated from both the social goals and the legitimate means of attaining them. Innovators, according to Merton's terminology, are those who accept the goals but seek to attain them by disapproved means such as prostitution, selling hard drugs, theft, dealing in stolen property,

embezzlement, price-fixing, or any of the numerous shortcuts that are disapproved by society. By rebellion Merton meant behavior patterns by which people express their rejection of both the goals and the major norms and values of conventional society and substitute their own. Members of communes, underground political radicals, and so-called Jesus freaks fit the rebel definition.

Rebellion (Merton): rejection of both socially approved goals and socially approved norms.

In each of Merton's categories the individual or group deals in a different way with the same situation: the separation between socially approved

Labeling theory: the theory that much persistent deviant behavior is the result of individuals' being labeled deviant by society.

goals and the possibility of achieving them. In this respect Merton's theory of anomie shades in with other theories of deviance. For example, the deviant subculture theory relates to three of Merton's categories.

Deviant Subcultures

A subculture, we have said, is a group that holds a set of norms and values that differ in important ways from those of the dominant culture. Just as people are socialized into the larger culture, others are socialized into the subculture. In the subculture of an urban ghetto or ethnic slum, for example, toughness, courage, and contempt for conventional authority may be the norms, as we discussed in Chapter 9.

A person who is socialized into such norms behaves perfectly acceptably in the context of the subculture but may be viewed as a deviant by the larger society, where respect for authority and for the property rights of others are the norms.[3] A person respected in the subculture may be condemned in the larger society as a juvenile delinquent, a pimp, a prostitute, a drug pusher, or a motorcycle bum. In Merton's terms, such a deviant is reacting with innovation.

Primary deviance (in labeling theory): behavior by an individual that violates social norms but that has not yet been detected by others and labeled deviant.

Labeling Theory

The third important theory of deviance, labeling theory, distinguishes between two types of deviance: primary and secondary.[4] An individual engaged in primary deviance violates cultural norms without being discovered. Such a deviant may well consider himself or herself basically normal. Whether the deviance is homosexual behavior, drug use, occasional shoplifting, or fraudulent advertising, the primary deviant is able to rationalize it as acceptable or as simply an eccentricity.

Secondary deviance (in labeling theory): deviant behavior that persists because the individual has been labeled a deviant.

Secondary deviation is behavior that follows the discovery of a primary deviance, according to labeling theory. That is, once a person is labeled a homosexual, an embezzler, an alcoholic, a drug addict, or a thief, he or she is affected in significant ways that may encourage continued or increased deviance.

A known homosexual may lose his or her job and friends, may feel compelled to change neighborhoods or even move to a distant city, and may become convinced, by public condemnation, that he or she is indeed funda-

[3]See J. L. Simmons, *Deviants* (Berkeley, Calif.: Glendessary Press, 1969), and Albert K. Cohen, *Delinquent Boys: The Culture of the Gang* (New York: Free Press, 1955).

[4]See Howard S. Becker, *The Outsiders* (New York: Free Press, 1963), and Erving Goffman, *Stigma* (Englewood Cliffs, N.J.: Prentice-Hall, 1963).

mentally deviant. Internal redefinition of the self as deviant, combined with public condemnation, may encourage the individual either to flee conventional society, perhaps by entering a deviant subculture in pursuit of lost acceptance or, on the contrary, to accept the deviant label and seek a cure for his or her "illness."

Women smokers were once considered deviants in our society but are no longer thought so. The same was true of women who sought the right to vote. Today women hold office in both houses of Congress, many state legislatures, and high executive branch positions.

Homosexuality was for a long time considered a sin or crime against nature; later it was thought to be a mental illness that could and should be cured; in 1974, the American Psychiatric Association declared it an alternative sexual orientation—no longer a mental illness. In the last six or seven years, homosexuals have sought the same public acceptance and the same rights under the law that heterosexuals enjoy.

Marijuana, once dubbed "the devil weed," has been condemned from many sides—chiefly as the first step on the ladder to depraved and criminal behavior, to addiction, and to the use of harder drugs such as heroin. No empirical evidence substantially and clearly supports these charges, and there is evidence to refute each. Moreover, despite the risks of detection and legal punishment, millions of persons have tried or regularly use marijuana. In 1976, California revised its laws to make possession of one ounce or less of marijuana a misdemeanor rather than a felony.

1. In each of these examples, a pattern of behavior once considered deviant in our society has come to be normal (such as women's participation in the democratic process) or at least somewhat more acceptable (such as homosexuality and marijuana use). Why do you think they were originally labeled deviant forms of behavior? How do you think changing definitions came about?

2. List and discuss several other previously deviant behaviors that are now largely acceptable and have become part of our conventional behavior. (Think, for example, of styles of dress for women and men, women in the labor force, interracial relationships, sexual and reproductive mores.)

Marijuana was legal in this country until some forty years ago. At that time it was used by few people, most of them in poor, black subcultures. In the recent past its use, though illegal, has grown rapidly–chiefly among middle-class and college-educated persons. It is persistently used by a broad spectrum of the populace, just as speakeasies and bootleggers flourished in the 1920s during Prohibition. How can such patterns of deviant behavior be explained?

CONFORMING TO DEVIANT PATTERNS

Whatever theory of deviant behavior one accepts, there seems to be common agreement that certain individuals or groups of individuals are sufficiently different from other members of society to be singled out. Not all react to this categorizing with disfavor. Street gang members, hippies, religious fanatics, and political revolutionaries often revel in their rebellion. They like the fact that others recognize their difference and hold them in awe. They feel truly a part of a deviant subculture.

In such a subculture, even among rebels and outlaws, certain rules must be learned and obeyed, certain patterns of behavior must be adopted, certain values must be accepted. Indeed, deviant subcultures often require strict *conformity* to the norms of the deviant group. Those who violate the code are often dealt with severely—as if they were deviant.

In recent years, for example, some young people from conventional homes have run off to join religious groups where they undergo a period of initiation, preparing them to recruit others to the following. Both parents and religious group leaders demand conformity to the norms they each consider right. Parents of such youngsters have sometimes gone to great lengths to find their children and bring them home. Often they are thwarted by group leaders or by the children themselves, who simply don't want to leave or who fear the punishment that is threatened for leaving the group and therefore claim they want to stay.

In both the process of becoming deviant, by internalizing the rules and roles appropriate to gangs or groups, and the process of reentering society after being a member of a deviant subculture, intensive retraining goes on. A person engaging in deviant behavior has to find models for that behavior outside the normal realm of significant others. The individual will be socialized by conforming members of society and resocialized by deviant models. To reenter mainstream society, the deviant often undergoes resocialization again. The agents of resocialization, whether they are gang leaders on the streetcorner, drill instructors in a basic training camp, psychiatrists in a mental hospital, or guards in a prison, profoundly reshape the individual's life.

Total institutions, or controlled environments: places in which the individual has no autonomy, has little or no privacy, performs most activities with other inhabitants, and is required to follow the instructions of a powerful central authority.

IN CONTROLLED ENVIRONMENTS: INTENSIVE RESOCIALIZATION

What happens to people who go through a resocialization process designed to give them new self-concepts, values, and norms? Resocialization, as we noted, usually occurs in special contexts, often in special places. Some sociologists, such as Erving Goffman, call them *total institutions;* we prefer to call them *controlled environments* because the term *institution* generally has a different meaning in sociology.

Controlled environments are established for a variety of purposes. Some exist to help or force people who are considered deviant to come back into society. Prisons and mental hospitals are examples. Others are designed to prepare people for new and different roles in specialized subcultures, such as military or monastery life. Whatever the purpose, so elaborate are the requirements and so all-encompassing are the activities that controlled environments often represent miniature social systems. They have their own hierarchies of authority, codes of conduct, and patterns of socialization. When successful in attaining their goals, they are able to block out most other aspects of life for the recruits, nuns, or inmates.

In this section we examine the resocialization that takes place within several of these environments, exploring both similarities and differences among them. There are important differences, for example, between the places a person enters voluntarily in order to be "remade" and the places he or she enters involuntarily. The range of voluntary entrants is wide: from the young drifter who decides to let the army turn him into a fighting man, to the devout Catholic adolescent who chooses the rigors of a career in the clergy, to the mentally disturbed person who seeks psychiatric help by entering a mental hospital.

The degree of voluntarism affects the entire resocialization process. For example, it is easier to resocialize people into becoming armed fighters if that is what they want to be than if they have to be forced into the role. Thus, the armed forces voluntary enlistment program may have an easier time producing trained troops than the draft. Similarly, it is far easier to help persons with emotional problems who are seeking assistance than it is to cure reluctant, confused, or belligerent people who have been committed by others.

In some instances, of course, voluntarism does not exist at all. The most extreme controlled environments, such as prisoner-of-war camps or concentration camps, make no pretense of remaking people in a more positive image. Rather, in the interests of political or military authorities, inmates are simply controlled or are actually destroyed as we see later in this chapter.

Shared Characteristics of Controlled Environments

Although controlled environments are established for different purposes (and different inmate groups), they do tend to share certain characteristics. Erving Goffman, who studied these environments, noted four common traits.[5] First, all aspects of life are conducted in the same place and are under the control of the same authority. Most people interact in a variety of settings. They assume

[5]Erving Goffman, *Asylums* (New York: Doubleday Anchor, 1961).

Controlled environments exhibit four common characteristics: (1) all activities are performed in one setting under the same authority; (2) there is maximum contact with others and minimal privacy; (3) all activities are imposed and scheduled by the authorities; (4) all activities have one goal–to fulfill the purpose of the institution.

many roles. No matter how successful their socialization to these roles is, there is always competition from the demands of the others. "Sorry I can't stay and listen to music. I have to get to work," or, "Hello, Pat. I'll be late getting home from school because I'm staying for practice."

All of us depend on getting time out from the demands of a particular setting. "Thank God, it's Friday," exclaim workers, teachers, and students alike. What they really mean is, "I want to get away from work. I'd like to do some other things, interact with different people."

In a controlled environment, whether it is a merchant ship or a monastery, the inmates eat, work, and sleep in the same place with the same authorities regulating their lives. Usually a large number of people are managed by a small staff, and the interaction among role-players in different positions is carefully regulated.

A second characteristic of controlled environments is that all aspects of daily life are conducted in the company of others who are in the same circumstances. Army recruits, novices in a convent, and prisoners generally enjoy little privacy. They spend most of their days with others in similar circumstances. Contact with the outside world is regulated and occurs under conditions specified by the establishment's authorities.

A third characteristic is that all activities are scheduled by the authorities without consulting the participants. Very often a formal routine prescribes such details of life as when to get up and go to bed, what to wear, when and what to eat, the work to do, and the leisure activities offered.

Finally, the activities in a controlled environment are all designed to meet the same goal: to fulfill the purpose of the organization. Physical training, harassment by authorities, strict enforcement of rules and regulations, and limitations on contact with the outside world are all used by military authorities, for example, to transform civilians into fighting men. Similarly, all activities in a monastery are centered around prayer and communion with God, while prison activities are designed to keep antisocial people in order, if not to change their antisocial attitudes.

Ideal type: a description of a complex phenomenon that incorporates all its essential traits and excludes the incidental variants found in real-world examples of the phenomenon.

In the remainder of this chapter we examine in detail the intense resocialization process in four environments—the army, the mental hospital, the prison, and the concentration camp. These establishments do not share every element of a controlled environment to the same degree. Some allow inmates to have passes, while others do not, for example. What distinguishes these settings from other places, however, is, as Goffman points out, "that each exhibits to an intense degree many items in this family of attributes."[6] That

[6]Ibid., p. 5.

is, each sufficiently resembles the ideal type to be classified as a controlled environment.

Boot Camp

The armed forces prepare men (and some women) to endure hardship, obey orders, have group solidarity, and acquire the skills and attitudes necessary for war. To do this, military authorities demand that recruits leave behind their families, possessions, ideas—indeed, their whole civilian selves—and forge new identities as military personnel. How this occurs is well described by Steven Warner, a young man who had been given a conscientious objector designation by his local draft board but nevertheless was drafted by the marine corps. Warner, like the other recruits, found that many of his previous beliefs were challenged as the corps attempted to turn him from a citizen who hated war into a soldier who would obey on command. Warner was quickly labeled a deviant by his superiors and singled out for special harassment. The experience had a deep impact on him.

> Our Greyhound drove onto Parris Island at ten that night. A few seconds after we stopped, a staff sergeant wearing the Smokey Bear hat all drill instructors wear came on the bus and said: "You're on Parris Island. There are two ways to leave here: on a bus like this in eight or nine weeks or in a box. . . . If you have any cigarettes, put them out. If you have any gum, swallow it. . . . You have ten seconds to get into that building. . . . Move!"
>
> A staff sergeant began . . . telling us how we were to behave from that moment on. . . .
>
> Recruits must stand at attention at all times. Recruits will not eyeball. Recruits will double-time everywhere. Recruits will do nothing without permission: they will not speak or swat bugs or wipe off sweat or faint without permission. Recruits will call everyone, except other recruits, "Sir." Recruits will never use the word "you" because "you" is a female sheep and there are no ewes on Parris Island. Recruits will never use the word "I" because "I" is what a recruit sees with, not what he calls himself.[7]

Depersonalization: treatment of the individual in ways that minimize or destroy his or her sense of uniqueness and, often, worth; the term is also used for the result of this treatment.

An initial part of the resocialization process began with *depersonalization.* The young men were no longer called by their names. Their possessions were taken away, and a hundred rules or new norms were thrown at them. Merging with the group was stressed, rather than individual identity. Recruits were no longer treated as individuals, but had to speak, look, and act like every other

[7]Steven Warner, "A Conscientious Objector at Parris Island," *Atlantic,* June 1972, p. 46. Copyright © 1972 by The Atlantic Monthly Company, Boston, Mass., reprinted by permission, and by permission of Paul R. Reynolds, Inc., 12 East 41st Street, New York, N.Y., 10017

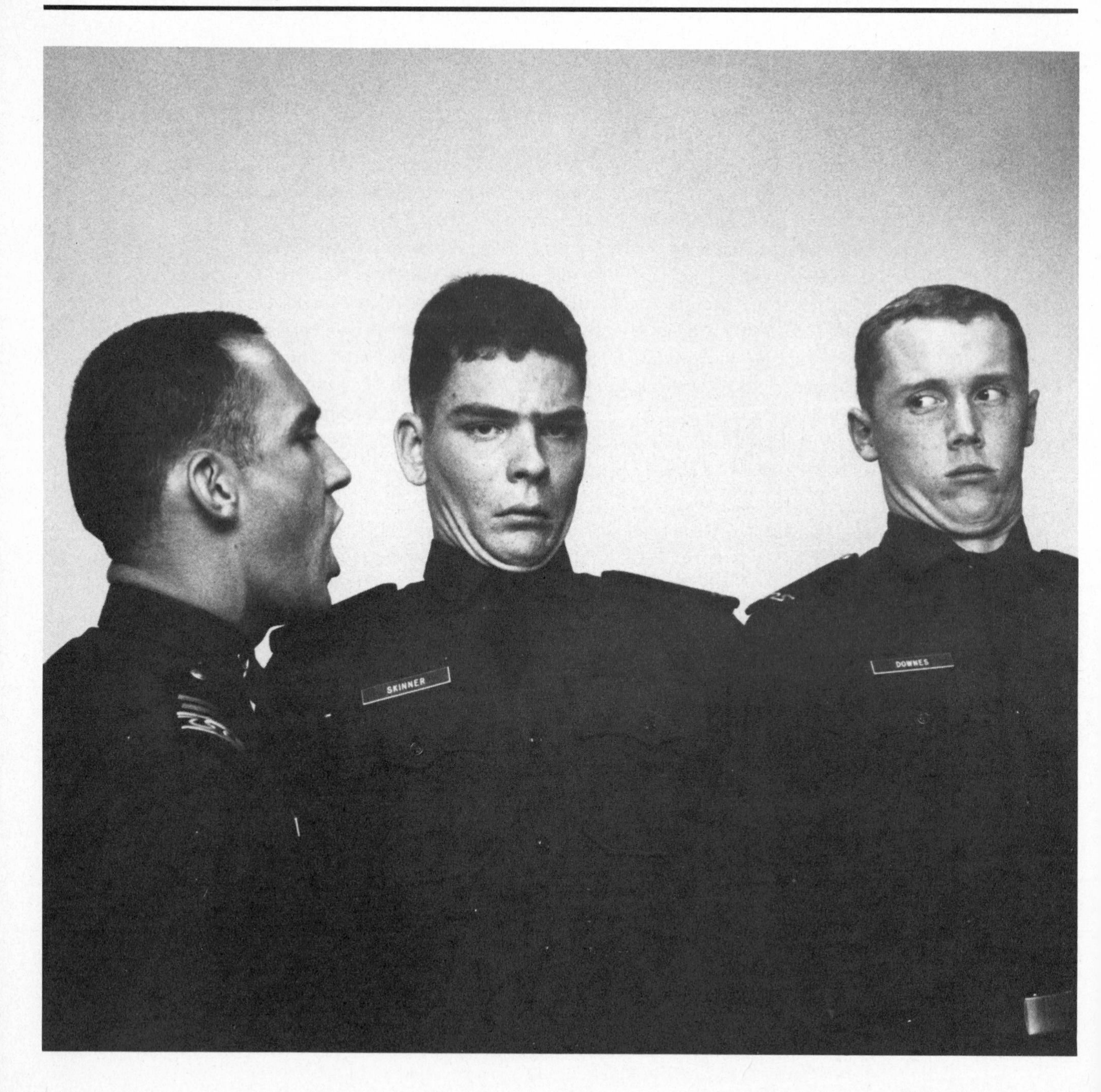
SKINNER
DOWNES

recruit—or else. Uniforms and haircuts were important components of that transformation. To accomplish the depersonalization, the men had to do some *unlearning*. It no longer mattered whether a recruit had been a high school baseball star, a talented carpenter, a big man on campus, or his parents' pride and joy. Former roles and identities simply did not count. The sooner they were forgotten, the better the recruit would get along.

The resocialization process included another crucial component made clear by Warner's first exposure to the marines. The drill instructor (DI) immediately became the recruits' most imporant *significant other*. The welcoming speech not only set out a whole series of new norms but also established that the DI controlled rewards and punishments. If the recruit did not live up to his role obligations, he would be observed and quickly reprimanded. The DI's opinion and reactions were what counted now. He and his fellow DIs were in control.

This was made abundantly clear when the men were ordered to pick up their gear and follow their DI after the initial speech. Those recruits who couldn't keep the double time pace were cajoled, cursed, and ultimately punished. The message was clear. Tough days were ahead. The DIs had the difficult task of turning soft-bellied individual civilians into a disciplined fighting unit. It may not have been a task they relished, but it was necessary, and they did it in a relentless manner.

The DIs' definition of their own roles seemed abundantly clear and reflected their sensitivity to the process of resocialization. The recruits brought with them a vast baggage of previous roles and cultural definitions. It was the assumption of the armed forces that all of these had to be broken down and discarded if the recruits were to become military men capable of responding to orders, working as a group, and living together. New norms had to be repeated continually and appropriate behavior demanded. No exceptions could be made. The DIs' role demanded that they be constantly alert for infractions of the rules and be ready to "chew out" or "ream" offenders. The DIs' vigilance and consistency in playing their roles were important defenses against letting the recruits slide into former civilian patterns of behavior.

Each DI's vigilance also served to remind his men that he represented the authority of the entire military chain of command. His legitimacy stemmed from his position in the military hierarchy, and he had clearcut obligations to his superiors to bear down hard. The DI, as well as the men, was judged by the unit's efficiency in performing its tasks.

Warner's training continued. Physical exercise was peppered with constant harassment and emphasis on the cunning and toughness of North

Primary group: a group in which intimate, spontaneous, emotionally significant relations are characteristic (discussed in Chapter 5).

Vietnamese soldiers. Although Warner came to training camp with no fear of or ill will toward the "enemy" in Southeast Asia, exposure to the training sessions instilled such fear in him. The controlled environment was having its effect. Other things were also happening. A sense of group solidarity was beginning to take hold. The men reached out to help each other in time of trouble and provided comfort. As in actual combat situations, the recruits came to act out the belief that they could depend on their buddies. Primary group relations were clearly developing under the supervision of the authorities.

> Since the first days of boot camp, we had been warned about the PRT (Physical Readiness Test) we would take during the last week. This would be our initiation into the Marine Corps. . . .
>
> We climbed some ropes in full gear, carried one another over our shoulders for a while, crawled a lot. . . . Then came the last hurdle: a three-mile run in full gear—steel helmet, boots, pack, rifle.
>
> Everyone was grim. Our commanding officer, also in full gear, ran in front of the company. Gordon [the DI] was in front of our platoon. . . . We ran silently for a while. The only sounds were heavy breathing and boots hitting the ground. Then Gordon started us on our chants: ''Here we go-o! HERE WE GO-O! Long Road! LONG ROAD! Hard Road! HARD ROAD! Won't Stop! WON'T STOP! Gimme More! GIMME MORE! Marine Corps! MARINE CORPS!''
>
> Two or three recruits were having a hard time. They had run the distance many times before, but now they gasped for air and stumbled trying to keep up. Other recruits took turns, carrying their rifles, their packs, and even their helmets. If the stragglers continued to fade, they were held up by the arms, even carried. . . . The point was, the platoon kept on running, and no one was left behind. We had learned our lesson.
>
> When it was over, everybody was grins and back-slapping. Gordon, sweating more than I had ever seen before, came into the barracks and gave us a small smile and said: ''MARINES . . . take a shower.'' It was the first time he had ever called us that.[8]

This episode includes some telling points about the process of resocialization. The men's new status required far more than putting aside previous statuses. It required them to forge a new identity, a new set of role definitions to go along with their new status as marines. A positive identity was developing. This identity included the belief that the recruit could overcome difficult physical challenges, that he must and could make sure that the others made it as well, that this successful outcome came under the leadership of competent authorities. The reward was a shared satisfaction that the unit had succeeded and that each member could take personal pride in the achievement.

[8]Ibid., p. 51.

Later in this chapter we see that this consistency of values is not present in some other controlled environments, such as prisons. The resistance of inmates to resocialization is then greater, and the process is more difficult.

Thus, while former statuses had been suppressed in the process of resocialization, the new one—marine—once achieved, made all the sacrifices easier to bear.

In this effort, the peer group had played a central part. Feelings of "We're doing it together" or "We can make it, if we stick together" reflect a sense of interdependence that reinforces the value of the authorities that the unit is more important than the individual. In essence, resocialization of each participant is attained more effectively if the peer group comes to support the values of the authorities.

How do the characteristics of a controlled environment that we described earlier apply to the military basic training situation? All aspects of the recruit's life are conducted at one particular place—the military base—and under the control of one authority—the DI. All aspects of the recruit's life are conducted in the company of other recruits who are in the same circumstances and playing the same role. All activities of the day are scheduled by the authorities without the consent of the recruits. No one asks them what time they care to get up, what they would like to wear or eat during the day, or which tasks they prefer to perform. Finally, the activities were designed to fulfill the main purpose of the military—to prepare men to fight in wars. This means socializing men to do tasks and respond to authority even when their lives are at stake. Behavior that had been perfectly acceptable in civilian life was now defined as deviant and subject to punishment. Even a conscientious objector like Steven Warner found his previous beliefs undermined. His last statement is particularly revealing, for he writes that, if his own son ever has to be in the armed forces, he hopes the boy will serve in the marines.[9]

Warner's experiences in marine basic training show us several other characteristics of controlled environments. For one thing, depersonalization is a central component of resocialization. It forces the recruit to leave behind former positions and the roles and identities associated with them. Warner's experience also shows that unlearning former role behavior is a painful procedure that people are likely to resist. Significant others are crucial in the unlearning process. They are more likely to have their expectations met when these are set out clearly and consistently and when resources are available to reward conformity and punish deviance. An individual is more willing to play new roles if these roles are shown to have some relation to past definitions of the self. Thus, recruits may vehemently dislike obeying orders, but they are more likely to do so if they can be convinced that this shows they "can take

[9]Ibid., p. 52.

it," "are growing up," or are now fit to be called "marine." In essence, resocialization occurs more easily if conformity to the roles of the new position is shown as competence rather than subservience. Finally, resocialization proceeds more smoothly if the individual finds new groups with which to identify within the controlled environment. This occurred in Warner's marine basic training. As we see next, it can also occur in mental hospitals.

The Mental Hospital

The patient in a mental hospital, like the military recruit, must learn a new set of behaviors and attitudes for interactions with a variety of new persons. Like boot camp, the mental hospital has a goal: to take people who have been defined—by their physicians, their families, or themselves—as emotionally disturbed and transform them, if they are capable of responding to therapy, into functioning members of the larger society.

The mental patient spends virtually all his or her time in the hospital, is cut off from playing former roles, and is usually deprived of regular clothing and possessions. The patient experiences the depersonalization process in many subtle and obvious ways. Yet the experience in a mental hospital is much more individualized than that in basic training. Patients do not enter or leave as a group. Though similar behavior is demanded of the patients, each patient must adjust on his or her own to the new setting, and each must progress individually to a healthier condition in order to be released.

Sociologist Lewis Killian described his experience as an actual patient in a small mental hospital in New England. He was suffering from severe depression, and his psychiatrist had recommended hospitalization.

> I remember my admission to the hospital only in fragments. I kissed my wife goodbye and heard the appalling words, "No visitors for 72 hours," and then I was alone among strangers. I didn't care: I wanted to be alone. . . . But immediately the [staff] began to break through my shell. "Have you eaten supper, Lewis?" "We all use first names here—patients and staff; I'm Helen, I'm a nurse". . . .
>
> We inventoried everything I had brought into the hospital. I was required to give my keys to the nurse for safe keeping because the small knife on my key chain constituted a "sharp" in the lingo of the ward, and all sharps had to be kept behind the nurses' station. I was reminded by this that I really was suspect—I did not just imagine that I was in a somewhat abnormal state. I could accept this, though, for I wasn't sure that I might not harm myself. After I went to bed that night it reassured rather than disturbed me to realize that an attendant looked in on me every hour throughout the night. . . .
>
> The power vested in the staff was so evident that one of my first reactions to the ward was, "This is like a prison!" When I found that a staff member had to

> accompany me on the short walk down the corridor to the lavatory; when I saw patients with "hospital privileges" asking the charge nurse for a pass to go to the gift shop; when I realized that I was forbidden to go out the doors of the ward without permission, I was reminded of the pervasive system of control which I had observed in a maximum security military prison while training there as a reserve officer. For me as for our prisoners "being out of place" was an offense against the norms of the total institution.[10]

Despite the apparent differences between Killian's first hours in the mental hospital and the marines' initial exposure to basic training, there are important similarities. In both instances the authorities have a clear-cut goal and a method that they believe is effective in resocializing people in accordance with the goal. They are confident that, in the context of a highly structured and even authoritarian environment, they can reshape individuals' behavior and conceptions of themselves. At first, individuals go along, because they are made acutely aware of the imbalance of power. But this is not sufficient. Ultimately, in order to create well-motivated fighting men or cured patients, the authorities must convince those in their charge that the establishment's goals and methods are appropriate:

> My conception of the power of the staff changed as I reacted to their behavior. I came to feel that it was . . . essentially supportive rather than threatening. A patient saw his therapist only two or three times a week, and then for an hour at a time. On the other hand, at least one member of the nursing staff was on the floor at all times, and usually there were three present. . . .
>
> This almost constant observation and intervention made it very difficult for a patient to withdraw and nurse his troubles in private—something I was certainly inclined to do when I entered the community. . . . I soon reached the conclusion that it was easier to keep active and involved with other people than it was to justify going into a shell. This change of behavior pattern was, of course, just what I needed to break the cycle of my depression, and it came about without anyone's explicitly prescribing it for me.[11]

Lewis Killian's ability to understand himself increased as he became an active participant in the hospital community. He grew to feel close to both staff and patients. For a short but crucial period, the hospital became his home. Patients shared their problems and helped each other find new strength. Killian thrived in an environment where people could freely discuss what was

[10] Lewis M. Killian and Sanford Bloomberg, "Rebirth in a Therapeutic Community: A Case Study, " *Psychiatry* 38 (1975): 43–45.

[11] Ibid., pp. 48–49.

The custodial role of many mental institutions illustrates Merton's distinction between manifest (intended) functions—here, therapy—and latent (unintended) functions—here, keeping patients isolated from the rest of society. (Manifest and latent functions are discussed in Chapter 2.)

troubling them. There was no need to fool themselves or each other. In effect, the authorities fostered the development of primary group relations. It was important for the therapeutic method that close bonds develop among people of diverse ages, backgrounds, and interests who could support each other in the rehabilitation process. Perhaps Killian's last sentence best captures his feeling. When friends say they are sorry to hear he was in the hospital, he replies: "Thank you—but it was one of the most wonderful experiences of my life."[12]

Killian's experience shows that secondary deviance—being defined by others as emotionally ill—can have positive consequences. It was only in the company of others who were similarly defined that he was able to come to terms with his illness. The hospital staff provided the social structure in which his "rebirth" would take place.

Other mental patients have encountered very different experiences, however. Not all mental hospitals are so clearly directed toward healing as the one described by Killian. Patients may not know of such a place, or they may not be able to afford one. Also some patients are too difficult to control in such a setting. These people are most likely to be placed in facilities that emphasize management, control, and caretaking. Here the depersonalization and powerlessness are not as likely to produce beneficial results for the patient as they did for Killian in his setting.

In a project directed by D. L. Rosenhan, a number of graduate students and professionals studied mental hospitals by pretending to be patients.[13] The researchers were interested in finding out how easily they could be diagnosed as mentally ill and admitted to a mental hospital, and how easily they could obtain their discharge. All understood that once they entered the hospital they would be released only when they convinced the staff that they were sane. This turned out to be no simple task.

Each went to the admitting office of a mental hospital and claimed to be hearing unfamiliar voices. All were admitted to their chosen hospitals. No researcher was recognized as a pretender by the staff. At all times they were treated as real patients. Other patients, however, frequently noticed that the researchers did not seem ill. They asked if they were journalists or professors.

Rosenhan's description of what the researchers experienced tells us a great deal about the resocialization process in a mental hospital. As you read it, compare this resocialization experience with Steven Warner's account of boot camp.

[12]Ibid., p. 52.
[13]D. L. Rosenhan, "On Being Sane in Insane Places," *Science* 179 (1973): 250–58.

Consider the structure of the typical psychiatric hospital. Staff and patients are strictly segregated. Staff have their own living space, including their dining facilities, bathroom, and assembly places. The glassed quarters that contain the professional staff, which the pseudopatients came to call "the cage," sit out on every dayroom. The staff emerge primarily for caretaking purposes—to give medication, to conduct a therapy or group meeting, to instruct or reprimand a patient. Otherwise, staff keep to themselves. . . .

. . . It has long been known that the amount of time a person spends with you can be an index of your significance to him. If he initiates and maintains eye contact, there is reason to believe that he is considering your requests and needs. If he pauses to chat or actually stops and talks, there is added reason to infer that he is [treating you as an individual]. In four hospitals, the pseudopatient approached the staff member with a request which took the following form: "Pardon me, Mr. [or Dr. or Mrs.] X, could you tell me when I will be eligible for grounds privileges?" (or " . . . when I will be presented at the staff meeting?" or " . . . when I am likely to be discharged?"). . . . Care was taken never to approach a particular member of the staff more than once a day, lest the staff member become suspicious or irritated. . . .

. . . By far, their most common response consisted of either a brief response to the question, offered while they were "on the move" and with head averted, or no response at all.[14]

This kind of response reduces the patient to childlike status. The question is not worthy of an answer. The doctor's answer is almost like a pat on the head. Rosenhan concludes:

No data can convey the overwhelming sense of powerlessness which invades the individual as he is continually exposed to the *depersonalization* of the psychiatric hospital. . . .

Powerlessness was evident everywhere. The patient is deprived of many of his legal rights. . . . His freedom of movement is restricted. . . . Personal privacy is minimal. Patient quarters and possessions can be entered and examined by any staff member, for whatever reason. . . . The water closets may have no doors. . . .

On the ward, attendants delivered verbal and occasionally serious physical abuse to patients in the presence of other observing patients. . . . Abusive behavior, on the other hand [ended quickly] when other staff members were known to be coming.[15]

Rosenhan's critique echoes those made by other researchers,[16] civil liber-

[14]Ibid., pp. 254–55.

[15]Ibid., p. 256.

[16]For a recent statement, see Martha R. Fowlkes, "Business as Usual—At the State Mental Hospital," *Psychiatry* 38 (1975): 55–64.

tarians, and public officials. Most mental hospitals seem far more capable of giving custodial care than of providing therapy. Their patients most often are resocialized to play a passive and apathetic role rather than an active one in an effort to change troublesome patterns of feelings and behavior. Depersonalization and powerlessness make patients easier to handle. Authority figures often do not use these techniques to achieve therapeutic goals as they did in the hospital described by Killian.

1. Imagine that you are a mental hospital administrator accused of running an organization where patients are treated in an "impersonal" and "powerless" manner. How would you defend the actions of your staff when questioned by a local news reporter?

2. Construct a conversation between a marine DI and a hospital psychiatrist, each of whom is having trouble resocializing an unruly charge. Would they find that they treated recruits or patients in the same manner? Would they use the same techniques for bringing a problem individual into line? In what ways might they disagree about the best treatment for their charges?

3. Put yourself into the role of Dr. Sanford Bloomberg who treated Lewis Killian. What criticism would he have of the hospital settings studied by Rosenhan and his associates?

The Prison

Prisons, unlike mental hospitals, have long been a favorite subject of movie makers. Striped uniforms, marching men, the tough, good-guy warden have all been part of the scenario. Yet these films give the audience only a glimpse of prison life. They cannot fully detail the years of boredom, the meaningless work, the fear of violence, the deprivation of heterosexual activity, and the humiliation of forced homosexual participation that often characterize a prison sentence.

In the 1950s Gresham Sykes wrote a detailed account of a maximum security prison in New Jersey.[17] Several years later Willard Gaylin did a study of a group of conscientious objectors who were serving time in a minimum security federal prison.[18] The settings differed, and the men were in prison for

[17]Gresham M. Sykes, *The Society of Captives* (Princeton, N.J.: Princeton University Press, 1958).

[18]Willard Gaylin, *In the Service of Their Country: War Resisters in Prison* (New York: Viking Press, 1970).

The two faces of mental hospitals: custodial and therapeutic. Ideally these two functions are not at cross-purposes, but in practice they often are. The depersonalization of patients accentuates their illnesses, rendering effective therapy more difficult.

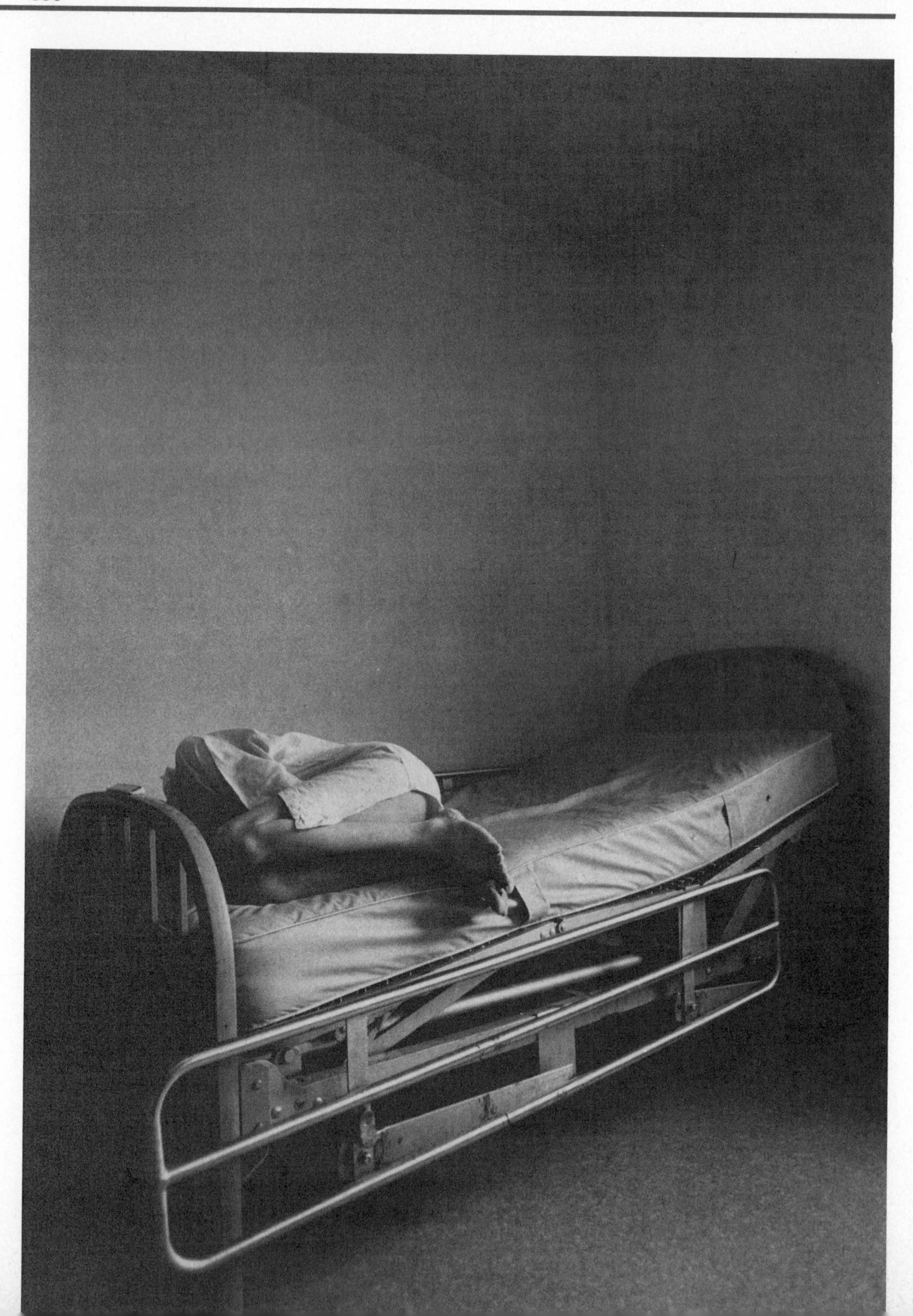

entirely different reasons, yet the experiences were alike in many ways.

In both studies, the prisoners learned that prison means loss of self-expression. Prisoners are allowed little sense of individuality. Closely cropped hair and prison uniforms strip inmates of the personal distinctions that help tell them who they are. They are thoroughly searched upon arrest and are deprived of any privacy. Prisoners who attempt to gain rights or organize others to do so may be singled out for swift and often cruel punishment.

For centuries prisons have been places of incarceration and punishment. Only in modern times has the idea of rehabilitation of society's deviants become a central task. However, programs designed to accomplish the preparation of prisoners for life on the "outside" have had limited success. As evidence of the failure of rehabilitation, critics point to the high proportion of ex-convicts who return to their former activities and end up back in prison. Of the 228,032 adults arrested for federal crimes during 1970–72, 25 percent had one previous conviction, 9 percent two, 5 percent three, and 8 percent four or more. The percentages of recidivism (return to criminal behavior) by type of crime are shown below.

RECIDIVISM BY TYPE OF CRIME, 1970–71

Type of Crime	*Percentage of Adults Arrested Who Are Repeaters*
Robbery	77
Forgery	74
Auto theft	73
Burglary	71
Fraud	69
Assault	68
Gambling	65
Weapons (illegal possession)	62
Larceny	61
Narcotics	60
Embezzlement	34
All others	66
Average for all	65

Source: Federal Bureau of Investigation, *Uniform Crime Report* (Washington, D.C.: U.S. Government Printing Office, 1972), pp. 37, 38.

Other critics say it is not the idea of rehabilitation that is at fault but the inadequate training of prison personnel and insufficient funding to support effective programs. Moreover, some suggest, most prison authorities still see their jobs as keeping inmates securely behind bars and maintaining order.

Is it necessary for prisoners to be treated so differently from the rest of us in our everyday lives? Prisons have been established by the larger society to control and isolate men and women convicted of breaking some law. Does the attempt to control prisoners require guards to play their role in a certain way? As husbands, fathers, or friends, these same men may be kind and gentle. Yet most guards seem to believe that such traits are a weakness in the prison community and therefore a threat to the order they are hired to maintain.

An experiment in intensive resocialization. To understand more about how guards and prisoners learn to play their roles, a group of social scientists set up a mock prison in the basement of a building at Stanford University as an experiment.[19] Into this prison they sent ten "prisoners" and eleven "guards."

[19]Philip G. Zimbardo, W. Curtis Banks, Craig Haney, and David Jaffe, "A Pirandellian Prison," *New York Times Magazine*, April 8, 1973, p. 38.

All the men were actually ordinary college students who had answered an ad offering them the chance to make fifteen dollars a day by participating in an experiment. The interaction between prisoners and guards was carefully recorded by hidden recorders and video tape.

The people chosen to play the role of prisoner agreed to remain in the jail for two weeks, and each was arrested and booked by the local Stanford police, who cooperated in the experiment. Prisoners wore special smocks for uniforms and nylon stocking caps to imitate short haircuts. Guards were dressed in uniforms and sunglasses (to avoid eye contact), and carried billy clubs, whistles, and handcuffs. They were told that they were responsible for maintaining law and order. They were informed that the situation was dangerous.

Prisoners were not allowed to write letters, smoke cigarettes, or go to the bathroom without first obtaining permission. Roll-call was held during each of three guard shifts, and prisoners were often awakened for special counts. Prisoners had to remain silent during rest periods, meals, and outdoor activities, and after lights-out. They were required to address each other by ID numbers only and to address guards as "Mr. Correctional Officer."

Here are three possible outcomes of the prison experiment.

Scenario 1. Although the guards and prisoners interacted within the prison setting, none of them could actually play the assigned roles. The guards did not treat the prisoners as inmates. Indeed, they were as kind to the prisoners as they were to their friends on the outside. All the guards were determined to be good guys and thus win the cooperation of the prisoners.

The prisoners didn't take their roles seriously. They knew they would be released in two weeks. They didn't feel afraid of the prison environment or the guards.

The experiment showed that it is not possible to create a true prison atmosphere without the belief that prisoners have violated social norms and actually need resocializing.

Scenario 2. The prisoners played their role with great seriousness. The prison atmosphere, their uniforms, their mock shaved heads all made them feel that they were actually "doing time." They followed the regulations carefully and did everything possible to cooperate with the guards. The prisoners seemed determined to show that they could maintain their dignity behind bars.

The guards also quickly stepped into an unfamiliar role. They had been told to keep order, and they did. They treated the prisoners with consideration, being careful not to abuse them. The guards decided that prisoners could be treated firmly but fairly. They acted this out, and the prison ran smoothly.

The experiment showed that the prisoner role could be played with dignity and that guards could control prisoners while treating them fairly as human beings.

Scenario 3. The prisoners panicked when they were arrested, searched, and locked up. They felt trapped by the bars, the guards' clubs, and the rules governing their behavior. They resented having to be told when they could smoke, use the toilet, or write a letter. They felt that the frequent prisoner counts, which even awakened them at night, were unnecessary.

Several prisoners could not adjust to the controlled setting. They quickly became depressed, cried constantly, and exhibited fits of rage. The authorities released them within the first few days, long before the scheduled end of the experiment. Other prisoners rebelled and destroyed the furniture in their cells.

The guards quickly responded to the prisoners' actions. Guards felt threatened by the prisoners' hostility to their confinement. They decided that they could control the prisoners only by strict enforcement of rules. Prisoners were treated roughly and insulted on many occasions. A revolt was put down by spraying fire extinguishers at the prisoners. The guards punished all the rebellious prisoners and set aside a special cell for those who decided to cooperate.

1. Which scenario do you think actually happened? Explain why.

2. If you were to participate in such an experiment, how do you think you would react in the roles of guard, prisoner, and superintendent making the rules?

Scenario 3 is correct. The experiment revealed that normal college students placed in a prison setting quickly assumed behavior that actual prisoners and guards display. When interviewed by the researchers, guards said how angry they became with prisoners who resisted their control. The guards enjoyed feeling the power they held over the prisoners and resented any attempt by the prisoners to stand up to them. One guard, for example, told how he listened to a conversation a prisoner had with a visitor. The guard interrupted whenever he disagreed with anything the prisoner said. The guard reported that he relished the feeling of superiority. Yet this same guard described himself as a pacifist and was deeply surprised by his own actions.

Most of the guards were sorry when the experiment ended. They did not like giving up the money they were making by participating in the experiment. But, even more important, they had really enjoyed their sense of power.

Prisoners, on the other hand, were glad when it was all over. In their cells they had talked almost constantly about the prison—the food, their treatment, how they could escape. Prison had been a real and deeply troubling experience for them. Very quickly they learned to play passive roles, accommodating themselves to unjust rules, finding it easier not to assert themselves or stick up for their rights. The experiment revealed that the prison affected the volunteers the way it does actual prisoners. They were afraid, hated their guards, and tried to rebel. They seemed to forget that they were to be there for only two weeks. Finally, they adjusted to their environment, became passive, and began to toe the line.

The guards, too, responded much the way real guards do to hostile, threatening prisoners. Some were kinder than others, but no guards ever stopped their colleagues from treating prisoners cruelly.

In fact, the study concluded, even normal, healthy, educated young men can be transformed or resocialized under the pressures of the prison environment. It did not seem to matter that the situation was an artificial one. Nor did it matter that the subjects had individual personalities at the outset. Once put into their prison roles, they responded very similarly to others in those roles. Philip Zimbardo, the chief researcher, concluded that

> the mere act of assigning labels to people and putting them into a situation where those labels acquire validity and meaning is sufficient to elicit pathological behavior. . . . The prison situation, as presently arranged, is guaranteed to generate severe enough pathological reactions in both guards and prisoners as to debase their humanity, lower their feelings of self-worth and make it difficult for them to be part of a society outside their prison.[20]

Zimbardo's conclusion, based on a carefully conducted experimental study of a small group of students, is supported by numerous official reports published over the years. A recent effort focused on the Attica prison uprising in which forty-three prisoners and hostages were killed by New York State police on September 9, 1971.[21] The report of the New York State Commission on Attica strongly criticized this nation's entire prison system. Massive establishments like Attica, with 2,200 prisoners, are unlikely to provide an environment in which prisoners can be treated humanely, it contended. (We might say the same of large-scale mental hospitals.)

The New York commission found that confinement and security were far more important to Attica authorities than rehabilitation. Shortages of staff and funds prevented the prison from offering education or job training programs for prisoners. Rarely were guards and other officials trained to

[20]Philip G. Zimbardo, "Pathology of Imprisonment," *Society,* April 1972, p. 6.

[21]*Attica: The Official Report of the New York State Commission on Attica* (New York: Bantam Books, 1972).

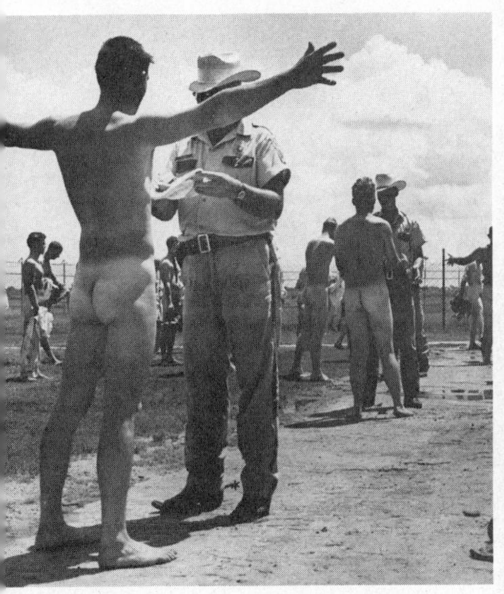

Our prisons have had a bad track record in rehabilitation, but many critics maintain that the high failure rate is due to the conditions in prisons. They claim that the structured patterns of prison interaction work toward depersonalization, which makes rehabilitation unlikely. The debate over prison reform is bound to continue until systematic experiments with alternative methods of treating criminal deviants are conducted.

communicate with prisoners in a meaningful way. Personnel did not think it was part of their job to understand the inmates. Facilities were so crowded that it was even difficult to maintain personal cleanliness and health. Most prisoners could shower only once a week, change their clothes only once a week, and rarely replace worn-out clothing.

It was impossible for prisoners to distinguish between incompetence and harassment. They became less and less willing to cooperate with authorities and less and less convinced that the resocialization process was beneficial to them. Inmates defined the bureaucracy as the enemy. One inmate, for example, received much-needed undershorts and pajamas from his family; unfortunately, the underwear was blue, which was prohibited. He raged, "How can you tell a grown man that he is violating security by wearing a blue pair of shorts? . . . They actually think that we believe that? You know why that rule was made? For harassment and for harassment only."[22]

Under the severe limitations of inadequate clothing, minimal food, lack of spending money, and endless regulations, many prisoners adapted by "hustling." Unlike the therapeutic community, in prison primary groups were not organized by the authorities to help reshape or train their charges. Rather prisoners themselves created these groups to get around the authorities. For example, the Attica commission reported that, to get clean laundry, prisoners "bought a laundry man" (someone working in the laundry) for a carton of cigarettes a month. Many deals were made to meet sexual needs. Because of the lack of women and the denial of visits by wives and sweethearts, many formerly heterosexual men in prisons turn to homosexuality. Small prostitution and pimping groups emerged in Attica, the report found. Similar groups developed for production and distribution of "moonshine," drugs, and medicines.

Throughout the history of prisons, inmates have gone on hunger strikes, invented codes to communicate with and help one another, made implements out of the most primitive materials, and organized internal social systems to get around the rules. An elaborate system of theft and bribes in prisons and other controlled environments helps make life a bit more bearable for the inmates. In his book *Asylums,* sociologist Erving Goffman referred to this phenomenon as "make-do's"—a response that he claims characterizes people in all highly controlled environments.[23] This seems especially true where little effort is made to reshape people to a positive identity, and where the environment is geared toward isolation and control.

[22]Ibid., p. 46.
[23]Goffman, *Asylums,* p. 207.

1. Interview an individual who has lived in a controlled environment (prison, military base, convent or monastery, mental hospital) to learn what make-do's were created by those inside. Begin by asking what rules the inmates had to follow. Ask your respondent which were the most important, the less important, and the least important rules. Find out how inmates felt about these rules. If the respondent begins to express dissatisfaction with or disapproval of the rules, ask if he or she obeyed them. If not, how did the respondent get around the rules? How did others? This will tell you something about the make-do's. If inmates were deprived of certain things, did they create make-do's to replace what they lacked?

Try to distinguish which make-do's were accepted by the authorities and which were not.

2. Have three members of the class play the roles of marine recruit, mental hospital patient-researcher, and prisoner. The three meet after their release and discuss the initiation processes they underwent. How were they resocialized to accept new roles and give up their identification with their former roles? What part did such factors as clothing and daily routine play in their resocialization?

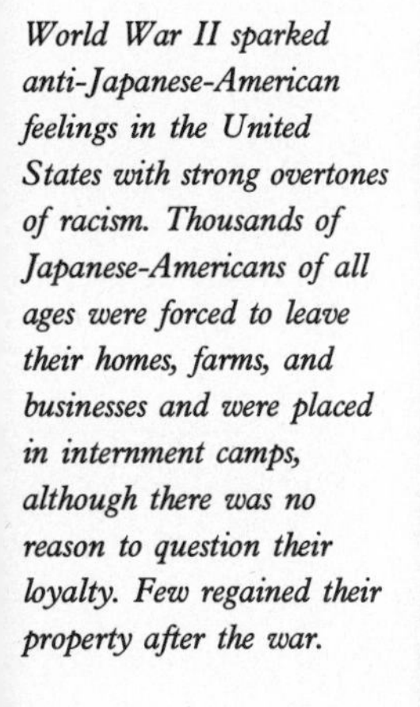

World War II sparked anti-Japanese-American feelings in the United States with strong overtones of racism. Thousands of Japanese-Americans of all ages were forced to leave their homes, farms, and businesses and were placed in internment camps, although there was no reason to question their loyalty. Few regained their property after the war.

The Concentration Camp

Many modern societies have had internment camps, occasionally or as a constant feature. An internment camp in many ways resembles a prison, except that its purpose is neither punishment nor rehabilitation. It is designed to hold people who have been removed from the general society in times of unrest or war because they are considered a threat to the social or political order. For example, at the outset of World War II, as hostile feelings against the Japanese rose, Americans adopted an official policy of holding all Japanese-Americans in internment camps.[24]

These people—most of whom were living in California—had committed no crimes. Many had been born in this country and had always been loyal to it. One Japanese-American battalion that was later formed distinguished itself for bravery in European combat, suffering the highest casualty rate of any battalion and boasting the lowest desertion rate in military history—zero. Yet Japanese-Americans had their property confiscated and were denied all civil liberties and rights, without charges, trial, or conviction. Official histories tend to ignore or underplay this episode, because it is now recognized as cruel, unnecessary, and nakedly racist—no Germans or Italians were interned even though their ancestral nations were also declared enemies of the United States in that war, and some German-Americans had formed organizations to promote sympathy for Nazism before the war.[25]

These American internment camps have been compared to the Nazi concentration camps of the 1930s and early 1940s. Yet there is an essential difference: the Nazi camps were engaged in a program of genocide (annihilation of a whole people considered racially or morally degenerate). In both kinds of camps, there was no training of recruits for army service as in the boot camp, no treatment of illness as in the mental hospital, no rehabilitation of prisoners or even simply holding inmates captive until they had served their sentences as in the prison. But the Nazi concentration camps had one extremely significant additional feature: they were established to work the inmates to death or to kill them outright if they became unfit to labor for the German war machine. Those who were not sent immediately to the gas chambers soon saw how worthless their lives were in the eyes of their captors. They learned the techniques of adaptation quickly or not at all. Bare survival was the only reward of the lucky few.

[24]See Alexander H. Leighton, *The Governing of Men* (Princeton, N.J.: Princeton University Press, 1945).

[25]Audrie Girdner and Anne Loftis, *The Great Betrayal: The Evacuation of Japanese Americans during World War Two* (New York: Macmillan, 1969).

The systematic brutalization and destruction of European Jews by the Nazis has received enormous attention from philosophers, religious writers, and social scientists. The Nazis were not the first to persecute the Jews, nor were the Jews the only people to be interned in concentration camps. But the six million Jews who were exterminated outnumbered all other groups combined. Shown here are survivors of Buchenwald liberated after the defeat of Germany, and two of the ovens at Dachau used to cremate those who died of disease, overwork, or malnutrition or were deliberately killed in gas chambers.

The inmates of the concentration camps included political activists and intellectuals who had resisted the Nazis, prisoners from invaded countries such as Poland and Russia, and Jews from many lands—including Germany, its allies, and occupied countries. Thus, although Italy under Mussolini fought on the side of Hitler's armies, Italian Jews were rounded up by their own countrymen and shipped to German concentration camps far across Europe.

Among these Italians was Primo Levi, a young man who fled to the mountains when the arrest of Italian Jews began but was captured by the Italian militia. His story illustrates how resocialization occurs in the most extreme form of controlled environment.

> A dozen SS men stood around, legs akimbo, with an indifferent air. At a certain moment they moved among us, and in a subdued tone of voice, with faces of stone, began to interrogate us rapidly, one by one, in bad Italian. They did not interrogate everybody, only a few: "How old? Healthy or ill?" And on the basis of the reply they pointed in two different directions. . . .
>
> In less than ten minutes all the fit men had been collected together in a group. What happened to the others, to the women, to the children, to the old men, we could establish neither then nor later: the night swallowed them up, purely and simply. Today, however, we know that in that rapid and summary choice each one of us had been judged capable or not of working usefully for the Reich; we know that of our convoy no more than ninety-six men and twenty-nine women entered the respective camps of Monowitz-Buna and Birkenau, and that of all the others, more than five hundred in number, not one was living two days later. . . .[26]

The initiation rite continued. Heads were shaved, the people were thrown in boiling showers, then immediately forced to run, naked and barefoot, in the icy snow. Finally they were given uniforms to put on.

> There is nowhere to look in a mirror, but our appearance stands in front of us, reflected in a hundred livid faces, in a hundred miserable and sordid puppets. . . .
>
> Then for the first time we became aware that our language lacks words to express this offense, the demolition of a man. In a moment, with almost prophetic intuition, the reality was revealed to us; we had reached the bottom. It is not possible to sink lower than this; no human condition is more miserable than this nor could it conceivably be so. Nothing belongs to us anymore; they have taken away our clothes, our shoes, even our hair; if we speak, they will not listen to us, and if they listen, they will not understand. They will even take away our

[26]From *Survival in Auschwitz* by Primo Levi, translated by Stuart Woolf. Copyright © 1959 by The Orion Press, Inc. All rights reserved. Reprinted by permission of Grossman Publishers, a division of The Viking Press, Inc.

name; and if we want to keep it, we will have to find in ourselves the strength to do so, to manage somehow so that behind the name something of us, as we still were, still remains. . . .

Driven by thirst, I eyed a fine icicle outside the window, within hand's reach. I opened the window and broke off the icicle but at once a large, heavy guard prowling outside brutally snatched it away from me. "Warum?" I asked him in my poor German. "Hier ist kein warum" (there is no why here), he replied, pushing me inside with a shove.

The explanation is repugnant but simple: in this place everything is forbidden, not for hidden reasons, but because the camp has been created for that purpose. . . .

And we have learnt other things, more or less quickly, according to our intelligence: to reply *"Jawohl,"* never to ask questions, always to pretend to understand. We have learnt the value of food; now we also diligently scrape the bottom of the bowl after the ration and we hold it under our chins when we eat bread so as not to lose the crumbs. We, too, know that it is not the same thing to be given a ladleful of soup from the top or the bottom of the vat, and we are already able to judge, according to the capacity of the various vats, what is the most suitable place to try and reach in the queue when we line up.

We have learnt that everything is useful: the wire to tie up our shoes, the rags to wrap around our feet, waste paper to (illegally) pad out our jackets against the cold. We have learnt, on the other hand, that everything can be stolen, in fact is automatically stolen as soon as attention is relaxed; to avoid this, we had to learn the art of sleeping with our head on a bundle made up of our jacket and containing all our belongings, from the bowl to the shoes.

. . . The prohibitions are innumerable: to approach nearer to the barbed wire than two yards; to sleep with one's jacket; or without one's pants, or with one's cap on one's head; to use certain washrooms or latrines . . . .

We Italians had decided to meet every Sunday evening in a corner of the Lager, but we stopped it at once, because it was too sad to count our numbers and find fewer each time, and to see each other ever more deformed and more squalid. And it was so tiring to walk those few steps and then, meeting each other, to remember and to think. It was better not to think.[27]

1. What methods were used by the Nazis to break their prisoners? Look over Primo Levi's account, and list the techniques used to resocialize the newly arrived inmates.

2. Levi also wrote, "if I find a spoon lying around, a piece of string, a button which I can acquire without danger of punishment, I pocket them and consider them mine by full right." What values does this reveal? How are these new values different from those you think he formerly held?

[27]Ibid., pp. 21–34.

We have stated that socialization is the process of learning the ways of society and that resocialization is the process of relearning codes of conduct and patterns of behavior appropriate to new circumstances. Often, intensive resocialization in controlled environments has some supposedly positive goal for those undergoing the process. This is true of boot camp, where citizens are trained to be soldiers, and mental hospitals, where people are presumably helped to adjust to or overcome their psychological difficulties. Even prison officials sometimes claim that they are rehabilitating people found guilty of violating its rules. But the goal of the concentration camp had no positive value for the inmates. Those who were not physically destroyed were mentally broken. Hitler succeeded in annihilating millions of those confined, and nearly succeeded in eradicating European Jewry.

Controlled environments are found in every modern society. They are inevitably problematic. Governments seem to have found no other way to resocialize people intensively. No military establishment in the world would consent to have recruits simply take a few classes and read some books about soldiering, and then consider them "combat-ready." Similarly, societies almost always demand that people defined as mentally disturbed or dangerous to themselves and others be isolated in highly controlled environments.

These places invariably violate the inmates' individual liberties and rights. They succeed more often in controlling people than in rehabilitating them. And when people are confined strictly for political reasons, as in internment or concentration camps, the most reprehensible features of controlled environments predominate. Societies in which large numbers of citizens are subjected to or threatened by this kind of punishment for political activities are defined as totalitarian. In more democratic systems, there is a continual tension between those who seek to solve social problems by the use of controlled environments and those who fight to preserve the civil liberties of inmates—mental patients, the elderly in nursing homes, prisoners, and military recruits. Some contend that intensive resocialization in controlled environments tends to worsen existing problems rather than solve them.

SUMMARY

Deviance is any behavior that violates social norms to an intolerable degree. It is relative—to a particular society at a particular time. Behavior may be tolerated or even considered normal now that was once considered deviant.

Some theorists consider deviance to be a feature of modern societies—a result of the competing values and norms in a heterogeneous society. Others see deviance as a strategy for dealing with a world in which only a few people can achieve the goals that everyone wants. A third theory suggests that some forms of behavior considered deviant by "mainstream" society are normal ways of gaining acceptance with a subculture. Another theory maintains that practitioners of deviant behavior come to think of themselves as deviants only after society has discovered their behavior and labeled them deviant.

Some deviants experience resocialization, the process of learning new roles, or adapting known roles to new needs, and unlearning previous values, norms, and roles. Some forms of resocialization occur in controlled environments designed to promote rapid, drastic changes in a person's behavior. Prisons, mental institutions, military training camps, convents and monasteries, concentration camps, and prisoner-of-war camps are examples of controlled environments.

Despite many differences in their details of administration, the voluntariness of entry, and the establishment's goals, they share certain basic features of institutions engaged in extreme resocialization. In each, the identity (or definition of self) of inmates is assaulted by techniques of depersonalization and denial of autonomy. The individual is deprived of most personal possessions and most distinguishing features of appearance. He or she can perform few tasks or functions without first obtaining permission, and punishments for infractions of rules are chosen and administered by the authorities. These techniques are planned to replace the inmate's old identity with a new one that is submissive to the demands and goals of the environment.

Virtually every person on earth is a member of one or more groups: family, tribe, friendship, work, recreation, political, or other groups. And almost everyone lives with others in a human settlement, whether a village, town, city, or suburb. When people share a living place, a sense of belonging, and organized ways of interacting, they develop what sociologists call a sense of community. Communities tend to provide their members with stability, passing the culture from one generation to the next and resisting change.

Not all human settlements have a sense of community. The size of a group affects the patterns of interaction within it. In larger groups and settlements members have fewer chances to interact intimately with all fellow members. Communities are characterized by intimate, informal relationships based on shared beliefs, values, and norms, and a strong sense of group membership. The opposite characteristics—impersonal, formal, object-oriented relationships among people who feel a weak sense of social bond—seem to predominate in urban living.

Cities have always been places of comparative cultural diversity, specialization, division of labor, and exchange. While some sociologists stress the isolation and impersonality of city life today, others find a sense of community in small sectors and neighborhoods within the metropolis.

Cities have been undergoing extensive changes recently in this country. Since the turn of the century an overwhelming proportion of the population has moved into urban areas. Since World War II much of that urban population has moved into suburban areas. Many central cities have been abandoned to the poor. Since these residents require more public services and contribute less tax revenue, cities have been thrown into a financial crisis. It will take some drastic changes to solve the urban dilemma.

Change is a fact of life in human societies, although drastic changes do not occur often. Beliefs, values, norms, social roles, and social institutions are all subject to change. Social change has many sources: geographical changes, new ideas and ideologies, new technology, and exchanges between cultures.

Social change in contemporary life is often brought about by social movements. People join together to promote a change in the patterns of social interaction. Social movements share certain basic traits: each has an ideology—a set of beliefs and values by which current social patterns are judged; a set of goals; tactics; and leaders. Usually a movement is represented by several organizations representing somewhat different positions.

5

12 THE NATURE OF COMMUNITY

Although everyone inhabits some form of human settlement, not everyone can be said to live in a *community,* by some definitions of the word. In this chapter community means a settlement that has geographical, psychological, and organizational dimensions. That is, a community occupies a place, yields its members "a sense of community," and incorporates social patterns of interaction that support and express that sense.

This definition of community is akin to the folk society, a model devised by anthropologist Robert Redfield, who placed the folk society and the urban society at the opposite ends of a continuum. Also relevant for a study of community as an ideal type is the commune or intentional community, which usually seeks to encourage what are apparent opposites: social harmony and individual self-fulfillment.

In the village of Olympos, in Karpathos, Greece, villagers share an intimate community life. They participate together in everyday tasks and joyous celebrations. Here villagers beach a fishing vessel and celebrate the breaking of the Lenten fast on the Monday after Easter.

THE DIMENSIONS OF COMMUNITY

When a combat soldier, a traveling salesman, or a foreign student thinks of home, three things may come to mind: a place—perhaps a street, or neighborhood, a small town, a village, or a city; people—friends, relatives, neighbors, and townsfolk who intimately share many of his or her basic values and beliefs; and a sense of belonging.

The feelings for home that we have listed describe what most sociologists call a *sense of community.* To them, a community is where place and people and a special sense of belonging combine. Participants in a community are conscious of interacting as parts of a larger whole. This sociological notion uses Weber's idea of the *ideal type* as a starting point for describing the real world. In actuality, communities vary in how closely they resemble the ideal type.

The place people think of when they think of home usually has a name, such as Middletown, Easthampton, Westport, Kalgoorlie, or Anatevka. The name often evokes a very special feeling. It is "*my* town," "*my* village," "*my* neighborhood."

> Anatevka, Anatevka . . .
> Where I know everyone I meet . . .
> Dear little village,
> Little town of mine. . . .[1]

Anatevka, the little village portrayed in the musical play and movie *Fiddler on the Roof,* is an example of an ideal, if not idyllic, community. It is a composite portrait of the villages that thousands of Eastern European Jews populated in Czarist Russia. Located in Eastern Russia, mythical Anatevka was inhabited by people who shared a sense of "fellow feeling." They knew what it meant to have a home. When they were driven out, they knew what it meant to lose it. They knew one another, and knew where each stood in relation to the other villagers. They also knew how they all stood in relation to people from beyond the boundaries of their community.

The Jews of Eastern Europe, often forced to live in isolation from others in shtetls or rural villages, built a self-contained life. All social institutions—family, education, economics, politics, and religion—were geared to satisfying the needs of the community's members. Thousands and thousands

[1]"Anatevka" by Sheldon Harnick and Jerry Bock from the dramatico-musical play *Fiddler on the Roof.*

Community: as used in this text, human settlements in which patterns of interaction approximate primary relations more than secondary relations. (The primary-secondary continuum is discussed in Chapter 5.)

of real villages with many of the same structural if not the same specific cultural features as Anatevka exist throughout the world. Others, larger and smaller, also exist with differing structures but whose inhabitants also possess that special sense of community.

The word *community* stems from the Latin word *communis,* meaning in common or sharing. Because community denotes sharing, people use it in a variety of ways. We speak of "the community of scholars" or "the community of nations." Here the word means sharing scholarly interests and techniques or sharing nationhood, the status of sovereignty.

Sociologists generally give the term a more specialized meaning. By *community* sociologists mean a human settlement and the people who share life in such a place, bound together by mutual participation in social institutions.

Such a community can vary considerably in size. As we saw in our discussion of groups in Chapter 5, the size of a group affects the patterns of interaction within it. Communities have many grouplike characteristics, and they too are affected by size. The larger they are, the less likely it is that individuals will know one another. Reliance on secondary relations will increase, and the spirit that binds individuals will decrease.

In Chapter 13 cities are discussed in terms of their size and density and their influence on patterns of interaction.

Obviously some communities are held together more tightly than others. Our focus in this chapter is on close-knit communities because they so clearly highlight certain sociological characteristics of the ideal type of community. Many of these characteristics can appear, to different degrees, in a wide variety of communities, however.

What, then, are the characteristics of a community in the sociological sense? Our thoughts of home at the beginning of this chapter give a clue. Community has three dimensions: geographical, psychological, and organizational.

The Geographical Dimension

Communities are settlements. They can usually be located on maps.

Wellfleet, Massachusetts. Pop. 1,743. Between Eastham and Truro, fifteen miles south of Provincetown, straddling Route 6 on the northern end of Cape Cod.

Aztec, New Mexico. Pop. 3,354. Forty miles south of the Colorado border and 120 miles from the Arizona line in northwestern New Mexico.

Mason City, Iowa. Pop. 32,642. At the intersection of Highways 18 and 65, 135 miles south of Minneapolis, 125 miles north of Des Moines.

Hudson Street, Greenwich Village, New York. A neighborhood in lower Manhattan, bordered by St. Luke's School to the south, St. Veronica's to the west, and Public School 41 to the east.

The Tuareg of the Atlas Mountains, in Algeria, and these gypsies in Spain are two examples of nomadic communities: neither has a fixed place of settlement but each travels as a group, establishing temporary camps.

Sacred (Nisbet): ways of behaving that are valued in and for themselves; roughly synonymous with tradition, in which things draw their value from their longevity in the past.

These places—and thousands of others around the world—are enduring settlements. Some nomadic communities are more difficult to locate. Their people move from place to place with the seasons to hunt or to graze their livestock. But even nomadic people often have a permanent village or campsite where they always stay part of the year.

The Psychological Dimension

The people of an ideal type community share a common culture—a common set of beliefs, values, and norms. In addition, they unthinkingly sense the warmth of sharing these elements of culture.

To better understand the psychological dimension of community, sociologist Robert Nisbet's dichotomy of the sacred and the secular is useful. By the *sacred* Nisbet means "the mores, the non-rational, the religious and ritualistic ways of behavior that are valued beyond whatever utility they may possess." The secular, on the other hand, involves "the utilitarian, the profane (in Durkheim's momentous wording)." (The word *profane,* which normally means not concerned with religious purposes, here also means rational, nonritualistic ways of behaving.)

Secular (Nisbet): utilitarian (use-centered) values and norms governed by the rational.

The psychological dimension of the ideal type community is much more akin to the sacred than to the secular, whereas the city, as an ideal type, is

closer to embodying the secular. In the community the generalized other against which members evaluate their behavior is much more uniform than in the city. Even the deviants within the community serve to strengthen the sense of community. The expressions "the town drunk," "the village idiot," and "the local freethinker (or atheist)" show how an individual can achieve high visibility in a community by not conforming to its cultural demands.

Émile Durkheim theorized that such visible deviants against community norms actually served to reinforce the norms. Because community members can see the difference between their own role performance and that of the deviant, can experience disapproval of the deviant, and can witness the visibility the deviant is subjected to, they may become more committed to the norms.

Springdale, a small village in upstate New York, is the sort of place we think of as a typical "Mainstreet, U.S.A." Sociologists Arthur Vidich and Joseph Bensman present a portrait of Springdale:

The people of Springdale . . . like to think of themselves as "just plain folks." The editor of the paper, in urging people to attend public meetings or in reporting a social event, says "all folks with an interest" should attend or "the folks who came certainly had a good time." Almost any chairman of a public gathering addresses his audience as folks—"all right, folks, the meeting will get underway"

The psychological dimension of the American community tends more to the sacred than to the secular in Nisbet's continuum. The "sacred" elements need not be strictly religious, however. The Fourth of July, for example, can be an occasion to reaffirm the community's ties to its traditions, to the patriotic ideals that the holiday symbolizes. This shared tradition sustains the group's sense of community in its everyday life.

—and the interviewer in his work frequently encounters the same expressions—"the folks in this community," "the townfolk," "the country folk," "good folks," and "bad folks." Depending on context, the term carries with it a number of quite different connotations.

First and foremost, the term serves to distinguish Springdalers from urban dwellers, who are called "city people," an expression which by the tone . . . implies the less fortunate, those who are denied the wholesome virtues of rural life. City people are separated from nature and soil, from field and stream, and are caught up in [a] . . . web of impersonality and loneliness, of which the public statement in Springdale is: "How can people stand to live in cities?" . . .

The [term] "folk" includes everyone in the community; . . . it excludes neither the rich nor the poor . . . . To be one of the folks requires neither money, status, family background, learning, nor refined manners. It is, in short, a way of referring to the equalitarianism of rural life.

The term also includes a whole set of moral values: honesty, fair play, trustworthiness, good-neighborliness, helpfulness, sobriety, and clean-living. To the Springdaler it suggests a wholesome family life, a man whose spoken word is as good as a written contract, a community of religious-minded people, and a place where "everybody knows everybody" and "where you can say hello to anybody."[2]

[2]Arthur J. Vidich and Joseph Bensman, *Small Town in Mass Society: Class, Power and Religion*, 2d ed. (Princeton, N.J.: Princeton University Press, 1968), pp. 29–30.

From this profile of Springdalers, we can see that their community depends for its existence on a high degree of cultural homogeneity (sameness among members) and a sense that they embody the right values and norms. Small town people like the Springdalers often heap scorn on cities not only as places of loneliness, impersonality, and isolation from nature but also as places where different groups with different values and norms are thrown together. Cultural diversity is seen as weakening the good old values.

Members of a small town or village can enforce their norms easily, because each individual is so visible and exposed to any criticism by others. The entire community, as a body, demands informally but effectively that members follow the accepted norms. They let their judgments be known and use gossip, ridicule, or ostracism (isolating the person who breaks a norm from friendly interaction) as the chief means of keeping members from misbehaving.

This is why many small towners seem able to resist change so well. This does not mean that homogeneous, tightly knit communities do not experience a great deal of conflict. They do—between families, between social classes, and between old settlers and recent arrivals, for example. Such conflicts characterize Springdale, too, as Vidich and Bensman found.

The Organizational Dimension

Societies and the institutions within them are collections of norms and roles that govern and channel social interaction. In a whole society, the network of norms and roles can be vast and widely dispersed. We may interact with or be aware of only some small part of it at a time. The same is true of a city. We may do our banking at a firm in which not one employee or fellow customer goes to the same school, attends the same church, or has the same friends as we do.

Communities, at least as ideal types, are different. Virtually all members of a community participate in almost all the social institutions within it. Of course, not everyone in a community is a Republican, a Presbyterian, or an Elk. But there is considerable overlap of memberships from group to group in the community, so that the distinctions between primary and secondary group relations are blurred—acquaintances are likely to become friends because they share so many activities. The elements of the institutional structure of the community—its organizational dimension—are more visible to the members than they are in a larger settlement, such as a city, or in the society as a whole.

Community members are expected to be familiar with the entire system of norms and roles. They are supposed to know how to behave and how far they can depart from any norms without upsetting others. Members are supposed to perform certain tasks, to "pull their weight." They also have to know more subtle norms, such as where they stand in relation to others in the social pecking order and how to adjust their personal desires to the rhythms of community life. These norms are clear expressions of social values and standards.

In Springdale both rich and poor were "just plain folks." Yet despite the image of equality presented, Vidich and Bensman found clear evidence of rank ordering among the people. Certain "folks" were of high status, and others were low. Certain people were pretty much assured of attaining high prestige and power, while others learned to content themselves with lower aspirations.

Real communities are only approximations of the ideal type we have described. They match the sociological definition of community to varying degrees.

1. So far, our study of the community has looked chiefly at small towns and villages. Poll your class on how many students come from such communities and how many do not. Have those who come from small communities rate them against the ideal type just described for each dimension—do they show great similarity, some, or little?

2. Poll the students from larger settlements (cities, suburbs) on their feelings about the ideal type community described. Ask several questions, such as how the students feel about the high visibility of the individual and the informal systems of maintaining uniformity of norms. Ask students from the small communities the same questions. How do their answers compare?

HOW CHANGE AFFECTS COMMUNITIES

In all industrial societies change is an inevitable fact of life. Change can threaten the stability of many tightly knit communities. Isolated towns and villages are vulnerable to any number of social, political, and economic forces —some obvious, others subtle.

Organizational Changes

Communities may change geographically. They may die, for example, like ghost towns of the West and Southwest, when their source of economic livelihood disappears. They may be forcibly uprooted, like villagers in Poland

and other Eastern European countries during Hitler's rampages before and during World War II. They may change geographically by growth. Two or more may expand until they merge. Los Angeles, for example, is a collection of former communities.

Before these communities became part of Greater Los Angeles, many of them lost their separate, self-sufficient status and became suburbs. Usually this changes the organizational dimension of a community most directly, although the geographical dimension (encroachment by a larger settlement) precipitates the change. The people's means of livelihood and sources of income change as farms, ranches, and orchards become housing tracts whose inhabitants work chiefly in the city. As the population increases, small schoolhouses are replaced by larger schools, part of consolidated or unified school districts. Downtown stores decline as shopping centers spring up, offering larger stocks of standard brand foods, clothing, furniture, and other goods. The town hall becomes a

A bustling town can lose its sense of community through changes in the organizational or geographical dimensions. It can be swallowed up by an encroaching city, disappearing beneath the onward march of characterless suburbs; or it can die and become a ghost town. When patterns of land use change (for example, when housing projects are built on land that was formerly used for farms and orchards), a town that flourished by serving the old patterns will no longer have a function.

city hall, and its bureaucracy expands. More public services (schools, police force, fire department, hospitals) are needed. School and property taxes are raised to pay for them, and tax assessment and collection staffs expand. Within a decade or less, the small, intimate community that was first there may be buried from view in the complex suburb.

Psychological Changes

Such changes cannot occur without affecting the psychological dimension. The loss of intimacy can be felt in many ways by residents witnessing the transformation of their community. The town banker retires or expands the bank to meet competition from new branches of bigger banks. Other small proprietors retire or close shop when much of their business is lost to the shopping malls. The town newspaper goes out of business or yields its social and political influence to the "big city" dailies. Virtually all the community ways of institutional interaction yield to suburban or city ways. The subjective sense of being part of an intimate whole is replaced by a larger, more impersonal framework.

Organizational changes brought by encroachments or merger are not the only source of psychological changes. Many cultural forces in our society work against the community's sense of protective isolation. In an industrial, urban, consumption-oriented society, young people from small towns are often sent away to colleges. There they are exposed to political, religious, philosophical, economic, and social values and norms quite different from those of their early socialization in the community. Those who return may be an unsettling cultural force within their towns. Those who migrate to cities after college diminish the pool of young adults needed by the community to sustain its future life. (This dilemma was voiced in the early 1920s in a song about American soldiers overseas, entitled "How You Gonna Keep 'Em Down on the Farm After They've Seen Paree?")

Another source of cultural forces that may introduce changing ideas to the community is mass communication. Everyone is exposed to network radio and television programs created in Hollywood or New York. Whether national news, variety shows, situation comedies, dramas, or broadcasts of films and plays, television programming tends to present urban values and norms. Even when a rural setting is used, the dramas often depict the values and concerns of the urban middle class. For example, let's assume that in real life children in a small farming community are taught to accept responsibilities and are socialized to norms by a mixture of reasoning and physical coercion. A television program in this setting might present the growing up process as a

Residence Patterns of College Graduates by Size of Community

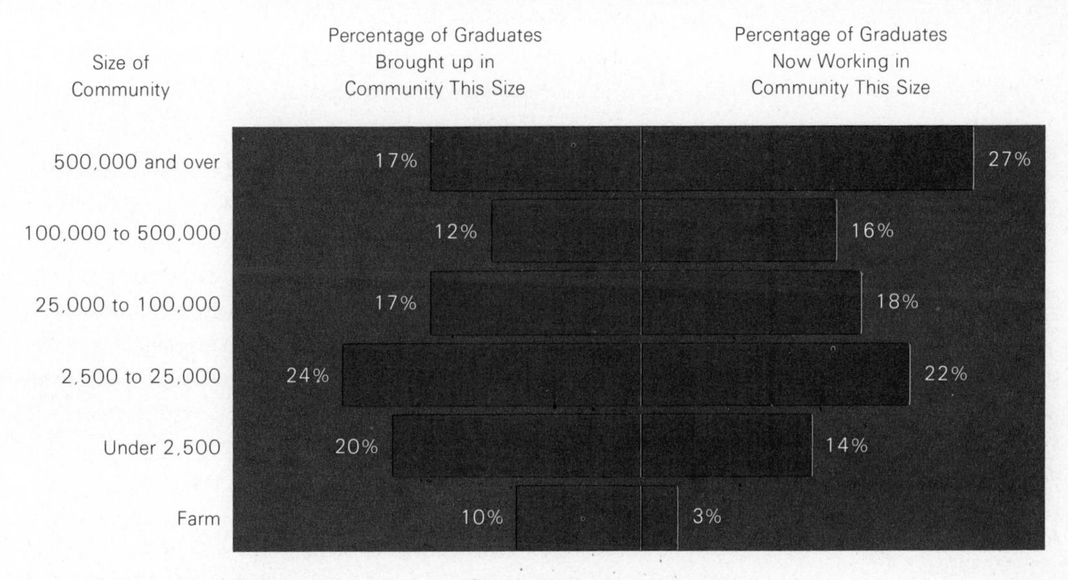

Source: *They Went to College* by Ernest Havemann and Patricia Salter West, published by Harcourt, Brace and Co., Inc. © 1952 by Time Inc. Reprinted by permission.

conflict between the set ways of adults and the youngsters' sensitive, confused searching for identity.

Generally television dramas present an initial conflict. It is eventually resolved when each character tries to achieve some understanding of the needs of others. (Critics of such programs often accuse their creators of a formula called "pop-Freudianism.") This way of resolving conflicts may never be used in a real rural community. In fact, few such conflicts surface where the norms dictate that parents give the orders and children follow them. Thus, in our hypothetical instance, the values of a social class whose children undergo a prolonged process of preadult socialization are presented to people in a community whose children are socialized to adapt quickly and smoothly to early adult roles. The rural setting of the television program may be familiar to the audience in the small community, but the values and norms may be quite foreign.

The program we just described is only one of a broad variety of offerings whose values and norms may not coincide with those of a particular community. National news and consumer magazines are other sources of outside ideas. Travel may have the same effect, whether the townspeople travel to other parts of the world or tourists from elsewhere visit their communities. In either case they may be exposed to values different from their own. No single source of cultural difference is a threat to the community, but a combined assault from the outside world may weaken it.

Loss of Identity

Many small towns in our society are hundreds of miles from the nearest city. They are in little danger of being annexed by a city or wiped out by a natural disaster. They are not likely to suffer extinction from a steady dose of television programs about urban detectives, rape, abortion, international espionage, and big city hospitals. Nevertheless, a community may gradually be deprived of much of its identity, its psychological dimension. Members may no longer feel what the Springdalers we discussed earlier believed about themselves in contrast to city dwellers. They may come to question their own traditional values.

Gemeinschaft (Toennies): a system of relationships characterized by intimacy, spontaneity, lack of specialization, prevalence of interdependence, and stability.

Many questions still need to be answered about the function and future of communities in our society today. Will a community's loss of cultural isolation, through the mass media, college education of the young, and travel, destroy its psychological dimension? Are small town people, like the Springdalers, right or wrong in believing that the community is the constant source and guardian of our basic values and norms? Or do the values and norms peculiar to communities make up a subculture that is functional in small, rural settlements but dysfunctional in larger, industrial settlements? Finally, does the decline of the small town and village mean the loss of community in a complex, industrial, urbanized society? The answers to these questions are of considerable concern to sociologists and anthropologists and are a principal focus of much current research.

THE FOLK-URBAN CONTINUUM

Gesellschaft (Toennies): a system of relationships characterized by formal, contractual bonds, impersonality, rationality in ways of doing things, and instability of interactions.

In the late nineteenth and early twentieth centuries several large-scale conceptual frameworks gained wide acceptance among sociologists. These frameworks have long influenced sociological thinking on the questions we just asked, especially the last question. The German sociologist Ferdinand Toennies, in 1887, formulated two related but opposite concepts of social organization: *gemeinshaft* and *gesellschaft.*[3] The German word gemeinschaft meant roughly community; it was characterized by many of the traits of primary groups. In a gemeinschaft relationship, people are united by feelings, they share traditional goals, beliefs, values, and norms, and they have a sense

[3]Ferdinand Toennies, *Community and Society* (East Lansing: Michigan State University Press, 1957).

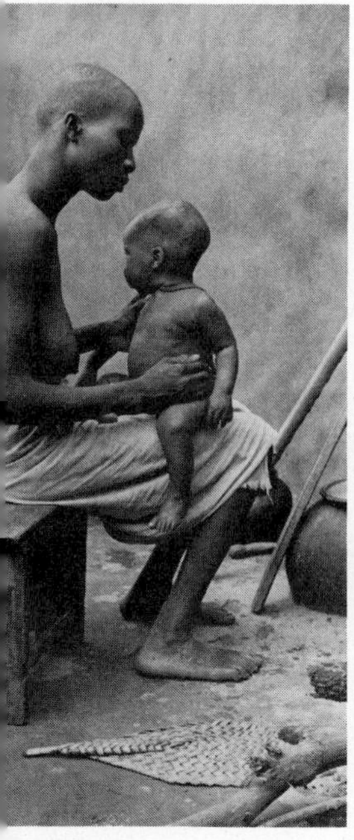

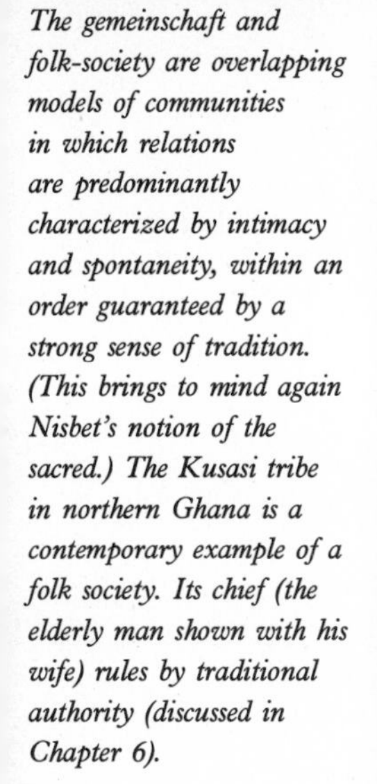

The gemeinschaft and folk-society are overlapping models of communities in which relations are predominantly characterized by intimacy and spontaneity, within an order guaranteed by a strong sense of tradition. (This brings to mind again Nisbet's notion of the sacred.) The Kusasi tribe in northern Ghana is a contemporary example of a folk society. Its chief (the elderly man shown with his wife) rules by traditional authority (discussed in Chapter 6).

Mechanical relationships (Durkheim): social bonds maintained by tradition, intimacy, and a sense of shared community and lacking differentiation in skills or tasks among members.

Organic relationships (Durkheim): social bonds that are utilitarian, are based on division of labor, and satisfy the need for interdependence by contractual relations.

Folk society (Redfield): a small, nonliterate, traditional society in which social relations are intimate, spontaneous, and emotionally involving.

of a strong common bond as a result. Their interactions reflect the importance of the group; they willingly share a concern for every member's welfare.

A gesellschaft relationship is characterized by impersonal patterns of interaction. Contractual (written, formal) agreements replace tradition as a social bond. Utilitarian values prevail: objects or activities are valued not as a part of a tradition but for their usefulness, measured on a scale of gain or loss. Concern for the welfare of the group is correspondingly diminished.

Toennies considered both gemeinshaft and gesellschaft as ideal types that were more useful for guiding research than for describing any society in the real world. Nevertheless, he associated the gemeinshaft with small rural societies and the gesellschaft with complex urban societies. The sociologist Émile Durkheim made a similar distinction.[4] He called the two opposite types of relationships *mechanical* and *organic.* The mechanical, corresponding to the gemeinschaft, characterizes societies in which members experience a strong sense of collective identity and minimal differentiation in skills. In organic relations, which correspond to the gesellschaft, members have specialized skills and depend on each other to satisfy the needs they cannot meet with their own skills. Today these words have connotations that may make Durkheim's uses puzzling to us: organic now suggests "natural," mechanical the opposite.

Folk Societies

Durkheim's pair of contrasted concepts contributed to the research of anthropologist Robert Redfield in the Yucatán peninsula of Mexico. Redfield, strongly influenced by Durkheim, formulated another ideal type, which echoed the notions of both Toennies and Durkheim. He called it the *folk society,* and described it in these terms: "Such a society is small, isolated, nonliterate, and homogeneous, with a strong sense of group solidarity. The ways of living are conventionalized into that coherent system which we call 'a culture.' Behavior is traditional, spontaneous, uncritical, and personal.[5]

With the exception of the word *nonliterate* (meaning that the people do not have a written language), Redfield's terms come very close to our earlier description of the dimensions of community.

Urban Societies

In writing about folk society, Redfield contrasted it with another type of society, urban society. Although he did not create an ideal type for urban

[4]Émile Durkheim, *The Division of Labor in Society* (Glencoe, Ill.: Free Press, 1947) (originally published in 1893).

[5]Robert Redfield, "The Folk Society," *American Journal of Sociology* 52 (1947): 294.

Urban society: the implied opposite of Redfield's ideal type of the folk society; relations are impersonal, contractual, rational, and motivated by self-interest.

society, he implied that such a society would be the opposite, in every respect, of folk society.

If folk societies are small, isolated, and homogeneous, with a strong sense of group solidarity, then urban societies are large, cosmopolitan, and heterogeneous, with a weak sense of group solidarity. If folk societies are similar to ideal communities, urban societies must lack communal feeling and have a sense of estrangement or alienation.

Contrast and Continuum

Redfield and others often portrayed this contrast by showing the two types at the extremes of a continuum (the ends of a line). Many sociologists who have

Folk Society____Urban Society

studied modern, urban, industrial societies claim that this contrast is reflected in reality. They suggest that life in cities and in areas influenced by city values is sharply different from life in self-contained hamlets or villages. The people behave differently and have very different feelings about themselves and others. Some sociologists even find ample evidence that three principal effects of urban living are the breakdown of collective feelings, the lack of guidance about norms, and the sense of loneliness everywhere. Thus, in answer to the last question we raised in the previous section, it does seem that a sense of community is lost, that city life rises at the expense of community life.

Urban Villages

Other sociologists disagree with this answer. While they do not deny that cities are different from rural villages, they maintain that cities are actually collections of communities. For all their resemblance to the gesellschaft ideal type, many cities possess "folk" characteristics.

In his classic study, *The Ghetto,* Louis Wirth described a Jewish neighborhood in Chicago.[6] It had many of the characteristics of the Eastern European villages these Jews had lived in before they immigrated to the United States. The language, the folklore, the religious beliefs, the family structure, the humor, and the sadness that we now associate with *Fiddler on the Roof,* with the people of Anatevka, were found on Chicago's bustling Halsted and Maxwell Streets.

Herbert Gans used the term *urban villages* to describe such communities in a city. Gans studied the Italian-American neighborhood in the West End of

[6]Louis Wirth, *The Ghetto* (Chicago: University of Chicago Press, 1956).

Boston that we discussed in Chapter 9 on socialization. In describing this city neighborhood as an urban village, he wrote:

Everyday life in the West End was not much different from that in other neighborhoods, urban or suburban. The men went to work in the morning, and, for most of the day, the area was occupied largely by women and children—just as in the suburbs. There were some men on the street, the older, retired ones, as well as the young and middle-aged ones who either were unemployed, worked on night shifts, or made their living as gamblers. In the afternoon, younger women could be seen pushing baby carriages. Children of all ages played on the street, and teen-agers would "hang" on the corner, or play ball in the school yard. . . . Many women went shopping every day, partly to meet neighbors and to catch up on area news in the small grocery stores, and partly to buy foods that could not be obtained in the weekly excursion to the supermarket. On Sunday mornings, the streets were filled with people who were visiting with neighbors and friends before and after church. . . . A few people had moved into the area to hide from the world. . . . Generally speaking, however, neighbors were friendly and quick to say hello to each other, although more intense social contact was limited to neighbors and friends. . . .

The sharing of values was also encouraged by the residential stability of much of the population. Many West Enders had known each other for years, if only as acquaintances who greeted each other on the street. Everyone might not know everyone else; but, as they did know something about everyone, the net effect was the same, especially within each ethnic group. Between groups, common residence and sharing of facilities—as well as the constant struggle against absentee landlords—created enough solidarity to maintain a friendly spirit. Moreover, for many families, problems were never far away. Illnesses, job layoffs, or school or discipline problems among the children occurred regularly. Alcoholism, mental illness, desertion, the death of a loved one, serious financial difficulties, and even violence were familiar to everyone. If they did not take place in one's immediate family, they had happened at some time to a relative or a neighbor. Thus when emergencies occurred, neighbors helped each other readily; other problems were solved within each ethnic group.

For most West Enders, then, life in the area resembled that found in the village or small town . . . .[7]

1. Gans suggests that, despite their poor education, their problems of trying to eke out a living, and their other difficulties, the people of the West End had "by and large a good place to live." What features in this community support his view?

2. Examine Gans's description of the West End both here and in Chapter 9. In what ways does the neighborhood resemble the ideal

[7]Herbert J. Gans, *The Urban Villagers* (Glencoe, Ill.: Free Press, 1962), pp. 14–16.

The stereotyped impersonality and anonymity of the city is belied by a closer look at many urban neighborhoods. Often they have patterns of interaction that suggest a community. Especially in neighborhoods with a strong ethnic unity, traditions may maintain a strong hold—perhaps precisely because they contribute to a sense of identity that gives community members comfort from the sense of anonymity they feel outside the neighborhood.

type of community, such as a rural small town? In what ways does it differ?

3. Are you persuaded by Gans that the Italian-Americans in the West End form a community? Why or why not? (In answering, deal with each of the three dimensions of community.)

4. Where would you place your neighborhood or town on the folk society–urban continuum? What criteria would you use?

5. Gans says, "other problems were solved within each ethnic group." Why is an urban village that is composed mainly of one ethnic group more likely to be a community than a city neighborhood with no single distinctive ethnic population?

ALIENATION IN URBAN LIFE

In describing the West End of Boston as an urban village, Gans himself cautioned that not all neighborhoods qualify as what we have been calling communities. Many urban sociologists feel that Halsted Street and other urban villages are becoming increasingly rare in cities. They point to our rising rate of physical mobility, which tears people away from their "roots." Rarely do these people find a sufficient substitute for the security offered by the place they used to call home.

Joseph Lyford has described one large area on the West Side of Manhattan as "an airtight cage." His description fits any number of places characterized by alienation and anomie. The individual and the group have lost the sense of having clear guides for behavior. Lyford writes:

> People convey the feeling that they have no community worth talking about. [An] attitude survey . . . reported that West Siders then had only the vaguest idea of where they would turn in case of need. They almost never mentioned political organizations, government agencies, or elected officials, and no single institution was mentioned more than a handful of times. . . . The only people who talk about community as if they believe in it are the people who are paid to be community organizers.
>
> The one [point of agreement] is that there is no community. The group that cuts across all class lines is the army of noninterferers who remain passive while violence is committed on another human being, and who will tolerate the destruction of a neighborhood itself because they are resigned to its destruction.[8]

[8]Joseph Lyford, *The Airtight Cage* (New York: Harper and Row, 1966), pp. 321–22.

Such a neighborhood seems to embody Durkheim's prediction that in a large, complex society the sense of community will break down. People are caught up in their own concerns. They are afraid to befriend anyone or even to help out in an emergency. An extreme example of this lack of communal feeling was illustrated by the celebrated case of Kitty Genovese, a young New Yorker murdered in the streets several years ago. Assaulted and repeatedly stabbed, she screamed and cried for help for some time. At least thirty-eight people are known to have heard her, but none came to her assistance. Not one even lifted the phone to call the police. Kitty died, and her assailant got away. Later, during the investigation of the crime, when witnesses were asked why they had done nothing, they replied as if with one voice, "We didn't want to get involved."

Kitty Genovese's death was not the first of such occurrences in cities, of course, but it became a turning point for many people. The fact that thirty-eight people had failed to aid a person in distress indicated how vulnerable and alone each individual was. This affected the way many people viewed the large cities they inhabited. More than this, though, it forced them to do some soul-searching. People had to ask themselves what they would have done if they had witnessed the attack.

Alienation and anomie are difficult social phenomena to measure. And it is difficult to believe that these conditions alone would inhibit people from helping another person in a situation like Kitty Genovese's violent death. In fact, the onlookers were not indifferent but horrified. Why then their passivity?

One possibility is that in many situations the greater the number of witnesses the more passivity is likely. Conformity is at work. People look to others for cues to action and when none is forthcoming nobody does anything. This hypothesis has been given repeated experimental testing and seems amply confirmed.[9] Nevertheless, the question remains why the behavior model that people often conform to is inaction rather than action.

INTENTIONAL COMMUNITIES

In the last decade, many members of our society deliberately tried to establish living arrangements that restore a sense of community. Often younger people, they distrusted "the establishment"—those holding power in business, government, education, and religious institutions. They criticized "the system," arguing that those in control of our institutions valued money and material

[9]John Darley and Bibb Latané, "Bystander Intervention in Emergencies: Diffusion of Responsibility," *Journal of Personality and Social Psychology* 8 (1968): 377–83; Bibb Latané and John Darley, "Group Inhibition of Bystander Intervention in Emergencies," *Journal of Personality and Social Psychology* 10 (1968): 215–21.

Utopian or intentional communities have a venerable history in our society. Not all early communes were explicitly religious, but many were. The Shaker family posing in the doorway is an example of a nineteenth-century religious community intended to fully realize Christian principles in every detail of daily life. The Mennonite women and child crossing a Virginia field are modern survivors of another religious communal movement. Many of today's communes are founded on the same effort to realize a utopia, based on similar fundamental Christian principles and rejection of an industrialized, materialistic, consumption-oriented society. Shown facing is the Lama community, a religious commune in northern New Mexico.

Counterculture: a system of values and norms set up by persons opposed to those of the larger, "mainstream" culture.

progress more than human relations. They saw bigness as a curse, whether it was big business, big labor, or big government. In one degree or another, they and their social arrangements represented a *countercultural* response: they developed a system of values and norms in opposition to those of the mainstream society.

To live by the values and norms of the counterculture, they set up *communes*—group living arrangements in which responsibilities and benefits are shared. Sociologists have devoted much attention to communes, or intentional communities, not because a significant portion of any population has membership in them but because of their unique goals and structures. Virtually every commune represents an effort to achieve the utopian community, where "humankind's deepest yearnings, noblest dreams, and highest aspirations come to fulfillment, where all physical, social, and spiritual forces work together in harmony, to permit the attainment of everything people find necessary and desirable."[10]

Commune: an intentional community, established to achieve relationships that approximate the ideal type of the community.

Although Americans today associate communes with the hippies of the 1960s, such social arrangements go back centuries to the first monastic communities of medieval times. In the early and middle nineteenth century, religious communities resembling communes flourished in the United States, some for more than twenty-five years. Many nonreligious communities also were founded to accomplish what recent communes are seeking: gemeinschaft relationships in as many of their social interactions as possible.

[10]Rosabeth M. Kanter, *Commitment and Community: Communes and Utopias in Sociological Perspective* (Cambridge: Harvard University Press, 1972), p. 3.

Commune Organization

Despite their beliefs that organizational systems are inherently alienating, commune members find they must establish some system of their own if their communities are to survive. One member, writing of his experiences in a New England commune, called attention to five major aspects of commune organization.[11]

Personal involvement. Commune members were critical of the specialized roles that most people played in different sectors of their lives. They wanted each member to be an individual, to be at ease in the group, and to be himself or herself. They saw the commune as a substitute for the family, a setting where relations should have the characteristics of those in a primary group.

Work as a group experience. The commune struggled with the issue of whether to assign certain tasks. It ultimately rejected this in favor of an agreement that members would do work as it came up. Most important, the members felt that work represented the chance not only to get chores done but also to be together. In that sense, work was much like play, and specific assignments were theoretically not necessary.

Limited property ownership. The commune members knew that the issue of economic sharing was always a central one in the development of communes. What norms should prevail in their community about private property? This was very difficult to resolve. It was finally decided to share food but not other economic assets. In some communes, all property is shared.

Consensus. The commune members quickly discovered that resolving conflicts was crucial. They rejected the possibility of having a leader make the final decision. They also turned down majority rule. They opted instead for full and continuing debate on an issue until some resolution was achieved. This was no easy matter. Thorough and honest discussion was required. Often a member had to judge his or her needs against those of the others in the dispute. Whose needs were greater? This was often difficult to determine, but the effort kept communication open among members and helped to cement a community feeling.

Influence. The commune members believed in their way of life but did not believe in imposing it or their way of organizing it on others. People must come to their own decisions about how they want to live, the members felt.

[11]Randy Huntsberry, "Transcendence, Non-violence, and Communitarianism," mimeographed (1971).

The commune might serve as an influence on others, but members should never try to force others to change.

This commune operated according to an explicit set of rules that were binding on the members. Clearly organizational principles are necessary to the survival of such a community.

1. Would you expect a commune to have a greater sense of community than, say, a new town house development in the suburbs? Suppose, in both cases, that very few of the residents were acquainted with each other before coming to the new locality. Consider the effects of size, type of local governing body, and diversity of social class backgrounds in making your comparison. Explain your answer.

2. Compare our brief description of a commune with the previous discussions of a rural community (Springdale) and of Redfield's folk society. In what ways does it resemble both? In what ways does it resemble one but not the other? In what ways does it resemble neither?

3. With other members of your class draw up a plan for a commune. Decide on its location, size, and organizational structure. Anticipate major problems, and conduct a role-playing session to work them out within your rules. Assess the results.

THE IMPORTANCE OF COMMUNITY

Rosabeth Kanter summarized the organizational problems of utopian communities as follows:

1. How to get the work done, but without coercion.

2. How to assure that decisions are made, but that they are to everyone's satisfaction.

3. How to build close, fulfilling relationships, but without exclusiveness.

4. How to choose and socialize new members.

5. How to regulate a degree of autonomy, individual uniqueness, and even deviance.

6. How to achieve agreement and shared perceptions around community functioning and values.[12]

[12]Kanter, *Commitment and Community,* Chaps. 5–6.

Mass society: a society characterized by large numbers of persons who are anonymous to one another and do not share a broad sense of common interests or goals.

In each of these items, except 4, the problem is clearly one of achieving a a balance of opposites. As ideal types the community and the city are opposites, the community realizing Nisbet's concept of the sacred and the city his concept of the secular. In a modern, secular society like that of the United States few people would choose an environment that embodied the sacred because its living conditions are too limiting and claustrophobic: most persons want to preserve more individual autonomy. At the same time, most find the city in actuality too lonely—a place where individuality verges into anomie, the condition of normlessness.

The city is the characteristic settlement in mass society. Can a mass society, one in which secondary relations and anonymity prevail, be the basis for an eventual synthesis of balanced opposites? For several reasons, this is a question of some urgency. As we see in the next chapter, the cities have suffered from long-standing crises for which no lasting solutions have been unanimously accepted. It seems likely that we will adopt new ways of using energy and resources in the future that in turn may require us to make fundamental changes in social arrangements.

SUMMARY

Communities, in the sociological sense, possess three interrelated dimensions: place; a sense of belonging; and organization. A community in this sense is a human settlement whose members have a strong sense of belonging that is embodied in the structure of the settlement. In the small town or village these dimensions are evident.

A delicate balance of conditions in all three dimensions maintains a community. Communities may change and remain communities. But change often destroys one or more of the dimensions, or leads to further change that is destructive. If a settlement grows to enormous size or becomes incorporated into an encroaching settlement, the organizational dimension is affected, and the psychological sense of community may be lost.

Researchers often relate the concept of community to Toennies's gemeinschaft–gesellschaft distinction, and to Redfield's folk society–urban society continuum. At the gemeinschaft–folk-society end are found small groups with a strong sense of solidarity among members who share the bonds of tradition. At the gesellschaft–urban-society end are found large, complex settlements in which group solidarity is weak or absent and in which impersonal, contractual relationships replace the bonds of tradition.

Nevertheless, large urban settlements often contain communities, as Gans demonstrated with his concept of urban villages. Urban groups often develop the psychological bonds that turn their neighborhoods into communities within the larger, impersonal city.

13 URBAN LIVING

In the last chapter we saw that some human settlements more or less approximate the ideal type of the community, a geographical settlement in which primary relations characterize many of the patterns of social interaction. In this chapter we examine how cities approximate an ideal type that is the opposite of the community. In cities secondary relations and anonymity prevail, and these may be accompanied by a tendency toward anomie, or normlessness.

We also look at sociological models of urban growth, the historical process of suburbanization, and the consequent decay of the core city as the middle class abandoned it to the poor. The increasing failure of the city as a satisfactory place to live and probable changes in our use of energy and resources both invite and demand us to develop new models for human settlements.

THE CITY AND MASS SOCIETY

Andy Warhol, the pop artist, once whimsically suggested that, if he were in charge of society, each person would be given the chance to be famous for half an hour. Famous for what? Warhol didn't say. Presumably we would just be ourselves, but for a half hour each of us would be known to millions of people who have never heard of us.

Warhol's idea, as crazy as it may seem on the surface, suggests many things about our culture and social patterns. We might consider a half hour of fame as a mass-society metaphor for the sense of belonging that people in smaller societies—communities—accept as a natural part of their lives. As we saw in Chapter 12, members of communities, at least ideal type communities, experience primary relations in almost all their institutional roles. In contrast, many sociologists see cities as overwhelmingly representative of what Toennies called gesellschaft relationships—interactions in which anonymity and impersonality predominate.[1]

A series of social arrangements in which most forms of interaction have

[1]The sociologist who best expresses this point of view is Louis Wirth, whose work is discussed at length later in this chapter. His thesis is presented in the article "Urbanism as a Way of Life," *American Journal of Sociology* 44 (1938): 1–24.

lost their primary quality, have become impersonal and formal, is what sociologists have come to call *mass society.* The notion of mass society is not related merely to the size of a society. Sociologist Melvin DeFleur notes:

> There are many societies of the world, for example, India, that have astronomical numbers of people, but are still more or less traditional in their organization. Mass society refers to the relationship that exists between an individual member and the social order around him. In mass society . . . the individual is presumed to be in a situation of psychological isolation from others, impersonality is said to prevail in his interactions with others and he is said to be relatively free from the demands of binding social obligations.[2]

Cities are the characteristic or predominant human settlements in a mass society. They embody gesellschaft relations geographically. We work in one place and live in another; in both places we are surrounded by many more people than we could ever come to know.

In folk societies, such as those discussed by Redfield[3] (see Chapter 12), the force of tradition governs interactions, and the individual feels comfortable as an unquestioning part of that tradition. But in our complex society the value of *individualism* conflicts with many of the patterns of social requirements. This is, perhaps, what gives Andy Warhol's idea its crazy charm: it offers us a brief fling of individualism. It allows us to be somebodies in a context in which, too often, we feel like anonymous nobodies.

THE ANCIENT ROOTS OF THE CITY

Cities, as we mentioned in our discussion of the economic institution, in Chapter 6, began in ancient times. The first cities took root about 8,000 years ago. Ancient cities, like all modern ones, were both products of change and vehicles for change. Cities could arise only when permanent human settlements were common and cultivation of domesticated plants and animals (agriculture) had advanced to the point where surpluses were produced. Thus the first cities arose in fertile river valleys. A well-developed power structure was also required, for "without an effective political apparatus through which power can be exerted, cities could not derive sustenance from the hinterland."[4]

Cities quickly became the homes of artisans and craftsmen, and trade flourished between these workers and the outlying farmers. Trade also grew

[2]Melvin S. DeFleur, *Theories of Mass Communication* (New York: McKay, 1966), p. 111.

[3]Robert Redfield, "The Folk Society," *American Journal of Sociology* 52 (1947): 293–308.

[4]Gideon Sjoberg, *The Preindustrial City* (Glencoe, Ill.: Free Press, 1960), p. 68.

among distant cities. As regular trade routes became established, the role of the city as a source of cultural diversity grew. Traders and travelers from distant cultures brought foreign ideas with them. Once introduced into a city, many of these ideas were transmitted to the surrounding countryside. Thus trade brought differing beliefs, values, norms, and ways of doing things—technological ideas and tools for farming or crafts.

The city was a source of changes in social interactions as well as of ideas. As we noted in Chapter 5, the size of a group affects the patterns of interaction within it. When the first cities developed, the surrounding countryside had low-density occupancy (few people spread out over large areas) and uniform activity—farming. The cities were areas of high density by comparison and of diversity of skills and occupations. People needed to have stated patterns of organization for city living—different chains of command or authority had to be established. Social stratification became more evident, as differences among people in wealth and prestige increased. The ruling and priestly classes were at the top, the craftworkers below them, and the struggling poor still further below.

Thus, from their very beginnings cities displayed characteristics and fulfilled social functions that we associate with modern cities.[5] They began with one technological revolution—the agricultural—and developed in the next major technological revolution—the industrial. Urbanization was a steady but slow process until the middle of the eighteenth century, when Western society began a period of incredibly rapid technological and social change.

Social change is discussed at length in Chapter 14.

PERCENTAGE OF WORLD'S POPULATION LIVING IN CITIES

Year	*Cities of 20,000 or More*	*Cities of 100,000 or More*
1800	2.4	1.7
1850	4.3	2.3
1900	9.2	5.5
1950	20.9	13.1

Source: Kingsley Davis, "The Urbanization of the World," *American Journal of Sociology* 60 (1955): 429–37.

[5]See, for example, Lewis Mumford, *The City in History* (New York: Harcourt, Brace, 1961), for a general history of the city; see also Kingsley Davis, "The Origin and Growth of Urbanization in the World," in *Neighborhood, City, and Metropolis,* ed. Robert Gutman and David Popenoe (New York: Random House, 1970), pp. 120–30; V. Gordon Childe, "The Urban Revolution," *Town Planning Review,* April 1950, pp. 3–17.

From their beginnings cities were centers of production and trade. They were also administrative centers and fortresses. Note the massive walls evident in the painting of the medieval Italian city of Siena, the moat in the aerial photograph of Palma Nuova, a Renaissance Italian city, and the mountaintop location of Machu Picchu, an ancient Peruvian city that the Incas finally had to abandon when the Spanish invaded Peru in the sixteenth century.

Details of American Urbanization Since 1900

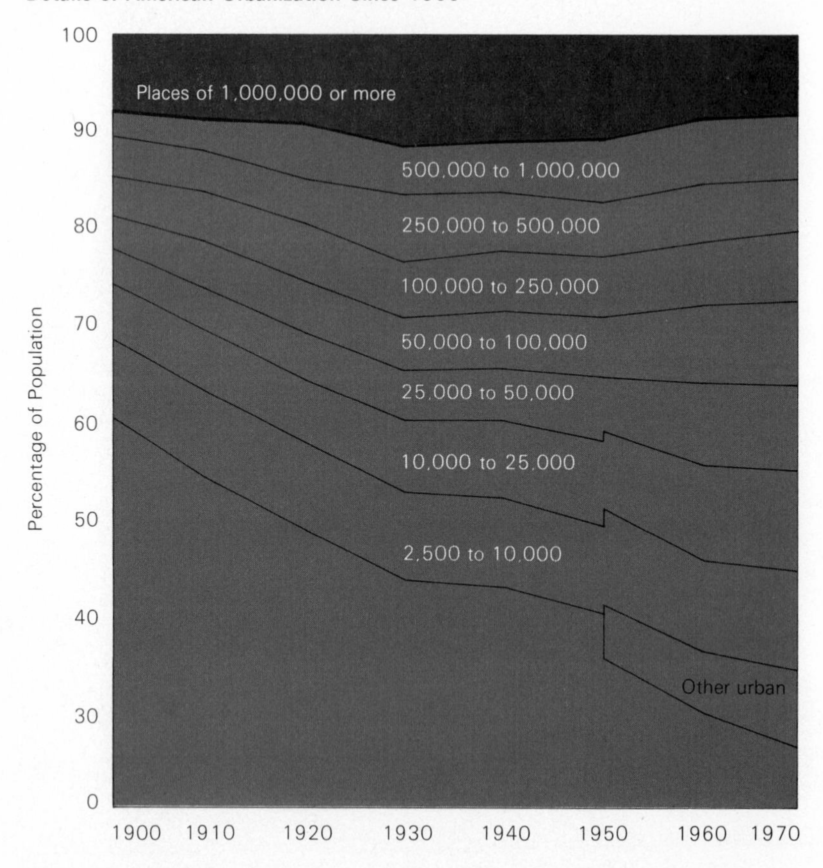

Source: *Social Indicators 1973* (Washington, D.C.: U.S. Government Printing Office, 1974), p. 242.

Methods of mass production using machines operated by unskilled labor vastly increased the output of goods. New methods of transportation–railroads and steamboats–sped up the process of exchange and expanded the possibilities for trade. The new technology created its own needs, not only for more raw materials with which to make consumer products but also for heavy industry–plants to manufacture machines, trains, boats, mills, and smelters.

Cities grew, because of a push-pull effect. As agricultural methods improved, fewer people were needed on farms. Successful farms commonly swallowed up surrounding, poorer farms. Many people were therefore being pushed off the land. At the same time, manufacturers in cities were rapidly in-

Urban and Rural Population Growth in The United States, 1900–70

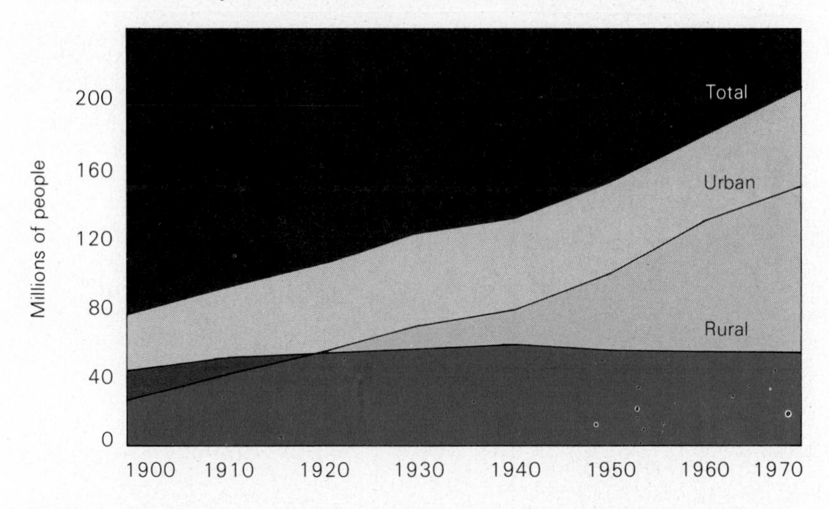

Source: *Encyclopedia of Sociology* (Guilford, Conn.: Dushkin Publishing Group, 1974), p. 217.

creasing in number and hiring multitudes of unskilled laborers. People were therefore being pulled to the cities by the magnet of jobs. The rapid growth in technological possibilities was matched by an accumulation of raw materials, labor, and markets.

In the last hundred years we have witnessed a new phenomenon in the development of cities: suburbanization. This is the only development that does not trace back to the cities of ancient times.

CHARACTERISTICS OF MODERN CITIES

City: a relatively large, densely populated, permanent human settlement characterized by cultural heterogeneity.

The urbanization trend in industrial or industrializing societies has been dramatic. In the United States alone, the portion of the population living in urban areas has gone from about 6 percent in 1800 to 73.5 percent in 1970.[6] These figures may be deceptive, however, for they are based on the United States Census Bureau's definition of an urban area—any place with a population of 2,500 or more. To many of us, a place that small is a town, not a city. European countries, for example, often define a city as a place having 20,000 people or more.

In trying to decide what is a city and what is not, any population figure

[6]United States Department of Commerce, Bureau of the Census, *Statistical Abstract of the United States, 1974* (Washington, D.C.: U.S. Government Printing Office, 1974), p. 16.

is arbitrary. Other characteristics must be used as well. One distinguishing feature is that the economic livelihood of the settlement is not primarily agricultural. Beyond that, we can rely on the definition supplied by the urban sociologist Louis Wirth in the late 1930s: "A city may be defined as a relatively large, dense, and permanent settlement of socially heterogeneous individuals."[7]

Wirth's three definitional elements—size, density of population, and heterogeneity—appeared in our description of the earliest cities. Now let us apply each to modern urban settlements.

[7]Wirth, "Urbanism as a Way of Life," p. 5; see also id., *The Ghetto* (Chicago: University of Chicago Press, 1928), and Albert Reiss, ed., *Louis Wirth on Cities and Social Life* (Chicago: University of Chicago Press, 1964), for Wirth's interpretation of city life.

Although cities possess the same three dimensions as communities—geographical, psychological, and organizational—their determining features are size and density of population.

Size

Because experts do not agree on how many people make a city, most urban sociologists avoid using a fixed number. Instead they use other indications of size. For example, a city has many more people than can easily know one another. True bonds of kinship and neighborliness are still formed in the city, as we noted in Chapter 12. There may be many communities, or urban villages, within its borders. But, because of the number of people and size of the area, common services are needed by the city as a whole that cannot be supplied simply by neighbors and friends.

These public services, provided by a wide variety of city agencies, are directly related to the size of the population. Instead of a volunteer fire brigade, for example, there is a professional fire department. A fire in one apartment in a large building or row of joined buildings endangers many more lives and much more property than a fire in an isolated farmhouse. The residents need the speed and expertise of trained professional firefighters. The locations of firehouses must be planned to offer coverage of and access to all neighborhoods. Thus, an administrative organization is needed.

For the same reasons, instead of a local sheriff and a few deputies, a city needs a highly organized police department. Instead of the one or two schools that a small town or rural area has, city children need a complex school system.

Little communities can get by without big government. Cities simply cannot. To best understand the problem of coping with sheer size, imagine how different the results would be if the fire brigade in a small town and a fire department in a major city both decided to strike. In the first instance, it is likely that volunteers could deal with most emergencies. In the second, it would be silly to think that they could. Similar contrasts can be made about police services, garbage disposal, or even schooling. The number of public services required by a large city imposes the need for a city government. The services must be coordinated, their responsibilities defined and interrelated, and their administrators hired. The costs of the services must be raised by taxes on property, businesses, and income. Therefore a tax assessment and collection agency must be formed. Clearly, the sheer size of the modern city necessitates bureaucracies.

Population Density

People in most cities are crowded into small areas compared to rural towns and villages. Thus density of population, the number of people occupying a given land area, is greatest in cities. However, density can vary greatly from city to city and from neighborhood to neighborhood within a city.

DENSITY OF UNITED STATES CITIES

City	*Population per Square Mile*	*City*	*Population per Square Mile*
New York	26,343	St. Louis	10,167
Manhattan	67,808	Cleveland	9,893
Jersey City, N.J.	17,255	Oakland	6,771
Paterson, N.J.	17,241	Seattle	6,350
San Francisco	15,764	Los Angeles	6,025
Philadelphia	15,164	Honolulu	3,872
Chicago	15,126	Dallas	3,179
Washington, D.C.	12,321	New Orleans	3,011
Detroit	10,953	Phoenix	2,346

Source: United States Department of Commerce, Bureau of the Census, *Statistical Abstract of the United States, 1974* (Washington, D.C.: U.S. Government Printing Office, 1974), pp. 23–25.

Density is not directly related to size of population, either. For example, look at the table of people per square mile in various cities. From these figures San Francisco may seem larger than Dallas. The reverse is true, but the smaller city has five times the population density of the larger one. Although cities have an image as places of overcrowding, some are not so closely packed.

An extreme example of urban crowding is found in the city of Hong Kong. Hundreds of thousands of people there are crammed into housing that allows as little as twenty-four square feet of space (equal to four feet by six feet) per adult and only half that amount for children. A family of nine to twelve members may live together in a single room of only one hundred twenty square feet (equal to ten feet by twelve feet).[8]

No American cities match the population density of Hong Kong. However, some parts of our major urban areas are extremely congested. Manhattan has nearly 68,000 people per square mile. The New York metropolitan area, which includes the five boroughs of New York City plus nearby parts of Long Island, New Jersey, and Connecticut, contains more people than the combined populations of Arizona, Delaware, Idaho, Maine, Montana, Nevada, New Hampshire, New Mexico, North Dakota, South Dakota, Rhode Island, Utah, Vermont, and Wyoming.[9]

Diversity of People and Cultures

Cities are not only large centers of dense population; they are also, in the

[8]Marcia Burick Goldstein, "The Rectification of a Mistake: A Study of the Hong Kong Government's Plan to Rehabilitate the Shek Kip Mei Estate" (M.A. thesis, Smith College, Northampton, Mass., 1974), Chap. 1

[9]Wilfred Owen, *The Metropolitan Transportation Problem* (Garden City, N.Y.: Doubleday Anchor, 1966), p. 10.

words of Louis Wirth, "settlements of socially heterogeneous individuals." People come to the city from a variety of cultures and subcultures. They often bring part of those other worlds with them when they migrate. Thus they have varying ideas about life and the way to live it. They differ in who they are, what they think, and what they do. This diversity means that city residents can observe and enjoy a wide range of life-styles.

Perhaps the most obvious forms of diversity in American cities are racial and ethnic. Our cities, and many others throughout the world, are checkerboards of different racial and ethnic groups. People from many lands who came to the United States often settled in seaboard towns or new cities springing up along transportation lines. In city after city we find fairly distinct ethnic neighborhoods with names like Little Italy, Germantown, and Chinatown or with names that give no clue to the ethnic makeup: in New York, the Lower East Side (once predominantly inhabited by Jewish immigrants) and Hell's Kitchen (almost all Irish-Americans at one time). We also find segregated living patterns between blacks and whites. (Such segregation is not unique to the cities, however. It is one characteristic that many smaller towns share with cities.)

In Hong Kong the population density on land is almost rivaled by that on water. Multitudes of inhabitants live in the harbor.

1. Think of the large city that you know best. It might be where you live, a place you often visit, or a nearby city from which you see the local television news. What kinds of racial and ethnic neighborhoods does it have? What are some of the special foods, crafts, religious services, or other attractions made available by and for the various peoples of that city?

2. Draw a map of a city that you know well, and designate the ethnic and racial ghettos or neighborhoods. Why do you think this city developed the way it did?

Racial diversity and ethnic diversity are not the only kinds of heterogeneity to be found in cities. Our sketch of the earliest cities showed that diversity is built into the nature of the city. This is especially true of cities in an industrial society. City dwellers differ by level and kind of education, by occupation, income, and prestige, by social class background, by religous beliefs, by political affiliations, by the length of their family history as city dwellers or as members of a particular society, by their exposure to other cultures through business or travel, and by many other cultural and individual traits.

You can see that some of these areas of diversity have to do with where city people have come from (rural areas, other cultures, different social classes) and what they do for a living (plumbing, law, banking, bus driving). The *possibility* of such diversity, however, comes from the size of the city. As we saw in Chapter 12, the small size of a town increases the visibility of each individual. Thus communities have informal means of social control for preserving their cultural unity. The largeness of a big city, on the other hand, reduces the pressure for such conformity by bestowing anonymity on its inhabitants.

We have seen the Italian-Americans of Boston's West End in Chapters 9 and 12. Gans stated that only a few West Enders had been born in Italy. Yet they maintained their subculture over several generations. Was this possible because they lived in a city? To explore the answer, imagine that two or three West End families move to a small midwestern farm town. What do you think would happen to the subculture of these families in the next generation or two? Why? Be as detailed as you can.

Organizational and Institutional Specialization

Even within occupations, size and density of the city population help to explain why the city has so much diversity. The large and crowded population not only demands but also can support a wide range of goods and services of all degrees of specialization. For example, both the village and the city need doctors. But the village may have to get along with one doctor having a general practice. The city has all kinds of medical specialists. Why? Because, although the same illnesses are found in both countryside and city, those requiring a specialist will be far fewer in the small town, not enough to support a specialist's practice. Suppose that 5 percent of the people must see a heart specialist for treatment in a year. In a town of 1,800 people, 5 percent is 90 patients. Even a specialist who was willing to survive on the small income from so few patients would lack sufficient hospital and lab facilities to do the job right. In a city of, say, 25,000 people, 5 percent comes to 1,250 patients, enough to support a couple of specialists, and at least one adequately staffed and equipped hospital.

Specialists in the city also provide services to those who live in the countryside. Retail merchants from small towns come to the city to select from the assortment of available goods. Many families make regular shopping trips to a nearby city to buy specialty items or to have a wider selection of goods.

Often the main products of a city are sent out across the nation and the world. Detroit, for example, is the automobile center. Besides its car assembly plants, it has many producers of auto parts. The economic well-being of Detroit is tied to the demand for cars throughout the nation. When the country buys fewer cars, as happened in 1975, Detroit's workers suffer layoffs. In 1975, Detroit auto workers had a higher unemployment rate than those of any other industry.

Such a grim fact underlines the economic nature of the cities–a characteristic they have had since their beginnings. Cities are places of manufacturing, trade, and related activities–transportation, banking, corporate and business law, and so on. They also serve as the dwelling places of the multitudes engaged in those activities. Thus, the economic institution coexists with all the other social institutions required by the population. This coexistence produces spatial patterns, as you might expect: industrial areas; railroad yards and docks; business districts; financial districts; civic centers (city hall, courthouses); entertainment centers; educational complexes; and residential areas.

Later in this chapter we discuss urban ecology and models of urban growth.

The folk society was discussed in Chapter 12. It represents the sacred (in Nisbet's terminology) as opposed to the city, which embodies the secular.

URBAN INTERACTION: A GESELLSCHAFT MAZE?

Louis Wirth, whose definition of the city we examined earlier, saw the city as an embodiment of Toennie's gesellschaft model. In fact, such a view of the city was shared by most of the well-known theoreticians and researchers of the late nineteenth and early twentieth centuries, among them Émile Durkheim and Max Weber.[10] Anthropologist Robert Redfield implied the same view of the city in his ideal type of the folk society: relations in the city were the opposite of the cohesive, primary group interactions found in folk societies.

The Need for Secondary Relationships

Wirth, in presenting his concept of the ideal type of urban society, attributed the characteristic patterns of urban interaction to the very nature of the city: its size, density, and heterogeneity. The vast number of relationships that any city dweller must have, according to Wirth, demands formality, superficiality, and impersonality in human encounters in the city.[11] Because the informal social controls that are supposedly so effective in a community are impossible in a city, formal controls must be established: regulations, law codes, and vigilant police departments. The anonymity of the individual in an urban setting perhaps weakens the internalization of norms. The heterogeneity of values and norms in the city also weakens internalization.

In a folk society, people are intimately involved with each other in all aspects of community life. In the ideal sense, the residents pray with the same people they work with, play with, study with, buy from, and live near. Some sociologists contend that in the ideal type of mass society, people participate in various secondary groups or associations with totally different sets of people.

Test this point of view. List the secondary groups to which you belong. Then list the people who belong to more than one of these groups. How many did you find?

The growing crime rates in the inner cities and the passive reactions of witnesses to attacks such as the fatal assault on Kitty Genovese (discussed in Chapter 12) seem to support Wirth's claims. Many city dwellers share Wirth's judgment. Others do not. Consider the following statements:

[10]See Émile Durkheim, *The Division of Labor in Society* (New York: Free Press, 1947); Max Weber, *The Theory of Social and Economic Organization* (New York: Oxford University Press, 1947).

[11]See Wirth, "Urbanism as a Way of Life."

Me, I can't stand the city. It's crowded, dirty, and dangerous. I spend three-quarters of my time jammed on subways and buses, choked by pollution, and jostled by rude crowds. I don't even know the names of the people in neighboring apartments. I think if I fell down and broke a leg in front of my apartment house, people would just trip over me and hurry along their own way.

I think there's no place better than the city. Take last Sunday, for example. We went for a long walk in the park and stopped to watch skating at the rink. Then we visited a marvelous exhibit of ancient art, while the kids were looking at the dinosaur skeletons in the Museum of Natural History. We have so many movies, television stations, stores, and restaurants to choose from. All the great show people appear here sometime during the year. It's really exciting. I know I'd die from boredom in some little hick town.

Sometimes I really hate the city and sometimes I love it. I mean, like, two weeks ago three people got mugged on the next block. And all the time you read in the papers about corruption in the city government, problems of poor people, welfare cheats, race riots. Who needs it? But then I think, I'd never leave. This is my home. If you want to see the latest styles, you have to come to the city. If you want to have a choice of things to do and places to go and people to meet, you have to come to the city. And people in the city aren't really as bad as a lot of other people say. Sure, everyone's always in a hurry, but if you really need some kind of help, a lot of people will take the time.

Let's face it, there's nothing like a city, even one like this. I guess you have to take the good with the bad.

Primary Groups within the Maze

Sociologists, of course, substitute research methods for personal impressions. On the basis of research, several sociologists have challenged Wirth's description of the city. No sociologist contests the prevalence of secondary relations in urban life. On the job and in many everyday dealings with others, city people interact in superficial, formalized ways. But they have primary interactions with relatives and friends and often become friendly with at least a few neighbors.

Herbert Gans, whose study of the West End of Boston demonstrated the survival of communities within the cities, criticized Wirth's conclusions on the ground that they were based on research in only one particular kind of neighborhood.[12] For the transient, poor, inner-city neighborhood that Wirth's research was based on, his conclusions were correct. But, for other kinds of

[12]Herbert J. Gans, "Urbanism and Suburbanism as Ways of Life: A Re-evaluation of Definitions," in *Human Behavior and Social Processes,* ed. Arnold Rose (New York: Houghton Mifflin, 1962), pp. 625–48.

CROME & GOLDSCHMIDT

To many people, city dwellers among them, the city is a place of loneliness in the midst of crowds. People seem to be self-absorbed and fearful of intimacy with strangers. The heterogeneity of life in a modern city contributes to what Durkheim called anomie, a decay of norms stemming from the abundance of competing norms. Anomie further weakens the social fabric by reducing the element of predictability in the conduct of others.

residential areas with stable populations, they were incorrect. In its entirety, the city may display heterogeneity, but in many neighborhoods people experience homogeneous relations with "their own kind."

On the basis of his own research, Gans maintains, in fact, that many interactions in stable, working- and middle-class neighborhoods are neither secondary nor primary but somewhere in between. Jane Jacobs, a student of urban life, gives supporting evidence of this. She describes activity on Hudson Street in New York City as ballet—as ritual. This suggests formality, for ballet is choreographed: each dancer must precisely follow certain steps and be in certain places at certain times. The same is true of any ritual. Yet behind her use of this metaphor is deep feeling. Like the art of ballet and ritual, activities on Hudson Street are moving experiences. Jacobs writes:

> The stretch of Hudson where I live is each day the scene of intricate sidewalk ballet. I make my own first entrance into it a little after eight when I put out the garbage can. . . . as the droves of junior high school students walk by the center of the stage dropping candy wrappers. . . .
>
> While I sweep up the wrappers I watch the other rituals of morning: Mr. Halpert unlocking the laundry's handcart from its mooring to a cellar door, Joe Cornacchia's son-in-law stacking out the empty crates from the delicatessen, the barber bringing out his sidewalk folding chair. Mr. Goldstein arranging the coils of wire which proclaim the hardware store is open. . . . Now the primary children, heading for St. Luke's, dribble through to the south; the children for St. Veronica's cross, heading to the west, and the children for P.S. 41, heading toward the east. Two new entrances are being made from the wings: well-dressed and even elegant women and men with brief cases emerge from doorways and side streets. Most of these are heading for the bus and subways, but some hover on the curbs, stopping taxis which have miraculously appeared at the right moment, for the taxis are part of a wider morning ritual: having dropped passengers from midtown in the downtown financial district, they are now bringing downtowners up to the midtown. Simultaneously, numbers of women in housedresses have emerged and as they crisscross with one another they pause for quick conversations that sound with either laughter or joint indignation, never, it seems, anything between. It is time for me to hurry to work too, and I exchange my ritual farewell with Mr. Lofaro, the short, thick-bodied, white-aproned fruit man who stands outside his doorway a little up the street, his arms folded, his feet planted, looking solid as earth itself. We nod; we each glance quickly up and down the street, then look back to each other and smile. We have done this many a morning for more than ten years, and we both know what it means: All is well. . . .
>
> On Hudson Street, the same as in the North End of Boston or in any other animated neighborhoods of great cities, . . . we are the lucky possessors of a city order that makes it relatively simple to keep the peace because there are plenty of eyes on the street. But there is nothing simple about that order itself,

or the bewildering number of components that go into it. Most of those components are specialized in one way or another. They unite in their joint effect upon the sidewalk [the community itself], which is not specialized in the least. That is its strength.[13]

1. In Jane Jacobs's description of a normal early morning on Hudson Street we see her interact with only one person, Mr. Lofaro, and their interaction is limited to a nod, a glance at the street, and a smile. What kind of relation do they share—primary, secondary, or other? Explain.

They have performed their ritual for ten years, yet it does not include speaking to one another. Why do you think this is so?

2. Do some content analysis (as described in the Appendix, "The Research Process"). Consider the language Jacobs uses to describe her perception of her street in early morning. What feelings does it express? For example, she mentions women she does not seem to know personally yet she describes them, as if from many repeated observations, pausing "for quick conversations that sound with either laughter or joint indignation, never, it seems, anything between." What do you think she feels toward these women?

3. Look at Jacobs's last paragraph. Why does she feel the community's strength is the fact that it isn't specialized? How is this neighborhood like a small town, and how is it different?

URBAN ECOLOGY: THEORIES OF URBAN GROWTH

Communities, as we saw in Chapter 12, can grow or change in any or all of their three dimensions—geographical, psychological, and organizational. Cities can change, too, in the three dimensions we are studying—size, density, heterogeneity—and they do. In the 1920s, sociologists began studying cities in earnest. Chief among those urban sociologists were many at the University of Chicago who came to be known in sociology circles as the Chicago School. They studied and developed theories on how and why cities change.

Urban ecology: the study of how people in urban settlements interact with each other and their environment, affecting and being affected by those interactions.

For much of the last decade the word *ecology* has been very fashionable as an idea suggesting conservation of the natural environment, the fight against pollution, and the effort to stop the waste of precious resources. Properly

[13]Jane Jacobs, "Community in the City Streets," in *The Search for Community in Modern America*, ed. E. Digby Baltzell (New York: Harper and Row, 1968), pp. 90–91, 93.

speaking, ecology is one of the natural sciences: it is the study of how organisms interact with their natural environment and other organisms that share it.

Ecology stresses the fact that not only does the environment modify people's behavior but also people's behavior reshapes their environment. The natural environment, for example, may influence where we will build our cities —at the mouth of a great river, perhaps, or on a fertile plain. Cultural values, social pressures, and economic conditions influence human use of the environment, thereby shaping the human landscape. For example, agricultural land adjoining growing suburbs may be taxed on its higher value of development property for homes or industry. Farmers who can't afford to pay those taxes and still make a living must sell the land, which then becomes an extension of the suburbs. In turn, as cities and suburbs spread outward, the culturally favored use of private cars rather than government-subsidized mass transit may create air pollution problems and the blight of more and more freeways crisscrossing the area.

The Chicago sociologists, led by Robert Park, sought to apply the conceptual framework of ecology to the study of the human urban environment. They saw the city itself as an environment that, like its natural counterpart, undergoes change. Thus, they saw that the city is more than the people who live in it. For example, the Chicago sociologists studied the ways in which "neighboring" was often influenced by natural and artificial boundaries: rivers, lakes, roads, and railroad tracks.

These sociologists also reviewed the history of urban development, looking for common themes and patterns. Like others before them, they noted that cities are often market villages grown up. The villages that became cities were often located at the bend in a river, on the edge of a natural harbor, by an oasis, or at a major crossroad. That is, the selection of cities that grew and prospered was not generally a matter of arbitrary human choice. Natural circumstances favored some and disfavored others. Often, though, technology would swing the balance. Because of the railroads, many cities grew that would never have developed otherwise. For example, the railroads made Kansas City, Missouri, and Omaha, Nebraska, become important cities because they were available as railheads for our cattle trade.

Three Models of City Growth

The Chicago sociologist Ernest Burgess proposed one of three models of urban growth that are associated with the Chicago School. His model, called the *concentric zone* model, presented the city as a set of circles, each one ringing the smaller one within it. At the center is the business district, where

Models of Urban Growth

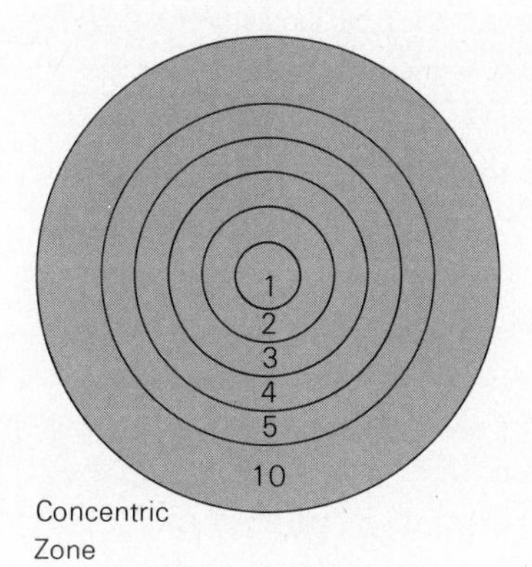

Concentric Zone

Sector

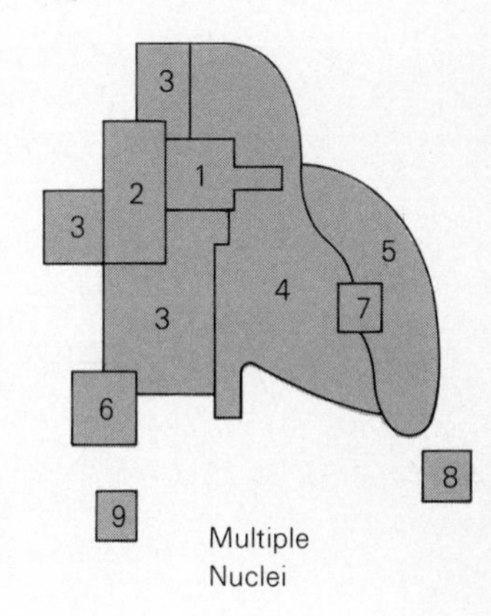

Multiple Nuclei

1. Central business district
2. Wholesale, light manufacturing
3. Low-class residential
4. Medium-class residential
5. High-class residential
6. Heavy manufacturing
7. Outlying business district
8. Residential suburb
9. Industrial suburb
10. Commuter zone

Source: Reprinted from "The Nature of Cities" by C. D. Harris and E. L. Ullman in volume 242 of *The Annals of The American Academy of Political and Social Science.* Copyright © 1945 by the American Academy of Political and Social Science. Reprinted by permission.

property values favor the income-earning uses of land. The only residents there are transients living in rundown hotels. The next zone, ringing the center, is the zone in transition. Once decent housing, it has been blighted by the encroachment of the business center. As its residential acceptability declines, and as housing is neglected by owners who anticipate selling their property to business interests, this area becomes the home of the poor and minorities. Next outside this area is a zone of working-class homes. Beyond are the middle-class homes. And those, in turn, are encircled by an outer ring of upper-class homes.

Burgess proposed this model only as a basis for testing. Many people, however, adopted it uncritically as an accurate general description of all urban growth. In fact, it fits Chicago, but the growth of many other cities cannot be described by this pattern.

Homer Hoyt produced an alternative—the *sector model.* This model proposes that some cities grow, not in ever-expanding circles, but in segments or sectors. Often the growth pattern follows the topography of the land or the most favored transportation routes—rail, boat, horse and buggy (at one time), automobile, bus, and truck. A river cutting through the city may encourage the development of an industrial sector that stretches for miles right through the middle of town. Or three hills at different points may be the sites for wealthier residential neighborhoods, while working-class homes fill in the valleys between them. Boston and Philadelphia are best described by the sector model.

Chauncey Harris and Edward Ullman proposed still a third model, the *multiple-nuclei* model. According to them, particular kinds of land use are found in separate, distinct areas. Industrial areas are located near the transportation routes needed for shipments of raw materials and finished goods. Thus, in a harbor city industrial areas may concentrate around or near the port. Similar users of land in other fields may flock together because the proximity of all of them favors each. This happens in financial or shopping districts. Still other land users congregate away from their opposites. The wealthy choose residential areas that command the best views and most scenic landscapes perhaps. But they certainly select areas that are as far as possible from the pollution and grime of the industrial district and the congestion and bustle of the business district. Still other land users locate wherever property values allow them to go; they can afford no better. Thus, low-income housing may crop up between an industrial district and a business district. So may warehouses and other activities requiring large areas of space but yielding a low return.[14]

Obtain a map of the city your college is in or closest to. As a class, undertake a field research project on the entire city. Describe each of its areas in terms of use, condition, and population. If a field trip is not possible, use the yellow pages of the phone book to locate industrial, business, and other areas and mark them on the map.

How will you find the residential areas? Will you decide that areas with no representation in the yellow pages are residential? How can you learn what economic or social class they represent? (Remember: it is not scientific to assume their social class from the kind of area that is near them. That would be assuming the truth of part of a theory.) Hint: Where are the medical specialists, fine restaurants, and gourmet specialty shops located?

[14]For further descriptions of the concentric zone, sector, and multiple-nuclei theories, see C. D. Harris and E. L. Ullman, "The Nature of Cities," *Annals of the American Academy of Political and Social Science* 242 (1945): 7–17.

From your field work or telephone book research, decide which model seems to describe this city best. When the class is polled, is there general agreement? If not, discuss.

Urban Succession

Urban succession: the replacement of one social class, ethnic group, or economic function in an urban area by another.

A major component of the Chicago School theories of urban ecology is the concept of urban succession.[15] Cities and the areas within them change over time. A wealthy neighborhood may gradually decline to a slum. Later it may be renovated to its original condition or replaced by new middle- or high-income housing. An industrial area may expand into neighboring areas or be abandoned because of technological obsolescence. Shopping districts lose significant business to shopping centers, become more and more run-down, and sprout vacant or boarded-up store fronts.

Urban succession is the term used for these changes. It indicates that a different social class, ethnic or racial group, or economic function has entered and ultimately taken over a given area of the city. Succession can occur in many ways. A common form is the replacement of one ethnic group in a slum by another. Say that a wave of Italian immigrants moved into a city slum in the 1870s. In a couple of generations most of those families improve their economic means and gradually move elsewhere, to working-class or middle-class neighborhoods. Meanwhile, other ethnic or racial groups have been migrating to the city, such as blacks from the rural South. The economic circumstances of the newcomers—and, for blacks, patterns of discrimination—give them little choice about where to live. They move into the slum, as the Italian-Americans move to better housing. Once the Italian-Americans have virtually been replaced by the blacks, urban succession has taken place.

The Chicago School sociologists contended that the time of arrival of immigrants to this country influenced the urban succession pattern. That is, the first groups to come to a port city like New York lived in the least desirable areas of town—near the harbor. They moved out as they became adjusted to American life and became more successful. Then newer, less fortunate immigrants took their place.

This theory seems true except for black immigrants. Although

[15]See Roderick D. McKenzie, "The Ecological Approach to the Study of the Human Community," in *The City,* ed. Robert E. Park, Ernest W. Burgess, and Roderick D. McKenzie (Chicago: University of Chicago Press, 1925), pp. 63–79. McKenzie outlined three ecological processes: segregation, invasion, and succession.

This street on the Upper West Side of Manhattan illustrates urban succession. Two decades ago it was part of a long-standing neighborhood of comfortably middle-class people. Now it is occupied by lower middle-class and working-class people of various ethnic backgrounds. The earlier inhabitants have become suburbanities.

they were among the earliest settlers in the United States, blacks today still live in some of the least desirable areas of town. Why do you think this is so?

What parts do these factors play in the breakdown of this succession theory: race, opportunities, group cohesion, type of work available, politics, family life, economics, and education?

Much of urban succession is begun because of *social mobility,* the upward (or downward) movement of people among the strata of society. As people increase their wealth or social prestige they often move to neighborhoods or suburbs that offer them more comfort or have a better reputation. The Italian-Americans in our example illustrate this. Their initial movement makes room for another group to succeed them.

1. Evidence of succession patterns may be found in the histories of many cities. Clues are offered by the names of some streets and shops that are legacies of earlier groups. Succession is evident in the changing character of some buildings—for example, churches that became synagogues and later changed into churches again. It is also seen in the names of the pupils at neighborhood schools: over a long period of time, the ethnic flavor of the names shifts.

2. Interview a member of your own family to trace movements that might be related to urban succession. Try to discover any personal moves from one place or neighborhood to another because of social mobility—for example, because of a better job or because members of other racial or ethnic groups were moving into the old neighborhood. If the person interviewed had no personal experiences of this kind, ask whether he or she can tell you about the experience of another family member.

SUBURBANIZATION: THE MOVE OUTWARD

Since the industrial revolution, the push-pull effect we mentioned earlier has drawn people from rural areas, where little work was to be found, to cities, where many opportunities for self-improvement were known or rumored to exist. Since the late 1950s, patterns of urban succession have occurred that threaten the economic survival of the city. While migration from rural to urban areas has declined, and migration of blacks from the South to northern cities has decreased, many cities have nevertheless become progressively poorer. This is because more and more members of the middle and upper classes have abandoned the cities to the poor of all races and ethnic backgrounds.

Decline of the Cities

The poor, by the very nature of their poverty, must rely heavily on public services for everything from transportation and schooling to medical care and hospitalization. Their limited incomes give them little buying power to keep businesses going in the city. As business declines, the tax revenues that the

Population Changes in Metropolitan Areas by Race, 1950–70

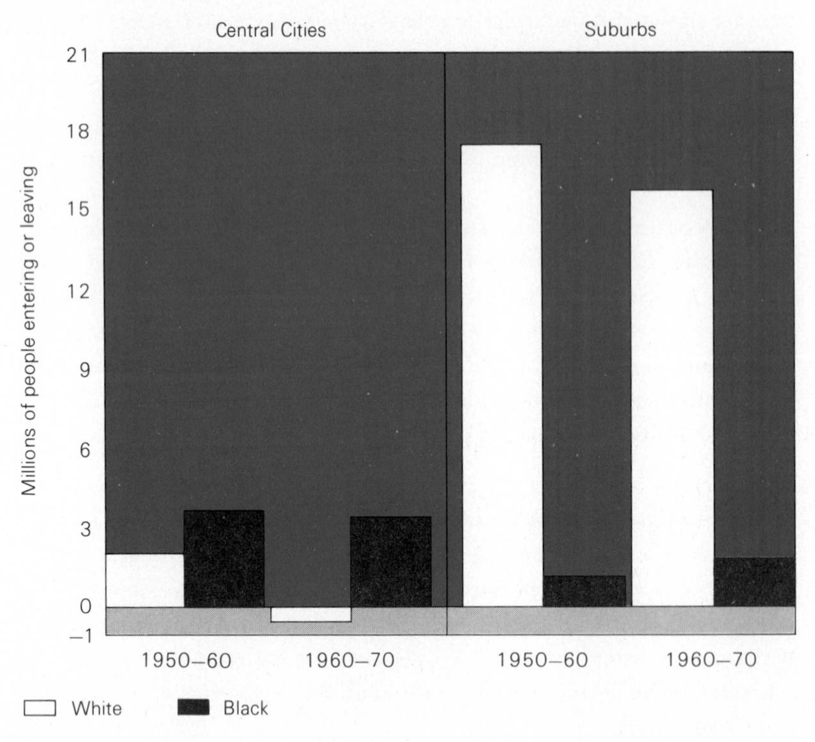

Source: *Encyclopedia of Sociology* (Guilford, Conn.: Dushkin Publishing Group, 1974), p. 35.

city needs to maintain services also go down. Income from property taxes declines because property values are lower—since fewer upper-class homes are located in the city. Thus, in recent years, many cities have suffered a pattern of urban succession that threatens to bankrupt them.

Recent writers Stanley Aronowitz and Harry Braverman have pointed to various other structural reasons that have led to the decline of the city.[16] In many of the older, industrial cities—Chicago, Detroit, New York, Providence, and Fall River, Massachusetts—major industries that supported much of the economy began to move out, leaving the cities vulnerable to unemploy-

[16]Stanley Aronowitz, *False Promises: The Shaping of American Working Class Consciousness* (New York: McGraw-Hill, 1973); and Harry Braverman, *Labor and Monopoly Capital: The Degradation of Work in the Twentieth Century* (New York: Monthly Review Press, 1974).

ment and economic decay. In these older cities, labor unions often held a great deal of power, perhaps too much for the liking of the corporations. The garment industry, for example, relocated from northern cities to southern communities where unions were weak or did not exist. Similarly, the shoe and textile industries left New England cities and often relocated in places where they could find cheap labor. They moved not only to other areas of the country but also to other countries, such as Spain, Brazil, Taiwan, Korea, and the Philippines.

1. If urban succession continues, and much-needed city revenue is increasingly drawn out of the urban core by fleeing businesses and residents, what problems will increase or develop for cities?

2. If you were to tackle the urban financial crisis, how would you judge the feasibility of each of the following suggestions:

> **Renew and revitalize the inner city area through urban renewal and building programs, an urban promotion campaign to draw businesses back into the city, tax incentives for industries to move into the city, training programs for lower-class members, and financial support for the arts.**
>
> **Redraw the city boundaries to include affluent suburbs that will then bring needed revenue and citizens into the city.**
>
> **Cut down on services within the city.**
>
> **Relocate the urban poor in outlying suburban areas by offering low-cost housing there.**

What other solutions would you suggest to help bring money back into the city, so that it can continue to function and supply the urban poor with the social services they need?

Suburb: a settlement neighboring a central city and economically and culturally dependent upon it.

The Dream of the Suburbs

Where did the middle and upper classes go when they abandoned the cities in such numbers? As everyone knows, they went to the suburbs. Suburbs have been defined by William Dobriner as "those urbanized, residential communities which are outside the corporate units of a large central city, but which are culturally and economically dependent upon the central city."[17] Leo F. Schnore

[17]William Dobriner, *The Suburban Community* (New York: Putnam, 1958), p. xvii.

A block picnic in a Northern California suburb shows the effort of residents to reclaim a sense of community. Do they have a better chance of achieving this goal than the urban villagers (discussed in the previous chapter)? Consider the definition of community, and compare it with what you know of the suburbs.

further distinguishes between "residential" and "employing" suburbs—those where people live and those where people work.[18]

The economic boom following World War II enabled multitudes of middle-class city dwellers for the first time to buy their piece of the American dream in suburbia: a home of their own; fresh air, space, and sunlight; clean, uncrowded schools for the kids; friendly neighbors; a front lawn and a backyard. For many people, this approximation of the real or imagined rural roots of our society had an irresistible appeal.

[18]Leo F. Schnore, "Satellites and Suburbs," *Social Forces* 36 (1957): 121–29.

Population in Central Cities and Surrounding Areas

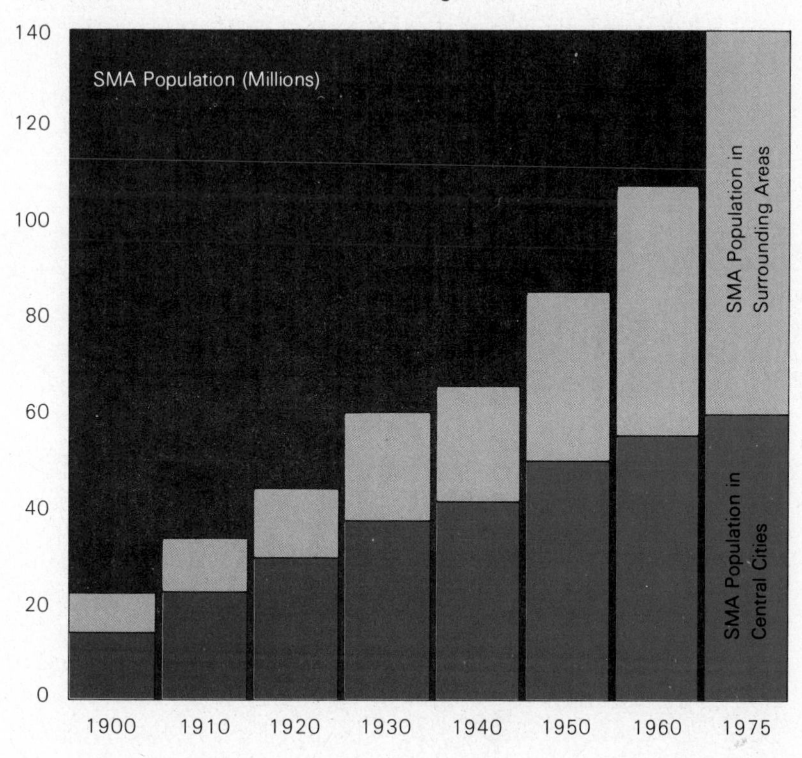

Source: Committee for Economic Development, Research and Policy Committee, *Guiding Metropolitan Growth: A Statement on National Policy* (n.p., n.d.), p. 15.

Suburbs themselves are not entirely a recent phenomenon. Larger cities, such as New York and Chicago, had them more than a hundred years ago, but the percentage of the population that lived in them was very small. By 1970, the population of the suburbs had surpassed that of the inner cities.

The postwar economic boom was only one cause of this phenomenal growth. Technology, the fuse for the urban population explosion of the last two centuries, helped make the suburbs dominant in our social landscape, in turn. When horse-drawn vehicles gave way to motorized transport, people no longer had to live so close to their jobs. Some chose to have a single-family house and yard beyond the city limits.

The growth of automobile sales spurred the movement outward. No longer did people have to think about living near the trolley line, which often stopped at the edge of the city. In the United States in the 1920s auto ownership grew rapidly. Towns and villages near cities took on new life. People could live there and still work in the city. New housing developments were started. Commuter trains further encouraged the growth of these settlements.

Suburban movement slowed during the depression of the 1930s. Then World War II made building materials and gasoline for private cars scarce. In 1945, when the war ended, the accumulated buying power that was released started a suburban boom. Suburban growth was also stimulated by lack of housing in the central cities, low-cost housing loans, government road-building projects, and a rising birth rate.

The Suburban Push-Pull Effect

In the twenty years after 1950, the American population grew by nearly fifty-two million. Nearly all of that growth took place in urban areas—the rural population remained steady. But while our central cities (of fifty thousand people or more) added a little over ten million persons, suburbia grew by over thirty-three million. In 1950 the suburbs had less than 14 percent of the population; by 1970 they had over 37 percent.[19]

We have seen that a number of factors spurred the growth of suburbs. Flanking the boundaries of the cities was land for housing. Government programs made housing loans available at relatively low interest rates. Shopping centers with big parking lots made the suburbs more attractive. Some business firms moved their offices and plants to the suburbs. New highways made it easier to enjoy the city's advantages (jobs, theaters, sports events) while living outside. Rising incomes gave families more choices of where to live.

Sociologist David Riesman has suggested that working- and middle-class families moved out not so much in imitation of the rich as in quiet revolt against city life and industrialization.[20] The cities became notorious in the postwar years as hotbeds of crime—not the political corruption or big time syndicated crime of the 1920s but "street" crime: muggings, rapes, murders, burglaries of homes. When New Yorkers were asked, "What are the two or three problems or issues of greatest concern to you personally that you would most like to see the new city administration do something about?" a large majority answered, "Crime," as the following table indicates:

[19]United States Department of Commerce, Bureau of the Census, *Statistical Abstract of the United States, 1974* (Washington, D.C.: U.S. Government Printing Office, 1974), p. 17.

[20]David Riesman, "The Suburban Dislocation," *Annals of the American Academy of Political and Social Science* 314 (1957): 138.

PROBLEMS OF GREATEST CONCERN TO NEW YORKERS

Problem Cited	*Percentage of Respondents*
Crime	63
Drugs	28
High cost of living, inflation	20
Transportation, 35¢ fare	19
Housing	13
Problems of the aged	11
Schools	11
Unemployment	9
Quality of city services	9
Corruption in government	9
Pollution	9
Welfare abuse	7
The courts	7
Garbage collection	7
Energy shortages	7
Health care	6
Deteriorating neighborhoods	5
Traffic	4
Racial discrimination	3

Source: Adapted from the *New York Times,* January 16, 1974, p. 1. © 1974 by The New York Times Company. Reprinted by permission.

People of all socieconomic classes wanted to flee these urban problems, but not all had the ability to flee.

Suburbia seemed a safer and more open place to raise a family. The social atmosphere seemed friendlier than that in the city. People could take pride in their yards and gardens. There were various organized activities for children and teenagers.

Thus, a push-pull effect was again at work: the flaws in city life gave city dwellers reasons to leave, and the absence of such flaws in suburbia, plus the unique charms of life there, attracted growing numbers of people. City planner Edmund Bacon summed it up:

> The rapid spread of this suburban image came about, I think, because valid dissatisfaction with life in the city led to acceptance of the idea that the . . . exact opposite was obviously the best thing achievable. So came the idea that low density was good, therefore, lower density was better, and the more space around each home, the higher the state of culture it represented.[21]

[21]Edmund Bacon, untitled paper in the series "Cities and Suburbs" (delivered at Goucher College, Baltimore, Maryland, 1960).

Cracks in the Suburban Image

To many Americans, suburbia was the end of the rainbow. Critics, however, claimed that too many people were seeking the same pot of gold. So many new housing developments kept springing up that the country was blighted by suburban sprawl instead of enhanced by planned, orderly growth. Traffic arteries between city and suburbs were increasingly the scene of tie-ups during rush hours and on weekends. Systems of mass transit were often unable to attract enough commuters to break even financially. Public funds favored roads and disfavored these failing commuter lines. The effect was to stack cars up not only on commuter arteries but on city streets as well.

Critics also described a sort of "suburban sadness." The general argument was that, even though suburbanites had access to the advantages of the city, life in suburbia was very dull, suffocating in routine work and highly organized play. Since many suburban neighborhoods consisted of tract homes selling within a narrow price range, they were in effect restricted to people of only one class. In sum, many critics saw the suburbs as possessing neither the community characteristics of the small town nor the cultural diversity of the central city.

Others disagree, claiming that such arguments are based on the value positions of the writers and not of the people about whom they are writing. Suburbs, they say, are as varied as the cities to which they are attached. Like their city cousins, suburbanites differ about whether they feel a sense of fulfillment or emptiness. That debate continues.[22]

1. Think of the suburbs that you have observed. Are most of them one-class or multiple-class communities? Do any have a highly diversified population?

2. If possible, interview three city dwellers and three suburbanites. Try to get a range of race, social class, sex, and age of both sets of respondents. Ask both sets to describe as many important characteristics of suburban life as they can. (The city dwellers may be describing what they *think* life in the suburbs is like, if they have never lived there.) Ask the suburbanites how long they have lived in the suburbs, and ask the urban dwellers if they have ever lived in the suburbs.

[22]See, for example, Herbert J. Gans, "Effects of the Move from City to Suburb," in *The Urban Condition,* ed. Leonard J. Duhl (New York: Basic Books, 1963).

In good part the modern suburb is the product of technology and a high standard of living (as measured by patterns of consumption).

Many social critics and environmental planners maintain that the suburbs are as much a social blight as the inner cities, except for a few areas enjoyed mainly by the very affluent. Suburban crime rates are still lower than urban rates, and the suburbs do not have the physical squalor of the inner cities, but they offer neither the delights of the countryside nor the cultural diversity of the city.

Compare their answers. Do the city dwellers generally have the same ideas about life in suburbia? Do the suburbanites? Do long-term suburbanites differ from newcomers in their responses? Do people of the same age group, or race, or sex tend to feel the same way about the suburbs?

What conclusions can you draw about people's perceptions of the suburbs?

Metropolitan Area Model

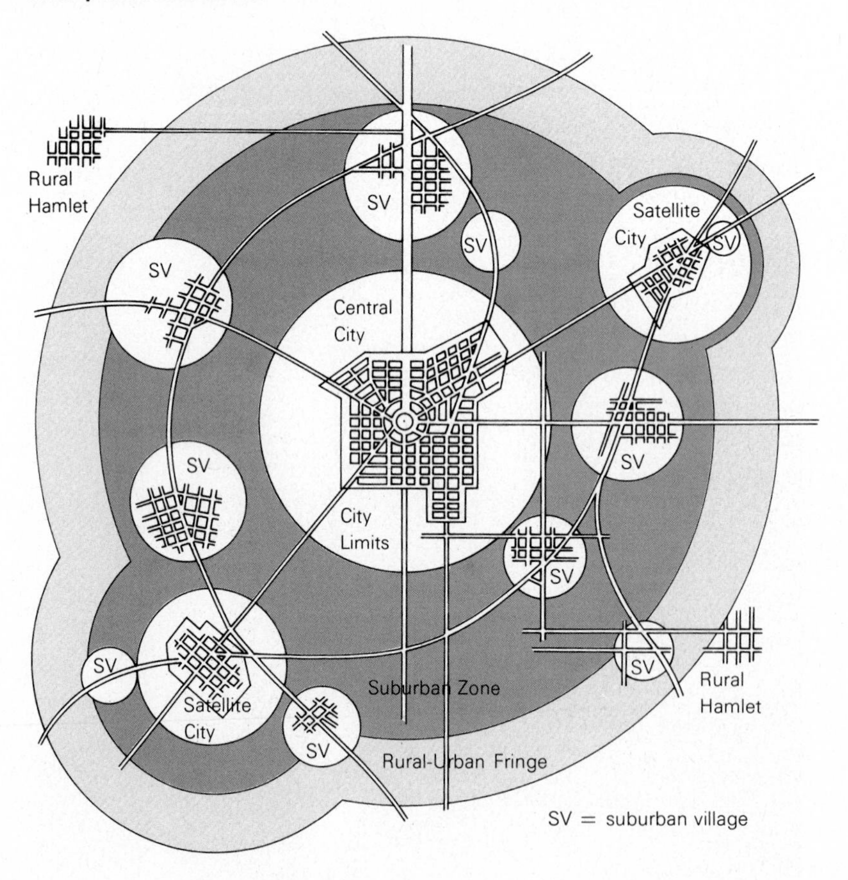

Source: William M. Dobriner, *Class in Suburbia,* © 1963, p. 154. Reprinted by permission of Prentice-Hall, Inc., Englewood Cliffs, New Jersey.

NEW URBAN—SUBURBAN MODELS

The predominance of suburbs in modern society has created problems beyond the practical ones of transportation and revenue distribution. Recent patterns of urban growth have made old urban definitions and models obsolete. No longer can a neat distinction between city and countryside be applied broadly by sociologists or government planners. New models have been created to fit new needs.

The *metropolitan area model* fits the extended city that has burst its boundaries.[23] The diagram of this model shows a central city with two satellite cities near it. Around these cities are suburban villages. Farther out is a rural–urban fringe, an area that is neither truly suburban nor isolated and rural. Although it consists mainly of rural villages and farms, it may be inhabited by part-time farmers who work in the city and other city workers or retirees who choose to live in the country. Networks of roads tie the various places in the area together.

No metropolitan area fits this diagram exactly, but the various elements are real. A few metropolitan areas have two or more central cities abutting each other. Examples are Minneapolis–St. Paul; Gary–Hammond–East Chicago; and Kansas City in Missouri and Kansas.

A metropolis was traditionally defined as the chief city of a country, state, or region, or as a center of trade and activity. Today, however, the term usually refers to a major city and its satellite suburbs. We often distinguish the total entity from the core by using the adjective *greater.* Thus we speak of Greater Boston, Greater Atlanta, and Greater New York.

SMSAS: Defining Metropolitan Areas

A central city has precise borders—its political boundaries. A metropolitan area does not. If a metropolitan area is a large city and its urban-oriented fringe, where does the edge of one fringe end and another begin? The boundary is seldom clear.[24] To get around this difficulty, the Bureau of the Census came up with the term *Standard Metropolitan Statistical Area* (SMSA), which it defined as a county or group of continguous counties containing at least one central city of 50,000 inhabitants or more, or "twin cities" with a combined population of 50,000. (New England is made an exception to this definition; there, towns and cities rather than counties are used in defining SMSAS.)

[23]See William M. Dobriner, "The Growth and Structure of Metropolitan Areas," appendix to *Class in Suburbia* (Englewood Cliffs, N.J.: Prentice-Hall, 1963) pp. 143–66.

[24]Ibid.

GROWTH OF TOP FIFTY CITIES

Rank	City	Population 1970	1950	1900	1850	1750
1	New York, N.Y.	7,894,862	7,891,957	3,437,202	696,115	49,401
	Bronx borough	1,471,701	1,451,277	200,507	8,032	1,781
	Brooklyn borough	2,602,012	2,738,175	1,166,582	138,882	4,495
	Manhattan borough	1,539,233	1,960,101	1,850,093	515,547	33,131
	Queens borough	1,986,473	1,550,849	152,999	18,593	6,159
	Richmond borough	295,443	191,555	67,021	15,061	3,835
2	Chicago, Ill.	3,369,357	3,620,962	1,698,575	29,963	
3	Los Angeles, Calif.	2,809,813	1,970,358	102,479	1,610	
4	Phila., Pa.	1,949,996	2,071,605	1,293,697	121,376	28,522
5	Detroit, Mich.	1,513,601	1,849,568	285,704	21,019	
6	Houston, Tex.	1,232,802	596,163	44,633	2,396	
7	Baltimore, Md.	905,787	949,708	508,957	169,054	13,503
8	Dallas, Tex.	844,401	434,462	42,638	. . .	
9	Washington, D.C.	756,510	802,178	278,718	40,001	
10	Cleveland, Ohio	750,879	914,808	381,768	17,034	
11	Indianapolis, Ind.	746,302	427,173	169,164	8,091	
12	Milwaukee, Wis.	717,372	637,392	285,315	20,061	
13	San Francisco, Calif.	715,674	775,357	342,782	34,776	
14	San Diego, Calif.	697,027	334,387	17,700	. . .	
15	San Antonio, Tex.	654,153	408,442	53,321	3,488	
16	Boston, Mass.	641,071	801,444	560,892	136,881	18,320
17	Memphis, Tenn.	623,530	396,000	102,320	8,841	
18	St. Louis, Mo.	622,236	856,796	575,238	77,860	
19	New Orleans, La.	593,471	570,445	287,104	116,375	
20	Phoenix, Ariz.	581,562	106,818	5,544	. . .	
21	Columbus, Ohio	540,025	375,901	125,560	17,882	
22	Seattle, Wash.	530,831	467,591	80,671	. . .	
23	Jacksonville, Fla.	528,865	204,517	28,429	1,045	
24	Pittsburgh, Pa.	520,117	676,806	321,616	46,601	
25	Denver, Colo.	514,678	415,786	133,859	. . .	
26	Kansas City, Mo.	507,330	456,622	163,752	. . .	
27	Atlanta, Ga.	497,421	331,314	89,872	2,572	
28	Buffalo, N.Y.	462,768	580,132	352,387	42,261	
29	Cincinnati, Ohio	451,455	503,998	325,902	115,435	
30	Nashville, Tenn.	447,877	174,307	80,865	10,165	
31	San Jose, Calif.	446,537	95,280	21,500	. . .	
32	Minneapolis, Minn.	434,400	521,718	202,718	. . .	
33	Fort Worth, Tex.	393,476	278,778	26,688	. . .	
34	Toledo, Ohio	383,105	303,616	131,822	3,829	
35	Newark, N.J.	381,930	438,776	246,070	38,894	
36	Portland, Oreg.	379,967	373,628	90,426	. . .	
37	Oklahoma City, Okla.	368,377	243,504	10,037	. . .	
38	Louisville, Ky.	361,706	369,129	204,731	43,194	200
39	Oakland, Calif.	361,561	384,575	66,960	. . .	
40	Long Beach, Calif.	358,879	250,767	2,252	. . .	

GROWTH OF TOP FIFTY CITIES

		Population				
Rank	*City*	*1970*	*1950*	*1900*	*1850*	
41	Omaha, Nebr.	346,929	251,117	102,555	. . .	
42	Miami, Fla.	334,859	249,276	1,681	. . .	
43	Tulsa, Okla.	330,350	182,740	1,390	. . .	
44	Honolulu, Hawaii	324,871	248,034	39,306	. . .	
45	El Paso, Tex.	322,261	130,485	15,906	. . .	
46	St. Paul, Minn.	309,714	311,349	163,065	1,112	
47	Norfolk, Va.	307,951	213,513	46,624	14,326	2,959
48	Birmingham, Ala.	300,910	326,037	38,415	. . .	
49	Rochester, N.Y.	296,233	332,488	162,608	36,403	
50	Tampa, Fla.	277,753	124,681	15,839	. . .	

Source: *The World Almanac and Book of Facts 1975* (New York: © Newspaper Enterprise Association, Inc., 1974), p. 150.

SMSAs OF OVER ONE MILLION PEOPLE, 1974

SMSA	*Rank*	*Population*
New York, N.Y.-N.J.	1	9,973,577
Los Angeles-Long Beach, Calif.	2	7,032,075
Chicago, Ill.	3	6,978,947
Philadelphia, Pa.-N.J.	4	4,817,914
Detroit, Mich.	5	4,431,390
San Francisco-Oakland, Calif.	6	3,109,519
Washington, D.C.-Md.-Va.	7	2,908,801
Boston, Mass.	8	2,899,101
Nassau-Suffolk, N.Y.	9	2,553,030
St. Louis, Mo.-Ill.	10	2,410,163
Pittsburgh, Pa.	11	2,401,245
Dallas-Fort Worth, Tex.	12	2,377,979
Baltimore, Md.	13	2,070,670
Cleveland, Ohio	14	2,064,194
Newark, N.J.	15	2,054,928
Houston, Tex.	16	1,999,316
Minneapolis-St. Paul, Minn.-Wis.	17	1,965,159
Atlanta, Ga.	18	1,597,816
Seattle-Everett, Wash.	19	1,421,869
Anaheim-Santa Ana-Garden Grove, Calif.	20	1,420,386
Milwaukee, Wis.	21	1,403,688
Cincinnati, Ohio-Ky.-Ind.	22	1,384,851
San Diego, Calif.	23	1,357,854
Buffalo, N.Y.	24	1,349,211
Kansas City, Mo.-Kan.	25	1,271,515
Miami, Fla.	26	1,267,792
Denver-Boulder, Colo.	27	1,237,208
Riverside-San Bernardino-Ontario, Calif.	28	1,143,146
Indianapolis, Ind.	29	1,109,882
Tampa-St. Petersburg, Fla.	30	1,088,549
San Jose, Calif.	31	1,064,714
New Orleans, La.	32	1,045,809
Columbus, Ohio	33	1,017,847
Portland Oreg.-Wash.	34	1,009,129

Source: United States Department of Commerce, Bureau of the Census, "1970 Census of Population and Housing," PHC(2), *General Demographic Trends for Metropolitan Areas, 1960 to 1970, Characteristics of the Population,* Part 1, *United States Summary;* and id., *Current Population Reports,* series P–25, no. 505 (Washington, D.C.: U.S. Government Printing Office, 1973).

In 1974 there were 263 SMSAs in the United States. The largest were New York, Los Angeles–Long Beach, Chicago, Philadelphia, Detroit, San Francisco–Oakland, and Washington, D.C.

The division of metropolitan areas into the central city (where much of the money is earned) and the suburbs (where much of it is spent) has created the recent dilemma known as "the crisis of the cities." Many solutions have

In this aerial view we seem to see a large city bisected by a river. Wrong: we are looking at several cities (spanning two states). In the foreground is Manhattan. Across the Hudson River are Jersey City, Bayonne, and Hoboken, divided by invisible boundaries. To refer to this (and hundreds of square miles not shown) as the Greater New York Metropolitan Area gives a false sense of unity. There is only a tenuous political affiliation among these many urban centers. Prevailing winds inflict much of New Jersey's pollution problem on New Yorkers, but New York has no legal jurisdiction over the polluters. Taxes and commuter transit are two more areas in which people affected can exercise little or no control over conditions affecting them.

been proposed but few have been tried, chiefly for lack of cooperation from the suburbs. The arrangement, at least in the short term, favors the suburbs, and they are not about to share their wealth with the cities voluntarily.

Ultimately some workable solution will have to be found, however, or both city and suburb are seriously threatened. The central cities may decay to the point where they fail to serve even the self-interest and needs of the suburbanite.

In *The Unheavenly City,* Edward Banfield presented these two contrary views of the city today:

That we face an urban crisis of utmost seriousness has in recent years come to be part of the conventional wisdom. We are told on all sides that the cities are uninhabitable, that they must be torn down and rebuilt or new ones must be built from the ground up, that something drastic must be done—and soon—or else.

On the face of it this "crisis" view has a certain plausibility. One need not walk more than a few blocks in any city to see much that is wrong and in crying need of improvement. It is anomalous that in a society as technologically advanced and as affluent as ours there should be many square miles of slums and even more miles of dreary blight and chaotic sprawl. And when one considers that as many as 60 million more people may live in metropolitan areas in 1980 than lived there in 1960, it seems clear that unless something drastic is done things are bound to get worse.

There is, however, another side to the matter. The plain fact is that the overwhelming majority of city dwellers live more comfortably and conveniently than ever before. They have more and better housing, more and better schools, more and better transportation, and so on. By any conceivable measure of material welfare the present generation of urban Americans is, on the whole, better off than any other large group of people has ever been anywhere. What is more, there is every reason to expect that the general level of comfort and convenience will continue to rise at an even more rapid rate through the foreseeable future.[25]

Evaluate Banfield's positive description. Are the factors he lists as "plain fact" true—in every city and for everyone in a city? Operationalize several of the details he lists, and draw up a plan of study for testing his assertions in your own or a nearby city. (For example, how would you measure the improvement in quality of transportation services and schools?)

[25]Edward C. Banfield, *The Unheavenly City* (Boston: Little, Brown, 1970), pp. 3–4.

FUTURE SETTLEMENTS IN A MASS SOCIETY

As we've seen, the enduring problems of the inner cities and the shortcomings of the urban–suburban balance have created great frustrations. Some people have coped by fleeing the metropolitan areas entirely, going "back to the land" to escape the rat race of modern living. In a mass society like ours, however, such a solution is beyond the reach of most people. We congregate where the jobs are, and few jobs are to be found outside the metropolitan areas.

Realistic solutions to the metropolitan dilemma must deal with the inevitability of cities and seek to reduce their problems while expanding their advantages. Urban planners, sociologists, other social scientists, and government agencies have been sources of proposals on how to do this in recent years. Some are short-term solutions, such as giving an entire metropolitan area a unified government to ensure fairer distribution of political authority and tax money. Other solutions are long term, such as redistributing much of our population in numerous planned cities of lower density and smaller size than our present swollen metropolitan areas. These and other proposals face immense obstacles.

Local Independence or Regional Cooperation?

What are the reactions of suburbanites to the possibility of an influx of poorer residents from the city?

Citizens in the suburb of Midvale, northeast of Central City, are concerned about a developer's proposal to build a 100-unit apartment complex for low- and middle-income families. The town planning board is wrestling with the issue. Many people fear that education, welfare, and other costs would far exceed any taxes that the new complex would pay. Others say that they just don't want low-income families from Central City as neighbors.

Some people in Midvale urge approval of the project, usually because they have friends or relatives who need moderate-cost housing, and a few because they believe the town has a moral responsibility to give low-income people a chance for decent housing. They say that crowding the poor into the cities hurts the whole region.

1. Where would you stand on this issue, if it faced your community or neighborhood? Why?

2. Role-play a hearing by the town planning board. The board must take action on the developer's application for a building permit. Have class members take the roles of board members, the developer, and citizens for and against the project.

Many communities in the United States regulate land use by means of zoning. A master plan designates certain areas to be used for businesses, others for industry, others for single-family homes, and others for multiple-family dwellings. Some suburban towns limit new housing to expensive dwellings on lots of a half acre or more. This has the effect of keeping out all but upper-income families.

Subjects for regional action. Few local governments initiate projects and programs that might benefit an entire urban area. There are many programs that could be beneficial in an urban area but are frequently viewed as undesirable by individual communities. Some recent ones that have been debated include a proposal that low-income housing be scattered throughout the cities and towns of a metropolitan area rather than being concentrated in the central city. Another proposal sought to make the public schools of a metropolitan area truly integrated by busing some minority students out of the central city into the suburbs. Reverse busing—from suburbs to city schools—has also been suggested. A less controversial proposal called for regional public transit systems, subsidized by all the towns and cities in a metropolitan area, to reduce traffic congestion in and around the central city. Regional waste-disposal systems have also been proposed to handle wastes more economically.

Models of regional governance. Today our metropolitan areas typically have ten or twenty separate local governments—and some have more than a hundred. Getting agreement among them to handle a regional problem may be close to impossible. Several ways of furthering cooperation have been tried.

For example, a few places have a combined city-county government. Another model is the *special-district* approach, in which a regional agency is created to handle a specific problem or set of problems. A group of cities and towns may join forces in setting up a sanitation district to handle waste disposal. The Port of New York Authority handles numerous transportation facilities (harbors, bridges, airports, bus depots) around New York City and northern New Jersey.

Under the *metropolitan federation* approach, local governments in an area turn over some activities and powers to a central council, while they continue to handle others locally. Toronto in Canada and Miami-Dade County in Florida use this system. Several other places have tried to install federations, but they were turned down by voters or ran into other difficulties.

Most of the efforts at regional cooperation have been aimed at setting up special regional authorities (special districts) to handle single activities (such as sanitation) or groups of related activities (such as roads, bridges, tran-

The Thirteen Major Strip Cities in the United States

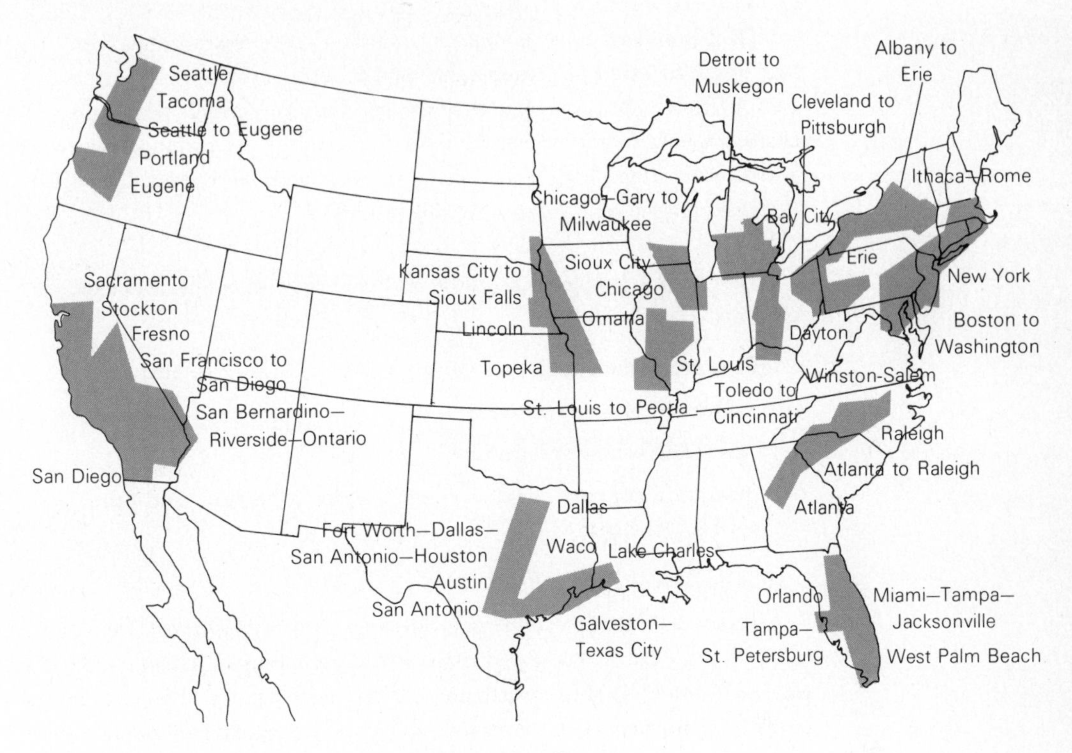

Source: United States Department of Commerce, Bureau of the Census.

sit, and harbors). Other efforts have been made to consolidate or federate the governments of a single county. However, many of our urban areas extend across county and state lines, making this solution inadequate.

Megalopolis. To further complicate the problem, many metropolitan areas virtually merge together. The great urban region from Portland, Maine, to south of Washington, D.C., is sometimes called a *megalopolis,* or giant city. Another term is *strip city.* One strip extends from north of San Francisco down the California coast to Mexico. Another, around the Great Lakes, includes Milwaukee, Chicago, South Bend, Fort Wayne, Toledo, Detroit, Cleveland, and Buffalo. Still another runs from Jacksonville almost to Key West on the eastern coast of Florida. Some European and Asian cities have formed similar patterns, for example in the Ruhr Valley in Germany, on the southwest coast of Sweden, and on the east coast of Japan from north of Tokyo to south of Kobe.

If it is difficult to get cooperation within a single metropolitan area, think of the challenge of getting a thousand or more separate governments to coordinate their efforts on common problems. On some matters people do achieve a unified effort through the federal government. In pollution control, for example, national and regional standards have been worked out. Federal grants encouraged localities to solve this problem.

1. What urban problems seem to require regional cooperation for solution?

2. What are some conflicting values on the following issues:

scattered low-cost housing

areawide school integration

areawide support of mass transit, waste collection, and other public services?

Revitalized Inner Cities

By the mid-1970s the spread of suburbia appeared to have slowed. The cost of a new single-family house had risen beyond the means of most people in search of housing. In many places housing developers tended to build duplexes or high-rise apartments rather than single homes. Rising costs of gasoline and fuel oil encouraged some people to move back into cities.

New apartment houses and refurbished neighborhoods in some cities are also drawing some people. By restoring old houses, groups and individuals have brought run-down areas to life once again. They have poured in money. They have organized block communities. The Georgetown section of Washington, Society Hill in Philadelphia, and Pioneer Square in Seattle are a few of many examples.

These changes, although encouraging, do not go far toward solving the overwhelming problems of urban areas. In many inner cities, remodeled middle-class housing simply displaces the poor, who are forced to go elsewhere—usually to even less desirable quarters—in the city. Many city dwellers bitterly equate "urban renewal" with "minority removal."

Meanwhile, in some suburban areas, communities of apartment complexes are growing up as a kind of compromise between city and suburban living. They often have restaurants and shops, and some have recreational and religious centers: they are towns within towns. But, again, unless population

Plan of Columbia, Maryland

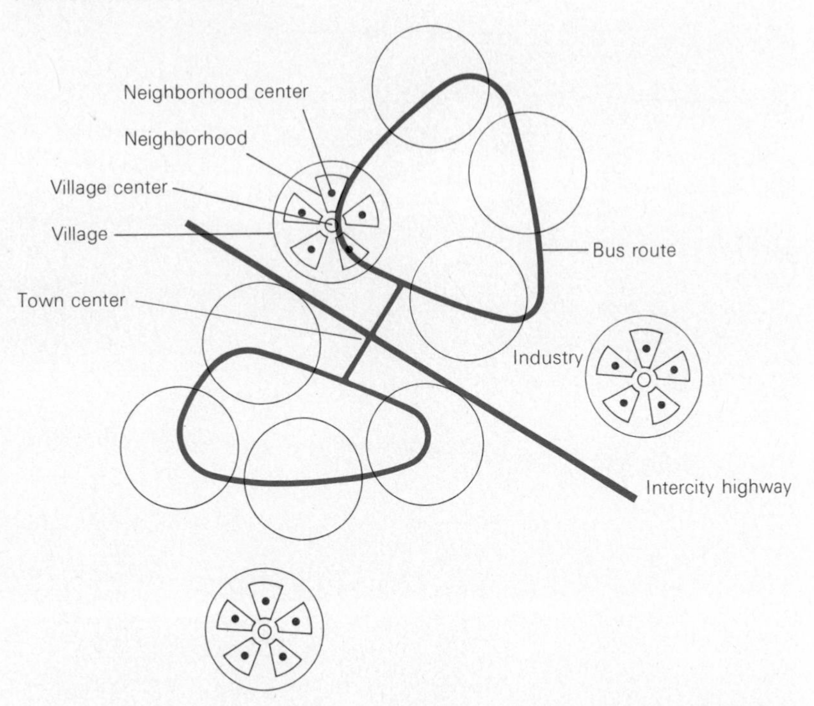

Source: *Society Today*, 2d ed. (Del Mar, Calif.: CRM Books, 1973), p. 409. © 1973 by Communications Research Machines, Inc. Reprinted by permission of CRM Books, a Division of Random House, Inc.

distribution is changed along with population density, no ultimate solution has been approached. The poor and the inner cities must be freed from one another. If these moderate density suburban complexes remain middle-class, the urban–suburban problems are not relieved.

Planned Cities

In several countries around the world, whole new planned cities and towns have been built in the last thirty years. One of the best examples of such a project is Tapiola, located twenty minutes from downtown Helsinki, Finland. It is a planned residential community with apartments at a wide range of prices and rents. It has shopping centers, recreational facilities, parks, woodlands, a lake for all to share, and convenient, inexpensive public transportation to the central city.[26]

[26]For a further description, see Heikki von Hertzen, *Building a New Town: Finland's New Garden City, Tapiola* (Cambridge, Mass.: MIT Press, 1971).

Some of these photographs might seem to be of particularly attractive, affluent suburbs, but this impression is incorrect. All of these photographs are of New Towns or planned communities. What's the difference? Chiefly that the designers of planned communities seek to deal comprehensively with the patterns of interaction essential to meeting social needs. These communities can be seen as attempts to satisfy all four dimensions of Yinger's model of human behavior (discussed in Chapter 1): cultural, structural, psychological, and biological. By their location, the facilities they provide, and the spatial arrangements among the facilities, planned communities try to approximate ideal human settlements.

In the United States several planned cities something like Tapiola have been built, and others are proposed. Two of the best known are Reston, Virginia, and Columbia, Maryland. The master plan for Columbia (as of 1972–73) called for ten "villages," each one divided into five neighborhoods. Each village and neighborhood has its own center. Eight of the villages are served by buses. The other two are for residents who wish to use cars. Industry is set apart from residential areas, and there is open space between villages. Offices, recreational and religious facilities, stores, schools, and industrial firms are located in convenient, appropriate areas throughout the city.

While many Americans are fascinated by the ideas for new cities, they often feel that these efforts do not come to grips with the realities of our society. Enormous amounts of capital are needed to build a new town according to plan—and the investment can be recovered only when the developer has sold or rented the properties.

Suburban developers in the past engaged in some planning. They laid out streets, put up model houses, and sometimes even put restrictions on the kinds of dwellings that could be built. But typically they sold the lots one by one, and built the houses only after financing had been arranged. Schools and other public facilities were generally left to the new residents to finance and build. This approach requires much less capital by developers than building a whole town and then selling or leasing the properties.

Thus, planned cities and towns require large-scale government commitments—in both subsidies for building them and agencies for overseeing them. If the costs of constructing and operating such communities were passed on to the residents they would make living in planned cities too expensive for working-class, lower-class, and even many middle-class families. Their effectiveness as a remedy for urban blight therefore depends on large, continuous government subsidies.

Such solutions are acceptable in other societies, such as those in Finland, Sweden, and England, but they are unpopular in our society. Large-scale government investment in real estate and urban planning is seen by many as unfair competition with private enterprise or as "creeping" socialism. Such fears, plus national and world economic problems in recent years, have prevented meaningful experimentation with planned communities in the United States.

Meanwhile the inner cities continue to deteriorate, and the problems of metropolitan areas continue to grow in number and complexity. Looming energy shortages and present pollution problems, the costliness of mass transit systems and the glut of traffic, the economic contributions of the cities and

The dark towers standing against the sky like dominoes are part of the city of Brazilia, now an acknowledged failure among planned cities. It is spacious and luxurious in design, but it lacks a human scale. Built to be the future capital city of Brazil, it remains virtually uninhabited today, a decade after its conception.

their inadequate operating budgets—all are problems that urgently demand changes in our patterns of human settlement. But our economic values and political attitudes inhibit many possible solutions.

SUMMARY

The city as a human settlement is as ancient as history. Some two hundred years ago, at the dawning of the industrial age, cities began to house masses of people. From their very beginnings, they have shared certain characteristics: they have always been relatively large, dense, and permanent settlements of socially heterogeneous individuals.

Today the majority of our society lives in metropolitan areas (cities and their surrounding areas). Hence, sociology, the study of society, is predominantly the study of urban life. Many sociologists attribute the patterns of social interaction within cities to the size, density, and diversity of urban areas. These patterns of interaction in modern cities often fit Toennie's gesellschaft model of society: impersonal superficial interactions among contractual participants, in which secondary relationships predominate and alienation and anomie are experienced. Some sociologists, however, have found evidence of warm, gemeinschaft communities within city neighborhoods.

Urban ecologists of the Chicago School studied the growth of cities and noted a pattern of change they called urban succession: the replacement of one distinct population group by another in a city area. Since World War II, the rural poor of the United States have flocked to cities in search of jobs and a higher standard of living. At the same time white middle-class city dwellers were moving in droves to the suburbs in search of space, quiet, and a piece of property to call their own. The central cities have become impoverished, as poor residents needing public services increased and middle-class taxpayers decreased.

Modern cities face seemingly insurmountable problems. Their political boundaries give them no power over the middle-class populations who earn their living in the city but live outside it. Some short-term solutions that have been proposed involve redistributing political authority through areawide governmental bodies or special districts to share control and costs of certain services to residents and businesses.

Planned towns and cities are a long-term solution to the urban crisis. They are designed to keep a careful balance among the residential, business, industrial, and recreational functions of an urban area, to provide the best environment for all inhabitants. These cities require vast capital investments, however, that businesses and governments seem unwilling to expend.

14

SOCIAL CHANGE

Human history is the story of change—much of it spectacular, much of it barely discernible. Wars and their aftermaths have wrought immense changes, but so have unimposing devices like the cotton gin and abstruse specialized theories like Keynes's solution to economic depressions. These and an infinite variety of other occurrences have brought social change: changes in a society's structure, in its patterned social relationships and the ways of doing things.

What happens when Vietnamese villagers, tilling their plots, suddenly hear "monsters in the sky"? Two governments, remotely located, have decided that this village is a strategic outpost in their battle for power. Bombs begin to fall. The village is devastated. Those who survive pack their meager belongings, leave the graves of their ancestors, and move out into an unknown world.

What does it mean to people who have lived in a neighborhood all their lives to hear that it is going to be torn down to make room for a new expressway? They gather on streetcorners to talk about the threat. They organize and take their pleas to city hall. But the need to accommodate increasing traffic prevails, the protest fails, and the demolition plans proceed. Residents are dispersed, shops closed, and personal relationships severed.

How do high school graduates react, after observing campus activism from the sidelines for several years, when they come to college only to find that political activism has evaporated? The revolution is over, and students are back to the books. A few campus political organizations struggle for support but cannot stimulate much enthusiasm. "Everything is different now," the would-be leaders say. "It is almost like the silent fifties."

Social life seems to go on because people normally know what to expect from others and know what others expect of them. While this stability is important, it is also true that nothing really stays the same. We grow up, move out, meet new people. In fact, much of our socialization is preparation for new situations and new positions. When this preparation is faulty, it leads to problems of adaptation, as our discussion of aging revealed (see Chapter 10).

Almost every chapter of this book contains accounts of social change.

Social change: significant and enduring alterations of the structure of a society or its cultural characteristics or both.

We have seen how the growth of suburbs and the emergence of metropolitan areas have changed urban life, making new demands on inhabitants. We have also seen how the position of minority groups in the social stratification system of this country has been modified over time.

EXAMPLES OF CHANGE IN MODERN SOCIETIES

Today social change is such a constant element in our lives that people in modern, industrial societies often take it for granted. Let's look at a few recent examples of social change in our society. Then we'll take a closer look at the different sources of social change.

Throughout the text there have been many examples of social change. Think back to the ones you thought were important to you. Why were they important? How do those changes affect you (or don't they)? What were the reasons for the changes? How did they affect other aspects of society or social living (or didn't they)?

Sociologists are most interested in understanding changes that influence existing patterns of social interaction. They are concerned with changes in values, norms, roles, and institutions. In the following three cases, we show people in families, neighborhood groups, and larger communities undergoing changes in some facets of their lives. As you read the descriptions, try to identify the sociological changes that are occurring.

Case 1. A Day-Care Center

Over a hundred parents attended a meeting about beginning a day-care center in Greenacres, a middle-class suburban community. "This surprisingly large turnout shows how much demand there is for new forms of child-care," said one of the organizers in an opening speech. "Twenty years ago very few mothers of young children in Greenacres were working. They were full-time homemakers. The trend for young women to work has been very noticeable in the past few years. There seem to be new ideas in the air. Women now are bus drivers, computer programmers, telephone installers, X-ray technicians, and store managers. We have one mother who drives a taxi, one policewoman, and one woman in our neighborhood running for the state assembly."

A survey of those at the meeting showed that the men as well as the women had changed. Now most of the fathers expected their wives to participate in some activity out of the house. The men also expected to help with housework.

"I never saw my father dry a dish or change a diaper," explained one man, a lawyer with two youngsters. "But I've become quite proficient at vacuuming, dusting, shopping, and taking care of the children. My wife is a chemist. Both of us are busy, so we share housework and child-care. It is a new kind of family life, but we enjoy sharing the work. It brings me closer to my children than my father ever was to his."

Other men echoed these ideas and told how they were developing new family relationships because women no longer spent all of their time doing housework and child-care activities. Now the community wanted to go one step further. It wanted to organize a center where preschool children could have good care and enjoy themselves while parents worked. Several ideas were presented. The one that was most popular was to form a cooperative in which each couple would work four hours a month. A committee began to hunt for a location and to look into state and local licensing regulations.

Among the current student population on any campus are numbers of men and women with small children. These students have decided to begin or continue their studies while fulfilling the responsibilities of parenthood. Seek out two or three of these people. Ask them why they have decided to become students, how they support themselves, what arrangements they have made for the care of their children.

Case 2. The Energy Crisis

The time was early in the year 1974. Mark Stebert was up before sunrise. His usual routine of a morning shower, breakfast, and drive to work had changed. He now had a long wait at the local gas station. Like his neighbors, Stebert knew that he had to buy gas early in the morning or risk going without it.

Adapting to the energy crisis had changed more than his early morning routine. Before the gas shortage, he enjoyed the ride to work for the time it gave him to be alone. Now he was part of a car pool with four neighbors who worked in his plant. The company had assigned the best parking places to cars carrying three or more employees.

Stebert had also decided to trade in his eight-cylinder car for a compact model that would get better gas mileage. He and his wife talked it over and agreed that their big car was simply too hard to maintain now that gas was scarce and expensive. This was a tough decision, because the big car had been a source of pride for the family. They all felt pleased that they could afford one of the most prestigious cars produced in Detroit.

There was a general controversy about whether the energy crisis was real or just created by the oil companies, but the Steberts were convinced that, even if the crisis was a phony this time, in the future there would be a real one. Nearly everyone agreed on that. The Steberts decided they had better begin to change certain of their habits to cut down their consumption of increasingly scarce resources.

The Steberts were not alone in their decisions. A survey by newspaper reporters had found hundreds of families cutting back on heat consumption in their homes, reducing the amount of gasoline they bought, and carefully considering any new purchases of appliances such as air-conditioners and dishwashers. Again and again, reporters heard the same expressions:

Gasoline, electricity, and oil are so expensive that we've had to cut back on their use. We think it's a shame that the utility companies still favor heavy users in the rates they charge. That only encourages energy waste.

We didn't believe there was such a thing as the energy crisis until shortages here began to affect our own daily lives. We don't know if the shortage is real or a trick of the oil companies, but we sure can't find much fuel.

I was lucky. Some workers have lost their jobs because companies have cut back production when the energy crisis accelerated the economic recession. I guess Americans should have seen the problem coming. We've been living as if there were no tomorrow, as if the good things would last forever.

We used to think we were making progress every time we bought a new appliance. Guess that's part of the American dream. Now we feel we are making a move in the right direction when we decide to do without some new gadget.

The government will have to impose rationing to make sure that everyone gets a fair share of the gasoline that is available. Without rationing, the people with plenty of money can go on using as much gas as they want, while the rest of us won't be able to get what we need.

Government rationing of fuel is the wrong way to control consumption. It distorts prices and discourages the oil companies from producing. Besides, there'll be a black market in gasoline anyway. The free enterprise system is the only efficient way to deal with energy problems, the same as for all other problems in the distribution of goods and services.

Energy has become a driving force in our society. The oil embargo of 1973 illustrated how important oil is to the maintenance of a mechanized way of life.

Assume for a moment that our nation's overseas sources of oil were stopped, and we could rely on only the sources we have within our own boundaries. What types of controls would be placed on Americans? What effect would the restrictions have on our patterns of interaction, our consumption patterns, our way of life?

Establish a list of priorities among users for the allocation of fuel. Defend your rankings.

Case 3. School Desegregation

The question of equality among the races had been a central issue of American life for generations. In 1954, the Supreme Court ruled in *Brown* v. *Board of Education* that the existence of separate schools meant that black children were receiving an inferior education. The Court ordered school boards to develop plans to end the segregation of black and white children.

The Supreme Court decision meant a major change in the southern and border states. Although black and white children had played together and often had much closer contact there than in other parts of the country, their social interactions would now take place in a very different setting. Children of both races were now, ideally, to be educated in the same manner and given equal opportunities to become qualified for desirable positions as adults.

There were important changes in the educational institutions in states that had maintained segregated schools. Many deeply held values were challenged as black children entered formerly all-white schools. New roles resulted for students, teachers, and administrators. The norms and values of institutional racism were now rendered invalid by the courts. Many whites had to either change their beliefs or behave in ways that were contrary to those beliefs. In many parts of the South, desegregation met with massive resistance, much of it violent. Subsequently, resistance occurred in the North as school desegregation became a nationwide phenomenon.

Robert Coles, a psychiatrist and social scientist, spent many years studying the people involved in the struggle to integrate the public schools. He studied the black children who first entered desegregated schools and often had to be escorted by their parents or federal marshals through hostile white crowds. Coles also studied the white parents who boycotted the schools, refusing to allow their children to learn with blacks. These parents set up privately funded schools in many places to maintain segregated education. Coles recorded the fears of the whites and their determination to resist change.

Cole's account of the struggle to integrate the schools emphasized the courage of the black children and sympathetic southern whites in changing social patterns that had existed for generations. Many black adults had seen their own dreams destroyed by the barrier of racial discrimination. They were often willing to risk their jobs and even the safety of their children to break that barrier. The federal government backed their efforts with federal marshals and sometimes the National Guard. Black and white civil rights workers from all over the country also participated in their fight.[1]

In each of the three cases above, what changes in values, role interactions, and institutions occurred? What were the underlying causes of these changes? Can you spell out the precise nature of the resistance to the changes described? If these are not presented in the statements, what resistance would you predict might arise and from whom?

[1]See Robert Coles, *The South Goes North* (Boston: Little, Brown, 1971), pp. 421–535; id., *Children of Crisis* (Boston: Little, Brown, 1967).

COMPONENTS OF SOCIAL CHANGE

As individuals, we each have our own attitudes and personal values. These often change over time. So do those that characterize our society. For example, a study of attitudes toward the sensitive issue of voluntary male and female sterilization shows an increased acceptance of this form of contraception.

APPROVAL OF MALE AND FEMALE STERILIZATION, 1965 AND 1970

	Approving Male Sterilization		*Approving Female Sterilization*	
Category	*1965*	*1970*	*1965*	*1970*
Total	34%	52%	37%	54%
Race				
White	34	54	37	55
Black	30	34	39	46
Education				
Under 12 years	32	43	37	48
12 years	34	52	36	54
College	36	62	43	61
Religion among whites				
Non-Catholic	42	59	44	60
Mixed Catholic	24	47	32	49
Both Catholic	17	40	20	39

Source: Larry L. Bumpass/Harriet B. Presser, "The Increasing Acceptance of Sterilization and Abortion" in *Toward the End of Growth: Population in America*, Charles F. Westoff ed., © 1973, pp. 33–46. Adapted by permission of Prentice-Hall, Inc., Englewood Cliffs, New Jersey.

From the table, let's examine the exact nature of the change between 1965 and 1970. Which categories of people changed their views most in the five-year period? Who were most favorable to male and female sterilization in 1970? Who were least favorable? Can you formulate any hypotheses explaining the attitude changes of these groups? What norms and role relationships might be affected by these changes?

Until recently Americans rarely challenged the values that women should manage the home, should be in charge of child-care, and should support their husbands' career advancement. A norm that reflected these values was that even most working women remained in charge of household and child-care arrangements. One study showed, for example, that future professional men wanted an educated wife but not one whose career would interfere with her home responsibilities.[2]

[2]Cynthia F. Epstein, *Woman's Place, Options and Limits in Professional Careers.* (Berkeley: University of California Press, 1971), pp. 100–101, 116.

In the last several years, under the influence of the feminist movement, some women have asserted that they should be able to combine marriage and careers more effectively. Thus far, although husbands have taken a greater role in child-care and housekeeping and do feel pride in their wives' accomplishments, studies conducted on two-career families nevertheless reveal that the wife's career continues to be highly dependent on active support from the husband.

Despite some role changes on the husbands' part, very few of the families studied were truly equalitarian—with both sexes sharing family duties uniformly. Rather, many women pursuing careers continued to accommodate their work lives to family responsibilities and to define their family obligations as primary. These women often worked part-time when their children were young. They felt they could become totally involved in their professions only "at the expense" of their families. At the same time, these women defined their new situation as a positive one. They believed they were better mothers because they worked and had outside interests.[3]

Despite these research findings, there are also signs of more radical changes in traditional family life. For example, some innovative two-career families have worked out elaborate commuting arrangements or communal child-care and living arrangements. No systematic study of these pioneering arrangements has yet been made to reveal whether the marital relationships are truly equalitarian and what changes result from the new arrangements.

Our society's definitions of the appropriate roles for married women are changing. Some families are adopting an equalitarian value system that is substantially different from the values of traditional American families. In most families, however, many traditional norms and values about the mother's obligations still have salience. Thus new norms coexist with established ones in thousands of two-career families attempting to answer the challenges created by changing values and roles.

Similarly, as black people in the South fought to achieve integrated schools and other civil rights, they also engaged in a new set of role relationships with whites. Blacks have stopped behaving submissively in their dealings with whites. Black leaders have taken complaints against whites into court.

[3]See Margaret M. Paloma, "Role Conflict and the Married Professional Woman," in *Toward a Sociology of Women,* ed. Constantina Safilios-Rothschild (Lexington, Mass.: Xerox College Publishing, 1972), pp. 187–98. See also Lynda Lytle Holmstrom, *The Two-Career Family* (Cambridge, Mass.: Schenkman, 1973). For a British study, see Rhona Rapaport and Robert N. Rapaport, *Dual-Career Families* (Harmondsworth, England: Penguin Books, 1971).

Blacks have begun to play active political roles in their communities for the first time.

When values, norms, and roles undergo change, so do social institutions. For example, changes in educational philosophy have made many American schools considerably different from those of a generation or two ago. Some elementary schools have more individualized programs than they used to. In such schools, not all the students in a class are working on the same lesson at once, as happened in traditional classes. Each student works on his or her own program in reading, mathematics, social studies, and the like. Teachers and aides serve as resource people and consultants, offering information and advice as individual students require them. Formal instruction is given to the class as a group only occasionally. Such programs are intended to give children a chance to develop their independence. Instead of forcing each student to keep up with—or hold back to—the pace of everyone else, each finds a comfortable rate of progress.

Technology has provided society with effective methods of birth control that are being used by more and more young women and men. How has this brought social changes to the following institutions:

economic

religious

educational

family

political

What institutions are affected most by effective family planning and a declining birth rate?

GENERATORS OF SOCIAL CHANGE

Change is rarely isolated. Change produced in one element of society by a new idea, invention, or discovery or by a new set of values can produce change in other aspects of the social system. Remember, for example, the series of changes in the family that we noted in Chapter 6 as results flowing from the industrial revolution. Among other variables, the urbanization of industrial societies and the development of consumer economies reduced the extended family to the nuclear family and then reduced the average number of children in the nuclear family. Because social change is so far-reaching and complex, it is useful to break down its causes into several major categories.

Environmental Change

The way of life in any society is bound to be affected by the society's natural habitat. Soil characteristics, water supply, landforms (mountains, plains, and so on), climate, natural resources, and other ecological features have a direct effect on a society's economic institutions in particular—how the people make a living. Let's see what might happen if the natural habitat were to undergo a swift, dramatic change.

A small Mexican village subsists economically on the farming of corn. Most of the people live a simple peasant life. Then a nearby, long-dormant volcano suddenly erupts and makes the villagers' land useless for farming. The spectacular display soon brings many tourists. Former peasants now provide services to tourists, set up inns, and start making and selling crafts. They learn some English, earn some cash. Many townspeople, influenced by visitors from Mexican cities and the United States, begin to wear clothing very different from their traditional garb. Their new life-styles continue for a few years until the volcano stops erupting. Then the tourists no longer visit, but the land is still not fit for farming. The villagers are forced to adjust to a new and devastating poverty. Young people leave the village to seek work in the cities. Old-timers pick up any work they can find, chiefly continuing to make craft articles for sale in other tourist areas.

Just as a natural disaster may produce dramatic social change, so may the discovery of a natural resource. A rich mining strike or the discovery of oil and natural gas has often had remarkable effects on a society. Think of the changes occurring in the oil-rich nations of the Middle East and North Africa. Because of the heavy dependence of the industrial West on their natural resources, various countries that used to be small and underdeveloped now have new, immense economic and political power.

Change in the natural environment may also occur slowly and still have far-reaching effects. The change may be brought by human actions or natural events. Land may be torn up by strip-mining or worn down by harmful farming practices or by drought. Erosion may slowly wash away rich farming lands, leaving dust bowls. These developments that slowly impoverish the land impose hardship on the people and cause mass migrations, as happened in the southern United States in the 1930s and is happening in sub-Saharan Africa in the 1970s. Air and water pollution and shortage of fuels and other materials may become severe enough to trigger new norms and laws on how producers and consumers may use resources and dispose of waste.

1. In addition to antipollution laws, what social changes have been created in our society because of damage we have done to the natural environment?

2. Have you ever lived in a place that was hit by a natural disaster? See if you can talk to someone who has had such an experience. What social changes occurred? Which changes were short-term adjustments? Which were longer lasting?

Population Growth

Demography: the study of population and the interrelationships between population changes and social structures.

Major growth or decline of the population of a society is likely to generate other social changes. The population size of any region or nation depends on the birth rate, the death rate, and the rate of movement in or out of the area. Slow rises or declines in population have a slight immediate impact on social institutions. But population growth in recent decades has been what social demographers call explosive. Demographers are social scientists who study population size, its growth or decline, and the social causes and consequences of size changes. For example, demographers see the truly alarming population rise in some nations as resulting mainly from sharply reduced infant and child mortality rates while birth rates remain unchanged. People in such countries as India have as many babies as earlier generations did but fewer children die at birth or in early childhood.

A rapid rise in population puts new demands on a society's economic and political institutions. More of everything is needed: food, clothing, housing, schools, hospitals, government agencies. Peasants in many parts of the world have been able for years to grow barely enough food for themselves on small plots of land. Population growth in these areas creates enormous pressure for change. Families need to produce more to feed the larger number of surviving children. Some of the wealthier farmers turn to technology—machinery, fertilizers, insecticides—to increase the productivity of their crowded land.

POPULATION GROWTH AND DOUBLING TIME BY COUNTRY

Country	*Annual Percentage Rate of Growth*	*Number of Years for Population to Double*
Developed countries		
Australia	2.0	35
Canada	1.6	44
Czechoslovakia	0.5	140
France	0.9	78
Israel	2.9	24
Japan	1.1	64
Union of Soviet Socialist Republics	1.1	64
United Kingdom	0.6	117
United States	1.2	58
West Germany	1.0	70
Less-developed countries		
Algeria	3.0	23
Brazil	3.0	23
Chad	1.5	47
China (mainland)	1.4	50
India	2.5	28
Kenya	2.0	35
Pakistan	2.1	33
Peru	3.1	23
United Arab Republic	2.5	28
Venezuela	3.5	20

Source: *Encyclopedia of Sociology* (Guilford, Conn.: Dushkin Publishing Group, 1974), p. 217.

Other, poorer peasants turn for the first time to regional cities and towns for employment or for markets to sell their surplus produce.

If this process of change is successful, population growth can produce a rise in the standard of living. If productive resources are so strained that they cannot accommodate the rapidly rising population, this can cause a decline in the standard of living. What promotes population growth, and what factors determine whether beneficial or harmful social changes will follow from it?

Often, marked population growth has been the result of modern medical and agricultural technology brought into a country by a colonial administration. Improved medical care and food consumption reduce the death rates. However, if social patterns are not open to change, misery can follow this initial improvement. If religious beliefs, political values, and the distribution of land and wealth remain unchanged, the society may not be able to cope

India has always been a populous nation, but in recent generations its overpopulation has been a source of perpetual crisis for government leaders and most Indians. In some cities thousands have no home but the streets.

with its population growth. Periodic famines and constant hardship in both cities and rural areas may result, as we have seen in recent decades in India.

The Indian dilemma makes a sharp contrast with developments in the People's Republic of China in the last twenty-five years. There, drastic changes in all the social patterns of interaction—economic, political, religious, educational, and family—have enabled the world's largest population to erase starvation and malnutrition.

Whether or not an area can support a sharp rise in population, the rise will affect the natural environment. It will create faster use of resources, more waste to get rid of, and less open space.[4] And we saw earlier in this chapter how changes in the natural environment bring about social changes.

[4]See Paul R. Ehrlich, *The Population Bomb* (New York: Ballantine, 1971).

In the People's Republic of China, the communist ascent to power in 1949 was followed by sweeping social change. Among many broad programs was one for controlling family size. This has helped improve the general standard of living among the populace.

1. At present rates of growth some countries will double in size in about thirty-five years. What are some likely effects if such growth continues?

2. Assume that leaders in a rapidly growing country foresee the problems of growth. What social and cultural forces would have to be overcome to bring about the changes needed to deal with these difficulties?

3. For about twenty years after World War II the American population grew rapidly; then growth slowed down. Name some social changes that resulted *in part* from this rise and decline in the birth rate.

Migration

We are properly called a nation of immigrants. Native Americans make up a tiny percentage of our present population. Immigration and internal migration (the westward movement, the movement from farms to cities, the movement from cities to suburbs) have had profound effects on American society. The migration of large numbers of people into or within any society produces social change.[5]

Immigration provided a mighty stimulus to American economic development. Blacks from Africa and the West Indies, brought here as unwilling immigrants, and farmers from Europe, willing immigrants, were the chief sources of labor for American agriculture. To a large extent immigrant labor built the railroads, mined the coal, and operated the factory machinery in this nation's industrial revolution.

Immigrants not only contributed their energy and skills but also enriched American culture. Americans whose ancestors had arrived earlier sometimes worried about the impact of alien values and norms brought by later waves of immigrants. Organizations to help integrate the immigrants into American life became common. The purpose of these groups was to safeguard "American" culture by teaching it quickly to the newcomers—before they could influence it with their own. Nevertheless, important changes occurred as people with quite different values, norms, and institutions mingled and eventually intermarried.[6]

The United States was also characterized by much internal movement. Two migration patterns have had a particularly strong impact on social change in recent years: southern blacks in large numbers have moved to northern cities, and whites in large numbers have moved to the suburbs. With these twin movements have come many other changes in American life. For example, urban blacks took the lead in the civil rights revolution of the 1960s. Black mayors won elections in several large northern cities and some southern towns and cities as well. Congress authorized new agencies to serve the urban poor.

Meanwhile, stores, factories, and offices tended to move to the urban fringe. Commuting became a way of life for suburban residents. Working people often had to allow more than an hour for travel to their jobs. Some observers contend that the suburbanite was more friendly with neighbors, more community-minded, and more politically active than the typical city resident. In the suburbs the white middle class came close to isolating itself from other social classes and ethnic minorities. We saw in Chapters 8 and 13 the social

[5]See, for example, Oscar Handlin, *The Uprooted* (New York: Grosset and Dunlap, 1951); id., *The Newcomers* (Garden City, N.Y.: Doubleday, 1962); John F. Kennedy, *A Nation of Immigrants* (New York: Popular Library, 1964).

[6]See Horace M. Kallen, *Culture and Democracy in the United States: Studies in Group Psychology of the American Peoples* (New York: Boni and Liveright, 1924).

changes that have followed from the urbanization of minorities and the suburbanization of much of the white middle class.

We must be careful, of course, not to think that one kind of change (internal migration) was solely responsible for these social changes. Most social change results from a variety of factors. Nevertheless, population movement has a profound influence on it.

Technology

Some sociologists believe that technology is the single most important source of social change. In the middle of the eighteenth century technological progress occurred so rapidly that the changes have been called an industrial revolution. In England and the United States, which were both in the forefront of the revolution, the number of people working in agriculture dropped, and the number employed in factories rose. Thus, the economic institutions underwent major changes. Since most factories were located in the cities, large numbers of people moved there from the country in search of employment. They found different housing arrangements and were confronted by new environmental problems. For many people, rural poverty was replaced by urban misery.[7]

Since then, new products, new methods of production, and new means of distribution have emerged as the fruits of technology. Think of the impact on social behavior of such inventions as telephones, penicillin, television, automobiles, tractors, and railroads.

1. Ask ten people of your parents' generation to name the three inventions that they think brought the greatest social change to the United States in the twentieth century. What impact do they think these changes had on their own lives and on social life in general? Compare the results. Is there a measure of social consensus among the respondents?

2. In your own lifetime you have seen many social changes. Think back over some of these changes. Which ones stand out in your mind? Why? What particular significance did they have on your life, the lives of your friends, your nation, or the world?

[7]See, for example, W. Fred Cottrell, "Death by Dieselization, a Case Study in the Reaction to Technological Change," *American Sociological Review* 16 (June 1951): 358–65.

Despite the efforts of some to keep our society "English"—dominated by the culture of the British colonists—a constant influx of people from various other nations of the world has given our society a pluralist character.

Technological changes have both positive and negative consequences. The automobile and the airplane speed up travel so that we can visit relatives and friends who live far away, send a letter in a matter of days, have food and other products flown in from all over the world, and participate in foreign travel and commerce. The telephone enables us to speak directly to people on

Technological innovation has been a major source *of social change and, like all sources of change, also a* product *of change. The conversion of nomadic peoples to settled farmers was the first major social change. The earliest cities were possible only because improved farming methods yielded surpluses to feed city inhabitants. The cities, in turn, stimulated further innovation by centralizing and encouraging crafts and trade. The effects of these are seen in modern-day farming throughout the world, where machinery vastly improves human efficiency.*

the other side of the nation or even the globe. Similarly, medical technology has drastically reduced mortality rates throughout much of the world and has wiped out many deadly diseases in advanced societies. In these and many other ways technology has increased our freedom of action.

But jet planes and cars have also been the cause of serious pollution, thousands of injuries and deaths, energy shortages, and the blight of freeway and highway networks. The medical advances that keep more people alive today are a major cause of overpopulation problems in Third World countries, where birth rates remain unchanged. At the same time cancer and various heart conditions are on the rise, leading many to suspect that they are by-products of advanced technology.

Social changes that follow technological advances can have a serious economic impact. In the last hundred years economic power in the marketplace has increasingly been concentrated in large corporations. Frequently they were the only organizations that could afford the massive investments for machinery required by the new technology. The inability to raise the needed capital often drove competitors out of business, leaving the market to the unchallenged control of a few large corporations. In recent years many of these organizations have grown to such size and power that they extend beyond national boundaries. Multinationals, as they are called, often meddle in the relations between countries or within them as a way of protecting or furthering their own commercial interests. The attempt of ITT to prevent the Marxist Salvador Allende from assuming the presidency of Chile in 1970 is but one instance of such interference.[8]

Some sociologists believe technological developments produce major social tensions because they inevitably result in cultural lag. William Ogburn, who coined the term *cultural lag,* wrote: "A cultural lag occurs when one of two parts of culture which are correlated changes before or in a greater degree than the other part does, thereby causing less adjustment between the two parts than existed previously."[9] For

[8]See, for example, Richard J. Barnet and Ronald E. Muller, *Global Reach: The Power of the Multinational Corporations* (New York: Simon and Schuster, 1975); United States Senate, Committee on Foreign Relations, Subcommittee on Multinational Corporations, *Hearings: Multinational Corporations and United States Foreign Policy,* Parts I and II, *The International Telephone and Telegraph Company and Chile, 1970–71* (Washington, D.C.: U.S. Government Printing Office, 1973).

[9]William F. Ogburn, "Cultural Lag as Theory," *Sociology and Social Research* 41 (1957): 167.

example, our society has produced extensive equipment for industrial production, but it has not yet developed the social commitment to prevent these industrial plants from polluting our water supplies.

1. Describe in detail several other examples of cultural lag that exist today.

2. Atomic energy has been available for the past thirty years, because of modern technology. Is there cultural lag in our society's adjustment to its use?

3. Some institutions respond more quickly to change than do others. Which major institutions respond most quickly to change in other sectors of society? Think, for example, of the family and such representative components of the political institution as the courts, the prisons, the military, local government, and state government.

Theories that Challenge Contemporary Beliefs

Theories about how to make work easier and life more comfortable bring about technological change that causes social change. But other kinds of theories are powerful sources of social change too. Down through the ages many of the arguments of religious prophets, philosophers, natural scientists, and social scientists have had profound effects on values and behavior.

Charles Darwin's investigations of evolution—how animal species adapt over long periods of time to changes in the environment—led to new theories on the origins of life. His views clashed with the biblical account of the creation of the earth and humanity. The religious faith of many people was shaken by Darwin's theories. Established religions have since accommodated their teachings to the findings that followed from Darwin's work.[10]

Sigmund Freud's research generated theories about the nature and development of the personality. Initially his ideas influenced the treatment of people with severe emotional problems. His writings have also affected the child-rearing and educational practices of many people. His reports on the healing effect of bringing hidden thoughts into the open promoted new

[10]See Charles Darwin, *Charles Darwin's Autobiography*, ed. Francis Darwin (New York: Schuman, 1950); id., *The Origin of Species* (New York: Modern Library, 1953); David L. Hull, *Darwin and His Critics* (Cambridge: Harvard University Press, 1973).

attitudes and values about sexual behavior.[11]

Social scientists' research and writings have also challenged old values and resulted in social change. Until two generations ago, for example, economists and political leaders believed that a national government should not spend more than it collected in taxes, except in such emergencies as wars. In other words, they contended that the national budget should be balanced each year. This time-honored judgment was challenged in the 1930s by a British economist, John Maynard Keynes.[12] He argued that government could do a great deal to prevent serious business depressions by spending more than it collected when business was sluggish. On the other hand a vigorous business boom that threatened to cause inflation could be slowed down by collecting more and spending less. This idea had in fact been put into practice by the Franklin Roosevelt administrations during the Great Depression, but it did not win wide public acceptance until the 1960s.

While Keynes's theories were encouraging deficit spending and increased government involvement in the economy, our social patterns of consumption were also changing. Once we considered it foolhardy to buy things we could not afford to pay for in full. Today most people borrow money not only to buy houses but also to buy cars, appliances, clothes, and smaller items. Many of us use credit cards habitually, always spending before earning. If we were to return to our old values ("Neither a borrower nor a lender be," in Shakespeare's words), the economy would suffer a severe blow.

Research by social scientists also played a part in the historic 1954 Supreme Court school desegregation decision. Until this decision the courts had ruled that the requirements of equality were adequately met through social arrangements that were "separate but equal." As long as members of each race attended schools or used public facilities that were equally funded and maintained, then segregation of the races was not in violation of the United States Constitution. So the courts had reasoned. But, in the 1954 case, psychologists and sociologists reported evidence to the Court on the effects of racial segregation on children's self-concepts and learning. In the Court's unanimous opinion, Chief Justice Earl Warren wrote that segregated education was inherently unequal and harmed black children. The decision noted that, even if

[11]See, for example, Bartlett H. Stoodley, *The Concepts of Sigmund Freud* (Glencoe, Ill.: Free Press, 1959); Sigmund Freud, *The Standard Edition of the Complete Psychological Works of Sigmund Freud* (London: Hogarth Press, 1953–74).

[12]John Maynard Keynes, *The Collected Writings of John Maynard Keynes* (London: Macmillan, 1971).

Today labor unions are an established part of our social landscape, but generations ago organizers were hated and feared—virtually outlaws. Here strikers against a Philadelphia railroad car manufacturer, in 1919, are attacked by police. The philosophy of Social Darwinism, though not known by name to most people, governed the thinking of those in power. Many believed that allowing workers to organize and bargain collectively would damage society by upsetting the "natural" balance of power in which survival of the fittest occurred. A more equalitarian ideology motivated workers to seek power through force of numbers. Thus, conflict among ideologies often characterizes social change.

separate facilities were in fact equal in every respect, the evidence showed that the fact of segregation was psychologically and socially damaging and therefore submitted the ostracized race to unequal treatment.[13]

Ideology

Darwin's theory of evolution, as we saw, challenged the biblical description of

[13]See Albert P. Blaustein and Clarence Clyde Ferguson, Jr., eds., *Desegregation and the Law,* 2d ed. (New York: Vintage, 1962), especially Chap. 9.

creation and the special status of humans in the scheme of things. Because of this, it was disturbing to churchmen and religious believers. However, some people in nineteenth-century industrial societies enthusiastically embraced Darwin's theory that the process of evolution depended on "the survival of the fittest." In any natural environment, Darwin argued, the strong survived and the weak perished. Thus, the species transmitted only those traits most favorable to its survival.

In the United States and England in the late nineteenth century, a powerful movement, Social Darwinism, applied this theory to human affairs. Supporters of Social Darwinism warned that the human species would maintain its vigor only by following the principle of survival of the fittest without interference. In business, this principle was used to support the growth of monopolies and trusts. Government control of business activities and the formation of labor unions were denounced as interference with the natural course of events.

Ideology: a set of beliefs and related values that justify social conditions or that provide a unified criticism of those conditions and justify opposition to them in favor of other, stated goals (discussed further in Chapter 15).

Thus, a scientific theory that had been tested empirically was translated into an ideology—a set of beliefs and values that serve to justify certain political, social, and class interests. The ideology spells out the norms of conduct for the various groups. In the above example, the norms had to do with how industrialists could run their businesses and how workers could and could not behave. If the workers were allowed to organize into unions and engage in strikes, collective bargaining, and other means of exerting their will, the weak would have power to hamper the strong. This, said the Social Darwinists, would impair survival of the fittest, the condition for improvement of the human species. In essence, the Social Darwinists developed an entire system of belief to bring meaning to social life and to provide the rationale for the stratification system of that time.[14]

Social Darwinism is only one of many ideologies that have assumed importance in the modern world. Karl Marx, an early conflict theorist, as we noted, has had probably the broadest impact on social change in this century. His ideas about capitalism and its effect on social life have served as the underpinning for most socialist ideologies. Without greatly oversimplifying, we can divide the world today into those nations that have embraced and applied his ideas about history, economics, and politics, and those that have rejected them. The cold war, which dominated international relations for more than a decade following World War II, divided nations along this ideological differ-

[14]See Richard Hofstadter, *Social Darwinism in American Thought* (Boston: Beacon, 1955); Charles Page, *Class and American Sociology: From Ward to Ross* (New York: Dial, 1940); R. J. Wilson, *In Quest of Community, 1860–1920* (New York: Wiley, 1968).

ence. In the West it was common to say the struggle was between the free world and the communist powers; communist nations said it was between people's republics and imperialistic, capitalistic powers.[15]

The adherence of Americans to electoral politics and representative democracy depends on our belief in democratic principles such as equality. Likewise, our capitalist economic system rests on the belief that society benefits most from private ownership of property and of the means of production.

Ideologies are also the cornerstone of stability, usually to the detriment of change. The predominant norms in a society are supported by a set of beliefs and values that are persuasive for most members of that society. Ideology is a source of social change only when one set of beliefs and values replaces or modifies another. This produces a change in the predominant norms. We see a little later in this chapter why such changes can occur and why they often do not.

Cultural Diffusion

Cultural diffusion: the (voluntary or involuntary) adoption of traits from one culture by another culture.

It's common to hear people say that modern technology has shrunk the globe. Jet air transport of people and cargo has made worldwide exchanges of goods and cultural experiences quicker, easier, and less expensive than ever before. International exchange of television programs and the introduction of transistor radios to remote villages in Africa and Latin America have provided new opportunities for what sociologists call *cultural diffusion:* the acceptance of elements of one culture by members of another. Cultural elements can range from material objects and technologies to beliefs and ideas.

Our era abounds with examples of cultural diffusion. For example, the nations of Africa that have achieved independence in the last fifteen years evolved their leadership and administrative structures not from the tribal monarchies and alliances native to their regions but from the structures of foreigners who colonized the continent. Likewise, African political and economic ideologies, ranging from Marxism to modifications of capitalism, are importations of European ideologies. Nationalism itself—consciousness of nationhood and identification of individual welfare with the well-being of the nation—is usually a foreign importation.

Before the colonial period, political boundaries and alliances in Africa were usually tribal. Much of the civil turmoil in emerging African nations has

[15]See, for example, Shlomo Avineri, *The Social and Political Thought of Karl Marx* (London: Cambridge University Press, 1968); David McLellan, *The Thought of Karl Marx* (New York: Harper and Row, 1972); Raymond Aron, *Main Currents in Sociological Thought* (Garden City, N.Y.: Basic Books, 1968), 1:145–236.

In Stockholm, Sweden, an area is set aside for graffiti on any issue. It is periodically whitewashed for reuse. In terms of Kornhauser's model of societal types, is this wall more suggestive of the pluralist society or the mass society?

arisen from the failure of present national borders to reflect earlier tribal territorial borders. The cultural diffusion of European ideas has often been more successful in imposing new administrative techniques and technology than in erasing old beliefs and values. The fact that the old ideas hang on indicates that much of the cultural diffusion the native Africans experienced was forced on them.

A good deal of cultural diffusion, however, occurs voluntarily—two cultures exchange beliefs, values, and techniques willingly. For example, the early settlers of North America adopted from the native Indians the use of corn, tobacco, and potatoes. The Indians adopted the use of the horse and, later, the rifle. Although many Indians were converted to Christianity by missionaries, no Indian religious beliefs made any headway with the European settlers or their descendants. Although Europeans were eager to learn of new crops to farm, few Indians were interested in adopting European farming techniques. Many tribes preferred to improve their hunting abilities by using horses.

During times of political isolationism, Americans have often looked down on "foreign" ideas and goods. They then express a belief that American ways and things are best. Anthropologist Ralph Linton found ironies in this notion, in an article he called "One Hundred Per Cent American":

There can be no question about the average American's Americanism or his desire to preserve this precious heritage at all costs. Nevertheless, some insidious foreign ideas have already wormed their way into his civilization without his realizing what was going on. Thus dawn finds the unsuspecting patriot garbed in pajamas, a garment of East Indian origin; and lying in a bed built on a pattern which originated in either Persia or Asia Minor. He is muffled by the ears in un-American materials: cotton, first domesticated in India; linen, domesticated in the Near East; wool from an animal native to Asia Minor; or silk whose uses were first discovered by the Chinese. All these substances have been transformed into cloth by methods invented in Southwestern Asia. If the weather is cold enough he may even be sleeping under an eiderdown quilt invented in Scandinavia.

On awakening he glances at the clock, a medieval European invention, uses one potent Latin word in abbreviated form, rises in haste, and goes to the bathroom. Here, if he stops to think about it, he must feel himself in the presence of a great American institution: he will have heard stories of both the quality and frequency of foreign plumbing and will know that in no other country does the average man perform his ablutions in the midst of such splendor. But the insidious foreign influence pursues him even here. Glass was invented by the ancient Egyptians, the use of glazed tiles for floors and walls in the Near East, porcelain in China, and the art of enameling on metal by Mediterranean artisans of the Bronze Age. Even his bathtub and toilet are but slightly modified copies of Roman originals. The only purely American contribution to the ensemble is the steam radiator, against which our patriot very briefly and unintentionally places his posterior.

In this bathroom the American washes with soap invented by the ancient Gauls. Next he cleans his teeth, a subversive European practice which did not invade America until the latter part of the eighteenth century. He then shaves, a masochistic rite first developed by the heathen priests of ancient Egypt and Sumer. The process is made less of a penance by the fact that his razor is of steel, an iron-carbon alloy discovered in either India or Turkestan. Lastly, he dries himself on a Turkish towel.[16]

Linton traces the foreign origins of the American's clothes, breakfast, and even newspaper, concluding:

As he scans the latest editorial pointing out the dire results to our institutions of accepting foreign ideas, he will not fail to thank a Hebrew God in an Indo-European language that he is a one hundred percent (decimal system invented by the Greeks) American (from Americus Vespucci, Italian geographer).[17]

[16]Ralph Linton, "One Hundred Per Cent American," *American Mercury* 60 (1937): 427–28.

[17]Ibid., p. 429.

ACCEPTANCE OF CHANGE AND RESISTANCE TO CHANGE

Why did the early settlers coming to America adopt new crops but not religious beliefs from the Indians, and why did the Indians adopt the Christian religion (with modifications) and the horse but little else of European culture? Why are there strong Communist parties, representing Marxist ideas, in Italy, France, and Portugal but not in England or West Germany? Why has divorce become much more acceptable to recent generations of Americans than it was to their parents and grandparents? In short, why are some possible forms of social change accepted by a society and other forms rejected or resisted?

Many times social change of drastic proportions can be imposed. The Africans who were brought to this country in captivity as slaves had to endure bondage for centuries. Not only their occupations and dwelling places but also their beliefs, values, and behavior were imposed on them by the slaveowner society. Similarly, in the nineteenth century, the surviving American Indians underwent forcible social change when they were put on reservations under the jurisdiction of the Bureau of Indian Affairs. Their children were sent to so-called Indian schools–often boarding schools located far from the reservations –where they were made to speak only English and were taught none of their own heritage.

Many social changes, however, are not forced on one culture by another. They can be accepted or rejected or accepted with modifications by a society according to the importance it sees in the innovation. In our own society, for example, technological changes have been more readily accepted than changes in social patterns.

In some instances change is resisted because it conflicts with other values. The oil embargo of 1973–74 made Americans painfully aware of their growing dependence on foreign oil, and gave them reason to believe the warnings of experts that many natural resources were finite and rapidly dwindling. Nevertheless, most have not taken to mass transit and given up their cars.

Why has this resistance to changing patterns of travel occurred? In part, because other options, such as adequate mass transport systems, are not always available. But such resistance is also based on cultural values. The automobile appeals to many people as a symbol of prestige. It fits our values of individualism, privacy, and mobility. Furthermore, we cannot believe that new technology will not solve the energy crisis somehow without forcing us to change our habits drastically. Some experts believe only changes in the social structure–such as fuel rationing or new taxes on "gas guzzlers"– will force new patterns of behavior.

Only a few of the Native Americans in this turn-of-the-century picture are in Indian dress. The others are barely distinguishable from their white teachers in this school for reservation children. For many generations, United States policy has been to wean Indians away from their native customs and social structures, thereby promoting involuntary social change.

Other changes are resisted because they threaten the interests of powerful groups that are able to keep things the way they are through lobbying and propaganda. For example, Britain, Canada, Sweden, and several other Western democracies have socialized medicine, a program in which physicians are paid salaries by the government from tax revenues, and patients then receive free or very inexpensive medical care. Yet when socialized medicine is proposed here as a solution to our problems in health care delivery, it is roundly condemned as "creeping socialism," harmful to the rights of doctor and patient alike.

Why, then, do some people propose socialized medicine for our society? Because the poor and more and more middle-class families can no longer afford adequate medical care even if they have medical insurance plans. If this is true, then why is socialized medicine resisted? Partly because many of us are convinced that our values of free enterprise and individual rights should apply to the norms of medical practice. Doctors should be able to earn incomes that reflect their abilities and their years of arduous training, and patients should be able to choose their doctors rather than be assigned them by a bureaucracy. The majority of United States physicians heartily agree with that argument, and their professional organization, the American Medical Association, has long fought to keep this belief an American norm. These doctors have a *vested interest* in keeping the present structure of medical practice; any change in the pattern will harm their interests. Thus the AMA becomes a force resisting this social change.

Vested interests are common in society and in the lives of most individuals. Homeowners have a vested interest in keeping residential property taxes down and having other taxpayers—such as commercial property owners and consumers—pay a greater share into government revenues. Housing contractors and construction workers have a vested interest in a healthy rate of housing growth. Working parents have a vested interest in the creation of well-staffed day-care centers. Veterans have a vested interest in a GI Bill, providing support for them to pursue higher education.

Many people, however, can have vested interests in seeing that social changes come about, rather than resisting changes. Working-class and poor people might see great advantages in a socialized medicine program that provided them with the quantity and quality of medical care they cannot now afford. Migrant farm workers have a vested interest in obtaining the benefits of union representation. Workers once had a vested interest in the establishment of a federal minimum wage.

Thus, vested interests can be a source of both resistance to and promotion of change. As we saw in Chapter 7, many social theorists find that societies like ours are composed of interest groups competing against one another to attain their own goals. Social stability and social change, in this view, depend on whether the dominant group in the controversy over an issue maintains its dominance or is forced to yield to a competing group. Often these competing groups form what sociologists call *social movements,* which we discuss in the following chapter.

Migrant farm workers have been fighting for years to organize unions. In 1975 California farm workers finally secured legislation guaranteeing their right to choose a collective bargaining agent by secret-ballot elections and enforcing the power of that agent to make contracts with the growers. What vested interests do the workers have in union representation? What vested interests do the growers have in keeping their workers unorganized?

SUMMARY

Throughout this book we have cited innumerable instances of social change: changes in values, norms, roles, and social institutions. All societies and social groups exhibit such change, for change has many diverse sources. Chief among them are geographical change, population growth, and migration.

Inventions and new technologies promote new ways of doing things, or even new things to do. Scientific discoveries, philosophical advances, and new religious ideas can alter our systems of beliefs and values. Yet while change is a fact of life, societies tend to resist its occurrence, because the social structure harbors groups with vested interests in the status quo.

15

SOCIAL MOVEMENTS

Forces for social change can range, as we saw in the previous chapter, from the spectacular and catastrophic to the minute. Nature can impose the need to change, but most change is of human origin: inventions, discoveries, new ideas, ideologies. Many times, of course, social change is an unintended consequence of these. But change often results from deliberate effort by groups of like-minded persons organized into social movements.

CHARACTERISTICS OF SOCIAL MOVEMENTS

Social movement: a more or less loosely organized collection of individuals and groups intended to promote or resist social change.

Social movements have been a highly visible part of our social landscape in recent decades. A social movement is defined by sociologists as a continuing collective effort to promote or resist social change. Various social movements spring readily to mind: the civil rights movement; the antiwar movement; the women's liberation movement; the ecology environmentalist movement; the gay liberation movement.

Social movements range from loosely organized to tight-knit groups. One movement may be virtually without an organizational structure or may have several organizations competing to impose their point of view on the movement. The antiwar movement of the 1960s and 1970s is an example. Occasionally, for limited periods of time, the movement may be dominated by a single organization. The movement to organize farm workers until very recently was dominated by the United Farm Workers union.

Pluralist society (Kornhauser): a society in which the elites are accessible and the nonelites are not readily available for agitation, because "intermediate relations" (community, voluntary association, and occupational groups) are strong.

Social movements should not be confused with formal organizations. A social movement has supporters and members who may not be members of the organization or organizations within it. Members come and go, now being active, now giving only moral support. Leaders of the movement achieve their positions by popular acclaim, not by formal means as they do in organizations. And social movements may rely on tactics that other kinds of groups rarely or never use—sit-ins, demonstrations, and other visible forms of protest or disruption.

Thus a social movement is a group of people working together over some length of time to promote or resist social change. In Chapter 6 we discussed William Kornhauser's model for the continuum of societal types.

Kornhauser distinguished the pluralist and mass societies, in his model, by the relative accessibility or inaccessibility of elites and availability or nonavailability of nonelites. He concluded that the key distinction was the strength of intermediate relations between elite and nonelite, "notably the local community, voluntary association, and occupational group." Voluntary associations are long-standing formal organizations that recruit memberships among people with shared interests: Elks clubs, PTAs, the NAACP, the American Red Cross.

Mass society (Kornhauser): a society in which the elites are accessible and the nonelites are readily available to be mobilized for action, because intermediate relations are weak.

Thus, according to Kornhauser, when the community is strong, the economy is stable, and people are channeling their energies into voluntary associations, nonelites show low availability—they cannot easily be agitated by social issues into collective action. When social movements flourish, on the other hand, this indicates the prevalence of mass society characteristics, for the nonelites can be motivated to organize around immediate issues and seek short-term, and often sweeping, goals.

A brief survey of several social movements should help to delineate their characteristics and their variety. Try to note their similarities and differences in underlying ideologies, goals, and tactics.

VOTE

The birth of the civil rights movement is often traced to the Montgomery, Alabama, bus boycott in 1955. Blacks there attempted to influence the social structure by direct pressure rather than by appeals for justice and equality. In the 1960s "freedom riders" challenged segregation of public facilities serving interstate transit. They frequently met with violent attacks and fire bombings and sometimes received protection from National Guard troops. Voter registration drives were directed toward overcoming the well-founded black fear of asserting constitutional rights. Martin Luther King, Jr., achieved national prominence through his charismatic ability to rally blacks, and many whites, to action in the movement.

Issues

In 1955, black people in Montgomery, Alabama, decided to boycott buses until the city bus company ended its policy of forcing blacks to ride in the back of the bus. The black demonstrators were publicizing the fact that they would no longer accept segregated seating. They were demanding a change in city transportation regulations. This was a major event in the development of the civil rights movement. Victory in Montgomery made the chief organizer of the boycott, Martin Luther King, a national leader. He stood for the use of nonviolent tactics to bring about social change. The media publicized his efforts nationally, exposing people throughout the country to his ideas, his goals, and his ability to inspire support against tough odds.

The peace movement, organized to oppose United States involvement in the Vietnam war, ultimately involved hundreds of thousands of Americans in the late 1960s and early 1970s. Many marched repeatedly in Washington and other cities, signed newspaper ads calling for troop withdrawal, and urged members of Congress to vote against war legislation and to draft antiwar legislation. A smaller group of people within the peace movement often took more militant action. They engaged in civil disobedience: they deliberately broke laws to protest the war. They risked arrest by sitting-in at military bases or

The antiwar movement was composed of a tiny, barely visible minority in the early 1960s. The Vietnam war did not command much general attention until 1964. Only in the later 1960s did the opposition spread to large numbers of diverse people, ranging from college students and professors (who had been among the first to oppose the war) to businesspeople and eventually politicians. The differing groups in the movement were barely united by the goal of ending the war. There was often as much disagreement within the movement as there was between opponents and supporters of United States involvement in the war. The movement spanned the political spectrum not only in ideologies but also in approved tactics for expressing opposition and in definitions of the goal, ranging from "out now" to "peace with honor."

draft boards. Some young men burned their draft cards; other protesters burned American flags. A few ransacked draft board offices. Thousands of young men fled the country rather than serve in what they considered an unjust war.

Social movements have also been organized around other issues. Few issues have aroused greater intensity of feeling in recent years than the abortion question. In 1973 the United States Supreme Court, following the precedents of other state and federal courts, declared antiabortion laws an unconstitutional infringement of personal liberties. This decision was the culmination

Organizers for the United Farm Workers fought growers for years in the Southwest for the right of migrant workers to bargain collectively on issues such as wages, working conditions, and living conditions. Their goals resembled those of the labor movement as a whole in its early years of struggle, and they used some of the same tactics—the strike and the boycott. Ironically, once the UFW won collective bargaining agreements from several California growers, an established union, the Teamsters, usurped these victories by offering growers contracts more appealing to their interests. In 1975 California law gave farm workers the right to elect by secret ballot whether to join a union and which union to join, the UFW or the Teamsters.

The goals and tactics of the civil rights movement were adopted by several other groups in the late 1960s and early 1970s. Individuals organized on the basis of their shared struggle against exploitation or discrimination. Homosexuals today are confronting entrenched beliefs about the nature of their sexual orientation. In trying to abandon their protective secrecy without suffering discrimination, homosexuals face the same two problems that confronted women, blacks, and other racial and ethnic minorities: they must win their legal rights and change ancient beliefs.

of a social movement to remove these laws. Members of the movement argued that the decision to have an abortion must, by rights, be made by the pregnant women, not by society or the government. The Court decision spurred a new social movement, however—this time against abortion and in favor of restoring strict abortion laws. The two movements disagree about when life begins (that is, when a fetus acquires legal human status), what rights the human fetus should be guaranteed, and how these rights balance against those of the pregnant woman.

Since the early 1800s, American workers have tried to organize unions to improve their wages and working conditions. In the 1930s legislation was passed guaranteeing most workers the right to organize. Farm owners were successful in convincing Congress that farm workers should be excluded because they were performing an essential service in feeding the nation. If workers were to strike at harvest time, the argument ran, an entire crop could be ruined. In recent years, however, farm workers have organized and won recognition of their bargaining rights. They have gone on strike during critical harvest periods and have picketed against the employment of nonunion workers by the growers. They have also asked the general public to support their efforts by refusing to buy nonunion farm products. Organizing a boycott is one way in which unions and other social movements have sought to pressure organizations to accept social change.

Classification by Types of Goals

As we have seen, social movements can have a wide variety of goals. Sociologists have distinguished a number of types of social movements according to what they hope to accomplish. Louis Wirth[1] suggested a useful system for classifying social movements.

Pluralist movement (Wirth): a movement seeking to improve the social acceptance of a distinctive category of persons without obliterating that distinctiveness.

Pluralist movements. Pluralist movements are organized to obtain recognition and satisfaction of the needs of a segment of the society. A pluralist movement might seek toleration for a religious minority. An ethnic group might organize to pressure the schools to recognize its language as the children's primary language in school. Other movements emerge among groups who have been ridiculed, shunned, or harassed by others. Homosexuals in our society are currently battling for a change in social values that will allow them to "come out of the closet," publicly admit their sexual identity, and play legitimate roles in all social institutions without being penalized or harassed.

Pluralist movements share the primary goal of being allowed to practice their own traditions and live a style of life acceptable to themselves. They do not necessarily seek to convert others to their beliefs and values.

Assimilationist movements. Many social movements strive for the right to be included. History is full of examples of people who banded together to demand access to powers and privileges that have been denied them. The labor

[1]See Louis Wirth, "Types of Minority Movements," in *Collective Behavior,* ed. Ralph H. Turner and Lewis M. Killian (Englewood Cliffs, N.J.: Prentice-Hall, 1957), pp. 321–30.

Assimilationist movement (Wirth): a movement seeking to improve the social status of particular categories of individuals.

movement in this country has not sought to destroy the factory system or, with some exceptions, to abolish capitalism, but rather, to win good pay and fringe benefits for workers, safe working conditions, compensation for the injured, and pensions for retired workers. The labor movement is built on the premise that the workers should share more of the profits from their productive labor.

The civil rights and women's movements were organized to combat discrimination against blacks and women respectively. They want access to good jobs, equal pay, and better education for these groups. In recent years Mexican-Americans and Native Americans have been struggling for public recognition of their underprivileged position and for access to the more highly rewarded roles in American society for their members.

Reform movement: a movement that seeks to change a specific set of values, norms, roles, or institutional patterns of interaction.

Reform movements. Although Louis Wirth did not include this type in his classification system, many social movements are organized around the goal of changing some specific aspect of social life. The temperance, conservation, zero population growth, abortion, and right to life movements all sought to change a specific set of values, roles, or institutional arrangements. Reform social movements do not intend to make sweeping, fundamental changes in the social system. They generally believe that certain problems can be solved by educating the public and by pressuring the government to respond. The suffrage movement, for example, was a widespread reform movement in the late nineteenth and early twentieth centuries, advocating women's right to vote. Leading proponents of woman suffrage argued that this reform would aid those in government to do a better job. Suffragists believed that women were able and necessary participants in American government. Their program did not advocate radical changes in the governing process.

Secessionist movement: a movement seeking separation of its members from social forces or from an entire society that it considers discriminatory.

Secessionist movements. Secessionist movements have the goal of separating their members from some source of injustice or discrimination. One of the best examples is the movement that culminated in the American Revolution. As resistance to English treatment of the colonies grew, more and more colonists began to advocate separation from England, dissolution of the colonies, and the formation of a new nation. Later the southern states sought to secede as a block from the Union on the grounds that the northern states were exploiting them and discriminating against them economically. What we generally call the Civil War was then called by southerners the War for Secession.

Secessionist movements have arisen all over the world in recent history. Independence movements have appeared throughout Asian and African colonies. Frequently they were successful in forcing out the colonial powers and in

VOTES FOR US WHEN WE ARE WOMEN

WENTWORTH
CLEAN STREETS
AND
TO-THE-HOME-

Like the civil rights movement, the feminist movement in its early days of this century faced the major hurdle of obtaining women's right to vote. Blacks received the constitutional right to vote in 1869. By the 1890s, however, most states in the South had passed local voter registration laws that effectively kept almost all blacks from exercising this right. It took the civil rights movement of the 1960s to break through these voting barriers. Women obtained the right to vote in 1919, after bitter struggles, but over fifty years later many women believe an additional constitutional amendment is needed to break other political and social patterns of discrimination against them. They reason that the social attitudes treating women as inferior can be changed only if women have the legal right to demonstrate their equality with men. Institutional racism and the cultural dimension of prejudice, discussed in Chapter 8, can be applied to sexism.

establishing independent governments. Other secessionist movements have become allied with or swallowed up by revolutionary movements, which we discuss next. In Indochina immediately after World War II a secessionist movement was organized to prevent the French from returning to the area as a colonial power, after the Japanese colonialists were ousted. After eight years of struggle, the French were defeated. But in the cold war atmosphere of the 1950s the French were able to persuade the United States government to become involved, and, in the years of continuous war that followed, revolutionary movements overshadowed the earlier secessionist goals.

Revolutionary movement: a movement seeking to make major, sweeping changes in all the social institutions by taking power in the political institution.

Revolutionary movements. In many societies political groups can be found that believe they must overthrow the existing government in order to achieve their desired changes. Their goal is *revolution:* the complete change of the social system, usually by sudden and often by violent means. Revolutions may be attempted when large, organized groups become convinced that their needs will never be met in the existing political system. For a revolutionary movement to develop, people must feel not only that their political institutions are failing to bring about necessary changes but also that they can defeat the government in power.

Revolutionaries want to control and direct massive changes in the system. They are usually willing to use force to win the necessary power. Frequently they also use force to bring their changes about once they are in power. In the Cuban Revolution of 1959, for example, thousands of Cubans from all levels of society took up arms against the government of the dictator Fulgencio Batista. When Batista realized that he had lost the support of almost all sections of the society and found that his army had been defeated by the rebel forces led by Fidel Castro, he fled the country. The victorious revolutionaries had succeeded in ousting a repressive government by the use of arms. They had resorted to arms after all other political means had failed, and it had become apparent that Batista was intent on keeping power despite strong and growing popular opposition.

Later, Castro used both his great personal appeal among the peasantry and the urban working class and the power of his rebel army to maintain control of the government despite the growing opposition of middle-class people to the changes that he wanted to bring about in Cuba's economic and social institutions.[2]

[2]See, for example, Wyatt MacGaffey and Clifford Barnett, *Twentieth-Century Cuba: The Background of the Castro Revolution* (Garden City, N.Y.: Doubleday, 1965); Maurice Zeitlin, *Revolutionary Politics and the Cuban Working Class* (Princeton, N.J.: Princeton University Press, 1967).

Revolutionaries must take political power so that their new government can direct the changes it seeks, even if there is substantial resistance among some sectors of the population. The government then exercises control over the values people hold, the roles they play, and the structure of their social institutions. The workplace, the family, the school, and the church are among the institutions affected.

Alex Inkeles, a sociologist who studied the Russian Revolution of 1917, described the radical transformation of the Russian countryside wrought later by Joseph Stalin's program of collectivization. Economic relations were changed. Peasant families no longer cultivated a small plot of land for their landlords. Instead they were part of collectives. A new, state-run political and economic administration regulated the workday, decided the acceptable rate of production, established a bonus system, built houses and communal buildings, started an education program, and controlled the mass media. In short, the revolutionary government changed virtually every important aspect of life for millions of people living in the countryside of the Soviet Union.

> Some 25 million farm families, constituting more than 100 million souls, were forced in the span of a few short years radically to change the whole pattern of their lives. Five million of these people, those in the families designated as "kulak," [wealthy peasants] were dispossessed outright of their land and property, and a large proportion forcibly transplanted to other parts of the country. The Russian countryside glowed red, the sky with flames of burning peasant huts and government buildings, the ground with the blood of cattle slaughtered by the peasants and peasants slaughtered by the militia and by the flying squads of Communist workers and the agitated peasant "Committees of the Poor." Between 1928 and 1933, the cattle population fell from 70 to 38 million, sheep and goats from 147 to 50 million, and pigs from 26 to 12 million. . . . Once again famine stalked the land.[3]

COMPONENTS OF SOCIAL MOVEMENTS

Every social movement, no matter what type, has certain components: an ideology, a program or set of goals, tactics for achieving its program, and leaders.

Ideology

An ideology, as we saw in Chapter 14, embodies the movement's perception of current social circumstances and their causes, why change is necessary, and how it can be attained. A movement's ideology defends or asserts its interests.

[3]Alex Inkeles, "The Great Social Experiment," in *The Soviet Experience,* ed. Daniel R. Brower (New York: Holt, Rinehart and Winston, 1971), pp. 69–70.

Revolution is difficult to define operationally with any unanimity. The Russian revolution of 1917 was clearly a revolution, culminating in Russia's swift progress from a true feudal monarchy to a "dictatorship of the proletariat." Social change was rapid and sweeping. But what of other revolutions or revolutionary movements? Some historians, for example, argue that the American revolution was not a true revolution but simply a violent struggle over who would hold power—the British king or the colonists. They contend that our Constitution was purposely designed to maintain the social, political, and economic privileges in the hands that held them before and during the revolution. Perhaps because there was no real redistribution of power then, many in our society today fear any hint of redistribution and refuse to consider equalizing ideas on their merits, condemning them as "un-American." Thus, ideas that in other industrial societies are considered reformist are here considered revolutionary, and many would-be reformers are forced—or choose—to adopt the stance of "revolutionaries," as commonly happened in the 1960s.

Ideology: a set of beliefs and values that justify social conditions or that provide a unified criticism of those conditions and justify alternative patterns.

The ideology of the farm workers' movement, for example, sets forth its general belief in American principles of equality of opportunity and equality before the law. Farm workers argue that they have been discriminated against for years and have been denied the quality of life that all Americans desire. Only if they are represented by a strong union can these workers win the protections and benefits that other American workers have. The movement's ideology pointedly states its faith in the current American social and economic system and in the nation's ability to uplift its most underprivileged members. In essence, the ideology of César Chavez and his followers draws heavily on the American creeds of justice for all citizens and of giving particular help to those who have benefited least from the nation's abundance.

The ideology of the ecology movement holds that natural resources are limited and may be forever ruined if people do not exercise greater care to protect them. Progress and economic growth must always be balanced against their cost to the natural environment. According to the movement, private owners do not have the right to deplete or abuse natural resources in any way they see fit.

Some social movements encompass such a variety of groups and viewpoints that no single, consistent set of beliefs and values can be presented as its ideology. The women's liberation or feminist movement is one example.[4] All members share the ideological position that throughout history women have been exploited in almost every society. There is less agreement on the reasons for this exploitation, however. Some movement members assert that, since men have been the beneficiaries of the exploitation, they must be the source of it. Men are the opposition and will fight to maintain their favored position, these feminists contend. Others argue that men are also victimized by the present structure of sex roles: the fact that many men see equality between the sexes as threatening to their masculinity indicates that they suffer from a "false consciousness" just as unliberated women do. In other words, men too are operating under a false set of ideas and need to be liberated from these notions as much as women.

The values underlying the women's movement are equally diverse. Everyone in the movement holds the value of equality between the sexes—equality of educational and job opportunities, equal pay for equal work, and equal legal status (in matters such as financial credit). Some also put a high value on equality of rights and responsibilities in household work, child-care, family income, and other obligations. Others give less value to an equal divi-

[4]See, for example, Shulamith Firestone, *The Dialectic of Sex: The Case for Feminist Revolution* (New York: Morrow, 1970).

sion of these duties and are satisfied with a more traditional division of labor. Some feminists value sexual separatism. They declare men to be the enemy and intend to have little or nothing to do with them. Others value sharing their lives with men in equal partnership.

Clearly, the values underlying an ideology are related to the beliefs. If a woman believes that men suffer from sexism nearly as much as women do, she is more likely to value an equal partnership between the sexes and liberation of both sexes from false ideas. If a woman believes that men knowingly maintain sex discrimination, she is likely to reject partnership as inevitably unequal and to value sexual separatism as the means to equality or liberation.

Goals

Goals: the specific, defined conditions that a movement seeks to achieve.

While its ideology may embody general beliefs and values, such as justice, equality, morality, democracy, or peace (or elitism, fascism, or the glorification of war), a social movement must set forth specific goals that its leaders and members can easily understand and strive for on a day-to-day basis. The farm workers' movement speaks of social justice. Its major goal is to win for farm workers the right to organize into unions and bargain collectively with their employers. The civil rights movement was motivated by the ideology of equality. Its specific goal was to end segregation and discrimination in public facilities, housing, voting rights, education, and jobs.

The feminist movement expressed its goals in the following statement:

> We demand.
>
> I. That the U.S. Congress immediately pass the Equal Rights Amendment to the Constitution to provide that "Equality of Rights under the law shall not be denied or abridged by the United States or by any State on account of sex" and that such then be immediately ratified by the several States.
>
> II. That equal employment opportunity be guaranteed to all women, as well as men, by insisting that the Equal Employment Opportunity Commission enforces the prohibitions against racial discrimination.
>
> III. That women be protected by law to ensure their rights to return to their jobs within a reasonable time after childbirth without loss of seniority or other accrued benefits, and be paid maternity leave as a form of social security and/or employee benefit.
>
> IV. Immediate revision of tax laws to permit the deduction of home and child-care expenses for working parents.
>
> V. That child-care facilities be established by law on the same basis as parks, libraries, and public schools, adequate to the needs of children from the pre-school years through adolescence, as a community resource to be used by all citizens from all income levels.
>
> VI. That the right of women to be educated to their full potential equality with men be secured by Federal and State legislation, eliminating all discrimi-

nation and segregation by sex, written and unwritten, at all levels of education, including colleges, graduate and professional schools, loans and fellowships, and Federal and State training programs such as the Job Corps.

VII. The right of women in poverty to secure job training, housing, and family allowances on equal terms with men, but without prejudice to a parent's right to remain at home to care for his or her children; revision of welfare legislation and poverty programs which deny women dignity, privacy, and self-respect.

VIII. The right of women to control their own reproductive lives by removing from the penal code laws limiting access to contraceptive information and devices, and by repealing penal laws governing abortion.[5]

Choose a social movement we have not yet discussed, and spell out its ideology and goals. To what extent do you agree with its ideology? Are its goals realistic—that is, what do you think are the chances that they can be realized?

Tactics

Tactics: the specific, day-to-day actions taken to achieve stated goals.

Just as a movement must define its goals, so it must determine its tactics. The farm workers' union organized a national boycott of lettuce and grapes picked by strikebreakers. This tactic was used to put economic pressure on the growers and force them to accept the union. Peace groups and civil rights groups often held massive rallies in Washington to influence the president and Congress to change certain policies. The Women's Christian Temperance Union, which opposed the sale and use of alcohol, would march into taverns singing and praying, to interrupt business there. Gandhi and his followers used strikes, fasts, and refusal to obey laws to pressure the British to grant India independence. Some revolutionary movements have used terrorism or armed fighting when they felt legal mechanisms were ineffective. Others, including some Marxist movements, have sought power through democratic processes, using what are considered legitimate means by the existing social structure. We can classify the wide variety of tactics into three major types.

Educational tactics. Most movements include some form of public education as part of their tactics. They may issue leaflets, deliver speeches, or put on television and radio programs to inform the public of their positions. By these methods they hope to win support for their movement and to undercut the strength of any opposition.

[5]National Organization for Women, "Bill of Rights," adopted at NOW's first national conference, Washington, D.C., 1967, reprinted in *Sisterhood Is Powerful,* ed. Robin Morgan (New York: Vintage, 1970), pp. 513–14.

Boycotts and protest demonstrations are two tactics of social movements. The goal of the boycott is to exert direct pressure on the source of resistance to change, as this farmworker seeks to do. An effective boycott is designed to deprive the organization being boycotted and thus force the opponent to negotiate with the boycotters. Protest demonstrations generally seek to persuade, if not by force of argument then by force of numbers.

In 1969 the antiwar movement, frustrated by years of ineffectiveness in influencing government policy despite steadily growing popular support, tried briefly to combine the demonstration and the boycott by holding one-day moratoriums in which people opposed to the war were to abstain from "business as usual," refusing to work or to spend money.

Education campaigns are one tactic of social movements that are shared by voluntary organizations (the League of Women Voters, for example). Educational tactics are implicit in tactics such as the protest and the boycott, as well. To broaden support for and increase the effectiveness of the movement, leaders must persuasively inform others of their points of view.

Political tactics. Supporters of a movement often feel that education alone is not enough. They seek to enforce their views through the political system. They may send lobbyists to state and national capitals to pressure legislators to vote for the laws that will aid their cause. They campaign for candidates who are sympathetic to the cause. Demonstrations at the seats of government, delivering petitions to government officials, and organizing letter-writing campaigns to the president are further examples of political tactics.

Direct action. The most militant tactics usually involve some form of direct action. Here, members of the movement decide who is "the enemy" or the main obstacle to their cause and take action against that particular set of role-players. Unions organize strikes against employers. Members of the civil rights movement staged sit-ins at lunch counters and other public facilities until owners or officials ended their segregation practices. Women in the temperance movement, blaming saloon keepers for encouraging drunkenness and alcoholism, marched into taverns singing hymns and sometimes smashed bottles and furniture. Revolutionary movements use the most drastic forms of direct action to accomplish their goals. They have often organized their supporters into fighting (guerrilla) units and sometimes commit acts of terrorism. These are intended to disrupt the social structure and ultimately, the group hopes, to overthrow those in power.

Leadership

Charisma: exceptional personal appeal that is useful for attracting adherents to a social movement (also discussed in Chapter 7, under types of authority).

Decisions have to be made in social movements. Day-to-day work must be assigned to members and carried through. Speeches and articles must be written to explain the movement to others. Negotiations must be held with authorities for contracts, new laws, and fair treatment. Overall strategies and specific tactics must be chosen. Those who speak in the name of the group, help guide its efforts, serve as role models, and inspire the rank and file are the leaders of the movement.

Styles of leadership vary in different movements. Some leaders are *charismatic* figures: in the eyes of their followers they are exceptional people, embodying the most valued human qualities.[6] The charismatic leader is usually believed to have an acute understanding of the contemporary situation, its historical roots, the future possibilities, and how they can be achieved.

[6]For a classical sociological explanation of charismatic authority, see Hans H. Gerth and C. Wright Mills, *From Max Weber* (New York: Oxford University Press, 1970), pp. 245–52; see also Reinhard Bendix, *Max Weber, an Intellectual Portrait* (Garden City, N.Y.: Doubleday Anchor, 1962), pp. 298–328.

Followers believe that their leader can be trusted to help the members achieve their goals, that he or she is a strong person who cannot be conned or bought off by the opposition. Many times leaders with charisma are able to attract large followings, guide their movements through crises, and keep others committed to the cause, through personal magnetism. Martin Luther King had such qualities; so did Lenin, Joan of Arc, Hitler, Gandhi, Dorothea Dix, and Malcolm X.

1. Write a brief description of one of these leaders analyzing his or her role in the movement. What ideology did this leader follow? How effective was the leader in achieving the goals of the movement? What tactics were employed? Would you agree that this person was charismatic? Why or why not?

2. Think of other charismatic leaders you have studied or read about. What do you think their special qualities were? What did they have in common?

Some social movements develop a different type of leadership. They favor shared or rotating leadership, in which no one person holds a great deal of power or responsibility. These leaders might not have charismatic qualities but instead may have an exceptional ability to analyze and describe the movement's ideology or goals; that is, they provide *intellectual* leadership. Other leaders may have little charisma or intellectual ability but have fine administrative ability. They excel, for example, at overseeing the publication of the movement's newspaper or keeping its office functioning and its records up to date.

A social movement needs various kinds of leaders if it is to gain members, followers, and sympathizers and if it is to survive and work toward its goals over a period of time, despite opposition. Leaders must develop an ideology that can be communicated in everyday language. They must organize the long-term efforts needed to bring about changes in values, roles, and institutions. Some observers believe that the New Left movement of the 1960s suffered from the refusal of its adherents to develop such forms of leadership. High value was placed on "participatory democracy," in which everyone was supposed to have an equal voice in decisions. Strong, concentrated leadership was incompatible with this value. As a result, however, people with particular leadership skills were deprived of the opportunity to exercise them in sharpening and expressing the movement's ideology, devising strategies and tactics, and handling administration.

John L. Lewis was a formidable leader who rallied mine workers in the prolonged, fierce battle against mine owners from the 1930s, to the 1950s. Much of his effectiveness as a union organizer came from his personal charisma. Malcolm X was a rival of Martin Luther King's for leadership of the civil rights movement, until Malcolm's assassination in 1965. Although politically and socially more radical than King, and therefore less popular with whites sympathetic to the cause, Malcolm X possessed great charisma.

DIVERSITY WITHIN SOCIAL MOVEMENTS

Sometimes those who seek a particular kind of social change join in a united effort, with the same ideology, goals, leadership, and tactics. It is as common, however, for a movement to be made up of a number of groups or organizations that differ from one another on one or another of these components. Diverse organizations may also emerge within a movement at various times or in different parts of the country. For example, the civil rights movement of the 1960s incorporated many different kinds of organizations of the past and present—from the NAACP (begun in 1910), and CORE (1940), to SCLC (1959), and SNCC (1960), among others. The separate groups within a movement often unite to sponsor special activities and programs, despite their differences on various issues.

The ecology movement includes such organizations as the Sierra Club, National Wildlife Federation, Friends of the Earth, and Save the Redwoods League. Some of these organizations are more than fifty years old. Over the years substantial ideological disagreements have arisen among leaders of the movement. John Muir, one of the founders of the Sierra Club, believed that wilderness areas had to be preserved in their natural state for beauty and "strength for body and soul." Other conservationists want wise public management of natural resources but are willing to allow public development of reservoirs in preserved wilderness areas. Such issues have aroused great controversies in the movement and led to some splits. In later years differing groups formed coalitions on certain issues, but the ecology movement still harbors organizations that disagree about priorities, leadership, and tactics. Some are concerned chiefly with wildlife preservation; others monitor national energy-use policies; and others emphasize a global approach that looks beyond national boundaries.

Sometimes a movement has a collection of differing groups because each group started at a different period and reflects the norms and values of its early days. But often splinter groups are formed within a movement because of disagreements about certain details of ideology, tactics, or leadership within the group that previously represented the movement. The Black Panther party, which has national headquarters in Oakland, California, began as an offshoot of the Lowndes County Freedom Organization formed in Alabama in 1966. Originally the group advocated black power, but it later adopted a modified Maoist ideology. From its roots as a voter registration organization, it evolved into a somewhat revolutionary organization.

Social movements that encompass a variety of organizations generally must accommodate diverse points of view on ideology, goals, and tactics. The various organizations can usually agree or compromise on one or a few elements long enough to strive for shared goals in an immediate program. Often the goals of the movement are broad enough to neutralize many differences and promote a fairly long-lived coalition. In the late 1960s and early 1970s, for example, the antiwar movement included people and organizations of many political persuasions. At one extreme were revolutionaries who maintained that United States capitalists were promoting the war in Indochina to serve their business interests. But many opponents of the war were businessmen, investors, and stockbrokers, who wanted prosperity for business but nevertheless opposed the war.

Interview a parent, friend, or acquaintance who has been involved at some time in a social movement. Ask such questions as these: Why did you join? How active were you? What were the goals of the movement? What tactics were used? What changes did the movement help bring about? What goals were not met?

SUMMARY

A key generator of social change is the tension in the social order caused by unmet needs and the discrepancies between ideal and actual conditions of living. When groups of individuals come to believe that their interests are not being met within current institutional arrangements, they may organize social movements to achieve change in their roles or their share in society, or in the social values, role relationships, and institutional structures that characterize the society. In United States society in recent generations, these organized efforts have focused on the struggle for peace, civil rights, women's liberation, environmental protection, the right to abortion or opposition to abortion, and labor unionization.

Whatever the fundamental issue, each social movement is characterized by an ideology (its set of beliefs and values), goals (its definitions of the social arrangements it seeks to achieve), tactics (its methods of achieving social change), and leadership. The spectrum of types of movements includes pluralist and assimilationist movements, striving for greater acceptance of their members' way of life or beliefs; secessionist movements seeking independence; those seeking social reform; and revolutionary movements, seeking total social transformation. Social movements often encompass a variety of groups that are on the same side of the barricades but have different conceptions of the scope of the problem and the most effective methods for achieving the movement's goals. It is not uncommon for members of a movement to engage in internal debate while they simultaneously struggle against a common adversary.

A SOCIOLOGICAL DEBATE

The United States was two hundred years old in 1976. The people celebrated the bicentennial of the founding of the nation. Many traveled to Boston, Philadelphia, Washington, and Williamsburg. Special charter flights brought tourists to visit the historic sites.

Teachers spent extra time discussing the meaning of "the American dream"; preachers gave sermons about the freedoms granted under the Bill of Rights and the religious bases of many of our ideals; politicians declaimed about the uniqueness of the American way; merchants and travel agents cashed in on the business of patriotism; and social scientists debated the character of the American system.

The American system, is, indeed, fascinating to social scientists. Ours is a land of complexities and contradictions, a nation of many nations—a melting pot to some and a seething caldron to others. It is a "house that we call freedom" and "the home of liberty"; it is also both racist and sexist. Ours is a culture in which success is often seen as the ultimate value, in which achievement and drive are most highly rewarded, yet it has a tradition of rooting for the underdog, and a number of its young people today are dropouts from the materialist, dog-eat-dog world.

These contradictions are known to most Americans. Indeed, we grow up learning about them—and living them. It is this point that intrigues both supporters and critics of the United States, those sociologists who see it as a functioning whole and those who view it as a stage for conflict between the masses and certain power elites who manipulate the press, public opinion, and major institutions for their own benefit.

In recent years much has been written and said about the American system by social scientists. A shelf of books with a variety of intriguing titles discuss the dilemmas of democracy: S. M. Lipset's *The First New Nation,* Max Lerner's *America as a Civilization,* Jean François Revel's *Without Marx or Jesus,* Raymond Mack's *Transforming America,* Maurice Zeitlin's *American Society, Incorporated,* Henry Etzkowitz's *Is America Possible?* Vance Packard's *A Nation of Strangers,* William Manchester's *The Power and the Glory,* and Andrew Hacker's *The End of the American Era.*

The issues are debated day and night on talk shows. The following hypothetical talk show is fairly typical. The setting is a studio in Washington, D.C., an early winter evening in 1976. Three sociologists have been invited to join moderator Tom Kelly to discuss the subject "America at Two Hundred: Sociological Perspectives."

A gag or a case of oversocialization? Many social critics saw the commercialism of the American bicentennial celebration as another instance of symbol triumphing over substance—outward shows of patriotism instead of a reappraisal of our values and our past and present performance in relation to those values.

Moderator: Good evening. I'm Tom Kelly, and this is the National Public Broadcasting Corporation's "Weekly Forum." This is the second program in our bicentennial series "America at Two Hundred." Last week three noted historians looked at the history of the United States. The discussion was lively, to say the least, and you may have wondered at times whether our three guests were talking about the same country. While one kept insisting that ours was the first new nation to have had a truly democratic revolution, another said the nation was new but the revolution was far from democratic. And the third, in case you missed her, said that the founding fathers purposely gave power to the privileged, and left the majority—including women and racial minority groups—powerless. All conceded that social changes had occurred. But, again, they differed on how to interpret them.

Tonight I am pleased to have with me three sociologists noted for their work on American society and culture. Professor Cyrus Wyckham teaches at Warren University here in Washington, his specialty is political sociology, and he has recently published a two-volume work entitled *Freedom and Control: The American Contradiction.*

Our second guest is Janice Fisher, professor of sociology at Blaine College. Professor Fisher has written extensively on American social structure. Her well-known books include *Meritocracy* and *Democracy: A Functionalist Analysis.*

And, finally, we have Professor Terry Jordan, a sociologist on the staff of St. George University. Professor Jordan also teaches courses on American social structure, with emphasis on the American people themselves. She is the author of *Peasants to Parvenus* and *The Plural Society*, and her latest book is an edited volume called *Consensus and Dissensus: The American People at Bicentennial.*

As we agreed when the three sociologists were invited to participate, each is to make a brief statement summarizing his or her position regarding the nature of the American system today. Professor Fisher, will you begin?

Fisher: This bicentennial year is a substantial documentation of how I see American society—as a functioning system whose mechanisms are constantly at work trying to solve major social issues. I should stress that all sociologists know how problematical it is to maintain the social order. There are constantly new members to be socialized, deviant behaviors to be controlled, tensions to be managed, needs to be met, decisions to be made, resources to be allocated, physical and social environments to be adapted to. This is such a complicated undertaking that it is impressive that any modern industrial society can continue functioning at all while providing the freedom to its members that ours does. It can only do so if there is substantial agreement on basic values and structural arrangements to support them. The United States is effectively held together by such cultural and social factors.

The founding fathers created a unique set of social institutions whose norms underscored the values they felt were pertinent in achieving what sociologist Seymour Martin Lipset has called "the first new nation." Freed from the legacy of feudalism that restricted most European nations, the United States emphasized individual achievement, not birthright, equality before the law, an open marketplace relatively free from restraints, and an enlightened public who could participate in the processes of government.

What was created was a system, or series of systems, designed to carry out both lofty and mundane goals. While few of the founding fathers anticipated the changes that would affect the course of national development—the influx of millions of immigrants, the challenge to the practice of involuntary servitude, the problems of urbanization and industrialization—they did provide the cement in the mosaic that was to become the modern United States. That cement—the core values of the society—has been amazingly resilient.

To my way of thinking, a society must be judged by the extent to which it establishes and maintains a meaningful equilibrium among its various parts. This equilibrium depends in very large measure on a general agreement about what the priorities should be and how to achieve them. In judging American society, I would say the structures have served their functions well and that we have an extraordinarily stable society. A concrete example should help make my perspective clearer.

Within the last two decades this nation has suffered the removal of two presidents: Kennedy by assassination, Nixon by forced resignation. Events like these are sufficiently grave to undermine almost any nation's stability. But our people held firm. Our values and laws supported the peaceful transfer of power. Widespread consensus and commitment to the system were clearly evident. In other countries, takeovers by the military would have been the order of the day. And many were certain that the United States was also going to succumb to the rule of the generals. What they failed to understand was the ability of American political institutions to adapt to crisis.

I am not suggesting that a society of more than two hundred million people does not have serious problems. Nowhere in human history is there evidence of a true utopia free from conflict. What I do look at in my analysis of this country is the ability of its various components to work together smoothly and to correct the society's course where necessary without destroying its basic structure.

In contrast to some of my colleagues, I would argue that the persistence of the "American way" is based far more on the will of the people, the masses of people, than on pressures by some powerful elite of bankers, politicians, and military leaders. We can test that assumption by asking the people their views. The majority will agree with my view that, by and large, we are doing very well.

Moderator: Thank you. Professor Fisher has argued that this country is basically sound, that the American system, for all its problems, "works." What do you say, Professor Wyckham?

Wyckham: Professor Fisher is what we sociologists call a functionalist. To me, functionalism avoids asking certain very serious questions. I see society—any society—from a rather different point of view. Every sociologist knows that these bicentennial programs are patriotic rituals. Traditional societies reaffirm their values and their group solidarity at annual group rituals and festivals; this year we Americans are gathering together on weekly television shows to pay tribute to our past and our future.

Tonight I'd like to introduce another function to this ritual—one that is perhaps more appropriate to the state of our society on its two hundredth birthday. I'd like to propose a little more introspection, to probe the overwhelming problems that surround us. Frankly, I think the issue is one of survival, and I want to point to the critical problems that may spell our decline.

The first is racial violence. Despite the Supreme Court decision in 1954 ordering desegregation of public schools and despite the vast civil rights movement of the 1960s, I see little evidence that our racial problems can be solved—or even that the system is working toward solving them. We are faced with the fact that busing children from black ghettos to decent white schools leads to violence, riots, and hatred, and further encourages the white exodus to the suburbs. Many blacks are still confined to the decaying centers of cities and are increasingly alienated. They hold little hope of improving their lot in the system. The same is true of millions of Puerto Ricans, Chicanos, and Native Americans. This despair has brought us the highest rate of violent crime in the history of the nation—from terror in city subways to gun battles on Indian reservations. Perhaps even worse is the hopelessness and apathy that pervade broken neighborhoods and families.

I think we have neither the will nor the way to solve the problems of race, urban decay, and national violence. As a sociologist I would say that the social structure inhibits meaningful changes. The socialization process transmits the beliefs and values of the past to the social participants of the future. This is true in any society, of course. But it means that the social structure perpetuates itself. And, unfortunately, the values that most members of our society hold do not encourage them to make sacrifices to achieve equality or justice—or, in fact, even to support the Bill of Rights. The results of some studies show that many people rejected the contents of the Bill of Rights when they appeared, reworded, on a questionnaire.

I think that our society is dominated by the profit motive. Great power is concentrated in the hands of corporations and their military and political allies. It may be in their interests to overthrow unfriendly governments in foreign countries, but it isn't in their interests to increase the power and opportunities available to poor people here or abroad.

Most of the rest of us are trapped by our commitment to the system's values and rules. We don't want to give up a promotion in order to let someone from a deprived group get ahead. We don't want our kids going to integrated schools for fear that they won't get as good an education—even though it would improve the educational opportunities for minority kids. We don't want our "property values" to go down because other, less privileged people have moved into the neighborhood.

These are the social values we live by, and they seem so reasonable. Yet the difficulty is that they're based on an incorrect assessment of the situation. Many of us are taught to blame the victims for their poverty, their lack of skills, their violent outrage. But even among those of us who see poverty as a structural part of our society, rather than as the fault of the poor, few blame those in power for this structural inequality. We accept the system, so we go on defending the interests of the powerful against the weak.

I realize my time is running short, but I want to give one more example of our inability to make the basic changes we so desperately need. This is the richest country in the world. We are only 6 percent of the world's population, but we consume 50 percent of the world's annual output of natural resources. These resources are limited. So what happens in the face of an energy crisis?

First of all, you've got to remember that our entire economy is geared toward the ever-increasing production of consumer goods—from toasters to automobiles. Any immediate cutback would result in a deepened recession, more unemployment, and falling profits. This structural problem could be averted only by massive reorganization of the economy. It would amount to a virtual revolution, which simply does not appear in the offing.

The government is so big and so influenced by vested interests that it cannot come up with decent policies to deal with the energy crisis, pollution, or the production of dangerous products. We used to worry about destroying ourselves through a nuclear holocaust. That's still a possibility; but I think we are more in danger of choking ourselves to death from smog, poisoning ourselves from cancer-producing materials in the water supply, or spraying ourselves to death with aerosol cans.

Cigarette companies don't care about lung cancer. They care about profits. Oil companies have used the oil shortage to raise prices and profit margins and to lobby for tax benefits and unrestrained offshore drilling. They don't care about the rest of society. Unfortunately, profit is the name of their game.

I'll close by saying the problems are getting worse—and bigger. Unfortunately, the solutions are not keeping pace.

Moderator: You sociologists differ as much in your interpretations of modern American society as the historians did in their views of its history. Professor Wyckham's society is very different from Professor Fisher's. Wouldn't you say so, Professor Jordan?

Jordan: Frankly, no. Their differences represent two basic perspectives of society that sociologists have debated for years. To my way of thinking, my two colleagues would look at any society from either a "functionalist" view or a "conflict" view. But, of course, our concern here is with the United States. No, they are not looking at different societies, but they're looking at this country from different angles of vision and different theoretical positions.

My own view is that the United States is not so easily praised or damned. It is a tension-ridden social system, and in those tensions lie both its promises and its problems. This has been true for a long time. The United States is a vast land. It is many peoples with many voices. It is a nation of contradictions. It is held together by powerful interests that often appear more concerned with the private good than with the public welfare. But it is also a place where the dream of mobility has proved to be more than a slogan, more than a catchphrase. It is also a society that can change and has changed.

Changes in American society have rarely come about through the good will of those in power. But they have occurred. The pressure of the people has been the primary motivating force. What was not accomplished by the ballot box was often accomplished in the streets. Voices in the wilderness—labor agitators, civil rights demonstrators, feminists, student radicals—who

The everts of recent decades of our history have presented an especially strong challenge to both of the traditional sociological perspectives—structural-functionalism and conflict theory. The structural-functionalist works from the assumption that every structural component of a society exists because it fulfills a function, which it is the sociologist's job to analyze. The conflict theorist works from the assumption that social patterns evolve through conflict among groups seeking to achieve their own specific goals. In this Epilogue we witness sociologists enacting a debate as to the merits of each perspective as a means of describing and analyzing contemporary social structures and their problems—not only the obvious problems of poverty, racism, and sexism, but also the issues surrounding social stratification, faith in material progress, and other enduring structural and cultural features. Is either perspective adequate to explain contemporary phenomena?

TRANS AM
GOODYEAR

STAND
UP FOR

BEANS
BY THE
STATES
AGRICULTURE

first met with hostility and violence, were not easily stilled. In time—and admittedly it was often a long time—others joined them. Little movements grew into great campaigns, and time and again the employers and the government officials and the representatives of other powerful sectors of the society began to make concessions. Indeed, what is most interesting to me is the willingness of the opponents of change to change themselves, once they recognize that the force of public opinion is running against them.

Now, to be sure, there are areas where progress has been slow. And there are areas where we have not yet found the way or the will to make broader changes that will affect all who suffer from some of our greatest problems. Our cities are decaying and unmanageable; our environment is becoming polluted; economic recessions have caused thousands of publicly and privately employed citizens to be laid off. Perhaps these problems, which are not unique to the United States, are unavoidable in postindustrial societies. Perhaps they are so enormous that we cannot deal with them all. But so far such a view is not widespread in our society. There is still a fundamental optimism about our ability to deal with adversity.

Moderator: You feel, then, Dr. Jordan, that the American people think they are capable of solving their own problems?

Jordan: I do. While many Americans are frightened of what they see around them, they still seem to have a fundamental belief in the soundness of the system. Of course, this may be naive on their part. As I tried to point out, the problems that confront us today are far greater and more ominous than those we have faced in the past.

Fisher: I disagree. The problems of today are not greater, they are different. There were very great problems in the earlier days of this country, and most were solved quite successfully. They were solved because of a common spirit that almost everyone—rich and poor—felt. It was a spirit or belief that no problem was too big to handle.

Jordan: You really think Americans can do just about anything?

Fisher: Perhaps I was overdramatizing, but I do think that too much is said about how we've failed and not enough is said about the strengths and successes of this country. Those successes are not based on some abstract notion of patriotism but on a combination of institutional forms and values that bind us together in an integrated society. Even those who are most removed from the mainstream have a sense of their Americanness.

Frankly, I am concerned by those who continually promote the idea that there are no common interests, that there is no strength in the social fabric. I think they give people false expectations that complex problems are the fault of a wicked conspiracy. I think it is irresponsible to undermine the emotional bonds that give us a sense of interdependence. The "hyphenated Americans"—Irish-Americans, Polish-Americans, Jewish Americans, even black Americans—feel it. At the core of whatever they are is something that binds them. After all, why do blacks prove to be among the most patriotic citizens in public opinion polls?

Jordan: I'll tell you why. It's not because they're black but because they're southern. Southern Protestants, to be more accurate. And they're poor. Take those three variables, and you've got a winning combination for political conservatism. Of course, they're not conservative when it somes to racial or bread-and-butter issues. But on anything else they're conservative.

In fact, although it is hard for many critics to accept, members of the working class—whether white, black, or whatever—are more conservative on many issues than any other sector of society. Let me cite just a few examples. Studies of sexual attitudes and behavior reveal greater permissiveness among members of the middle class than among the working class. Opinion polls about desegregation and the rights of minorities reveal more support for these values among members of the middle class. Studies of attitudes toward the war in Vietnam also showed greater opposition to the war from the middle class than from those lower down the ladder.

Wyckham: But that doesn't mean that working-class people are enamored with the system. They may simply reflect a fear of the changes that other, more powerful people are always advocating at *their* expense. They stick to the straight and narrow because they are not really able to strike out at the system. They are taught to believe their problems are personal rather than political, they are encouraged to blame blacks or Puerto Ricans for slums and filth and crime. No one suggests to them that the big banks may have anything to do with urban decay. Sociologists call that "blaming the victim."

Jordan: It isn't entirely true that working-class people aren't able to fight the system. When members of the working class really want to mobilize around issues that are important to them, they can and have, as I tried to point out before. I wouldn't say working-class people were being manipulated.

Fisher: I believe they have accepted the values of the dominant culture and feel they can achieve something. They are not outsiders; rather, they are integrated into the wider society.

Moderator: Professor Fisher, why do you persist in saying this is an integrated society? It seems to me we have substantial evidence that the United States is still segregated.

Fisher: I mean integrated in the Parsonian sense. As sociologist Talcott Parsons would argue, the whole system functions fairly smoothly because of the harmonious intermeshing of its various parts. In this sense I believe that our society is integrated. If it were not, it wouldn't work—and ours works amazingly well. Our institutions mesh, our stratification hierarchy allows for considerable social mobility, our people find that, by and large, they are far better off than nine-tenths of the world's population.

As I said before, we have our problems, just as any modern, industrial society does. But everything is relative in two ways: relative to what others face and suffer, and relative to what existed before. Take the first. Can you think of any place that is as complex as our society, that has so many different groups of people from so many places, that has done better than we? The assimilation of millions of immigrants and their considerable mobility is but one example of the ability of this system to function and to adapt to change as needs arise. And, on the second point of comparison, think what life was like for the early settlers. They didn't land in a bed of roses; they landed in a wilderness. They worked and slaved, and many of them died trying to open up this country. The birth rate was high, but the death rate was, too. Most people lived only forty to fifty years—if they were lucky.

Today we have problems too: pollution, heart disease, the threat of nuclear holocaust. But, in the "good old days," the manure that piled up in city streets was a far worse menace than the auto fumes of today; the scourge of epidemics like dysentery, malaria, and tuberculosis hung over the people like the Sword of Damocles . . .

Jordan: But, isn't it true that many of the problems of those days still exist, Janice? You haven't even touched on some of the major ones Cy mentioned: poverty, racism, military power. These are the real issues that threaten to pull our society apart. The saving grace, I think, is that we are aware of them and have begun to deal with them. It isn't easy, but at least every American today is aware of the fact that so many are poor in this land of riches, that so many are discriminated against, that . . .

In the United States the descendants of many who came as impoverished immigrants (like these lodgers in a crowded tenement on the Lower East Side of New York) are now, a few generations later, experiencing the affluence that social mobility can yield, but often at the cost of assimilation. On the other hand, some groups achieve affluence while refusing to assimilate: these Hutterites, religious commune members, live in the Midwest on large, successful farmland and follow their sect's traditional norms and values.

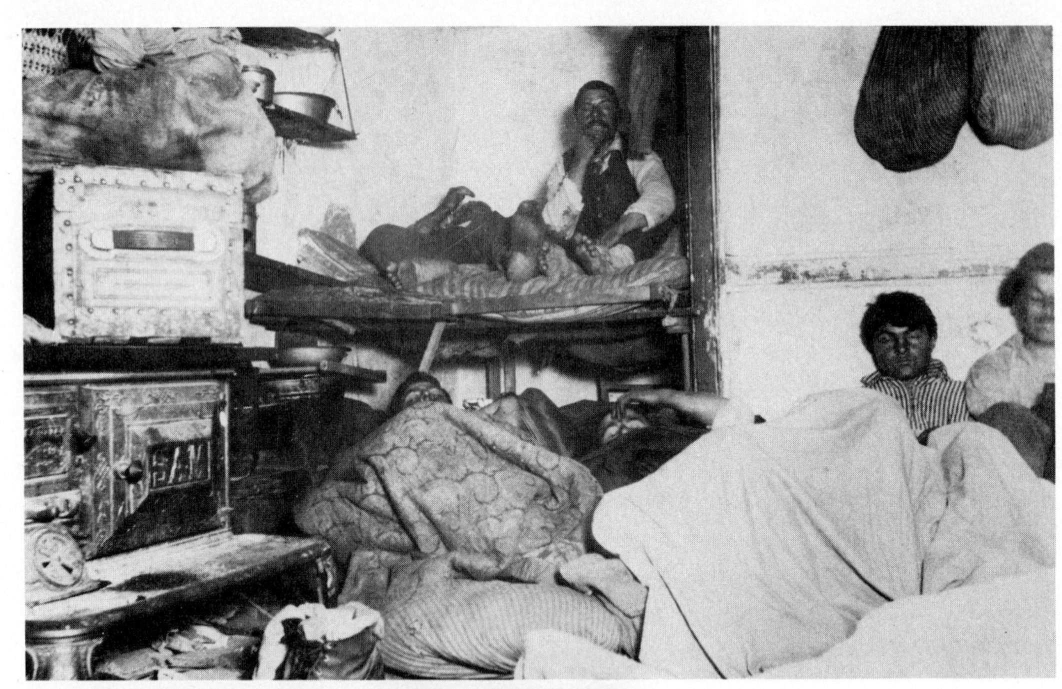

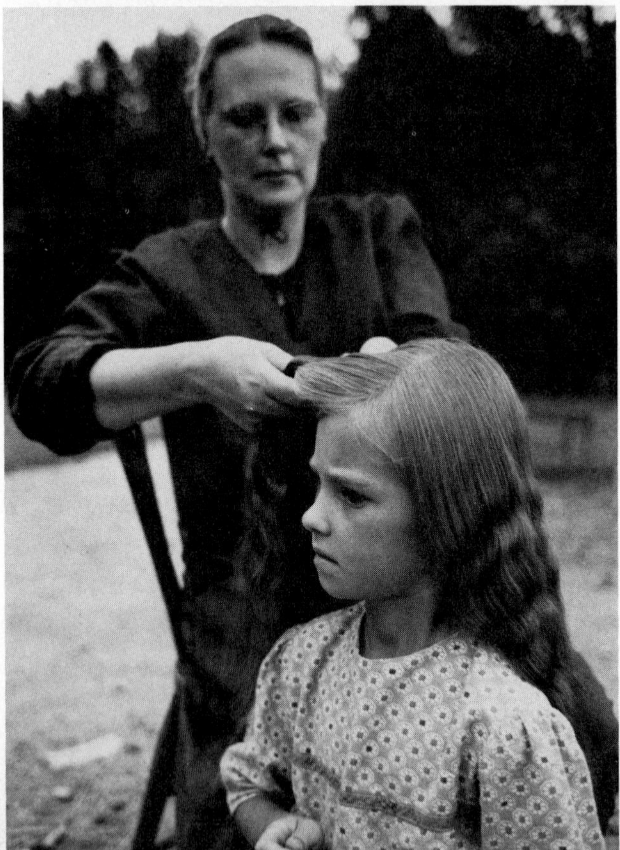

Wyckham: So they know. They still turn their backs, except when they are personally affected. When people get laid off themselves, *then* they begin to understand what it is not to work. When their own kids have to go to Vietnam, then they wake up to what we have been doing. When . . .

Fisher: Now just a minute. You know, better than any of us, Cy, that things can change. You were in the forefront of the civil rights movement. We've seen more changes on the racial front in the last fifteen years than in the previous hundred.

Wyckham: Right. And they came about when people were willing to stand up and be counted. When they really challenged the old system. But even that wasn't enough. What happened was that the people in power did what they always do in this country when there is real pressure: they engaged in tokenism. They gave a little to save a lot.

Fisher: I agree with you, in part; only I see that as the genius of the system. It says, in essence, "I don't agree with you, but I hear what you are saying. Let's work out a compromise." It says, "You cool it, and we will work something out." And often something is worked out. More jobs, perhaps. More access to the universities. More recognition. Maybe some new facilities.

Wyckham: That's cooptation. That's simply a slick way of conning some of the protesters into thinking they have made real gains and then using them to defuse the protest. What is really happening is an attempt to integrate a select few into the system.

Fisher: Precisely. And it works.

Wyckham: Come on, Janice. It "works" for how long? People can be part of an integrated system and still be on the short end of the stick. A functionalist like you should know that. What is important is that the system works, right? Equality has nothing to do with it—you've said that before. Face facts. This country is not so tolerant. It is an oppressive society where only the rich and powerful have any real clout. They are the gatekeepers. They decide who to let in—and how far. And they are not about to let anyone tear down the gates.

Jordan: But there are times when the people can have clout, too. If we have time I'd like to illustrate how changes have come about in this society by using three examples: the assimilation of immigrants, women's roles, and our sexual mores.

Moderator: Go ahead, Professor Jordan.

Jordan: In colonial times, this country was an Anglo-Saxon nation to which newcomers were "invited." They were welcome as long as they shed their foreign ways. Later on, when it was apparent that not all who came wished to assimilate so completely that they lost their former identities—when ethnic enclaves dotted the expanding maps, and when ethnic neighborhoods began to abound the cities—we began speaking of the United States as a "melting pot," a place where the ingredients of varied civilizations would be blended into a new social stew. This did happen to some extent through social mixing and intermarriage. At least, many people paid lip-service to the idea of the melting pot and prided themselves on their contribution to the overall heritage.

But, again, reality intruded. Many ethnic groups coexisted within the society but were not assimilated into it. This fact of persisting cultural pluralism led us to recognize that the nation was not so much a melting pot as, in Horace Kallen's words, an orchestra. Each group is like a section—strings, brass, percussion, woodwinds—with its own timbre and tonality. Together the various ethnic and religious groups provide the harmonies and dissonances of a vibrant society.

Thus, cultural pluralism was a fact in American society before it became a theory. Today, pluralism is recognized as a characteristic of American life.

Now, I recognize that our racial problems have not been resolved this way. In fact, until very recently, nonwhites had to try to adopt the characteristics of whites in order to be accepted. Pluralism for them was considered unacceptable separatism. Nevertheless, the civil rights and black power movements made great strides in getting political, business, and labor leaders to begin redressing the grievances of those discriminated against. Although in the past few years there has been a retreat on the commitment to civil rights, so that the goals have not been met, blacks have made headway against strong resistance. And it's undeniable that black people feel differently about themselves from the way they did fifteen years ago.

In the years ahead, I believe we will see a return to the commitment to the justice for all. It may well take another wave of unrest and civil disobedience, but it is inevitable.

My second example concerns American women. The colonists had rather traditional views of the role of women in the political life of societies. With some rare exceptions, women were considered beyond the pale of political activity. Despite the fact that they toiled at home and in the fields side by side with the menfolk, they were, on the one hand, put up on a pedestal and, on the other, put down by those who said they didn't have heads for making the tough decisions of life. They had no vote and few privileges of their own. Even the Bill of Rights expressed the view that all *men* were created—and to be treated—equal. Not women. In the 1840s and 1850s, spurred by their involvement in the antislavery campaign then going on, a number of women began to challenge the character of their own "servitude." Their women's rights movement won several skirmishes, but it was cut off by the Civil War. When women resumed their battle for equality at the end of the nineteenth century, they girded their efforts to the struggle for suffrage. Finally, in 1919, this culminated in passage of the nineteenth amendment to the Constitution.

The suffragist fight was the second wave of the struggle for "women's liberation." The movement of the 1960s and 1970s is the third and the most far-reaching. While women achieved many rights in law, they still faced discrimination in almost every sphere of life. In ten years their persistent pressure on institutions and organizations, on men in general and on husbands, fathers, brothers, and lovers in particular, has brought about significant changes. Consciousness-raising has stretched the old norms beyond their limits, and new norms—and ideas about women—have begun to replace the old.

Moderator: Are you saying that women are really different as a result of these pressures?

Jordan: Yes, I think we are. And I think men are too. I think society is different.

Wyckham: There is still ample evidence of sexism in our society. Just look at our training of future mechanics and future presidents.

Fisher: That's not the point. Women's liberation is great. Even I benefit from it. I've had more attractive job offers in the last two years than in the last twenty. But, as a professional, I really think that those who are impatient and want to change things too quickly are disrupting more than they realize. Plenty of men are unfairly discriminated against because quota systems are replacing qualifications. A backlash is setting in. If women start competing in earnest for scarce jobs, something's got to give. For men to be out of work is more devastating than for women. After all, our society is still oriented to having men be breadwinners and women take care of them. Those are still generally followed norms. And, the data indicate that, unlike middle-class women, many working-class women like it that way. They aren't too eager to work at some of the deadly dull jobs open to them.

Wyckham: But, if we had a different system, we wouldn't have to worry constantly about who was going to be laid off. If our system was designed to give priority to full employment, instead of to profiteering, women and men wouldn't be pitted against each other in a scramble for scarce jobs. We don't really know what working-class women would like if they weren't subjected to so much economic insecurity. No wonder they want their men to be breadwinners. Look at the alternatives open to these women—low-paid factory and service jobs. You yourself said they were "deadly dull."

Moderator: Let's go back to Professor Jordan. I'm going to ask for her third example, and then I want to pose one final question to you all.

Jordan: I mentioned changes with regard to ethnic groups and women's rights and roles. Let me take an even more loaded subject: sex.

For centuries a double standard has existed: males could sow their wild oats—so long as they did so on the other side of the tracks—and prove their masculinity by words and deeds. Women—"nice" women that is—were expected to be virginal, saving themselves for their husbands. Women's liberation has altered this view considerably, and premarital sex between men and women has become normative if not formally sanctioned.

But these changed mores are nothing compared to the changes in attitudes that have occurred relating to homosexual behavior. Until very recently, homosexuality was considered sinful, degenerate, and sick. No self-respecting man or woman could openly display sexual attraction to members of his or her own sex. Yet, in the wake of civil rights activities relating to racial minorities and to women, homosexuals began, in their own words, "to come out of the closet." Gay liberation, a movement that began in the late 1960s, has brought about profound changes not only in sexual behavior but also in attitudes toward it. Under pressure and publicity from people who no longer accept social views of what are proper and improper sexual relationships, homosexuals and their supporters have gained recognition for their cause.

Fisher: I'd like to comment on something that Terry suggests but does not say. It is an important sociological point that relates her examples to something about which I feel quite strongly. While it is true that changes of all kinds have occurred in recent years—the three she mentioned are but a sampling—many people seem to feel that these changes demonstrate the willingness of our society to stretch its tolerance limits to satisfy the needs of individuals who feel left out or discriminated against. That is true. But it is also true that the reason authorities are willing to do so—whether they be employers or college administrators or government officials—is because they see acquiescence as a means of preserving the system.

Wyckham: Exactly.

Fisher: Wait, Cy, I'm not finished. You see, you think it is a bad thing to try to absorb the dissidents. I don't. I think it is essential to the well-being of a society that reform be orderly and at a pace that the society can absorb. If not, the entire equilibrium of society can be upset and chaos can result in benefits for no group.

Wyckham: That is my basic disagreement with functionalists like Janice Fisher. I think there is a real question about whether you can gradually patch up a failing welfare system, an alienated labor force, a swollen military establishment, given the highly uneven distribution of power we have. Sure, the country will stay afloat a while longer, but it is destined to sink. That's the United States at two hundred years of age: a ship stuck together with bandaids.

Making your sort of concession to protesters simply cools them down. It's clever all right. Any attempt at genuine revolutionary change is dampened by expanding what is acceptable. The outsiders—blacks, women, homosexuals, and others—are taken into the fold and, feeling grateful for admittance, curb their zeal to overturn the system. What I think is less visible is the seething anger that most blacks still feel in their slums, the potential violence that may explode in a way we can't control—not because changes occurred too rapidly, but because unemployment, poverty, and racism continued at their present levels.

Moderator: I must get to that last question, since time is fleeting. Where are we going from here? I gather from Professor Wyckham's remarks that he thinks we are going nowhere, that the period some have called "the American era" is coming to a sad ending.

Wyckham: Not sad. Just an ending. As you know, I have little faith in this society. It uses warfare to build itself up and welfare to keep people thinking everything is just fine. It is built on a mystique of individualism that is belied by the very fact that the little guy can never run an even race. The United States was founded on lofty values and ideals that no one can fault: life, liberty, the pursuit of happiness. But it never seems able to realize its own proclaimed destiny. It is a society crying for a real revolution—not one like the war of 1776. That was really just a civil war between British monarchists and British republicans. I'm talking about a true revolution. And yet I fear it will never occur. There will be protest, violence, rebellion, but it will come to nothing, because the people are controlled by the powerful. The people are forever told that they really have the best of all possible worlds. You'd no doubt say the fabric is too strong.

Fisher: I think you've just admitted something that many of us have tried to say. Like it or not, the American system is an integrated society, and it's going to last a very long time. It will last, because it will continue to be what it has been in the past—a dynamic society that values its heritage. It recognizes that one of the most significant aspects of that heritage is a future orientation, a belief that the past was good, the present is better, and the future will be better still.

Jordan: I think we're in for some rough sledding and our famous future orientation will be undergoing some rude reorientations in the years ahead. In recent years the raw wounds of this society have been exposed. Our tensions and fears have been expressed. We have suffered—through misadventure or mismanagement or sheer bullheadedness—in foreign policy and domestically. But we've also proved that we can deal with defeat, disillusionment, even corruption in the highest places. As many people said in the wave of relief after the Nixon impeachment hearings, "The system works."

Moderator: Our time is up. Once again, we are left with a variety of views and no clear answers to our questions. What the three sociologists have done is to provoke our thinking about the nature of our society. That, I suppose they would all agree, is really the function of such discussions.

So I leave you with some questions I posed to them: Is the United States an integrated society? How does it deal with its many problems, and how should it deal with them? What is the future of this nation?

Our imaginary program raises a number of questions about the ways sociologists look at society, in this case our own society. Like the moderator, we note that there was only partial agreement. Yet all three sociologists used common concepts to analyze the problem they were given. They had to explore the nature of a social system, cultural norms and values, social relationships, institutional requirements, stratification and differentiation, the purposes and consequences of socialization, the sense of community, and the character of social change. Had they been asked to present scholarly papers, rather than speak off the top of their heads, they would have marshaled mounds of evidence to support their various positions. And they would have been considerably more precise in their exchanges with one another.

A SUMMARY AND AN ASSIGNMENT

In all the other chapters of this volume the text has been interspersed with activities challenging you to try to deal with a particular concept or technique or problem. So far, in this chapter, the questions have been posed by a hypothetical moderator to three imaginary sociologists. Obviously these sociologists are composites of individuals who range along the continuum discussed in Chapter 2. At one end is the person who takes an essentially *functional* approach, seeing society as an integrated whole in which the norms, values, and institutions mesh sufficiently well to form a relatively smoothly functioning system.[1] At the other end is the *conflict theorist,* who sees society as essentially divided into various factions that exist in a constant state of tension. Rather than consensus, coercion is the principal binding force. Relationships, according to conflict theory, are underscored not by mutual interest but by controlled antagonism.[2] Dominant groups invariably exercise control over those in subordinate positions.

In between these extremes of the continuum are many sociologists who argue that there is in fact an alternating rule of conflict and consensus. Robin Williams, for example, has written that "all interacting human populations show both coerced and voluntary conformity,"[3] and even the well-known functionalist A. R. Radcliffe-Brown has stated that "opposition, that is, organized and regulated antagonism, is, of course, an essential feature of every social system."[4] Richard Schermerhorn argues that each of these "ostensibly clashing theories" is equally applicable in many areas of investigation. Choosing the field of ethnic relations, Schermerhorn writes:

> The expansion of European peoples to other parts of the globe from the fifteenth to the nineteenth centuries was a succession of conquests overpowering innumerable "native" peoples by coercion. To a number of Western Hemisphere countries with such a historical past came millions of immigrants in the nine-

[1]For articulations of the functionalist view, see Talcott Parsons, *The Social System* (Glencoe, Ill.: Free Press, 1951), and Marion J. Levy, *Modernization and the Structure of Societies* (Princeton, N.J.: Princeton University Press, 1966).

[2]The conflict theory position is clearly expressed by Ralf Dahrendorf, *Class and Conflict in Industrial Society* (Stanford, Calif.: Stanford University Press, 1959), and Gerhard Lenski, *Power and Privilege: A Theory of Social Stratification* (New York: McGraw-Hill, 1966).

[3]Robin M. Williams, Jr., "Some Further Comments on Chronic Controversies," *American Journal of Sociology* 71 (1966): 718.

[4]A. R. Radcliffe-Brown, *Structure and Function in Primitive Society* (Glencoe, Ill.: Free Press, 1952), p. 181n.

teenth and twentieth centuries; yet in this latter invasion, strife and violence were exceptional rather than the rule. . . . Here are two contrasting social situations, conquest and migration, where quite opposite forms of social interaction ensue.[5]

In recent years a number of theorists have taken positions that are essentially similar to that expressed by Schermerhorn. Among them are Lewis Coser, Kingsley Davis, Robert K. Merton, and Pierre van den Berghe.[6] Like the hypothetical Terry Jordan, they generally argue that conflict, in the United States and elsewhere, may be functional for stimulating change or for enhancing cohesion, while consensus may be dysfunctional, leading to a kind of hardening of the social arteries.

The fact remains that there are sharp differences of opinion about the nature of society in general and American society in particular. Some favor the consensus model, others the conflict position, and others an interplay between the forces of consensus and the forces of conflict. Robin Williams sums up the view of many when he writes:

As we have seen, much controversy has raged over the question, which of these doctrines is correct? My own answer is quite direct: all are correct in part, all are partly wrong, none is wholly adequate. Actual societies are held together by consensus, by interdependence, by sociability, and by coercion. This has always been the case, and there is no reason to expect it to be otherwise in any foreseeable future. The real job is to show how actual social structures and processes operating in these ways can be predicted and explained. That task will require our best efforts for a long time to come.[7]

It will require the efforts of sociologists already practicing their profession and sociologists just being trained, people like you in fact, who may have their own ideas of how to apply the basic principles about the nature of society to actual ongoing social systems. If you go to the vast literature you will see how common are the references to the matters we have discussed

[5]Richard A. Schermerhorn, *Comparative Ethnic Relations* (New York: Random House, 1970), pp. 51–52.

[6]See Lewis A. Coser, *The Functions of Social Conflict* (Glencoe, Ill.: Free Press, 1956); Kingsley Davis, "The Myth of Functional Analysis as a Special Method in Sociology and Anthropology," *American Sociological Review* 24 (1959): 757–72; Robert K. Merton, *Social Theory and Social Structure* (Glencoe, Ill.: Free Press, 1949); and Pierre van den Berghe, "Dialectic and Functionalism: Toward a Theoretical Synthesis," *American Sociological Review* 28 (1963): 695–705.

[7]Williams, "Some Further Comments," p. 721.

throughout this text, how much sociologists rely on the basic concepts of culture and society, institution and group, role and position, how often they examine such processes as socialization, urbanization, and various forms of social change, to give them a point of departure for their own theoretical excursions. Even now you must be aware that Janice Fisher, Cyrus Wyckham, and Terry Jordan, like Talcott Parsons, Ralf Dahrendorf, and Pierre van den Berghe, are all "speaking the same language" despite their differing perceptions of the nature of society itself.

The only questions asked in this chapter were those presented by the moderator of the debate. Now suppose that you are on that panel.

1. From what you have learned about sociology, its conceptual underpinnings and its varying perspectives, write an introductory statement giving your sociological assessment of the American system at its two hundredth birthday. To make your arguments as clear as possible, note in the margins which points are based on facts, which ones are based on assumptions drawn from your understanding of American norms and values and various people's interpretations of them, and which are based on your own theoretical perspective.

2. Exchange papers with another class member, one whom you feel has a different theoretical position, and then write a rejoinder or rebuttal to each other's arguments.

OR

3. Stage your own debate, similar to the Fisher-Wyckham-Jordan panel we described.

APPENDIX

THE RESEARCH PROCESS

Sociological research covers almost every aspect of social life—child-rearing practices, voter behavior, population growth and control, crime and justice, religious affiliations or their absence, role conflict, communication among workers in large corporations, ethnic group loyalties, and thousands of other areas of investigation. Although some sociologists specialize in one research area, such as crime, education, or population, most do research in many areas. Research can be broad or narrow in scope, ranging from, say, the study of how social structures reflect culture to the modes of interaction in a group of rural teenagers.

The several ways of gathering and analyzing social research data follow the scientific model. In such a model, an issue or topic for research is identified; hypotheses are made; and data are gathered and analyzed to test the hypotheses. We will look at each of these components of the research process in some detail.

SELECTING AN AREA FOR RESEARCH

What motivates sociologists to choose a particular area of research? There are many possible reasons and combinations of reasons. One common motive is for researchers to understand their *personal experiences* better. A black person or Chicano who has known discrimination may be drawn to do research in intergroup relations. Ex-soldiers may decide to study sociological issues relevant to the military. People who have grown up in rural villages and watched them become suburbs of expanding cities might decide to study urban problems.

Public issues such as rising crime rates, pollution, interracial school busing, and political corruption also may spark the interest of researchers. Many sociologists, privately funded or supported by grants, do research on public issues to learn more than is commonly known about them and perhaps to contribute solutions or ideas for improvements.

Theoretical problems—many generated by the ideas of Karl Marx, Émile Durkheim, Max Weber, Robert Park, Talcott Parsons, and other sociologists mentioned in this book—often provide the bases for empirical research. Studies at the macrosociological level are frequently prompted by questions about the nature of society itself, about consensus and dissensus, about the causes and consequences of social change. Examples are found in comparative studies of various societies and in research on individual societies. Microsociological research is also often based on larger theoretical issues. Such matters as the meaning of friendship as a social process, the bases of group cohesion, and the workings of the socialization process are subjects.

FORMULATING QUESTIONS

Social scientists want to know what makes the society, the community, and the group tick. They want to be able to *describe* the patterns of social relationships they study, to *explain* what is going on, and to *predict* what might happen in the future. Sometimes they want to be able to *prescribe* particular courses of action or to find out what others would prescribe. The accuracy of a sociologist's predictions is a partial test of the correctness of his or her descriptions and explanations. Describing, explaining, predicting, and prescribing require four kinds of questions.

A *descriptive question* asks for factual information. How many people attended the Billy Graham Rally on October 31, 1974? What are the socioeconomic classes, ethnic groups, political affiliations, etc., of the people who support the Sierra Club?

An *explanatory question* asks why something happens. It starts from the answers to descriptive questions. Why did black leadership shift the emphasis from civil rights to black power in the mid-1960s? Why are an increasing number of American marriages ending in divorce today?

A *predictive question* asks about what will happen. Will the divorce rate continue to climb in the United States? (This may be combined with an explanatory question: Why or why not?) What will be the outcome of the school busing dispute?

A *prescriptive question* determines what ought to happen or be done. What should a school board do about the lack of funds for girls' sports? What should Congress do to get people to use less energy?

Later in this chapter we see how to apply knowledge of these types of questions in creating survey questionnaires.

1. Indicate whether each of the following questions is descriptive, explanatory, predictive, or prescriptive.

What should be done to prevent airplane hijacking?

Which branch of Congress has power to impeach the president?

Why did the price of oil rise so dramatically in the winter of 1974?

Who makes the financial decisions in the average American family?

When will there be a new election for president of your student body?

Should the president grant amnesty to war resisters?

Why do reported crime rates seem to rise and fall?

Who are the three most influential people in your town?

Are poor people more likely to become criminals than rich people?

Why is the burning of an American flag considered a crime?

2. Make up two more questions of each of the four types.

DEFINING KEY TERMS

Often the questions that social scientists raise contain terms that must be defined. For example, let's look at a question from the list above: Are poor people more likely to become criminals than rich people? This has three terms (*poor people, rich people, criminals*) that must be defined before the connections between wealth and criminal behavior can be studied. Getting an acceptable definition of rich and poor may give us some trouble. We could adopt the government definition of poverty, to classify people as poor. But what income figure would we use to define *rich?*

Defining *criminal* might be even more troublesome. Can you clearly define the term? Here are some possible definitions: a person who violates the law; a person convicted of committing any act defined by the state as a crime; a person with two (or three or four) criminal convictions.

Clearly, the first definition is too vague. People who have never violated the law would be hard to find. And many people would not accept the label criminal for a person with a single conviction. The conviction might be for a "crime of passion" or one committed while drunk. People would generally reserve the term for those who show a pattern of criminal behavior. But how many incidents make a pattern?

Another problem with using convictions as a measure of criminal behavior is that only a small proportion of all criminal acts lead to conviction. Many violators are never caught. Many others never come to trial. Other people receive a string of convictions for acts of civil disobedience—as part of their civil rights or antiwar protests—yet many would not consider these people criminals.

An early task in social research, therefore, is to define key concepts in terms of the operations used in performing them. For example, suppose a key concept in our proposed research is *heavy coffee drinker.* To qualify as a heavy coffee drinker in our study, we decide that a person must drink more than eight cups of coffee daily. These are the *operations* that define the participant in our study as a heavy coffee drinker. We have thus *operationalized* the term, so that a person wishing to repeat the study and test its accuracy can know exactly how it was done the first time.

A social scientist might choose to define a *criminal* as a person with two or more criminal convictions. If this operational definition of criminal is clearly stated in the report of the research or experiment, any person reading it knows precisely what set of people was included in the study. The reader can then raise the same questions we raised about the accuracy of the definition and can judge the experiment accordingly. To deal with data about criminals or any other key term, we must define the term so that it can be measured or counted.

1. In the following two questions, operationalize the terms in italics.

Are *business education students* more likely than other high school students of this state to take a course in economics?

Do college students coming from *small towns* get better grades than those from *big cities?*

2. Make up two more questions containing terms that need operationalizing in order to conduct social research. Then operationalize the terms.

FORMULATING HYPOTHESES

The two questions above whose terms we asked you to operationalize ask about relationships that might exist between two or more things. The first question asks about the possible relationship between enrollment in economics courses and enrollment in the business education curriculum. The second question asks about the relationship between a student's college grade average and the size of the student's home town.

Many of the questions asked by social scientists inquire about how one aspect of society relates to another, for example:

1. Are second marriages more likely than first marriages to end in divorce? (We studied this question in Chapter 1.)

2. Are alcoholics more likely than other people to have parents who are alcoholics?

3. Does the crime rate increase during periods of high unemployment?

4. Are boys more likely to start conversations with girls who look them directly in the eye?

In doing research, scientists often turn questions about relationships into statements. For example, the question "Are poor people more likely to become criminals than rich people?" can be turned into three alternative statements, or *hypotheses:*

1. Poor people are more likely to become criminals than rich people.

2. Rich people are more likely to become criminals than poor people.

3. Poor and rich persons are equally likely to become criminals.

A hypothesis is a hunch, or educated guess, about how two or more things are related. The task of the researcher is to test the hunch to see if it is true.

1. Take the four questions we gave as examples above and turn each into a hypothesis.

2. Your first hypothesis talks about the relationship between divorce rates and first and second marriages. What relationships do your other hypotheses ask about?

The parts of the relationship that make up a hypothesis are called *variables.* The variables in the hypothesis, "Poor people are more likely to become criminals than rich people," are *amount of wealth* and *criminality.*

In any research project there is at least one *dependent* variable and often more than one *independent* variable. A *variable* is a trait or characteristic that can vary or change in different cases. An independent variable is a characteristic that is considered to be the cause of something or to effect changes in something. A dependent variable is the factor that the independent variable is expected to change. For example, wealth is a variable because people can be poor, or rich, or in between. In our hypothesis it is the independent variable that is expected to affect criminality—the dependent variable. Three common social class variables are lower, middle, and upper. We saw in Chapter 7 that many social variables are related to social class. Infant mortality rates, years of education, age at time of marriage, and size of family are dependent variables in relation to the independent variable social class.

We have noted that hypotheses are guesses about the relationships between two or more variables. To test a hypothesis, sociologists must collect evidence and analyze the facts.

THE RESEARCH DESIGN

Social research requires a plan for gathering data and then sifting and analyzing them. The choice of a research design, or plan of action, is influenced by many factors. Most important, of course, are the questions that have to be answered. If, for example, you want to test a hypothesis about national attitudes toward political participation, face-to-face interviews would not be practical because your respondents are widely scattered. More than likely you would choose a questionnaire or survey to gather your data. If you are considering a historical hypothesis about colonial Americans, you would design a study that relies heavily on library resources (books, historical documents, and scholarly articles) rather than survey techniques.

In other research projects, in-depth interviews and observations of people might best fit your design. For example, the impact of technology on Amish customs and values could best be studied by a combination of observing the Amish life-style and interviewing Amish people about changes in their beliefs. Such information is not likely to be available in books, and Amish men and women might respond more readily to a personal interview than to a questionnaire. Thus, the type of question your hypothesis raises will favor particular techniques to help you answer it.

The research design consists of several steps. We have already looked at the first steps in some detail: to identify and operationalize the concepts or variables and to state the predicted relationship in the form of a hypothesis. Suppose we want to study the relationship between school work and sports activity. We think that football or any other sports activity probably interferes with school work, so we predict—or hypothesize—that "athletes are more apt to get lower college grades than nonathletes." We operationally define *athletes* as all members of college athletic teams. To test our hypothesis we must now collect evidence and analyze the facts. We have to gather information about the relative grade averages of college athletes and nonathletes.

The next step is to decide which sources of information and what sample of the available data to use. For example, we cannot study all college students in the world or even all those in the United States or in the area. But we might select four colleges in one big city and four in a large rural district as representative of the broader category of, say, colleges in the area, and get lists of all the athletes (according to the operational definition) and all the other students, the nonathletes. Then, using random selection (described later in this chapter), we could choose fifty from each list for each college, giving a total of 400 athletes and 400 nonathletes as representatives. Or we might use only ten athletes and ten nonathletes from a college, but draw samples from every college in the state.

GATHERING DATA

Suppose we have stated our hypothesis, identified and defined the variables, and devised a plan for collecting the facts to prove or disprove our "educated guess." The next step in designing a research plan is to select a procedure for collecting the information. Let's look at various techniques for gathering data.

Reading the Literature

Almost all studies begin with a review of what others interested in the same problem have written before. Researchers examine "the literature" in order to find out what others have learned—and haven't learned.

Suppose you want to study the relationship between the social class backgrounds of freshman students and their political attitudes. Before completing your research design, you ought to examine any studies done by others on student attitudes.

You could start with the *Reader's Guide to Periodical Literature*, an index of articles in some of the more general periodicals, to find writings on your subject. *Sociological Abstracts*, which offers brief summaries of articles, essays, and books on a variety of sociological subjects, is another good source. Specialized journals of education and politics and magazines such as the *Satur-*

day Review, *Society*, and *Psychology Today* often carry useful articles for the social science researcher.

Looking through the indexes of the *American Sociological Review* (the official journal of the American Sociological Association), the *American Journal of Sociology*, *Social Forces*, *Social Problems*, and the *Sociology of Education* can provide additional help. *Contemporary Sociology*, a journal of book reviews, is especially helpful because it examines recent books that might deal with the subject you wish to study. The library card catalog also lists books on the topic. Additonal help may be found in collections of research studies in sociology, such as the *Handbook of Sociology*. There are more specialized collections on specific topics—prison reform, race relations, and education, for example.

The practice of going to the literature is both useful and necessary. It is useful because previous reports can give you many ideas about methods that proved effective, pitfalls to avoid in operationalizing terms, and so on. It is necessary because you can avoid wasting time "reinventing the wheel"—duplicating work that other researchers have done. Their reports will tell you what their findings were.

Published findings can often be used as a frame of reference. If you find a 1960 study on your chosen subject, you could frame your own study not only to analyze how the political attitudes of today's college freshmen relate to their social class but also to compare their political attitudes with those of the 1960 freshmen. If you find a recent study that concentrates on one region of the country, you might compare the correlations between social class and political attitude in your region with those found in the other region.

There are times, of course, when a search through the literature turns up very little on your precise subject. Even then, however, you might find useful information and ideas in research on related matters. Although you may find little that bears directly on your study of the relationship between students' social classes and political attitudes, your search of the literature may produce useful information on overall changes in social class makeup and mobility or other influences on the political attitudes of students (ethnic background or urban versus rural upbringing, for instance).

Using Documents and Other Library Resources

The library can also provide you with general source materials. These include back issues of newspapers, original documents, collections of letters, and, in recent times, tapes and recordings.

Library research takes three principal forms. Social history research is simply the use of historical records as a source for describing the past. Such research is unlike the following two forms in that it is nonquantified (not translated into numbers), whereas they are quantified. The second form of library research, historical/statistical analysis, uses statistics drawn from the records of the past. (Durkheim's study of suicide, examined in Chapter 2, relied heavily on such analysis for data.) The third form of library research, content analysis, is an objective quantification of recurrent word patterns. For example, Stephen Sales[1] performed a comparative content analysis on comic strips in newspapers of the 1920s and 1930s for recurrent terms and phrases that he correlated to attitudes toward authority. He found much greater evidence of authoritarian notions in the 1930s, the period of the Great Depression when the federal government was very active in the economy and related social institutions. Likewise, Diana Scully and Pauline Bart[2] performed a content analysis of gynecology textbooks to discover changes in the attitudes these books indicated that gynecologists had about the female sex role and sexuality.

Formulate a hypothesis for a content analysis of

daytime soap opera scripts
army training manuals
lyrics to current rock/pop music

Observing People in Social Situations

Much social research involves "people-watching." If the researcher is personally involved in what he or she is observing, the method is called *participant observation.* If the researcher is an outside observer "looking on," the method is called *nonparticipant observation.*

Participant observation: getting involved. Investigators often conceal who they are from those being studied. This might be called *concealed* participant observation in contrast to *open* observation. Using the concealed observation method, the investigator disguises himself or herself as a member of the subject group in order to observe the situation more closely. A sociologist might go through basic police science training disguised as a cadet, or might join a Black Muslim temple or a Vermont commune to observe its inner workings.

[1]Stephen Sales, "Authoritarianism," *Psychology Today* 6 (November 1972): 94.

[2]Diana Scully and Pauline Bart, "A Funny Thing Happened on the Way to the Orifice: Women in Gynecology Texts," *American Journal of Sociology* 78 (January 1973): 1045–50.

One of the most effective uses of this technique was made by John Howard Griffin, a Texas newspaperman who wanted to experience racial prejudice as the southern black man experienced it.[3] Reaching that goal was far from simple. Being white, Griffin felt that he could never get black people to talk to him candidly. Nor did he think he could really understand their plight without facing their problems. He decided to become black.

Griffin shaved his head and altered the color of his skin through sun-lamp treatments and the use of dyes. For many weeks he moved, undetected, through the black world, learning to see his two selves (the one white, the other black) in new lights. By hitchhiking, applying for jobs, entering diners and hotels, he learned the stigma of black skin in the South of the late 1950s. In time, as the deep tan began to fade, he would move between the two worlds, one day as a white man, the next (sometimes with the aid of a bit more dye) as a black.

His report, first published in *Sepia* magazine and later in his book *Black Like Me,* offered his fellow whites a glimpse of people that many of them thought they knew but really did not. Among blacks who read it, there were mixed reactions. Most reviews praised his effort and his motive. Some, however, felt that even such an experience could never give an outsider a real sense of what it meant to be black in this predominantly white nation.

Another example of concealed observation was conducted by Muzafer Sherif in a study of a boys' camp.[4] To observe the interaction between campers, Sherif adopted the role of Mr. Muzee, the handyman. He could then observe every part of camp life without arousing suspicion.

Suppose you wanted to study conditions in the jail of the hall of justice. How would you get the information you needed? Would you consider having yourself imprisoned for a short time? If so, what would you tell the other inmates? How would you identify yourself?

Sociologists have wrestled for many years with ethical questions about concealed observation. Many feel that, no matter how effective it is, this technique is unfair. They argue that it is not very different from hiding a tape recorder in a committee meeting or wiretapping a telephone conversation, activities that are against the law under most circumstances in this country.

[3]John Howard Griffin, *Black Like Me* (Boston: Houghton-Mifflin, 1961).

[4]Muzafer Sherif and Carolyn W. Sherif, *Groups in Harmony and Tension: An Integration of Studies on Intergroup Relations* (New York: Harper, 1953).

Other sociologists disagree. They argue that the knowledge gained by use of these methods may be so valuable in helping our society understand itself that the methods used to obtain that knowledge are justified.

Sociologists who reject the use of concealed observation may use open observation. In that method, the researcher participates in the life of the group under study as a recognized and accepted outsider. The people being studied are aware of the researcher's purpose for being there.

A number of excellent community studies mentioned in this book used this method. In Chapter 12 we saw how Arthur Vidich and Joseph Bensman reported on life in a village in upstate New York. Ulf Hannerz used this method to report on a black community in Washington, D.C. John Lofland used it to study a fundamentalist group that believed in the imminent end of the world. He got the cooperation of group members because they were convinced they would convert him. William Foote Whyte's study of an Italian urban neighborhood is often cited as the best example of open observation.[5]

Whyte describes a section of an Italian-American neighborhood in Boston in the 1940s. The author could hardly pass for a member of the community he wanted to study, since he was a middle-class Protestant studying at Harvard. What he did was to impress on the neighborhood people his desire to learn something about their community. He moved into the area. He learned some Italian. Most important, he made friends with Doc, one of the leaders of the "Corner Boys." Doc became Whyte's guide, informant, and friend. With Doc, Whyte was able to move freely into what had been, to him, unfriendly territory.

Whyte wanted to understand the social organization of "Cornerville." He observed its people on the street, in their homes, in recreation halls, at political meetings, and in gambling joints. He constantly made mental notes of who spoke to whom, what was said, who were the leaders, and who were the followers. As soon as he returned to his room he wrote down and filed these observations. When he was unclear about a point, he continued to watch and listen.

During his three years of research, Whyte became interested in the Cornerville Social and Athletic Club, which included a number of influential

[5]See Joseph Bensman and Arthur Vidich, *Small Town in Mass Society: Class, Power, and Religion in a Rural Community* (Princeton, N.J.: Princeton University Press, 1958); Ulf Hannerz, *Soulside: Inquiries into Ghetto Culture and Community* (New York: Columbia University Press, 1969); John Lofland, *The Doomsday Cult* (Englewood Cliffs, N.J.: Prentice-Hall, 1966); William Foote Whyte, *Street Corner Society: The Social Structure of an Italian Slum* (Chicago: University of Chicago Press, 1943).

people. Whyte saw that there were two major groups in the club. He hoped to be able to tell which people sided with each faction so that he could later predict how people would line up on a major political issue.

Here I had a more complicated task than any I had faced before. The club had fifty members. Fortunately, only about thirty of them were frequent attenders so that I could concentrate on that smaller number, but even that number presented a [major] problem.

I felt I would have to develop more formal and systematic procedures than I had used when I had been hanging on a street corner with a much smaller group of men. I began with positional mapmaking. Assuming that the men who associated together most closely socially would also be those who lined up together on the same side when decisions were to be made, I set about making a record of the groupings I observed each evening in the club. . . .

When evening activities were going full blast, I looked around the room to see which people were talking together, playing cards together, or otherwise interacting. I counted the number of men in the room, so as to know how many I would have to account for. Since I was familiar with the main physical objects of the clubroom, it was not difficult to get a mental picture of the men in relation to tables, chairs, couches, radio, and so on. When individuals moved about or when there was some interaction between these groupings, I sought to retain that in mind. In the course of an evening, there might be a general reshuffling of positions. . . .

I managed to make a few notes on trips to the men's room, but most of the mapping was done from memory after I had gone home. At first, I went home once or twice for mapping during the evening, but, with practice, I got so that I . . . could do all of my notes at the end of the evening.

I found this an extremely rewarding method . . . . As I piled up these maps, it became evident just what the major social groupings were and what people [moved] between the two factions of the club. As issues arose within the club, I could predict who would stand where.

In the course of my observations I recorded 106 groupings. Upon inspecting the data, I divided the club tentatively into the two factions I thought I was observing. Then, when I re-examined the data, I found that only 40, or 37.7 per cent, of the groupings observed contained members of both factions. I found further that only 10 out of these 40 groupings contained two or more members of each faction. The other 30 were cases where a single individual of the other faction joined in the card game or conversation. I then divided the groupings into two columns, placing in one column those which were predominantly of one faction and in the other column those which were predominantly of the other faction. Then I underlined in red those names which did not "belong" in the column where I found them. Out of a total of 462 names, 75, or approximately 16 per cent, were underlined in red.[6]

[6]Whyte, *Street Corner Society*, pp. 333–35.

Nonparticipant observation: maintaining distance. William Whyte said that there were times when he tried to observe from afar. Looking out from behind the venetian blinds, he tried to watch the comings and goings of various club members.

There are many times when participation is not practical. Indeed, most of us carry on nonparticipant observation daily.

Try some observing.

1. Go to a busy intersection with two of your friends. Stand six to ten feet apart and have each person record everything observed across the street for ten minutes. Compare notes. Do you agree on what you each observed? Why or why not?

2. Now decide on some characteristics or events that you are all going to look *at* and *for*. Repeat the entire process. Compare your notes again.

More and more sociologists use videotape machines or tape recorders to observe and record various sorts of behavior. There is much controversy over the ethics of such scientific snooping. One study in the early 1950s was done by researchers from the University of Chicago who were interested in the American jury system. They wanted to know how the jury came to its decision after listening to the evidence given in court. After much debate, they decided that interviewing jury members or giving them questionnaires to fill out would not get the needed data. The researchers decided they had to record actual discussions among jury members who were unaware that they were being taped.

This turned out to be a difficult task. A number of judges were approached before one agreed to a project using a hidden recording device. The team and the judge who decided to cooperate set up a careful procedure to make sure that the recordings could not harm any defendant or jury member. Still, when the project became public knowledge some months later, many people criticized the taping. Members of the United States Senate accused the team of threatening a vital American institution by eavesdropping on what had always been secret discussions. The senators did not accept the argument that the team wanted to gather firsthand data in order to help improve the jury system.[7]

[7]For a discussion of the jury bugging and a variety of other ethical issues, see Myron Glazer, *The Research Adventure* (New York: Random House, 1972).

1. What is your opinion about the use of hidden recording devices for such purposes? Why? Do some library research on the issue, to learn the laws that apply and the constitutional principles involved. If law enforcement agencies are supposed to adhere to the laws governing wiretapping, can social scientists consider themselves immune to this law?

2. How do you feel about using the same techniques for studying alleged corruption in the office of a city treasurer or some other local agency?

3. How do you feel about "bugging" the conversations of civil rights workers in order to learn the nature of their operations?

Clearly, the answers to these questions of ethics are not easy. Many people approve of the technique in certain circumstances and only for certain purposes. Others say "never." They argue that, while limits might be set on use of such techniques, there would always be abuses. They maintain that the line between proper and improper use is not at all clear.

The Experimental Method

Sometimes sociologists conduct studies using the *experimental* method. These studies use two groups of subjects, an *experimental* group, which actively takes part in the experiment, and a *control* group, which does not. The control group is identical in all ways to the experimental group except that it doesn't participate. At the conclusion of the study the researcher can compare both groups to make sure that changes in the experimental group are the result of the experiment and are not changes that would have taken place anyway.

Here is an illustration of how this method works: Recruits at many military basic training camps used to be housed in open-bay barracks—quarters having beds placed around the walls of one large room. At one such base, the commanding officers noticed that many of the young recruits seemed depressed and lonely. They also tended to go on sick call a good deal to escape work. The officers felt a change was needed.

Relying on the research of Edward A. Shils on primary relations in the German army during World War II, one investigator suggested an experiment. In some of the large barracks, workmen would install partitions to divide the rooms into ten smaller cubicles having six beds each. This would reduce the amount of space in which the men would spend most of their time in the barracks and might help to create a feeling of closeness among them. Recruits would be assigned by random selection to either the new closed-bay barracks or the traditional open-bay ones. Later, judgments would be made about their adjustment to army life, their morale, and other issues.

The results of the study showed that changing the physical environment could affect the social structure and morale. The men in the closed-bay barracks appeared to adjust more rapidly to army life and to establish relationships with one another more easily than those in the open-bay barracks. They appeared to become dependent on a small group of persons, often fellow members of their bay. Since the control-group recruits in open-bay barracks did not show similar improvements in morale, the researcher concluded that the factor causing the change was the rearrangement of the barracks.

In other control-group experiments a "before" and an "after" test are given. For example, a researcher gives a group of students a questionnaire about racial prejudice. Then the group is divided in half at random, and one half is shown a film (or given a lecture) about what prejudice and discrimination can do to people. The other group does not see the film. When restudied (or retested) the experimental group (the group that saw the film) tends to show less prejudice than the control group.

Design a small experiment using two groups of your classmates, one to serve as the control. First ask students in both groups their attitudes toward such topics as the Arab-Israeli conflict, a local political issue, or drug abuse. Then provide the experimental group with propaganda stressing one side of the topic you have chosen. Do not give the same information to your control group. At the conclusion of the study ask both groups to describe their attitudes again. Look for any changes in attitude.

The Sample Survey

To learn in some detail the attitudes, opinions, or beliefs of a large number of people, sociologists often use a sample survey. This technique enables them to question a *cross section* of a population—that is, a portion of the population that can reasonably be expected to represent the thinking of the whole population that interests the researcher.

Suppose you wanted to know whether attitudes toward legalized abortion had any relationship to the region of the country from which people came, their religious beliefs, and their social class. To obtain this information you would want to question people from all parts of the country, making sure that you included people of many religions and social classes from each region. You couldn't very well ask every adult in the nation for his or her views.

Ordinarily it would be impossible even to ask all the adults in a single city. It would be too expensive and time-consuming. Instead you would take a randomly chosen *sample* of people from the total group (which is known as the *universe*).

The universe varies from one study to another. If you are interested in how the people in your community feel about a particular school bond issue, residents of your community are the universe from which you would draw your sample. If you are interested in how Americans in general feel about the financing of public education, all United States citizens are potential members of your study and would thus be your universe. Your sample would be drawn from a national universe.

Sampling techniques. *Sampling* refers to the selection of a small number of people to represent the views of a larger group. The only truly representative sample is one chosen at random, because in a *random sample* every person in the total group (the universe) has an equal chance of being selected.

The size of a sample depends on how much error can be tolerated by the investigator. According to George Gallup, one of the country's best known pollsters,

> formulae have been developed which give the range of error that may result from the size of the sample used for random sampling. Tables based on these formulae show the range of error at each stage as the size of the sample is increased. For example, if only 100 persons properly selected were interviewed in a national survey, the outside margin for error would be 15 per cent. That is to say, 997 times out of 1,000 on the average, the error would not go beyond 15 per cent. When 900 persons throughout the nation are interviewed, the outside limit of error due solely to the size of the sample is reduced to 5 per cent.[8]

If applied to questionnaires rather than interviews, this limit of error would, of course, be based on the assumption that all questionnaires mailed are returned (in other words, that the researcher receives a 100-percent response). Since this rarely occurs, the actual margins of error are higher than those given by the mathematical tables.

Now, let us say that you want to ask citizens of your community their opinions about certain local issues, such as health care and welfare. Your town has 20,000 families (a total of 50,000 adults), most of whom are in the city telephone directory. It would be too costly and time-consuming to poll all the

[8]George Gallup, *A Guide to Public Opinion Polls* (Princeton, N.J.: Princeton University Press, 1948), p. 17.

adults. Instead you decide to use a sample of 500, 1 percent of the 50,000. Using the city directory as your guide, you can pick every hundredth name.

Or you might want to study the views of all students in the two high schools in town. Suppose there are 2,500 in the two schools, and you want a sample of 500. You might write all the names on slips of paper, put them in a big box, mix them thoroughly, and then pick out 500. Or a computer can be programmed to select a sample at random from a list. The machine actually does the same sort of mixing and choosing that you would do in the big box.

Other kinds of samples are frequently used by social scientists: stratified samples, area samples, and quota samples. In a random sample every person in the total population under consideration has an equal chance of being selected. In a *stratified sample* the units to be sampled are first grouped according to certain characteristics that are important to the study, such as geographic location, age, or religion. Then random samples are drawn from each group or stratum. The procedure increases the likelihood that each group will be properly represented in the overall sample. Thus, a stratified sample of all states in the union would draw a proportionate number of sample representatives from each state, according to the ratio of its population to the whole population. A state with a large population, such as New York, would probably be well represented anyway, but a state with a small population, such as Nevada, might not receive any representation in a sample of all Americans without the use of stratification.

In *area sampling,* a geographic area (a region, a state, a county, a city, a neighborhood) is arbitrarily divided into sectors. Political boundaries may be used; so might roadways and streets. Random samples are then drawn from each sector marked off. These samples might be of households or individuals within households. Area sampling is often used in public opinion polls and market surveys. So is *quota sampling,* which selects representatives in proportion to the numerical size of their group. First the subject population is divided into its component parts or strata, such as occupation, age, and sex. Then a sample is drawn that represents each part in proportion to its total magnitude. Interviewers and other investigators must fill their quotas for each category within a given context. The context may be an area chosen by area sampling.

Probability and the sample survey. Random samples perfectly represent the universe from which they are drawn. The reason for this is explained by *probability theory:*

Pretend that you have a large container in front of you that holds a million marbles of equal size. Half the marbles are red and half are green. You select randomly 100 marbles from the container. According to probability theory, you are very likely, within a 3 percent margin of error, to select 50 green marbles and 50 red marbles. According to probability theory, you are very likely to obtain the same results if you repeat this activity again and again.[9]

This means that, if you went back to the box with the 2,500 names of high school students and chose another 500 by the same random selection method, the students selected would show the same divisions by sex and age and would give the same results in responding to your questions in the second sample as in the first. And both would accurately reflect the total group of students.

Using lists of counties, cities, and larger areas as their bases, the Gallup, Harris, and other polling organizations use random samples of fewer than 2,000 individuals to represent all the adults in the United States. The pollsters have found that this number of individuals, selected by either random methods or stratified random selection, generally provides an adequate sample to reliably represent the universes from which they were drawn.

Answering the question "How many persons have to be included in a poll to obtain reliable results?" George Gallup once wrote:

Size and accuracy are inextricably linked in the minds of most laymen. . . . Actually, the size of the sample (the number of persons interviewed) is far less important as a factor in achieving reliable results. . . . The number of persons who must be included in a sample or cross section can be determined by reference to the laws of probability, set out by Bernouilli in 1713. But even if the director of a polling organization had no knowledge of these laws, the exercise of common sense would prove to be a sufficiently good guide. All that he would have to do is to follow the simple plan of adding cases until those additions failed to make any important difference in the results.[10]

Gallup illustrated this with an example dealing with a survey of opinions of the nation's attitude toward prohibition as reported by the American Institute of Public Opinion in 1944:

The first national sample containing proper proportions of the various population groups included 1,327 interviews. To determine the extent of vari-

[9]Howard D. Mehlinger and John J. Patrick, *American Political Behavior* (Boston: Ginn, 1972), pp. 43–44.

[10]*A Guide to Public Opinion Polls,* by George Gallup (copyright © 1948 by Princeton University Press): selections from pp. 14, 15, 16, and 17. Reprinted by permission of Princeton University Press.

ations resulting solely from the number of persons reached, this sample was divided in a random manner into three groups of approximately the same size.

The first sample showed the following results:

Persons favoring the return of prohibition	137	or	31%
Persons opposing the return of prohibition	276	or	62%
Those without opinions or undecided	29	or	7%
Total	442		

When the results of the second and third samples are added to the figures given above, the following totals emerge:

	Favor Prohibition	*Oppose Prohibition*	*No Opinion*
First sample of 442	31%	62%	7%
First and second samples totaling 884	29%	63%	8%
First, second, and third samples totaling 1,327	30%	63%	7%

Additional surveys were conducted on this issue until a total of 12,494 persons had been interviewed, with results as follows:

	Favor Prohibition	*Oppose Prohibition*	*No Opinion*
When 2,585 persons had been interviewed	31%	61%	8%
When 5,255 persons had been interviewed	33%	59%	8%
When 8,253 persons had been interviewed	32%	60%	8%
When 12,494 persons had been interviewed	32%	61%	7%

. . . The important point demonstrated here is that this survey of the nation's attitude toward the return of prohibition might have included any number of persons from 442 up to 12,494 and the results would have been substantially the same.[11]

Survey researchers, however, must take precautions to assure that their universe is properly defined. For example, in 1936 the *Literary Digest* confidently predicted a landslide victory for the Republican Alf Landon over Democrat Franklin D. Roosevelt in the presidential election. Instead Roosevelt won by a landslide. Why was the magazine's prediction so wrong? The magazine's subscribers had been randomly surveyed by proper techniques, but the

[11]Ibid., pp. 14–16.

assumption that the universe of its subscribers represented the universe of all United States voters was incorrect. The editorial board had forgotten that, since the magazine generally favored the Republican party, its subscribers were far more likely to be Republicans than Democrats.

Developing the survey instrument. After determining the universe (and in most cases selecting a sample of subjects), researchers develop the survey instrument itself. Usually this consists of either an interview guide, a highly structured interview (like a questionnaire that is read to the subjects) or a questionnaire to be administered by mail.

Most interview guides and questionnaires ask the respondent (the person being questioned) a number of personal questions—age, sex, occupation, education, and the like—as well as inquiring about the survey topic. Then the researchers can analyze whether differences in these characteristics affect responses about the survey topic. Frequently questions are worded so that a single phrase or a check mark answers the question. Sometimes, however, the question calls for a longer reply. To obtain accurate information from respondents, questions must be stated clearly and without bias.

Here are ten questions. Some are clear and unbiased. Others are confusing, misleading, or "loaded" (biased for or against one point of view or assuming an opinion as fact). See if you can pick out the clear, unbiased questions. What is wrong with the others?

1. Where were you born?

2. Why do most delinquents come from broken homes?

3. How long does it take you to complete your paper route?

4. Do you think we should get our troops out of Vietnam and send them to the Middle East?

5. Are you male or female?

6. I hate television advertising, don't you?

7. Would you say you are more sympathetic, less sympathetic, or feel about the same way you did a year ago about equal rights for women?

8. Do you agree or disagree that enculturation is inhibited by libidinal deprivation?

9. In general, how do you feel about the president's foreign policy?

10. If it weren't for the Wright Brothers, air congestion would never have become an issue. How do you feel about that?

A researcher may solicit answers either face-to-face (by visiting the respondent and asking the questions directly) or by mail (sending a questionnaire that the respondent fills out and returns).

Face-to-face interviews ensure that the intended respondent is the one who actually answers the questions. They also have the advantage of allowing the investigator to probe or ask for further information, which cannot be done in a mailed survey. But face-to-face interviews also have several disadvantages. They are costly in time and effort. The respondent may react negatively to the interviewer's personality. Respondents may look for clues from the interviewer on how to answer each question, and the interviewer may unintentionally supply clues by his or her tone of voice, phrasing of the questions, or facial expressions, showing how he or she feels about the topic. Careful training of interviewers to avoid such things is helpful.

To gain some advantages of each technique and to compare the results for possible biases, researchers commonly interview a subsample (small number) of the larger sample in person and question the others by mail.

Conducting an interview. When you are conducting a face-to-face interview, a few basic steps should be followed. Introduce yourself, announce the research topic, and explain why you are doing the research. Assure the respondent of his or her anonymity in the report. Tell the respondent how much time the interview will take, and keep within that limit.

Be courteous and really listen to the respondent. Remain nonjudgmental or neutral about any beliefs, attitudes, or opinions the respondent may express. Do not inhibit responses or create hostility in the respondent by expressions that betray your own attitudes. Try to record the respondent's answers to open-ended questions in his or her own words. If you summarize what has been said, you may distort the meaning of the respondent's ideas or unconsciously take them out of context. Tell the respondent you are taking the time to do this because you need to record the answers accurately and fairly.

After the interview is completed, read the answers over carefully to be sure you understand them all clearly. If not, ask for further information.[12]

Suppose you want to study the influence of parents' social classes on children's future plans. You hypothesize that the parents' position influences

[12]See Margaret Branson, *Land of Promise* (Boston: Ginn, 1974), pp. 70–71.

their children's career ambitions. You would want to know the social class of the parents, what the children want to do for a living as adults, what they think their actual futures will be, and why they have these goals and these expectations. You would also want to gather enough data about the children and their parents to test for other factors that might be influencing their career ambitions (such as sex, race, ethnic background, or intellectual ability).

Suppose you are limiting your universe to the students of a given town. You have selected a sample of 300 students from the two high schools in town. You decide to interview 25 from each school personally and to send questionnaires to the other 275.

Survey-takers sometimes use identical questions for interviews and questionnaires. More often, however, the questions are posed in slightly different fashion for the two techniques. Questionnaires usually contain many questions answered by a check mark or a brief statement.

Next we offer two examples of survey questions used to gather the same information.

An interview guide. If you were to conduct a personal interview, you would first write down all the information you already have about the respondent, such as his or her name and sex. Immediately after the interview, you would write down other key data such as the respondent's approximate age and race.

You should inform the respondent that you are a sociology student doing a study of high school students and their plans for the future and that the respondent is one of a number of students randomly selected to participate. Explain that the responses will remain anonymous.

Here are the questions you might ask.

1. Where were you born?
2. Where was your father born? Your mother?
3. Where, specifically, do you live now?
4. Have you lived there most of your life? (If the answer is no, ask: Where did you live for most of your life?)
5. What school do you go to?
6. What year are you in there?
7. What course are you taking—business, college entrance, home economics?
8. Do you expect to graduate? (If not, why not?)
9. What do you expect to do when you leave school?
10. What do you expect to be doing about ten years from now?
11. What does your father do? How about your mother?
12. How far did your father go in school? What about your mother?

13. What do you think your parents would like you to be?
14. What do you think they expect you to be?
15. How accurate do you think their expectations are?
16. Do you have any brothers or sisters? (If yes, ask: How old are they? What do the older ones do? What do you think the younger ones will do when they grow up?)
17. In general, would you describe your parents as upper class, middle class, working class, or lower class?
18. Why would you place them in that particular category? (Be sure to write down the respondent's answer word for word.)
19. Would you describe yourself as upper class, middle class, working class, or lower class?
20. What social class do you think you will be in twenty years from now?

Look over your interview sheets quickly and see if you have responsive answers to all the questions posed. If you need further information, ask for it now. If not, thank the respondent for his or her time and cooperation.

Many of the same questions would be included in a questionnaire to be mailed to the rest of the sample.

A mailed questionnaire. Attach a cover letter to the questionnaire to explain that the respondent was selected at random to participate in a study of high school students and their future plans. Identify yourself and the sponsoring agency (the sociology class of North College). Urge the respondent to answer honestly, and point out that respondents are asked not to sign their names. Include a stamped, addressed envelope for returning the survey.

1. Where were you born?
   a. ______ In this community
   b. ______ Elsewhere. Please specify ______________

2. Where were your parents born?
   a. Father ______________
   b. Mother ______________

3. Where do you now live? Street ______________
   City ______________

4. How long have you lived in your present house?
   a. ______ Less than a year
   b. ______ One to three years
   c. ______ More than three years

5. Which high school do you attend?
   a. ______ East High School
   b. ______ West High School
6. What year are you in?
   a. ______ Senior
   b. ______ Junior
   c. ______ Sophomore
   d. ______ Freshman
   e. ______ Other. Please specify ____________
7. What is your main course of study?
   a. ______ Business administration
   b. ______ College entrance
   c. ______ Home economics
   d. ______ Secretarial science
   e. ______ Mechanical or vocational
   f. ______ Agricultural
   g. ______ Other. Please specify ____________
8. Do you expect to graduate from high school?
   a. ______ Yes
   b. ______ No. Why not? ____________________________
   ____
   ____
   ____
9. What do you expect to do when you leave school?
   a. ______ Go to college. In what field? ____________
   b. ______ Get some other advanced training. In what field? ____________
   c. ______ Get a job. Doing what? ____________
   d. ______ Other. Please specify ____________________
   ____
   ____
10. What do you expect to be in ten years? (Please try to be as specific as you can; for instance, a foreman in an auto factory, a surgeon, a bank teller, an officer in the marines, a court stenographer.) ____________
    ____
    ____
11. What do your parents do?
    a. Father ____________________________________
    ____
    b. Mother ____________________________________
    ____

12. How far did they go in school?

Father			Mother
a.	______	Less than eighth grade	aa. ______
b.	______	Some high school, didn't finish	bb. ______
c.	______	High school graduate	cc. ______
d.	______	Some college, didn't finish	dd. ______
e.	______	College graduate	ee. ______
f.	______	Further training, no higher degree	ff. ______
g.	______	Higher degree	gg. ______

13. What do you think your parents would like you to be?

____

____

14. What do you think they expect you to be? ______________________

____

____

15. Do you have brothers or sisters?

a. ______ No

b. ______ Yes. Please specify their ages and occupations:

a. ______ No

b. ______ Yes. Please specify their ages and occupations:

	Brothers	Age	Occupation*
c.	First brother	______	______
d.	Second brother	______	______
e.	Third brother	______	______
f.	Fourth brother	______	______
g.	Fifth brother	______	______

*If in school, state what school; if preschool, state so.

	Sisters	Age	Occupation*
h.	First sister	______	______
i.	Second sister	______	______
j.	Third sister	______	______
k.	Fourth sister	______	______
l.	Fifth sister	______	______

*If in school, state what school; if preschool, state so.

16. In general, how would you categorize your family?

a. ______ Upper class c. ______ Working class

b. ______ Middle class d. ______ Lower class

17. Why did you place them in the category you did?
(Please try to give as much detail as possible.)

____

____

____

____

18. How would you categorize yourself?
a. ______ Upper class c. ______ Working class
b. ______ Middle class d. ______ Lower class

19. What is your sex?
a. ______ Male
b. ______ Female

20. What is your race?
a. ______ Black d. ______ Red
b. ______ White e. ______ Yellow
c. ______ Brown f. ______ Other. Please specify ____________

21. What is your religion?
a. ______ Catholic d. ______ Other. Please specify ____________
b. ______ Jewish e. ______ None
c. ______ Protestant. Which denomination? __________

After the questionnaire is drafted, it should be tested; that is, it should be tried out on a number of people before being sent to your sample. This is one way of finding out if the questions are valid—if they are getting the information they are meant to get. If not, revisions should be made and the new version tested.

When the final version is ready, the next step is to send it to the chosen respondents. Various techniques are used to get people to respond. One of the most effective is to tell people (either in the cover letter that accompanies the questionnaire or in person) that they are part of a random sample and that everyone's response is needed for accurate results. Sometimes it is also effective to add, "We need your assistance to help tell *your* story accurately."

Tabulating responses. Once questionnaires have been returned, you are ready to start organizing the data, tabulating the results, and beginning the analysis. To allow researchers to transfer the information to punch cards, such as those used by computer firms, many questionnaires are precoded—that is, the answers are marked in such a way that they can be punched on cards.

These cards can then be fed into counting and sorting machines or into computers. This procedure is essential in complex studies and extremely useful in all kinds of survey research.

In small sample surveys, such as the one we have been discussing, punch cards are a useful tool but not a necessity. To tally the results by hand, you first count the number of times each response was given to each question. These are called the *marginals* because they are usually written down the side of a master copy of the questionnaire. For example, suppose we have 227 respondents from the total sample of 275. (This is a very high return rate.) Let's look at how data from three of the questions we used are translated into useful information about our hypothesis. First the marginals are added up. These sums are called *raw scores*, because nothing has yet been done to analyze them. The raw scores are next turned into percentages.

Question	*Number of Answers*	*Percentage of Respondents*
What is your sex?		
Male	152	67
Female	75	33
No answer	0	0
	227	100
Which high school do you attend?		
East High School	122	54
West High School	103	45
No answer	2	1
	227	100
In general, how would you categorize your family?		
Upper class	21	9
Middle class	85	38
Working class	79	35
Lower class	37	16
No answer	5	2
	227	100

The percentages are based on the number of respondents to a given question. Since some respondents may skip certain questions, the number that a percentage represents will vary from question to question. In the first case, 152 males from a total of 227 respondents is 67 percent. In another question a smaller number may constitute 67 percent of the total respondents.

Now you are ready to begin some simple *cross tabulations,* for example, comparing one item (or variable), such as sex, with another, such as plans after high school. You do this to determine what relationships between various categories of people or events are revealed by the answers to your questions.

Hypothetically, in the study of 275 high school students, of which 227 (152 males and 75 females) finally responded, you might find a breakdown like the following:

	Sex	
Plans After Leaving School	*Male (Number)*	*Female (Number)*
Go to college	65	32
Get some other advanced training	34	15
Get a job	40	15
Other	13	13
Total	152	75

These raw figures are difficult to interpret since the *bases* (the totals in each column) are quite different: looking at the first row across, at first glance it may seem that twice as many men as women plan to go to college after high school. But, if the responses are put in percentages, the picture changes.

	Sex			
	Male		*Female*	
Plans After Leaving School	*f**	*Percentage*	*f**	*Percentage*
Go to college	65	43	32	43
Get some other advanced training	34	23	15	20
Get a job	40	26	15	20
Other	13	8	13	17
Total	152	100	75	100

*The symbol *f* is used to mean the number answering the question or *frequency of response.*

If you compare the percentages, you see that an equal proportion of males and females who returned the questionnaires expect to go to college. How do the data on the category "Other" change when raw figures and percentages are compared?

In a report, this information would probably be presented in the following simplified table.

	Sex	
Plans After Leaving School	*Male (152)*	*Female (175)*
Go to college	43%	43%
Get some other advanced training	23%	20%
Get a job	26%	20%
Other	8%	17%
	100%	100%

Here's another cross tabulation drawn from the hypothetical study of parental social class and student goals.

	High School Attended	
Social Class of Parents (According to Respondent)	*East High (122)*	*West High (103)*
Upper class	5%	1%
Middle class	63%	24%
Working class	28%	68%
Lower class	4%	7%
	100%	100%

(Note that the total number of respondents here is 225 not 227. As we noted above, two individuals did not identify their school.)

1. **What percentage of the students attending East High considered their parents working class? Lower class?**

2. **Overall do students at West High see their parents as higher or lower in social-class position than students at East High?**

In the previous tables two variables were cross-tabulated, for example, school attended and social class of parents. In the next table there are three

variables: school attended, social class of parents, and plans on leaving school.

	High School Attended and Social Class of Parents			
	East High (122)		*West High (103)*	
Plans After Leaving School	*Upper and Middle (83)*	*Working and Lower (36)*	*Upper and Middle (26)*	*Working and Lower (77)*
Go to college	80%	32%	78%	13%
Get some other advanced training	8%	30%	14%	25%
Get a job	7%	31%	6%	44%
Other	5%	7%	2%	18%
	100%	100%	100%	100%

(Note that the total number of respondents here is 222 not 227. As noted above, five individuals did not indicate their social class position.)

1. What percentage of upper- and middle-class students planned to attend college?

2. What percentage of East High's working- and lower-class students had college plans?

3. Which school has the larger percentage of students who consider their parents working or lower class?

4. Does West High have more or fewer students of working- and lower-class families who plan to go to college?

5. How might the differences between East High and West High working- and lower-class students on college plans be explained?

ANALYZING THE DATA

The last two tables show a relationship between college attendance and social class of parents. They also show that East High has more middle- and upper-class students than West High does.

It seems clear from the last table that there is a relationship between parents' social class (as seen by the student) and the student's future plans. In both schools, a high proportion of upper- and middle-class students plan to go to college.

The school appears to exert an influence on those students who see their families as working and lower class. Going to a predominantly middle-class high school seems to raise the expectations of working-class students. More of them intend to prepare for careers that offer upward social mobility. Of the East High students with working-class parents, 32 percent plan to attend college, while only 13 percent of West High's working-class students do.

Correlation and Causation

The goal of the sociologist is to find causal connections. A causal connection is just what it sounds like: a relationship in which one event or variable causes or directly influences a second event or variable in a specific way. For example, as every dieter knows, there is a causal connection between the amount of food a person eats and how much the person weighs. In the table we just looked at, we might predict a causal relationship between parents' social class as seen by a student and the student's future plans.

Not all connections between variables are causal, however. *Correlation* is another relationship between two or more classes of events. Suppose we observed that the overweight men in our study all had short hair. In that case, we could say that there was a correlation between short hair and overweight, or that these variables correlated (existed together) in our study.

However, the fact that two characteristics of the people in our study—short hair and overweight—correlated does not indicate a causal relationship between them. We all know that weight is not affected by hair length or vice versa; there is no causal connection between them. The two factors merely existed together in this study. Yet the correlation was almost perfect. Wherever one trait appeared, the researcher found the other.

In many studies the correlation between two variables may be so high that the researcher may be tempted to think that one does indeed cause the other. There is a direct correlation, for example, between the amount of ice cream eaten at New York's largest beach, Coney Island, and the number of deaths by drowning on a given summer day. Is it a causal relationship as well? Remembering your mother's warning never to go swimming on a full stomach ("Wait at least one hour after you eat"), you might say, "Yes. It makes sense. If you eat ice cream and go into the water, you have a good chance of getting cramps and drowning." Perhaps. But few doctors today believe eating ice cream, which is easily digestible, causes cramps that lead to drowning. Behind a seeming causal connection lies the fact that both ice cream consumption and the number of people at the beach and in the water go up when it is hot. The temperature of the day is the principal factor accounting for a large attendance at the beach. And when it is hot, more people swim, therefore more are exposed to drowning.

Correlation is not causation. It is simply the observed fact that two variables are related to one another. They may be related in one of two ways: positively or negatively. In a *positive correlation*, as one variable increases, so does the other. For example, think of the simple relationship between increase in the size of a community and the amount of money needed to clean the streets, collect the garbage, and pay teachers. In a *negative correlation*, as one variable increases, the other decreases, or vice versa. For example, as the number of farms in the United States has decreased, the average size per farm has increased.

THE RESEARCH REPORT

Researchers have not completed their intellectual journey with the analysis of the data. They must still record their research experience in its entirety, so that others—colleagues, sponsors, students, and the general public—can benefit from their efforts. This record is known as the research report. It may appear in a professional journal, a full-length book, or perhaps a statement for circulation among members of a government agency or private firm.

The report usually contains an account of the nature of the problem; the available literature in the field; the major concepts and how they were operationalized; the hypotheses; the research design; the data collected, presented in tables, graphs, and other forms; the analysis; and the conclusions.

With this information, readers of the report are in a position to evaluate the importance of the research, its strengths and weaknesses. Conscientious researchers carefully spell out the particular problems encountered in implementing the research design and how they dealt with these difficulties. If respondents were resistant, for example, the author of the report is required to say what percentage of the sample actually completed the interviews or questionnaires and how substitutions were made for those who could not be located or who declined to participate. In this way, biases in the data can be evaluated not only by researchers themselves but also by the readers of the report. Serious researchers, in essence, will often give their potential critics sufficient evidence to "hang them." This is necessary as a built-in check on the validity and reliability of the research effort. Sociologists, after all, are presumably seeking to generate knowledge about society, not to make propaganda points. For this reason, any circumstances that might limit the reliability of the research must be forthrightly published with the findings themselves.

SUMMARY

Research is central to the work of sociologists. Sociological research can focus on any of a virtually infinite variety of possible issues, from the characteristics and importance of education in a given society, to the causes of worker alienation or the factors involved in mate selection. The researcher's choice of a subject of study may derive from his or her own personal experience, from pressing public concern about an issue, from a contract offered by a government or private agency, or from the need to complete the requirements of a professional degree.

In setting up the research design, a sociologist not only must set forth a question to be answered but also must operationalize key concepts contained in the question. Often the question takes the form of a hypothesis—an educated guess on how two or more factors or variables are related. An early step in the research process is a review of the relevant literature. This review may give the researcher clearer insight into the issue to be studied and may also cut down on effort wasted in duplicating completed research.

Once the researcher has specified the nature of the question, has set forth the hypothesis, and has operationalized its concepts, data can be collected. The sociologist's choice of a collection method from the many available is strongly influenced by the nature of the questions asked. Data collection procedures include library research, such as historical and content analysis; participant observation; nonparticipant observation; the experiment; and the sample survey (by questionnaire, interview, or both).

Each method contains a variety of potential problems. Participant observers face the ethical problem of violating the privacy of their subjects. Interviewers must be careful not to influence their respondents' answers to questions. Researchers using the sample survey must be sure that their methods of random selection yields a representative sample of the universe under investigation and that the universe is appropriate for the problem.

The data collected must be analyzed in light of the original question raised. The research report records the researcher's goals and methods and the conclusions to be drawn from the findings, as well as their possible theoretical and applied contributions to sociology and for society.

GLOSSARY

Achieved position: a position acquired by a person through individual effort.

Adolescence: a culturally defined period between childhood and adulthood.

Alienation (Marx): a condition of estranged detachment of industrial workers from their occupation or the goods they produce, and a resulting diminished sense of identity.

Anomie (Durkheim): a condition of normlessness.

Anticipatory socialization: behavior that prepares the individual for occupying future roles.

Ascribed positions: those assigned to a person by the society or by nature.

Assimilation: a minority's replacement of its distinctive ethnic or subculture traits with those of the dominant group.

Assimilationist movement (Wirth): a movement seeking to improve the social status of particular categories or individuals.

Authoritarian personality: a personality type that is very conventional, is intolerant of variants in behavior and custom, and believes in a strong central authority.

Authority: the formally recognized right to exercise power.

Avoidance: in relation to discrimination, patterns of interaction that minimize contact between one group and another or others.

Bureaucracy: a formal organization that incorporates clearly defined, separate tasks, assigned to positions, within an explicit hierarchy of authority.

Caste system: a closed stratification system usually sanctified by religion (as in India) in which a person's parentage determines his or her social position for life. "Castelike" systems also exist, often based on racial group membership instead of religion.

Charisma: exceptional personal appeal that is useful for attracting adherents to a social movement; also one source of authority.

City: a relatively large, densely populated, permanent human settlement characterized by cultural heterogeneity.

Closed stratification system: a system in which there is virtually no social mobility, where people remain in the social position of their parents.

Commune: an intentional community, established to achieve relationships that approximate the ideal type of the community.

Community: human settlements in which patterns of interaction approximate primary relations more than secondary relations.

Compartmentalization: isolation of competing or conflicting norms by considering two or more social roles as separate.

Controlled environments: places in which the individual has no autonomy, has little or no privacy, performs most activities with other inmates, and is required to follow the instructions of a powerful central authority.

Correlations: relationships asserted between two or more variables.

Counterculture: a set of norms and values that contradicts and rejects many or all norms and values of the mainstream culture.

Cultural diffusion: the voluntary or involuntary adoption of traits from one culture by another culture.

Cultural pluralism: the ideal of distinct ethnic groups living in harmony and equality in a society.

Cultural prejudice: prejudiced attitudes and stereotypes absorbed during socialization.

Cultural relativity: the acknowledged absence of absolute standards of behavior and the consequent need to judge behavior within its cultural setting.

Culture: the sum of a society's learned beliefs, values, norms, and ways of doing things.

Demography: the study of population and the interrelationships between population changes and social structures.

Denial: in relation to discrimination, avoidance achieved by excluding a minority group from participation in given social patterns.

Dependent variable: the variable believed to be affected by another variable in given circumstances; the effect variable.

Depersonalization: treatment of the individual in ways that minimize or destroy his or her sense of uniqueness and, often, worth; the term is also used for the result of this treatment.

Desegregation: removal of all legal and customary barriers to integration.

Deviance: the violation of a society's essential norms.

Dialectic: an ongoing interplay of opposing forces that produces constant change in each.

Discrimination: social patterns or behavior that disfavors members of a group or groups.

Ethnicity: the condition of being distinct from other groups in the society in race, national origin, or religion.

Ethnocentrism: the belief that our own group has superior moral standards, beliefs, or ways of behaving to those of others.

Extended family: a family structure that includes more than one nuclear family or includes three or more generations of people linked by birth.

Feudal system: a closed system of stratification in which social position is ascribed, strata are distinctly defined, mobility is difficult, and wealth is based heavily on land ownership.

Folk society (Redfield)**:** a small, nonliterate, traditional society in which social relations are intimate, spontaneous, and emotionally involving.

Folkways: less essential norms derived from tradition and custom.

Formal organization: a secondary group in which rules of interaction are explicit and there is a hierarchy of authority.

Functional prerequisites: the basic needs that must be met by a society if it is to survive.

Gemeinschaft (Toennies)**:** a system of relationships characterized by intimacy, spontaneity, lack of specialization, prevalence of interdependence, and stability.

Generalized other: the individual's notion of what behavior is expected of him or her by society in general.

Gesellschaft (Toennies)**:** a system of relationships characterized by formal, contractual bonds, impersonality, rationality in ways of doing things, and instability of interactions.

Group: two or more people who interact in patterned ways, share beliefs, values, and goals, and have a sense of membership.

Hypothesis: a statement of expected relationship between two or more variables or sets of variables to be tested by observation or experiment.

Ideal type: a description of a complex phenomenon that incorporates all its essential traits and excludes the incidental variants found in real-world examples of the phenomenon.

Ideology: a set of beliefs and related values that justify social conditions or that provide a unified criticism of those conditions and justify opposition to them in favor of other, stated goals.

Imitation: in relation to prejudice, the creation by a minority group of patterns of behavior that parallel those of the dominant group.

Independent variable: the variable believed to produce a change in particular circumstances; the causal variable.

Innovation (Merton)**:** acceptance of the broadly held social goals but use of illegitimate means to achieve them.

Institutional racism: enduring patterns of social interaction that express racist assumptions and enforce racial subordination.

Intergenerational mobility: change in a person's social class from that of his or her parents.

Internalization: the process of adopting a society's norms as part of the individual's personality and notion of self.

Intragenerational mobility: change of a person's social class within his or her own working life.

Labeling theory: the theory that much persistent deviant behavior is the result of individuals' being labeled deviant by society.

Language: any system of communication that uses signs or symbols whose meanings can be understood by others.

Laws: norms that are formally codified and enforced by police and courts.

Life chances: the statistical probability

of certain events or patterns of behavior occurring because of an individual's or group's set of social variables.

Looking-glass self: the self as a product of how we think others judge us and how we feel as a result of that judgment.

Mass society: a society characterized by large numbers of persons who are anonymous to one another and do not share a broad sense of common interests or goals; in Kornhauser's terms, a volatile society in which elites are accessible and nonelites are available for mobilization into social movements.

Mechanical relationships (Durkheim): social bonds maintained by tradition, intimacy, and a sense of shared community and lacking differentiation in skills or tasks among members.

Minority: a group sharing ethnic, racial, or social class status and subordinate to another group. (A "minority" group can actually have larger membership than the dominant group.)

Model: a description that incorporates the essential features of a complex phenomenon and excludes the unimportant or incidental variants.

Mores: the major essential norms of a culture.

Norms: the rules of behavior that govern members of a society.

Nuclear family: two parents and their children.

Open stratification system: a system of stratification in which social mobility is possible and is based on personal achievement.

Operationalize: to define a concept by observable specifics (for example, to define "rich" to mean "having an income of $35,000 or more per year") so that the concept can be used in empirical research.

Order: in science, the governing of phenomena by "natural laws"—accurate, general descriptions of how given phenomena occur and why.

Organic relationships (Durkheim): social bonds that are utilitarian, are based on division of labor, and satisfy the need for interdependence by contractual relations.

Peer group: collectively, the individual's peers in their role as a significant other.

Pluralism: in political sociology, the sharing of power by rival voluntary associations favoring different interests.

Pluralist movement (Wirth): a movement seeking to improve the social acceptance of a distinctive category of persons without obliterating that distinctiveness.

Pluralist society (Kornhauser): a society in which the elites are accessible and the nonelites are not readily available for agitation, because "intermediate relations" (community, voluntary association, and occupational groups) are strong.

Power: the ability to determine the behavior of others with or without their consent.

Power elite (Mills): in theory, an interlocking of elites sharing and protecting common interests by monopolizing political power.

Prejudice: negative attitudes toward all members of a given group.

Prestige: the degree of honor and respect accorded a person.

Primary deviance: in labeling theory, behavior by an individual that violates social norms but that has not yet been detected by others and labeled deviant.

Primary group: two or more persons who interact in intimate, spontaneous ways that provide emotional involvement.

Projection: in relation to prejudice, ascribing to members of another group traits we cannot admit to having ourselves.

Race: biologically, an aggregate of persons who share a composite of genetically transmissible physical traits; socially, a group of people who share physical traits, are considered different from others because of this, and are treated differently.

Racism: the assumption that those considered members of a given race are inferior to others in mental or moral capabilities.

Rebellion (Merton): rejection of both socially approved goals and socially approved norms.

Reference group: the people by whose standards we judge ourselves.

Reform movement: a movement that seeks to change a specific set of values, norms, roles, or institutional patterns of interaction.

Resocialization: a rapid and extreme

change in an individual's permitted behavior and a consequent change in his or her sense of self.

Retreatism (Merton): abandoning socially prescribed behavior along with the socially held goals.

Revolution: an abrupt, sweeping change in a social system, usually through the efforts—often violent—of a social movement; sometimes as a result of profound changes in one area of society that spread throughout.

Revolutionary movement: a movement seeking to make major, sweeping changes in all the social institutions by taking power in the political institution.

Rite of passage: any ceremony that marks an individual's transition to a further stage of growth or social acceptance.

Ritualism (Merton): going through the motions of a role with no hope of or interest in achieving its supposed goals.

Role conflict: conflict between opposing demands within a role or between two roles occupied by the same person.

Role loss: curtailment or reduction of a role that contributed to the individual's definition of self.

Role-playing: imitation by children or others of behavior they observe in the role occupants around them.

Role priorities: the ranking of role demands in order of importance to minimize role conflict and strain.

Role tolerance: the margin of acceptable variances in performance of a role.

Sacred (Nisbet): ways of behaving that are valued in and for themselves; roughly synonymous with tradition, in which things draw their value from their longevity in the past.

Scapegoat: in relation to prejudice, a group wrongly blamed as the source of problems or frustrations.

Scientific method: a set of premises and methods of observation and experimentation used to arrive at accurate, verifiable descriptions of events.

Secondary deviance: in labeling theory, deviant behavior that persists because the individual has been labeled a deviant.

Secondary group: a group in which participation and interaction tend to be impersonal, unspontaneous, and task-oriented.

Secular (Nisbet): utilitarian (use-centered) values and norms governed by the rational.

Segregation: maintaining separation of two or more groups by laws or strongly enforced customs.

Self: the ideas and attitudes of an individual about himself or herself.

Sex roles: the expected behavior of society's members according to whether they are male or female.

Significant others: those whose attitudes and judgments are important in the process of socialization.

Social change: significant and enduring alterations of the structure of a society or its cultural characteristics or both.

Social class: a number of people within a society who are grouped together because they have similar amounts of wealth, power, and prestige and have similar lifestyles.

Social control: the various methods of ensuring and reinforcing conformity to a society's norms.

Social institution: a system of norms and values that pattern behavior toward fulfilling some basic, enduring human need.

Socialization: the process of learning the beliefs, values, norms, and social roles of a culture and society.

Socially constructed reality: our perceptions of the physical and social world as governed by our learned beliefs, values, and expectations about it.

Social mobility: movement up or down in the system of social stratification.

Social movement: a more or less loosely organized collection of individuals and groups intended to promote or resist social change.

Social position: a position within a social structure that is accompanied by a set of expected behaviors.

Social rewards: the wealth, power, and prestige distributed among the members of a society.

Social role: the behavior expected in each of the many positions a person holds in a society, such as parent, worker, or student.

Social strata: levels within a society that are distinguished from one another by their share of social rewards.

Social structure: the recurrent pattern of

relations within a group or a society that constitutes its organization.

Social variables: those variations in social background (race, sex, age, ethnic and religious membership, social class) that influence individual and group behavior.

Socioeconomic status: a measurement of a person's position in a system of social stratification that does not have clearly defined classes.

Sociological perspective: the viewpoint that individual behavior is explainable as a product of group interaction and can be studied by systematic observation and experimentation.

Sociological racism: the belief that individual members of a racial minority are responsible for their disadvantaged status.

Sociology: the systematic study of society and patterns of human interaction.

Structural prejudice: economic, social, and political benefits that accrue to others through the exploitation of particular minorities.

Subculture: a cultural group that shares certain traits with the larger society but possesses important distinctive cultural traits of its own.

Submission: acceptance by a minority of the dominant group's stereotype of it.

Suburb: a settlement neighboring a central city and economically and culturally dependent upon it.

Symbols: things that stand for other things—usually ideas or values.

Total institutions: places in which the individual has no autonomy, has little or no privacy, performs most activities with other inmates, and is required to follow the instructions of a powerful central authority.

Urban ecology: the study of how people in urban settlements interact with each other and their environment, affecting and being affected by those interactions.

Urban society: the implied opposite of Redfield's ideal type of the folk society; relations are impersonal, contractual, rational, and motivated by self-interest.

Urban succession: the replacement of one social class, ethnic group, or economic function in an urban area by another.

Value-free sociology: the belief that sociologists can and should examine a society without allowing their values to influence their analysis in any way.

Value judgments: evaluation of facts or events according to a belief system.

Values: the preferred or desirable goals, conditions, and modes of behavior of a culture.

Variable: anything that is measurable and subject to change in such ways as to affect research findings.

Voluntary association: a formal organization of relatively prolonged duration in which members come together voluntarily because they share the association's values and goals.

SELECTED BIBLIOGRAPHY

CHAPTER 1 The Sociological Perspective

Berger, Peter L. *Invitation To Sociology.* Garden City, N.Y.: Doubleday, 1963.

A provocative commentary on the field of sociology and its humanistic concerns. Includes discussion of such classical sociologists as Weber and Durkheim in Europe and Cooley, Mead, Parsons, and Merton in the United States.

Chinoy, Ely, and Hewitt, John P. *Sociological Perspective.* 3d ed. New York: Random House, 1975.

A brief introduction to the field of sociology. Various approaches are discussed, including the historical method, structural-functional analysis, and symbolic interaction.

Marx, Gary T., ed. *Muckraking Sociology.* New Brunswick, N.J.: Transaction Books, 1972.

A collection of articles drawn from the pages of the journal *Society.* Shows how research can be used to analyze major social problems. Issues range from the area of justice to social class to education and, finally, to problems in the availability and distribution of health services.

Merton, Robert K. *Social Theory and Social Structure.* Glencoe, Ill.: Free Press, 1957.

A distinguished sociologist's thoughts on a variety of issues, from the causes of deviance to the nature of reference groups. His discussion of functionalism stands as a major statement.

Nisbet, Robert A. *The Sociological Tradition.* New York: Basic Books, 1966.

The development of the field of sociology seen as centering around certain "unit-ideas": community, authority, status, the sacred, and alienation.

Rose, Peter I., ed. *The Study of Society.* 4th ed. New York: Random House, 1977.

Close to sixty essays drawn from sociological books and journals, on the major themes of sociological analysis.

Truzzi, Marcello, ed. *The Classic Statements.* New York: Random House, 1971.

Excerpts from the works of the "masters" of sociological thought. Includes Durkheim's statement on social facts, Toennies on gemeinschaft and gesellschaft, and many others.

CHAPTER 2 Methods, Models, and Theories

Bart, Pauline, and Frankel, Linda. *The Student Sociologist's Handbook.* Cambridge, Mass.: Schenkman, 1971.

A guide to source material and a commentary on the literature of sociology with special attention to various "schools," including functionalism, Marxism, and radical sociology.

Blau, Peter M., ed. *Approaches to the Study of Social Structure.* New York: Free Press, 1975.

A collection of recent essays on the study of society written by many of our foremost sociologists.

Hammond, Philip E., ed. *Sociologists at Work.* Garden City, N.Y.: Doubleday, 1967.

A collection of studies illustrating the variety of research activities in which sociologists engage.

Madge, John H. *The Origins of Scientific Sociology.* Glencoe, Ill.: Free Press, 1962.

A sophisticated review of research schools and major research projects; an excellent source book.

Shostak, Arthur B., ed. *Putting Sociology to Work.* New York: McKay, 1974.

The application of sociological theory and research to the solution of problems in urban and rural development, race relations, deviance, social conflict, and other areas.

Wiseman, Jacqueline P., and Aron, Marcia S. *Field Projects for Sociology Students.* Cambridge, Mass.: Schenkman; San Francisco: Canfield Press, 1970.

Introduces the student to a wide array of basic sociological research tools and techniques.

CHAPTER 3 Symbols and Substance

Benedict, Ruth. *Patterns of Culture.* New York: Houghton Mifflin, 1934.

A comparison of American lifeways and those of three non-

Western nonliterate societies. Originally published in 1934, this study is now available in many editions.

Botkin, B. A., ed. *Sidewalks of America.* Indianapolis: Bobbs-Merrill, 1954.

Folklore, legends, sagas, traditions, customs, songs, stories, and sayings of the nation's city folk.

Hall, Edward T. *The Hidden Dimension.* Garden City, N.Y.: Doubleday, 1966.

The cultural meaning of "territoriality" is the subject of this imaginative book. Hall discusses the use of space in public and private in different parts of the world.

———. *The Silent Language.* Garden City, N.Y.: Doubleday, 1959.

Culture seen as a complex of message systems, in a stimulating and highly readable book about manners and behavior.

Henry, Jules. *Culture Against Man.* New York: Random House, 1963.

The values of American society analyzed. Family, educational, and advertising concepts are among those examined.

Lewis, Oscar. *The Children of Sanchez.* New York: Random House, 1961.

"The culture of poverty" explored through the lives and autobiographies of members of a Mexican family. Lewis details the importance of belief systems in maintaining the culture from one generation to the next.

Turnbull, Colin M. *The Mountain People.* New York: Simon and Schuster, 1972.

The complete disintegration of a people's values under the impact of exile and deprivation, which make individual survival life's central goal.

Zborowski, Mark, and Herzog, Elizabeth. *Life Is with People.* New York: International Universities Press, 1952.

A detailed study of the culture of the *shtetl,* the village of East European Jews.

CHAPTER 4 Values and Norms

Dolbeare, Kenneth M., and Dolbeare, Patricia. *American Ideologies.* Chicago: Markham, 1971.

Concisely summarizes competing political beliefs in contemporary American society. Commentaries on capitalism, liberalism, black liberation, the New Left, American Marxism, and conservatism.

Hoggart, Richard. *The Uses of Literacy.* Boston: Beacon Press, 1957.

A study of the effects of mass media on the values of members of the English working class.

McGiffert, Michael, ed. *The Character of Americans.* Rev. ed. Homewood, Ill.: Dorsey Press, 1970.

A book of readings on American society and "national character."

Mead, Margaret. *Culture and Commitment: A Study of the Generation Gap.* New York: American Museum of National History Press, 1970.

The noted anthropologist looks at the past, present, and future character of American norms and values.

Scott, John Finley. *Internalization of Norms: A Sociological Theory of Moral Commitment.* Englewood Cliffs, N.J.: Prentice-Hall, 1971.

A sophisticated theoretical study of the process by which norms and internalized commitments are maintained and deviance is generated.

Williams, Robin M. *American Society.* 2d ed. New York: Knopf, 1960.

A sociological interpretation of the United States. Of special significance is the chapter on "Values and Beliefs in American Society."

CHAPTER 5 Roles and Relationships

Banton, Michael. *Roles.* New York: Basic Books, 1965.

An excellent introduction to the study of role theory by an English sociologist. Deals with role conflict, role change, and other processes.

Biddle, Bruce J., and Thomas, Edwin J., eds. *Role Concepts and Research.* New York: Wiley, 1967.

One of the most comprehensive collections dealing with the concept of role. Presents the development of the concept, its various usages, and its application in analyzing a wide variety of social behaviors.

Blau, Peter M. *Bureaucracy in Modern Society.* Rev. ed. Chicago: University of Chicago Press, 1973.

An introduction to the study of formal organizations in the tradition of Max Weber.

Crozier, Michael. *The Bureaucratic Phenomenon.* Chicago: University of Chicago Press, 1964.

Bureaucracy in France compared with that in other societies.

Etzioni, Amitai. *Complex Organizations.* New York: Free Press, 1961.

A theoretical model for the examination of large organizations using the concept of role-compliance.

Goffman, Erving. *Interaction Ritual.* Garden City, N.Y.: Doubleday, 1967.

Six essays by the author of the famous study, *The Presentation of Self in Everyday Life,* are presented. All deal with face-to-face behavior.

Homans, George C. *The Human Group.* New York: Harcourt, Brace, 1950.

A comprehensive examination of social interaction and group life, interweaving theory and analysis. Homans examines the significance of custom and what he sees as the basic characteristics of social groups: activity, interaction, and sentiment.

Olmstead, Michael S. *The Small Group.* New York: Random House, 1959.

An introduction to the study of small groups with case illustrations.

CHAPTER 6 Social Institutions

Birnbaum, Norma, and Lenzer, Gertrud. *Sociology and Religion.* Englewood Cliffs, N.J.: Prentice-Hall, 1969.

A collection of essays analyzing religious ideas and institutions in historical and contemporary perspective. A very useful reference work.

Clark, Burton R. *Educating the Expert Society.* San Francisco: Chandler, 1962.

A systematic study of American education.

Dabaghian, Jane, ed. *Mirror of Man.* 2d ed. Boston: Little, Brown, 1975.

A collection of readings in sociology and literature. Of special interest is Part 5, "Human Institutions."

Ehrensaft, Philip, and Etzioni, Amitai, eds. *Anatomies of America: Sociological Perspectives.* New York: Macmillan, 1969.

Fifty-three essays by sociologists, most dealing with American social institutions.

Goode, William J. *World Revolution and Family Patterns.* New York: Free Press, 1963.

A prize-winning study of family structures and the changes that are occurring in various parts of the world.

Gordon, Michael, ed. *The American Family in Social-Historical Perspective.* New York: St. Martin's Press, 1973.

Family life from the eighteenth century to the present. Childhood and youth, sex and sex roles, demographic trends, and other issues pursued in this valuable collection of essays.

Hacker, Andrew, *The Corporation Take-over.* New York: Harper and Row, 1964.

The nature of the corporation explored. Corporate powers, responsibility, and irresponsibility analyzed by a group of sophisticated contributing authors.

Hollander, Paul. *Soviet and American Society.* New York: Oxford University Press, 1973.

An unusual and ambitious effort to compare the two societies. The author emphasizes the similarities as well as the differences that characterize the two societies.

Lipset, Seymour Martin. *Political Man.* New York: Doubleday, 1963.

The social bases of politics are considered in this volume of essays and research reports.

Parsons, Talcott. *The Social System.* Glencoe, Ill.: Free Press, 1951.

A leading structural-functional theorist in the United States makes the analysis of social institutions one of the principal concerns of this landmark book.

Poll, Solomon. *The Hasidic Community of Williamsburg.* New York: Schocken Books, 1969.

A comprehensive analysis of an unusual community still thriving in modern American society. The religious basis of Hasidic life and the importance of economic, educational, and family institutions in the Hasidic community are discussed.

Riesman, David; Gusfield, Joseph; and Gamson, Zelda. *Academic Values and Mass Education.* New York: McGraw-Hill Paperbacks, 1975.

An empirical study of two colleges founded in the United States in the post-Sputnik era. The dream and the reality are both clearly analyzed.

Skolnick, Jerome H., and Currie, Elliot, eds. *Crisis in American Institutions.* Boston: Little, Brown, 1970.

Major American institutions and their problems are scrutinized. Education, social services, justice, and the military are among the institutions probed.

CHAPTER 7 Social Stratification

Aronowitz, Stanley. *False Promises.* New York: McGraw-Hill, 1973.

A radical view of the shaping of American working-class consciousness.

Baltzell, E. Digby. *Philadelphia Gentleman.* Glencoe, Ill.: Free Press, 1958.

A study of the social bases of upper-class power and privilege in a major American city.

Bendix, Reinhard, and Lipset, Seymour Martin, eds. *Class, Status, and Power.* Rev. ed. Glencoe, Ill.: Free Press, 1966.

A comprehensive collection of papers on the sociology of social stratification.

Blau, Peter M., and Duncan, Otis Dudley. *The American Occupational Structure.* New York: Wiley, 1967.

A study of occupation and mobility in the United States. Contains lengthy discussions and tables on ways of measuring mobility.

Blumberg, Paul, ed. *The Impact of Social Class.* New York: Crowell, 1972.

Thirty-two articles discussing complex issues associated with the study of social stratification. Classic statements by Marx, Engels, and Weber are included.

Caudill, Harvey M. *Night Comes to the Cumberlands.* Boston: Little, Brown, 1962.

A sympathetic account of the plight of coal miners in a depressed area.

Finifter, Ada W., ed. *Alienation and the Social System.* New York: Wiley, 1972.

The various uses of the concept of alienation are presented. Alienation in academia, in the world of work, in the political system are all discussed.

Howell, Joseph T. *Hard Living on Clay Street.* New York: Doubleday Anchor Books, 1973.

A sensitive portrayal of family life among blue-collar workers.

Kohn, Melvin L. *Class and Conformity: A Study in Values.* Homewood, Ill.: Dorsey Press, 1969.

The focus is on the different values of various social classes concerning punishment of children, attitudes toward work, aspirations, and other issues.

Lenski, Gerhard. *Power and Privilege.* New York: McGraw-Hill, 1966.

A theory of social stratification that imaginatively integrates many of the classic statements.

Mills, C. Wright. *The Power Elite.* New York: Oxford University Press, 1956.

One of the best-known works of modern sociology. Mills presents a theory of power in American society indicating the interlocking character of civilian and military control.

Spiro, Melford E. *Kibbutz: Venture in Utopia.* New York: Schocken Books, 1970.

An augmented edition of the well-known research study on kibbutz life. Includes some of the author's further thoughts, written in 1970.

Young, Michael. *The Rise of Meritocracy.* New York: Random House, 1959.

Social-science fiction about a new order of society in which "meritocratic" principles of personal achievement prevail.

CHAPTER 8 Race and Ethnicity

Abramson, Harold J. *Ethnic Diversity in Catholic America.* New York: Wiley, 1973.

Analysis of a wealth of data on the Catholic population of the United States. Emphasis on diversity among Catholic ethnic groups.

Allport, Gordon W. *The Nature of Prejudice.* Cambridge, Mass.: Addison-Wesley, 1954.

This book, available in various editions, is a social-psychological assessment of prejudice.

Banks, James A., and Grambs, Jean D., eds. *Black Self Concept.* New York: McGraw-Hill, 1972.

Challenging papers written in the early 1970s, on development of the self-concept among black children. Policy implications of social science findings are spelled out.

Blackwell, James E., and Janowitz, Morris, eds. *Black Sociologists.* Chicago: University Chicago Press, 1974.

Original essays discussing the historical and contemporary perspectives of black sociologists from W. E. B. DuBois to Nathan Hare and other sociologists.

Glazer, Nathan, and Moynihan, Daniel P., eds. *Ethnicity.* Cambridge: Harvard University Press, 1975.

A series of essays by leading scholars on ethnic identity. Theoretical articles are written by Harold Isaacs, Talcott Parsons, Milton M. Gordon, and Daniel Bell. In addition, descriptive essays deal with ethnicity in the Old World, the New World, and the Third World.

Gordon, Milton M. *Assimilation in American Life.* New York: Oxford University Press, 1964.

The role of race, religion, and national origin in American society. Of special note is Gordon's thesis about the relationship between class and ethnicity.

Greeley, Andrew M. *Why Can't They Be Like Us?* New York: Dutton, 1971.

A study of white ethnic groups and their attitudes toward nonwhites in the United States.

Killian, Lewis M. *The Impossible Revolution: Phase II.* New York: Random House, 1975.

An updated analysis of "Black Power and the American Dream."

Myrdal, Gunnar. *An American Dilemma.* New York: Harper and Row, 1962.

Originally published in the 1940s, this classic study examines the hypothesis that there is a discrepancy between creed and conduct in the white American's views of blacks. Especially noteworthy are the excellent descriptions of the "etiquette" of race relations.

Novak, Michael. *The Rise of the Unmeltable Ethnics.* New York: Macmillan, 1971.

A commentary on the attitudes and behavior of white ethnics, especially Catholics, as they observe the changes brought about by the black power movement in the United States.

Rose, Peter I. *They and We.* 2d ed. New York: Random House, 1974.

An introduction to the sociology of intergroup relations and an assessment of racial and ethnic relations in the United States.

———, ed. *Nation of Nations.* New York: Random House, 1972.

A collection of essays and articles on the American ethnic experience and the racial crisis.

Scanzoni, John H. *The Black Family in Modern Society.* Boston: Allyn and Bacon, 1971.

A volume based on a sample of 400 black households in Indianapolis.

Shibutani, Tomatsu, and Kwan, Kian W. *Ethnic Stratification.* New York: Macmillan, 1965.

A comparative approach to the study of racial and ethnic relations.

Simpson, George E., and Yinger, J. Milton. *Racial and Cultural Minorities.* 4th ed. New York: Harper and Row, 1972.

One of the best texts on the subject of prejudice and discrimination.

CHAPTER 9 Early Socialization

Billingsley, Andrew. *Black Families in White America.* Englewood cliffs, N.J.: Prentice-Hall, 1968.

An analysis of the historical roots of the black family and the nature of black achievement.

Bronfenbrenner, Urie. *Two Worlds of Childhood.* New York: Russell Sage, 1970.

The results of a comparative study of child-rearing in the United States and the Soviet Union.

Clausen, John A., ed. *Socialization and Society.* Boston: Little, Brown, 1969.

A valuable reference work analyzing childhood and adult socialization. The development of moral values and competence are discussed in detail.

Coleman, James, et al. *Equality of Educational Opportunity.* Washington, D.C.: U.S. Government Printing Office, 1972.

An ambitious empirical study focusing on the impact of schooling on the opportunity for young people to acquire the skills essential for social mobility.

Goodman, Paul. *Growing Up Absurd.* New York: Random House, 1960.

A critical view of American socialization in the 1950s. The author became a leading "guru" of the New Left movement in the following decade.

Linton, Ralph. *The Cultural Background of Personality.* New York: Appleton-Century-Crofts, 1945.

Linton's famous lectures on the relationship between culture and character.

Scarr-Salapatek, Sandra, and Salapatek, Philip, eds. *Socialization.* Columbus, Ohio: Merrill, 1973.

Sex and social-class factors in socialization are considered in detail.

Swerdloff, Peter, and the editors of Time-Life Books. *Men and Women.* New York: Time-Life Books, 1975.

A lively discussion of sex roles in society.

Whiting, John, and Child, Irwin L. *Child Training and Personality.* New Haven, Conn.: Yale University Press, 1958.

Based on comparative studies of child-rearing in different societies and the effects of culture on personality development.

Williams, Thomas Rhys. *Introduction to Socialization.* St. Louis: Mosby, 1972.

Brings together a wealth of information on the socialization process in a variety of cultures.

CHAPTER 10 The Adult Years: Family, Work, and Retirement

Bradbury, Will, and the editors of Time-Life Books. *The Adult Years.* New York: Time-Life Books, 1976.

An overview of life from marriage, the first child, and the first job until death. Particular emphasis on middle age and the "golden years."

Braude, Lee. *Work and Workers.* New York: Praeger, 1975.

Survey of the world of work, with an analysis of the American labor force and a summary of various occupational categories.

Cherry, Mike. *On High Steel.* New York: Quadrangle Books, 1974.

A breezy account of the steelworker's life by someone who has partaken of it.

Chinoy, Ely. *Automobile Workers and the American Dream.* Garden City, N.Y.: Doubleday, 1955.

A classic study of the lives, work experiences, and aspirations of men working in a Ford Motor plant.

Freeman, Jo, ed. *Women: A Feminist Perspective.* Palo Alto, Calif.: Mayfield, 1975.

A fine collection of recent essays on issues related to women. There is an especially useful section on working women.

Friedson, Eliot. *Profession of Medicine.* New York: Dodd, Mead, 1972.

A book-length examination of the medical profession, dealing with its formal organization, professional performance, and the social construction of illness.

Komarovsky, Mirra. *Blue-Collar Marriage.* New York: Random House, 1964.

An empirical study of blue-collar marriages that predates the contemporary women's movement yet remains one of the most important books on the subject.

Skolnick, Arlene E., and Skolnick, Jerome H., eds. *Family in Transition.* Boston: Little, Brown, 1971.

A reference book on the cultural basis of the family, its social organization, its variations in different societal contexts, and alternatives to its current structure.

Smuts, Robert W. *Women and Work in America.* New York: Schocken Books, 1971.

This book was first published in 1959 and was reissued in 1971. Although many of the statistics are dated, it remains an important volume raising many issues about women and work.

Steinberg, Rafael, and the editors of Time-Life Books. *Man and the Organization.* New York: Time-Life Books, 1975.

A highly readable and visually attractive introduction to the sociology of occupations and the study of men and women in the work force.

Terkel, Studs. *Working: People Talk about What They Do All Day and How They Feel about What They Do.* New York: Pantheon Books, 1974.

A series of interviews with and commentaries about working Americans.

CHAPTER 11 Conformity, Deviance, and Resocialization

Akers, Ronald L. *Deviant Behavior.* Belmont, Calif.: Wadsworth, 1973.

A theoretical statement that emphasizes "a social learning approach" to deviant behavior. White-collar crime, professional crime, and organized crime are examined as well as drug use and deviant sexual behavior.

Bryant, Clifton D. *Deviant Behavior.* Chicago: Rand McNally, 1974.

This collection of essays focuses on deviant behavior in the occupations. Professionals, blue-collar workers, and military personnel are among those studied.

Clinard, Marshall D., ed. *Anomie and Deviant Behavior: A Discussion and Critique.* New York: Free Press, 1964.

A collection of essays exploring and elaborating on a central concept in sociological thought.

Cohen, Elie A. *Human Behavior in the Concentration Camp.* New York: Universal Library, 1953.

A former inmate describes the camp in vivid detail.

Ennis, Bruce, and Siegel, Loren. *The Rights of Mental Patients.* New York: Avon Books, 1973.

This book, written under the auspices of the American Civil Liberties Union, is intended to offer a basic guide to a mental patient's rights.

Gaylin, Willard. *Partial Justice.* New York: Knopf, 1974.

A troubling account of the sentencing procedure in the American judicial system. Using psychoanalytic techniques, the author interviewed over forty judges.

Geis, Gilbert, ed. *White Collar Criminal.* New York: Atherton Press, 1968.

Theoretical and empirical statements about deviance among

the respectables. Geis's article on price-fixing in the electrical industry raises an array of disturbing questions.

Hawkins, Richard, and Tiedeman, Gary. *The Creation of Deviance.* Columbus, Ohio: Merrill, 1975.

A text that emphasizes the organizational and interpersonal forces leading to deviance.

Merton, Robert K., and Nisbet, Robert A., eds. *Contemporary Social Problems.* New York: Harcourt Brace Jovanovich, 1971.

A series of essays by leading sociologists about social problems and deviant behavior.

Rubington, Earl, and Weinberg, Martin S. *Deviance: The Interactionist Perspective.* 2d ed. New York: Macmillan, 1973.

Deviance is in the eye of the beholder. How acts come to be labeled deviant. The reactions of those designated deviants.

CHAPTER 12 The Nature of Community

Arensberg, Conrad. *The Irish Countryman.* Garden City, N.Y.: Natural History Press, 1968.

This reprint of Arensberg's study, first published in 1937, offers another opportunity to read an outstanding monograph about life in a close-knit Irish community.

Baltzell, E. Digby, ed. *The Search for Community in Modern Society.* New York: Harper and Row, 1969.

A collection of essays by historians and sociologists.

Cheever, Julia. *Your Community and Beyond.* Palo Alto, Calif.: Page-Ficklin Publications, 1975.

Intended for students interested in analyzing and changing major problems in community life. Worksheets integral to the text provide readers with easily available research tools.

Goodman, Percival, and Goodman, Paul. *Communitas: Means of Livelihood and Ways of Life.* Chicago: University of Chicago Press, 1947.

An architect and a social critic consider the nature of community and offer their views for preserving old values in the face of modernization and change.

Roberts, Ron E. *The New Communes.* Englewood Cliffs, N.J.: Prentice-Hall, 1971.

Traces early American communes and alternative approaches to the good life. A variety of contemporary communes are sympathetically presented.

Stein, Maurice R. *The Eclipse of Community.* Princeton, N.J.: Princeton University Press, 1960.

An interpretation of problems and prospects of American community life using sociological field studies of communities done in the twentieth century.

West, James. *Plainville, U.S.A.* New York: Columbia University Press, 1945.

A study of an American town beginning to undergo the strains of modernization and urbanization.

Wirth, Louis. *The Ghetto.* Chicago: University of Chicago Press, 1928.

A comprehensive portrait of the Jewish ghetto in Europe and in America.

CHAPTER 13 Urban Living

Chinoy, Ely, ed. *The Urban Future.* New York: Atherton Press, 1973.

A series of controversies about the future of the American city. Includes a splendid introductory essay by the author, "Trends and Prospects."

Gans, Herbert J. *The Levittowners.* New York: Pantheon, 1967.

A participant observer's account of life and social structure in a newly built suburb.

Gutman, Robert, and Popenoe, David, eds. *Neighborhood, City, and Metropolis.* New York: Random House, 1970.

One of the most comprehensive of the readers on urban sociology. Gutman and Popenoe include many of the classic articles, including those by Weber, Simmel, Wirth, Mumford, and Gans.

Keller, Suzanne. *The Urban Neighborhood.* New York: Random House, 1968.

The nature of the urban neighborhood and the character of life within it. The author discusses the importance of the neighborhood concept for city planning.

Lewis, Michael. *Urban America.* New York: Wiley, 1973.

A systematic overview of urban institutions and problems with an important chapter on "The Failure of Professional Reform."

Lynch, Kevin. *The Image of the City.* Cambridge, Mass.: M.I.T. Press, 1960.

A consideration of the visual character of urban areas. Many comparisons are made between old European and modern cities.

Miller, Delbert C. *Leadership and Power in the Bos-Wash Megalopolis.* New York: Wiley, 1975.

Megalopolis defined and major cities explored. Leaders are identified and their base of power specified. An ambitious undertaking.

Mumford, Lewis. *The Urban Prospect.* New York: Harcourt Brace Jovanovich, 1968.

A collection of the famed urbanologist's views on the city of the past—and of the future.

Sennett, Richard. *The Uses of Disorder.* New York: Knopf, 1970.

An exciting book about how too much order stifles creativity and rigidifies behavior. Sennett looks at personal identity and the problems of city life.

Walton, John, and Carns, Donald E., eds. *Cities in Change: Studies on the Urban Condition.* Boston: Allyn and Bacon, 1973.

A collection of forty-three essays discussing urban life and problems in comparative perspective. Focus is on cities in the United States and in developing countries.

CHAPTER 14 Social Change

Anderson, Robert T., and Anderson, Barbara Gallatin. *Bus Stop for Paris.* Garden City, N.Y.: Doubleday, 1965.

A study of the effect of modernization on Wissous, a village just outside Paris.

Apter, David. *The Politics of Modernization.* Chicago: University of Chicago Press, 1965.

A functional approach to the comparative study of modernization.

Hagopian, Mark N. *The Phenomenon of Revolution.* New York: Dodd, Mead, 1975.

An effort to continue the work of the early theorists of revolution. A final section deals with the relationship between counterrevolution and revolution.

Lauer, Robert H. *Perspectives on Social Change.* Boston: Allyn and Bacon, 1973.

Socio-psychological theories of social change are analyzed. A variety of other perspectives, including the materialistic, the idealistic, and the interactional, are also presented.

Migdal, Joel M. *Peasants, Politics, and Revolution.* Princeton, N.J.: Princeton University Press, 1974.

An analysis of the pressures for social change in the developing world. A wide range of ethnographic material is covered.

Moore, Wilbert E. *Social Change.* Englewood Cliffs, N.J.: Prentice-Hall, 1963.

An introduction to the sociological study of social change.

CHAPTER 15 Social Movements

Denisoff, R. Serge, ed. *The Sociology of Dissent.* New York: Harcourt Brace Jovanovich, 1974.

A collection bringing together some of social science's best articles on social movements.

Jackson, Larry R., and Johnson, William A. *Protest by the Poor.* Lexington, Mass.: Lexington Books, 1974.

The welfare rights movement in New York City and its relation to the civil rights movement are the focus.

London, Joan, and Anderson, Henry. *So Shall Ye Reap.* New York: Crowell, 1970.

A highly sympathetic account of the rise of the United Farm Workers Union and its leader, César Chavez.

Roberts, Ron E., and Kloss, Robert Marsh. *Social Movements: Between the Balcony and the Barricade.* St. Louis: Mosby, 1974.
The concept of social movement is defined in the first chapter. The remainder of the volume focuses on efforts by sociologists to analyze social movements in the United States and elsewhere.

Smelser, Neil J. *Theory of Collective Behavior.* New York: Free Press, 1963.
A systematic approach to the study of social movements. The author distinguishes between norm-oriented and value-oriented movements.

Turner, Ralph H., and Killian, Lewis M. *Collective Behavior.* Englewood Cliffs, N.J.: Prentice-Hall, 1972.
An impressive amount of material ranging from the analysis of crowd behavior to the nature of social movement organization and leadership. An excellent reference source, offering case material and conceptual development in the vast field of collective behavior.

Useem, Michael. *Conscription, Protest and Social Conflict.* New York: Wiley, 1973.
An analysis of the draft resistance movement that flourished in the late 1960s and early 1970s.

APPENDIX The Research Process

Babbie, Earl R. *The Practice of Social Research.* Belmont, Calif.: Wadsworth, 1975.
A straightforward and well-organized "cookbook" to guide the beginning student through the research process.

Glazer, Myron. *The Research Adventure.* New York: Random House, 1972.
A discussion of the process and ethics of field research in sociology.

Hyman, Herbert H., et al. *Interviewing in Social Research.* Chicago: University of Chicago Press, 1975.
A revised version of the famous textbook on the interviewing process and its many facets.

Lewis, George H., ed. *Fist-Fights in the Kitchen.* Pacific Palisades, Calif.: Goodyear, 1975.

A multitude of lively articles on various problems in sociological research.

Riley, Matilda White, and Nelson, Edward E., eds. *Sociological Observation.* New York: Basic Books, 1974.
A collection of essays analyzing virtually every aspect of the research process.

Sanders, William B., ed. *The Sociologist as Detective.* New York: Praeger, 1974.
A wide range of field research methods are covered. Pertinent introductions are followed by essays by practitioners of each technique of data collection.

Simon, Julian. *Basic Research Methods in Social Science.* New York: Random House, 1969.
A fine reference guide to major research tools.

Sjoberg, Gideon, ed. *Ethics, Politics, and Social Research.* Cambridge, Mass.: Schenkman, 1967.
A variety of authors set forth the challenges of empirical research.

Photographic Acknowledgments—*continued*

343 *bottom* Ken Heyman
344 John Dunlop
346 Elliott Erwitt, Magnum
347 *top* Charles Harbutt, Magnum
347 *bottom* John Dunlop
357 *top* Ellen Pines, Woodfin Camp
357 *bottom* Leo Hetzel
358 *top* Bruce Davidson, Magnum
358 *bottom left* Burk Uzzle, Magnum
358 *bottom right* Ken Heyman
359 *top* St. Louis Post Dispatch, Black Star
359 *bottom left* Ken Heyman
359 *bottom right* Eve Arnold, Magnum
360 *top* Paul Conklin
360 *bottom* Bruce Davidson, Magnum
365 Leonard Freed, Magnum
369 Paul Almasy, W.H.O.
370 The Society of California Pioneers
371 Jeffrey Blankfort, BBM Associates
374 Paul Conklin
377 Burk Uzzle, Magnum
380 Ken Heyman
381 Burk Uzzle, Magnum
390 Burk Uzzle, Magnum
391 Burk Uzzle, Magnum
396 Danny Lyon, Magnum
397 Danny Lyon, Magnum
399 National Archives
400 U.S. Army
408 Constantine Manos, Magnum
409 Constantine Manos, Magnum
412 George Rodger, Magnum
413 Leo Hetzel
414 Burk Uzzle, Magnum
415 Bruce Davidson, Magnum
418 Library of Congress
419 *top* Bob Adelman, Magnum
419 *bottom* Roger Lubin, Jeroboam
423 Leo Hetzel
427 *top* Charles Gatewood, Magnum
427 *bottom* Abigail Heyman, Magnum
430 *top* Professor Elmer Pearson, Illinois Institute of Technology, Chicago
430 *bottom* Ruth Silverman, BBM Associates
431 Dennis Stock, Magnum
436 Charles Harbutt, Magnum
440 *top* The Mansell Collection
440 *bottom* Aerofilms
441 Ken Heyman
444 Charles Harbutt, Magnum
445 Sepp Seitz, Magnum
448 Dennis Stock, Magnum
449 Burt Glinn, Magnum
454 *top* Charles Gatewood, Magnum
454 *bottom* Leo Hetzel
455 Charles Gatewood, Magnum
462 Bob Henriques, Magnum
466 Bill Owens, BBM Associates
471 *top* Bill Owens, BBM Associates
471 *bottom* Bob Adelman, Magnum
475 Andy Mercado, Jeroboam
477 Erich Hartmann, Magnum
484 Consulate of Finland
485 *top* Ken Heyman
485 *bottom* Information Canada Photothèque
487 Elliott Erwitt, Magnum
491 Peeter Vilms, Jeroboam
498 Jeanne Thwaites, BBM Associates
499 Abigail Heyman, Magnum
503 Ken Heyman
504 Caprasse, Asia Photo
507 Photo by Byron, Museum of the City of New York
508 Leo Hetzel
509 Henri Cartier-Bresson, Magnum
513 Brown Brothers
516 Leif Skoogfors, Woodfin Camp
519 Western History Collections, University of Oklahoma Library
523 Charles Harbutt, Magnum
524 Dan Budnik, Woodfin Camp
525 *top* Bruce Davidson, Magnum
525 *bottom* Leonard Freed, Magnum
526 Roger Malloch, Magnum
527 Charles Harbutt, Magnum
528 Paul Fusco, Magnum
529 Leonard Freed, Magnum
532 Library of Congress
533 Suzanne Arms, Jeroboam
536 Brown Brothers
537 Charles Harbutt, Magnum
541 *top* Carol Simowitz
541 *bottom* Ken Heyman
542 Ken Heyman
545 *left* United Mine Workers
545 *right* Eve Arnold, Magnum
549 U.P.I.
555 Kent Reno, Jeroboam
556 Leonard Freed, Magnum
557 *top* Bill Owens, BBM Associates
557 *bottom* Hap Stewart, Jeroboam
558 *top* Hiroji Kubota, Magnum
558 *bottom* Ken Heyman
562 *top* Photo by Jacob Riis, Museum of the City of New York
562 *bottom* Ken Heyman
569 Jeffrey Blankfort, BBM Associates

INDEX